HP
Certified Systems
Administrator

HP-UX 11i v3

EXAM
HP0-A01

Training Guide and Administrator's Reference

3rd Edition
October 2008

Asghar Ghori

Lightning
Source

1246 Heil Quaker Blvd., La Vergne, TN USA 37086
Chapter House, Pitfield, Kiln Farm, Milton Keynes, UK MK11-3LW
www.lightningsource.com

Technical Reviewers: Mehmood Khan, Ming Zhao, Asif Zuberi and Kurt Glasgow
Cover Design: Endeavor Technoloiges Inc.
Printers and Distributors: Lightning Source Inc.

Printed in the United States of America and the United Kingdom.

ISBN: 978-1-60643-654-7

Printed and Distributed by: Lightning Source Inc.

To order in bulk, please contact the author:
asghar_ghori2002@yahoo.com

Preface

Here is the third edition of the book. The objective to publish this edition is based on the fact that HP recently revised the Certified Systems Administrator exam. The new exam HP0-A01 (which has replaced HP0-095) covers several additional topics. At the same time, some topics have been taken out from the list of exam objectives. This edition of the book reflects the updates and provides a single, comprehensive resource that equips you with enough knowledge to pass the exam. Moreover, the book furnishes procedures to help configure and manage an HP-UX-based computing environment effectively, efficiently and successfully. Most of the contents are based on initial HP-UX 11i v3 which was released in February, 2007. Later, HP released updates 1 and 2 in September 2007 and March 2008, respectively. This book includes some information from there too.

I have put together 863 exam questions to help you prepare for the CSA exam. My suggestion to you is to take this quiz once you finish studying the entire book along with all installation, configuration and administration tasks presented. Passing the exam does not mean that you become an expert in the area. You need to perform hands-on practice on actual HP-UX systems as much as possible to master the concepts learnt. If a command does not produce desired results, see what message it generates and try to resolve it. Minor issues such as wrong path prevent commands from running. Sometimes there are syntax errors in the command construct. HP-UX manual pages prove helpful and are useful in comprehending commands and their syntax. There is a whole bunch of commands, options, daemons and configuration files in the operating system; discussing all of them is not possible within the scope of this book.

There are three areas where you should focus to gain expertise with HP-UX – grasping concepts, mastering step-by-step implementation procedures and learning commands, configuration files and service daemons. An excellent understanding of which command involves and updates which files, which daemon provides what service, etc. must also be developed. This way you develop a better overall understanding of what exactly happens in the background when a command is executed. This book provides all that knowledge. Troubleshooting becomes easier when concepts are clear and working knowledge is solid.

I am maintaining *www.getitcertify.com* website where errors reported in the book, additional exam information and links to useful resources are made available. I encourage you to visit this website. I am also going to make the topics included in the 2nd edition but removed from this edition, available on this website as a downloadable pdf file.

At the end, I would like to ask you to forward your feedback, negative or positive, to my personal address at *asghar_ghori2002@yahoo.com* about the content, structure, layout, consistency, clarity and flow of the book. Please also let me know if you come across any errors or mistakes. Improvement is a continuous process and I am sure your feedback will help me publish a better and improved fourth edition, as it helped me with this third edition.

Good luck in your endeavors.

Asghar Ghori
September 2008
Toronto, Canada

Acknowledgments

I am grateful to God who enabled me to write and update this book successfully.

I would like to thank my friends, colleagues, students and peers who supported and encouraged me to write this book. I am also grateful for their tremendous feedback from previous editions of this book that assisted me to come up with a better, updated third edition. I am thankful to all of them for their invariable support, constant encouragement, constructive feedback and valuable assistance.

Finally, I would like to pay my special thanks to my wife, two daughters and son, who endured me through the lifecycle of this project and extended their full assistance, support and love. I would not be able to complete this project without their cooperation and support.

Asghar Ghori

About the Author

Currently working as an independent technical consultant, Asghar Ghori has been in the IT industry for 18 years. He started his career as a UNIX support engineer working with SCO UNIX and SCO XENIX, visiting customers and providing UNIX technical support services. He has worked with various flavors of the UNIX operating system including HP-UX, SUN Solaris, IBM AIX, Microsoft XENIX, AT&T UNIX, SGI's IRIS, ISC UNIX, DYNIX/ptx and Stratus UNIX in addition to SCO UNIX and XENIX, and Linux system such as Red Hat Linux. He has worked in different capacities such as UNIX support engineer, UNIX administrator, UNIX specialist, technical lead, solution design lead and technology consultant serving business and government customers. In addition, he has architected and deployed solutions around HP-UX, Sun Solaris and Linux that involved enterprise disk and tape storage subsystems, Storage Area Networks, clustering technologies such as HP Serviceguard, Veritas Cluster Server and Sun Cluster, and systems management software.

Asghar Ghori has been involved in planning, developing and executing IT infrastructure disaster recovery procedures for multiple large corporations.

Asghar Ghori holds a BS in Engineering and has delivered and attended numerous training programs. He has been delivering courses on UNIX for the past eight years at local colleges in Toronto, Canada. He teaches UNIX as a sessional faculty at Algoma University. He is HP Certified Systems Administrator (HP0-A01, HP0-095, HP0-091, HP0-002), HP Certified Systems Engineer (HP-UX Operations lab), SUN Certified System Administrator (SCSA) for various Solaris versions, IBM Certified Specialist for AIX, Certified Novell Engineer (CNE) and holds Project Management Professional (PMP) certification designation.

Conventions Used in this Book

The following typographic and other conventions are used throughout this book:

Book Antiqua Italic is used in text paragraphs for special words, phrases, acronyms and abbreviations that are emphasized. For example:

> "HP-UX, like other UNIX operating systems, is a *multi-user, multi-tasking, multi-processing* and *multi-threading* operating system meaning that a number of users can access an HP-UX machine simultaneously and share its resources."

Times New Roman Bold is used for commands and command line arguments that the user is expected to type at the command prompt. For example:

$ ls –lt

Times New Roman Italic is used for commands, daemons, usernames, group names, hostnames, printer names, file and directory names and URLs in text paragraphs.

All headings and sub-headings are bold.

`Courier New` is used for `Ctrl`, `Enter` and `Esc` keys.

`Ctrl+x` key sequence means that you hold the `Ctrl` key down on the keyboard and then press the other key.

Light grey background is used to differentiate output generated by commands and shell scripts from surrounding text.

Command outputs have been edited and/or formatted for enhanced readability.

. . . . Single dotted line is used to show the continuation of text in command outputs.

"\" The backslash character at the end of a command line represents that the rest of the command is on the next line.

Many places in the book refers to situations where he and/or she is used. For example: "when another user attempts to change his or her password while you are editing the file, he or she is denied permission to change the password." Throughout the book only "his" is used which covers both he and she.

 Indicates additional information.

Indicates a task performed using HP-UX System Management Homepage (SMH).

About this Book

Like the first two editions of this book, the third edition also covers the three main objectives – to provide a comprehensive resource to individuals including novice, IT/Non-HP-UX administrators and HP-UX administrators who intend to take the new HP Certified Systems Administrator exam HP0-A01 and pass it; to provide a quick and valuable on-the-job resource to HP-UX administrators, administrators of other UNIX operating systems, IT managers, and programmers and DBAs working in the HP-UX environment; and to provide an easy-to-understand guide to novice and IT/non-HP-UX administrators who intend to learn HP-UX from the beginning.

This book contains 36 chapters and is structured to facilitate readers to grasp concepts, understand implementation procedures, learn command syntax, configuration files and daemons involved, and understand basic troubleshooting. The 36 chapters are divided into three key areas: UNIX Fundamentals, HP-UX System Administration and HP-UX Network Administration. These chapters cover topics that are on HP's recommended certification courses – UNIX Fundamentals, System and Network Administration I, System and Network Administration II, and HP-UX for Experienced UNIX System Administrators – as well as on official exam objectives list.

1. **UNIX Fundamentals** (chapters 1 to 6, and 22) covers the basics of UNIX and HP-UX. Most information is not specific to a particular UNIX flavor, rather, includes general UNIX concepts, file manipulation and security techniques, vi editor, shell and awk programming, basic commands and other essential topics. Unlike many other similar books, a chapter on shell scripting is presented after covering HP-UX System Administration area. This is done purposely to provide readers with practical examples based on the knowledge they gain from UNIX Fundamentals and HP-UX System Administration chapters.

2. **HP-UX System Administration** (chapters 7 to 21) covers the HP-UX-specific system administration concepts and topics including server hardware information and mass storage stack; virtualization technologies and HP-UX installation; software and patch management; user and group administration; LVM and file system administration; EVFS and swap management; system shutdown and startup procedures; kernel configuration and management techniques; backup and restore functions; printer and print request management, job automation and process control; and system logging and performance monitoring.

3. **HP-UX Network Administration** (chapters 23 to 36) covers HP-UX network and security administration concepts and topics such as OSI and TCP/IP reference models; network hardware overview and LAN interface administration; IP subnetting and routing techniques; basic network testing and troubleshooting; internet services and sendmail; time synchronization (NTP) and resource sharing (NFS, AutoFS and CIFS) services; naming (DNS, NIS and LDAP) services and automated installation techniques; and high-availability concepts and system security tools and practices.

Each chapter begins with a list of key topics covered and ends with a summary. Throughout the book figures, tables, screen shots and examples are given for explanation purposes. The background of the output generated from running commands and shell scripts is highlighted in light grey to differentiate from surrounding text.

The book includes several appendices, one of which contains 863 exam review questions. Answers to exam review questions, and tables of commands, important files and service daemons are included in appendix area as well.

About the HP CSA Exam (HP0-A01)

The Certified Systems Administrator (CSA) certification exam from Hewlett-Packard is designed for UNIX professionals. There is only one exam to pass to get this certification. There are total 60 questions on the exam. Question format includes multiple choice, drag-and-drop and graphical. A minimum score of 70% is required to pass the exam in 90 minutes. The official exam objectives are given below, and are covered in various chapters throughout the book.

Objective 1: HP-UX architecture and structure (17%)
1. Describe the HP-UX OS architecture
2. Describe the HP-UX processor families
3. Describe the major hardware components found in HP's current systems
4. Describe the features and benefits of HP disk management solutions
5. Describe the significance of basic LVM concepts and structure
6. Describe virtualization technologies and concepts
7. Describe the concept and benefits of the Mass Storage Stack
8. Describe 11i v3 performance and capacity improvements and workload benefits

Objective 2: HP-UX user environment, basic commands and utilities (15%)
1. Login and logout of an HP-UX system
2. Determine basic information about a system
3. Execute HP-UX commands from the command line
4. Manage and manipulate files and directories
5. Define and describe the attributes of basic system components
6. Demonstrate the tools and techniques used to identify, monitor and terminate programs and processes
7. Identify and explain how and when to use advanced shell features
8. Describe and demonstrate how to communicate with system users
9. Describe when and how to access basic network services

Objective 3: HP-UX system administration and operational tasks (26%)
1. Boot, reboot and shutdown an HP-UX system or partition
2. Connect and configure HP-UX hardware
3. Describe, configure and manage HP-UX device files
4. Configure and manage disks and partitions
5. Maintain file and file system integrity and design
6. Backup and recover data on an HP-UX system
7. Create and manage swap space
8. Create and manage user/group environments
9. Configure and reconfigure the HP-UX kernel
10. Describe common areas of performance bottlenecks
11. Describe SYS-V IPC services and their use
12. Describe SAM and its use
13. Describe System Startup model and its use
14. Describe /etc/default and its use
15. Monitor system activity and events
16. Implement HP partitioning solutions
17. Describe Web-Based Enterprise Management (WBEM) and its use
18. Describe HP Systems Insight Manager (HP SIM) and its use
19. Describe System Management Homepage (SMH) and its use

Objective 4: HP-UX system network administration tasks (23%)

1. Describe MAC addressing and its use
2. Describe IP addressing and its use
3. Enable DHCP for NIC address configuration
4. Check local connectivity to a known neighbor by IP or by MAC address
5. Describe set_parms and its use
6. Describe common network configuration files and their use
7. Describe network monitor utilities and their use
8. Configure and monitor network services
9. Describe the HP CIFS product suite and its use
10. Describe the ONC suite of network services and their use
11. Describe LDAP and its use
12. Describe DNS and its use
13. Describe sendmail and its use as a MTA and MDA
14. Describe NTP and its use

Objective 5: HP-UX installation, upgrade and recovery tasks (6%)

1. Perform an HP-UX installation from local installation media
2. Perform HP-UX installation from an SD-UX server
3. Install HP-UX patches
4. Describe the features and benefits of Ignite-UX

Objective 6: HP-UX security administration tasks (11%)

1. Cite 'users level' security settings
2. Describe how to implement system access restrictions
3. Describe common system security concerns
4. Describe ssh and its use
5. Describe PAM and its use
6. Describe available security tools
7. Describe common administrative security tasks
8. Explain how various network architectures/features can affect a system security policy
9. Use Bastille for system hardening
10. Use Encrypted Volume and File System (EVFS)
11. Identify Identity Management features and functions
12. Use Install-time Security
13. Identify new security features (new to 11i v3)
14. Use the Software Assistant (SWA)
15. Describe Local User Administration

Objective 7: Describe HP-UX high availability and clustering features (2%)

1. Explain Key HA Terms
2. Identify the Risks with SPOF

Visit *www.hp.com/go/certification* for up-to-date and more in-depth information about the exam requirements.

HP Student ID

If you have not taken an HP exam before, you must obtain an HP Student ID to register for the CSA HP0-A01 certification exam. Visit *www.hp.com/certification/americas/student_id.html* and follow the procedure.

Exam Fee and How to Register for the Exam

The exam fee is US$150. To register for the exam, obtain a list of Authorized Prometric Testing Centers (APTCs) in your area where you can take the exam or get regional contact infromation, visit *www.prometric.com*. You are required to provide your HP student ID when registering for the exam.

TABLE OF CONTENTS

08. Virtualization Technologies **157**

List of Figures

List of Tables

## 01

Introduction to UNIX and HP-UX

This chapter covers the following major topics:

- ✓ A brief history of the UNIX system
- ✓ HP-UX 11i releases
- ✓ Structure and features of HP-UX
- ✓ How to login and logout
- ✓ Command line components and how to build a command
- ✓ General HP-UX commands and how to execute them
- ✓ HP-UX online help

1.1 Introduction

The UNIX operating system is a set of tools created by programmers for programmers at the AT&T Bell laboratories in 1969 when Ken Thompson, Dennis Ritchie and others developed an early version of the system on a PDP-7 computer in *B* language. UNIX, spelled UNICS, is an acronym for *UNiplexed Information and Computing System* and was derived from another earlier version operating system called *MULTiplexed Information and Computing System* (MULTICS). UNIX was later re-written in *C* language for portability purposes, among others.

Programmers at the University of California at Berkeley made significant updates to the original source code in the mid 1970s and brought out a new version of the UNIX system called *Berkeley Software Distribution* (BSD) UNIX. BSD UNIX allowed the operating system to function in a networked environment.

Presently, there are several flavors of UNIX available from various vendors, and although conceptually UNIX flavors are similar, features and services implemented and used in individual operating systems vary.

HP-UX was developed in the early 1980s and the first version was released in 1983. HP-UX was initially derived from AT&T version of the UNIX system, but today it includes the best from both AT&T and BSD versions, as well as scores of enhancements from HP development team.

1.1.1 UNIX and Standards

Beginning in the late 1980s, an open operating system standardization effort provided a common baseline for all operating systems. This effort is now known as *Portable Operating System Interface eXchange* (POSIX). The *Institute of Electrical and Electronic Engineers* (IEEE) created a series of standards committees to develop standards for an industry recognized UNIX operating systems interface. On the other hand, the *X/Open Consortium* brought together various UNIX-related standards, including the *Common Open System Environment* (COSE) specification, and published a series of specifications called the *X/Open Portability*. The consortium eventually became the *Single UNIX Specification* managed by *The Open Group*. The MOTIF user interface is one popular standard to emerge from this effort. Later, IEEE and The Open Group provided a common definition of POSIX and Single UNIX Specification. The US government has specified a series of standards based on XPG and POSIX.

1.1.2 HP-UX Release Names and Identifiers

Beginning with HP-UX 11i v1 in 2000, HP-UX was made Internet-enabled and available as integrated OE bundles. Versions 11.0 and earlier were referred to as *Operating Systems*. *Operating Environment* (OE) includes operating system as the core product, which acts as the most essential and critical component. Operating system comprises of core HP-UX functionality, while an operating environment includes additional components and functionalities such as Online JFS, MirrorDisk/UX, GlancePlus and virtualization technologies. These components were purchased separately with 11.0 and older versions.

Table 1-1 lists all HP-UX OE releases.

Release Name	Release Identifier	Release Year	Supported Processor Architecture
HP-UX 11i v1	B.11.11	2000	PA-RISC
HP-UX 11i v1.5	B.11.20	2001	Intel Itanium
HP-UX 11i v1.6	B.11.22	2002	Intel Itanium
HP-UX 11i v2	B.11.23	2003	Intel Itanium and PA-RISC
HP-UX 11i v3	B.11.31	2007	Intel Itanium and PA-RISC

Table 1-1 HP-UX 11i Release Names and Identifiers

1.1.3   HP-UX System Structure

The structure of an HP-UX system is comprised of three main components: the kernel, the shell and the hierarchical directory structure. These components are illustrated in Figure 1-1 and explained below.

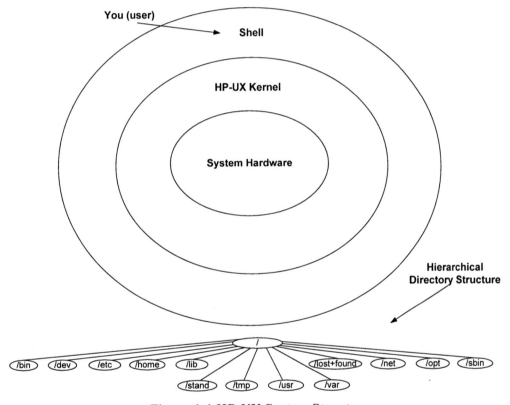

Figure 1-1 HP-UX System Structure

The HP-UX Kernel

The *kernel* controls everything inside-out on a machine that runs HP-UX. It controls all associated system hardware including memory, processors, disks, I/O (Input/Output) and internal/external devices. It receives instructions from the shell, engages appropriate hardware resources and acts as instructed.

The Shell

The *shell* is the interface between a user and the kernel. User provides instructions (commands) to the shell, which are interpreted and passed to the kernel for processing. The shell handles input and output, keeps track of data stored on disks, and communicates with peripheral devices such as monitors, hard disk drives, tape devices, CD/DVD drives, printers, modems and terminals. Chapter 05 "The Shells" discusses shells in detail.

The Hierarchical Directory Structure

HP-UX uses a conventional *hierarchical directory structure* where directories can contain both files and sub-directories. Sub-directories may further contain more files and sub-directories. A sub-directory, called *child directory*, is a directory located under a *parent* directory. That parent directory is a sub-directory of some other higher-level directory. In other words, the UNIX directory structure is similar to an inverted tree where the top is the root of the directory and branches and leaves are sub-directories and files, respectively. The root of the directory is represented by the forward slash (/) character, which is also used to separate directories as shown below:

　　/home/user1/dir1/subdir1

In this example, *home* sub-directory (child) is located under root (/), which is parent directory for *home*. *user1* (child) is located under *home* (parent). Similarly, *dir1* (child) is located under *user1* (parent), and at the very bottom *subdir1* (child) is located under *dir1* (parent).

Each directory has a parent directory and a child directory with the exception of the root (/) and the lowest level directories. The root (/) directory has no parent and the lowest level sub-directory has no child.

 The term sub-directory is used for a directory that has a parent directory.

The hierarchical directory structure keeps related information together in a logical fashion. Compare the concept with a file cabinet that has several drawers with each storing multiple file folders.

1.1.4　HP-UX Features

HP-UX, like other UNIX operating system flavors, is a *multi-user, multi-tasking, multi-processing* and *multi-threading* operating system. This means that a number of users can access an HP-UX system simultaneously and share available resources. The system allows each logged in user to run any number of programs concurrently. The kernel is capable of using multiple processors (CPU) installed in the system and breaking large running programs into smaller, more manageable pieces, called *threads*, for increased performance.

 A resource may be a hardware device or a software program or service.

The kernel allows *time-sharing* among running programs, and runs programs in a round-robin fashion to satisfy processing requirements of all running processes on the system.

HP-UX, like most other UNIX systems, is *immune* to viruses and remains up and running in the event a file containing a virus enters the system.

HP-UX is a *file-based* operating system. Hardware devices are accessed through corresponding *device special files* that are managed and controlled by the system kernel.

1.2   Logging In and Out

A user must login to an HP-UX system to use it. The login process identifies a user to the system. There are three common ways of logging in – at the system console, via *Common Desktop Environment* (CDE) login screen and over the network using *telnet*, *rlogin* or *ssh* command. The following sub-sections show how to login at the system console and via the *telnet* command. Logging in using *rlogin* and *ssh* is covered later in the book. CDE is beyond the scope of this book.

1.2.1   Logging In and Out at the System Console

A console is a serial text terminal (a.k.a. *dumb* or *ASCII* terminal) device connected to the serial console port on the back of the system.

All new HP-UX systems come with a LAN console port. Connecting a PC or laptop to the LAN console port via a network cable enables you to run a system console session on a Windows machine using, for example, MS Windows Hyper Terminal program.

When a console is connected to the system, login prompt appears by hitting a key on the console keyboard. The default console login prompt looks like:

GenericSysName [HP Release B.11.31] (see /etc/issue)
Console Login:

Enter a valid username and password to access the system. Both username and password are case sensitive. Suppose there is a user account *user1* on the system with password *user1234*, messages similar to the following will be displayed when you login as this user:

Please wait...checking for disk quotas
(c)Copyright 1983-2006 Hewlett-Packard Development Company, L.P.
(c)Copyright 1979, 1980, 1983, 1985-1993 The Regents of the Univ. of California
(c)Copyright 1980, 1984, 1986 Novell, Inc.
. . . .
under vendor's standard commercial license.
$

To end the login session, use the *exit* command or press Ctrl+d key combination.

1.2.2   Logging In and Out Using telnet

The second method to login is by using the *telnet* command from a Windows or another UNIX system on the network. The *telnet* command requires either an IP address of the HP-UX system or its hostname to be specified. A login prompt similar to the following will be displayed when you attempt to access the system (*hp01* for instance):

```
$ telnet hp01
HP-UX hp01 B.11.31 U 9000/800 (ta)
login:
```

Enter the username and press the Enter key. Then enter the password and press the Enter key again.

Use the *exit* command or press Ctrl+d to log out.

When you login using one of the methods mentioned above, you are placed into a directory, referred to as your *home* directory. Each user on the system is assigned a home directory where the user normally keeps private files.

1.3   Common HP-UX Commands

This section provides an understanding on how commands are formed and describes several common HP-UX commands frequently used in routine system administration work.

1.3.1   What is the Command Line?

The *command line* refers to the operating system command prompt where you enter commands for execution. The command may or may not have arguments supplied with it. Arguments are used with commands for better, restricted or enhanced output, or a combination. The basic syntax of a command is:

$ command argument1 argument2 argument3 ......

where:

> Command: specifies what to do
> Argument: is usually a file or directory name, some text or an option

Not every command requires an argument. Many commands run without one specified. Some commands do require that you specify one or more arguments, or a fixed number of them.

The following examples use arguments. The text on the right tells if and how many arguments are supplied with the command.

> **$ cal 2005**   (one argument)
> **$ cal 10 2005**   (two arguments)
> **$ ls**   (no arguments)
> **$ ls –l**   (an argument, which is an option)
> **$ ls directory_name**   (one argument)
> **$ ls –l directory_name** (two arguments of which the first one is an option)

1.3.2   The ls Command and its variants

The *ls* (or *lc*) (list) command displays a list of files and directories. It has several options available to it. Some common options are listed in Table 1-2 along with a short description of each.

Option	Description
–a	Lists hidden files also. If the name of a file starts with the period (.) character, it is referred to as a hidden file. For the *root* user, this option displays hidden files by default so there is no need to specify it.
–F	Displays file types. Shows (/) for directories, (*) for executable files, (@) for symbolic links and nothing for text files.
–l	Displays long listing with detailed file information including file type, permissions, link count, owner, group, size of file, date and time of last modification, and name of the file.
–ld	Displays long listing of the specified directory, but hides contents of it.
–R	Lists contents of the specified directory and all sub-directories (recursive listing).
–t	Lists all files sorted by date and time with the newest file first.
–tr	Lists all files sorted by date and time with the oldest file first.

Table 1-2 *ls* Command Options

The following examples help you understand the impact of options used with the *ls* command.

To list files in the current directory:

```
$ ls
.profile     .ssh     bin     home          net     stand     var
.secure      .sw      dev     lib           opt     tmp
.sh_history  .swa     etc     lost+found    sbin    usr
```

To list files in the current directory with detailed information, use any of the following:

```
$ ll
$ ls –l
total 160
-r--r--r--    1   bin    bin    965     Feb 15 2007    .profile
drwx------    3   root   root   96      Apr 8 11:53    .secure
-rw-------    1   root   sys    5520    Apr 10 14:39   .sh_history
drwxr-xr-x    2   root   sys    96      Apr 8 11:46    .ssh
drwxr-xr-x    6   root   sys    96      Apr 8 09:07    .sw
drwxr-xr-x    3   root   root   96      Apr 8 11:55    .swa
lrwxr-xr-x    1   bin    bin    8       Apr 8 09:07    bin -> /usr/bin
dr-xr-xr-x    20  bin    bin    8192    Apr 10 09:45   dev
dr-xr-xr-x    38  bin    bin    8192    Apr 10 11:41   etc
drwxr-xr-x    6   root   root   96      Apr 8 11:41    home
lrwxr-xr-x    1   bin    bin    8       Apr 8 09:07    lib -> /usr/lib
drwxr-xr-x    2   root   root   96      Apr 8 08:58    lost+found
dr-xr-xr-x    1   root   root   1       Apr 10 09:33   net
dr-xr-xr-x    84  bin    bin    8192    Apr 8 11:47    opt
dr-xr-xr-x    16  bin    bin    8192    Apr 8 11:52    sbin
dr-xr-xr-x    7   bin    bin    1024    Apr 10 09:33   stand
```

drwxrwxrwt	4	root	root	8192	Apr 10 14:29	tmp
dr-xr-xr-x	22	bin	bin	8192	Apr 8 11:41	usr
dr-xr-xr-x	30	bin	bin	8192	Apr 8 11:54	var

To display all files in the current directory with their file types, use any of the following:

```
$ ls –F
$ lsf
```

.profile	.ssh/	bin/	home/	net/	stand/	var/
.secure/	.sw/	dev/	lib/	opt/	tmp/	
.sh_history	.swa/	etc/	lost+found/	sbin/	usr/	

To list all files in the current directory with detailed information and sorted by date and time with the newest file first:

```
$ ls –lt
```
total 160

-rw-------	1	root	sys	5542	Apr 10 14:40	.sh_history
drwxrwxrwt	4	root	root	8192	Apr 10 14:29	tmp
dr-xr-xr-x	38	bin	bin	8192	Apr 10 11:41	etc
dr-xr-xr-x	20	bin	bin	8192	Apr 10 09:45	dev
dr-xr-xr-x	7	bin	bin	1024	Apr 10 09:33	stand
dr-xr-xr-x	1	root	root	1	Apr 10 09:33	net
drwxr-xr-x	3	root	root	96	Apr 8 11:55	.swa
dr-xr-xr-x	30	bin	bin	8192	Apr 8 11:54	var
drwx------	3	root	root	96	Apr 8 11:53	.secure
dr-xr-xr-x	16	bin	bin	8192	Apr 8 11:52	sbin
dr-xr-xr-x	84	bin	bin	8192	Apr 8 11:47	opt
drwxr-xr-x	2	root	sys	96	Apr 8 11:46	.ssh
dr-xr-xr-x	22	bin	bin	8192	Apr 8 11:41	usr
drwxr-xr-x	6	root	root	96	Apr 8 11:41	home
drwxr-xr-x	6	root	sys	96	Apr 8 09:07	.sw
lrwxr-xr-x	1	bin	bin	8	Apr 8 09:07	bin -> /usr/bin
lrwxr-xr-x	1	bin	bin	8	Apr 8 09:07	lib -> /usr/lib
drwxr-xr-x	2	root	root	96	Apr 8 08:58	lost+found
-r--r--r--	1	bin	bin	965	Feb 15 2007	.profile

To list all files, including the hidden files, in the current directory with detailed information:

```
$ ls –la
```
total 192

drwxr-xr-x	17	root	root	8192	Apr 10 09:33	.
drwxr-xr-x	17	root	root	8192	Apr 10 09:33	..
-r--r--r--	1	bin	bin	965	Feb 15 2007	.profile
drwx------	3	root	root	96	Apr 8 11:53	.secure
-rw-------	1	root	sys	5558	Apr 10 14:41	.sh_history
drwxr-xr-x	2	root	sys	96	Apr 8 11:46	.ssh
drwxr-xr-x	6	root	sys	96	Apr 8 09:07	.sw
drwxr-xr-x	3	root	root	96	Apr 8 11:55	.swa

lrwxr-xr-x	1	bin	bin	8	Apr 8 09:07	bin -> /usr/bin
dr-xr-xr-x	20	bin	bin	8192	Apr 10 09:45	dev
dr-xr-xr-x	38	bin	bin	8192	Apr 10 11:41	etc
drwxr-xr-x	6	root	root	96	Apr 8 11:41	home
lrwxr-xr-x	1	bin	bin	8	Apr 8 09:07	lib -> /usr/lib
drwxr-xr-x	2	root	root	96	Apr 8 08:58	lost+found
dr-xr-xr-x	1	root	root	1	Apr 10 09:33	net
dr-xr-xr-x	84	bin	bin	8192	Apr 8 11:47	opt
dr-xr-xr-x	16	bin	bin	8192	Apr 8 11:52	sbin
dr-xr-xr-x	7	bin	bin	1024	Apr 10 09:33	stand
drwxrwxrwt	4	root	root	8192	Apr 10 14:29	tmp
dr-xr-xr-x	22	bin	bin	8192	Apr 8 11:41	usr
dr-xr-xr-x	30	bin	bin	8192	Apr 8 11:54	var

To list contents of a directory and sub-directories recursively for the */etc* directory, use any of the following:

$ ls –R /etc
$ lsr /etc
< a very long output will be generated >

1.3.3 The pwd Command

The *pwd* (present working directory) command displays a user's current location in the directory tree. The following example shows that *user1* is in the */home/user1* directory:

$ pwd
/home/user1

1.3.4 The cd Command

The *cd* (change directory) command is used to navigate the directory tree. Do the following examples as *user1*:

To change directory to */usr/bin*:

$ cd /usr/bin

To go back to the home directory, do either of the two:

$ cd
$ cd ~

To go directly from */etc* into *dir1*, which is a sub-directory under *user1*'s home directory, perform the following:

$ cd ~/dir1

tilde (~) is used as an abbreviation for absolute pathname to a user's home directory. Refer to Chapter 02 "Files and Directories" to understand what an absolute path is.

To go to the home directory of *user2* from anywhere in the directory structure, use the ~ character and specify the login name. Note that there is no space between ~ and *user2*.

$ cd ~user2

Usage of ~ character, as demonstrated in previous examples, is called *tilde substitution*. Refer to Chapter 05 "The Shells" for more information.

To go to the root directory, use the forward slash character:

$ cd /

To go one directory up to the parent directory, use period twice:

$ cd ..

To switch between current and previous directories, repeat the *cd* command with the dash (-) character.

$ cd –

1.3.5   The tty and pty Commands

Both commands display pseudo terminal where you are currently logged in.

$ pty
$ tty
/dev/pts/4

1.3.6   The who Command

The *who* command displays information about all currently logged in users.

$ who
user1	pts/3	Feb 25 13:50	
user2	Console	Feb 25 13:51	:0

where:

user1	name of the real user
pts/3	the third pseudo terminal session
console	system console screen
Feb 25 13:50	date and time the user logged in
(:0)	the user is logged in via CDE/GUI

The *who* command shows information only about the user that runs it if executed with "am i"' arguments. For example:

```
$ who am i
user1          pts/4      Feb 25 13:50      :0
```

1.3.7   The w Command

The *w* (what) command displays information similar to the *who* command but in more detail. It also tells how long the user has been idle for, his CPU utilization, and what he is currently doing. It displays on the first line of the output the current system time, how long the system has been up for, how many users are currently logged in and what the current average load on the system is over the past 1, 5 and 15 minutes.

```
$ w
8:01am up 1 day, 23:17,  1 user,  load average: 0.67, 0.72, 0.95
user        tty        login@  idle      JCPU    PCPU   what
root        pts/ta     8:01am                            w
```

 The *uptime* command with –w option displays exact same output. Try running it and compare results

1.3.8   The whoami Command

The *whoami* (who am i) command displays the username of the user who executes this command. The output may either be the current or the effective username. The current username is the name of the user who logs in and runs this command. When this user uses the command *su* to switch to a different user, he becomes the effective user.

```
$ whoami
user1
```

1.3.9   The logname Command

The *logname* (login name) command shows the name of the real user who logs in initially. If that user uses the *su* command to switch to a different user account, the *logname* command, unlike the *whoami* command, still shows the real username.

```
$ logname
user1
```

1.3.10   The id Command

The *id* (identification) command displays a user's UID (*user identification*), username, GID (*group identification*), group name and all secondary groups that the user is a member of.

```
$ id
uid=110(user1) gid=20(users)
```

Each user and group has a corresponding number (called UID and GID, respectively) in UNIX for identification purposes. See Chapter 12 "Users and Groups" for more information.

1.3.11   The groups Command

The *groups* command lists all groups that the user is a member of.

> **$ groups**
> users other

The first group listed is the primary group for the user, all others are secondary (or supplementary) groups. Consult Chapter 12 "Users and Groups" for further details.

1.3.12   The uname Command

The *uname* command produces basic information about the system. Without any options, this command displays the operating system name only. You can use the –a option to get more information.

> **$ uname**
> HP-UX
> **$ uname –a**
> HP-UX hp01 B.11.31 U 9000/800 3937816409 unlimited-user license

where:

HP-UX	operating system name
hp01	hostname
B.11.31	OE release identifier
U	current version level of the OE
9000/800	machine hardware type. It would be "ia64" for Itanium-processor based systems
3937816409	system's host id
unlimited-user license	OE license level

Try running *uname* with –l, –r, –n, –m, –s, –v and –i options. Each of these options displays specific information.

1.3.13   The hostname Command

The *hostname* command displays the system name.

> **$ hostname**
> hp01

1.3.14   The model and getconf Commands

The *model* and *getconf* commands display hardware model of the system. The following displays output of the two commands when executed on an rp7410 server:

```
$ model
$ getconf MACHINE_MODEL
9000/800/rp7410
```

1.3.15   The machinfo Command

The *machinfo* (machine information) command prints information about the system. The following displays the output when the command is invoked on an rp7410 server:

```
# machinfo
CPU info:
  4 PA-RISC 8700/8750 processors (750 MHz, 1.5 MB)
      CPU version 5
Memory:                    8184 MB (7.99 GB)
Firmware info:
  Firmware revision:       17.8
  IPMI is not supported on this system
.Platform info:
  Model:                   "9000/800/rp7410"
  Machine ID number:       Z3e109d8aeab64f59
  Machine serial number:   USE43388DW
OS info:
  Nodename:                hp01
  Release:                 HP-UX B.11.31
  Version:                 U (unlimited-user license)
  Machine:                 9000/800
  ID Number:               3937816409
  vmunix _release_version:
 _release_version:
  @(#) $Revision: vmunix:  B.11.31_LR FLAVOR=perf
```

1.3.16   The clear Command

The *clear* command clears the terminal screen and places the cursor at the beginning of the screen.

```
$ clear
```

 You must have proper terminal type set in order for this command to produce desired results.

1.3.17   The date Command

The *date* command displays the current system date and time. You can also use this command to modify system date and time.

```
$ date
Thu Apr 10 14:45:12 EDT 2008
```

1.3.18   The cal Command

The *cal* (calendar) command displays calendar for the current month.

```
$ cal
            April 2008
   S    M   TU   W   TH    F    S
             1    2    3    4    5
   6    7    8    9   10   11   12
  13   14   15   16   17   18   19
  20   21   22   23   24   25   26
  27   28   29   30
```

1.3.19   The uptime Command

The *uptime* command shows a system's current time, how long it has been up for, number of users currently logged in and average number of processes over the past 1, 5 and 15 minutes. For example, output of the *uptime* command below shows that the current system time is 9:19am, system has been up for 1 day, 11 hours and 29 minutes, there is currently one user logged in, and average number of processes over the past 1, 5 and 15 minutes is 0.56, 0.54 and 0.54, respectively.

```
$ uptime
9:19am  up 1 day, 11:29,  1 user,  load average: 0.56, 0.54, 0.54
```

1.3.20   The banner Command

The *banner* command prints a banner of the text passed to it as an argument. For example, the following command will print the banner "HP-UX" on the screen:

```
$ banner HP-UX
#    # #####        #     # #    #
#    # #    #       #     # #    #
#    # #    #       #     # # ##
#### ##### #### #   #    #
#    # #    #       #     # # ##
#    # #    #       #     # # #  #
#    # #    #      ####  #    #
```

1.3.21   The which and whence Commands

When the name of a command is specified with either the *which* or the *whence* command, it shows the absolute path of the command that is executed if run without using the absolute path. For example:

```
$ which cat
$ whence cat
/usr/bin/cat
```

The system returns */usr/bin/cat*, which means that the *cat* command is executed from */usr/bin* directory if you run it without specifying its full path.

1.3.22   The whereis Command

When a command name is specified with the *whereis* command, it gives full pathnames of the source, the command and its manual page sections. For example:

$ whereis cat
cat: /sbin/cat /usr/bin/cat /usr/share/man/man1.Z/cat.1

1.3.23   The wc Command

The *wc* (word count) command displays number of lines, words and characters contained in a text file. For example, when you run this command on the */etc/profile* file, you will see output similar to the following:

$ wc /etc/profile
129   383   2459   /etc/profile

where:

the 1st column shows the number of lines in */etc/profile* (129)
the 2nd column shows the number of words in */etc/profile* (383)
the 3rd column shows the number of characters in */etc/profile* (2459)
the 4th column shows the file name (*/etc/profile*)

You can use the options listed in Table 1-3 to obtain desired output.

Option	Action
–l	Prints line count.
–w	Prints word count.
–c	Prints byte count.
–m	Prints character count.

Table 1-3 *wc* Command Options

The following example displays only the number of lines in */etc/profile*:

$ wc –l /etc/profile
129   /etc/profile

Try running *wc* with other options and view the results.

1.3.24   The diff Command

The *diff* (difference) command enables a user to find differences between contents of text files and prints line-by-line differences in the output. Two options are commonly used: –i to ignore letter case and –c to produce a list of differences in three sections.

For example, assume that you have two text files, *testfile1* and *testfile2*, with the following contents:

testfile1	testfile2
apple	apple
pear	tomato
mango	guava
tomato	mango
guava	banana

When the –c option is used with the *diff* command to find differences, the results are displayed in three sections:

```
$ diff –c testfile1 testfile2
*** testfile1  Tue Nov 29 16:20:18 2005
--- testfile2   Tue Nov 29 16:20:37 2005
***************
*** 1,5 ****
  apple
- pear
- mango
  tomato
  guava
--- 1,5 ----
  apple
  tomato
  guava
+ mango
+ banana
```

The first section shows the file names being compared along with time stamps on them and some fifteen asterisk (*) characters to mark the end of this section.

The second section tells the number of lines in *testfile1* that differs from *testfile2* and the total number of lines *testfile1* contains. Then actual line entries from *testfile1* are printed. Each line that differs from *testfile2* is preceded by the (–) symbol.

The third section tells the number of lines in *testfile2* that differs from *testfile1* and the total number of lines *testfile2* contains. Then actual line entries from *testfile2* are printed. Each line that differs from *testfile1* is preceded by the (+) symbol.

In short, to make the contents of the two files identical, you need to remove entries for pear and mango from *testfile1* and append entries for mango and banana to *testfile1*.

You can also use the *diff* command to find differences in directory contents. The syntax is the same.

1.3.25   The write Command

The *write* command allows you to send a message to another logged in user as listed in the */etc/utmps* file. It is a uni-directional user communication tool. For example, if you are logged in as *user1* and you wish to send a message to *user2*, type the following on your terminal screen:

$ write user2

How are you, user2?
```
Ctrl+d
```

The message will be displayed on *user2*'s terminal screen after pressing the `Enter` key followed by `Ctrl+d`. Before *user2* gets any messages on screen, *user2* needs to run "*mesg* y" command to enable receiving messages from other parties.

1.3.26   The talk Command

The *talk* command initiates a screen-oriented two-way communication session between users. The users can be on the same or on different systems. For example, if you are logged in as *user1* and want to initiate a talk session with *user2* who is also logged on to the same system, type the following at your terminal screen:

$ talk user2

user2 will see the invite on his screen requesting to issue the *talk* command with specified arguments. After *user2* enters the *talk* command, the terminal screens of both users will split into two sections and a two-way interactive communication session is established. Either user may press `Ctrl+d` to disconnect. Before *user2* sees any messages on his screen, he needs to run "*mesg* y" command on his screen to enable receiving messages from other parties.

1.3.27   The wall Command

The *wall* command is used to broadcast a message to either all logged in users on the system or all logged in users that are members of a particular group.

To broadcast a message to all logged in users, type the *wall* command and hit the `Enter` key. Start typing a message and press `Ctrl+d` when finished to broadcast it.

wall

To broadcast a message to all logged in members of group *users*:

wall –g users

To broadcast a message stored in */tmp/message.out* file to all logged in users:

wall –f /tmp/message.out

1.4   Online Help

While working on the system you require help to understand a command, its usage and options available. HP-UX offers online help via manual (or man) pages. man pages are installed as part of the HP-UX OE installation, and provide detailed information on commands, options, usage, system configuration files, their syntax, etc.

Use the *man* command to view help on a command. The following example shows how to check man pages for the *passwd* command:

```
$ man passwd
passwd(1)                                        passwd(1)
NAME
     passwd - change login password and associated attributes
SYNOPSIS
     passwd [name]
     passwd -r files [-F file] [name]
     passwd -r files [-e [shell]] [-gh] [name]
     passwd -r files -s [-a]
     passwd -r files -s [name]
     passwd -r files [-d|-l] [-f] [-n min] [-w warn] [-x max] name
     passwd -r nis [-e [shell]] [-gh] [name]
     passwd -r dce [-e [shell]] [-gh] [name]
Standard input
```

While you are in man pages, some common keys listed in Table 1-4 help you navigate efficiently.

Key	Action
Spacebar or f	Moves forward one page.
Enter	Moves forward one line.
b	Moves backward one page.
d / u	Moves down / up half a page.
g / G	Moves to the beginning / end of the man pages.
:f	Displays line number and bytes being viewed.
q	Quits the man pages.
/pattern	Searches forward for the specified pattern.
?pattern	Searches backward for the specified pattern.
n / N	Finds the next / previous occurrence of a pattern.
h	Gives help on navigational keys.

Table 1-4 Navigating within *man* Pages

1.4.1   man Sections

There are several sections within man pages. For example, section 1M refers to system administration commands, section 4 refers to system configuration files and so on. The default is section 1. A list of key sections is presented in Table 1-5 along with a brief description.

Section	Information
1	User commands.
1M	System administration commands.
2	UNIX and C language system calls.
3	C language library routines.
4	File formats and conventions for configuration files.
5	Miscellaneous.
7	Device special files.
9	General information and glossary.

Table 1-5 *man* Sections

To look for information on a configuration file */etc/passwd*, do the following:

$ man 4 passwd

passwd(4)   passwd(4)
NAME
   passwd - password file
SYNOPSIS
   #include <pwd.h>
DESCRIPTION
   /etc/passwd contains the following information for each user:
      + login name
      + encrypted password
      + numerical user ID
      + numerical group ID
      + reserved gecos ID
      + initial working directory
      + program to use as shell
   This is an ASCII file. Each field within each user's entry is
   separated from the next by a colon. Each user is separated from the
   next by a newline. This file resides in the /etc directory. It can
   and does have general read permission and can be used, for example, to
   map numerical user IDs to names.
Standard input

1.4.2   Searching by Keyword

Sometimes you need to use a command but you do not know the name of it. HP-UX allows you to perform keyword search on all available man pages. Use the –k option with the *man* command and specify a keyword. The *man* command lists names of all man pages that contain the specified keyword. In order to use this feature, you must run a utility called *catman* one time on the system to generate a database to enable this feature. Specify the –w option when running the command. The database is created in */usr/share/lib* directory by the name *whatis*.

 # catman –w
$ man –k password

keytab (1m)   - A dcecp object that manages server passwords on DCE hosts
pam_dce("5")   - authentication, account, and password management PAM functions for DCE
passwd_export ("1m")   - Creates local password and group files
passwd_import ("1m")   - Creates registry database entries based on information in UNIX group and
password files
. . . .

When you run *man* to look at manual pages, it looks for help in several man page directories and displays requested information. These directory paths are defined in a variable called MANPATH. Run the following to see all directories where the *man* command searches for help:

$ echo $MANPATH

/usr/share/man/%L:/usr/share/man:/usr/contrib/man/%L:/usr/contrib/man:/usr/local/man/%L:/usr/local/man:/opt/ldapux/share/man/%L:/opt/ldapux/share/man:/opt/ipf/man:/opt/ldapux/ypldapd/man:/opt/samba/man:/opt/samba/WTEC_Support_Tools/man:/opt/samba/cfsm_man:/opt/cifsclient/share/man:/opt/rdma/share/man:/opt/openssl/man:/opt/openssl/prngd/man:/opt/wbem/share/man:/opt/hpsmdb/pgsql/man:/opt/ssh/share/man:/opt/mx/share/man/%L:/opt/mx/share/man:/opt/graphics/common/man:/opt/amgr/man:/opt/amgr/man/%L:/opt/sec_mgmt/share/man:/usr/dt/share/man:/opt/drd/share/man/%L:/opt/drd/share/man:/opt/dsau/man:/opt/resmon/share/man/%L:/opt/resmon/share/man:/opt/gnome/man:/opt/perf/man/%L:/opt/perf/man:/opt/ignite/share/man/%L:/opt/ignite/share/man:/usr/contrib/kwdb/share/man:/opt/perl_32/man:/opt/perl_64/man:/opt/prm/man/%L:/opt/prm/man:/opt/sfmdb/pgsql/man:/opt/sfm/share/man:/opt/swm/share/man/%L:/opt/swm/share/man:/opt/sec_mgmt/share/man/%L:/opt/spb/share/man:/opt/swa/share/man/%L:/opt/swa/share/man:/opt/VRTS/man:/opt/gwlm/man/%L:/opt/gwlm/man

Summary

In this chapter basics of UNIX and HP-UX was covered. You were provided with an overview of the structure and components that make up the core of the UNIX system. You looked at some of the common features associated with HP-UX. You learned how to login to a system using various methods.

You saw how to construct a command; then you executed a number of basic HP-UX commands. These commands displayed information such as directory path, directory and file listing, directory navigation, user login names, logged in user information, user identification information, basic system and hardware information and so on.

Finally, you learned how to access online help on commands and system configuration files. You performed keyword search on all available man pages that listed commands and configuration files whose manual pages contained the keyword.

## 02

Files and Directories

This chapter covers the following major topics:

✓ HP-UX directory structure
✓ Static and dynamic directories
✓ Access files using absolute and relative pathnames
✓ Types of files
✓ Naming convention for files and directories
✓ Manage and manipulate files and directories including creating, listing, displaying, copying, moving, renaming and removing them
✓ Search for text within files
✓ Search for files in the directory system
✓ Sort contents of text files
✓ Create file and directory links

2.1   File System Tree

HP-UX files are organized in a logical fashion to ease administration. This logical division of files is maintained in hundreds of directories. These directories reside in larger containers called *file systems*.

The HP-UX file system structure is like an inverted tree with the root of the tree at the top and branches and leaves at the bottom. The top-level is referred to as *root* and represented by the forward slash (/) character. This is the point where the entire file system structure is ultimately connected to.

Seven file systems are created, by default, when HP-UX is installed on a machine. These are */, /stand, /var, /usr, /tmp, /opt* and */home*. The main directories under the root and other file systems are shown in Figure 2-1. Some of these directories hold *static* data while others contain *dynamic* (or *variable*) information. The static data refers to file contents that are not usually modified. The dynamic or variable data refers to file contents that are modified as required. Static directories usually contain commands, library routines, kernel files, device special files, etc. while dynamic directories hold log files, status files, configuration files, temporary files, etc. A brief description of some of the directories is provided in the following sub-sections.

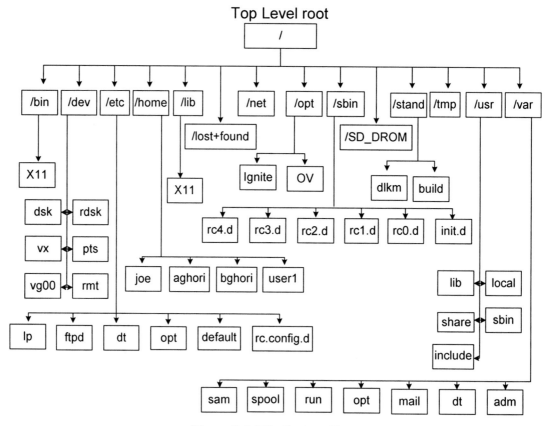

Figure 2-1 File System Tree

2.1.1   The Root File System (/)

The *root* file system contains many higher-level directories with each holding specific information. Some of the more important directories under the root are:

The Binary Directory (/bin)

The *binary* directory contains user executable commands. This directory is linked to */usr/bin* directory and holds static data files.

The *X11* sub-directory under */bin* contains X windows related files.

The Devices Directory (/dev)

The *devices* directory contains hardware device files. UNIX kernel communicates with system hardware devices through corresponding device files that are located here.

There are two types of device files: *character* special device files (a.k.a. *raw* device files) and *block* special device files. The kernel accesses devices using one or both types of device files.

Character devices are accessed in a serial manner, meaning that a stream of bits is transferred during kernel and device communication. Examples of such devices are serial printers, terminals, hard disk devices, tape drives, etc.

Block devices are accessed in a parallel fashion, meaning that data is transferred between the kernel and the device in blocks (parallel) when communication between the two happens. Examples of block devices are hard disk devices, CD/DVD drives, parallel printers, etc.

 Some utilities access hard disk devices as block devices while others access them as character special devices.

Some key sub-directories under */dev* are: *dsk, disk, rdsk, rdisk, rmt, rtape, pts* and *vg00*. These sub-directories contain block device files for disks including hard disks and CD/DVD drives (*dsk* and *rdisk*), character device files for hard disks and CD/DVD drives (*rdsk* and *rdisk*), tape device files (*rmt* and *rtape*), pseudo terminal session device files (*pts*) and root volume group device files (*vg00*).

The */dev* directory holds static data files.

The Library Directory (/lib)

The *library* directory contains shared library files required by programs. It contains sub-directories that hold library routines. The */lib* directory can also be accessed using */usr/lib* directory path since both are linked and point to identical information.

In Figure 2-1, *X11* sub-directory under */lib* refers to library files used by X Window system.

The */lib* directory holds static data files.

The System Binary Directory (/sbin)

Most commands required at system boot are located in the *system binary* directory. In addition, most commands that require *root* privileges to run are also located in this directory. This directory

---

does not contain commands intended for regular users (although they still can run a few of them) and hence */sbin* is not included in normal users' default search path.

In Figure 2-1, *init.d, rc0.d, rc1.d, rc2.d, rc3.d* and *rc4.d* refer to directories where system boot and shutdown scripts are located. The contents of these directories are explained in detail in Chapter 16 "HP-UX Shutdown and Startup".

The */sbin* directory holds static data files.

The Etcetera Directory (/etc)

The *etcetera* directory holds most system configuration files. Some of the more common sub-directories under */etc* are: *rc.config.d, default, opt, dt, ftpd, lp, lvmconf, mail, sam* (smh), *skel* and *vx*. These sub-directories contain, in that sequence, configuration files for system startup scripts, system operations and user account defaults, additional software installed on the machine, CDE desktop environment, file transfer, printers, HP Logical Volume Manager, mail subsystem, System Administration Manager (System Management Homepage), user profile templates and Veritas volume manager.

The */etc* directory contains dynamic data files.

The lost+found Directory (/lost+found)

This directory is used to hold files that become orphan after a system crash. An *orphan* file is a file that has lost its name. A detailed discussion on orphan files is covered in Chapter 14 "File Systems".

If the *lost+found* directory is deleted, it should be re-created with the *mklost+found* command as follows:

 # mklost+found
creating slots...
removing dummy files...
done

This directory is automatically created at the file system creation time.

The /net Directory

If AutoFS is used to mount NFS file systems using a special map, all available NFS file systems on the network are mounted by default beneath */net* under their corresponding hostnames. AutoFS and the special map are explained in detail in Chapter 29 "AutoFS".

2.1.2   The Kernel File System (/stand)

The kernel files are located in the */stand* file system. Files that contain HP-UX kernel code, boot device information, kernel parameter and module information, etc. are stored here.

This directory is only altered when an update to the kernel is performed. More information is provided in Chapter 17 "Kernel Management".

2.1.3   The Variable File System (/var)

/var contains data that frequently change while the system is up and running. Files holding log, status, spool and other dynamic data are typically located in this file system.

Some common sub-directories under */var* are briefly discussed below:

/var/adm: Most system log files are located here. This directory contains system logs, su logs, user logs, mail logs, etc.
/var/dt: This directory contains CDE related log files.
/var/mail: This is the location for user mailboxes.
/var/opt: For additional software installed in */opt* file system, this directory contains log, status and other variable data files for that software.
/var/spool: Directories that hold print jobs, cron jobs, email messages and other queued work before being sent to their proper destination are located here.
/var/tmp: Large temporary files or temporary files that need to exist for extended periods of time than what is allowed in */tmp* are stored here. These files survive across system reboots and are not automatically deleted.

2.1.4   The UNIX System Resources File System (/usr)

This file system contains general files related to the system. Usually, this file system occupies more space than others on the system.

Some of the more important sub-directories under */usr* are briefly discussed below:

/usr/sbin: Additional system administration commands.
/usr/local: System administrator repository to keep commands, and tools that they download from the web or obtain elsewhere. These commands and tools are not generally included with original HP-UX OE distributions. In particular, */usr/local/bin* holds executable files, */usr/local/etc* contains their configuration files and */usr/local/man* holds related man pages.
/usr/include: Header files for the C language.
/usr/share: Directory location for man pages, documentation, etc. that may be shared on multi-vendor UNIX platforms with heterogeneous hardware architectures.
/usr/lib: Libraries pertaining to programming sub-routines.

2.1.5   The Temporary File System (/tmp)

This file system is a repository for temporary files. Many programs create temporary files as they run. Some programs delete the temporary files that they create after they are finished, while others do not. These files do not survive across system reboots and are removed.

2.1.6   The Optional File System (/opt)

This file system typically holds additional software installed on the system. A sub-directory is created for each installed software.

In Figure 2-1, two sub-directories are shown under */opt*. One contains HP OpenView software binaries and the other HP Ignite-UX binaries.

2.1.7   The Home File System (/home)

This file system is designed to hold user *home* directories. Each user account is assigned a home directory for keeping personal files. Each home directory is owned by the user the directory is assigned to. No other user usually has access to other user's home directory.

In Figure 2-1, users *joe, aghori, bghori* and *user1* have their home directories located under */home*.

The directories discussed thus far are HP-UX system related. It is highly recommended that you create separate file systems for data and applications. A detailed discussion on file systems and how to create and use them is covered in Chapter 14 "File Systems".

2.2   Absolute and Relative Paths

A *path* is like a road map which shows how to get from one place in the directory tree to another. It uniquely identifies a particular file or directory by its absolute or relative location in the directory structure.

At any given time, you are located in one directory within the directory tree, which is referred to as your *present* (or *current*) working directory. When you login to the system, the *current directory* is set to your home directory by default. Use the *pwd* command to verify after you are in.

2.2.1   Absolute Path

An *absolute path* (a.k.a. *full path* or *fully qualified path*) points to a file or directory in relation to root (/). An absolute path must always start with a forward slash (/) character. The *pwd* command displays your current location in the tree.

> **$ pwd**
> /home/user1/dir1/scripts

This example shows that you are in */home/user1/dir1/scripts* directory. This represents the full path with respect to root (/).

2.2.2   Relative Path

A *relative path* points to a file or directory in relation to your current location in the directory tree. A relative path never begins with the forward slash (/) character; it always begins with one of the following three ways:

With a period: A period represents the current working directory. For example, if you are located in */home/user1/dir1/scripts* directory and wish to run a script *file1* from this directory, you would type:

> **./file1**

With a pair of periods: A pair of period characters represents the parent directory in relation to your current working directory. A parent directory is one level higher than the current working directory.

To go back one level up to parent directory, type:

> **$ cd ..**

With a sub-directory name: Let us say you are currently in */home/user1* directory and you want to go to the *scripts* sub-directory under *dir1*. Do the following:

> **$ cd dir1/scripts**

2.3   File Types

HP-UX supports several different types of files. Some of the common file types are regular files, directory files, executable files, symbolic link files, device special files, named pipe files and socket files, and are described in the following sub-sections.

2.3.1   Regular Files

Regular files may contain text or binary data. These files can be shell scripts or commands. When you do an *ll* on a directory, all line entries for files in the output that begin with " – " represent regular files.

> **$ ll /bin**

```
. . . . . . . .
-r-xr-xr-x  2 bin    bin    36864   May 23 2007    /bin/w
-r-xr-xr-x  1 bin    bin      158   Feb 15 2007    /bin/wait
-r-xr-xr-x  1 bin    bin    28672   Feb 15 2007    /bin/wc
-r-xr-xr-x  1 bin    bin    73728   Jan 12  2007   /bin/wdutil
-r-xr-xr-x  1 bin    bin    28672   Feb 15 2007    /bin/what
-r-xr-xr-x  1 bin    bin    32768   Feb 15 2007    /bin/whereis
-r-xr-xr-x  1 bin    bin      654   Feb 15 2007    /bin/which
-r-xr-xr-x  1 bin    bin    53248   Feb 15 2007    /bin/who
-r-xr-xr-x  1 bin    bin    20480   Feb 15 2007    /bin/whoami
-r-xr-xr-x  1 bin    bin    28672   Feb 15 2007    /bin/whois
-r-xr-xr-x  1 bin    bin    28672   Feb 15 2007    /bin/write
```

You can use the *file* command to determine the type of a file. For example, the following shows that */home/user1/.profile* contains ascii text:

> **$ file /home/user1/.profile**
> /home/user1/.profile: ascii text

2.3.2   Directory Files

Directories are logical containers that hold files and sub-directories. Do an *ll* on the root (/) directory and the output similar to the following will be displayed:

> **$ ll /**

```
dr-xr-xr-x   14   bin    bin    8192   Nov 16 16:11   dev
dr-xr-xr-x   36   bin    bin    8192   Nov 16 16:17   etc
drwxr-xr-x    5   root   root     96   Nov 24 14:34   home
drwxr-xr-x    2   root   root     96   Mar 29 2005    lost+found
dr-xr-xr-x    1   root   root    512   Nov 16 16:10   net
dr-xr-xr-x   68   bin    bin    8192   Nov 24 14:09   opt
```

dr-xr-xr-x	13	bin	bin	8192	May 6 2005	sbin
dr-xr-xr-x	11	bin	bin	1024	Nov 16 16:11	stand
drwxrwxrwx	23	bin	bin	8192	Nov 24 16:30	tmp
dr-xr-xr-x	25	bin	bin	8192	Apr 5 2005	usr
dr-xr-xr-x	34	bin	bin	8192	May 20 2005	var

The letter "d" at the beginning of each line entry indicates a directory. Use the *file* command to determine the type. For example:

$ file /home/user1
/home/user1:   directory

2.3.3   Executable Files

Executable files could be commands or shell scripts. In other words, any file that can be run is an executable file. A file that has an "x" in the 4th, 7th or the 10th field in the output of the *ll* command is executable.

$ ll /bin

. . . .
-r-xr-xr-x	2 bin	bin	36864	May 23 2007	/bin/w
-r-xr-xr-x	1 bin	bin	158	Feb 15 2007	/bin/wait
-r-xr-xr-x	1 bin	bin	28672	Feb 15 2007	/bin/wc
-r-xr-xr-x	1 bin	bin	73728	Jan 12 2007	/bin/wdutil
-r-xr-xr-x	1 bin	bin	28672	Feb 15 2007	/bin/what
-r-xr-xr-x	1 bin	bin	32768	Feb 15 2007	/bin/whereis
-r-xr-xr-x	1 bin	bin	654	Feb 15 2007	/bin/which
-r-xr-xr-x	1 bin	bin	53248	Feb 15 2007	/bin/who
-r-xr-xr-x	1 bin	bin	20480	Feb 15 2007	/bin/whoami
-r-xr-xr-x	1 bin	bin	28672	Feb 15 2007	/bin/whois
-r-xr-xr-x	1 bin	bin	28672	Feb 15 2007	/bin/write

Use the *file* command to identify the type. For example:

$ file /bin/who
/bin/who: PA-RISC1.1 shared executable dynamically linked -not stripped dynamically linked

2.3.4   Symbolic Link Files

A *symbolic link* (or *soft link* or simply *symlink*) may be considered as a shortcut to another file or directory. When you do an *ll* on a symbolically linked file or directory, you will notice two things. One, the line entry begins with the letter "l" and two, there is an arrow pointing to the linked file or directory. For example:

$ ll /bin
lrwxr-xr-x 1 bin   bin   8   Apr 8 09:07   /bin -> /usr/bin

The *file* command does not tell if the specified file or directory is linked, rather, it tells you the type based on contents.

$ file /bin
/bin: directory

2.3.5   Device Special Files (DSFs)

Each piece of hardware in the system has an associated file used by the kernel to communicate with it. This type of file is called a *Device Special File* (DSF). There are two types of DSFs: *character* (or *raw*) DSFs and *block* DSFs. The following outputs from the *ll* command display them:

$ ll /dev/disk

brw-r-----	1 bin	sys	1	0x000000	Apr 8 08:59	disk2
brw-r-----	1 bin	sys	1	0x000009	Apr 9 09:11	disk22
brw-r-----	1 bin	sys	1	0x00000a	Apr 9 09:11	disk23
brw-r-----	1 bin	sys	1	0x00000b	Apr 9 09:11	disk24
brw-r-----	1 bin	sys	1	0x00000c	Apr 9 09:11	disk25
brw-r-----	1 bin	sys	1	0x000001	Apr 8 08:59	disk3
brw-r-----	1 bin	sys	1	0x000006	Apr 8 10:26	disk5

$ ll /dev/dsk

brw-r-----	1 bin	sys	31	0x006000	Apr 8 08:59	c0t6d0
brw-r-----	1 bin	sys	31	0x0a0000	Apr 9 09:11	c10t0d0
brw-r-----	1 bin	sys	31	0x0a0100	Apr 9 09:11	c10t0d1
brw-r-----	1 bin	sys	31	0x0a0200	Apr 9 09:11	c10t0d2
brw-r-----	1 bin	sys	31	0x0a0300	Apr 9 09:11	c10t0d3
brw-r-----	1 bin	sys	31	0x0c0000	Apr 9 09:11	c12t0d0
brw-r-----	1 bin	sys	31	0x0c0100	Apr 9 09:11	c12t0d1
brw-r-----	1 bin	sys	31	0x0c0200	Apr 9 09:11	c12t0d2
brw-r-----	1 bin	sys	31	0x0c0300	Apr 9 09:11	c12t0d3

$ ll /dev/rdisk

crw-r-----	1 bin	sys	11	0x000000	Apr 8 09:07	disk2
crw-r-----	1 bin	sys	11	0x000009	Apr 9 09:11	disk22
crw-r-----	1 bin	sys	11	0x00000a	Apr 9 09:11	disk23
crw-r-----	1 bin	sys	11	0x00000b	Apr 9 09:11	disk24
crw-r-----	1 bin	sys	11	0x00000c	Apr 9 09:11	disk25
crw-r-----	1 bin	sys	11	0x000001	Apr 8 08:59	disk3
crw-r-----	1 bin	sys	11	0x000006	Apr 8 10:26	disk5

$ ll /dev/rdsk

crw-r-----	1 bin	sys	188	0x006000	Apr 8 08:59	c0t6d0
crw-r-----	1 bin	sys	188	0x0a0000	Apr 9 09:11	c10t0d0
crw-r-----	1 bin	sys	188	0x0a0100	Apr 9 09:11	c10t0d1
crw-r-----	1 bin	sys	188	0x0a0200	Apr 9 09:11	c10t0d2
crw-r-----	1 bin	sys	188	0x0a0300	Apr 9 09:11	c10t0d3
crw-r-----	1 bin	sys	188	0x0c0000	Apr 9 09:11	c12t0d0
crw-r-----	1 bin	sys	188	0x0c0100	Apr 9 09:11	c12t0d1
crw-r-----	1 bin	sys	188	0x0c0200	Apr 9 09:11	c12t0d2
crw-r-----	1 bin	sys	188	0x0c0300	Apr 9 09:11	c12t0d3

The first character in each line entry tells if the file is block or character special. A "b" denotes a block and a "c" stands for character DSF. The *file* command shows their type as follows:

```
$ file /dev/disk/disk2
/dev/rdisk/disk2:     character special (11/0)
$ file /dev/rdisk/disk2
/dev/disk/disk2:      block special (1/0)
$ file /dev/dsk/c0t6d0
/dev/rdsk/c0t6d0:     character special (188/24576)
$ file /dev/rdsk/c0t6d0
/dev/dsk/c0t6d0:      block special (31/24576)
```

2.3.6   Named Pipe Files

A *named pipe* allows two unrelated processes running on the same machine or on two different machines to communicate with each other and exchange data. Named pipes are uni-directional. They are also referred to as FIFO because they use *First In First Out* mechanism. Named pipes make *Inter Process Communication* (IPC) possible. The output of the *ll* command shows a "p" (highlighted) as the first character in each line entry that corresponds to a named pipe file.

```
# ll /etc/opt/resmon/pipe
prw-------  1 root    root        0  Apr 10 15:37      1533300606
prw-------  1 root    root        0  Apr 10 12:53      1573980217
prw-------  1 root    root        0  Apr  8 11:56      1761189933
prw-------  1 root    root        0  Apr 10 15:37      1885281202
prw-------  1 root    root        0  Apr 10 15:37      1998375097
```

IPC allows processes to communicate directly with each other. They tell each other how to act by sharing parts of their virtual memory address space and then reading and writing data stored in that shared virtual memory.

The *file* command shows the type of named pipe file as fifo. See the following example:

```
$ file /etc/opt/resmon/pipe/1533300606
/etc/opt/resmon/pipe/1533300606:      fifo
```

2.3.7   Socket Files

A *socket* is a named pipe that works in both directions. In other words, a socket is a two-way named pipe. It is also a type of IPC. Sockets are used by client/server programs. Notice an "s" (highlighted) as the first character in the output of the *ll* command below for each socket file:

```
$ ll /var/spool/sockets/pwgr
srwxrwxrwx  1 root    mail        0  Apr 10 09:41      client1446
srwxrwxrwx  1 root    root        0  Apr 10 09:44      client1554
srwxrwxrwx  1 root    root        0  Apr 10 09:44      client1556
srwxrwxrwx  1 root    root        0  Apr 10 09:44      client1557
```

The *file* command shows the type of socket file as follows:

```
$ file /var/spool/sockets/pwgr/client1446
/var/spool/sockets/pwgr/client1446:    socket
```

2.4   File and Directory Operations

This section discusses file and directory naming rules and describes various operations on files and directories that users perform. These operations include creating, listing, displaying contents of, copying, moving, renaming and deleting files and directories.

2.4.1   File and Directory Naming Convention

Files and directories are assigned names when they are created. There are certain rules, listed below, that you should remember and follow while assigning names. A file or directory name:

✓ Can contain a maximum of 255 alphanumeric characters (letters and numbers).
✓ Can contain non-alphanumeric characters such as underscore (_), hyphen (–), space and period (.).
✓ Should not include special characters such as asterisk (*), question mark (?), tilde (~), ampersand (&), pipe (|), double quotes ("), single back quote ('), single forward quote (`), semi-colon (;), redirection symbols (< and >) and dollar sign ($). These characters hold special meaning to the shell.
✓ May or may not have an extension. Some users prefer using extensions, others do not.

2.4.2   Creating Files and Directories

Files can be created in multiple ways, however there is only one command to create directories.

Creating Files Using the *touch* Command

The *touch* command creates an empty file. If the file already exists, the time stamp on it is updated with the current system date and time. Do the following as *user1*:

```
$ cd
$ touch file1
$ ll file1
-rw-rw-rw-  1 user1    users       0 Nov 25 15:30      file1
```

As indicated in the output, the fifth field is 0 "zero" meaning that *file1* is created with zero bytes. Now, if you run the command again on *file1* you will notice that the time stamp is updated.

```
$ touch file1
$ ll file1
-rw-rw-rw-  1 user1    users       0 Nov 26 11:13      file1
```

Creating Files Using the *cat* Command

The *cat* command allows you to create short text files.

```
$ cat > newfile
```

Nothing will be displayed when you execute this command. The system expects you to input something. Press Ctrl+d when done to save what you have typed to a file called *newfile*.

Creating Files Using the *vi* Command

The *vi* command invokes the vi editor. System users and administrators frequently use the vi editor to create and modify text files.

Refer to Chapter 04 "The vi Editor and Text Processors" on usage details.

Creating Directories Using the *mkdir* Command

The *mkdir* command is used to create directories. The following example shows you how to create a new directory by the name *scripts1* in *user1*'s home directory (*/home/user1*):

```
$ cd
$ pwd
/home/user1
$ mkdir scripts1
```

You must have appropriate permissions to create a directory, otherwise, you will get an error message complaining about lack of permissions.

You can create a hierarchy of sub-directories using the *mkdir* command with the –p option. In the following example, *mkdir* creates a directory *scripts2* in *user1*'s home directory. At the same time, it creates a directory *perl* as a sub-directory of *scripts2* and a sub-directory *perl5* under *perl*.

```
$ mkdir –p scripts2/perl/perl5
```

2.4.3 Listing Files and Directories

To list files and directories, use the *ls* or *ll* command. The following example runs *ll* as *user1* in *user1*'s home directory:

```
$ ll
total 608
-rw-rw-rw-  1    user1    users      1089 Feb  4 22:56    file1
-rw-rw-rw-  1    user1    users      2426 Feb  4 22:56    file2
-rw-rw-rw-  1    user1    users    270336 Feb  4 22:57    file3
-rw-rw-rw-  1    user1    users        11 Feb  4 22:57    file4
-rw-rw-rw-  1    user1    users        67 Feb  4 22:57    file5
-rw-rw-rw-  1    user1    users        21 Feb  4 22:57    file6
drwxrwxrwx 2    user1    users        96 Feb  4 22:55    scripts
drwxrwxrwx 2    user1    users        96 Feb  4 22:55    scripts1
drwxrwxrwx 2    user1    users        96 Feb  4 22:55    scripts2
drwxrwxrwx 2    user1    users        96 Feb  4 22:55    subdir1
```

Notice that there are nine columns in the output. These columns contain:

Column 1: The 1st character tells the type of file. The next 9 characters indicate permissions. File permissions are explained at length in Chapter 03 "File and Directory Permissions".
Column 2: Displays how many links the file or the directory has.

Column 3: Shows owner name of the file or directory.

Column 4: Displays group name that the owner of the file or directory belongs to.

Column 5: Gives file size in bytes. For directories, this number reflects number of blocks being used by the directory to hold information about its contents.

Columns 6, 7 and 8: List month, day of the month and time the file or directory was created or last accessed/modified.

Column 9: Name of the file or directory.

2.4.4   Displaying File Contents

There are several commands that HP-UX offers to display file contents. Directory contents are simply the files and sub-directories within it. Use the *ll, ls* or the *lc* command to view directory contents as explained earlier.

The *cat, more, pg, head, tail, view, vi* and the *strings* commands are available to display file contents. Following text explains each one of them.

Using the *cat* Command

The *cat* command displays the contents of a text file. In the example below, */home/user1/.profile* is displayed using the *cat* command:

$ cat /home/user1/.profile

```
. . . . . . . .
# Set up the terminal:
     if [ "$TERM" = "" ]
     then
             eval ` tset -s -Q -m ':?hp' `
     else
             eval ` tset -s -Q `
     fi
     stty erase "^H" kill "^U" intr "^C" eof "^D"
     stty hupcl ixon ixoff
     tabs

# NOTE: '.' is added to $PATH for compatibility reasons only. This
#       default will be changed in a future release. If "." is not
#       needed for compatibility it is better to omit this line.
#       Please edit .profile according to your site requirements.

# Set up the search paths:
     PATH=$PATH:.

# Set up the shell environment:
     set -u
     trap "echo 'logout'" 0

# Set up the shell variables:
     EDITOR=vi
     export EDITOR
```

Using the *more* Command

The *more* command displays the contents of a long text file one page at a time. In the example below, */etc/profile* is shown with the *more* command. Notice that the *more* command shows the percentage of the file being displayed in the last line.

$ more /etc/profile

```
# @(#)B.11.31_LR

# Default (example of) system-wide profile file (/usr/bin/sh initialization).
# This should be kept to the bare minimum every user needs.

# Ignore HUP, INT, QUIT now.

    trap "" 1 2 3

# Set the default paths - Do NOT modify these.
# Modify the variables through /etc/PATH and /etc/MANPATH

        PATH=/usr/bin:/usr/ccs/bin:/usr/contrib/bin
        MANPATH=/usr/share/man:/usr/contrib/man:/usr/local/man

# Insure PATH contains either /usr/bin or /sbin (if /usr/bin is not available).

    if [ ! -d /usr/sbin ]
    then
        PATH=$PATH:/sbin

    else   if [ -r /etc/PATH ]
        then
profile (23%)
```

The navigation keys in Table 2-1 would prove helpful when viewing a large file with *more*.

Key	Purpose
Spacebar or f	Scrolls to the next screen.
Enter	Scrolls one line at a time.
b	Scrolls to the previous screen.
d / u	Scrolls down / up half a screen.
h	Displays help.
q	Quits and returns to the shell prompt.
/string	Searches forward for string.
?string	Searches backward for string.
n / N	Finds the next / previous occurrence of string.

Table 2-1 Navigating with *more*

The *more* command is used for viewing man pages by default.

Using the *pg* Command

The *pg* command displays the contents of a file page-by-page as does the *more* command. It shows the colon (:) character at the bottom of the screen.

$ pg /etc/profile

```
# @(#)B.11.31_LR
# Default (example of) system-wide profile file (/usr/bin/sh initialization).
# This should be kept to the bare minimum every user needs.
# Ignore HUP, INT, QUIT now.

    trap "" 1 2 3

# Set the default paths - Do NOT modify these.
# Modify the variables through /etc/PATH and /etc/MANPATH

    PATH=/usr/bin:/usr/ccs/bin:/usr/contrib/bin
    MANPATH=/usr/share/man:/usr/contrib/man:/usr/local/man

# Insure PATH contains either /usr/bin or /sbin (if /usr/bin is not available).

    if [ ! -d /usr/sbin ]
    then
        PATH=$PATH:/sbin
    else   if [ -r /etc/PATH ]
        then
:
```

The navigation keys listed in Table 2-2 would prove helpful when using *pg*. You need to hit the Enter key after every command.

Key	Purpose
Enter	Scrolls to the next screen.
l	Displays the next line.
d	Scrolls down half a page.
.	Redisplays the current page.
h	Displays help.
q	Quits and returns to the shell prompt.
+/string/	Searches forward for the string.
$	Scrolls to the last page.

Table 2-2 Navigating with *pg*

Using the *head* Command

The *head* command displays the first few lines of a text file. By default, the first 10 lines are displayed. The following example displays the first 10 lines from the */etc/profile* file:

$ head /etc/profile

@(#)B.11.31_LR

Default (example of) system-wide profile file (/usr/bin/sh initialization).
This should be kept to the bare minimum every user needs.

Ignore HUP, INT, QUIT now.

    trap "" 1 2 3

Supply a number with the *head* command as an argument to view a different number of lines. The following example displays the first fifteen lines from the */etc/profile* file:

$ head –15 /etc/profile

@(#)B.11.31_LR

Default (example of) system-wide profile file (/usr/bin/sh initialization).
This should be kept to the bare minimum every user needs.

Ignore HUP, INT, QUIT now.

    trap "" 1 2 3

Set the default paths - Do NOT modify these.
Modify the variables through /etc/PATH and /etc/MANPATH

    PATH=/usr/bin:/usr/ccs/bin:/usr/contrib/bin:/usr/contrib/Q4/bin:/opt/perl/bin
    MANPATH=/usr/share/man:/usr/contrib/man:/usr/local/man

Using the *tail* Command

The *tail* command displays the last few lines of a file. By default, the last 10 lines are displayed. The following example shows the last 10 lines from the */etc/profile* file:

$ tail /etc/profile
    echo "Please change the backup tape.\n"
    rm -f /tmp/changetape
  fi

  fi   # if !VUE

Leave defaults in user environment.

    trap 1 2 3

You can specify with *tail* a numerical value to display different set of lines. The following example displays the last 17 lines from */etc/profile*:

$ tail −17 /etc/profile
```
      then news -n
      fi

  # Change the backup tape

      if [ -r /tmp/changetape ]
      then   echo "\007\nYou are the first to log in since backup:"
           echo "Please change the backup tape.\n"
           rm -f /tmp/changetape
      fi

  fi                          # if !VUE

# Leave defaults in user environment.

   trap 1 2 3
```

The *tail* command also allows you to view all lines in a text file starting from the specified line number to the end of the file and skips all previous lines. In the following example, the first 101 lines are skipped from */etc/profile* and the remaining are shown:

$ tail +101 /etc/profile
```
  # Notify if there is mail

      if [ -f /usr/bin/mail ]
      then
           if mail -e
           then   echo "You have mail."
           fi
      fi

  # Notify if there is news

      if [ -f /usr/bin/news ]
      then news -n
      fi

  # Change the backup tape

      if [ -r /tmp/changetape ]
      then   echo "\007\nYou are the first to log in since backup:"
           echo "Please change the backup tape.\n"
           rm -f /tmp/changetape
      fi
```

```
        fi                          # if !VUE
```

Leave defaults in user environment.

```
    trap 1 2 3
```

The *tail* command proves to be very useful when you wish to view a log file while it is being updated. The –f option enables this function. The following example shows how to view the HP-UX system log file */var/adm/syslog/syslog.log* in this manner. Try running this command on your system and notice the behavior.

$ tail –f /var/adm/syslog/syslog.log

Using the *view* and *vi* Commands

The *view* command opens up a text file as read-only in the vi editor.

$ view /home/user1/.profile

The *vi* command invokes the vi editor. Refer to Chapter 04 "The vi Editor and Text Processors" for detailed information on vi.

Using the *strings* Command

The *strings* command finds and displays legible information embedded within a non-text or binary file. For example, when you run the *strings* command on */usr/bin/cat*, you will observe output similar to the following:

$ strings /usr/bin/cat
```
usrvbnte
Usage: cat [-benrstuv] [-|File ...]
cat: Cannot get status on standard output.
cat: Cannot open
cat: Cannot get status on
cat: Cannot close the file
cat: Cannot use %s as both input and output.
cat: Cannot close the file
cat: Cannot write to output.
cat: read error
cat: Cannot close the file
cat: Cannot write to output
cat: Cannot open
cat: Cannot get status on
cat: Cannot close the file
cat: Cannot use %s as both input and output.
cat: Cannot close the file
. . . . . . . .
cat: read error
cat: Cannot close the file
cat: Cannot write to output
```

2.4.5 Copying Files and Directories

The copy operation duplicates a file or directory. There is a single command called *cp* which is used for this purpose. Here is how to use it.

Copying Files

The *cp* command copies one or more files to either current or another directory. If you want to duplicate a file in the same directory, you must give a different name to the target file. If you want to copy a file to a different directory, you can either use the same file name as the original file or assign it a different name. Consider the following examples:

To copy *file1* in the same directory by the name *newfile1*:

 $ cp file1 newfile1

To copy *file1* into another directory called *subdir1* by the same name:

 $ cp file1 subdir1

By default, when you copy a file, the destination is overwritten and a warning message is not generated. In order to avoid such a situation you can use the –i option with the *cp* command, which prompts for confirmation before overwriting.

 $ cp –i file1 file2
 overwrite file2? (y/n)

Copying Directories

The *cp* command copies a directory and its contents to another location. Use the –r (recursive) option to perform this operation. In the following example, *scripts1* directory is copied under *subdir1*:

 $ cp –r scripts1 subdir1

You may wish to use the –i option with *cp* if needed.

2.4.6 Moving and Renaming Files and Directories

The move operation copies a file or directory to an alternate location and deletes the original file or directory. The rename operation simply changes the name of a file or directory. Here is how to perform move and rename operations.

Moving and Renaming Files

The *mv* command is used to move files or rename them. The –i option can be specified for user confirmation if the destination file exists. The following example moves *file1* to *subdir1* and prompts for confirmation if a file by the same name exists in *subdir1*:

 $ mv –i file1 subdir1
 remove subdir1/file1? (y/n)

To rename *file3* as *file4*, do the following:

> **$ mv file3 file4**

You may want to use the –i option with *mv* command if needed.

Moving and Renaming Directories

To move a directory along with its contents to some other directory location or simply change the name of the directory, use either the *mv* or the *mvdir* command. For example, moving *scripts1* under *scripts2* (*scripts2* must exist), do one of the following:

> **$ mv scripts1 scripts2**
> **# mvdir scripts1 scripts2**

> By default, *mvdir* does not have execute permission set for normal users other than *root*. This prevents normal users from running this command. If execute permission is set, a normal user would be able to run it as well. See Chapter 03 "File and Directory Permissions" on how to modify permissions.

To rename *scripts1* as *scripts10* (*scripts10* must not exist), do one of the following:

> **$ mv scripts1 scripts10**
> **# mvdir scripts1 scripts10**

You may like to use the –i option with *mv* command. This option is not supported with *mvdir*.

2.4.7   Removing Files and Directories

The remove operation deletes a file or directory. Here is how you would do it.

Removing Files

You can remove a file using the *rm* command. The *rm* command deletes one or more specified files at once. The –i option can be used to prevent accidental file removal. The option prompts for confirmation before removing. The following example prompts for confirmation to delete *file1* and *file2*:

> **$ rm –i file1 file2**
> rm: remove file1: (y/n) ? y
> rm: remove file2: (y/n) ? y

Removing Directories

There are two commands available to remove directories. They are demonstrated by the following examples:

To remove an empty directory, use the *rmdir* command:

> **$ rmdir /home/user1/subdir100**

To remove a directory that contains files or sub-directories, or both, use *rm* with –r option:

$ rm –r /home/user1/subdir1

Use the *rm* command with –i option to interactively remove directories and their contents:

$ rm –ir subdir1
directory subdir1: ? (y/n) y
directory subdir1/subdir2: ? (y/n) y
subdir1/subdir2: ? (y/n) y
directory subdir1/subdir3: ? (y/n) y
subdir1/subdir3: ? (y/n) y
subdir1: ? (y/n) y

2.4.8   Summary of File and Directory Operations

Table 2-3 lists commands for file and directory operations you just learned.

Command to	File	Directory
Create	*cat, touch, vi*	*mkdir*
List	*ll, ls, lc* and variants	*ll, ls, lc* and variants
Display	*cat, more, pg, head, tail, view, vi, strings*	*ll, ls, lc* and variants
Copy	*cp*	*cp*
Move	*mv*	*mv, mvdir*
Rename	*mv*	*mv, mvdir*
Remove	*rm*	*rm –r, rmdir*

Table 2-3 Summary of File and Directory Operations

2.5   Searching for Text within Files

HP-UX provides a powerful tool to search the contents of one or more text files for a pattern (also called *regular expression* or *pattern matching*). A pattern can be a single character, a series of characters, a word or a sentence. You must enclose in double quotes if the pattern contains one or more white spaces.

The tool is called *grep* and stands for *global regular expression print*. It searches contents of one or more specified files for a regular expression. If found, it prints every line containing the expression on the screen without changing the original file contents. Consider the following examples.

To search for the pattern "user1" in the */etc/passwd* file:

$ grep user1 /etc/passwd
user1:vdelFV.f/fU0M:110:20::/home/user1:/usr/bin/ksh

To search for all occurrences of the pattern "root" in both the */etc/passwd* and */etc/group* files:

```
$ grep root /etc/passwd /etc/group
/etc/passwd:root:/af/4dEOdgkpY:0:3::/:/sbin/sh
/etc/group:root::0:root
/etc/group:other::1:root,hpdb
/etc/group:bin::2:root,bin
/etc/group:sys::3:root,uucp
/etc/group:adm::4:root,adm
/etc/group:daemon::5:root,daemon
/etc/group:mail::6:root
/etc/group:lp::7:root,lp
/etc/group:users::20:root
```

To display only the names of those files that contain the pattern "root" from the specified file list, use the –l option:

```
$ grep –l root /etc/group /etc/passwd /etc/hosts
/etc/group
/etc/passwd
```

To search for the pattern "root" in */etc/group* along with associated line number, use the –n option:

```
$ grep –n root /etc/group
1:root::0:root
2:other::1:root,hpdb
3:bin::2:root,bin
4:sys::3:root,uucp
5:adm::4:root,adm
6:daemon::5:root,daemon
7:mail::6:root
8:lp::7:root,lp
11:users::20:root
```

To search for the pattern "root" in */etc/group* and exclude the lines in the output that contain this pattern, use the –v option:

```
$ grep –v root /etc/group
tty::10:
nuucp::11:nuucp
nogroup:*:-2:
smbnull::101:
ids::102:
sshd::103:
tftp::104:
hpsmc::105:
hpsmh::106:
```

To search for all lines in the */etc/passwd* file that begin with the pattern "root". The POSIX shell treats the caret (^) sign as a special character which marks the beginning of a line or word. This is useful, for instance, if you want to know whether there are more than one users by that name.

$ grep ^root /etc/passwd
root:/af/4dEOdgkpY:0:3::/:/sbin/sh

To list all lines from the */etc/passwd* file that end with the pattern "ksh". The POSIX shell treats the dollar ($) sign as a special character which marks the end of a line or word. This is useful, for example, to determine which users are using the Korn shell.

$ grep sh$ /etc/passwd
user1:vdelFV.f/fU0M:110:20::/home/user1:/usr/bin/ksh

To search for all empty lines in the */etc/passwd* file, do the following:

$ grep ^$ /etc/passwd

To search for all lines in the */etc/passwd* file that contain only the pattern "root":

$ grep ^root$ /etc/passwd

To search for all lines in the */etc/passwd* file that contain the pattern "root". The –i option used with the *grep* command here ignores letter case. This is useful to determine if there are *root* user accounts with a combination of lowercase and uppercase letters.

$ grep –i root /etc/passwd
root:/af/4dEOdgkpY:0:3::/:/sbin/sh

To print all lines from the output of the *ll* command that contain either "bin" or "root" pattern, run either of the following:

 # ll | grep –E 'bin | root'
 # ll | egrep 'bin | root'

-r--r--r--	1	bin	bin	965	Feb 15 2007	.profile
drwx------	3	root	root	96	Apr 8 11:53	.secure
-rw-------	1	root	sys	6540	Apr 10 15:56	.sh_history
drwxr-xr-x	2	root	sys	96	Apr 8 11:46	.ssh
drwxr-xr-x	6	root	sys	96	Apr 8 09:07	.sw
drwxr-xr-x	3	root	root	96	Apr 8 11:55	.swa
lrwxr-xr-x	1	bin	bin	8	Apr 8 09:07	bin -> /usr/bin
dr-xr-xr-x	20	bin	bin	8192	Apr 10 09:45	dev
dr-xr-xr-x	38	bin	bin	8192	Apr 10 15:26	etc
drwxr-xr-x	7	root	root	96	Apr 10 15:26	home
lrwxr-xr-x	1	bin	bin	8	Apr 8 09:07	lib -> /usr/lib
drwxr-xr-x	2	root	root	96	Apr 8 08:58	lost+found
dr-xr-xr-x	1	root	root	1	Apr 10 09:33	net
dr-xr-xr-x	84	bin	bin	8192	Apr 8 11:47	opt
dr-xr-xr-x	16	bin	bin	8192	Apr 8 11:52	sbin
dr-xr-xr-x	7	bin	bin	1024	Apr 10 09:33	stand
drwxrwxrwt	4	root	root	8192	Apr 10 14:52	tmp
dr-xr-xr-x	22	bin	bin	8192	Apr 8 11:41	usr
dr-xr-xr-x	30	bin	bin	8192	Apr 8 11:54	var

To print all lines from the */standcurrent//system* file that contain the character " * ". Note that with −F, " * " is treated as a regular character and not as a wildcard character. Run any of the following:

> **$ grep −F '*' /stand/current/system**
> **$ fgrep '*' /stand/current/system**
> *
> * Created on Thu Apr 10 09:33:17 2008
> *
> *
> * Module entries
> *
> *
> * Dump entries
> *
> *
> * Tunables entries
> *

2.6   Finding Files in the Directory Structure

Sometimes you need to find one or more files or directories in the file system structure based on criteria. To enable you to perform this function, HP-UX offers a command called *find*. The *find* command recursively searches the directory tree, finds files that match the specified criteria and optionally performs an action. This powerful tool can be customized to look for files in a number of ways. The search criteria may include searching for files by name, size, ownership, group membership, last access or modification time, permissions, file type and inode number. Here is the command syntax:

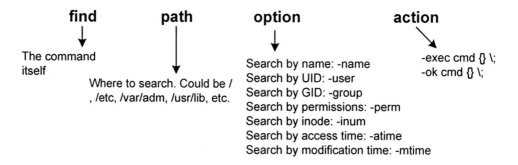

With the *find* command, files that match the specified criteria are located and the full path to each file is displayed. Let us look at a few examples.

To search for *file2* in *user1*'s home directory */home/user1*:

> **$ cd**
> **$ find . −name file2 −print**
> ./file2
> ./subdir6/subdir54/subdir20/subdir1/file2

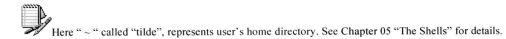–print is optional. The *find* command, by default, displays results on the screen. You do not have to specify this option.

To search for files and directories in */dev* directory that begin with "vg". Run this command as *root*.

 # find /dev –name vg*
/dev/vg00
/dev/vg01
/dev/vg02

The (*) character is used as a wildcard character. It means any files or directories that begin with the pattern "vg" followed by any characters.

To find files larger than 1000 blocks in size (one block equals 512 bytes) in *user1*'s home directory:

$ find ~ –size +1000

Here " ~ " called "tilde", represents user's home directory. See Chapter 05 "The Shells" for details.

To find files in */home* owned by *user1*. Run it as *root*.

 # find /home –user user1

To find files in */etc/rc.config.d* directory that were modified more than 120 days ago:

 # find /etc/rc.config.d –mtime +120

To find files in */etc/rc.config.d* directory that have not been accessed in the last 90 days:

 # find /etc/rc.config.d –atime –90

To search for character DSFs in */dev* directory with permissions 700:

 # find /dev/rdisk –type c –perm 700

In the above example, two criteria are defined. Files that match both criteria are displayed. The criteria are to look for files that are character DSFs and having read/write/execute permissions for the file owner and no permissions to any other users.

To search for symbolic link files in */usr* directory with permissions 777:

 # find /usr –type l –perm 777

To search for core files in the entire directory tree and delete them as found without prompting for confirmation:

find / –name core –exec rm {} \;

 The pattern "{} \;" is part of the syntax and must be defined that way.

To search for core files in the entire directory tree and prompt to delete them as found:

find / –name core –ok rm {} \;

2.7   Sorting File Contents

Sorting allows you to arrange columns of text in the specified order. The *sort* command is used for this purpose. It sorts contents of a file and prints the result on the screen. You can specify multiple files for sort. Also, you can sort file contents in either alphabetic (default) or numeric order.

Let us look at a few examples to understand the usage of *sort*.

Consider a file, *file10*, in *user1*'s home directory with the following text in two columns. The first column contains alphabets and the second contains numbers.

```
Maryland 667
Mississippi 662
Pennsylvania 445
Missouri 975
Florida 772
Montana 406
Massachusetts 339
```

To sort this file alphabetically:

$ sort file10
Florida 772
Maryland 667
Massachusetts 339
Mississippi 662
Missouri 975
Montana 406
Pennsylvania 445

To sort this file numerically, use the –n option and specify the column number:

$ sort –n +1 file10
Massachusetts **339**
Montana **406**
Pennsylvania **445**
Mississippi **662**
Maryland **667**
Florida **772**
Missouri **975**

To sort *file10* numerically (–n option) but in reverse order (–r option):

$ sort –rn +1 file10

Missouri **975**
Florida **772**
Maryland **667**
Mississippi **662**
Pennsylvania **445**
Montana **406**
Massachusetts **339**

To sort the output of the *ll* command ran on *user1*'s home directory:

$ ll | sort

-rw-rw-rw-	1	user1	users	11	Feb 4 22:57	file4
-rw-rw-rw-	1	user1	users	21	Feb 4 22:57	file6
-rw-rw-rw-	1	user1	users	67	Feb 4 22:57	file5
-rw-rw-rw-	1	user1	users	1089	Feb 4 22:56	file1
-rw-rw-rw-	1	user1	users	2426	Feb 4 22:56	file2
-rw-rw-rw-	1	user1	users	270336	Feb 4 22:57	file3
drwxrwxrwx	2	user1	users	96	Feb 4 22:55	scripts
drwxrwxrwx	2	user1	users	96	Feb 4 22:55	scripts2
drwxrwxrwx	2	user1	users	96	Feb 4 22:55	scripts1
drwxrwxrwx	2	user1	users	96	Feb 4 22:55	subdir1
drwxrwxrwx	2	user1	users	96	Feb 4 22:55	subdir2
total 608						

To sort on the 5th column (month column) of the *ll* command output ran on */etc/skel* directory:

$ ll –a /etc/skel | sort +5M

total 80						
-r--r--r--	1	bin	bin	334	Feb 15 2007	.login
-r--r--r--	1	bin	bin	347	Feb 15 2007	.exrc
-r--r--r--	1	bin	bin	700	Feb 15 2007	.profile
-r--r--r--	1	bin	bin	832	Feb 15 2007	.cshrc
dr-xr-xr-x	38	bin	bin	8192	Apr 10 15:26	..
drwxrwxr-x	2	root	sys	96	Apr 8 11:41	.

By default, output of *sort* is displayed on the screen. If you would like to save the output into a file, you may redirect it using –o option. The example below saves the output in */tmp/sort.out* file and does not display it on the screen:

$ ll /etc/skel | sort +5M –o /tmp/sort.out

To sort on the 5th and then on the 6th column. This is an example of multi-level sorting.

```
$ ll –a /etc/skel | sort +5M +6n
total 80
-r--r--r--    1        bin     bin   334      Feb 15  2007     .login
-r--r--r--    1        bin     bin   347      Feb 15  2007     .exrc
-r--r--r--    1        bin     bin   700      Feb 15  2007     .profile
-r--r--r--    1        bin     bin   832      Feb 15  2007     .cshrc
drwxrwxr-x  2        root    sys   96       Apr  8 11:41     .
dr-xr-xr-x  38       bin     bin  8192     Apr 10 15:26     ..
```

There are numerous other options available with the *sort* command. Try them to build a better understanding. Refer to the command's man pages.

2.8 Linking Files and Directories

Each file in HP-UX has a unique number assigned to it at the time it is created. This number is referred to as its *inode* (index node) number. All file attributes such as the name, type, size, permissions, ownership, group membership and last access/modification time are maintained in that inode. Moreover, the inode points to the exact location in the file system where the data for the file sits. See Chapter 14 "File Systems" for details on inodes.

Linking files (or directories) means that you have more than one file (or directory) name pointing to the same physical data location in the directory tree.

There are two types of links: *soft* links and *hard* links.

2.8.1 Soft Link

A *soft* link (a.k.a. *symbolic* link or *symlink*) makes it possible to associate one file with another. It is similar to a "shortcut" in MS Windows where the actual file resides somewhere in the directory structure but you may have multiple "shortcuts" or "pointers" with different names pointing to that file. This means accessing the file via the actual file name or any of the shortcuts would yield the same result. Each soft link has a unique inode number.

A soft link can cross file system boundaries and can be used to link directories.

To create a soft link for *file1* as *file10* in the same directory, use the *ln* command with –s option:

    $ cd /home/user1
    $ ln –s file1 file10

where:

    file1 is an existing file
    file10 is soft linked to *file1*

After you have created this link, do an *ll* with –i option. Notice the letter "l" as the first character in the second column of the output. Also notice an arrow pointing from the linked file to the original file. This indicates that *file10* is nothing but a pointer to *file1*. The –i option displays associated inode numbers in the first column.

$ ll –i

48 -rwxr--r--	1	user1	users	101	May 10 12:13	file1
49 lrwxrwxrwx	1	user1	users	5	May 10 12:13	file10 -> file1

If you remove the original file (*file1* in this example), the link (*file10*) stays but points to something that does not exist.

2.8.2   Hard Link

A *hard* link associates two or more files with a single inode number. This allows the files to have the same permissions, ownership, time stamp and file contents. Changes made to any of the files are reflected on the linked files. All files will actually contain identical data.

A hard link cannot cross file system boundaries and cannot be used to link directories.

The following example uses the *ln* command and creates a hard link for *file2* located under */home/user1* directory to *file20* in the same directory. *file20* does not currently exist, it will be created.

> **$ cd /home/user1**
> **$ ln file2 file20**

After creating the link, do an *ll* with –i option.

$ ll –i

18 -rw-rw-rw-	2	user1	users	412	Nov 25 15:38	file2
18 -rw-rw-rw-	2	user1	users	412	Nov 25 15:38	file20

Look at the first and the third columns. The first column indicates that both files have identical inode numbers and the third column tells that each file has two hard links. *file2* points to *file20* and vice versa. If you remove the original file (*file2* in this example), you still will have access to the data through the linked file (*file20*).

Summary

In this chapter you got an overview of the HP-UX file system structure and significant higher level sub-directories. Those sub-directories consisted of either static or variable files, which were further logically grouped into lower level sub-directories. The files and sub-directories were accessed using path relative to either the top-most directory of the file system structure or your current location in the tree.

You learned about different types of files and a set of rules to adhere to when creating files or directories. You looked at several file and directory manipulation tools such as creating, listing, displaying, copying, moving, renaming and removing them.

Searching for text within files and searching for files within the directory structure using specified criteria provided you with an understanding and explanation of tools required to perform such tasks.

Finally, you studied how to sort contents of a text file or output generated by executing a command in ascending or descending order. The last topic discussed creating soft and hard links between files and between directories.

## 03

File and Directory Permissions

This chapter covers the following major topics:

- ✓ File and directory permissions assigned to owners, members of owner's group, and others
- ✓ Types of permissions based on read, write and execute requirements
- ✓ Modes of permissions based on adding, revoking or assigning permissions
- ✓ Modify file and directory permissions using symbolic and octal notations
- ✓ Set default permissions on new files and directories
- ✓ Modify ownership and group membership on files and directories
- ✓ Configure special permissions on executable files and directories by setting setuid, setgid and sticky bits

3.1 Determining Access Permissions

In HP-UX, permissions are set on files and directories to prevent access by unauthorized users. Users are grouped into distinct categories, and each user category is then assigned required permissions. The following sub-sections elaborate on file and directory permissions.

3.1.1 Permission Classes

Users on the system are categorized into three distinct classes for the purpose of maintaining file security through permissions. These classes are described in Table 3-1.

Permission Class	Description
User (u)	Owner of file or directory. Usually, the person who creates a file or directory is the owner of it.
Group (g)	A set of users that need identical access on files and directories that they share. Group information is maintained in the /etc/group file and users are assigned to groups according to shared file access needs.
Others (o)	All other users that have access to the system except the owner and group members. Also called *public*.

Table 3-1 Permission Classes

3.1.2 Permission Types

Permissions control what actions can be performed on a file or directory and by whom. There are four types of permissions as defined in Table 3-2.

Permission Type	Symbol	File	Directory
Read	r	Displays file contents or copies contents to another file.	Displays contents with the *ll* command.
Write	w	Modifies file contents.	Creates, removes or renames files and sub-directories.
Execute	x	Executes a file.	*cd* into the directory.
Access Denied	-	None.	None.

Table 3-2 Permission Types

3.1.3 Permission Modes

A permission mode is used to add, revoke or assign a permission type to a permission class. Table 3-3 shows various permission modes.

Permission Mode	Description
Add permissions (+)	Gives specified permission(s).
Revoke permissions (-)	Removes specified permission(s).
Assign permissions (=)	Gives specified permission(s) to owner, group members and public in one go.

Table 3-3 Permission Modes

The output of the *ll* command lists files and directories along with their type and permission settings. This information is shown in the first column of the command's output where 10 characters are displayed. The first character indicates the type of file: d for directory, – for regular file, l for symbolic link, c for character DSF, b for block DSF, n for named pipe, s for socket and so on. The next nine characters – three groups of three characters – show read (r), write (w), execute (x) or none (-) permissions for the three user classes: user, group and others, respectively.

Figure 3-1 illustrates the *ll* command output and its various components.

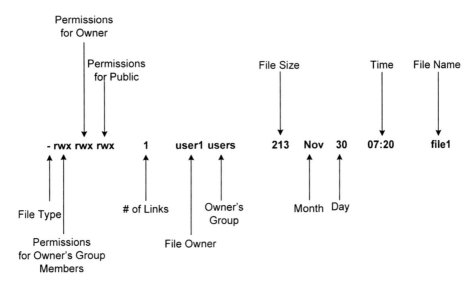

Figure 3-1 Permission Settings

From Figure 3-1, it is obvious who the owner (3rd column) of the file is and which group (4th column) the owner belongs to.

3.2   Changing Access Permissions

The *chmod* command is used to modify access permissions on files and directories. *chmod* can be used by *root* or file owner, and can modify permissions specified in one of two methods: *symbolic* or *octal*.

3.2.1   Using Symbolic Notation

Symbolic notation uses a combination of letters and symbols to add, revoke or assign permissions to each class of users. The following examples and their explanation provide an understanding on how to set file permissions. It works in an identical fashion on directories.

Suppose there is a file called *file1* with read permission for the owner, group members and others. This file is owned by *user1* who will be modifying permissions in the following examples.

```
-r--r--r--  1 user1    users       0 Nov 30 07:20 file1
```

To add execute permission for the owner:

$ chmod u+x file1
```
-r-xr--r--  1 user1    users       0 Nov 30 07:20 file1
```

To add write permission for the owner:

$ chmod u+w file1
```
-rwxr--r--  1 user1    users       0 Nov 30 07:20 file1
```

To add write permission for group members and public:

$ chmod go+w file1
```
-rwxrw-rw-  1 user1    users       0 Nov 30 07:20 file1
```

To remove write permission for public:

$ chmod o-w file1
```
-rwxrw-r--  1 user1    users       0 Nov 30 07:20 file1
```

To assign read, write and execute permissions to all three user categories:

$ chmod a=rwx file1
```
-rwxrwxrwx  1 user1    users       0 Nov 30 07:20 file1
```

3.2.2   Using Octal (or Absolute) Notation

The octal notation uses a three-digit numbering system that ranges from 0 to 7 to specify permissions for the three user classes. Octal values are given in Table 3-4.

Octal Value	Binary Notation	Symbolic Notation	Explanation
0	000	---	No permissions.
1	001	--x	Execute permission only.
2	010	-w-	Write permission only.
3	011	-wx	Write and execute permissions.
4	100	r--	Read permission only.
5	101	r-x	Read and execute permissions.
6	110	rw-	Read and write permissions.
7	111	rwx	Read, write and execute permissions.

Table 3-4 Octal Permission Notation

From Table 3-4 it is obvious that each "1" corresponds to an "r", a "w" or an "x" and each "0" corresponds to the " – " character for no permission at that level. Figure 3-2 shows weights associated with each digit location in the 3-digit octal numbering model. The right-most location has weight 1, the middle location has weight 2 and the left-most location has weight 4. When you assign a permission of 6, for example, it would correspond to the two left-most digit locations. Similarly, a permission of 2 would mean only the middle digit location.

Figure 3-2 Permission Weights

The following examples and their explanation provide an understanding on how to set file permissions using octal method. It works in an identical fashion on directories.

Suppose you have a file called *file2* with read permission for the owner, group members and others. This file is owned by *user1* who will be modifying permissions in the following examples.

```
-r--r--r--  1 user1     users        0 Nov 30 07:23  file2
```

The current permissions on *file2* in the octal notation are 444, where each digit represents one class of users. The first digit 4 is for file owner, the second for owner's group members and the third for everyone else.

To add execute permission for the owner:

```
$ chmod 644 file2
-rw-r--r--  1 user1     users        0 Nov 30 07:20  file2
```

To add write permission for the owner:

```
$ chmod 744 file2
-rwxr--r--  1 user1     users        0 Nov 30 07:20  file2
```

To add write permission for group members and others:

```
$ chmod 766 file2
-rwxrw-rw-  1 user1     users        0 Nov 30 07:20  file2
```

To revoke write permission from public users:

```
$ chmod 764 file2
-rwxrw-r--  1 user1     users        0 Nov 30 07:20  file2
```

To assign read, write and execute permissions to all three user categories:

```
$ chmod 777 file2
-rwxrwxrwx  1 user1     users        0 Nov 30 07:20  file2
```

3.3   Setting Default Permissions

The system assigns *default permissions* to a file or directory when it is created. Default permissions are calculated based on the *umask* (user mask) permission value subtracted from a pre-defined value called *initial* permissions.

The umask is a three-digit value that refers to read/write/execute permissions for owner, group and other. Its purpose is to set default permissions on new files and directories. In HP-UX, the default umask value is set to 022. Run the *umask* command without any options to display the current umask value:

$ umask
022

Run the *umask* command with the –S option to display the current umask in symbolic notation:

$ umask –S
u=rwx,g=rx,o=rx

The umask value is shown differently in different shells. It is shown as 022 in the POSIX and Korn shells, and 22 in the C shell.

The pre-defined initial permission values are 666 (rw-rw-rw-) for files and 777 (rwxrwxrwx) for directories.

3.3.1   Calculating Default Permissions

Here is how you would calculate default permission values on files:

Initial Permissions	666	
umask	– 022	(subtract)
==========================		
Default Permissions	644	

This indicates that every new file will have read and write permissions assigned to owner and read-only permission to owner's group members and public.

To calculate default permission values on directories:

Initial Permissions	777	
umask	– 022	(subtract)
==========================		
Default Permissions	755	

This indicates that every new directory will have read, write and execute permissions assigned to owner and read and write permissions to owner's group members and public.

If you wish to have different default permissions set on new files and directories, you need to modify umask. First, determine what default values are needed. For example, if you want all your new files and directories to have 640 and 750 permissions, respectively, run *umask* and set the value to 027:

$ umask 027

The new umask value becomes effective right away. Note that the new umask is applied only one the files and directories created after the umask is changed. The existing files and directories will remain intact. Create a file, *file10*, and a directory, *dir10*, as *user1* under */home/user1* to test the effect of the change.

```
$ touch file10
$ ll file10
-rw-r-----  1 user1     users        0  May 18 15:01  file10
$ mkdir dir10
$ ll –d dir10
drwxr-x---  2 user1     users       96  May 18 15:01  dir10
```

The above examples show that new files and directories are created with different permissions. The files have (666 – 027 = 640) and directories have (777 – 027 = 750) permissions.

The umask value set at the command line is lost as soon as you log off. In order to retain the new setting, place it in one of the shell initialization files. Customizing shell initialization files is covered in Chapter 12 "Users and Groups".

3.4   Changing File Ownership and Group Membership

In HP-UX, every file and directory has an owner associated with it. By default, the creator becomes the owner. The ownership can be altered if required, and allocated to some other user.

Similarly, every user is a member of one or more groups. A group is a collection of users that have similar privileges on a file or directory. By default, the owner's group is assigned to a file or directory.

For example, below is the output from the *ll* command on *file1*:

```
$ ll file1
-rw-r--r--  1 user1     users        0  Nov 30 14:04  file1
```

This output indicates that the owner of *file1* is *user1* who belongs to group *users*.

Use the *chown* and *chgrp* commands to alter ownership and group membership on files and directories. You must be either the file owner or *root* to make this modification. Consider the following examples.

To change ownership from *user1* to *user2*:

```
$ chown user2 file1
$ ll  file1
-rwxr--r--  1 user2     users      101  May 18 15:09  file1
```

To change group membership from *users* to *other*:

```
# chgrp other file1
# ll file1
-rwxr--r--   1 user2    other       101  May 18 15:09  file1
```

To modify both ownership and group membership in one go:

```
$ chown user1:users file1
$ ll file1
-rwxr--r--   1 user1    users       101  May 18 15:09  file1
```

To modify recursively all files and sub-directories under *dir1* to be owned by *user2* and *group* users:

```
$ chown –R user2:users dir1
```

3.5   Special Permissions

There are three special types of permissions available in HP-UX for executable files and directories. These permissions may be assigned if required. These are:

- ✓ The *setuid* (set user identification) bit
- ✓ The *setgid* (set group identification) bit
- ✓ The *sticky* bit

3.5.1   The setuid Bit

The *setuid* bit is set on executable files at the file owner level. When this bit is enabled, the file will be executed by other users with exact same privileges as the file owner has on it. For example, the *su* command is owned by *root* with group membership set to *bin*. This command has setuid bit enabled on it by default. See the highlighted "s" in the owner's permission class below:

```
$ ll /usr/bin/su
-r-sr-xr-x  1 root     bin       24576  Nov 14  2000  /usr/bin/su
```

When a normal user executes this command, it will run as if *root* (the owner) is running it and, therefore, the user is able to run it successfully and gets the desired result.

> The *su* (switch user) command allows a user to switch to some other user's account provided the switching user knows the password of the user he is trying to switch to.

Now, let us remove the setuid bit from *su* and replace it with an "x":

```
# chmod 555 /usr/bin/su
# ll /usr/bin/su
-r-xr-xr-x  1 root     bin       24576  Nov 14  2000  /usr/bin/su
```

The file is still executable, but when a normal user runs it, he will be running it as himself and not as *root*. Here is what will happen when *user1* tries to su into *user2* and enters a valid password:

```
$ su – user2
Password:
su: Invalid ID
```

user1 gets the "Invalid ID" message even though he entered correct login credentials.

To set setuid bit back on *su* or on some other file:

```
# chmod 4555 /usr/bin/su
# ll /usr/bin/su
-r-sr-xr-x  1 root     bin        24576 Nov 14 2000 /usr/bin/su
```

When digit 4 is used with the *chmod* command in this manner, it sets the setuid bit on the file. Alternatively, you can use the symbolic notation to get exact same results:

```
# chmod u+s /usr/bin/su
```

To search for all files in the system that have setuid bit set on them, use the *find* command:

```
# find / –perm –4000
```

3.5.2   The setgid Bit

The *setgid* bit is set on executable files at the group level. When this bit is enabled, the file will be executed by other users with exact same privileges that the group members have on it. For example, the *write* command is owned by *bin* with group membership set to *bin*. This command has setgid bit enabled on it. See the highlighted "s" in the group's permission class below:

```
$ ll /usr/bin/write
-r-xr-sr-x  1 bin      bin        16384 Nov 14 2000 /usr/bin/write
```

When a normal user executes this command, it will run as if *bin* is running it and, therefore, the user is able to run it successfully and gets the desired result.

To set the setgid bit on */home/user1/file1*:

```
# chmod 2555 /home/user1/file1
# ll
-r-xr-sr-x  1 user1    user1        101 May 18 15:09 file1
```

When digit 2 is used with the *chmod* command in this manner, it sets the setgid bit on the file. Alternatively, you can use the symbolic notation to get exact same results:

```
# chmod g+s /home/user1/file1
```

To search for all files in the system that have setgid bit set, use the *find* command:

```
# find / –perm –2000
```

You may wish to set the setgid bit on a directory shared by users of a group. This will allow the group members to be able to create files in that directory, but the files created will not have group membership of the creator's group, rather, they will be members of the group which the directory belongs to.

To set the setgid bit on a shared directory, issue the *chmod* command the same way as you did when you enabled setgid on files.

3.5.3 The Sticky Bit

The *sticky* bit is set on public writable directories to protect files and sub-directories of individual users from being deleted by other users. This is typically done on */tmp* and */var/tmp* directories. Normally, all users are allowed to create and delete files and sub-directories in these directories. With default permissions, any user can remove any other user's files and sub-directories.

Here is how you would set sticky bit on */tmp* and */var/tmp*:

> # **chmod 1777 /tmp**
> # **chmod 1777 /var/tmp**

When digit 1 is used with the *chmod* command in this manner, it sets the sticky bit on the specified directory. Alternatively, you can use the symbolic notation to do exactly the same:

> # **chmod o+t /tmp**
> # **chmod o+t /var/tmp**

After setting sticky bits on the directories above, do an *ll* and you will notice the character "t" in other's permissions. This indicates that sticky bit is enabled.

> # **ll –ld /tmp /var/tmp**
> drwxrwxrwt 6 bin   bin   8192 Nov 30 15:30 tmp
> drwxrwxrwt 4 bin   bin   6144 Nov 30 15:30 var/tmp

To search for all directories in the system that have sticky bit set, use the *find* command:

> # **find / –type d –perm –1000**

Summary

In this chapter you learned about file and directory permissions assigned to their owners, members of the group that the owner belonged to, and other users on the system. You looked at types and modes of permissions and how to modify those using symbolic and octal notations.

You studied how default permissions could be setup for new files and directories and the role of umask value in determining new default permissions.

Then you saw how a user could alter his primary group membership temporarily and how a user or root could modify ownership and group membership on files and directories.

Finally, you learned about setting special permissions on executable files and directories.

The vi Editor and Text Processors

This chapter covers the following major topics:

- ✓ Modes of operation for the vi editor
- ✓ Start and quit the vi Editor
- ✓ Navigate within vi
- ✓ Manipulate text
- ✓ Save modifications
- ✓ Customize vi settings
- ✓ Manipulate columns of text using the awk text processor
- ✓ Manipulate rows of text using the sed text processor

4.1   The vi Editor

The *vi* editor is an interactive *visual* text editor tool that enables a user to create and modify text files. It was written by Bill Joy in the mid 1970s. All text editing with the vi editor takes place in a buffer (a small chunk of memory used to hold updates being done to a file). Changes can either be written to the disk or discarded.

It is essential for system administrators to master vi editor skills. The following sub-sections provide details on how to use and interact with vi.

4.1.1   Modes of Operation

The vi editor has three basic modes of operation:

1. Command mode
2. Edit mode
3. Last line mode

Command Mode

The *command* mode is the default mode of vi. The vi editor places you into this mode when you start it. While in the command mode, you can carry out tasks such as copy, cut, paste, move, remove, replace, change and search on text, in addition to performing navigational tasks. This mode is also known as the *escape* mode as the Esc key is pressed to enter it.

Input Mode

In *input* mode, anything you type at the keyboard is entered into the file as text. Commands cannot be run in this mode. The input mode is also called the *edit* mode or the *insert* mode. To return to the command mode, press the Esc key.

Last Line Mode

While in the command mode, you may carry out advanced editing tasks on text by pressing the colon (:) character. Pressing the colon places the cursor at the beginning of the last line of the screen and hence referred to as the *last line* mode. This mode is considered a special type of command mode.

4.1.2   Starting the vi Editor

You can start vi in one of the ways described in Table 4-1.

Method	Description
vi	Starts vi and opens up an empty screen for you to enter text. You can save or discard the text entered later as you wish.
vi existing_file	Starts vi and loads the specified file for editing or viewing.
vi new_file	Starts vi and creates the specified file when saved.

Table 4-1 Starting The vi Editor

4.1.3 Inserting text

To start entering text, issue one of the commands described in Table 4-2 from the command mode to switch to the edit mode.

Command	Action
i	Inserts text before the current cursor position.
I	Inserts text at the beginning of the current line.
a	Appends text after the current cursor position.
A	Appends text at the end of the current line.
o	Opens up a new line below the current line.
O	Opens up a new line above the current line.

Table 4-2 Inserting Text

Press the Esc key when done to return to the command mode.

4.1.4 Navigating within vi

Table 4-3 elaborates key sequences that control cursor movement while you are in the vi editor. You must be in the command mode to move around.

Command	Action
h, left arrow, Backspace or ctrl+h	Moves left (backward) one character.
j or down arrow	Moves down one line.
k or up arrow	Moves up one line.
l, right arrow or Spacebar	Moves right (forward) one character.
W or w	Moves forward one word.
B or b	Moves backward one word.
E or e	Moves forward to the last character of the next word.
M	Moves to the line in the middle of the page.
$	Moves to the end of the current line.
0 (zero) or ^	Moves to the beginning of the current line.
Enter	Moves down to the beginning of the next line.
ctrl+f	Moves forward to the next page (scrolls down).
ctrl+d	Moves forward one-half page (scrolls down).
ctrl+b	Moves backward to the previous page (scrolls up).
ctrl+u	Moves backward one-half page (scrolls up).
G or]]	Moves to the last line of the file.
(	Moves backward to the beginning of the current sentence.
)	Moves forward to the beginning of the next sentence.
{	Moves backward to the beginning of the preceding paragraph.
}	Moves forward to the beginning of the next paragraph.
1G or [[or :1	Moves to the first line of the file.
:11 or 11G	Moves to the specified line number (such as line number 11).
ctrl+g	Tells you what line number you are at.

Table 4-3 Navigating Within vi

4.1.5   Deleting Text

Commands listed in Table 4-4 are available to perform delete operations. You must be in the command mode to accomplish these tasks.

Command	Action
x	Deletes a character at the current cursor position. You may type a digit before this command to delete that many characters. For example, 2x would remove two characters, 3x would remove 3 characters and so on.
X	Deletes a character before the current cursor location. You may type a digit before this command to delete that many characters. For example, 2X would remove two characters, 3X would remove 3 characters and so on.
dw	Deletes a word or part of the word to the right of the current cursor location. You may type a digit before this command to delete that many words. For example, 2w would remove two words, 3w would remove 3 words and so on.
dd	Deletes the current line. You may type a digit before this command to delete that many lines. For example, 2dd would remove two lines, 3dd would remove 3 lines and so on.
D	Deletes at the current cursor position to the end of the current line.
:6,12d	Deletes lines 6 through 12.

Table 4-4 Deleting Text

4.1.6   Undoing and Repeating

Table 4-5 explains commands available to undo the last change you did and repeat the last command you ran. You must be in the command mode to perform the tasks.

Command	Action
u	Undoes the last command.
U	Undoes all changes at the current line.
:u	Undoes the previous last line mode command.
. (dot)	Repeats the last command you ran.

Table 4-5 Undoing and Repeating

4.1.7   Searching and Replacing Text

Search and replace text functions are performed using commands mentioned in Table 4-6. You must be in command mode to do these tasks.

Command	Action
/string	Searches forward for string.
?string	Searches backward for string.
n	Finds next occurrence of string. This would only work if you have run either a forward or a backward string search.
N	Finds previous occurrence of string. This would only work if you have run either a forward or a backward string search.

Command	Action
:%s/old/new	Searches and replaces the first occurrence of old with new on each line. For example, to replace the first occurrence of "profile" with "Profile", you would use ":%s/profile/Profile".
:%s/old/new/g	(Globally) Searches and replaces all occurrences of old with new in the entire file. For example, to replace all occurrences of "profile" with "Profile" in the file, you would use ":%s/profile/Profile/g".

Table 4-6 Searching and Replacing Text

4.1.8   Copying, Moving and Pasting Text

The *co* command writes copied text into a temporary buffer. The *P* or *p* command reads text from the temporary buffer and writes it into current file at the specified location. You can also do move and copy functions from the last line mode. See Table 4-7 for further information.

Command	Action
yy	Yanks the current line into buffer. You may specify a digit before this command to yank that many lines. For example, 2yy yanks two lines, 3yy yanks three lines and so on.
p	Pastes yanked line(s) below the current line.
P	Pastes yanked line(s) above the current line.
:1,3co5	Copies lines 1 through 3 and pastes them after line 5.
:4,6m8	Moves lines 4 through 6 after line 8.

Table 4-7 Copying, Moving and Pasting Text

4.1.9   Changing Text

Use commands given in Table 4-8 to change text. Some of these commands take you to the edit mode. To return to the command mode, press the Esc key.

Command	Action
cw	Changes a word (or part of a word) at the current cursor location to the end of the current word.
C	Changes at the current cursor position to the end of the current line.
r	Replaces character at the current cursor location with the character entered following this command.
R	Overwrites or replaces text on the current line.
s	Substitutes a string for character(s).
S or cc	Substitutes an entire line.
J	Joins the current line and the line below it.
xp	Switches position of the character at the current cursor position with the character to the right of it.
~	Changes letter case (uppercase to lowercase, and vice versa) at the current cursor location.

Table 4-8 Changing Text

4.1.10   Importing Contents of Another File

While working in vi you may want to insert contents of some other file. The vi editor allows you to do that. You must be at the last line mode to accomplish this. See Table 4-9.

Command	Action
:r file2	Reads *file2* and inserts its contents below the current line.

Table 4-9 Importing Contents of Another File

4.1.11   Customizing vi Edit Sessions

The vi editor supports settings to customize edit sessions to display line numbers, invisible characters and so on. Use the *set* command to control these options. Consult Table 4-10.

Command	Action
:set nu	Shows line numbers.
:set nonu	Hides line numbers.
:set ic	Ignores letter case when carrying out searches.
:set noic	Does not ignore letter case when carrying out searches.
:set list	Displays invisible characters such as Tab and End Of Line (EOL).
:set nolist	Hides invisible characters such as Tab and EOL.
:set showmode	Displays current mode of operation.
:set noshowmode	Hides mode of operation.
:set	Displays current vi variable settings.
:set all	Displays all available vi variables and their current settings.

Table 4-10 Customizing vi Settings

4.1.12   Saving and Quitting vi

When you are done with modifications, you will want to save them (or discard them if you want to). Commands listed in Table 4-11 would help.

Command	Action
:w	Writes changes into file without quitting vi.
:w file3	Writes changes into a new file called *file3*.
:w!	Writes changes into file even if file owner does not have write permission on the file.
:wq or :x or ZZ	Writes changes to file and quits vi.
:wq! or :x!	Writes changes into currently-opened file and quits vi even if file owner does not have write permission on the file.
:q	Quits vi if no modifications were made.
:q!	Quits vi if modifications were made, but you do not wish to save them.

Table 4-11 Saving and Quitting vi

4.1.13   Miscellaneous vi Commands

Table 4-12 describes additional commands available to perform specific tasks within vi.

Command	Action
ctrl+l or ctrl+r	Refreshes vi screen if proper terminal type is set.
:sh	Exits vi editor session temporarily. Type *exit* or `Ctrl+d` to come back.
:!command	Executes the specified command without quitting vi.

Table 4-12 Miscellaneous vi Commands

4.2   The Text Processors

HP-UX supports two famous UNIX text processors to perform functions on columns and rows of text. These are known as *awk* and *sed*, and both work on input taken either from a specified file or the output of a command such as *ll*. Neither text processor makes any modifications to files provided as input. They only read input files and display results on the screen. If you wish to save the result, you need to use output redirection (See Chapter 05 "The Shells" on how to use output redirection). Let us take a look at both and understand them with the help of examples.

4.2.1   The awk Processor

The name *awk* was derived from the first initial of the last names of those who developed it: Alfred **Aho**, Peter **Weinberger** and Brian **Kenigham**.

awk works on columns of text to generate reports. It scans a file, or input provided, one line at a time. It starts from the first line, searches for lines matching the specified pattern enclosed in quotes and curly braces, and performs selected action on those lines.

In order to understand the behavior of the *awk* utility, create a file by running the *ll* command and redirect its output to a file called *ll.out*. Then use this file as input to *awk* and examine results displayed on the screen. Before doing that, let us see how *awk* interprets columns. In other words how *awk* differentiates between columns. Let us run *ll* on *user1*'s home directory */home/user1*.

```
$ cd
$ ll
total 608
-rw-rw-rw-  1       user1    users     1089   Feb  4 22:56     file1
-rw-rw-rw-  1       user1    users     2426   Feb  4 22:56     file2
-rw-rw-rw-  1       user1    users   270336   Feb  4 22:57     file3
-rw-rw-rw-  1       user1    users       11   Feb  4 22:57     file4
```

awk automatically breaks a line into columns and assigns a variable to each one of them. A white space such as a tab, is used as the default delimiter between columns to separate them.

Each line from the *ll* command output contains nine columns of text. Figure 4-1 shows how *awk* represents each column with respect to its position. The figure shows that $1 represents the first column, $2 represents the second column, $3 represents the third column and so on. All columns are collectively represented by $0.

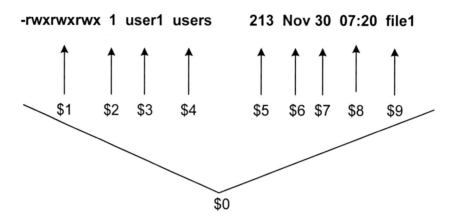

Figure 4-1 *awk* Command Arguments

Let us save the output of *ll* into *ll.out*.

$ ll > ll.out

The following examples help you develop an understanding on the usage of *awk*.

To display only the file name (column 9), file size (column 5) and file owner (column 3) in that sequence, do the following. Notice the space between variables in the *awk* statement. The output will not contain any spaces between columns. It will be printed as one single string of characters.

$ awk '{print $9 $5 $3}' ll.out
file11089user1
file22426user1
file3270336user1
file411user1

awk requires that you enclose the pattern in quotes and curly braces. The "print" function within curly braces is part of the syntax.

To place a single space between columns in the output, use a comma between variables:

$ awk '{print $9, $5, $3}' ll.out
file1 1089 user1
file2 2426 user1
file3 270336 user1
file4 11 user1

To provide for exact alignment between columns, insert a `tab` or two:

$ awk '{print $9 " " $5 "   " $3}' ll.out
file   11089   user1
file   22426   user1
file3   270336   user1
file4   11   user1

HP Certified Systems Administrator 11i v3

To re-arrange columns to display file owner, file size and file name in that order:

$ awk '{print $3,$5,$9}' ll.out
user1 1089 file1
user1 2426 file2
user1 270336 file3
user1 11 file4

To add text between columns:

$ awk '{print $9,"was last modified/accessed on",$6,$7,"at",$8}' ll.out
file1 was last modified/accessed on Feb 4 at 22:56
file2 was last modified/accessed on Feb 4 at 22:56
file3 was last modified/accessed on Feb 4 at 22:57
file4 was last modified/accessed on Feb 4 at 22:57

Note that when inserting text between columns, each text insert must be enclosed in double quotes and all but the last text inserted must be followed by a comma.

4.2.2   The sed Processor

Unlike *awk* that works on columns of text, the *sed* (stream editor) text processor works on rows of text. The following examples illustrate how *sed* works.

To search */etc/group* file for all lines containing the word "root" and hide them in the output. Note again that *sed* does not remove anything from the specified file. Let us first see what */etc/group* file contains.

$ cat /etc/group
root::0:root
other::1:root,hpdb
bin::2:root,bin
sys::3:root,uucp
adm::4:root,adm
daemon::5:root,daemon
mail::6:root
lp::7:root,lp
tty::10:
nuucp::11:nuucp
users::20:root
nogroup:*:-2:
smbnull::101:
ids::102:
sshd::103:
tftp::104:
hpsmc::105:
hpsmh::106:

Now run *sed* to get the desired result:

$ sed '/root/d' /etc/group
tty::10:
nuucp::11:nuucp
nogroup:*:-2:
smbnull::101:
ids::102:
sshd::103:
tftp::104:
hpsmc::105:
hpsmh::106:

/root/d is enclosed in single quotes. The "/root" portion of the command tells *sed* to search for the pattern "root" and the "/d" portion tells *sed* to delete that pattern from the output.

To remove all lines from the output of the *ll* command containing digit "3":

$ ll | sed '/3/d'
total 624
-rw-rw-rw-	1	user1	users	1089	Feb 4 22:56	file1
-rw-rw-rw-	1	user1	users	2426	Feb 4 22:56	file2
-rw-rw-rw-	1	user1	users	11	Feb 4 22:57	file4

To print all lines in duplicate that contain the pattern "root" in the */etc/group* file; all other lines will be printed one time.

$ sed '/root/p' /etc/group
root::0:root
root::0:root
other::1:root,hpdb
other::1:root,hpdb
bin::2:root,bin
bin::2:root,bin
sys::3:root,uucp
sys::3:root,uucp
adm::4:root,adm
adm::4:root,adm
daemon::5:root,daemon
daemon::5:root,daemon
. . . .

To print only those lines that contain the pattern "root" in */etc/group* file:

$ sed –n '/root/p' /etc/group
root::0:root
other::1:root,hpdb
bin::2:root,bin
sys::3:root,uucp
adm::4:root,adm
daemon::5:root,daemon

mail::6:root
lp::7:root,lp
users::20:root

To append the character string "HPUX" to the end of every line in the output of the *ll* command. In the following command, "s" is used for substitute and "$" represents end of line. Run the command as *user1* on *user1*'s home directory */home/user1*.

$ ll | sed 's/$/ HPUX/'

total 624 HPUX						
-rw-rw-rw-	1	user1	users	1089	Feb 4 22:56	file1 HPUX
-rw-rw-rw-	1	user1	users	2426	Feb 4 22:56	file2 HPUX
-rw-rw-rw-	1	user1	users	70336	Feb 4 22:57	file3 HPUX
-rw-rw-rw-	1	user1	users	11	Feb 4 22:57	file4 HPUX

To perform two edits on */etc/group* file where the first edit replaces all occurrences of "root" with "ROOT" and the second edit replaces "daemon" with "USERS".

$ sed –e 's/root/ROOT/g' –e 's/daemon/USERS/g' /etc/group

ROOT::0:ROOT
other::1:ROOT,hpdb
bin::2:ROOT,bin
sys::3:ROOT,uucp
adm::4:ROOT,adm
USERS::5:ROOT,USERS
mail::6:ROOT
lp::7:ROOT,lp
tty::10:
nuucp::11:nuucp
users::20:ROOT
nogroup:*:-2:
smbnull::101:
ids::102:
sshd::103:
tftp::104:
hpsmc::105:
hpsmh::106:

You can perform multiple edits using this method.

Summary

Chapter 04 discussed vi editor and text processors. You learned various vi editor operating modes and methods of starting. Within vi, you learned how to navigate, insert and delete text, undo and repeat previous commands, change text, search and replace text, copy, move and paste text, import contents from another file, customize vi settings, save modifications and exit out of it.

You also learned how to manipulate columns and rows of text using the *awk* and *sed* text processors and saw several examples that explained the usage in detail.

## 05

The Shells

This chapter covers the following major topics:

- ✓ Shells available in HP-UX
- ✓ Features associated with the POSIX shell
- ✓ Local and environment variables
- ✓ Set and unset variables
- ✓ View variable values
- ✓ Modify command prompt
- ✓ Get input from alternate source and send output and error messages to alternate destinations
- ✓ Filename completion, command line editing, command history command aliasing and tilde substitution
- ✓ Special characters and mask special meaning of some of those
- ✓ Pipes, and filters including tee, cut, pr and tr

5.1   The Shell

In the UNIX world, the *shell* is referred to as the command interpreter. It accepts instructions (or input) from users (or scripts), interprets them and passes to the kernel for processing. The kernel utilizes all hardware and software components required to process the instructions. When finished, the results are returned to the shell and displayed on the screen. The shell also displays appropriate error messages, if generated. In short, the shell operates as an interface between a user and the kernel.

The shell provides many services such as I/O redirection, filename expansion, pattern matching, environment variables, job control, command line editing, command aliasing, command history, tilde substitution, quoting mechanisms, conditional execution, flow control and writing shell scripts.

The shell is changeable providing a user with the flexibility to choose a command interpreter at any time.

5.1.1   Available Shells

There are four shells available in HP-UX: the POSIX shell, Korn shell, C shell and the Key shell. These are explained below.

The POSIX Shell

The *Portable Operating System Interface eXchange* (POSIX) shell is similar to the Korn shell in terms of features. This shell is standardized to conform with the POSIX standards. It is identified by the $ prompt and located in */sbin/sh* and */usr/bin/sh* files. The first file represents the self-contained POSIX shell, which does not require any additional library routines to work. It is designed this way to ensure that it is available if the system is in single-user mode. In contrast, */usr/bin/sh* is dependent on the library routines, which are located in the */usr/lib* directory, to work.

The POSIX shell is the default shell for all users including the *root* user. A restricted version of it is located in the */usr/bin/rsh* file which limits a user of the shell to his home directory. The user cannot *cd* out of the directory.

The Korn Shell

The *korn* shell is similar to the POSIX shell in terms of features. This shell is not standardized and there are differences among vendor versions. The korn shell was created by David Korn at the AT&T labs and its prompt is $. It resides in */usr/bin/ksh* file. A restricted version of it is located in */usr/bin/rksh* file which limits a user of the shell to his home directory. The user cannot *cd* out of the directory.

The C Shell

The *C* shell is mainly used by developers. It provides a programming interface similar to the C language and offers many POSIX and Korn shell functions in addition to numerous other features. Created by Bill Joy at the University of California at Berkeley for early BSD UNIX releases, the prompt for the C shell is % and it resides in */usr/bin/csh* file.

The Key Shell

The *key* shell is an extension to the korn shell. It presents an interactive interface to users where a softkey menu appears at the bottom of the screen. It provides context-sensitive help as you type commands at the prompt.

It is invoked by typing *keysh* at the command prompt. It loads a menu displayed at the bottom of the screen, as shown in Figure 5-1. You may want to assign this shell to users so whenever they login, this shell is invoked for them.

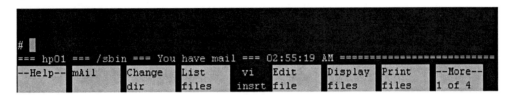

Figure 5-1 The Key Shell

5.2 POSIX Shell Features

The POSIX shell offers many features. These features are discussed in this chapter.

5.2.1 Variables

A *variable* is a temporary storage of data in memory. Variables contain information used for customizing the shell environment. Their values are used by many system and application processes to function properly. The shell allows you to store values into variables.

There are two types of variables: local and environment.

Local Variables

A *local* variable is private to the shell it is created in and its value cannot be used by processes that are not started in that shell. This introduces the concept of *current shell* and *sub-shell* (or *child shell*). The current shell is where you execute your programs from, whereas a sub-shell is created by a running program. The value of a local variable is available only in the current shell, and not in the child shell.

Environment Variables

The value of an *environment* variable, however, is passed from current shell to sub-shell. In other words, the value stored in an environment variable is passed from parent process to child process. The environment variable is also called *global* variable. Some variables are set automatically through system and user initialization files when you login to the system. Variables may also be set in shell scripts or at the command line as required.

5.2.2 Setting, Unsetting and Viewing Variables

To set, unset or view shell variables, consult Table 5-1. Two variables – V1 and V2 – are used as examples. It is recommended that you use uppercase letters for variable names to distinguish them from the names of any commands or programs that you might have on the system.

Action	Local Variable	Environment Variable
Setting variables	Syntax: V1=value Examples: **$ V1=college** **$ V2="I am using HP-UX"**	Syntax: V1=value; export V1 or export V1=value Examples: **$ V1=college; export V1** **$ V2="I am using HP-UX"; export V2** or **$ export V1=college** **$ export V2="I am using HP-UX"**
Displaying variable values	**$ print $V1** or **$ echo $V1**	
Listing set variables	**$ set** **$ env** **$ export**	
Unsetting variables	**$ unset V1** **$ unset V2**	

Table 5-1 Setting, Unsetting and Viewing Variables

To set a local variable, V1, to contain the value "college", simply define it as shown in Table 5-1. Note that there must not be any spaces either before or after the equal (=) sign. To make V1 a global variable, use the *export* command. Another example sets a variable, V2, containing a series of space-separated words. Make sure to enclose them in double quotes.

To display the value of a variable, use either the *print* or the *echo* command.

The *set* command lists current values for all shell variables including local and environment variables. The *export* and *env* commands list only environment variables.

```
$ set
COLUMNS=80
EDITOR=vi
ERASE=^H
ERRNO=0
FCEDIT=/usr/bin/ed
HOME=/home/user1
IFS='
LINENO=1
LINES=24
LOGNAME=user1
MAILCHECK=600
MANPATH=/usr/share/man/%L:/usr/share/man:/usr/contrib/man/%L:/usr/contrib/man:/usr/local/man/%L
:/usr/local/man:/opt/ldapux/share/man/%L:/opt/ldapux/share/man:/opt/ipf/man:/opt/ldapux/ypldapd/man:/
opt/samba/man:/opt/samba/WTEC_Support_Tools/man:/opt/samba/cfsm_man:/opt/cifsclient/share/man:/o
```

pt/rdma/share/man:/opt/openssl/man:/opt/openssl/prngd/man:/opt/wbem/share/man:/opt/hpsmdb/pgsql/ma
n:/opt/ssh/share/man:/opt/mx/share/man/%L:/opt/mx/share/man:/opt/graphics/common/man:/opt/amgr/ma
n:/opt/amgr/man/%L:/opt/sec_mgmt/share/man:/usr/dt/share/man:/opt/drd/share/man/%L:/opt/drd/share/m
an:/opt/dsau/man:/opt/resmon/share/man/%L:/opt/resmon/share/man:/opt/gnome/man:/opt/perf/man/%L:/
opt/perf/man:/opt/ignite/share/man/%L:/opt/ignite/share/man:/usr/contrib/kwdb/share/man:/opt/perl_32/m
an:/opt/perl_64/man:/opt/prm/man/%L:/opt/prm/man:/opt/sfmdb/pgsql/man:/opt/sfm/share/man:/opt/swm/
share/man/%L:/opt/swm/share/man:/opt/sec_mgmt/share/man/%L:/opt/spb/share/man:/opt/swa/share/man
/%L:/opt/swa/share/man:/opt/VRTS/man:/opt/gwlm/man/%L:/opt/gwlm/man
OPTARG
OPTIND=1
PATH=/usr/bin:/usr/ccs/bin:/usr/contrib/bin:/usr/contrib/Q4/bin:/opt/perl/bin:/opt/ipf/bin:/opt/nettladm/bin
:/opt/fcms/bin:/opt/wbem/bin:/opt/wbem/sbin:/opt/rdma/bin:/opt/ssh/bin:/opt/mx/bin:/opt/graphics/commo
n/bin:/opt/atok/bin:/usr/bin/X11:/usr/contrib/bin/X11:/opt/sec_mgmt/bastille/bin:/opt/drd/bin:/opt/dsau/bin
:/opt/dsau/sbin:/opt/resmon/bin:/opt/firefox:/opt/gnome/bin:/opt/perf/bin:/opt/ignite/bin:/usr/contrib/kwdb/
bin:/opt/mozilla:/var/opt/netscape/server7/shared/bin:/var/opt/netscape/server7/bin:/opt/perl_32/bin:/opt/p
erl_64/bin:/opt/prm/bin:/usr/sbin/diag/contrib:/opt/sfm/bin:/opt/swm/bin:/opt/sec_mgmt/spc/bin:/opt/java1
.4/jre/bin:/opt/spb/bin:/opt/swa/bin:/opt/hpsmh/bin:/opt/thunderbird:/opt/gwlm/bin:.
PPID=24668
PS1='$ '
PS2='> '
PS3='#? '
PS4='+ '
PWD=/home/user1
RANDOM=27394
SECONDS=3
SHELL=/sbin/sh
TERM=xterm
TMOUT=0
TZ=EST5EDT
_=clear

$ env
_=/usr/bin/env
MANPATH=/usr/share/man/%L:/usr/share/man:/usr/contrib/man/%L:/usr/contrib/man:/usr/local/man/%L
:/usr/local/man:/opt/ldapux/share/man/%L:/opt/ldapux/share/man:/opt/ipf/man:/opt/ldapux/ypldapd/man:/
opt/samba/man:/opt/samba/WTEC_Support_Tools/man:/opt/samba/cfsm_man:/opt/cifsclient/share/man:/o
pt/rdma/share/man:/opt/openssl/man:/opt/openssl/prngd/man:/opt/wbem/share/man:/opt/hpsmdb/pgsql/ma
n:/opt/ssh/share/man:/opt/mx/share/man/%L:/opt/mx/share/man:/opt/graphics/common/man:/opt/amgr/ma
n:/opt/amgr/man/%L:/opt/sec_mgmt/share/man:/usr/dt/share/man:/opt/drd/share/man/%L:/opt/drd/share/m
an:/opt/dsau/man:/opt/resmon/share/man/%L:/opt/resmon/share/man:/opt/gnome/man:/opt/perf/man/%L:/
opt/perf/man:/opt/ignite/share/man/%L:/opt/ignite/share/man:/usr/contrib/kwdb/share/man:/opt/perl_32/m
an:/opt/perl_64/man:/opt/prm/man/%L:/opt/prm/man:/opt/sfmdb/pgsql/man:/opt/sfm/share/man:/opt/swm/
share/man/%L:/opt/swm/share/man:/opt/sec_mgmt/share/man/%L:/opt/spb/share/man:/opt/swa/share/man
/%L:/opt/swa/share/man:/opt/VRTS/man:/opt/gwlm/man/%L:/opt/gwlm/man
PATH=/usr/bin:/usr/ccs/bin:/usr/contrib/bin:/usr/contrib/Q4/bin:/opt/perl/bin:/opt/ipf/bin:/opt/nettladm/bin
:/opt/fcms/bin:/opt/wbem/bin:/opt/wbem/sbin:/opt/rdma/bin:/opt/ssh/bin:/opt/mx/bin:/opt/graphics/commo
n/bin:/opt/atok/bin:/usr/bin/X11:/usr/contrib/bin/X11:/opt/sec_mgmt/bastille/bin:/opt/drd/bin:/opt/dsau/bin
:/opt/dsau/sbin:/opt/resmon/bin:/opt/firefox:/opt/gnome/bin:/opt/perf/bin:/opt/ignite/bin:/usr/contrib/kwdb/
bin:/opt/mozilla:/var/opt/netscape/server7/shared/bin:/var/opt/netscape/server7/bin:/opt/perl_32/bin:/opt/p

```
erl_64/bin:/opt/prm/bin:/usr/sbin/diag/contrib:/opt/sfm/bin:/opt/swm/bin:/opt/sec_mgmt/spc/bin:/opt/java1
.4/jre/bin:/opt/spb/bin:/opt/swa/bin:/opt/hpsmh/bin:/opt/thunderbird:/opt/gwlm/bin:.
COLUMNS=80
EDITOR=vi
LOGNAME=user1
ERASE=^H
SHELL=/sbin/sh
HOME=/home/user1
TERM=xterm
PWD=/home/user1
TZ=EST5EDT
LINES=24
```

Finally, to unset a variable, use the *unset* command and specify the variable name. It will remove the variable.

5.2.3   Pre-Defined Environment Variables

Some environment variables are defined by the shell on login. You may define more environment variables as needed. Some of the common environment variables are EDITOR, HOME, LOGNAME, PATH, PWD, PS1, PS2, SHELL, TERM, MAIL, TZ, DISPLAY, HISTFILE and HISTSIZE. Here is a brief description of each one of these in Table 5-2.

Variable	Description
EDITOR	Defines default editor. It is usually set to the vi editor.
HOME	Contains home directory path.
LOGNAME	Stores login name.
PATH	Defines a colon separated list of directories to be searched when a user executes a command.
PWD	Stores current directory location.
PS1	Defines primary command prompt. It is # for *root* by default.
PS2	Defines secondary command prompt. It is > by default.
SHELL	Holds absolute path of primary shell.
TERM	Holds terminal type value.
MAIL	Contains path to user mail directory. For example, it would be */var/mail/user1* for *user1*.
TZ	Contains timezone value including offset from *Universal Time Coordinated* (UTC).
DISPLAY	Stores hostname or IP address to display graphics.
HISTFILE	Defines file name where shell stores a history of all commands as you execute them.
HISTSIZE	Defines maximum size for HISTFILE to grow to.

Table 5-2 Pre-Defined Environment Variables

5.2.4   Command and Variable Substitution

The primary command prompt for the *root* user is the # sign. The primary command prompt for the users of POSIX and Korn shells is the $ sign and for the C shell is the % sign. Customizing the primary command prompt to display useful information such as who you are, system you are currently logged on to and your current location in the directory tree, is a good practice. The following example shows how to modify *user1*'s primary prompt from the default $ sign to the one below:

$ **export PS1="< $LOGNAME@`hostname`:\$PWD > "**

user1's command prompt will now look like:

< user1@hp01:/home/user1 >

The value of the PWD variable will reflect the directory location in *user1*'s prompt as he navigates the directory tree. This is called *variable substitution*. For example, if he moves to */usr/bin*, the prompt will change to:

< user1@hp01:/usr/bin >

Also, the value of LOGNAME variable is used to display *user1*'s login name in this example.

Running the command *hostname* and assigning its output to a variable is an example of a shell feature called *command substitution*. Note that the command the output of which you want to assign to a variable must be enclosed in single forward quotes.

5.2.5   Input, Output and Error Redirection

Many programs in HP-UX read input from the keyboard and write output to the terminal window where they were initiated. If any errors are encountered, they are displayed on the terminal window too. This is the default behavior. What if you do not wish to take input from the keyboard or write the output to the terminal window? The POSIX shell allows you to redirect input, output and error messages. Programs or commands will read input from something other than the keyboard and send output and error messages to something other than the terminal window.

The default (or the standard) locations for input, output and error are referred to as *stdin*, *stdout* and *stderr*, respectively. Table 5-3 demonstrates that each of the three has an association with a symbol and a digit. These symbols and digits are used at the command line and in shell scripts for redirection purposes.

File Descriptor	Symbol	Associated Digit	Description
stdin	<	0	Standard input
stdout	>	1	Standard output
stderr	>	2	Standard error

Table 5-3 I/O/E Redirection Symbols

The following text explains how redirection of input, output and error takes place.

Redirecting Standard Input

Input redirection instructs a command to read required information from an alternate source such as a file, instead of the keyboard. For example, do the following to have the *mailx* command mail the contents of *file1* to *user2*:

$ mailx user2 < file1

In order for *mailx* to work properly, Sendmail must be configured and running. See Chapter 26 "Internet Services and Sendmail" on how to configure and use Sendmail.

Redirecting Standard Output

Output redirection sends the output generated by a command to an alternate destination such as a file, instead of sending it to the terminal window. For example, do the following to direct the *sort* command to send the sorted output of *file1* to a file called *sort.out*. This will overwrite any *sort.out* file contents. If *sort.out* does not exist, it will be created.

$ sort file1 > sort.out

To direct the *sort* command to append output to *sort.out*, use the >> symbols:

$ sort file1 >> sort.out

Redirecting Standard Error

Error redirection sends any error messages generated to an alternate destination such as a file, instead of sending them to the terminal window. For example, do the following to direct the *find* command to send any error messages generated to */dev/null*. The */dev/null* file is a special system file used to discard data.

$ find / –name core –print 2> /dev/null

This command will search for all occurrences of files by the name "core" in the entire root directory tree. Error messages will be generated when a directory where the user does not have rights is accessed with normal user privileges. These error messages will be discarded and sent to garbage.

Redirecting both Standard Output and Error

Do the following to redirect both stdout and stderr to the file called *testfile1*:

$ ls /etc /cdr 1> testfile1 2>&1

This example will produce a listing of the */etc* directory and saves the result in *testfile1*. At the same time, it will generate an error message complaining about non-existence of */cdr* directory. This error message will also be sent to the same file and saved.

5.2.6   Filename Completion, Command Line Editing and Command History

Filename completion or *filename expansion* is a POSIX shell feature whereby typing a partial filename at the command line and then hitting the Esc key twice, completes a filename if there are no other possibilities. If there exists multiple possibilities, it will complete up to the point they have in common.

Command line editing allows you to edit a line of text right at the command prompt. Pressing the Esc+k key combination brings at the prompt the last command you executed. Pressing the letter k repeatedly scrolls backward to previous commands in reverse chronological order. The letter j scrolls forward through the command history in chronological order. When you get the desired command, you may edit it right at the command prompt using the vi editor commands (refer to Chapter 04 "The vi Editor and Text Processors" to learn about the vi editor commands). If you do not wish to edit it or done with editing, simply press the Enter key to execute it.

Command history, or simply *history*, keeps a log of all commands that you run at the command prompt. The shell stores command history in a file located in user's home directory. You may retrieve these commands, modify them at the command line and re-run them using the command line editing feature.

There are three variables that enable the features you just learned. These variables are listed below along with sample values:

HISTFILE=~/.sh_history
HISTSIZE=1000
EDITOR=vi

The HISTFILE variable tells the POSIX shell to store all commands run by a user in *.sh_history* file in that user's home directory. This file is created automatically if it does not exist. Each command, along with options and arguments, is stored on a separate line.

The HISTSIZE variable controls the maximum number of commands that can be stored in HISTFILE. The default is 128.

The EDITOR variable defines what text editor to use. If this variable is not set, issue the following to be able to use the filename expansion, command line editing and command history features:

$ set −o vi

The three variables discussed are usually defined in user initialization files. Refer to Chapter 12 "Users and Groups" on how to define variables in user initialization files to customize the behavior.

HP-UX provides the *history* command to display previously executed commands. This command gets history information from *.sh_history* file. By default, the last 16 entries are displayed.

$ history
488   vi mailservs
489   /sbin/init.d/sendmail stop
490   /sbin/init.d/sendmail start
491   ps -eaf|grep send
492   kill -9 17388 17366
493   clear
494   ps -eaf|grep send
495   mailx user1 < /etc/profile
496   pwd
497   more mails*
498   cd
499   clear

```
500   exit
501   clear
502   history
503   su - user1
```

Let us use some of the *history* command options to alter its behavior.

To display the command history without line numbers:

$ history –n

To display this command and 25 commands preceding it:

$ history –25

To display command history in reverse order:

$ history –r

To display all commands between the most recent occurrence of one command (*mv* in the following example) and the most recent occurrence of another command (*cp* for example):

$ history mv cp

To re-execute a command by its line number (line 38 for example) in history file:

$ r 38

To re-execute the most recent occurrence of a command that started with a particular letter or series of letters (ch for example):

$ r ch

To repeat the most recent occurrence of a command beginning with letters "ch", perform a simple edit and execute the modified command:

$ chown user1 file1
$ r file1=file2

5.2.7   Alias Substitution

A *command alias,* or simply an *alias*, allows you to create shortcuts for lengthy commands. When an alias is run, the POSIX shell executes the corresponding command. This saves you time typing the same command repeatedly.

The POSIX shell contains several pre-defined aliases that you can view by running the *alias* command. Any new aliases that you have defined are also displayed.

```
$ alias
autoload='typeset -fu'
command='command '
functions='typeset -f'
history='fc -l'
integer='typeset -i'
local=typeset
nohup='nohup '
r='fc -e -'
stop='kill -STOP'
suspend='kill -STOP $$'
type='whence -v'
```

These aliases are explained in Table 5-4.

Alias	Value	Definition
autoload	"typeset –fu"	Defines how to load a function automatically.
command	"command"	Executes a command.
functions	"typeset –f"	Displays defined functions.
history	"fc –l"	Lists command history.
integer	"typeset –i"	Displays integer variables.
local	"typeset"	Defines a local attribute for variables and functions.
nohup	"nohup"	Keeps background jobs running even if you log off.
r	"fc –e –"	Re-executes the last command.
stop	"kill –STOP"	Suspends a job.
suspend	"kill –STOP $$"	Suspends the current job.
type	"whence –v"	Tells how it is interpreted if used as a command name.

Table 5-4 Pre-Defined Command Aliases

There are two commands available to work with aliases. These are *alias* and *unalias*. The *alias* command displays and sets an alias while the *unalias* command unsets it. Let us look at a few examples.

Create an alias "f" to abbreviate the *find* command. Use either single or double quotes to enclose multiple words. Do not leave any spaces before and after the = sign.

$ **alias f="find / –name core –exec rm {} \;"**

Now, when you type an "f" at the command prompt and hit the Enter key, the shell replaces the alias "f" with what is stored in it. Basically, you created a shortcut to that lengthy command.

Sometimes you create an alias by a name that matches the name of a system command. In this situation, the shell gives the alias precedence over the command. This means the shell will run the alias and not the command. For example, you know that the *rm* command deletes a file without giving any warning. To prevent accidental deletion of files with *rm*, you may create an alias by the same name.

```
$ alias rm="rm –i"
$ rm file1
file1: ? (y/n)
```

When you execute *rm* now, the shell will run what you have stored in the *rm* alias and not the command *rm*. If you wish to run the *rm* command, run it with a preceding \ character:

$ \rm file1

Use the *unalias* command to unset an alias if you no longer need it:

$ unalias f
$ unalias rm

5.2.8   Tilde Substitution

Tilde substitution (or *tilde expansion*) is performed on words that begin with the tilde (~) sign. The rules are:

1. If used as a standalone character, the shell refers to the $HOME directory of the user running the command. The following example displays the $HOME directory of *user1*:

    $ echo ~
    /home/user1

2. If used prior to the + sign, the shell refers to the current directory. For example, if *user1* is in */etc/rc.config.d* directory and does ~+, the output will display the user's current directory location (which is */etc/rc.config.d*):

    $ echo ~+
    /etc/rc.config.d

3. If used prior to the – sign, the shell refers to the last working directory. For example, if *user1* changes to */usr/share/man* directory from */etc/rc.config.d* and does ~–, the output will display the user's last working directory location (which was */etc/rc.config.d*):

    $ echo ~–
    /etc/rc.config.d

4. If used prior to a username, the shell refers to the $HOME directory of that user:

    $ echo ~user2
    /home/user2

You can use the tilde substitution with any command that refers to location in the directory structure. Such commands include *cd*, *ls* and *echo*.

5.2.9 Special Characters

Special characters are the symbols on keyboard that possess special meaning to the shell. These characters are also referred to as *metacharacters* or *wildcard* characters. Some of these such as dash (−), tilde (~) and redirection symbols (< >) have been discussed earlier in this chapter. Four additional special characters: asterisk (*), question mark (?), square brackets ([ ]) and semicolon (;) will be discussed in this sub-section.

The Asterisk (*) Character

The asterisk character matches zero to unlimited number of any characters, except the leading period in a hidden file. See the following examples to understand its usage.

To list names of all files that begin with letters "fi" followed by any characters:

$ ls fi*
file1.txt file2.txt file3.txt file4 file5 file6

To list names of all files that begin with letter "d". You will notice in the output that contents of *dir1* and *dir2* sub-directories are also listed.

$ ls d*
date1 date2 date3
dir1:
scripts1 scripts2
dir2:
newfile1 newfile2 newfile3 newfile4

To list names of all files that end with the digit "4":

$ ls *4
file4

To list names of all files that have a period followed by letters "txt" at the end:

$ ls *.txt
file1.txt file2.txt file3.txt

The Question Mark (?) Character

The question mark character matches exactly one character, except the leading period in a hidden file. See the following example to understand its usage.

To list all files that begin with characters "file" followed by one character only:

$ ls file?
file4 file5 file6

The Square Bracket ([]) Characters

The square brackets can be used to match either a set of characters or a range of characters for a single character position.

When you specify a set of characters, order is unimportant. Hence, [xyz], [yxz], [xzy] and [yxz] are treated alike. The following example encloses two characters within square brackets. The output will include all files and directories that begin with either of the two characters followed by any number of characters.

```
$ ls [cf]*
car1  car2  file1.txt  file2.txt  file3.txt  file4  file5  file6  fruit  fruit2
```

A range of characters must be specified in proper order such as [a-z] or [0-9]. The following example matches all file and directory names that begin with any alphabet between "a" and "f":

```
$ ls [a–f]*
alpha1  beta2  car1  car2  data1  data2  echo.txt  file1  file.1  file.3  file2  file4

dir1:
fruit  trees
dir2:
scripts  korn
```

The Semicolon (;) Character

The semicolon character separates commands. It enables you to enter multiple commands on a single command line. The following example shows three commands: *cd*, *ls* and *date* separated by semicolon. The three commands will be executed in the order they are specified.

```
$ cd; ls fil*; date
file1.txt  file2.txt  file3.txt  file4  file5  file6
Fri Dec  9 16:50:10 EST 2005
```

5.2.10 Masking Special Meaning of Some Special Characters

Sometimes you are in a situation where you want the shell to treat a special character as a regular character. There are three special characters that disable the meaning of other special characters when properly used with them. These characters are \, ' and ", and are described below.

The Backslash (\ ) Character

The backslash character forces the shell to mask the meaning of any special character that follows it. For example, if a file exists by the name * and you wish to remove it with the *rm* command, you will have to ensure that the \ character is specified right before *.

```
$ rm \*
```

If you forget \, all files in the directory will be deleted.

The Single Quote (') Character

The single quote character forces the shell to mask the meaning of all enclosed special characters. For example, LOGNAME is a variable and you use the *echo* command to display the value stored in it:

```
$ echo $LOGNAME
user1
```

If you enclose $LOGNAME within single quote characters, the *echo* command will display what is enclosed instead of the value of the variable.

```
$ echo '$LOGNAME'
$LOGNAME
```

Similarly, the backslash character is echoed when enclosed within single quotes.

```
$ echo '\'
\
```

The Double Quote (") Character

The double quote character forces the shell to mask the meaning of all but three special characters: \, $ and '. These special characters retain their special meaning if used within double quotes. Look at the following examples to understand the concept.

```
$ echo "$SHELL"
/usr/bin/sh
$ echo "\$PWD"
$PWD
$ echo "\"
\
^c
```

5.3   Pipes and Filters

This section talks about pipes and filters often used at the command line and in shell scripts.

5.3.1   Pipes

The *pipe*, represented by the | character and resides with \ on the keyboard, is a special character that sends output of one command as input to another command.

The following example uses the *ll* command to display contents of the */etc* directory. The output is piped to the *more* command, which displays the listing one screen at a time.

```
$ ll /etc | more
total 2112
-r--r--r--    1 bin    bin    1039 Apr  8 11:45   MANPATH
-r--r--r--    1 bin    bin     715 Apr  8 11:45   PATH
-r--r--r--    1 bin    bin     151 Apr  8 11:35   SHLIB_PATH
drwxr-xr-x    2 bin    bin      96 Apr 10 09:44   SnmpAgent.d
-r--r--r--    1 bin    bin      21 Apr  8 11:47   TIMEZONE
drwxr-xr-x    9 bin    bin    8192 Apr  8 11:41   X11
drwxr-xr-x    2 bin    bin      96 Apr  8 11:30   acct
-r--r--r--    1 root   sys      36 Feb 15 2007    acps.conf
lrwxr-xr-x    1 root   sys      17 Apr  8 11:40   aliases -> /etc/mail/aliases
--more—
```

Another example runs the *who* command and pipe its output to the *nl* command to display associated line numbers.

```
$ who | nl
     1  root    pts/0    May 12 10:16
     2  root    pts/1    May 12 11:17
```

The following example creates a pipeline whereby the output of *ll* is sent to the first *grep* command, which filters out all lines that do not contain the pattern "root". The new output is then sent to the second *grep* command which filters out all lines that do not contain the pattern "apr". Finally, the output is numbered and displayed on the screen. A structure like this with multiple pipes is referred to as a *pipeline*.

```
$ ll /etc | grep root | grep –i apr | nl
     1  lrwxr-xr-x  1 root  sys     17   Apr  8 11:40   aliases -> /etc/mail/aliases
     2  lrwxr-xr-x  1 root  bin     13   Apr  8 09:06   arp -> /usr/sbin/arp
     3  -rw-------  1 root  sys     34   Apr  9 12:45   auto_master
     4  -rw-r--r--  1 root  root    86   Apr 10 09:32   auto_parms.log
     5  -rw-r--r--  1 root  sys    219   Apr 10 09:25   auto_parms.log.old
. . . . . . . .
```

5.3.2   The tee Filter

The *tee* filter is used to send output to more than one destination. It can send one copy of the output to a file and another to the screen (or some other program) if used with pipe.

In the following example, the output from *ll* is numbered and captured in */tmp/ll.out* file. The output is displayed on the screen too.

```
$ ll /etc | nl | tee /tmp/ll.out
```

Do a *cat* on */tmp/ll.out* and you will notice that the file contains the exact information that was displayed on the screen when you executed the command.

By using –a with *tee*, the output is appended to the file, rather than overwriting existing contents.

```
$ date | tee –a /tmp/ll.out
```

5.3.3   The cut Filter

The *cut* filter is used to extract selected columns from a line. The default column separator used is white space such as a tab. The following example command cuts out columns 1 and 4 from the */etc/group* file as specified with the –f option. The colon character is used as a field separator.

$ cut –d : –f 1,4 /etc/group
root:root
other:root,hpdb
bin:root,bin

. . . .

5.3.4   The pr Filter

The *pr* filter is used to format and display the contents of a text file. The output may be piped to a printer if one is configured.

By default, the *pr* command prints file name, time stamp on it, page number and file contents. For example, to display the contents of */etc/group* file:

$ pr /etc/group

Apr 11 09:03 2008 /etc/group Page 1

root::0:root
other::1:root,hpdb
bin::2:root,bin
sys::3:root,uucp
adm::4:root,adm
daemon::5:root,daemon

. . . .

Options listed in Table 5-5 are available with the *pr* command for enhanced readability.

Option	Purpose
+page	Begins printing from the specified page number.
	$ pr +2 /etc/group
–column	Prints in multiple columns.
	$ pr –2 /etc/group
–d	Prints with double line spacing.
	$ pr –d /etc/group
–l lines	Changes page length (default is 66 lines).
	$ pr –l 20 /etc/group
–m	Prints specified files side-by-side in separate columns.
	$ pr –m /etc/group /etc/passwd /etc/hosts
–h header	Replaces filename in the output.
–t	Suppresses the filename and time stamp on it.

Option	Purpose
–n	Assigns a number to each line in the output.

Table 5-5 *pr* Command Options

The following example prints the */etc/group* file in two columns with double spacing between lines, the header title "My PR Command Test" and the page length not more than 20 lines.

> **$ pr –2dh "My PR Command Test" –l 20 /etc/group**

5.3.5   The tr Filter

The *tr* filter translates specified input characters and displays the output on the screen. Following are a few examples.

To remove all but one space between columns in the output of the *w* command. Note that there is a single space between double quotes in the command below:

$ w | tr –s '' "
```
2:28am up 12 days, 4:38, 1 user, load average: 0.50, 0.52, 0.53
user            tty       login@ idle     JCPU    PCPU    what
user1           pts/ta    2:28am                          tr -s
```

To remove all digits from the output of the *w* command:

$ w | tr –d '[0-9]'
```
:am  up  days,  :,  user,  load average: ., ., .
user            tty       login@ idle     JCPU    PCPU    what
user            pts/ta    :am                             tr -d [-]
```

To display all letters in uppercase:

$ w | tr '[a-z]' '[A-Z]'
```
2:31AM  UP 12 DAYS, 4:41,           1 USER,  LOAD  AVERAGE: 0.52, 0.52, 0.53
USER   TTY         LOGIN@           IDLE            JCPU   PCPU   WHAT
USER1   PTS/TA                      2:28AM                        TR [A-Z] [A-Z]
```

Summary

Chapter 05 discussed shells and shell features in detail. You looked at shells available in HP-UX; features of the POSIX shell including setting, unsetting and displaying contents of local and environment variables, modifying command prompt to display useful information, getting input from non-default sources, sending output and error messages to alternate destinations, defining and undefining shortcuts to lengthy commands; using tilde substitution; and setting required variables to enable filename completion, command line editing and command history features.

You learned about special characters and how to mask special meanings of some of them.

Finally, you studied the use of the pipe (|) character and the commands – *tee, cut, pr* and *tr* – for use as filters.

## 06

System Processes and Job Control

This chapter covers the following major topics:

✓ Understand system and user executed processes
✓ Display processes
✓ View process tree
✓ View process states
✓ Nice value and how to start a process with a non-default nice value
✓ Modify nice value of a running process
✓ Signals and how to use them
✓ Manage jobs in the POSIX shell
✓ Run a command immune to hang-up signals

6.1   Understanding Processes

A *process* is created in memory when a program or command is executed. A unique identification number, known as *process identification* (PID), is allocated to it, which is used by the kernel to manage the process until the program or command it is associated with terminates. When a user logs on to the system, shell is started, which is a process. Similarly, when a user executes a command or opens up an application, a process is created. Thus, a process is any program that runs on the system.

At system boot up, several processes are started. Many of these sit in memory and wait for an event to trigger a request to use their service. These background system processes are called *daemons* and are critical to system functionality.

6.1.1   Viewing System Processes

There are two commands commonly used to view currently running processes. These are *ps* (process status) and *top*.

The *ps* command, without any options or arguments, lists processes specific to the terminal where the *ps* command is run:

```
$ ps
PID         TTY     TIME    COMMAND
21938       pts/ta  0:00    ps
21924       pts/ta  0:00    sh
21923       pts/ta  0:00    telnetd
```

The output has four columns: PID of the process in the first column, terminal the process belongs to in the second column, cumulative time the process is given by the system CPU in the third column and actual command or program being executed in the last column.

Two options –e (every) and –f (full) are usually used to generate detailed information on every process running in the system. Check the *ps* command man pages for more options.

```
# ps –ef
    UID     PID    PPID   C    STIME       TTY     TIME    COMMAND
    Root    0      0      0    15:03:30    ?       0:02    swapper
    root    8      0      0    15:03:31    ?       0:00    supsched
    root    9      0      0    15:03:31    ?       0:00    strmem
    root    10     0      0    15:03:31    ?       0:00    strweld
    root    11     0      0    15:03:31    ?       0:00    strfreebd
    root    2      0      0    15:03:31    ?       0:00    vhand
    root    1      0      0    15:03:32    ?       0:01    init
    root    18947  18919  8    06:45:56    pts/ta  0:00    ps -ef
. . . . . . . .
```

The output shows more details about running processes. Table 6-1 describes content type of each column.

Title Heading	Description
UID	User ID of process owner.
PID	Process ID of process.
PPID	Process ID of parent process.
C	Process priority.
STIME	Process start time.
TTY	Terminal where process was started. Console represents system console. ? indicates a daemon running in the background.
TIME	Cumulative execution time for process.
COMMAND	Command or process name.

Table 6-1 *ps* Command Output Explanation

Notice in the output of the *ps* command above that there are scores of daemon processes running in the background that have association with no terminal. Also notice PID and PPID numbers. The smaller the number, the earlier it is started. The process with PID 0 is started first at system boot, followed by the process with PID 1 and so on. Each PID has a PPID in the 3rd column. Owner of each process is also shown along with the command or program name.

Information on each running process is kept and maintained in a process table, which the *ps* and other commands read to display output.

The other command to view process information is the *top* command, which displays additional information including CPU and memory utilization. A sample output from a running *top* session is shown below:

```
$ top
System: hp01                          Thu Dec 29 10:14:40 2005
Load averages: 0.52, 0.53, 0.53
127 processes: 105 sleeping, 22 running
Cpu states:
CPU  LOAD  USER  NICE   SYS   IDLE   BLOCK  SWAIT  INTR  SSYS
0    0.03  0.0%  0.0%  0.0%  100.0%  0.0%   0.0%   0.0%  0.0%
1    1.00  0.0%  0.0%  0.0%  100.0%  0.0%   0.0%   0.0%  0.0%

---  ----  - - - - - - - - -----
avg  0.52  0.0%  0.0%  0.0% 100.0%  0.0%   0.0%  0.0%  0.0%


Memory: 100144K (55512K) real, 350304K (248828K) virtual, 758248K free  Page# 1/11
CPU TTY  PID  USER PRI  NI  SIZE    RES    STATE TIME  %WCPU %CPU CMD
 1   ?  1474  root 152  20  4900K  6916K   run   6:57   1.15  1.15 prm3d
 0   ?    34  root 152  20    0K   336K    run   0:52   0.36  0.36 vxfsd
 1   ?   993  root 152  20  1596K  1944K   run   0:02   0.23  0.23 dmisp
 1   ?  1772  root 152  20  1076K  1956K   run   0:02   0.10  0.10 samd
```
Press Ctrl+c to quit.

6.1.2   Viewing Process Tree

There is a new tool called *ptree* which you can use to print the process hierarchy of running processes. It identifies parent and child processes in the first column and displays associated process names on the right. Here is an example output:

```
# ptree
391      /sbin/fs/fsdaemon -f 0
1245     /usr/sbin/syncer
1249     /usr/sbin/utmpd
1306     /usr/sbin/evmd
  1325      /usr/sbin/evmlogger -o /var/run/evmlogger.info -l /var/evm/adm/
  1326      /usr/sbin/evmchmgr -l /var/evm/adm/logfiles/evmchmgr.log
1494     /usr/sbin/syslogd -D
1499     /usr/sbin/ptydaemon
1513     /usr/sbin/hotplugd /var/adm/hotplugd.log trunc
1527     /usr/lbin/nktl_daemon 0 0 0 0 0 1 -2
1537     /usr/lbin/ntl_reader 0 1 1 1 1000 2 /var/adm/nettl /var/adm/con
  1538      /usr/sbin/netfmt -C -F -f /var/adm/nettl.LOG000 -c /var/adm/con
1702     /opt/ssh/sbin/sshd
  3124     sshd: root@pts/0
   3128      -sh
    4548       ptree
1712     /usr/sbin/rpcbind
. . . . . . . .
```

The output indicates that PID 1702 is associated with the *sshd* daemon, which has a child process "sshd:root@pts/0" running. Within the child process, the shell is running with PID 3128. The *ptree* command that you just ran had the PID 4548.

6.1.3   Process States

After a process is started, it does not run continuously. It may be in a non-running condition for a while or waiting for some other process to feed it with information so it continues to run. There are five process states: running, sleeping, waiting, stopped and zombie.

- ✓ The *running* state determines that the process is currently being executed by system CPU.
- ✓ The *sleeping* state shows that the process is currently waiting for input from user or another process.
- ✓ The *waiting* state means that the process has received input it has been waiting for and it is now ready to run as soon as its turn arrives.
- ✓ The *stopped* state indicates that the process is currently halted and will not run even when its turn comes, unless it is sent a signal.
- ✓ The *zombie* state determines that the process is dead. A zombie process exists in process table just as any other process entry, but takes up no resources. The entry for zombie is retained until the parent process permits it to die. A zombie process is also called a *defunct* process.

6.1.4   Process Priority

Process priority is determined using the *nice* value. The system assigns a nice value to a process when it is initiated to establish priority.

A total of 40 nice values exist with 0 being the highest. Most system-started processes use the default nice value of 20. A child process started by a parent process inherits the parent's nice value.

Use the *ps* command and specify the –l option to determine nice values of running processes. See associated nice values for each process under the "NI" column in the following example:

```
# ps –efl
F    S  UID   PID  PPID  C  PRI  NI  ADDR      SZ  WCHAN   STIME   TTY  TIME   COMD
1003 S  root  0    0     1  127  20  e0c228    0   b84064  May 22  ?    23:29  swapper
1003 S  root  8    0     0  100  20  72840040  0   114a0b0 May 22  ?    0:00   supsched
1003 S  root  9    0     0  100  20  72840180  0   db87d8  May 22  ?    0:00   strmem
```

A different priority may be assigned to a program or command at the time it is initiated. For example, to run *smh* with lower priority:

```
# nice –2 smh
```

The value assigned with *nice* is relative to the default nice value. The number –2 is added to 20, which means the specified program will run at a lower priority since its nice value is 22. If you wish to run the same program at a higher priority, say 18, use a pair of minus signs:

```
# nice --2 smh
```

Programs started to run in the background get the default nice value of 24. For example, to run *smh* in the background with nice value -10:

```
# nice –14 smh &
```

The priority of a running program can be altered as well using the *renice* command. For example, to change the nice value of the running *smh* program from -10 to +5, specify its PID (24854) with the *renice* command:

```
# renice –n 5 24854
24854: old priority -10, new priority 5
```

Add 20 to –10 to get the previous nice value, which was +10. The new priority is actually 25 (20 + 5) but the system shows 5.

To alter nice values of all processes owned by members of a particular group, you can use the –g option with *renice*. Similarly, to alter nice values of all processes owned by a particular user, use the –u option with it. Check *renice* command's man pages on usage.

6.2 Signals and Their Use

A system runs several processes simultaneously, and at times it is necessary to pass a notification to a process alerting it of an event. A user or the system uses a signal to pass that notification to a process. A signal contains a signal number and is used to control processes.

There are a number of signals available for use but most of the time you deal with only a few of them. Each signal is associated with a unique number, a name and an action. A list of available signals can be displayed with the *kill* command using the –l option.

kill –l

1) HUP	16) USR1	31) RESERVED
2) INT	17) USR2	32) bad trap
3) QUIT	18) CHLD	33) XCPU
4) ILL	19) PWR	34) XFSZ
5) TRAP	20) VTALRM	35) bad trap
6) IOT	21) PROF	36) bad trap
7) EMT	22) POLL	37) RTMIN
8) FPE	23) WINCH	38) RTMIN+1
9) KILL	24) STOP	39) RTMIN+2
10) BUS	25) TSTP	40) RTMIN+3
11) SEGV	26) CONT	41) RTMAX-3
12) SYS	27) TTIN	42) RTMAX-2
13) PIPE	28) TTOU	43) RTMAX-1
14) ALRM	29) URG	44) RTMAX
15) TERM	30) LOST	

Table 6-2 describes signals that are more often used.

Number	Name	Action	Response
1	HUP	Hang up signal causes a phone line or terminal connection to drop. Also used to force a running daemon to re-read its configuration file.	Exit
2	INT	Interrupt signal issued from keyboard, usually by ^c.	Exit
9	KILL	Kills a process abruptly by force.	Exit
15	TERM	Sends a process a soft termination signal to stop it in an orderly fashion. This signal is default.	Exit

Table 6-2 Some Key Signals

The commands used to pass a signal to a process are *kill* and *pkill*. These commands are usually used to terminate a process. Ordinary users can kill processes they own, while *root* can kill any process.

The syntax of the *kill* command to kill a process is:

kill PID
kill –s <signal name or signal number> PID

Specify multiple PIDs if you wish to kill all of them in one go.

The syntax of the *pkill* command to kill a process is:

pkill process_name
pkill –s <signal name or signal number> process_name

Specify multiple process names if you wish to kill all of them at once.

Let us look at a few examples.

To pass the soft terminate signal to the printing daemon *lpsched*, use one of the following to determine PID of it:

```
# ps –ef | grep lp
lp 1230    1  0 Dec 23 ?      0:08  /usr/sbin/lpsched
# pgrep lpsched
1230
```

Now pass signal 15 to the process using any of the following:

```
# kill 1230                  # kill –s 15 1230           # kill –15 1230
# kill –s SIGTERM 1230       # kill –SIGTERM 1230
# pkill lpsched              # pkill –s 15 lpsched       # pkill –15 lpsched
# pkill –SIGTERM lpsched
```

Using the *kill* or *pkill* command without specifying a signal name or number sends default signal of 15 to the process. This signal usually causes the process to terminate.

Some processes ignore signal 15 as they might be waiting for an input from some source to continue processing. Such processes can be terminated by force using signal 9:

```
$ kill –s 9 1230
$ pkill –9 lpsched
```

6.3   Managing Jobs in the POSIX Shell

A *job* is a process started by a user in the background and controlled by the terminal where it is spawned. It is assigned a PID by the kernel and a job ID by the shell. It does not tie up the terminal window where it is initiated, as a normal process does. This enables you to run some other program from the same terminal window.

The POSIX shell allows running multiple jobs simultaneously including transferring large amounts of data and running application programs in the background.

Jobs running in the background can be brought to foreground, taken to the background, suspended or stopped. The management of several jobs within a shell environment is called *job control*.

The shell offers some commands and control sequences for administering jobs. See Table 6-3.

Command	Description
jobs	Displays jobs currently running.
bg %*job_ID*	Places a job in the background.
fg %*Job_ID*	Places a job in the foreground.
ctrl+z	Suspends a job running in the foreground.
stop %*job_ID*	Stops a background job.

Table 6-3 Job Control

To run a job in the background type the command followed by the ampersand (&) character.

The examples below run commands *top*, *glance* and *vi* in the background. The shell displays job IDs enclosed in square brackets and associated PIDs for each command. The job IDs allow you to control the jobs. The PIDs are used by the kernel to manage the processes.

```
$ top &
[1] 4635
$ glance &
[2] 4696
$ vi file1 &
[3] 4767
```

Issue the *jobs* command to view all running jobs:

```
# jobs
[1] – Stopped        top &
[2] – Stopped        glance &
[3] + Running        vi file1 &
```

To bring job ID 1 to the foreground:

```
# fg %1
```

Before going to the next example, set an *stty* command option "susp" as follows:

```
# stty susp ^z
```

To suspend job ID 1 and sends it to the background again, press ^z followed by the following command to get the command prompt back:

```
# bg %1
```

To stop job ID 3:

```
# stop %3
```

A message is displayed when a job finishes indicating that the background job has been completed.

```
[3] + Done vi file1 &
```

6.4   Executing a Command Immune to Hang Up Signals

When a command or program is executed, it ties itself to the terminal session where it is initiated. It does not release the control of the terminal session to the shell until the command or program finishes execution. During this time, if the terminal session is closed or terminated, the command or program that was running there is also terminated. Imagine a large file transfer of several GBs was occurring and was about to finish when this unwanted termination occurred. This would be very frustrating.

To avoid such a situation, use the *nohup* (no hang up) command to execute commands or programs that need to run for extended periods of time without being interrupted. For example, to copy */opt/data1* directory containing 4GB of data to */opt/data2*, issue the *cp* command as follows:

nohup cp –rp /opt/data1 /opt/data2 &

Summary

You studied about processes in this chapter. A good understanding of what user and system processes are running is vital for performance and general system administration. You learned how to display processes, process tree and the five process states.

You studied nice values and how they were used to compute priority for a given process. You may either execute a process or command with the default nice value or assign one when you run it. You can always modify nice value of a process at any time in future while the process is still running.

Next, you looked at signals and understood what they did when passed to processes via the *kill* or *pkill* command.

Finally, you learned how to manage background jobs and run commands immune to hangup signals.

## 07

System Administration and HP-UX Server Hardware

This chapter covers the following major topics:

- ✓ Responsibilities of an HP-UX system administrator
- ✓ Help resources available to the HP-UX system administrator
- ✓ Web-Based Enterprise Management and how to use it
- ✓ HP Systems Insight Manager and how to use it
- ✓ System Management Homepage and how to use it
- ✓ Restricted access to System Management Homepage
- ✓ Overview of hardware components found in HP servers that run HP-UX
- ✓ Overview of HP Integrity and HP 9000 servers
- ✓ Overview of HP BladeSystem
- ✓ Understand Mass Storage Stack
- ✓ Legacy and persistent DSFs
- ✓ Major and minor numbers
- ✓ Create, display and remove DSFs
- ✓ View hardware diagnostic messages

7.1   HP-UX System Administration Overview

System administration is a series of management tasks that a person referred to as *system administrator*, is responsible to carry out on a routine basis. The computing environment which the system administrator is responsible for may comprise one or more networked HP-UX systems. Administration on standalone HP-UX machines is referred to as *system administration* and administration of services that involve more than one system is referred to as *network administration*. In the HP-UX world, the term *HP-UX system administrator* is commonly used for an individual that performs both system and network administration tasks on HP-UX systems.

7.1.1   System Administrator Responsibilities

The HP-UX system administrator is responsible for installing, configuring and supporting servers that run HP-UX in a networked environment. This includes hardware integration and management, server partitioning and HP-UX installation, and administration and support of software and patches, users and groups, LVM and VxVM, file systems and swap spaces, system shutdown and startup, kernel and backups, printing and scheduling, logging and performance, network interfaces and routing, internet services and sendmail, time and resource sharing, naming and boot services, automated installation and system recovery, high availability and clustering, and security and server hardening.

The system administrator requires data center access and *root* user privileges to configure and support HP-UX based computing infrastructure.

7.1.2   System Administrator Resources

There are certain resources available to the system administrator to help perform system and network administration tasks effectively and efficiently. Some of the key resources are:

Online man pages

The online manual pages are typically loaded on the system as part of HP-UX installation. See Chapter 01 "Introduction to UNIX and HP-UX" on usage and details.

www.docs.hp.com

This site contains documentation on current and previous HP-UX releases, server and workstation hardware and so on. Visit this site to access up-to-date technical material. Figure 7-1 shows portion of the main web page.

www.itrc.hp.com

This is HP's *Information Technology Resource Center* (ITRC) site that provides detailed maintenance and support information on HP software and hardware products. This site contains technical knowledge base and information on patch management as well as a free forum where thousands of HP-UX administrators exchange technical knowledge and discuss technical issues. Figure 7-2 displays portion of the main ITRC web page.

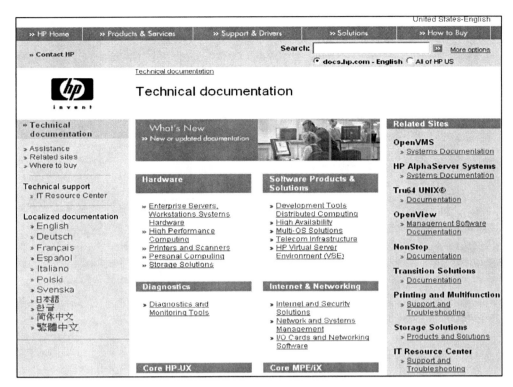

Figure 7-1 *www.docs.hp.com*

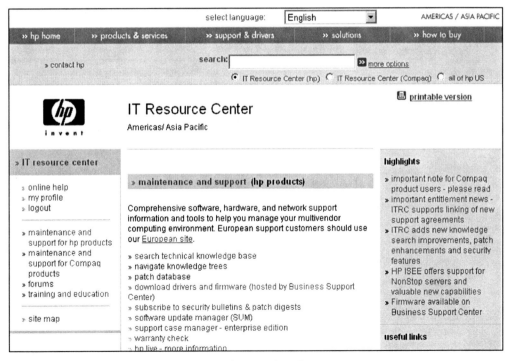

Figure 7-2 *www.itrc.hp.com*

7.1.3 System Administration Tools

HP-UX offers powerfull tools to manage systems proficiently and effectively. These tools are:

- ✓ HP Web-Based Enterprise Management (WBEM)
- ✓ HP Systems Insight Manager (SIM)
- ✓ HP System Management Homepage (SMH) [Previously called System Administration Manager (SAM)]

The following sections explain these tools in detail.

7.2 HP Web-Based Enterprise Management (WBEM)

Web-Based Enterprise Management (WBEM) is a set of management and internet standard technologies based on *Common Information Model* (CIM) and developed by the *Distributed Management Task Force* (DMTF), a vendor-neutral body, to integrate the administration of multi-vendor hardware platforms and operating systems for superior operational efficiency.

Based on the WBEM standards, HP offers "HP WBEM Services for HP-UX" software product that includes standard WBEM *providers* and *clients*.

7.2.1 WBEM Providers

WBEM providers provide configuration data and information about a device or service and performs a requested action on it. There are seven standard providers included in the WBEM Services software as listed and explained in Table 7-1. Additional providers for nPartition, PCI subsystem, FC HBA, LVM and kernel may be obtained from *www.software.hp.com*.

WBEM Provider for	Description
Computer system	Provides basic system information such as computer name, status and admin contact information.
OS	Provides information such as OS type, version, last boot up time, system date and time, number of logged on users, swap size and free physical memory.
Process and process statistics	Provides process name, PID, priority, execution state and process resource utilization statistics.
IP	Provides information about system's configured IP addresses with associated LAN interfaces, and routes.
DNS, NTP, NIS	Separate providers for DNS, NTP and NIS. Provide information about DNS, NTP and NIS.

Table 7-1 WBEM Providers

7.2.2 WBEM Clients

WBEM clients are WBEM-enabled management applications that receive data from providers and allow you to perform needed management operations. HP offers two WBEM clients – HP SIM and HP SMH – in addition to basic clients that come with HP WBEM Services software.

7.2.3 CIM Server and CIM Repository

HP WBEM Services includes a server component that acts as an intermediary between the client and providers. All communication between the client and providers passes through it. The server component is based on CIM and, therefore, referred to as *CIM server*. Key configuration files for the CIM server are *cimserver_current.conf* and *cimserver_planned.conf* located the in */var/opt/wbem* directory.

The CIM server consults *CIM repository*, a directory location that stores definitions of classes and instances for managed resources provided by providers. The CIM repository, located in the */var/opt/wbem/repository* directory, also contains and maintains relationship information about managed resources.

7.2.4 How WBEM Works

When the client issues a request to retrieve data from a managed hardware or software resource, the request goes to the CIM server which looks into the CIM repository for the information. If the requested information is available, the CIM server simply sends it back to the client. In case the information is unavailable, it engages appropriate providers. The providers obtain the information and return it to the CIM server, which updates the repository and forwards the information to the client.

7.2.5 WBEM Daemons and Commands

WBEM daemons and key administration commands are given in Table 7-2.

Daemon	Description
cimservera	Works with PAM to provide authentication services to *cimserverd*.
cimserverd	Main daemon. Interacts with *cimservera* for PAM authentication. Uses port 5988 for non-secure and 5989 for secure communications.
Command	
cimconfig	Sets, unsets and gets CIM server properties.
cimprovider	Disables, enables and removes registered CIM providers and associated modules.
cimserver	Starts, stops and manages daemons.

Table 7-2 WBEM Daemons and Commands

7.2.6 Downloading and Installing HP WBEM Services Software

Follow the instructions to download a copy for your HP-UX 11i v3 system and install it:

1. Go to *www.software.hp.com* → Security and manageability → HP WBEM Services for HP-UX → Receive for Free. Fill out the form and download the software.
2. The downloaded software is in SD-UX depot format. Store the depot file in a directory such as */var/tmp*.
3. Install the software using the *swinstall* command:

   # swinstall –s /var/tmp/WBEMSvcs_A.02.07_HP-UX_B.11.31_IA_PA.depot

4. Verify the installation with the *swverify* command:

```
# swverify WBEMServices WBEMSvcs
======= 04/14/08 08:41:53 EDT BEGIN swverify SESSION
   (non-interactive) (jobid=hp01-0012)
    * Session started for user "root@hp01".
    * Beginning Selection
    * Target connection succeeded for "hp01:/".
. . . . . . . .
    * The analysis phase succeeded for "hp01:/".
    * Verification succeeded.
. . . . . . . .
```

7.2.7   Starting and Stopping WBEM CIM Server

To start the WBEM CIM server, perform any of the following:

```
# cimserver
# /sbin/init.d/cim_server start
CIM cimserver started
```

To stop the WBEM CIM server, run any of the following:

```
# cimserver –s
# /sbin/init.d/cim_server stop
PGS10019: CIM server is stopped.
```

To ensure WBEM service automatically starts at each system reboot, set the CIMSERVER variable to 1 in the *etc/rc.config.d/cimserver* file:

```
CIMSERVER=1
```

7.2.8   Performing a Query Using WBEM Client

To check the basic functionality of WBEM, perform a query using a client called *osinfo*. The *osinfo* command pulls information about the operating system and displays it on the screen:

```
# osinfo
OperatingSystem Information
 Host: hp01
 Name: HP-UX
 Version: B.11.31
 UserLicense: Unlimited user license
 Number of Users: 2 users
 Number of Processes: 158 processes
 OSCapability: 64 bit
 LastBootTime: Apr 10, 2008  9:31:46 (-0400)
 LocalDateTime: Apr 14, 2008  8:14:44 (-0400)
 SystemUpTime: 340979 seconds = 3 days, 22 hrs, 42 mins, 59 secs
```

7.2.9 Checking Registered Providers

Several providers are loaded as part of the HP WBEM Services software installation. Run the *cimprovider* command to list them:

```
# cimprovider –l –s
MODULE                    STATUS
OperatingSystemModule     OK
ComputerSystemModule      OK
ProcessModule             OK
IPProviderModule          OK
DNSProviderModule         OK
NTPProviderModule         OK
NISProviderModule         OK
SDProviderModule          OK
. . . . . . . .
```

7.3   HP Systems Insight Manager (SIM)

The HP *Systems Insight Manager* (SIM) is a WBEM-enabled management tool that allows you to administer several networked systems centrally and efficiently. HP SIM can be used to configure and administer Linux- and Windows-based systems in addition to HP-UX systems from both graphical and command line interfaces. Some key features of SIM are listed and described in Table 7-3.

Feature	Description
Automatic discovery and identification	Automatically discovers and identifies devices on the network.
Fault management and event handling	Provides notification of component failure; allows you to define policies to forward event information, run scripts and notify users of faults.
Central management	Executes a command concurrently on several systems.
Secure management	Uses SSL and SSH to encrypt communication with managed systems.
Reporting	Collects data from managed systems and produces inventory reports.
Administrative delegation	Delegates a portion of administrative control to normal users. Normal users are added to HP SIM and given authorization to perform certain administrative functions.
Configuration comparison	Compares servers for configuration differences.
Service essentials remote support	Automatically and securely sends hardware event notifications to HP.

Table 7-3 HP SIM Features

7.3.1   Management Domain

HP SIM has a *management domain* which includes a *Central Management Server* (CMS) and several *managed systems*. CMS is responsible for overall SIM operation and administration of all managed systems including itself. It maintains a database to store detailed information about managed systems, authorized users allowed to use SIM and so on.

Managed systems may be grouped based on the operating system type, hardware type or administrative functions required to be performed on them. This grouping allows a single task to be performed on a group of systems in one go.

7.3.2   HP SIM Daemons and Commands

HP SIM daemons and key administration commands are given in Table 7-4.

Daemon	Description
mxdomainmgr	Interacts with HP SIM database and the *Distributed Task Facility* (DTF).
mxdtf	Runs commands remotely on managed systems.
Command	
mxagentconfig	Configures an agent to work with CMS.
mxinitconfig	Performs an initial HP SIM server configuration.
mxnode	Adds, lists, identifies, modifies and removes nodes.
mxpassword	Adds, lists, modifies and removes HP SIM user passwords.
mxstart	Starts HP SIM.
mxstop	Stops HP SIM.
mxuser	Adds, lists, modifies and removes HP SIM users.
mxtool	Adds, lists, modifies and removes tools.

Table 7-4 HP SIM Daemons and Commands

7.3.3   Downloading and Installing HP SIM

Follow the instructions to download a copy for your HP-UX 11i v3 system and install it:

1. Go to *www.software.hp.com* → Security and manageability → HP Systems Insight Manager 5.x – HP-UX → Receive for Free. Fill out the form and download the software.
2. The downloaded software is in SD-UX depot format. Store the depot file in a directory such as */var/tmp*.
3. Install the software using the *swinstall* command. The system will reboot after the install to complete the configuration.

    # **swinstall –s /var/tmp/HPSIM-HP-UX_C.05.02.01.00_11.31.depot**

4. Verify the installation with the *swverify* command:

```
# swverify HPSIM-HP-UX
======= 04/14/08 08:40:26 EDT  BEGIN swverify SESSION
    (non-interactive) (jobid=hp01-0011)
  * Session started for user "root@hp01".
  * Beginning Selection
. . . . . . . .
  * The analysis phase succeeded for "hp01:/".
  * Verification succeeded.
. . . . . . . .
```

7.3.4　Initializing HP SIM

After the installation is complete, you need to initialize HP SIM to make it work. Ensure that WBEM Services is already installed and functional on managed systems in order for HP SIM to administer them.

Run the *mxinitconfig* command with −l option to check if all the pre-requisites are met:

> # **mxinitconfig −l**
> Listing current status of server components (15):
>   1. Check Kernel Parameters ..OK
> Status   : Unconfigured
>   2. Node Security File ..OK
> Status   : Configured
>   3. Server Property File ..OK
> Status   : Unconfigured
>   4. Server Authentication Keys ..OK
> Status   : Unconfigured
>   5. SSH Keys ..OK
> Status   : Unconfigured
>   6. Status Property File ..OK
> Status   : Unconfigured
>   7. Task Results Output Cleanup ..OK
> Status   : Unconfigured
>   8. Database Configuration ..OK
> Status   : Unconfigured
>   9. Database Content ..OK
> Status   : Unconfigured
>   10. Web Server ..OK
> Status   : Unconfigured
>   11. Setup Property File ..OK
> Status   : Unconfigured
>   12. JBoss Setup ..OK
> Status   : Unconfigured
>   13. Agent Configuration ..OK
> Status   : Unconfigured
>   14. Management Services ..OK
> Status   : Unconfigured
>   15. Initialization and Database Population ..OK
> Status   : Unconfigured
> Completed all tasks successfully.
>
> Details can be found in the log files at: /var/opt/mx/logs

Re-run the *mxinitconfig* command with −a option to initialize HP SIM:

> # **mxinitconfig −a**
> Checking Requisites (15):
>   1. Check Kernel Parameters ..OK
>   2. Node Security File ..OK

---

        3. Server Property File ..OK
        4. Server Authentication Keys ..OK
        5. SSH Keys ..OK
        6. Status Property File ..OK
        7. Task Results Output Cleanup ..OK
        8. Database Configuration ..OK
        9. Database Content ..OK
        10. Web Server ..OK
        11. Setup Property File ..OK
        12. JBoss Setup ..OK
        13. Agent Configuration ..OK
        14. Management Services ..OK
        15. Initialization and Database Population ..OK
Requisite scan completed successfully.

Configuring Server Components (15):
        1. Check Kernel Parameters ..Done
        2. Node Security File ..Done
        3. Server Property File ..Done
        4. Server Authentication Keys ..Done
        5. SSH Keys ...Done
        6. Status Property File ..Done
        7. Task Results Output Cleanup ..Done
        8. Database Configuration ....Done
        9. Database Content ..Done
        10. Web Server ..Done
        11. Setup Property File ..Done
        12. JBoss Setup ..Done
        13. Agent Configuration ..Done
        14. Management Services ...Done
        15. Initialization and Database Population ....
          - Configuring tools and populating tools database ....Done
          - Initializing database ....Done
          - Compiling MIB and populating MIB database ....Done
Completed all tasks successfully.

Details can be found in the log files at: /var/opt/mx/logs

7.3.5   Starting and Stopping HP SIM Server

To start the HP SIM server, perform any of the following:

> # **mxstart**
> # **/sbin/init.d/hpsim start**

To stop the HP SIM server, run any of the following:

> # **mxstop**
> # **/sbin/init.d/hpsim stop**

To ensure HP SIM automatically starts at each system reboot, set the START_HPSIM variable to 1
in the *etc/rc.config.d/hpsim* file:

    START_HPSIM=1

7.3.6 First Time Wizard

The first time you start HP SIM GUI by typing either the hostname or IP address of the HP SIM server in a web browser, as shown below, it brings up the "Introduction" window of the *First Time Wizard*, see Figure 7-3, which allows you to do some initial settings.

http://hp01:280

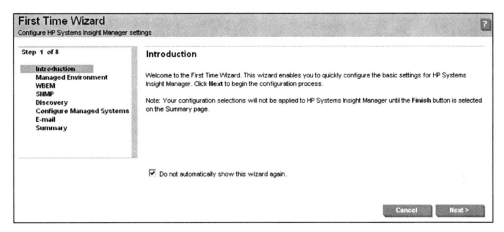

Figure 7-3 HP SIM First Time Wizard – Introduction

There are six windows available for you to configure settings. These are:

Managed Environment – Choose operating systems to be managed. Choices are Windows, Linux and HP-UX.
WBEM – Enter username and password for WBEM. If you wish to use *root*, then its information.
SNMP – Specify the SNMP community string to be used. Default is "public". SNMP is the default protocol that HP SIM uses to communicate with managed systems.
Discovery – Schedule automatic discovery of systems.
Configure Managed Systems – Configure username, password, SNMP, WBEM and secure shell access to be used to automatically configure new discovered systems.
E-mail – Enter an SMTP server name and an email address to be used to send event notifications.

A summary of configuration settings will be displayed on the "Summary" window. Press Finish to continue.

7.3.7 HP SIM Graphical Interface

The main web page for HP SIM is shown in Figure 7-4.

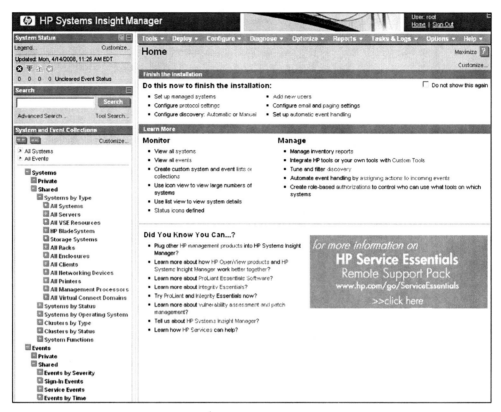

Figure 7-4 HP SIM Main Web Page

The main page can be divided into six areas. These are:

Home – HP SIM Home page.
System Status – Displays system health status and an alarm to notify of certain events and status changes.
Search – Enables you to search for matches by system name or attributes.
System and Event Collections – Enables you to view known systems and events.
Menu Bar – Provides access to tools that allow you to perform tasks on remote systems such as pulling system information, running SMH, executing commands, running glance, installing or recovering remote systems via Ignite-UX, installing, listing, verifying, removing and copying software and software depots, managing partitions, configuring MPs, managing patches, running WLM and PRM, generating reports and viewing logs. You can customize SIM as well.
Learn More – Provides short cuts to some administration tasks.

7.4   HP System Management Homepage (SMH)

The *System Management Homepage* (SMH) is a program that enables you to perform HP-UX administration tasks without the knowledge of HP-UX commands. SMH may be run graphically in a web browser or an X Window terminal. It may also be run as a menu-driven program in text mode and at the command prompt. This tool allows you to manage a single HP-UX 11i v3 system.

In HP-UX 11i v3, this tools has replaced *System Administration Manager* (SAM). Invoking SAM will now automatically start SMH. SAM is deprecated in HP-UX 11i v3 and will no longer be available in a future version. Some SAM functional areas have been retired and are not available in SMH. Similarly, some functions have been removed, enhanced or modified.

SMH daemon *smhstartd* must be running to use SMH.

SMH can be started on a system, *hp01* for example, as follows:

1. In a browser by typing the URL *http://hp01:2301*.
2. In a browser by typing the URL *https://hp01:2381* if configured to autostart at system boot.
3. By executing the following (if the daemon is not already running) and then entering the URL *http://hp01:2301*.

   # **/opt/hpsmh/lbin/hpsmh start**

4. By running *smh* at the command prompt. If DISPLAY environment variable is correctly set and a browser such as Firefox is installed, SMH will start in a browser window, otherwise, the text-based interface will appear.

The default startup mode is #1. If you wish to change it, execute the */opt/hpsmh/bin/smhstartconfig* command with –b on/off option for the second method, –t on/off for the fourth method or switch back to the first method using the –a on/off option.

Start SMH as instructed and enter a username and password to get in. The following will appear if started in a browser. See Figure 7-5.

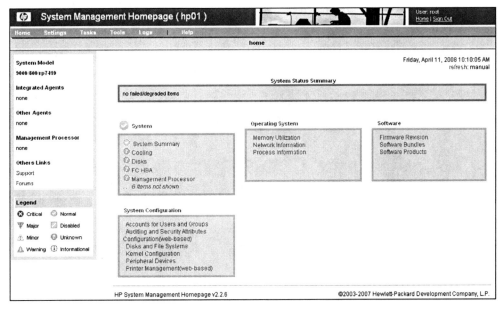

Figure 7-5 SMH – Browser Mode

This is the main SMH window. It contains three major sections:

✓ The main menu bar across the top provides six choices – Home, Settings, Tasks, Tools, Logs and Help. Clicking Home takes you to the main SMH page; clicking Settings allows you to add or remove custom menu items, display license certificate information for open source components included in HP-UX 11i v3 and configure access restrictions to SMH; clicking Tasks allows you to launch an X application or run a command on the system; clicking Tools presents you with a list of several administration tasks that can be performed on the system; clicking Logs lets you view logs for events, partitions, system and so on; and clicking Help displays detailed information on topics and categories available in SMH.

✓ The status bar beneath the menu bar, identifies where you are within SMH. It changes as you move around within SMH.

✓ In the large window, four sub-categories – System, Operating System, Software and System Configuration – are visible. System is where you can obtain general information about the system such as processors, memory, disks, Fibre HBAs, SCSI HBAs, power, voltage, cooling, temperature and MP; Operating System allows you to view memory utilization, network configuration information and process information; Software gives you information about system firmware revision, software bundles and software products currently installed in the system; and System Configuration allows you to run tools to carry out system administration tasks. These and several other management tasks can also be performed by clicking Tools and choosing a task from there. All available tasks are shown in Figure 7-6 and described in Table 7-5.

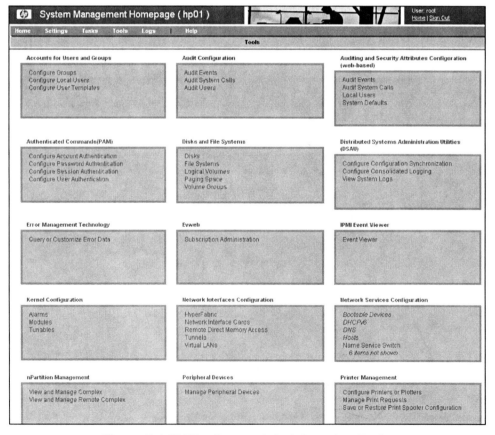

Figure 7-6 SMH – System Administration Tasks

Item	Function
Accounts for Users and Groups	Allows you to perform user and group account management tasks on local users and groups including creating, viewing, modifying and removing users and groups, activating and deactivating users, setting password aging attributes on user accounts, and configuring user templates.
Audit Configuration	Allows you to perform auditing and security management tasks including auditing events, system calls and users.
Auditing and Security Attributes Configuration (web-based)	Allows you to perform auditing and security management tasks including setting system default security policies and auditing events, system calls and users.
Authenticated Commands (PAM)	Allows you to configure and manage authentication at the account, password, session and user levels via PAM.
Disks and File Systems	Allows you to view and manage disks, LVM, file systems and swap. File systems include VxFS, HFS, CDFS, CIFS and NFS.
Distributed Systems Administration Utilities (DSAU)	Allows you to configure configuration synchronization and consolidated logging from several HP-UX boxes. System log is viewable from here as well.
Error Management Technology	Allows you to query and customize error data.
Evweb	Allows you to perform event subscription administration tasks such as creating, modifying, deleting and viewing subscription.
IPMI Event Viewer	Allows you to view hardware events.
Kernel Configuration	Allows you to view and modify kernel configuration by tuning kernel parameters, and adding, changing and removing kernel modules, dump device, device drivers and subsystems.
Network Interfaces Configuration	Allows you to create and manage LAN interfaces, IP tunnels and virtual LANs.
Network Services Configuration	Allows you to perform network-related configuration tasks on bootable devices, DHCP, DNS, NIS, NFS, AutoFS, /etc/hosts file, /etc/nsswitch.conf file, routing, internet services including rlogin, and NTP.
nPartition Management	Allows you to view and manage local and remote nPars.
Peripheral Devices	Allows you to configure and manage OLRAD cards and view I/O tree.
Printer management (web-based)	Allows you to define and administer local, remote and network printers, and manage print requests.
Resource Management	Allows you to configure and manage *Event Monitoring Service* (EMS), which is used to monitor system resources.
Resource Monitors	Allows you to configure and manage monitor and X server.
Software Management	Allows you to perform software management tasks including listing, installing, copying, viewing and removing software; depot management tasks such as copying, listing and removing depots and software in depots; and updating HP-UX.

Table 7-5 SMH Administration Tasks

The SMH may be started in text mode by running the *smh* command in a text terminal. Figure 7-7 shows the text interface. In text mode, tasks listed in Table 7-5 are grouped slightly differently. Navigate the interface to get yourself familiar with it.

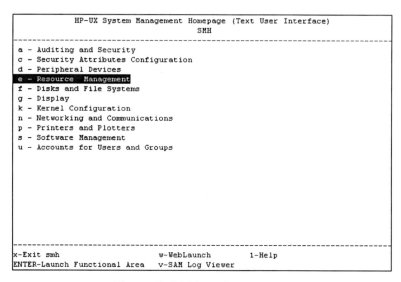

```
          HP-UX System Management Homepage (Text User Interface)
                               SMH
--------------------------------------------------------------------------------
a - Auditing and Security
c - Security Attributes Configuration
d - Peripheral Devices
e - Resource  Management
f - Disks and File Systems
g - Display
k - Kernel Configuration
n - Networking and Communications
p - Printers and Plotters
s - Software Management
u - Accounts for Users and Groups




--------------------------------------------------------------------------------
x-Exit smh                    w-WebLaunch        1-Help
ENTER-Launch Functional Area  v-SAM Log Viewer
```

Figure 7-7 SMH – TUI Mode

Use the keyboard in text mode for navigation purposes. Table 7-6 lists common navigational keys.

Key	Action
Up and down arrows	Move up and down through the list.
Left and right arrows	Scroll to the left and right.
Enter	Selects an item.
Esc	Takes back to a higher-level menu.

Table 7-6 Navigating Within SMH

There are several configuration files that affect the behavior of SMH. Two of them */opt/hpsmh/lbin/envvars* and */opt/hpsmh/conf/timeout.conf* are important in the sense that they set general configuration and timeout. General configuration include JAVA_HOME which is defined in the *envvars* file. A variable called TIMEOUT_SMH is defined in the *timeout.conf* file which sets, in minutes, the user inactivity period after which HP SMH automatically stops.

7.4.1   SMH (SAM) Log

SMH logs all actions and activities in the */var/sam/log/samlog* file, which can be viewed by clicking Logs in the main menu bar in the web interface or pressing v in text mode. Figure 7-8 shows a sample SMH (SAM) log view in text mode.

Alternatively, you may view it by running the following command. It will produce the exact same result.

> **# /usr/sam/bin/samlog_viewer**

```
Current Filters:
    Message Level:  [ Detail         ->]   [ User(s)... ] All
  [ Time Range... ] START: Beginning of Log (Wed 03/12/2008 15:38:05)
                    STOP: None


                  [ Save... ]     [ Search... ]    [ ] Include Timestamps
Filtered SAM Log                               [X] Automatic Scrolling

          lpmgr -l -xcols=1
      * lpmgr done, exit value is 0.
  ===== Tue Mar 25 11:10:15 2008 Exiting SAM area "Printer and Plotters
      (hp01)".
      * DISPLAY= /usr/sbin/swinstall
      * DISPLAY= /opt/swm/bin/swm oeupdate -i
      * /usr/sam/bin/samlog_viewer
      * /usr/sam/bin/samlog_viewer


[   OK   ]                                          [  Help  ]
```

Figure 7-8 SMH (SAM) Log Viewer

7.4.2   Restricted SMH Access to Users

By default, normal users cannot execute SMH as it requires *root* privileges. However, users or groups of users can be permitted to run SMH and perform one or more administration tasks without *root* privileges This gives *restricted SMH access* to normal users. You need to execute *smh* as *root* with –r option to start it in restricted builder mode. The privileges set for normal users from SMH text mode do not apply to SMH GUI. You need to go to Settings → Security in SMH GUI to configure the access for normal users.

To configure restricted access for *user1*, start SMH in restricted mode. Highlight *user1* and hit the Enter key to select it.

smh –r

        SMH->Restricted SMH->Select users

Login users	Primary Group	Has SAM privileges
daemon	daemon	No
bin	bin	No
sys	sys	No
adm	adm	No
uucp	sys	No
lp	lp	No
nuucp	nuucp	No
....		
sshd	sshd	No
tftp	tftp	No
user1	**users**	**No**

<-- > SCROLL ∨

x-Exit smh   ENTER-Select   /-Search
r-Remove Privileges   g-Display Groups

The next screen will display a list of available administrative functions:

```
            SMH->Restricted SMH->Functional Areas
Selected user : user1
------------------------------------------------------------------------
Functional Areas                     Access Status
========================================================================
    Resource  Management             Disabled
    Disks and File Systems           Disabled
    Display                          Disabled
    Kernel Configuration             Disabled
    Printers and Plotters            Disabled
    Networking and Communications    Disabled
    Peripheral Devices               Disabled
    Security Attributes Configuration  Disabled
    Software Management              Disabled
    Auditing and Security            Disabled
    Accounts for Users and Groups    Disabled
------------------------------------------------------------------------
    x-Exit smh  Esc-Back   s-Save Privileges  D-Disable All
    e-enable    d-disable  E-Enable All
```

Highlight the administrative function that you wish *user1* to have and press e to enable it for him. If you wish to allocate *user1* administrative access to all tasks, press E. Press s to save the configuration and exit out by pressing x when done.

7.4.3   SMH and SIM Integration

As SMH is a single-system management tool and SIM a multi-system tool, the two may be integrated to allow SMH to be invoked from within SIM GUI and run on a remote system. The integration allows you to:

✓ Manage several systems centrally from HP SIM.
✓ Help identify what, if any, corrective measures are required and by which system component.
✓ Choose an appropriate tool to run to fix an identified issue.

7.5   Server Hardware Component Overview

This section briefly examines hardware components found in HP servers that run HP-UX. An understanding of these is paramount in the sense that it would help you interact with a system in a better way.

7.5.1   I/O Slot

An *I/O slot* (or simply a *slot*) is a receptacle for installing an interface card. Figure 7-9 shows a system board with multiple I/O slots.

Figure 7-9 I/O Slots

The *olrad* (online replacement / addition / deletion) command displays configuration and status information of PCI slots. Run this command with –q option.

 # olrad –q

Slot	Path	Bus Num	Max Spd	Spd	Pwr	Occu	Susp	Driver(s) Capable OLAR	OLD	Max Mode	Mode
0-0-0-1	0/0/8/0	64	66	66	On	Yes	No	Yes	Yes	PCI	PCI
0-0-0-2	0/0/10/0	80	66	66	On	Yes	No	Yes	Yes	PCI	PCI
0-0-0-3	0/0/12/0	96	66	66	On	Yes	No	Yes	Yes	PCI	PCI
0-0-0-4	0/0/14/0	112	66	33	On	Yes	No	Yes	Yes	PCI	PCI
0-0-0-5	0/0/6/0	48	66	33	On	Yes	No	Yes	Yes	PCI	PCI
0-0-0-6	0/0/4/0	32	66	66	On	Yes	No	Yes	Yes	PCI	PCI
0-0-0-7	0/0/2/0	16	66	66	Off	No	N/A	N/A	N/A	PCI	PCI
0-0-0-8	0/0/1/0	8	66	66	Off	No	N/A	N/A	N/A	PCI	PCI

The output indicates that there are 8 PCI slots in the system. It shows each slot's number, hardware path, bus number, maximum and current speeds, power status, occupied or not, suspended or not, whether slot supports OLRAD functionality, and slot type (PCI or PCI-X).

7.5.2   Disk Array

An external data storage subsystem that contains several hard drives is referred to as a *disk array*. Disk arrays usually have redundant and hot-swappable power supplies, fans and I/O controllers. Disk arrays can be categorized in three groups – *Direct Attached Storage* (DAS), *Network Attached Storage* (NAS) and *Storage Area Network* (SAN). DAS are connected directly to one or limited number of servers providing dedicated bandwidth to them. NAS is attached to an IP network and the storage is made available over the network using NFS, CIFS or a proprietary protocol. SAN is typically fibre channel-based, and combines the benefits offered by both DAS and NAS technologies in addition to other benefits.

Figure 7-10 Disk Arrays

7.5.3   Logical Unit Number (LUN)

LUN, stands for *Logical Unit Number,* is a logical storage entity defined on RAID array devices by allocating some or all parts of one or more disk drives. When presented to a server, the LUN is seen as a standalone disk drive. A LUN can be of any size.

7.5.4   Storage Area Network (SAN)

A design technique whereby several computer systems are connected to one or more disk, tape and optical storage devices via fibre-channel switches is referred to as *Storage Area Network* (SAN). SAN storage devices offer thousands of terabytes of disk storage to be shared by a number of systems connected to the storage network. Moreover, huge tape libraries enable hundreds of servers to be backed up over SAN links.

7.5.5   PCI, PCI-X and PCIe Cards

PCI stands for *Peripheral Component Interconnect,* PCI-X stands for *PCI eXtended* and PCIe stands for *PCI Express.*

PCI provides a shared data path between CPUs and I/O adapters. It runs at 33MHz and 66MHz speeds and supports both 32-bit and 64-bit data paths. Figure 7-11 shows a picture of a PCI card.

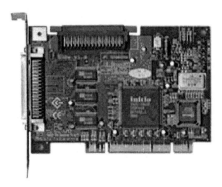

Figure 7-11 PCI Card

PCI-X is an enhanced version of PCI and is backward compatible. It runs at 133MHz and 266MHz speeds and supports both 32-bit and 64-bit data paths. The 64-bit PCI-X adapters are longer in size than their PCI counterparts and are almost twice as fast.

PCIe was primarily designed to replace both PCI and PCI-X. PCIe is faster than the other two.

All three types of cards can be installed and removed using HP-UX OLRAD functionality while the machine is up and running. OLRAD can be performed either via SMH or the *olrad* command. SMH performs *Critical Resource Analysis* (CRA) too that lists any potential impact due to replacing a card. The *olrad* command does not do CRA. It simply does the job quietly. Check the man pages of *olrad* for details.

To use SMH for an OLRAD task, follow steps below:

☞Go to SMH → Peripheral Devices → OLRAD Cards. Choose the slot that has the card to be replaced, and press Enter. Press c to perform CRA. If you are certain that the selected slot has the card to be deinstalled, press d to delete it, or r to replace it.

Alternatively, you can use the *pdweb* command, which is a short cut to "SMH → Peripheral Devices".

7.5.6   Interface Card

An *interface card* is either integrated onto the system board or plugs into one of the system slots. It enables the system to communicate with external hardware devices. Different types of interface cards are available to connect fibre channel, SCSI, LAN and other types of external devices. Interface cards are also referred to as *host adapters, device adapters* and *controller cards*. Figures 7-11 through 7-15 show different types of interface cards.

7.5.7   Network Interface Card (NIC)

A *Network Interface Card* (NIC) connects a system to the network. It is usually built-in to the system board and also available as an interface card. A NIC is also known as a *LAN card* or a *LAN adapter*. Multiport LAN cards are also available that provide 2 or 4 ports on a single physical NIC. Throughout this book the term "LAN interface" is used to identify a single-port LAN card or a port on a multiport card. Figure 7-12 shows pictures of 1-port and 4-port NICs.

Figure 7-12 Network Interface Cards

7.5.8   Small Computer System Interface (SCSI) Card

Small Computer System Interface (SCSI) (pronounced scuzzy) was developed in 1986 and has since been widely used in computers. SCSI is an I/O bus technology controlled by a set of protocols. It allows several peripheral devices (including hard drives, tape drives and CD/DVD drives) to be connected to a single SCSI controller card – also called SCSI *Host Bus Adapter* (HBA). Figure 7-13 shows a picture of a SCSI HBA.

Figure 7-13 SCSI Card

Many types of SCSI HBAs are available, and they differ based on factors such as bandwidth, data transfer speed and pin count on the connector. Table 7-7 lists and compares them.

Type	Bus Width	Max Speed
SCSI	8 bit	5 MB/second
Wide SCSI	16 bit	10 MB/second
Fast SCSI	8 bit	10 MB/second
Fast Wide SCSI	16 bit	20 MB/second
Ultra SCSI	8 bit	20 MB/second
Ultra Wide SCSI	16 bit	40 MB/second
Ultra2 SCSI	8 bit	40 MB/second
Ultra2 Wide SCSI	16 bit	80 MB/second
Ultra160 (Ultra 3)	16 bit	160 MB/second
Ultra320	16 bit	320 MB/second
Ultra640	16 bit	640 MB/second

Table 7-7 SCSI Chart

When working with SCSI devices and SCSI cards, make sure that the two are of the same type. For example, an Ultra3 SCSI DVD drive requires that the HBA it is connected to is also Ultra3 SCSI.

7.5.9   Fibre Channel (FC) Card

A *fibre channel* (fc) *card* provides servers optical connectivity to fibre channel-based network and storage devices such as switches, disk storage and tape libraries.

FC cards are available in 1Gbps (gigabits per second), 2Gbps and 4Gbps speeds. The FC cards with 1Gbps speed have the connector type called *Siemens Connector* (SC); the higher speed cards have a different type of connector called *Lucent Connector* (LC).

The FC cards – also called FC HBAs – are available in single and dual ports. Figure 7-14 shows both types with LC connector interface.

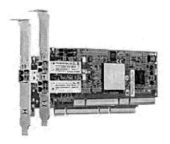

Figure 7-14 Fibre Channel Card

7.5.10   Multi-I/O (MIO) Card

A *multi-I/O* (MIO) *card* is a card that has the capability built in to it to perform more than one function concurrently. Such cards are commonly used in servers to save on slots. Some examples of multi-I/O cards include:

✓ Cards with a combination of LAN (Ethernet) and SCSI ports.
✓ Cards with a combination of LAN and Fibre Channel (FC) ports.
✓ Cards with a combination of SCSI and FC ports.
✓ Cards with a combination of LAN and modem ports.
✓ Cards with LAN console, serial console and SCSI ports.

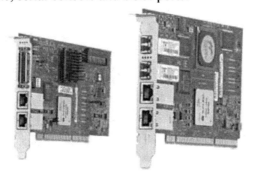

Figure 7-15 Multi-I/O Cards

7.5.11   Bus

All hardware components such as processors, memory and interface cards in the system communicate with one another through electrical circuits called *buses*. Data flows between processor and memory, memory and disk, memory and interface cards and so on. Busses can be internal or external. Internal busses facilitate data movement within the system while external buses allow external devices to become part of the system through interface adapters.

7.5.12   Bus Converter

There are different types of hardware components installed in the system. Some are very fast, others are slower or too slow. When a higher speed component talks to a slower speed component or device, a *bus converter* is used to facilitate data transmission. A bus converter is represented by the forward slash (/) character in the hardware path of a device.

7.5.13   Processor/Core

HP-UX runs on two types of hardware architectures – Integrity and 9000.

The Integrity server family uses 64-bit *Itanium* processors. The Itanium processors are based on the *Explicitly Parallel Instruction Computing* (EPIC) technology. Majority of the current Itanium processors are dual-cored, meaning that a single physical processor chip has two independent processing units called *cores* on it that share the chip connections to the system (or cell) board.

The 9000 server family uses 64-bit *Precision-Architecture Reduced Instruction Set Computing* (PA-RISC) processors. Most of the current PA-RISC processors are also dual-cored.

To understand how many processors and cores are in a given server, partition or on a cell board, a convention "xP/yC" is typically used. In this convention, "x" and "y" refer to the maximum number of processors and cores, respectively. For example:

- ✓ A server defined as a 1P/1C server represents one processor with a single core.
- ✓ A server defined as a 2P/4C server represents two processors and four cores.
- ✓ A server with four cell boards, each containing eight dual-core processors is a 32P/64C server (each cell board is 8P/16C).

7.5.14   Cell Board

A *cell board* (or *cell*) holds processors and memory. The newer cell boards support up to 4 dual-core processor modules and 128GB of memory per cell board. The largest HP-UX server complex supports up to 16 cell boards and 2TB of memory. Figure 7-16 shows a picture of a cell board.

Figure 7-16 Cell Board

Each cell is connected to one I/O chassis at a time, which cannot be shared with another cell.

7.5.15   I/O Chassis

I/O chassis (or *I/O card cage*) holds a set of 12 PCI and PCI-X slots for HP Superdome and rp/rx84xx servers. I/O chassis for rp/rx74xx servers holds 8 PCI and PCI-X slots. An I/O chassis has its own power supplies. You can add more slots to a server in multiples of 12 or 8 depending on the server model. One cell handles up to 12 (or 8) PCI slots. If you need an additional 12 (or 8), you need to add a cell and an I/O chassis.

7.5.16   Core I/O

Each server, or an nPar within a server complex, must have a unique card called *core I/O* installed. This card always sits in slot 0 and has one serial and one LAN port for MP access into the server or nPar. This card also has UPS and modem ports, and may or may not have a SCSI port. The cell board whose I/O chassis contains the core I/O is referred to as the *core cell*.

Figure 7-17 Core I/O Card

A detailed discussion on nPars and MP is covered in Chapter 08 "Virtualization Technologies".

7.5.17   System Bus Adapter (SBA) / Local Bus Adapter (LBA)

The HP-UX system communicates with I/O devices through the *System Bus Adapter* (SBA) and *Local Bus Adapter* (LBA). Each SBA has one or more LBAs connected to it, which in turn has one or several I/O devices attached. Figure 7-18 shows the relationship of SBAs and LBAs with respect to the system and I/O devices.

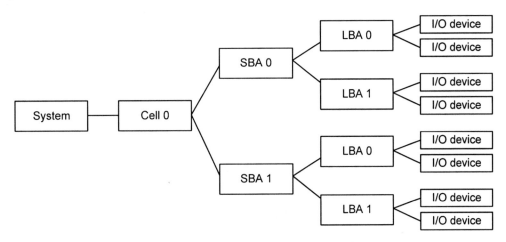

Figure 7-18 SBA/LBA Relationship

On non-cell board-based systems, the SBAs are directly connected to the system.

7.5.18   Power Supply

There are two types of power supplies in large and mid-range servers – *system power supplies* and *PCI power supplies*. System power supplies provide power to the entire system while PCI power supplies provide power to I/O chassis. All servers that run HP-UX come standard with at least two power supplies for redundancy purpose.

Entry-level servers come with system power supplies only.

7.5.19   Server Expansion Unit (SEU)

Mid-range servers can hold up to two cell boards and two I/O chassis units within the server. For growing requirements, you may need to add a pair of cell boards and I/O chassis units. These additional components are installed in a hardware unit external to the server. This hardware unit is referred to as the *Server Expansion Unit* (SEU). Once installed, an SEU becomes an integral part of the server. Figure 7-19 shows a picture of an SEU.

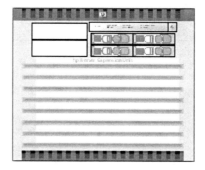

Figure 7-19 Server Expansion Unit

An SEU comes with its own power supplies and fan units. It has room to accommodate additional hard drives, tape drives and CD/DVD drives besides cell boards and I/O chassis.

7.5.20 Cabinet

The term *cabinet* is typically used with Superdome servers. Superdomes are the largest HP servers that run HP-UX with support for up to 16 cell boards and 16 I/O chassis units in addition to power supplies, fans and other hardware components. The base Superdome server fits into one cabinet space, but a fully loaded Superdome requires an additional cabinet. Figure 7-20 shows two cabinets of a Superdome server complex.

Figure 7-20 Superdome Server Complex Cabinets

7.5.21 Server Complex

A *server complex* is a complete physical hardware box including cell boards, power system, I/O chassis, server expansion unit, one or more cabinets and so on. Figure 7-21 displays a picture of a mid-range server complex.

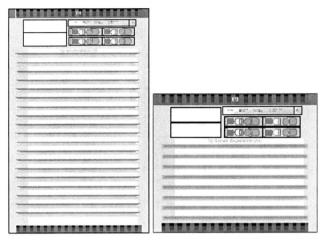

Figure 7-21 Server Complex

7.6　HP Integrity and 9000 Servers

There are two series of HP servers that run HP-UX. These are called Integrity and 9000. The following sub-sections provide an overview of both.

7.6.1　Integrity Servers

The *Integrity* series servers are powered by Intel Itanium processors and are capable of running multiple instances of HP-UX 11i v2, HP-UX 11i v3, MS Windows 2003 and Linux operating systems concurrently in separate nPars and vPars within a single server complex.

nPar (*node partition*) and vPar (*virtual partition*) are server partitioning techniques available on mid-range and high-end HP-UX servers. Both are covered in detail in Chapter 08 "Virtualization Technologies".

There are several server sizes available under this series and are classified as entry-level, mid-range and high-end. The servers are grouped based on factors such as maximum number of processors, amount of memory and number of PCI slots that they support. Table 7-8 provides summarized information. Visit *www.hp.com* for the latest and more accurate information.

Server	Max Processors / Cores	Max Memory	Max PCI Slots	Internal Disk	Cell Board	nPar	vPar	SEU	Class
rx2620	2/4	32GB	4	3 Disks	N/A	N/A	N/A	No	Entry
rx2660	2/4	32GB	3	8 Disks	N/A	N/A	N/A	No	Entry
rx3600	2/4	96GB	8	8 Disks	N/A	N/A	N/A	No	Entry
rx6600	4/8	192GB	8	16 Disks	N/A	N/A	N/A	No	Entry
rx7640	8/16	128GB	15	4 Disks	2	2	N/A	No	Midrange
rx8640	16/32	256GB	16	8 Disks	4	4	N/A	Yes	Midrange
Superdome	64/128	2TB	192	No Disks	16	16	N/A	Yes	Highend

Table 7-8 HP Integrity Server Models

Figure 7-22 displays front views of Superdome and rx7640 servers.

Figure 7-22 HP Superdome and rx7640 Servers

For your reference, some older Integrity server models that support HP-UX 11i v3 are listed in Table 7-9.

Server	Max Processors / Cores	Max Memory	Max PCI Slots	Internal Disk	Cell Board	nPar	vPar	SEU	Class
rx1620	2/2	16GB	2	2 Disks	N/A	N/A	N/A	No	Entry
rx4640	4/8	128GB	6	2 Disks	N/A	N/A	N/A	No	Entry
rx7620	16	128GB	15	4 Disks	2	2	N/A	No	Midrange
rx8620	32	256GB	16	8 Disks	4	4	N/A	Yes	Midrange

Table 7-9 Older HP Integrity Server Models

7.6.2   9000 Servers

The *9000 series servers*, on the other hand, are powered by PA-RISC processors. This server series supports all versions of HP-UX 11i. The 9000 servers may be divided into nPars and vPars where you can run multiple, independent instances of HP-UX.

There are several server sizes available under this series and are classified as entry-level, mid-range and high-end. The servers are grouped based on factors such as maximum number of processors, amount of memory and number of PCI slots that they support. Table 7-10 provides summarized information. Visit *www.hp.com* for the latest and more accurate information.

Server	Max Processors / Cores	Max Memory	Max PCI Slots	Internal Disk	Cell Board	nPar	vPar	SEU	Class
rp3410	1/2	6GB	2	3 Disks	N/A	N/A	N/A	No	Entry
rp3440	2/4	32GB	4	3 Disks	N/A	N/A	N/A	No	Entry
rp4410	2/4	128GB	6	2 Disks	N/A	N/A	N/A	No	Entry
rp4440	4/8	128GB	6	2 Disks	N/A	N/A	N/A	No	Entry
rp7440	8/16	128GB	15	4 Disks	2	2	16	No	Midrange
rp8440	16/32	256GB	32	8 Disks	4	4	32	Yes	Midrange
Superdome	64/128	2TB	192	No Disks	16	16	128	Yes	Highend

Table 7-10 HP 9000 Server Models

Figure 7-23 displays front views of Superdome and rp8440 servers.

Figure 7-23 HP Superdome and rp8440 Servers

For reference, some older 9000 server models that support HP-UX 11i v3 are listed in Table 7-11:

Server	Max Processors	Max Memory	Max PCI Slots	Internal Disk	Cell Board	nPar	vPar	SEU	Class
rp7410	8	32GB	15	8 Disks	2	2	8	No	Midrange
rp7420	8/16	128GB	15	4 Disks	2	2	16	No	Midrange
rp8400	16	64GB	16	8 Disks	4	4	16	Yes	Midrange
rp8420	16/32	256GB	32	8 Disks	4	4	32	Yes	Midrange

Table 7-11 Older HP 9000 Server Models

7.7   HP BladeSystem

The HP *BladeSystem* is a relatively new technology. This technology offers a complete infrastructure out of the box. The BladeSystem is powered by Itanium and Intel processors and supports HP-UX 11i v3, Microsoft Windows, SUN Solaris and Linux operating systems.

7.7.1   BladeSystem Components

A BladeSystem comprises of several hardware components. These components are explained below. Visit *www.hp.com* for the latest and more accurate information.

Enclosure

An *enclosure* is the box in which other components fit. It is available in two sizes to fit full-height and half-height server and storage blades. The maximum number of full-height blades in a single enclosure can be 8 and in a half-height enclosure 16. In other words, a full-height blade takes as much space as two half-height blades. Currently, there are two enclosure types available – c3000 and c7000; c3000 is ideal for small and medium size requirements and c7000 is suitable for enterprise requirements.

Figure 7-24 displays c3000 (rack-mountable and standalone models) on the left and c7000 (rack-mountable only) on the right.

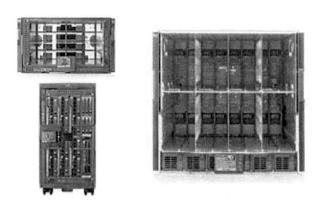

Figure 7-24 HP BladeSystem Enclosures

A comparison of the two types is given in Table 7-12.

	c3000	c7000
Device bays	4 full-height or 8 half-height blades	8 full-height or 16 half-height blades
Interconnect bays	4	8
Power supplies	6	6
Fans	6	10
Management	One Onboard Administrator	Dual Onboard Administrators

Table 7-12 HP BladeSystem Enclosures

Server Blade

A *server blade* can be thought of as a small form-factor computer. It is available in different models, most of which come with Intel processors to run Microsoft Windows, SUN Solaris or Linux operating system. For HP-UX, Itanium-based server blades – BL860c and BL870c – shown in Figure 7-25 are available.

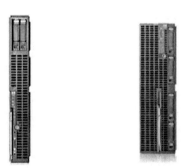

Figure 7-25 HP BladeSystem Server Blades

Both BL860c and BL870c are listed and compared in Table 7-13.

Blade	Max Processors	Max Memory	Max Disk Drives	# of Standard LAN Interfaces	Height	Max Mezzanine Slots
BL860c	2 single or dual core	48GB	2	4	Full	3
BL870c	4 dual core	96GB	4	4	Full	3

Table 7-13 HP Server Blade Models

Storage Blade

A *storage blade* allows for additional disk storage capacity. Two models – SB600c and SB40c – shown in Figure 7-26 are available.

Figure 7-26 HP BladeSystem Storage Blades

A comparison of the two is given in Table 7-14.

	SB600c	SB40c
Total storage	1.17TB	876GB
DVD / USB included	Yes	No
Max per enclosure	4	8
# of SAS/SATA Drives	8 x 146GB	6 x 146GB
Height	Half	Half

Table 7-14 HP BladeSystem Storage Blades

Interconnect

An *interconnect* is a device that provides additional LAN or SAN ports. There is a room for up to 8 such devices in a BladeSystem enclosure. Choice of interconnect devices include LAN switches with several 1Gbps and/or 10Gbps ports, Fibre Channel SAN switches with several 4Gbps ports and standalone LAN/SAN adapters.

PCI Expansion Blade

A *PCI expansion blade* allows an adjacent BladeSystem enclosure bay access to additional PCI adapters. Each PCI expansion blade can have either one or two PCI-X or PCIe adapters.

Figure 7-27 HP BladeSystem PCI Expansion Blade

7.7.2   BladeSystem Advantages

There are several advantages associated with using the BladeSystem solution. These are:

Scalability

You can start with a single blade in a BladeSystem enclosure with only one or two power supplies and fans, and grow to as many as 16 blades, 10 power supplies and 6 cooling fans in the enclosure.

Affordability

In contrast to any standalone rack server, the BladeSystem solution is more cost effective.

Flexibility

The BladeSystem is flexible in terms of adding and removing components.

Redundancy

Redundancy is built-in at every level in the BladeSystem. Each component is redundant or can be made redundant. From power supplies and cooling fans to interconnect devices and storage, all components are in pairs.

Less Power Consumption

The BladeSystem allows multiple server and storage blades to share power supplies and cooling fans, resulting in less power consumption, as compared to the same number of standalone servers in a rack.

Reduced Maintenance

Single, centralized management software is used to manage a BladeSystem environment, which reduces maintenance cost.

7.7.3   BladeSystem Management Software

Integrated management software called *onboard administrator* comes standard with the BladeSystem. This software runs locally on a BladeSystem and allows you to configure and manage it from a web browser. A more powerful product called *insight control* may be purchased and used for better control and manageability of a BladeSystem-based computing environment.

7.8 The Mass Storage Stack

In previous versions of HP-UX, hardware paths are used to represent mass storage devices such as disk and tape devices. These devices are bound to the path of the device. This representation of mass storage devices still exists in 11i v3, and is referred to as *legacy view*. Introduced in 11i v3 is a new representation of mass storage devices called *agile view*. With agile view, DSFs of a mass storage device are bound to the device's World Wide IDentifiers (WWID) rather than to the path of the device. In other words, the device is represented as an actual object. This makes the DSFs persistent, which means each LUN is uniquely identified by a single DSF irrespective of the number of paths to the device and independent of any physical path changes. With agile view, you do not need to worry about physical path changes. For example, if the path to a device is changed by relocating the device, HP-UX will continue to see the device as it was seeing it before. Moreover, this technique allows HP-UX to hide all but one path going to the same physical device. This way a single virtual path to the device is visible to the OS, and the I/O load is automatically distributed on all available paths. Both legacy and agile views can co-exist on the same server. Major advantages to using the agile view include scalability, agile addressing, multipathing and load balancing, adaptability and performance, and are discussed in brief in the following sub-sections.

7.8.1 Scalability

With mass storage stack, storage limits in a server have increased to new levels as compared to what they are in the older 11i versions. The bullets below highlight them:

- ✓ There is no limit to a LUN size as compared to 2TB in older 11i versions.
- ✓ There is no limit to the number of I/O busses as compared to 256 in older 11i versions.
- ✓ The number of supported LUNs has doubled to 16,384 from 8192.
- ✓ The number of alternate paths to a single LUN has quadrupled to 32 from 8.

7.8.2 Agile Addressing

Agile addressing (a.k.a. *persistent LUN binding*) creates one persistent DSF for each LUN even though the LUN uses multiple paths. This approach eliminates the need to encode the hardware path in the DSF's name and associated minor number as is the case in older versions. Persistent block DSFs are stored in the */dev/disk* directory and persistent raw DSFs in the */dev/rdisk* directory. A persistent DSF maps to the LUN's *World Wide IDentifier* (WWID) instead of to the LUN's hardware path, and does not contain any encoding of hardware path except the controller, SCSI target identifier or device specific option information. The WWID, similar to a serial number, is unique to the LUN and remains constant for the LUN even if it is relocated.

Benefits of agile addressing are:

- ✓ One DSF per LUN even though there are scores of paths to the LUN. In older versions, each path has a separate, unique DSF. This approach has simplified the management of disk storage subsystems using software such as LVM.
- ✓ No modifications are necessary if any of the paths to a LUN is altered, hence eliminating the need, for example, to update LVM configuration for the volume group.

When HP-UX 11i v3 is installed, both legacy and persistent DSFs are created, configured and enabled for each storage device by default.

7.8.3   Multipathing and Load Balancing

Multipathing is a feature that allows storage traffic to distribute over several physical connections between a server and a storage device. This is possible only if there are more than one physical connections. The distribution of storage traffic over several links is transparent to users and applications. In case one of the paths fails, the system automatically stops using the failed link; the other paths continue to function normally. As soon as the failed path is recovered, it is automatically and transparently re-added. This is equally true for any new paths added. As soon as a new path is discovered, the system automatically and dynamically adds it to the multipathing mechanism. Multipathing is enabled by default even if you use legacy DSFs.

Load balancing is a feature that essentially uses multipathing to balance the storage traffic load on multiple physical paths. This feature allows even distribution of traffic on all available paths. In case one of the paths fails, the system automatically stops using the failed path and balances the traffic load across the remaining paths. As soon as the failed path is recovered, it is automatically and transparently re-added and the traffic load distribution is adjusted accordingly. This is equally true for any new paths added. As soon as a new path is discovered, the system automatically and dynamically adds it to the load balancing mechanism.

With the availability of multipathing and load balancing natively in 11i v3, the need to purchase an add-on product to get these functionalities is abolished.

7.8.4   Adaptability

HP-UX 11i v3 responds to any hardware changes such as addition or modification of a LUN dynamically and adapts itself accordingly without a system reboot or software reconfiguration. Immediately after the system detects the presence of a new LUN, it creates for the LUN a persistent DSF automatically. Similarly, when the system detects any modifications such as the resize of an existing LUN or a change in its physical address or block size, HP-UX automatically, dynamically and transparently adjusts the parameters. In case of an increase in the size of a LUN which is part of an existing volume group, an LVM command can be used to reflect the expansion.

In previous 11i versions, OLRAD functionality is supported which allows you to add or replace a PCI card online. This functionality is enhanced in 11i v3. Now you can delete a PCI HBA online and replace it with a different PCI card too.

Similarly, in older versions, you have to remove individual device files manually or reboot the system to delete them after a device is physically detached. In 11i v3, you can run the *rmsf* command with –x option which removes all stale device files for you.

7.8.5   Performance

The mass storage stack offers the following benefits in terms of performance:

- ✓ Enhanced utilization of I/O channels with multipathing and load balancing.
- ✓ Increased parallel I/O results in reduced device scan and system boot time.
- ✓ Increased maximum I/O request size (from 1MB to 2MB).
- ✓ Improved performance monitoring tools such as *sar*.

7.8.6   New Commands and Command Options

Some new commands and several new options to existing commands have been added to HP-UX 11i v3 to manage mass storage stack efficiently and effectively. These commands and options are listed and described in Table 7-15.

Commands	Description
iobind	Binds a specific driver to a LUN.
iofind	Helps migrate from legacy to agile view.
io_redirect_dsf	Assigns a new LUN to an existing DSF.
scsimgr	Administers SCSI mass storage devices such as setting load balancing algorithm, enabling and disabling multipathing, and displaying statistics.
New Options	
glance	–U Displays HBA port-level statistics.
insf	Without any options, it creates persistent and legacy DSFs for new devices. –L Restores legacy DSFs. –Lv Displays whether legacy mode is enabled.
ioscan	–m dsf Displays mapping of persistent DSFs to their corresponding legacy DSFs, and vice versa. –m hwpath Displays mappings between a LUN's legacy, lunpath and LUN hardware paths. –m lun Displays mappings of a LUN hardware path to its lunpath hardware paths. –N Scans and displays persistent DSFs. –P Displays a device's property such as health status of a lunpath. –b Defers a binding operation until next reboot. –B Displays any pending deferred binding operations. –e Displays DSFs in EFI and BCH format on 9000 systems. –r Removes any pending deferred binding operations. –s Displays stale DSFs. –U Initiates a hardware scan on devices in UNCLAIMED state.
lssf	–s Displays stale DSFs.
rmsf	–L Removes all legacy DSFs and legacy configuration information. –x Removes stale DSFs and updates I/O configuration.
sar	–H Displays HBA port-level activity. –L Displays separate activity for each lunpath. –t Displays tape activity. –R Displays disk reads and writes in separate columns.

Table 7-15 New Commands and Command Options

7.9   Mass Storage Stack Terminology

Before jumping into the details of the mass storage stack, it is essential to get an understanding of various terms that will appear in the details.

7.9.1   Legacy Hardware Path

The standard and the only representation of hardware device paths used in HP-UX versions prior to 11i v3 is the *legacy hardware path*. This representation is still supported in 11i v3 but deprecated, and will be removed in a future HP-UX release. The following shows sixteen sample legacy hardware paths associated with four LUNs. Each LUN has four physical connections to the server.

```
0/0/10/0/0.120.16.19.0.0.0
0/0/10/0/0.120.16.19.0.0.1
0/0/10/0/0.120.16.19.0.0.2
0/0/10/0/0.120.16.19.0.0.3

0/0/10/0/0.120.17.19.0.0.0
0/0/10/0/0.120.17.19.0.0.1
0/0/10/0/0.120.17.19.0.0.2
0/0/10/0/0.120.17.19.0.0.3

0/0/12/0/0.119.16.19.0.0.0
0/0/12/0/0.119.16.19.0.0.1
0/0/12/0/0.119.16.19.0.0.2
0/0/12/0/0.119.16.19.0.0.3

0/0/12/0/0.119.17.19.0.0.0
0/0/12/0/0.119.17.19.0.0.1
0/0/12/0/0.119.17.19.0.0.2
0/0/12/0/0.119.17.19.0.0.3
```

Sample legacy hardware path for a tape device could be:

```
0/0/8/0/0/1/0.2.0
```

You can use the *ioscan* command to view the legacy hardware paths.

7.9.2   Lunpath Hardware Path

A *lunpath hardware path* represents each *lunpath* to a LUN. It is the same as a legacy hardware path down to the HBA level after which it includes a transport-independent target address and a LUN address which is represented in hexadecimal notation. One lunpath hardware path represents one legacy hardware path. The following demonstrates corresponding lunpath hardware path for each of the sixteen legacy hardware paths shown in the previous sub-section:

```
# ioscan –fnNk | grep lunpath
lunpath  8 0/0/10/0/0.0x5006016030201d6b.0x4000000000000000 eslpt CLAIMED LUN_PATH LUN path for disk22
lunpath  9 0/0/10/0/0.0x5006016030201d6b.0x4001000000000000 eslpt CLAIMED LUN_PATH LUN path for disk23
lunpath 10 0/0/10/0/0.0x5006016030201d6b.0x4002000000000000 eslpt CLAIMED LUN_PATH LUN path for disk24
lunpath 15 0/0/10/0/0.0x5006016030201d6b.0x4003000000000000 eslpt CLAIMED LUN_PATH LUN path for disk25
lunpath 11 0/0/10/0/0.0x5006016930201d6b.0x4000000000000000 eslpt CLAIMED LUN_PATH LUN path for disk22
lunpath 12 0/0/10/0/0.0x5006016930201d6b.0x4001000000000000 eslpt CLAIMED LUN_PATH LUN path for disk23
lunpath 13 0/0/10/0/0.0x5006016930201d6b.0x4002000000000000 eslpt CLAIMED LUN_PATH LUN path for disk24
lunpath 14 0/0/10/0/0.0x5006016930201d6b.0x4003000000000000 eslpt CLAIMED LUN_PATH LUN path for disk25
lunpath 20 0/0/12/0/0.0x5006016130201d6b.0x4000000000000000 eslpt CLAIMED LUN_PATH LUN path for disk22
lunpath 21 0/0/12/0/0.0x5006016130201d6b.0x4001000000000000 eslpt CLAIMED LUN_PATH LUN path for disk23
lunpath 22 0/0/12/0/0.0x5006016130201d6b.0x4002000000000000 eslpt CLAIMED LUN_PATH LUN path for disk24
lunpath 23 0/0/12/0/0.0x5006016130201d6b.0x4003000000000000 eslpt CLAIMED LUN_PATH LUN path for disk25
lunpath 16 0/0/12/0/0.0x5006016830201d6b.0x4000000000000000 eslpt CLAIMED LUN_PATH LUN path for disk22
lunpath 17 0/0/12/0/0.0x5006016830201d6b.0x4001000000000000 eslpt CLAIMED LUN_PATH LUN path for disk23
lunpath 18 0/0/12/0/0.0x5006016830201d6b.0x4002000000000000 eslpt CLAIMED LUN_PATH LUN path for disk24
```

7.9.3 LUN Hardware Path

LUN hardware path is a virtualized path presented as a single persistent DSF representing all lunpath hardware paths pointing to a single LUN. In the above two examples, sixteen legacy hardware paths and their corresponding sixteen lunpath hardware paths were shown. In the LUN hardware path format, these will be seen as four paths since each LUN hardware path has four physical connections going to the device.

64000/0xfa00/0x9	represents all 4 lunpath hardware paths for disk22
64000/0xfa00/0xa	represents all 4 lunpath hardware paths for disk23
64000/0xfa00/0xb	represents all 4 lunpath hardware paths for disk24
64000/0xfa00/0xc	represents all 4 lunpath hardware paths for disk25

7.9.4 Legacy DSF

A *legacy DSF* represents the old way of mass storage device special file format. Each hardware path to a multipathed LUN is represented as a separate DSF. You have to manually determine the paths pointing to the same LUN. In LVM, you have to use one of the paths to create/extend a volume group and then define other legacy paths as *alternate links* (or *physical volume links* – PV Links) to the LUN.

Block and character legacy DSFs for a sample LUN are shown below:

/dev/dsk/c10t0d0
/dev/rdsk/c10t0d0

A sample legacy DSF for a tape device could be:

/dev/rmt/c3t2d0

7.9.5 Persistent DSF

A *persistent DSF* is the LUN hardware path that represents all lunpath hardware paths to a single LUN. A persistent DSF remains unchanged even if the LUN it points to is relocated to another HBA. With persistent DSFs, there is no need to define PV links in LVM as the mass storage stack takes care of it automatically.

Block and character persistent DSFs for a sample LUN are shown below:

/dev/disk/disk22
/dev/rdisk/disk22

A sample persistent DSF for a tape device could be:

/dev/rtape/tape1_BEST

7.10 Legacy and Agile Views

In previous versions of HP-UX, hardware paths are employed to refer to storage devices. HP-UX 11i v3 uses agile view for this purpose. The old representation is now referred to as *legacy view* and

---

is still supported, but deprecated in 11i v3 and will no longer be available in a future HP-UX release.

Legacy view uses legacy DSFs and the agile view uses persistent DSFs. Both are explained in the following sub-sections.

7.10.1   Legacy View

Legacy view includes two types of DSFs: physical and logical. Each hardware component has a physical location where it can be reached at by the kernel when it needs to talk to it. This location is called *hardware address* or *physical address*.

The *ioscan* command allows you to view devices and associated addresses of all available devices on the system. A sample *ioscan* –f (full) output showing only mass storage devices – disk, DVD and tape – is displayed below:

```
# ioscan –f
```

Class	I	H/W Path	Driver	S/W State	H/W Type	Description
disk	0	0/0/0/3/0.6.0	sdisk	CLAIMED	DEVICE	HP 36.4GMAP3367NC
disk	4	0/0/4/0/0.0.0	sdisk	CLAIMED	DEVICE	HP 36.4GST336753LC
tape	0	0/0/8/0/0/1/0.2.0	stape	CLAIMED	DEVICE	HP C5683A
disk	1	0/0/8/0/0/1/0.4.0	sdisk	CLAIMED	DEVICE	HP DVD-ROM 305
disk	10	0/0/10/0/0.120.16.19.0.0.0	sdisk	CLAIMED	DEVICE	ABC ABC350WDR5
disk	11	0/0/10/0/0.120.16.19.0.0.1	sdisk	CLAIMED	DEVICE	ABC ABC350WDR5
disk	12	0/0/10/0/0.120.16.19.0.0.2	sdisk	CLAIMED	DEVICE	ABC ABC350WDR5
disk	13	0/0/10/0/0.120.16.19.0.0.3	sdisk	CLAIMED	DEVICE	ABC ABC350WDR5

There are seven columns in the output. Table 7-16 explains them:

Column	Explanation
Class	Device category. Examples are disk, tape, lan, processor, etc.
Instance	A unique number associated with a device or interface adapter within a class.
H/W Path	A series of digits separated by slash (/) and period (.) characters. Indicates the location of a physical device.
Driver	Software driver that controls the hardware. For example, "sdisk" is for SCSI disk and CD/DVD drives and "stape" is for the SCSI tape device.
S/W State	Software state is either CLAIMED or UNCLAIMED. CLAIMED means the driver for the device is successfully bound to it. UNCLAIMED means no driver is available for the device.
Hardware Type	An identifier for the hardware component.
Description	A short description.

Table 7-16 *ioscan* Output Explanation

The *ioscan* command output indicates that there are six hard drives – disk0, disk4, disk10, disk11, disk12 and disk13, one DVD drive – disk1, and one tape drive – tape0.

Run the *ioscan* command again as follows to view devices differently:

# **ioscan**	Scans entire system and lists all hardware found.
# **ioscan** –**fH 0/0/0/3/0.6.0**	Scans all devices at the specified hardware address.
# **ioscan** –**fn**	Scans entire system and also displays logical device files.
# **ioscan** –**fnk**	Same as "ioscan –fn" but gets information from the running kernel. This is much quicker.
# **ioscan** –**fnkCdisk**	Scans devices of the specified class. In this example, *ioscan* scans all devices of class "disk".

A different but simpler approach may be used instead to work with devices. This approach uses logical device files, which are mere pointers to their associated hardware device addresses.

Run the *ioscan* command to list all disk devices installed. Use the –n option to list logical device files.

ioscan –fnkCdisk

Class	I	H/W Path	Driver	S/W State	H/W Type	Description
disk	0	0/0/0/3/0.6.0	sdisk	CLAIMED	DEVICE	HP 36.4GMAP3367NC
		/dev/dsk/c0t6d0	/dev/rdsk/c0t6d0			
disk	4	0/0/4/0/0.0.0	sdisk	CLAIMED	DEVICE	HP 36.4GST336753LC
		/dev/dsk/c2t0d0	/dev/rdsk/c2t0d0			
disk	1	0/0/8/0/0/1/0.4.0	sdisk	CLAIMED	DEVICE	HP DVD-ROM 305
		/dev/dsk/c3t4d0	/dev/rdsk/c3t4d0			
disk	10	0/0/10/0/0.120.16.19.0.0.0	sdisk	CLAIMED	DEVICE	ABC ABC350WDR5
		/dev/dsk/c8t0d0	/dev/rdsk/c8t0d0			
disk	11	0/0/10/0/0.120.16.19.0.0.1	sdisk	CLAIMED	DEVICE	ABC ABC350WDR5
		/dev/dsk/c8t0d1	/dev/rdsk/c8t0d1			
disk	12	0/0/10/0/0.120.16.19.0.0.2	sdisk	CLAIMED	DEVICE	ABC ABC350WDR5
		/dev/dsk/c8t0d2	/dev/rdsk/c8t0d2			
disk	13	0/0/10/0/0.120.16.19.0.0.3	sdisk	CLAIMED	DEVICE	ABC ABC350WDR5
		/dev/dsk/c8t0d3	/dev/rdsk/c8t0d3			

The output displays the same information as did the previous *ioscan* command, but it shows the associated logical device files as well, which follows the convention illustrated in Figure 7-28.

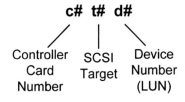

Figure 7-28 SCSI Disk DSF Naming Convention

Here, "c#" identifies the SCSI adapter number, "t#" identifies the SCSI target ID and "d#" identifies the SCSI disk number on the SCSI target.

The *ioscan* output indicates that the first hard drive is connected to the SCSI controller card number 0 (c0) having target SCSI ID 6. The SCSI disk device number is always 0 if there is no other device sharing the target ID.

The other disks shown are c2t0d0, c8t0d0, c8t0d1, c8t0d2 and c8t0d3 of which the first one is on controller 2 (c2) and the rest on controller 8 (c8). The DVD drive's DSF is c3t4d0 and is placed on a different SCSI controller card.

 Each SCSI disk must have a unique address on the SCSI bus, otherwise conflicts would occur.

All logical DSFs for disk and CD/DVD block devices are stored in the */dev/dsk* directory and their character counterparts in the */dev/rdsk* directory.

You can use the *lssf* command to view device characteristics. The following examples show attributes of */dev/rdsk/c0t6d0* and */dev/dsk/c3t4d0* legacy DSFs:

 # lssf /dev/rdsk/c0t6d0
sdisk card instance 0 SCSI target 6 SCSI LUN 0 section 0 at address 0/0/0/3/0.6.0 /dev/rdsk/c0t6d0
 # lssf /dev/dsk/c3t4d0
sdisk card instance 3 SCSI target 4 SCSI LUN 0 section 0 at address 0/0/8/0/0/1/0.4.0 /dev/dsk/c3t4d0

Note that a single disk drive with, say two connections to the system, is represented by two separate DSFs. Likewise, a separate pair of DSF is used for each additional path.

Tape devices are located in the */dev/rmt* directory. The first tape drive installed in the system is represented by the instance 0, followed by 1 for the next, 2 for the third and so on. The *ioscan* command below shows that there is only one tape drive in the system but with multiple logical legacy DSFs pointing to it:

 # ioscan –fnkCtape

Class	I	H/W Path	Driver	S/W State	H/W Type	Description
tape	0	0/0/8/0/0/1/0.2.0	stape	CLAIMED	DEVICE	HP C5683A
		/dev/rmt/0m		/dev/rmt/0mnb	/dev/rmt/c3t2d0BESTn	
		/dev/rmt/0mb		/dev/rmt/c3t2d0BEST	/dev/rmt/c3t2d0BESTnb	
		/dev/rmt/0mn		/dev/rmt/c3t2d0BESTb		

Figure 7-29 illustrates the naming convention followed for legacy tape DSFs.

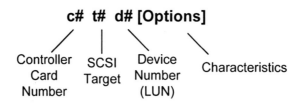

Figure 7-29 Tape DSF Naming Convention

This convention is similar to the one used for disks with the exception that it includes one or more options. For example:

/dev/rmt/c3t2d0BEST refers to the first tape drive and uses medium compression. It is hard linked to */dev/rmt/0m*.

/dev/rmt/c3t2d0BESTb is same as above but uses Berkeley-style behavior. It is hard linked to */dev/rmt/0mb*.

/dev/rmt/c3t2d0BESTn is same as the first one but does not rewind the tape after a backup is finished. It is hard linked to */dev/rmt/0mn*.

/dev/rmt/c3t2d0BESTnb is same as the previous one but uses Berkeley-style behavior. It is hard linked to */dev/rmt/0mnb*.

7.10.2   Legacy View Major and Minor Numbers

Every hardware device in the system has an associated device driver loaded in the HP-UX kernel. Some of the hardware device types are disks, DVD drives, printers, terminals, tape drives and modems. The kernel talks to hardware devices through their respective device drivers. Each device driver has a unique number called *major* number allocated to it by which kernel recognizes its type.

Furthermore, there is a possibility that more than one device of the same type is installed in the system. In this case the same driver will be used to control all of them. For example, SCSI device driver controls all SCSI hard disks and SCSI CD/DVD drives. The kernel in such a situation will assign another unique number called *minor* number to each individual device within that device driver category to identify it as a separate device. In summary, a major number points to the device driver and a minor number points to an individual device controlled by that device driver.

The major and minor numbers can be viewed using the *ll* command:

```
# ll /dev/dsk
total 0
brw-r-----   1 bin    sys     31 0x006000 Apr  8 08:59  c0t6d0
brw-r-----   1 bin    sys     31 0x0a0000 Apr  9 09:11  c10t0d0
brw-r-----   1 bin    sys     31 0x0a0100 Apr  9 09:11  c10t0d1
brw-r-----   1 bin    sys     31 0x0a0200 Apr  9 09:11  c10t0d2
brw-r-----   1 bin    sys     31 0x0a0300 Apr  9 09:11  c10t0d3
brw-r-----   1 bin    sys     31 0x0c0000 Apr  9 09:11  c12t0d0
brw-r-----   1 bin    sys     31 0x0c0100 Apr  9 09:11  c12t0d1
brw-r-----   1 bin    sys     31 0x0c0200 Apr  9 09:11  c12t0d2
brw-r-----   1 bin    sys     31 0x0c0300 Apr  9 09:11  c12t0d3
brw-r-----   1 bin    sys     31 0x020000 Apr  8 10:26  c2t0d0
brw-r-----   1 bin    sys     31 0x034000 Apr  8 08:59  c3t4d0
# ll /dev/rdsk
total 0
crw-r-----   1 bin    sys    188 0x006000 Apr  8 08:59  c0t6d0
crw-r-----   1 bin    sys    188 0x0a0000 Apr  9 09:11  c10t0d0
crw-r-----   1 bin    sys    188 0x0a0100 Apr  9 09:11  c10t0d1
crw-r-----   1 bin    sys    188 0x0a0200 Apr  9 09:11  c10t0d2
crw-r-----   1 bin    sys    188 0x0a0300 Apr  9 09:11  c10t0d3
crw-r-----   1 bin    sys    188 0x0c0000 Apr  9 09:11  c12t0d0
crw-r-----   1 bin    sys    188 0x0c0100 Apr  9 09:11  c12t0d1
crw-r-----   1 bin    sys    188 0x0c0200 Apr  9 09:11  c12t0d2
crw-r-----   1 bin    sys    188 0x0c0300 Apr  9 09:11  c12t0d3
crw-r-----   1 bin    sys    188 0x020000 Apr  8 10:26  c2t0d0
```

```
crw-r-----  1 bin      sys       188 0x034000 Apr  8 08:59  c3t4d0
```

Column 5 in the above outputs shows major numbers and column 6 shows minor numbers. The major number 31 always represents the block device driver for "sdisk" and major number 188 always represents the character device driver for "sdisk". All minor numbers are unique within the class. The output shows both block and character DSFs.

Another HP-UX command that displays major numbers for both character and block DSFs is the *lsdev* command. Run this command and *grep* for "sdisk":

 # lsdev | grep sdisk

Character	Block	Driver	Class
188	31	sdisk	disk

The first column lists major numbers associated with character devices, the second column shows major numbers associated with block devices, the third column displays the device driver used to control the devices and the last column signifies the device class. A –1 in either of the first two columns, indicates that a major number does not exist for that device class.

7.10.3 Agile View

Agile view displays a single persistent DSF for each LUN even though the LUN has several paths leading to it. Block persistent DSFs are stored in the */dev/disk* and */dev/rdisk* directories. Do an *ll* on the two directories to view current persistent DSFs:

 # ll /dev/disk
```
total 0
brw-r-----  1 bin      sys       1 0x000000 Apr  8 08:59  disk2
brw-r-----  1 bin      sys       1 0x000009 Apr  9 09:11  disk22
brw-r-----  1 bin      sys       1 0x00000a Apr  9 09:11  disk23
brw-r-----  1 bin      sys       1 0x00000b Apr  9 09:11  disk24
brw-r-----  1 bin      sys       1 0x00000c Apr  9 09:11  disk25
brw-r-----  1 bin      sys       1 0x000001 Apr  8 08:59  disk3
brw-r-----  1 bin      sys       1 0x000006 Apr  8 10:26  disk5
```
 # ll /dev/rdisk
```
total 0
crw-r-----  1 bin      sys       11 0x000000 Apr  8 09:07  disk2
crw-r-----  1 bin      sys       11 0x000009 Apr  9 09:11  disk22
crw-r-----  1 bin      sys       11 0x00000a Apr  9 09:11  disk23
crw-r-----  1 bin      sys       11 0x00000b Apr  9 09:11  disk24
crw-r-----  1 bin      sys       11 0x00000c Apr  9 09:11  disk25
crw-r-----  1 bin      sys       11 0x000001 Apr  8 08:59  disk3
crw-r-----  1 bin      sys       11 0x000006 Apr  8 10:26  disk5
```

If you wish to view the disk devices in agile view, use the –N option with *ioscan*:

 # ioscan –fNnk
```
Class   I H/W Path    Driver  S/W State  H/W Type   Description
================================================================
```

tgtpath 0 0/0/0/3/0.0x6 estp CLAIMED TGT_PATH parallel_scsi target served by c8xx driver
lunpath 0 0/0/0/3/0.0x6.0x0 eslpt CLAIMED LUN_PATH LUN path for disk2
tgtpath 3 0/0/4/0/0.0x0 estp CLAIMED TGT_PATH parallel_scsi target served by c8xx driver
lunpath 3 0/0/4/0/0.0x0.0x0 eslpt CLAIMED LUN_PATH LUN path for disk5
tgtpath 2 0/0/8/0/0/1/0.0x2 estp CLAIMED TGT_PATH parallel_scsi target served by c8xx driver
lunpath 2 0/0/8/0/0/1/0.0x2.0x0 eslpt CLAIMED LUN_PATH LUN path for tape1
tgtpath 1 0/0/8/0/0/1/0.0x4 estp CLAIMED TGT_PATH parallel_scsi target served by c8xx driver
lunpath 1 0/0/8/0/0/1/0.0x4.0x0 eslpt CLAIMED LUN_PATH LUN path for disk3
tgtpath 4 0/0/10/0/0.0x5006016030201d6b estp CLAIMED TGT_PATH fibre_channel target served by td driver
lunpath 4 0/0/10/0/0.0x5006016030201d6b.0x0 eslpt CLAIMED LUN_PATH LUN path for ctl1
lunpath 8 0/0/10/0/0.0x5006016030201d6b.0x4000000000000000 eslpt CLAIMED LUN_PATH LUN path for disk22
lunpath 9 0/0/10/0/0.0x5006016030201d6b.0x4001000000000000 eslpt CLAIMED LUN_PATH LUN path for disk23
lunpath 10 0/0/10/0/0.0x5006016030201d6b.0x4002000000000000 eslpt CLAIMED LUN_PATH LUN path for disk24
lunpath 15 0/0/10/0/0.0x5006016030201d6b.0x4003000000000000 eslpt CLAIMED LUN_PATH LUN path for disk25
tgtpath 5 0/0/10/0/0.0x5006016930201d6b estp CLAIMED TGT_PATH fibre_channel target served by td driver
lunpath 5 0/0/10/0/0.0x5006016930201d6b.0x0 eslpt CLAIMED LUN_PATH LUN path for ctl1
lunpath 11 0/0/10/0/0.0x5006016930201d6b.0x4000000000000000 eslpt CLAIMED LUN_PATH LUN path for disk22
lunpath 12 0/0/10/0/0.0x5006016930201d6b.0x4001000000000000 eslpt CLAIMED LUN_PATH LUN path for disk23
lunpath 13 0/0/10/0/0.0x5006016930201d6b.0x4002000000000000 eslpt CLAIMED LUN_PATH LUN path for disk24
lunpath 14 0/0/10/0/0.0x5006016930201d6b.0x4003000000000000 eslpt CLAIMED LUN_PATH LUN path for disk25
tgtpath 6 0/0/12/0/0.0x5006016130201d6b estp CLAIMED TGT_PATH fibre_channel target served by td driver
lunpath 6 0/0/12/0/0.0x5006016130201d6b.0x0 eslpt CLAIMED LUN_PATH LUN path for ctl1
lunpath 20 0/0/12/0/0.0x5006016130201d6b.0x4000000000000000 eslpt CLAIMED LUN_PATH LUN path for disk22
lunpath 21 0/0/12/0/0.0x5006016130201d6b.0x4001000000000000 eslpt CLAIMED LUN_PATH LUN path for disk23
lunpath 22 0/0/12/0/0.0x5006016130201d6b.0x4002000000000000 eslpt CLAIMED LUN_PATH LUN path for disk24
lunpath 23 0/0/12/0/0.0x5006016130201d6b.0x4003000000000000 eslpt CLAIMED LUN_PATH LUN path for disk25
tgtpath 7 0/0/12/0/0.0x5006016830201d6b estp CLAIMED TGT_PATH fibre_channel target served by td driver
lunpath 7 0/0/12/0/0.0x5006016830201d6b.0x0 eslpt CLAIMED LUN_PATH LUN path for ctl1
lunpath 16 0/0/12/0/0.0x5006016830201d6b.0x4000000000000000 eslpt CLAIMED LUN_PATH LUN path for disk22
lunpath 17 0/0/12/0/0.0x5006016830201d6b.0x4001000000000000 eslpt CLAIMED LUN_PATH LUN path for disk23
lunpath 18 0/0/12/0/0.0x5006016830201d6b.0x4002000000000000 eslpt CLAIMED LUN_PATH LUN path for disk24
lunpath 19 0/0/12/0/0.0x5006016830201d6b.0x4003000000000000 eslpt CLAIMED LUN_PATH LUN path for disk25
disk   2 64000/0xfa00/0x0   esdisk CLAIMED   DEVICE   HP 36.4GMAP3367NC
           /dev/disk/disk2 /dev/rdisk/disk2
disk   3 64000/0xfa00/0x1   esdisk CLAIMED   DEVICE   HP   DVD-ROM 305
           /dev/disk/disk3 /dev/rdisk/disk3
tape   1 64000/0xfa00/0x2   estape CLAIMED   DEVICE   HP   C5683A
           /dev/rtape/tape1_BEST   /dev/rtape/tape1_BESTn
           /dev/rtape/tape1_BESTb /dev/rtape/tape1_BESTnb
disk   5 64000/0xfa00/0x6   esdisk CLAIMED   DEVICE   HP   36.4GST336753LC
           /dev/disk/disk5 /dev/rdisk/disk5
disk   22 64000/0xfa00/0x9   esdisk CLAIMED   DEVICE   ABC   ABC350WDR5
           /dev/disk/disk22 /dev/rdisk/disk22
disk   23 64000/0xfa00/0xa   esdisk CLAIMED   DEVICE   ABC   ABC350WDR5
           /dev/disk/disk23 /dev/rdisk/disk23
disk   24 64000/0xfa00/0xb   esdisk CLAIMED   DEVICE   ABC   ABC350WDR5
           /dev/disk/disk24 /dev/rdisk/disk24
disk   25 64000/0xfa00/0xc   esdisk CLAIMED   DEVICE   ABC   ABC350WDR5
           /dev/disk/disk25 /dev/rdisk/disk25

The above output shows a wealth of information about mass storage devices. Each mass storage device is represented as a single LUN hardware path using a single persistent DSF even though it has several physical connections. The LUN hardware path begins with 64000, which is referred to as *virtual root address,* followed by virtual bus address and virtual LUN ID.

Each physical path to a LUN is called a *lunpath* and its hardware path a *lunpath hardware path.* These hardware paths are displayed as lunpaths with associated driver "sdisk" and persistent DSFs. The term *tgtpath* is used instead of *target* to represent a target device. Software drivers "estp", "eslpt" and "esdisk" are used for target paths, lunpaths and disks, respectively.

Use the *lssf* command to view device characteristics. The following example shows attributes of */dev/disk/disk22*:

> **# lssf /dev/disk/disk22**
> esdisk section 0 at address 64000/0xfa00/0x9 /dev/rdisk/disk22

Tape devices are located in the */dev/rtape* directory. The first tape drive installed in the system is represented by the digit 0, followed by 1 for the next, 2 for the third and so on. The following *ioscan* command output shows that there is only one tape drive in the system with multiple logical device files pointing to it:

> **# ioscan –fNnkCtape**
> Class   I H/W Path Driver S/W State H/W Type   Description
> ===
> tape   1 64000/0xfa00/0x2 estape CLAIMED   DEVICE   HP   C5683A
>   /dev/rtape/tape1_BEST /dev/rtape/tape1_BESTb /dev/rtape/tape1_BESTn /dev/rtape/tape1_BESTnb

This convention is similar to the one used for disks with the exception that it includes one or more options. For example:

> */dev/rtape/tape1_BEST* refers to the first tape drive and uses medium compression.
> */dev/rtape/tape1_BESTb* is the same as above but uses Berkeley-style behavior.
> */dev/rtape/tape1_BESTn* is the same as the first one but does not rewind the tape after a backup is finished.
> */dev/rtape/tape1_BESTnb* is the same as the previous one but uses Berkeley-style behavior.

7.10.4   Agile View Major and Minor Numbers

The major and minor numbers for persistent DSFs can be viewed using the *ll* command:

> **# ll /dev/disk**
> total 0
> brw-r----- 1 bin   sys   1 0x000000 Apr 8 08:59 disk2
> brw-r----- 1 bin   sys   1 0x000009 Apr 9 09:11 disk22
> brw-r----- 1 bin   sys   1 0x00000a Apr 9 09:11 disk23
> brw-r----- 1 bin   sys   1 0x00000b Apr 9 09:11 disk24
> brw-r----- 1 bin   sys   1 0x00000c Apr 9 09:11 disk25
> brw-r----- 1 bin   sys   1 0x000001 Apr 8 08:59 disk3
> brw-r----- 1 bin   sys   1 0x000006 Apr 8 10:26 disk5

```
# ll /dev/rdisk
total 0
crw-r-----  1 bin    sys    11 0x000000 Apr  8 09:07 disk2
crw-r-----  1 bin    sys    11 0x000009 Apr  9 09:11 disk22
crw-r-----  1 bin    sys    11 0x00000a Apr  9 09:11 disk23
crw-r-----  1 bin    sys    11 0x00000b Apr  9 09:11 disk24
crw-r-----  1 bin    sys    11 0x00000c Apr  9 09:11 disk25
crw-r-----  1 bin    sys    11 0x000001 Apr  8 08:59 disk3
crw-r-----  1 bin    sys    11 0x000006 Apr  8 10:26 disk5
```

Column 5 shows major numbers and column 6 shows minor numbers. The major number 1 always represents the block device driver for "esdisk" and major number 11 always represents the character device driver for "esdisk". All minor numbers are unique within that class. The output shows both block and character DSFs.

Use the *lsdev* command to display major numbers for both character and block devices. Run this command and *grep* for "esdisk".

```
# lsdev | grep esdisk
    Character     Block   Driver       Class
    11            1       esdisk       disk
```

The first column lists major numbers associated with character devices, the second column shows major numbers associated with block devices, the third column displays the device driver used to control the devices and the last column signifies the device class.

7.11   Other Types of DSFs

Besides mass storage DSFs, other hardware devices such as those connected to serial and parallel ports employ DSFs as well. These devices include modems, terminals, and serial and parallel printers. The following sub-sections examine these DSFs.

7.11.1   Serial and Modem DSFs

DSFs for serial ports are directly located under the */dev* directory. For example, an rp7410 server has two built-in serial ports for MP with each having three pseudo serial ports to support console, UPS and remote connectivity. The device files look similar to what the *ll* command displays below for the second serial port:

```
# ll /dev/tty1p*
crw--w--w-  1 bin    bin    1 0x010000 Mar 12 14:56  tty1p0
crw--w--w-  1 bin    bin    1 0x010100 Mar 12 14:56  tty1p1
crw--w--w-  1 bin    bin    1 0x010200 Mar 12 14:56  tty1p2
```

Do an *lssf* on one of the DSFs and you should be able to see its characteristics:

```
# lssf /dev/tty1p0
asio0 card instance 1 port 0 hardwired at address 0/0/0/0/1 /dev/tty1p0
```

Typical modem device files are */dev/cua0p0*, */dev/cu10p0* and */dev/ttyd0p0*.

7.11.2   Terminal DSFs

Device files for terminals are located under the */dev/pts* directory, as shown below:

```
# ll /dev/pts*
crw--w----  1 root    tty      157 0x000000 Apr 11 13:18 0
crw--w----  1 root    tty      157 0x000001 Apr 11 12:39 1
crw-rw-rw-  1 root    sys      157 0x00000a Apr  8 10:26 10
crw-rw-rw-  1 root    sys      157 0x00000b Apr  8 10:26 11
crw-rw-rw-  1 root    sys      157 0x00000c Apr  8 10:26 12
crw-rw-rw-  1 root    sys      157 0x00000d Apr  8 10:26 13
```

7.12   Creating, Displaying and Removing DSFs

DSFs may be created automatically when the system boots up or they may be created manually as desired. Similarly, you can remove them when devices associated with them are no longer accessible to the system. The following sub-sections shed light on creating and removing DSFs and how to view them.

7.12.1   Creating DSFs

All system hardware is scanned with the *ioscan* command and device files are created by the *insf* command during HP-UX installation process. All device information is then stored in the */etc/ioconfig* file. Each time the system is rebooted, the *ioinit* (i/o initialization) command calls the *insf* command, which automatically creates device files for any new devices it finds and updates */etc/ioconfig*. Similarly, it automatically removes device files for any devices it does not find and updates */etc/ioconfig*. This automatic process of creating and deleting device information is called *autoconfiguration*.

Sometimes it becomes necessary to create device files manually. You may use SMH or command line for this purpose.

At the command prompt, you can use *insf, mksf* or *mknod*. Let us see how these commands are used to create device files.

Creating DSFs with the *insf* Command

The *insf* (install special file) command creates device files under the */dev* directory for new devices that it finds. The following shows various examples.

To create device files for all existing and new devices:

```
# insf –e
insf: Installing special files for asio0 instance 1 address 0/0/0/0/1
insf: Installing special files for sdisk instance 0 address 0/0/0/3/0.6.0
. . . . . . . .
```

To create device files for all devices of class "disk" only:

```
# insf –C disk
```

To create device files for a specific device located at hardware address 0/0/0/3:

```
# insf –H 0/0/0/3 –e
insf: Installing special files for sdisk instance 0 address 0/0/0/3/0.6.0
insf: Installing special files for c8xx instance 0 address 0/0/0/3/0
insf: Installing special files for c8xx instance 1 address 0/0/0/3/1
```

Creating DSFs with the *mksf* Command

The *mksf* (make special file) command may be used to create device files for devices seen by the *ioscan* command but missing device files. The following example shows how to create a character special tape device file for the tape device located at 0/0/8/0/0/1/0.2.0 address with instance number 0 and hardware class type tape:

```
# cd /dev/rmt
# mksf –C tape –H 0/0/8/0/0/1/0.2.0 –I 0
# ll
crw-rw-rw-  1 bin      bin      205 0x032020 Apr  7 10:44 c3t2d0D0
```

Creating DSFs with the *mknod* Command

The *mknod* (make node) command can also be used to create device files. It requires that you supply major and minor device numbers. The following example shows how to create a character device file called *group* with major number 64 and minor number 0x010000:

```
# cd /dev
# mknod test c 64 0x010000
# ll test
crw-r-----  1 root     sys      64 0x010000 Apr  7 10:46 test
```

Creating DSFs with SMH

If you prefer using SMH (or *pdweb* command), go to SMH → Peripheral Devices → OLRAD Cards. Highlight the slot where the desired card is installed.

```
                    SMH->Peripheral Devices->OLRAD Cards

                                                                      8 Slots

          ----------------------------------------------------------------
Driver(s)
Capable
Slot       Path      Pwr   Occu   Susp   OLAR   OLD   Mode
========================================================================
0-0-0-1    0/0/8/0    On   Yes    No     Yes    Yes   PCI
0-0-0-2    0/0/10/0   On   Yes    No     Yes    Yes   PCI
0-0-0-3    0/0/12/0   On   Yes    No     Yes    Yes   PCI
0-0-0-4    0/0/14/0   On   Yes    No     Yes    Yes   PCI
0-0-0-5    0/0/6/0    On   Yes    No     Yes    Yes   PCI
0-0-0-6    0/0/4/0    On   Yes    No     Yes    Yes   PCI
```

| 0-0-0-7 | 0/0/2/0 | Off | No | N/A | N/A | N/A | PCI |
| 0-0-0-8 | 0/0/1/0 | Off | No | N/A | N/A | N/A | PCI |

----

x-Exit smh   ESC-Back   a-Add Chassis Online
ENTER-Select   t-Toggle Global Device View   Ctrl o-Other Actions

7.12.2   Displaying Stale DSFs

Stale DSFs represent hardware devices that have been removed from the system or become inaccessible. You can use the *lssf* command to list legacy and persistent stale DSFs.

 # lssf –s
Stale Character Device Files

/dev/rscsi/c6t0d0
/dev/rscsi/c8t0d0
/dev/rscsi/c12t0d0
/dev/rscsi/c10t0d0

7.12.3   Displaying Mappings for Persistent and Legacy DSFs

The *ioscan* command can be used to display mapping of a legacy DSF to its corresponding persistent path. The following shows an example:

 # ioscan –m dsf

Persistent DSF	Legacy DSF(s)
===	===
/dev/pt/pt1	/dev/rscsi/c7t3d0
	/dev/rscsi/c5t3d0
	/dev/rscsi/c11t3d0
	/dev/rscsi/c9t3d0
/dev/rdisk/disk2	/dev/rdsk/c0t6d0
/dev/rtape/tape1_BEST	/dev/rmt/c3t2d0BEST
/dev/rtape/tape1_BESTn	/dev/rmt/c3t2d0BESTn
/dev/rtape/tape1_BESTb	/dev/rmt/c3t2d0BESTb
/dev/rtape/tape1_BESTnb	/dev/rmt/c3t2d0BESTnb
/dev/rdisk/disk3	/dev/rdsk/c3t4d0
/dev/rdisk/disk5	/dev/rdsk/c2t0d0
/dev/rdisk/disk22	/dev/rdsk/c8t0d0
	/dev/rdsk/c6t0d0
	/dev/rdsk/c10t0d0
	/dev/rdsk/c12t0d0
/dev/rdisk/disk23	/dev/rdsk/c8t0d1
	/dev/rdsk/c6t0d1
	/dev/rdsk/c10t0d1
	/dev/rdsk/c12t0d1
/dev/rdisk/disk24	/dev/rdsk/c8t0d2
	/dev/rdsk/c6t0d2

	/dev/rdsk/c10t0d2
	/dev/rdsk/c12t0d2
/dev/rdisk/disk25	/dev/rdsk/c6t0d3
	/dev/rdsk/c8t0d3
	/dev/rdsk/c10t0d3
	/dev/rdsk/c12t0d3

7.12.4   Displaying Mappings for Hardware Paths

The *ioscan* command can be used to display mapping of a LUN hardware path, lunpath hardware path and legacy hardware path. The following shows an example:

```
# ioscan –m hwpath
```

Lun H/W Path	Lunpath H/W Path	Legacy H/W Path
===================	==	==============================
64000/0xfa00/0x0	0/0/0/3/0.0x6.0x0	0/0/0/3/0.6.0
64000/0xfa00/0x1	0/0/8/0/0/1/0.0x4.0x0	0/0/8/0/0/1/0.4.0
64000/0xfa00/0x2	0/0/8/0/0/1/0.0x2.0x0	0/0/8/0/0/1/0.2.0
64000/0xfa00/0x6	0/0/4/0/0.0x0.0x0	0/0/4/0/0.0.0
64000/0xfa00/0x8		
	0/0/10/0/0.0x5006016030201d6b.0x0	0/0/10/0/0.120.16.255.1.3.0
	0/0/10/0/0.0x5006016930201d6b.0x0	0/0/10/0/0.120.17.255.1.3.0
	0/0/12/0/0.0x5006016130201d6b.0x0	0/0/12/0/0.119.16.255.1.3.0
	0/0/12/0/0.0x5006016830201d6b.0x0	0/0/12/0/0.119.17.255.1.3.0
64000/0xfa00/0x9		
	0/0/10/0/0.0x5006016030201d6b.0x4000000000000000	0/0/10/0/0.120.16.19.0.0.0
	0/0/10/0/0.0x5006016930201d6b.0x4000000000000000	0/0/10/0/0.120.17.19.0.0.0
	0/0/12/0/0.0x5006016830201d6b.0x4000000000000000	0/0/12/0/0.119.17.19.0.0.0
	0/0/12/0/0.0x5006016130201d6b.0x4000000000000000	0/0/12/0/0.119.16.19.0.0.0
64000/0xfa00/0xa		
	0/0/10/0/0.0x5006016030201d6b.0x4001000000000000	0/0/10/0/0.120.16.19.0.0.1
	0/0/10/0/0.0x5006016930201d6b.0x4001000000000000	0/0/10/0/0.120.17.19.0.0.1
	0/0/12/0/0.0x5006016830201d6b.0x4001000000000000	0/0/12/0/0.119.17.19.0.0.1
	0/0/12/0/0.0x5006016130201d6b.0x4001000000000000	0/0/12/0/0.119.16.19.0.0.1
64000/0xfa00/0xb		
	0/0/10/0/0.0x5006016030201d6b.0x4002000000000000	0/0/10/0/0.120.16.19.0.0.2
	0/0/10/0/0.0x5006016930201d6b.0x4002000000000000	0/0/10/0/0.120.17.19.0.0.2
	0/0/12/0/0.0x5006016830201d6b.0x4002000000000000	0/0/12/0/0.119.17.19.0.0.2
	0/0/12/0/0.0x5006016130201d6b.0x4002000000000000	0/0/12/0/0.119.16.19.0.0.2
64000/0xfa00/0xc		
	0/0/10/0/0.0x5006016930201d6b.0x4003000000000000	0/0/10/0/0.120.17.19.0.0.3
	0/0/10/0/0.0x5006016030201d6b.0x4003000000000000	0/0/10/0/0.120.16.19.0.0.3
	0/0/12/0/0.0x5006016830201d6b.0x4003000000000000	0/0/12/0/0.119.17.19.0.0.3
	0/0/12/0/0.0x5006016130201d6b.0x4003000000000000	0/0/12/0/0.119.16.19.0.0.3

To display mapping of a specific hardware path at address 0/0/10/0/0.120.16.19.0.0.0, run the *ioscan* command as follows:

ioscan –m hwpath –H 0/0/10/0/0.120.16.19.0.0.0

Lun H/W Path	Lunpath H/W Path	Legacy H/W Path

64000/0xfa00/0x9
    0/0/10/0/0.0x5006016030201d6b.0x4000000000000000 0/0/10/0/0.120.16.19.0.0.0

To display mapping of a persistent hardware path at address 0/0/10/0/0.0x5006016030201d6b.0x4000000000000000, run the *ioscan* command as follows:

ioscan –m hwpath –H 0/0/10/0/0.0x5006016030201d6b.0x4000000000000000

Lun H/W Path	Lunpath H/W Path	Legacy H/W Path

64000/0xfa00/0x9
    0/0/10/0/0.0x5006016030201d6b.0x4000000000000000 0/0/10/0/0.120.16.19.0.0.0

To display mapping of a persistent hardware path at address 64000/0xfa00/0x9, run the *ioscan* command as follows:

ioscan –m hwpath –H 64000/0xfa00/0x9

Lun H/W Path	Lunpath H/W Path	Legacy H/W Path

64000/0xfa00/0x9
    0/0/10/0/0.0x5006016030201d6b.0x4000000000000000 0/0/10/0/0.120.16.19.0.0.0
    0/0/10/0/0.0x5006016930201d6b.0x4000000000000000 0/0/10/0/0.120.17.19.0.0.0
    0/0/12/0/0.0x5006016830201d6b.0x4000000000000000 0/0/12/0/0.119.17.19.0.0.0
    0/0/12/0/0.0x5006016130201d6b.0x4000000000000000 0/0/12/0/0.119.16.19.0.0.0

To display LUN hardware path to lunpath hardware paths mapping for all storage devices, run the *ioscan* command as follows:

ioscan –m lun

Class	I	Lun H/W Path	Driver	S/W State	H/W Type	Health	Description
disk	2	64000/0xfa00/0x0	esdisk	CLAIMED	DEVICE	online	HP 36.4GMAP3367NC
		0/0/0/3/0.0x6.0x0			/dev/disk/disk2	/dev/rdisk/disk2	
disk	3	64000/0xfa00/0x1	esdisk	CLAIMED	DEVICE	online	HP DVD-ROM 305
		0/0/8/0/0/1/0.0x4.0x0			/dev/disk/disk3	/dev/rdisk/disk3	
tape	1	64000/0xfa00/0x2	estape	CLAIMED	DEVICE	online	HP C5683A
		0/0/8/0/0/1/0.0x2.0x0			/dev/rtape/tape1_BEST	/dev/rtape/tape1_BESTb	
					/dev/rtape/tape1_BESTn	/dev/rtape/tape1_BESTnb	
disk	5	64000/0xfa00/0x6	esdisk	CLAIMED	DEVICE	online	HP 36.4GST336753LC
		0/0/4/0/0.0x0.0x0			/dev/disk/disk5	/dev/rdisk/disk5	
ctl	1	64000/0xfa00/0x8	esctl	CLAIMED	DEVICE	online	ABC ABC350
		0/0/10/0/0.0x5006016030201d6b.0x0					
		0/0/10/0/0.0x5006016930201d6b.0x0					
		0/0/12/0/0.0x5006016130201d6b.0x0					
		0/0/12/0/0.0x5006016830201d6b.0x0					
		/dev/pt/pt1					
disk	22	64000/0xfa00/0x9	esdisk	CLAIMED	DEVICE	online	ABC ABC350WDR5

```
                    0/0/10/0/0.0x5006016030201d6b.0x4000000000000000
                    0/0/10/0/0.0x5006016930201d6b.0x4000000000000000
                    0/0/12/0/0.0x5006016830201d6b.0x4000000000000000
                    0/0/12/0/0.0x5006016130201d6b.0x4000000000000000
                       /dev/disk/disk22   /dev/rdisk/disk22
disk   23 64000/0xfa00/0xa esdisk CLAIMED   DEVICE    online   ABC   ABC350WDR5
                    0/0/10/0/0.0x5006016030201d6b.0x4001000000000000
                    0/0/10/0/0.0x5006016930201d6b.0x4001000000000000
                    0/0/12/0/0.0x5006016830201d6b.0x4001000000000000
                    0/0/12/0/0.0x5006016130201d6b.0x4001000000000000
                       /dev/disk/disk23   /dev/rdisk/disk23
disk   24 64000/0xfa00/0xb esdisk CLAIMED   DEVICE    online   ABC   ABC350WDR5
                    0/0/10/0/0.0x5006016030201d6b.0x4002000000000000
                    0/0/10/0/0.0x5006016930201d6b.0x4002000000000000
                    0/0/12/0/0.0x5006016830201d6b.0x4002000000000000
                    0/0/12/0/0.0x5006016130201d6b.0x4002000000000000
                       /dev/disk/disk24   /dev/rdisk/disk24
disk   25 64000/0xfa00/0xc esdisk CLAIMED   DEVICE    online   ABC   ABC350WDR5
                    0/0/10/0/0.0x5006016930201d6b.0x4003000000000000
                    0/0/10/0/0.0x5006016030201d6b.0x4003000000000000
                    0/0/12/0/0.0x5006016830201d6b.0x4003000000000000
                    0/0/12/0/0.0x5006016130201d6b.0x4003000000000000
                       /dev/disk/disk25   /dev/rdisk/disk25
```

To display LUN hardware path to lunpath hardware paths mapping for a specific storage device, run the *ioscan* command as follows:

 # ioscan –m lun /dev/disk/disk22

```
Class    I Lun H/W Path     Driver  S/W State  H/W Type   Health  Description
====================================================================================
disk    22 64000/0xfa00/0x9 esdisk CLAIMED   DEVICE    online   ABC   ABC350WDR5
                    0/0/10/0/0.0x5006016030201d6b.0x4000000000000000
                    0/0/10/0/0.0x5006016930201d6b.0x4000000000000000
                    0/0/12/0/0.0x5006016830201d6b.0x4000000000000000
                    0/0/12/0/0.0x5006016130201d6b.0x4000000000000000
                       /dev/disk/disk22   /dev/rdisk/disk22
```

7.12.5   Listing, Initiating and Removing Deferred Bindings

To list deferred bindings, run the *ioscan* command as follows:

 # ioscan –B

To initiate deferred bindings, run the *ioscan* command as follows:

```
# ioscan –b
H/W Path      Class        Description
==========================================================
              root
0             cell
0/0           ioa          System Bus Adapter (804)
0/0/0         ba           Local PCI Bus Adapter (782)
0/0/0/0/0     tty          PCI BaseSystem (103c128d)
0/0/0/0/1     tty          PCI Serial (103c1048)
0/0/0/3/0     ext_bus      SCSI C1010 Ultra160 Wide LVD A6793-60001
0/0/0/3/0.6   target
0/0/0/3/0.6.0 disk         HP 36.4GMAP3367NC
. . . . . . . .
```

To remove deferred bindings for the specified hardware path, run the *ioscan* command as follows:

```
# ioscan –r –H 64000/0xfa00/0x9
```

7.12.6   Displaying Lunpath and LUN Status

To retrieve status information about a lunpath hardware path at 0/0/10/0/0.0x5006016030201d6b.0x4000000000000000, run the *scsimgr* command as follows:

```
# scsimgr get_info –H 0/0/10/0/0.0x5006016030201d6b.0x4000000000000000
     STATUS INFORMATION FOR LUN PATH :
0/0/10/0/0.0x5006016030201d6b.0x4000000000000000

Generic Status Information

SCSI services internal state              = UNOPEN
Open close state                          = ACTIVE
Protocol                                  = fibre_channel
EVPD page 0x83 description code            = 1
EVPD page 0x83 description association     = 0
EVPD page 0x83 description type            = 3
World Wide Identifier (WWID)               = 0x6006016051a015006ae307699405dd11
     . . . . . . . .
```

To retrieve status information about a LUN hardware path at 64000/0xfa00/0x9, run the *scsimgr* command as follows:

```
# scsimgr get_info –H 64000/0xfa00/0x9
     STATUS INFORMATION FOR LUN : 64000/0xfa00/0x9

Generic Status Information

SCSI services internal state              = UNOPEN
Device type                               = Direct_Access
EVPD page 0x83 description code            = 1
```

EVPD page 0x83 description association	= 0
EVPD page 0x83 description type	= 3
World Wide Identifier (WWID)	= 0x6006016051a015006ae307699405dd11
Serial number	= ABC0000000321
Vendor id	= ABC
Product id	= ABC350WDR5
Product revision	= HP03
Other properties	=
SPC protocol revision	= 4
Open count (includes chr/blk/pass-thru/class)	= 0
Raw open count (includes class/pass-thru)	= 0
Pass-thru opens	= 0
LUN path count	= 4
Active LUN paths	= 4
Standby LUN paths	= 0
Failed LUN paths	= 0
Maximum I/O size allowed	= 2097152
Preferred I/O size	= 2097152
Outstanding I/Os	= 0
I/O load balance policy	= round_robin

. . . .

7.12.7   Displaying Lunpath and LUN Statistics

To retrieve the statistics of a lunpath hardware path at 64000/0xfa00/0x9, run the *scsimgr* command as follows:

 # scsimgr get_stat −H 64000/0xfa00/0x9
       STATISTICS FOR LUN :64000/0xfa00/0x9

Generic Statistics:

Overall attempted opens	= 7
Overall successfull opens	= 1
Attempted Pass-thru opens	= 6
Successfull Pass-thru opens	= 6
Overall closes	= 7
Pass-thru closes	= 6
Offlines	= 0
Onlines	= 0
LUN path inititializations	= 4

. . . .

To retrieve the statistics of a LUN path at */dev/rdisk/disk22*, run the *scsimgr* command as follows:

 # scsimgr get_stat −D /dev/rdisk/disk22
       STATISTICS FOR LUN :/dev/rdisk/disk22

Generic Statistics:

```
Overall attempted opens        = 7
Overall successfull opens      = 1
Attempted Pass-thru opens      = 6
Successfull Pass-thru opens    = 6
Overall closes                 = 7
Pass-thru closes               = 6
Offlines                       = 0
Onlines                        = 0
LUN path inititializations     = 4
. . . . . . . .
```

7.12.8   Displaying Attributes

To display attributes such as WWID, serial number and LUN ID of a LUN at */dev/rdisk/disk22*, run the *scsimgr* command as follows:

 # scsimgr get_attr –D /dev/rdisk/disk22 –a wwid –a serial_number
```
     SCSI ATTRIBUTES FOR LUN : /dev/rdisk/disk22

name = wwid
current = 0x6006016051a015006ae307699405dd11
default =
saved =

name = serial_number
current = ABC0000000321
default =
saved =
```

7.12.9   Displaying Lunpaths of a LUN

To display all lunpaths of a LUN */dev/disk/disk22*, run the *scsimgr* command as follows:

 # scsimgr lun_map –D /dev/rdisk/disk22
```
     LUN PATH INFORMATION FOR LUN : /dev/rdisk/disk22

Total number of LUN paths    = 4
World Wide Identifier(WWID) = 0x6006016051a015006ae307699405dd11

LUN path : lunpath8
Class                        = lunpath
Instance                     = 8
Hardware path                = 0/0/10/0/0.0x5006016030201d6b.0x4000000000000000
SCSI transport protocol      = fibre_channel
State                        = UNOPEN
Last Open or Close state     = ACTIVE

LUN path : lunpath11
Class                        = lunpath
Instance                     = 11
```

```
Hardware path                 = 0/0/10/0/0.0x5006016930201d6b.0x4000000000000000
SCSI transport protocol       = fibre_channel
State                         = UNOPEN
Last Open or Close state      = ACTIVE

LUN path : lunpath16
Class                         = lunpath
Instance                      = 16
Hardware path                 = 0/0/12/0/0.0x5006016830201d6b.0x4000000000000000
SCSI transport protocol       = fibre_channel
State                         = UNOPEN
Last Open or Close state      = ACTIVE

LUN path : lunpath20
Class                         = lunpath
Instance                      = 20
Hardware path                 = 0/0/12/0/0.0x5006016130201d6b.0x4000000000000000
SCSI transport protocol       = fibre_channel
State                         = UNOPEN
Last Open or Close state      = ACTIVE
```

7.12.10   Removing DSFs

Use the *rmsf* (remove special file) command to remove any device files that you no longer need.
For example, to remove all device files that refer to tape device at hardware address
0/0/8/0/0/1/0.2.0, do the following:

 # rmsf –H 0/0/8/0/0/1/0.2.0

7.13   Viewing Hardware Diagnostic Messages

The *dmesg* (diagnostic messages) command gathers recent diagnostics messages from a system
buffer and displays them on the screen. These messages include messages generated when unusual
events occur in the system. This information may prove helpful in troubleshooting.

```
# dmesg
 . . . . . . . .
Memory Class Setup
-----------------------------------------------------------------
Class    Physmem         Lockmem         Swapmem
-----------------------------------------------------------------
System : 7784 MB         7784 MB         7784 MB
Kernel : 7783 MB         7783 MB         7783 MB
User   : 7399 MB         6559 MB         6585 MB
-----------------------------------------------------------------
 . . . . . . . .
0/0/10/0/0.0x5006016030201d6b.0x0 eslpt
0/0/10/0/0.0x5006016930201d6b.0x0 eslpt
0/0/10/0/0.0x5006016030201d6b.0x4000000000000000 eslpt
0/0/10/0/0.0x5006016030201d6b.0x4001000000000000 eslpt
0/0/10/0/0.0x5006016030201d6b.0x4002000000000000 eslpt
```

```
0/0/10/0/0.0x5006016930201d6b.0x4000000000000000 eslpt
0/0/10/0/0.0x5006016930201d6b.0x4001000000000000 eslpt
0/0/10/0/0.0x5006016930201d6b.0x4002000000000000 eslpt
0/0/10/0/0.0x5006016930201d6b.0x4003000000000000 eslpt
0/0/10/0/0.120 fcp
0/0/10/0/0.120.17.255.1 fcpdev
0/0/10/0/0.120.17.255.1.3 tgt
0/0/10/0/0.120.17.255.1.3.0 sctl
0/0/10/0/0.120.17.19.0 fcparray
0/0/10/0/0.120.17.19.0.0 tgt
0/0/10/0/0.120.17.19.0.0.0 sdisk
0/0/10/0/0.120.17.19.0.0.1 sdisk
0/0/10/0/0.120.17.19.0.0.2 sdisk
0/0/10/0/0.120.17.19.0.0.3 sdisk
0/0/10/0/0.0x5006016030201d6b.0x4003000000000000 eslpt
0/0/10/0/0.120.16.255.1 fcpdev
0/0/10/0/0.120.16.255.1.3 tgt
0/0/10/0/0.120.16.255.1.3.0 sctl
0/0/10/0/0.120.16.19.0 fcparray
0/0/10/0/0.120.16.19.0.0 tgt
0/0/10/0/0.120.16.19.0.0.0 sdisk
0/0/10/0/0.120.16.19.0.0.1 sdisk
0/0/10/0/0.120.16.19.0.0.2 sdisk
0/0/10/0/0.120.16.19.0.0.3 sdisk
. . . . . . . .
Memory Information:
    physical page size = 4096 bytes, logical page size = 4096 bytes
    Physical: 8380416 Kbytes, lockable: 6105060 Kbytes, available: 6951248 Kbytes
```

Summary

In this chapter you learned about the responsibilities of a system administrator in an HP-UX-based computing environment. You looked at available resources to seek help when required, and management tools such as Web-Based Enterprise Management, Systems Insight Manager and System Management Homepage that allowed you to manage one or several networked HP-UX servers. You were provided information on how to use them. You also looked at how SMH could be configured to delegate to normal users tasks that only superuser could otherwise perform.

The next set of topics covered in detail HP server hardware components including slot, PCI and PCI-X card, interface card, network card, SCSI card, bus, bus converter, processor/core, cell board, I/O chassis, core I/O, power supply, server expansion unit, cabinet and server complex. You were presented with HP-UX's online addition/replacement functionality. You looked at HP's Integrity and 9000 server families. You were given an overview about HP BladeSystems.

11i v3 introduced next generation mass storage stack and concept of persistent DSF. This chapter covered them in detail. You learned the concepts and associated features and benefits, and how to view, create and remove DSFs. You understood the concept of major and minor numbers. Finally, you saw how to display hardware diagnostic messages.

## 08

Virtualization Technologies

This chapter covers the following major topics:

✓ Understand HP-UX virtualization technologies
✓ Introduction to Management Processor
✓ Benefits of partitioning
✓ Node partitioning – concepts, create, modify and remove
✓ Virtual partitioning – concepts, create, modify and remove
✓ Virtual Machines partitioning – concepts
✓ Load balancing – instant capacity, pay per use, secure resource partitioning – concepts
✓ Virtualization management tools

8.1   Understanding HP-UX Virtualization Technologies

HP-UX *virtualization technologies* is a set of technologies that provides the flexibility to logically group or split physical resources of a server to function as several virtual resources. This allows for maximum utilization of physical resources. These technologies may be grouped into three areas:

1. Partitioning
2. Load Balancing
3. Clustering

Before getting into the details of virtualization technologies, let us study something called Management Processor.

8.2   Introduction to Management Processor (MP)

The *Management Processor* (MP) is part of all new HP Integrity and 9000 series servers. It is a hardware module installed in servers for system management, has its own processor and can be rebooted independent of the server in which it is installed without impacting the server operation. Through MP, you can perform management tasks such as:

- ✓ Access server or node partition (nPar) console.
- ✓ Access virtual partition (vPar) console.
- ✓ Power off, reset and send *Transfer Of Control* (TOC) signal to the system or nPar.
- ✓ Send event notification.
- ✓ View and log console messages, system events and error messages.
- ✓ View updated cell board and nPar status.
- ✓ View cell configuration information.
- ✓ View updated boot information through *Virtual Front Panel* (VFP).
- ✓ Display environment parameters such as electrical power and cooling.
- ✓ View and modify LAN MP TCP/IP settings for over the network *telnet* access.

In older server models, MP is called *Guardian Service Processor* (GSP). MP can be accessed via serial or LAN port. Both ports are part of the MP module and dedicated for MP access. For local MP access, you can physically connect a serial display device such as an HP dumb terminal to the serial MP port. On some server models, this port is referred to as *Console/Remote/UPS*. For remote, over the network MP access, you need to configure TCP/IP parameters for the LAN MP port. You also need to ensure that proper network connectivity is in place to access the MP remotely using the configured IP address.

It is important to understand the difference between LAN MP port and other network ports available in the server or nPar. Although both require configuring TCP/IP parameters, the LAN MP port is dedicated for MP operations and console access. It is accessible even if the server is down. In contrast, other network ports provide access into the server or nPar and only when the server or nPar is up and running. Users and applications employ these network ports.

8.2.1　Setting Serial MP Display Parameters

It is important to set correct parameter values on the serial console device to allow text and menus to be displayed correctly and navigated properly.

Follow the steps below to perform console settings on an HP dumb terminal device:

- ✓ Connect the HP dumb console terminal to the serial MP/console port on the system.
- ✓ Power it on.
- ✓ Press User/System key located in the middle of the top row on the console keyboard.
- ✓ Press F4 to select "Remote Mode". Ensure that the asterisk "*" character appears beside it.
- ✓ Press F8 to go to "Config Keys" and then F3 for "Datacomm Config". Set BaudRate to "9600", Parity/DataBits to "None/8", RecvPace to "Xon/Xoff" and XmitPace to "None". Press F1 to save when done.
- ✓ Press F8 again to go to "Config Keys" and then F5 for "Terminal Config". Set Datacomm/ExtDev to "Serial (1) / Serial (2)", Terminal Id "70096", Keyboard "USASCII", Language "ENGLISH", LocalEcho "off" and CapsLock to "off".

This completes the setup of the display terminal and now it should work well.

8.2.2　Setting LAN MP Parameters

If you wish to access MP over the network as well, connect the display terminal device to the serial MP port and login to MP (follow procedure in the next sub-section on how to login to MP). Go to the command mode by typing *cm* at the MP prompt (refer to Table 8-1 on commands and options available at the MP level). Execute the *lc* command to set appropriate network parameters such as IP address, subnet mask, default gateway and MP hostname. Execute the *xd* command when done to reset and restart MP.

You should now be able to access the server or nPar over the network via this interface.

8.2.3　Interacting with MP

To access MP via serial port, enter *Admin* as username and *Admin* as password at the MP login prompt. This username/password combination is the default. The MP> main menu will appear.

For over the network access, provide the LAN MP IP address to the *telnet* command to get the MP login prompt. Enter *Admin / Admin* to get the MP> prompt.

The following sample is taken from an rp8400 server:

```
MP login: Admin
MP password: *****
            Welcome to the
        Rp8400 Management Processor
(c) Copyright 1995-2002 Hewlett-Packard Co., All Rights Reserved.
            Version 4.20

 MP MAIN MENU:
   CO: Consoles
   VFP: Virtual Front Panel (partition status)
```

CM: Command Menu
CL: Console Logs
SL: Show chassis Logs
HE: Help
X: Exit Connection
MP:>

 If you are already connected and logged on to the MP, press Ctrl+b to get the MP prompt.

The main menu options are CO, VFP, CM, CL, SL, HE and X. Table 8-1 describes them.

MP Option	Description
CO	Takes you to the console of the connected system or nPar.
VFP	Displays diagnostic state of the system or nPar as it boots up.
CM	Displays available commands, which you can run from the CM sub-menu. Some of the key commands are: *bo* – Boots up the system or nPar. *cc* – Initiates a complex configuration. *cp* – Displays which cell is assigned to which nPar. *dc* – Resets parameters to factory defaults. *dl* – Disables LAN MP/console access. *el* – Enables LAN MP/console access. *lc* – Configures network parameters for LAN MP port. *ls* – Displays network parameters for LAN MP port. *ma* – Returns to the main menu. *pe* – Powers the system or nPar on or off. *ps* – Displays hardware and power configuration information. *rr* – Resets the system or nPar for reconfiguration. *rs* – Resets the system or nPar. *so* – Creates and manages MP user accounts and controls security. *tc* – Sends a TOC to the system or nPar. *xd* – Reboots MP. Also used to run MP diagnostics.
CL	Displays console logs.
SL	Displays hardware chassis logs.
HE	Displays help.
X	Exits out of MP.

Table 8-1 MP Commands

At times, it is necessary to press Ctrl+E+c+f to gain access to the console.

8.2.4   Accessing the VFP, Console Log and System Log

From the main MP menu, you can access the *Virtual Front Panel* by issuing the *vfp* command. VFP displays the diagnostic state of the system or nPar as it boots up. Any error messages generated are displayed on the screen and logged for a later review. A typical VFP view of an nPar is displayed below, which shows that HP-UX is running and no errors are reported:

```
PARTITION STATUS:  E indicates error since last boot
   Partition 1  state          Activity
   ------------------          --------
   HPUX heartbeat: *


# Cell state                   Activity
- ----------                   --------
0  Cell has joined partition
```

The error and diagnostic messages related to the console and system are logged. The console messages can be viewed using the *cl* command and the system messages with the *sl* command. Sample output from *cl* is displayed below:

```
MP> cl
   Partition Console Logs available:
   Part#  Name
   -----  ----
   1)  hp01
   C)  Clear a partition's console log.
   Q)  Quit


MP:VW> 1
          tty      16 0x00001c Mar 12 14:56 ptyqc
crw-rw-rw-  2 bin     tty      16 0x00001d Mar 12 14:56 ptyqd
crw-rw-rw-  2 bin     tty      16 0x00001e Mar 12 14:56 ptyqe
crw-rw-rw-  2 bin     tty      16 0x00001f Mar 12 14:56 ptyqf
crw-rw-rw-  2 bin     tty      16 0x000020 Mar 12 14:56 ptyr0


(N)ext or <cr>, (P)revious, ^B to exit to menu
```

With the *sl* command, you can display the activity log, error log or live chassis logs. You also have the option to clear all chassis logs. Here is the menu that you would see when you issue *sl*:

```
MP> sl
Chassis Logs available:
   (A)ctivity Log
   (E)rror Log
   (L)ive Chassis Logs
   (C)lear All Chassis Logs
   (Q)uit
```

8.2.5   Managing MP User Accounts and Access Levels

MP is accessed via user accounts. Up to 32 user accounts can be defined, with each user may be set to have different level of access to the server complex and MP commands. A powerful pre-configured user called *Admin* is available by default with full access to the entire server complex. Other user accounts that you may wish to create using the *so* MP command can have operator or nPar-specific access.

Here is how to create a new MP user account called *console_user* with administrator rights:

```
MP:CM> so
    1. MP wide parameters
    2. User parameters
        Which do you wish to modify? ([1]/2) 2
Current users:
    LOGIN           USER NAME           ACCESS          PART. STATUS
    1  Admin        Administrator       Admin
    2  Oper         Operator            Operator

1 to 2 to edit, A to add, D to delete, Q to quit : a
    Enter Login : console_user
    Enter Name : console_user
    Enter Organization : sys_admin
    Valid Access Levels:  Administrator, Operator, Single Partition User
    Enter Access Level (A/O/[S]) : a
    Valid Modes:  Single Use, Multiple Use
    Enter Mode (S/[M]) : m
    Valid States:  Disabled, Enabled
    Enter State (D/[E]) : e
    Enable Dialback ? (Y/[N]) n
    Enter Password :
    Re-Enter Password :
    New User parameters are:
    Login           : console_user
    Name            : console_user
    Organization    : sys_admin
    Access Level    : Administrator
    Mode            : Multiple Use
    State           : Enabled
    Default Partition :
    Dialback        : (disabled)

    Changes do not take affect until the command has finished.
    Save changes to user number 3? (Y/[N]) y
Current users:
    LOGIN           USER NAME           ACCESS          PART. STATUS
    1  Admin        Administrator       Admin
    2  Oper         Operator            Operator
    3  console_user console_user        Admin
1 to 3 to edit, A to add, D to delete, Q to quit : q
```

8.2.6   Resetting via the MP

A server or an nPar can be reset using either the *rr* or the *rs* command. The difference between the two commands is that *rr* resets a system or nPar if any hardware configuration is changed that requires a reconfiguration reboot. In contrast, *rs* only resets it. The *rs* command is useful to reset a hung system.

The *bo* command can be used to boot a server or nPar from the default (or an alternate) boot device.

8.3   Partitioning

HP-UX offers partitioning technologies that enable you to divide a server complex logically into several smaller computers, each of which is allotted dedicated (or shared) hardware resources and runs an independent HP-UX OE instance. Each of these virtual computers can be used to run a unique application completely independent of applications running in other virtual computers.

8.3.1   Supported Partitioning Technologies

Currently, three partitioning techniques are available:

1. **Node Partitioning** – used on both Integrity and 9000 cell-based servers.
2. **Virtual Partitioning** – used on both Integrity and 9000 mid-range and high-end servers.
3. **Virtual Machines Partitioning** – used on Integrity servers only.

8.3.2   Benefits of Partitioning

Partitioning technologies offer several benefits such as:

- ✓ Better system hardware resource utilization.
- ✓ Online allocation, de-allocation and administration of hardware resources.
- ✓ Separate, independent OE instance in each partition.
- ✓ Different patch level in each partition.
- ✓ Dissimilar kernel in each partition.
- ✓ Unique application in each partition with complete isolation from other running applications.
- ✓ Software fault isolation.

8.3.3   Available Hardware to Work with

In the next two sections, node and virtual partitioning techniques are discussed. In order to explain various administrative operations, example commands are executed on an rp8400 server and their outputs are displayed. Note that most tasks can be performed on Integrity machines the way they are performed on 9000 systems. The rp8400 server, where the example commands are run, has the following hardware configuration:

Hardware model: HP 9000 rp8400   Number of cabinets: 1
Number of server expansion units: 1   Number of cell boards: 4
Number of processors: 16 (4 on each cell board)   Memory on each cell board: 8GB
Total amount of memory: 32GB   Number of I/O chassis: 4
Number of I/O slots: 32 (8 in each I/O chassis)   Maximum nPars this server supports: 4
Maximum vPars this server supports: 16

8.4   Partitioning – nPars

Node partitioning is a hardware partitioning technique which is used to divide a cell-based server into several smaller computers called *node partitions* (nPars). Each nPar can then be used as a separate, independent, standalone server running HP-UX OE instance with its own dedicated processors, memory and I/O chassis. Depending on the hardware model, a server complex may be divided into as many electrically-separated nPars as the total number of cell boards in the complex. The minimum number of nPars that can be created in a server complex is 2 and the maximum in the largest server complex is 16. Each nPar must have at least one core I/O card installed in slot 0 of its I/O chassis. Figure 8-1 shows a logical nPar with December 2007 patch level and running two applications.

One or more cell boards with core I/O card
One or more I/O chassis
Boot disks
Applications
Patch level Dec 2007

Figure 8-1 nPar Logical

In the following sub-sections, nPar administration tasks such as creating the genesis partition, creating an nPar, renaming an nPar, adding a cell to an nPar, removing a cell from an nPar and removing an nPar, are explained. You can issue commands to perform these operations from any of the nPars within the server complex. Alternatively, you can run SMH in a web browser to perform these tasks. The *parmgr* command may be invoked instead. This command actually starts the partition manager portion of SMH in a web browser.

Some of the key nPar administration commands are given in Table 8-2.

Command	Description
parcreate	Creates the genesis partition and an nPar.
parmodify	Modifies an nPar including: ✓ Adding and removing cell boards, I/O chassis and so on ✓ Setting primary, HA alternate and alternate boot paths ✓ Renaming an nPar
parolrad	Activates / deactivates a cell online.
parremove	Removes an nPar.
parstatus	Displays status information of one or more nPars.

Table 8-2 nPar Administration Commands

8.4.1   Creating the Genesis Partition

The very first nPar created in a server complex is referred to as the *genesis partition*. It is a single-cell partition built via MP. Once created, you can load HP-UX into it.

To create the genesis partition, go to MP → CM → CC and choose option "G". Pick a cell that contains processors and memory, and is connected to an I/O chassis with a core I/O card installed. When created, use the *bo* MP command to boot the nPar. Insert the HP-UX installation DVD in the drive and follow the procedure outlined in Chapter 09 "HP-UX Installation" to do the install.

After the installation is over, login to the genesis partition and issue the *parstatus* command to check the status of the nPar and resources available in it.

```
# parstatus –w
The local partition number is 0.
# parstatus –Vp0
[Partition]
Partition Number         : 0
Partition Name           : Partition 0
Status                   : active
IP address               : 0.0.0.0
Primary Boot Path        : 0/0/0/2/0.6.0
Alternate Boot Path      : 0/0/0/3/0.6.0
HA Alternate Boot Path   : 0/0/0/0/0.0.0
PDC Revision             : 17.8
IODCH Version            : 5E40
CPU Speed                : 750 MHz
Core Cell                : cab0,cell0
Core Cell Choice [0]     : cab0,cell0
Total Good Memory Size   : 8.0 GB
Total Interleave Memory  : 8.0 GB
Total Requested CLM      : 0.0 GB
Total Allocated CLM      : 0.0 GB
GSM Sharing              : Disabled complex-wide
Hyperthreading Enabled   : yes
```

[Cell]

Hardware Location	Actual Usage	CPU OK/ Deconf/ Max	Memory (GB) OK/ Deconf	Connected To	Core Cell Capable	Use On Next Boot	Par Num
cab0,cell0	active core	4/0/4	8.0/ 0.0	cab0,bay0,chassis0	yes	yes	0

[Chassis]

Hardware Location	Usage	Core IO	Connected To	Par Num
cab0,bay0,chassis0	active	yes	cab0,cell0	0

By default, the genesis partition is called *Partition 0*.

As you can see from the output that there are 4 processors in the genesis partition and 8GB of memory. It also shows the primary and alternate boot disk paths.

8.4.2   Creating an nPar

After the genesis partition is formed, you can make additional nPars using unused cell boards and I/O chassis in the server complex.

Let us create a single cell nPar called *test_npar*. Login to the genesis partition and perform the following steps:

1.   Identify what cell board is available. Run the *parstatus* command:

```
# parstatus –AC
[Cell]
                              CPU     Memory                              Use
```

Hardware Location	Actual Usage	OK/ Deconf/ Max	(GB) OK/ Deconf	Connected To	Core Cell Capable	On Next Boot	Par Num
cab0,cell1	Inactive	4/0/4	8.0/0.0	cab0,bay0,chassis1	yes	-	-

2. Determine which I/O chassis is free:

parstatus –AI
[Chassis]

Hardware Location	Usage	Core IO	Connected To	Par Num
cab0,bay0,chassis1	Inactive	yes	cab0,cell1	-

3. Execute the *parcreate* command to create *test_npar*. Use cell board 1 and I/O chassis 1. Specify the nPar name with the –P option and cell number with the –c option. Values following each colon character are "base" (for cell type), "y" (to include the cell in next boot) and "ri" (reuse interleave – to reuse memory after a failure). Since these are default values, they are not exhibited in the following command line:

parcreate –P test_npar –c1:::
Partition Created. The partition number is: 1

4. Define primary (–b option) boot disk using the *parmodify* command. If you wish to use alternate boot disk as well, define it with the –t option:

parmodify –p1 –b 1/0/0/2/0.6.0 –t 1/0/0/3/0.6.0

5. Verify that the nPar is created successfully. Use the *parstatus* command.

parstatus –Vp1
[Partition]
Partition Number	: 1
Partition Name	: **test_npar**
Status	: active
IP address	: 0.0.0.0
Primary Boot Path	: **1/0/0/2/0.6.0**
Alternate Boot Path	: **1/0/0/3/0.6.0**
HA Alternate Boot Path	: 0/0/0/0/0.0.0
PDC Revision	: 17.8
IODCH Version	: 5E40
CPU Speed	: 750 MHz
Core Cell	: cab0,cell1

[Cell]
Core Cell Choice [0]	: cab0,cell0
Total Good Memory Size	: 8.0 GB
Total Interleave Memory	: 8.0 GB
Total Requested CLM	: 0.0 GB
Total Allocated CLM	: 0.0 GB
GSM Sharing	: Disabled complex-wide

```
Hyperthreading Enabled          : yes

                        CPU       Memory                              Use
                        OK/       (GB)                   Core         On
        Hardware Actual Deconf/   OK/                    Cell         Next   Par
        Location Usage  Max       Deconf   Connected To  Capable Boot Num
        ======== ====== ======    ======   ================ ====== ==== ===
        cab0,cell1 active core 4/0/4  8.0/ 0.0  cab0,bay0,chassis1  yes   yes   1

        [Chassis]
                                  Core  Connected    Par
        Hardware Location  Usage  IO    To           Num
        ================== ======= ==== =========== =====
        cab0,bay0,chassis1 active  yes  cab0,cell1   1
```

This nPar also has 4 processors and 8GB of memory.

```
# parstatus –P
[Partition]
Par              # of     # of I/O
Num  Status      Cells    Chassis    Core cell    Partition Name (first 30 chars)
===  ======      =====    =======    ========     ==========================
0    active      1        1          cab0,cell0   Partition 0
1    active      1        1          cab0,cell1   test_npar
```

You need to install HP-UX in the new nPar now. Use the *bo* MP command to boot the nPar. Make certain that you have the HP-UX installation DVD in the drive. Follow the installation procedure outlined in Chapter 09 "HP-UX Installation" to do the install.

8.4.3   Renaming an nPar

To rename the first (genesis) nPar from *Partition 0* to *prod_npar*, use the *parmodify* command. Verify the result with *parstatus* after the operation is complete.

```
# parmodify –p0 –P prod_npar
# parstatus –P
[Partition]
Par              # of     # of I/O
Num  Status      Cells    Chassis    Core cell    Partition Name (first 30 chars)
===  =====       =====    =======    ========     ==========================
0    active      1        1          cab0,cell0   prod_npar
1    active      1        1          cab0,cell1   test_npar
```

8.4.4   Adding a Cell to an nPar

To add a cell to an active nPar (say *test_npar*), use the *parmodify* command. Specify partition number with –p option and cell number with –a option. Ensure that the cell (cell 2 in this case) is available. The –B option reboots the nPar and activates the cell. You must reboot the nPar for reconfig (option –R with the *shutdown* command) before the modification takes place.

```
# parmodify –p1 –a2::y: –B
In order to activate any cell that has been newly added, reboot the partition with the -R option.
Command succeeded.
```

 # shutdown –Ry now

When the nPar is back up, execute *parstatus* and verify the added hardware:

```
# parstatus –P
[Partition]
Par         # of    # of I/O
Num  Status Cells   Chassis   Core cell    Partition Name (first 30 chars)
===  ====== ====    ======    =======      ========================
0    active 1       1         cab0,cell0   prod_npar
1    active 2       2         cab0,cell1   test_npar
```

To add a cell to an inactive nPar and boot it up to activate the cell, use the *parmodify* command as above. If you do not wish to boot the nPar and activate the cell, do not use the –B option. In either case, there is no need to reboot the nPar for reconfig.

8.4.5   Removing a Cell from an nPar

To remove an active cell from an active nPar, use –d option with *parmodify* and specify the cell number (cell 2 in this case). The nPar must be rebooted for reconfig (–R option with *shutdown*) for the changes to take effect.

 # parmodify –p1 –d2 –B
command succeded
 # shutdown –Ry now

To remove an inactive cell from an active or inactive nPar, use –d option and specify the cell number to delete. There is no need to specify –B option, or to reboot.

 # parmodify –p1 –d2

8.4.6   Removing an nPar

To remove an active nPar, run *parremove* from the nPar you wish to delete and supply –F option. This operation unassigns all cells from the nPar and destroys its partition definition. You must then shutdown and halt the nPar for the changes to take effect.

 # parremove –Fp1
Use "shutdown -R -H" to shutdown the partition.
The partition deletion will be effective only after the shutdown.
 # shutdown –RH now

To remove an inactive nPar, run *parremove,* as above, from an active nPar and specify the partition number of the nPar you wish to delete. No need to use –F option and no need to shutdown the inactive/deleted partition since it is already down.

8.4.7   Managing nPars Using SMH

The *partition manager* software is loaded as part of the HP-UX installation on supported servers. You can start the partition manager while you are in SMH. Follow the links below:

☞Go to SMH → Tools → nPartition Management → View and Manage Complex. Figures 8-2, 8-3 and 8-4 illustrate "Hardware", "nPartitions" and "General" tabs within the partition manager. Other tabs "Power and Cooling", "Cells" and "I/O" are self-explanatory. On the right hand side in the figures, several partition management tasks (some of them covered earlier) are listed, which you can click to perform. Note that these figures display nPar configuration on an rp7410 server and are provided for reference purposes only. Actual exercises earlier in this chapter were performed on an rp8400 server.

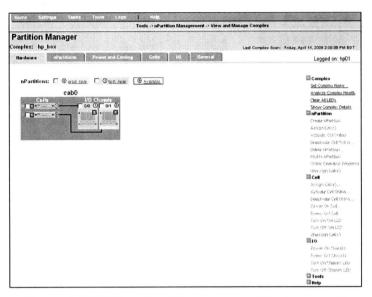

Figure 8-2 SMH – nPar Management (Hardware tab)

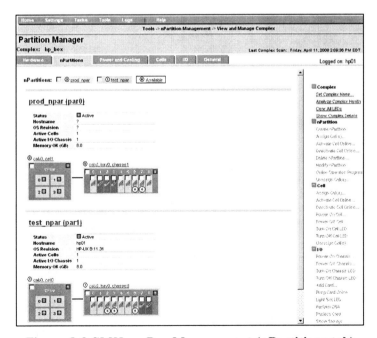

Figure 8-3 SMH – nPar Management (nPartitions tab)

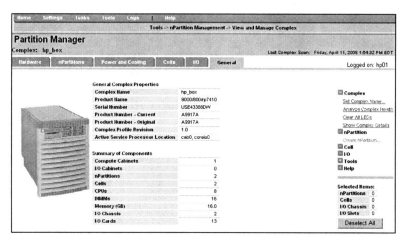

Figure 8-4 SMH – nPar Management (General tab)

8.5   Partitioning – vPars

Virtual partitioning is a software partitioning technique that is used to divide a server or an nPar into several virtual, smaller computers called *virtual partitions* (vPars). Each vPar can then be used as a separate, independent, standalone server running HP-UX instance with its own processor(s), memory and LBA(s). The number of vPars that can be created in a server or an nPar is equal to the number of processors the server or nPar has. In other words, each vPar requires at least one processor to be created. The minimum number of vPars supported in a server complex is 2 and the maximum in the largest server complex is 128. Figure 8-5 exhibits a server/nPar running two applications. This server/nPar is divided into two vPars (vPar0 and vPar1) each with different patch levels and running different applications.

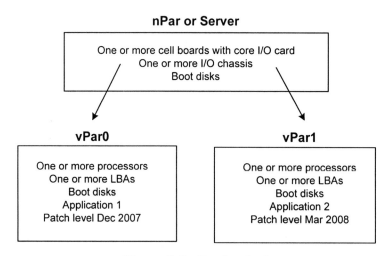

Figure 8-5 vPar Logical

When vPars are created, a software agent called *vpmon* is enabled, which sits between the server firmware and HP-UX instances running in vPars. At vPar boot up, vpmon looks into the vPar database */stand/vpdb* and loads HP-UX in the vPar. It uses the boot disks defined for the vPar and assigns the hardware components configured for it.

In the following sub-sections, vPar administration tasks such as creating a vPar, adding a processor to a vPar, removing a processor from a vPar, adding an LBA to a vPar, removing an LBA from a vPar, adding memory to a vPar, resetting a vPar and removing a vPar, are explained. You can issue commands to carry out these operations from any of the vPars within the server complex. Alternatively, you can use the *virtual partition manager* software to accomplish these tasks.

Some of the more common vPar administration commands you are going to be interacting with are given in Table 8-3.

Command	Description
vparboot	Boots a vPar.
vparcreate	Creates a vPar.
vparmodify	Modifies a vPar including adding and removing processors, LBAs, memory and so on.
vparremove	Removes a vPar.
vparreset	Resets a vPar.
vparstatus	Displays status information of one or more vPars.

Table 8-3 vPar Administration Commands

You can create vPars within an nPar. Make sure that you have T1335CC software installed in the nPar to create the first vPar in it. Issue the *swlist* command to check whether the software is loaded:

```
# swlist | grep T1335CC
T1335CC          A.05.02          HP-UX Virtual Partitions for 11.31
```

Install the software using the *swinstall* command if it is not already loaded. Consult Chapter 10 "Software Management" on how to install software.

8.5.1 Bound and Unbound Processors

When working with vPars, you can assign processors as either bound or unbound.

A processor assigned to a vPar to handle both normal processing as well as I/O interrupts is referred to as a *bound* processor. Every vPar must be assigned at least one bound processor. A processor should be allocated to a vPar as a bound processor if the vPar runs applications which require both processor and I/O horsepower. A processor can be added online to a vPar as a bound processor, however, a bound processor cannot be removed online from a vPar.

An *unbound* processor, on the contrary, is either not assigned to a vPar, or assigned but does not handle the vPar's I/O interrupts. A processor should be allocated to a vPar as an unbound processor if the application running in the vPar is processor-intensive but not I/O-intensive. An unbound processor can be added to or removed from a vPar online.

8.5.2 Creating the First vPar

To understand vPar operations, assume that an nPar containing 2 cells with 8 processors, 16GB of memory and 2 I/O chassis, is available in the rp8400. The hardware addresses of the processors are

41, 45, 101, 109, 141, 145, 201 and 209. Use the *vparcreate* command to create *test_vpar0* vPar with 1 bound and 1 unbound processors. Set the minimum and maximum limits on the number of processors this vPar can get to 1 and 2, respectively. Allocate 8GB of memory and define LBAs 1/0/0/2 and 1/0/0/3. Use 1/0/0/2/0.6.0 as the primary boot disk. With –B option, specify that the vPar searches automatically at each reboot for the bootable devices to boot off. All this configuration is stored in the vPar database located in */stand/vpdb* file when the following command is executed. This file is created if it does not already exist.

**vparcreate –p test_vpar0 –a cpu::2 –a cpu:::1:2 –a cpu:41 –a mem::8192 **
–a io:1/0/0/2 –a io:1/0/0/3 –a io:1/0/0/2/0.6.0:BOOT –B search –B auto

The options used with *vparcreate* are explained in Table 8-4:

Option	Description
–p	Name of the vPar.
–a cpu::2	Number of processors to be allocated.
–a cpu:::1:2	Minimum and maximum limits on processor allocation.
–a cpu:41	Hardware address of the processor to be bound. If not explicitly defined, the processor will be assigned as unbound.
–a mem::8192	Amount of memory, in MBs, to be allocated.
–a 1/0/0/2	All devices physically located on the LBA path will be allocated to this vPar.
–a 1/0/0/2/0.6.0:BOOT	Primary boot path.
–B search	Enables automatic search for the boot device at vPar boot.
–B auto	Enables automatic boot from the boot device.

Table 8-4 Options Used with *vparcreate*

The last three functions specified at the command line above can also be performed with the *setboot* or *vparmodify* command.

Modify the AUTO file on the primary boot path */dev/rdsk/c0t6d0* to make the nPar aware that vPars are implemented and ensure that the system will load vpmon first at next reboot before it starts loading the HP-UX kernel. Use the *mkboot* command to perform this.

On 9000 servers:

mkboot –a "hpux /stand/vpmon –a" /dev/rdsk/c0t6d0

On Integrity servers:

mkboot –a "boot vpmon –a" /dev/rdsk/c0t6d0

This creates a vPar within the nPar with 2 out of 8 processors and 8GB out of 16GB memory allocated to it. Now each time you reboot this nPar, it will come up as a vPar.

To manually boot *test_vpar0*, go to the nPar console, press Ctrl+a to get the *virtual console monitor* MON> prompt and run the *vparload* command:

MON> **vparload –p test_vpar0**

Alternatively, you can boot the vPar from ISL prompt (in case of an HP 9000 server):

ISL> **hpux /stand/vpmon vparload –p test_vpar0**

After *test_vpar0* is up and functional, run *vparstatus* to view status information:

vparstatus
[Virtual Partition]

Virtual Partition Name	State	Attributes	Kernel Path	Boot Opts
=================	=====	========	============	====
test_vpar0	Up	**Dyn,Auto**	/stand/vmunix	

[Virtual Partition Resource Summary]

Virtual Partition Name	CPU Min/Max	CPU Bound/ Unbound	Num IO devs	Memory (MB) # Ranges/ Total MB	Total MB
=================	=======	=======	====	=========	=======
test_vpar0	1/ 2	1 1	8	0/ 0	8192

Under Attributes column, two values – Dyn and Auto – are shown. "Dyn" means dynamic hardware configuration changes are allowed for the vPar and "Auto" indicates that the vPar is auto-bootable.

Run *vparstatus* again to display the information in a different way:

vparstatus –vp test_vpar0
[Virtual Partition Details]
Name   : test_vpar0
State   : Up
Attributes   : Dynamic,Autoboot
Kernel Path   : /stand/vmunix
Boot Opts   :

[CPU Details]
Min/Max   : 1/2
Bound by User [Path]   :
Bound by Monitor [Path]   : 41
Unbound [Path]   : 45
[IO Details]
    1.0.0.2
    1.0.0.3
    1.0.0.2.0.6.0 BOOT

[Memory Details]
Specified [Base /Range]   :
    (bytes) (MB)
Total Memory (MB)   : 8192

8.5.3   Creating Another vPar

At this point, you may wish to create another vPar using some or all available resources. Execute *vparcreate* command from *test_vpar0* to create *test_vpar1* with 1 bound processor and 8GB of memory:

```
# vparcreate –p test_vpar1 –a cpu::2 –a cpu:::1:2 –a cpu:101 –a mem::8192 –a io:2.0.0.2 \
–a io:2.0.0.3 –a io:2/0/0/2/0.6.0:BOOT –a io:2/0/0/3/0.6.0:ALTBOOT –B search –B auto
```

This creates *test_vpar1* within the nPar. Note that this command also sets up primary and alternate boot disk paths.

You now need to install HP-UX in *test_vpar1*. Make sure that you include vPar software when installing the OE. Shutdown *test_vpar0*, go to the BCH prompt and initiate HP-UX install on one of the boot disks assigned to *test_vpar1*. Use the DVD drive available to the nPar. When installation is complete, go to the virtual monitor prompt and boot *test_vpar0*:

```
MON> vparload –p test_vpar0
```

Login to *test_vpar0* when it is up and execute the *mkboot* command to modify the AUTO file contents on *test_vpar1*'s boot disks:

```
# mkboot –a "hpux /stand/vpmon –a" /dev/rdsk/c2t6d0
# mkboot –a "hpux /stand/vpmon –a" /dev/rdsk/c3t6d0
```

Now run *vparboot* from *test_vpar0* to bring *test_vpar1* up:

```
# vparboot –p test_vpar1
```

When *test_vpar1* is up, use *vparstatus* to verify the configuration and hardware allocation.

8.5.4   Adding a CPU to a vPar

The *test_vpar0* vPar currently has 1 bound (hw path 41) and 1 unbound (hw path 45) processors. In order to add a bound processor, you need to increase the maximum processor allocation limit to at least 3 from current 2 before doing the processor add. This operation requires that *test_vpar0* is down. Issue the following on *test_vpar0*:

```
# shutdown –hy now
```

Login to *test_vpar1* and execute the *vparmodify* command. The first command below increases the maximum limit to 3, the second adds the processor at hw path 101 as bound and the third command boots up *test_vpar0*:

```
# vparmodify –p test_vpar0 –m cpu:::1:3
# vparmodify –p test_vpar0 –a cpu:141
# vparboot –p test_vpar0
```

Run *vparstatus* with –vp options to verify the modifications after *test_vpar0* is back up.

To add a processor as unbound, you do not need to shutdown *test_vpar0*. Run the first command below to increase the processor limit to 4 (since you now have 3 processors assigned) and then the second to add a processor. When the hardware path of a processor is not explicitly defined, *vparmodify* adds a processor as unbound:

```
# vparmodify –p test_vpar0 –m cpu:::1:4
```

```
# vparmodify –p test_vpar0 –a cpu::1
```

8.5.5 Removing a CPU from a vPar

At this point, you have four processors assigned to *test_vpar0* (2 bound and 2 unbound). To remove a bound processor from this vPar, shut it down:

```
# shutdown –hy now
```

Then run *vparmodify* on *test_vpar1* and specify the target vPar name with –p option. Use –d to specify the hardware path (141 in this example) of the bound processor to be deleted. Restart *test_vpar0* when done:

```
# vparmodify –p test_vpar0 –d cpu:141
# vparboot –p test_vpar0
```

To remove an unbound processor, issue either of the following on *test_vpar0*:

```
# vparmodify –p test_vpar0 –m cpu::2
# vparmodify –p test_vpar0 –d cpu::1
```

This reduces the total number of processors in *test_vpar0* from 3 to 2. No need to shutdown.

Check the results using *vparstatus* with –vp options.

8.5.6 Adding an LBA to a vPar

To add an LBA to *test_vpar0*, shut *test_vpar0* down and execute the following on *test_vpar1*. Boot *test_vpar0* from *test_vpar1* when done. Check the results with *vparstatus* –vp:

```
# vparmodify –p test_vpar0 –a io:3.0.0.3
# vparboot –p test_vpar0
```

8.5.7 Removing an LBA from a vPar

To remove an allocated LBA from *test_vpar0*, shut it down and execute the following on *test_vpar1*. Boot *test_vpar0* from *test_vpar1* when done. Verify the results with *vparstatus* –vp:

```
# vparmodify –p test_vpar0 –d  io:3.0.0.3
# vparboot –p test_vpar0
```

8.5.8 Adding Memory to a vPar

To allocate additional 4GB of memory to *test_vpar0*, shut it down and execute the following on *test_vpar1*. Boot *test_vpar0* from *test_vpar1* when done. Check the results with *vparstatus* –vp:

```
# vparmodify –p test_vpar0 –a mem::4096
# vparboot –p test_vpar0
```

8.5.9   Resetting a vPar

A hung vPar can be reset from another running vPar. Use the *vparreset* command on *test_vpar1* to reset *test_vpar0* (assuming it is hung):

> # **vparreset –p test_vpar0**

8.5.10   Removing a vPar

A vPar can be removed from another running vPar. All resources allocated to it become free. Use the *vparremove* command on *test_vpar1* to remove *test_vpar0*:

> # **vparremove –p test_vpar0**

8.5.11   Rebooting vpmon

Periodically, it is necessary to stop and restart vpmon to perform maintenance tasks on the server or nPar that houses vPars. Follow the steps below to reboot vpmon:

1. Shut down all vPars. Go to the MON> prompt and verify. You should see the following:

    > MON> test_vpar0 has halted.
    > MON> test_vpar1 has halted.

2. Power off the server or nPar (if necessary).
3. Perform the maintenance tasks.
4. Power on the server or nPar (if powered off earlier).
5. Interact with BCH or EFI as appropriate.
6. Execute the *bo* command from the BCH prompt. On Integrity servers, perform the boot via EFI Boot Manager. See Chapter 16 "HP-UX Shutdown and Startup" for details.

    > Main Menu: Enter command or menu > **bo**

7. Interact with ISL and type the following:

    > ISL> **hpux /stand/vpmon**

8. Press Ctrl+a to go to MON> prompt and execute the following to boot all vPars:

    > MON> **vparload –all**

8.6   Partitioning – Virtual Machines

Virtual Machines (VM) is a software product designed to work on HP Integrity servers and nPars. With this software product, you can divide a server or an nPar into hundreds of virtual machines that run on top of the underlying HP-UX OE. Each virtual machine can be configured to run its own fully loaded, operational *guest* operating system instance such as HP-UX 11i v2, HP-UX 11i v3, MS Windows 2003 or Linux in an isolated environment. Application failures on one virtual machine do not affect other virtual machines.

Virtual machines virtualizes physical resources – processor, memory and I/O devices – and allows you to allocate these resources as virtual resources to virtual machines dynamically and on as-needed basis. Users, logged on to virtual machines, assume they are on separate, dedicated physical systems. Virtual machines can be created using either command line or GUI, and managed centrally from one VM console.

VM is similar to VMWare software, which provides comparable functionality on top of MS Windows based Intel x86 architecture computers.

Table 8-5 lists and describes some key commands pertaining to virtual machines.

Command	Description
hpvmclone	Clones virtual machines.
hpvmcollect	Collects virtual machines statistics.
hpvmcreate	Creates virtual machines.
hpvminfo	Displays information about virtual machines host.
hpvmmodify	Modifies virtual machines.
hpvmnet	Creates and modifies virtual networks.
hpvmremove	Removes virtual machines.
hpvmresources	Stipulates storage and network devices used by VMs.
hpvmstart	Starts virtual machines.
hpvmstatus	Displays guest status information.
hpvmstop	Stops virtual machines.

Table 8-5 Integrity VM Administration Commands

8.7   Load Balancing

Several load balancing solutions are available that provide the flexibility to allocate cores, memory and disk I/O bandwidth as needed. These solutions include Instant Capacity, Pay Per Use, PRM/WLM for Secure Resource Partitioning, and Processor Sets. Following sub-sections provide a brief overview of each one of them.

8.7.1   Instant Capacity (iCAP)

Instant Capacity (iCAP) allows you to purchase cores, memory and cell boards at a reduced price. These components are called *iCAP components*. Purchasing these components does not result in ownership, as they cannot be used until activated. These components act as standby components. They need to be activated in order to be used by purchasing the right-to-use in the form of a codeword for some or all of them. These components may be activated for a limited duration of time or permanently.

Temporary Instant Capacity (TiCAP) is same as iCAP except that it can only be valid for a predetermined amount of time, which is usually 30 days. The iCAP components are automatically deactivated after the time duration is elapsed. You may reactivate them by purchasing another right-to-use codeword for an additional 30 day period.

Global Instant Capacity (GiCAP) allows you to share right-to-use codewords among a group of servers so that the components may be used by any server within the group.

Several commands are available that enable you to administer iCAP. These commands are listed and explained in Table 8-6.

Command	Description
icapmanage	Manages GiCAP groups.
icapmodify	Activates and deactivates cores, modifies iCAP configuration and applies codewords.
icapstatus	Displays status, allocation and configuration information.
icapnotify	Turns notification and asset reporting on or off.

Table 8-6 iCAP Administration Commands

8.7.2   Pay Per Use (PPU)

Pay Per Use (PPU) is a pricing model that charges based on actual usage of computing resources. The concept is similar to the way you are charged for hydro, water, sewerage, phone, cable and other utilities. Charges are based on either percentage utilization of cores or number of active cores. A system called *utility meter* is installed which talks to the PPU agent running on the PPU server or nPar, gathers usage information and sends it to HP for a bill.

The key command for PPU configuration is *ppuconfig*, which can be used to view current configuration, set usage caps, set system information for sending usage reports to HP and specify a utility meter to be used.

8.7.3   Secure Resource Partitioning (PRM / WLM)

Secure resource partitioning technique is intended for resource and workload management on servers, nPars and vPars where several applications are typically run concurrently. Each of these applications may require varying amount of hardware resources such as processor, memory and disk I/O to operate well. Unlike nPars and vPars, resource partitions are not independent, standalone servers or partitions, rather, they work at the process and application level and allow you to allocate to applications resources they need. This way applications are guaranteed to have dedicated resources available to them at all times.

Secure resource partitioning can be implemented using *Process Resource Manager* (PRM) and *WorkLoad Manager* (WLM) software products.

PRM is a manual resource management tool. With this tool, groups, called *PRM groups*, are created and processes and users are assigned to them. Required resources are then allocated to these groups. Two benefits are achieved with this approach. One, processes are guaranteed dedicated resources and two, no processes or users that are part of the PRM group can use system resources other than what they are assigned. PRM can be configured using either commands or SMH.

WLM, on the other hand, is an automatic resource management tool used to monitor resources at regular intervals and adjust them automatically to keep up with changing application needs. With this tool, groups, called *workload groups*, are created and applications and user processes are assigned to them. Required resources are then allocated to these groups. This product is useful in an environment where system load, resource utilization or resource needs change frequently and unattended adjustments are necessary. WLM can be configured using commands, configuration wizard or GUI.

8.7.4   Processor Sets (PSets)

Typically used with PRM and WLM, *Processor Sets* (PSets) may be used on their own too.

A set of cores grouped together as an independent entity forms a processor set. This processor set is then assigned to one or more specific applications for their exclusive use at all times. Processor sets may be configured and modified dynamically.

The *psrset* command is used to create and manage processor sets.

8.8   Clustering

See Chapter 35 "Introduction to High Availability and Clustering" for detailed information.

8.9   Virtualization Management Tools

Several software tools in this space are available. These include HP's Systems Insight Manager, Integrity Essentials Capacity Advisor, Integrity Essentials Virtualization Manager and Integrity Essentials gWLM and WLM.

Systems Insight Manager was covered in an earlier chapter. Others are explained briefly in the following sub-sections.

8.9.1   Integrity Essentials Capacity Advisor

Integrity Essentials Capacity Advisor is designed to run on Integrity and 9000 servers. This tool is used for capacity planning purposes on HP-UX, Linux and MS Windows. Capacity Advisor simulates placement of application workloads to help improve utilization of a server's capacity. It allows you to view historical utilization graphically and match workloads to server resources by pre-testing several different scenarios before you make changes to critical applications. This tool can be integrated with Integrity Essentials Virtualization Manager.

8.9.2   Integrity Essentials Virtualization Manager

Integrity Essentials Virtualization Manager runs on Integrity and 9000 servers. This graphical tool is used for managing virtual servers running HP-UX, Linux and MS Windows. It displays available virtual resources, and their usage and status.

8.9.3   Integrity Essentials gWLM and WLM

Integrity Essentials Global Workload Manager (gWLM) is a graphical tool that runs on Integrity and 9000 servers. It is used for managing workloads on a number of servers running HP-UX and Linux, and allocating resources automatically among several workloads to improve server utilization.

Global Workload Manager helps pool and share computing resources for better utilization. It monitors workloads and automatically migrates processors from idle workloads to busy ones and from lower priority workloads to higher ones. It provides reports on resource usage as well.

WLM is covered earlier under the "Secure Resource Partitioning (PRM / WLM)" sub-section.

Summary

In this chapter you learned about virtualization technologies available on HP-UX platform. You learned the concepts and benefits associated with them. You studied management processor concepts and how to access it locally and remotely, and use it. You saw how a dumb console terminal could be setup to display correct text and menus. You learned the concepts of partitioning techniques and performed tasks to create, modify and manage them.

Finally, you were presented with an overview of Integrity virtual machines, resource partitioning techniques, and virtualization management tools.

## 09

HP-UX Installation

This chapter covers the following major topics:

- ✓ Types of HP-UX OE software bundles and what each include
- ✓ Plan HP-UX installation
- ✓ HP-UX installation using local DVD drive
- ✓ System configuration using the set_parms command

9.1 HP-UX Installation

This chapter explains how to perform a fresh installation of HP-UX on a server or partition. The install process requires prior planning regarding server or partition configuration. Key configuration items such as which disk drive to install HP-UX, disk management software to be used, types and sizes of file systems and networking information need to be identified before starting the load.

9.1.1 Types of HP-UX OE Software Bundles

The HP-UX OE software runs on 9000 and Integrity server families. Currently, the latest version of HP-UX is 11.31 and is commonly recognized as *HP-UX 11i v3*. Both 9000 and Integrity server families support this version. HP-UX 11i v3 is backward compatible with HP-UX 11i v1 and 11i v2.

The HP-UX 11i v3 OE software is available in four distinct bundles. These are referred to as *Base Operating Environment* (BOE), *Virtual Server Environment Operating Environment* (VSE-OE), *High Availability Operating Environment* (HA-OE) and *Data Center Operating Environment* (DC-OE). Depending on business and application needs, you can decide which bundle is appropriate for your environment. Table 9-1 lists the four bundles and components they include. For the latest and more accurate information, visit *www.hp.com*.

Component	BOE	VSE-OE	HA-OE	DC-OE
Core HP-UX Operating System including Networking, CDE, SD-UX, LVM, PERL, NFS, CIFS, Online Diagnostics, Ignite-UX, Auto Port Aggregator (APA), dynamic root disk, etc.	Yes	Yes	Yes	Yes
Host Intrusion Detection System	Yes	Yes	Yes	Yes
Java RTE, JDK, JPI, OOB Tuning Tools	Yes	Yes	Yes	Yes
IP Filter, IPSec, Bastille, OpenSSL, Secure Shell	Yes	Yes	Yes	Yes
LDAP-UX integration	Yes	Yes	Yes	Yes
Base Veritas file system and volume manager	Yes	Yes	Yes	Yes
Pluggable Authentication Module (PAM) Kerberos	Yes	Yes	Yes	Yes
Red Hat directory server	Yes	Yes	Yes	Yes
Mozilla web browser	Yes	Yes	Yes	Yes
HP-UX web server suite	Yes	Yes	Yes	Yes
Internet express	Yes	Yes	Yes	Yes
Partitioning providers and management tools	Yes	Yes	Yes	Yes
EMS framework	Yes	Yes	Yes	Yes
Software package builder	Yes	Yes	Yes	Yes
System Insight Manager	Yes	Yes	Yes	Yes
System Management Homepage	Yes	Yes	Yes	Yes
iCAP and PPU enablement	Yes	Yes	Yes	Yes
Install time security	Yes	Yes	Yes	Yes
Software assistant and security patch check	Yes	Yes	Yes	Yes
Distributed Systems Administration Utilities	Yes	Yes	Yes	Yes
PCI OL*	Yes	Yes	Yes	Yes
Native multipathing	Yes	Yes	Yes	Yes

Component	BOE	VSE-OE	HA-OE	DC-OE
Online JFS and MirrorDisk/UX	-	Yes	Yes	Yes
Process Resource Manager (PRM)	-	Yes	Yes	Yes
GlancePlus pak	-	Yes	Yes	Yes
Event Monitoring Services (EMS)	-	Yes	Yes	Yes
HA monitors	-	Yes	Yes	Yes
Virtual Server Environment (VSE) suite includes gWLM, WLM, Virtual Partitions, Virtualization Manager, Integrity Virtual Machines and Capacity Advisor	-	Yes	-	Yes
Serviceguard, Serviceguard NFS, and Enterprise Cluster Master (ECM) toolkits	-	-	Yes	Yes

Table 9-1 HP-UX OE Software Bundles

The OE bundles listed in Table 9-1 were referred to as *Foundation Operating Environment* (FOE), *Enterprise Operating Environment* (EOE), *Mission Critical Operating Environment* (MCOE) and *Technical Computing Operating Environment* (TCOE) in 11i v1 and 11i v2. The same bundle naming was used with the initial 11i v3 release and its first update. Starting 11i v3 update 2, these bundles have been renamed with changes based on software components they include.

- ✓ BOE includes what was previously included in FOE, plus enhancements
- ✓ VSE-OE includes entire BOE, original EOE and VSE suite
- ✓ HA-OE includes entire BOE, original EOE and Serviceguard
- ✓ DC-OE includes entire VSE-OE and HA-OE

9.1.2 Planning Installation

Installation of HP-UX 11i v3 on a server or partition requires that you have, at a minimum, the following information handy. You will need this information during the OE load to define system configuration:

- ✓ Type of OE to load (BOE, VSE-OE, HA-OE or DC-OE)
- ✓ Hard disk to be used (if there are several)
- ✓ Amount of primary swap space
- ✓ Disk management approach (whole disk, LVM or VxVM)
- ✓ Sizes of file systems
- ✓ Type(s) of file systems (HFS or VxFS)
- ✓ Size and location of dump device (default is the swap space)
- ✓ Hostname (unique 8 character alphanumeric string to identify the server or partition)
- ✓ IP address (unique 32-bit or 128-bit address)
- ✓ Subnet mask
- ✓ Root password
- ✓ Date and time
- ✓ Time zone
- ✓ Language
- ✓ Type of keyboard
- ✓ Any additional software to load

9.1.3   Installing HP-UX Using Local DVD

Let us perform an install of HP-UX 11i v3 OE using a local DVD drive. The install procedure on 9000 servers and nPars is the same, and so is the install procedure on Integrity servers and nPars.

The following are the steps to perform the install on a 9000 server. There are a few differences in the process on the two hardware platforms. The differences are highlighted.

1. Power the server on. In case of an nPar just created, login to MP and go to the command mode. Execute the *pe* command to power the nPar on.
2. Insert the first HP-UX 11i v3 installation DVD into the drive.
3. (Specific to 9000 servers and nPars) After the Power On Self Test (POST) on the hardware is complete, you will have 10 seconds within which you need to press any key to stop the autoboot process and interact with *Boot Console Handler* (BCH) menu. BCH is explained in Chapter 16 "HP-UX Shutdown and Startup".

```
    Attempting to boot using the primary path.
    --------------------------------------------------------------------------
     To discontinue, press any key within 10 seconds.
    Boot terminated.
    ---- Main Menu -----------------------------------------------------------
        Command                         Description
        --------------                  --------------

        BOot [PRI|HAA|ALT|<path>]       Boot from specified path
        PAth [PRI|HAA|ALT] [<path>]     Display or modify a path
        SEArch [ALL|<cell>|<path>]      Search for boot devices
        ScRoll [ON|OFF]                 Display or change scrolling capability
        COnfiguration menu              Displays or sets boot values
        INformation menu                Displays hardware information
        SERvice menu                    Displays service commands
        Display                         Redisplay the current menu
        HElp [<menu>|<command>]         Display help for menu or command
        REBOOT                          Restart Partition
        RECONFIGRESET                   Reset to allow Reconfig Complex Profile

        --------------
    Main Menu: Enter command or menu >
```

To proceed with installation on a 9000 server or nPar, jump to step 5.

4. (Specific to Integrity servers and nPars) Stop the autoboot process by pressing any key within 10 seconds. Select EFI Shell. EFI stands for *Extensible Firmware Interface* and is equivalent to BCH on 9000 servers. From the EFI Shell, issue the *map* command to list all available devices. Select the device name that points to the DVD drive such as Shell> fs1: and hit the Enter key to get to the fs1:\> prompt. Type "install" and press the Enter key to continue.
5. Search for bootable devices by running *search* or *sea* at the BCH main menu prompt:

```
Main Menu: Enter command or menu > sea
Searching for potential boot device(s)
This may take several minutes.
To discontinue search, press any key (termination may not be immediate).
                                    ODC
    Path#       Device Path (dec)   Device Type               Rev
    --------    ------------------------    ------------------    -----
    P0          0/0/0/3/0.6          Random access media       3
    P1          0/0/8/0/0/1/0.4      Random access media       3
    P2          0/0/8/0/0/1/0.2      Sequential access media   3
```

6. Choose the DVD path number (p1) from the list in the first column. Alternatively, you can specify the device path with the *boot* command. Commands at this level can be abbreviated such as *bo* for *boot*. Enter "n" when asked to stop at the ISL prompt prior to booting.

```
Main Menu: Enter command or menu > bo  p1
 BCH Directed Boot Path: 0/0/8/0/0/1/0.4
 Do you wish to stop at the ISL prompt prior to booting? (y/n) >> n
Initializing boot Device.
Boot IO Dependent Code (IODC) Revision 3
Boot Path Initialized.
HARD Booted.
ISL Revision A.00.44  Mar 12, 2003
ISL booting  hpux (;0):INSTALL

Boot
: disk(0/0/8/0/0/1/0.4.0.0.0.0.0;0):WINSTALL
21200896 + 4637920 + 8953352 start 0x22dc68
DoCalllist done
gate64: sysvec_vaddr = 0xc0002000 for 2 pages
Memory Class Setup
-------------------------------------------------------------------
Class    Physmem       Lockmem        Swapmem
-------------------------------------------------------------------
System :  7784 MB       7784 MB        7784 MB
Kernel :  7783 MB       7783 MB        7783 MB
User   :  7392 MB       6553 MB        6579 MB
. . . . . . . .
```

From this point onward, the installation procedure is identical on both 9000 and Integrity.

7. Select "Install HP-UX" and press Enter at the initial welcome screen as demonstrated in Figure 9-1. This screen also displays hardware inventory of the server or nPar. It displays total number of hard disk drives, CD/DVD drives, tape devices, LAN interfaces, memory, number of CPUs, etc.

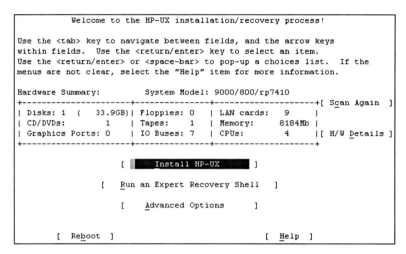

Figure 9-1 HP-UX Installation – Welcome Screen

8. Next, the system displays "User Interface and Media Options" window, as shown in Figure 9-2. Select "Media only installation" under "Source Location Options" to install from the DVD. Under "User Interface Options" choose "Advanced Installation". This option enables you to customize the installation. The "Guided Installation" option provides limited choices for customization and the "No user interface" option uses all system defaults, which we do not want. Use the Tab key to navigate and the Spacebar key to select an option. Select OK and hit the Enter key when done.

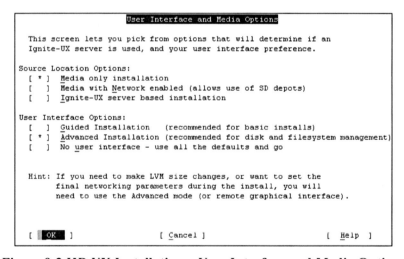

Figure 9-2 HP-UX Installation – User Interface and Media Options

9. On the next screen, the system provides you with an option to switch the install source. Choose "CD/DVD Installation" as illustrated in Figure 9-3 and press OK to continue.

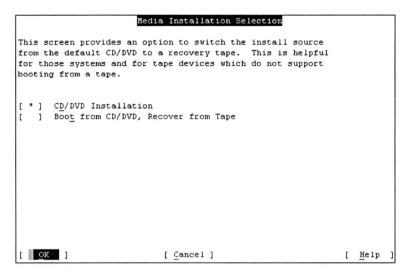

Figure 9-3 HP-UX Installation – Media Installation Selection

10. Next appears the screen as shown in Figure 9-4, which gives you an opportunity to do the customization. This screen appears when the install process executes the */opt/ignite/bin/itool* command. There are five sub-screens at this level: Basic, Software, System, File System and Advanced. Use the Tab key to navigate.

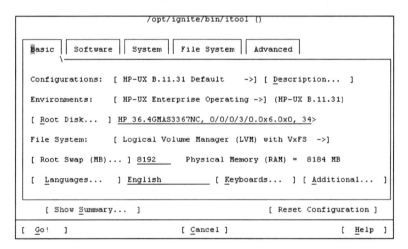

Figure 9-4 HP-UX Installation – Basic Configuration

11. On the "Basic" sub-screen, as shown in Figure 9-4, hang on to the "HP-UX B.11.31 Default" configuration choice. Next, choose an appropriate HP-UX 11i OE that you wish to install. If you have booted off with the DC-OE DVD, the choices here would include BOE, VSE-OE, HA-OE and DC-OE. Further down, you will see the disk that the installation process has picked up by default to install the OE on. This default disk is chosen based on the hardware scan performed in step 7. To select an alternate disk, highlight "Root Disk" and press Enter. Go to the next selection "File System" where you can choose the disk management technique and file system type to be used. You are provided with three choices, use the one that says "Logical Volume Manager (LVM) with VxFS" (Veritas Volume Manager with VxFS is

---

another option). The "Basic" sub-screen also shows amount of physical memory available on the server or nPar, and the swap space. The swap space is by default twice the size of physical memory, which the installation procedure picks up automatically. A detailed discussion on swap is covered in Chapter 15 "Swap Space". The "Language", "Keyboard" and "Additional" options should be left to their defaults unless there is a need to alter them.

12. On the next sub-screen "Software", select and include any additional software product that you wish to load as part of the install.

13. Move to the third sub-screen "System", which looks similar to what is shown in Figure 9-5.

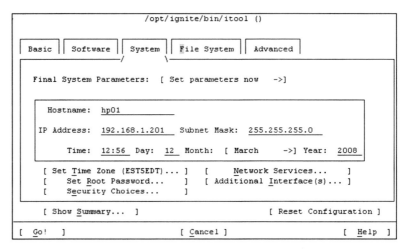

Figure 9-5 HP-UX Installation – System Configuration

Choose "Set parameters now" for "Final System Parameters" option. Enter hostname, IP address and subnet mask for this server or nPar. The date/time is usually shown correctly, otherwise you can modify it. You need to go to "Set Time Zone" and choose an appropriate time zone. For example, EST5EDT is US/Canada Eastern Time zone. Next, go to "Set Root Password" and type in a password for the *root* user account. "Security Choices" allows you to choose whether you wish to install security products such as "Install-Time security infrastructure" as shown in Figure 9-6.

```
                          Security Choices

        Marked ?   Product          Description

        Yes        Sec00Tools(OE)   Install-Time security infrastructure.
        No         Sec10Host(OE)    Host-Based Lockdown, without IPFilter confi
        No         Sec20MngDMZ(OE)  Lockdown + block most incoming traffic with
        Yes        Sec30DMZ(OE)     Host-Based and IPFilter Network Lockdown



        <                                                              >

        [   OK   ]                                           [  Help  ]
```

Figure 9-6 HP-UX Installation – Security Choices

These security options are referred to as *install-time security* options. By default, "Sec00Tools" and "Sec30DMZ" are selected. Here is what each of these options does:

Sec00Tools – installs the security infrastructure with optional security features disabled.
Sec10Host – installs a host-based lockdown system, without HP-UX IPFilter firewall. With this option chosen, most network services will remain disabled, but can be enabled using Bastille. A detailed discussion on Bastille and IPFilter is covered in Chapter 36 "HP-UX Security".
Sec20MngDMZ – installs a managed lockdown system that blocks most incoming traffic with an IPFilter firewall.
Sec30DMZ – installs a full DMZ lockdown system by implementing both host-based and IPFilter network lockdown.

If you do not wish to perform "Set parameters now", you can choose "Set parameters later" for "Final System Parameters" option. This will invoke the *set_parms* command at the first system reboot after the install is complete, and allows you to perform this customization. The usage of *set_parms* is explained later in this chapter.

14. Next, go to the "File System" sub-screen using the Tab key. The screen looks similar to the one shown below in Figure 9-7.

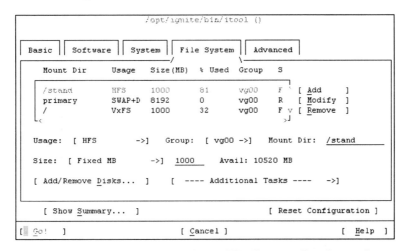

Figure 9-7 HP-UX Installation – File System Configuration

On this sub-screen you can add or remove file systems and modify their properties. Specify file system parameters as per your requirements. You may use sample file system properties given in Table 9-2 on a 36GB hard drive. Use the Tab key to move around. Leave "Add/Remove Disks" and "Additional Tasks" to defaults.

File System	Usage (FS Type)	Volume Group	Mount Dir	Size (Fixed MB)
lvol1	VxFS	vg00	/stand	1000 MB
lvol2 (Primary swap)	VxFS	vg00	N/A	8000 MB
lvol3	VxFS	vg00	/	1000 MB
lvol4	VxFS	vg00	/tmp	500 MB
lvol5	VxFS	vg00	/home	500 MB
lvol6	VxFS	vg00	/opt	7000 MB
lvol7	VxFS	vg00	/usr	4000 MB

File System	Usage (FS Type)	Volume Group	Mount Dir	Size (Fixed MB)
lvol8	VxFS	vg00	/var	4000 MB

Table 9-2 Sample HP-UX File System Properties

15. Leave to defaults selections on the next sub-screen "Advanced". This sub-screen allows you to specify any pre-install or post-install script, or both, to run before and/or after the install process.

16. Next, Tab to "Show Summary" option and hit Enter to view a summary of how your system will be configured based on the choices you have made. Verify your selections and press OK. You will see a message similar to the one shown in Figure 9-8.

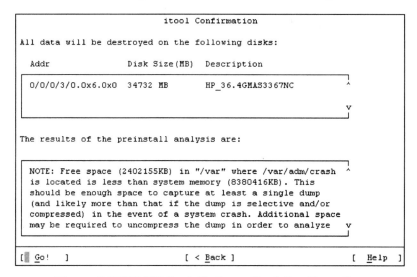

Figure 9-8 HP-UX Installation – itool Confirmation

17. Highlight the Go! button and press Enter to continue the install. The install process will prompt you to insert the second DVD in the drive to continue the installation process. Here is the message you will see on the console. Replace the DVD and press Enter.

```
* Please insert media number "2".
1) Continue.
Please pick from the choices above. (default: 1):
```

18. The install process will not prompt for any further information. The system will reboot following the installation and perform software configuration. When software configuration is complete, the system will complete the boot process and present you with the login prompt. You should also be able to login to the system using the *telnet* or *ssh* command.

19. Eject the DVD.

You are done with the installation.

9.2 Using set_parms

As mentioned in the note in step 13 of the installation process in the previous section, if "Set parameters later" under "Final System Parameters" option was chosen, the system would run the *set_parms* command with the argument "initial" at the first system boot after the installation was complete. In that case it would display the following:

```
                          Welcome to HP-UX!
Before using your system, you will need to answer a few questions.
The first question is whether you plan to use this system on a network.
Answer "yes" if you have connected the system to a network and are ready to link with a network.
Answer "no" if you:
    * Plan to set up this system as a standalone (no networking).
    * Want to use the system now as a standalone and connect to a network later.
Are you ready to link this system to a network?
Press [ y ] for yes or [ n ] for no, then press [ Enter ]
```

You would follow steps to configure system parameters given below. You would enter a "y" for yes and an "n" for no, as appropriate, when a question was asked:

- ✓ Hostname
- ✓ Physical location of the system such as option 1 for North America
- ✓ Time zone for the location such as option 3 for "Eastern Standard/Daylight"
- ✓ System date and time
- ✓ IP address
- ✓ Subnet mask and gateway IP addresses
- ✓ DNS domain name and DNS server name or IP address for DNS client setup, if appropriate
- ✓ NIS domain name and NIS server name or IP address for NIS client setup, if appropriate

Note that *set_parms* may be invoked anytime on a running system to modify any of the above.

Summary

This chapter presented information and enough knowledge to differentiate among various HP-UX OE software bundles available from HP. You studied the requirements to install HP-UX and learned how to perform an HP-UX installation using local DVD drive. Finally, you looked at the *set_parms* utility that allowed you to do initial system configuration.

## 10

Software Management

This chapter covers the following major topics:

✓ Software Distributor concepts and components
✓ Installed products database, software dependencies and protected software
✓ Administer software including listing, installing, verifying and removing them
✓ Software depot concepts and components including catalog files
✓ Administer software depots including copying software to a depot, registering and unregistering depot software, listing depots, listing and verifying depot contents, and removing depot software and depot

10.1   Software Distributor Concepts and Components

HP-UX provides a rich set of tools to administer software centrally in a multi-system HP-UX environment. This set of tools is called the *Software Distributor for HP-UX* (SD-UX). It enables you to install and manage software on local and remote machines. The software on an SD-UX server becomes accessible to the system itself as well as to other networked HP-UX systems.

SD-UX is a client/server functionality and only available in multi-user mode.

10.1.1   Software Structure

SD-UX commands operate on software objects that make up applications or software components. There are four such objects. Table 10-1 lists and describes them.

Object	Description
Fileset	Contains files and control scripts that make up a product. It can be part of a single product or included in other bundles or subproducts at the same time. A fileset is the lowest level of object managed by SD-UX.
Subproduct	A collection of filesets or other subproducts, or both, and control scripts.
Product	A grouping of filesets in a logical fashion. It is packaged and distributed for installation as a single entity. It can exist within a bundle or as a single, separate entity.
Bundle	Consists of groups of filesets or products, or both, packaged together for a specific purpose. It resides in a software depot and managed by SD-UX commands as a single entity.

Table 10-1 SD-UX Software Structure

10.1.2   Commands and Daemons

Several commands are included in SD-UX to perform software management functions. All these commands have similar syntax and options. Table 10-2 provides a list of most of the commands along with a short description of each. The table also lists associated log files.

Command	Description	Log File
swinstall	Installs or updates software. Runs in both GUI and TUI modes.	*/var/adm/sw/swinstall.log*
swlist	Lists installed software, software in a registered depot or software on media. Runs in both GUI and TUI modes.	N/A
swcopy	Copies software from one depot to another. Runs in both GUI and TUI modes.	*/var/adm/sw/swcopy.log*
swremove	Removes installed software, software in a depot or an entire depot. Runs in both GUI and TUI modes.	*/var/adm/sw/swremove.log*
swpackage	Creates software packages, which can then be used as a source for other SD-UX commands.	*/var/adm/sw/swpackage.log*

Command	Description	Log File
swconfig	Configures, reconfigures and unconfigures software.	*/var/adm/sw/swconfig.log*
swverify	Verifies the integrity of installed software by comparing IPD information with the files actually installed. Also used to verify depot contents.	*/var/adm/sw/swverify.log*
swmodify	Modifies the IPD and catalog files that contain information about the software on the system and in depots.	*/var/adm/sw/swmodify.log*
swreg	Registers or unregisters a depot. Registering makes a depot manageable by SD-UX commands.	*/var/adm/sw/swreg.log*

Table 10-2 SD-UX Commands

Table 10-3 provides a list of the SD-UX daemons along with a short description of each.

Daemon	Description	Log File
swagentd	Server daemon used by *swagent*.	*/var/adm/sw/swagentd.log*
swagent	SD-UX agent that communicates with *swagentd* on behalf of SD-UX commands to get the task done.	*/var/adm/sw/swagent.log*

Table 10-3 SD-UX Daemons

Although *swagentd* starts automatically when the system boots up to run level 2, it can be manually stopped, started or restarted if necessary.

To stop *swagentd*, do either of the following:

/usr/sbin/swagentd –k
/sbin/init.d/swagentd stop
The swagentd daemon is stopped.

To start *swagentd*, do the following:

/sbin/init.d/swagentd start

To restart a running *swagentd*, do the following:

swagentd –r

10.1.3   Installed Product Database

The *Installed Product Database* (IPD) is a set of files and sub-directories located under the */var/adm/sw/products* directory and contains detailed information about software products installed on the system. This information includes software product name, description, readme file, copyright information, revision information, operating system name/release/version, hardware machine type, vendor information, software state and part number. The IPD is maintained by the SD-UX utilities.

The IPD is updated automatically when install, configure, copy and delete operations are performed using the *swinstall*, *swconfig*, *swcopy*, and *swremove* commands, respectively. The *swlist* and *swverify* commands use IPD to list and verify installed software.

When the *swagent* client process is started, a file called *swlock* in the */var/adm/sw/products* directory is created to control multiple, simultaneous read/write accesses to software objects. This file is created to prevent more than one instance of the software agent from running to avoid any inconsistencies to occur in the IPD.

10.1.4   Software Dependencies

The successful installation of a software product requires certain files or products to be present or available. Similarly, many software products require certain files or products to be present in order for them to be able to run properly. This is called *software dependency* where a software depends on some other software in order to be installed or run properly. By default the *swconfig*, *swcopy*, *swinstall*, *swremove* or *swverify* commands select additional software to meet dependency requirements.

10.1.5   Protected Software

Some software products require that a codeword and customer ID be provided to be installed or copied. These software are known as *protected software*. This approach restricts the software to be installed on a specific system.

The *swinstall* and *swcopy* commands prompt to input codewords and customer ID when installing and copying a protected software.

10.2   Managing Software

This section talks about software management tasks including listing installed software, installing new software, verifying installed software and removing installed software.

10.2.1   Listing Installed Software

Information about software installed on the system is stored in the IPD. To see what is installed, use the *swlist* command. This command reads the IPD and displays requested information.

To display all software bundles installed on the system:

```
# swlist
# Initializing...
# Contacting target "hp01"...
# Target:  hp01:/
# Bundle(s):
  B2491BA           B.11.31           MirrorDisk/UX (Server)
  B3701AA           C.04.62.000       HP GlancePlus/UX Pak for 11.31
  B3835DA           C.03.03.01        HP Process Resource Manager
  B3929EA           B.11.31           HP OnLineJFS (Server)
  . . . . . . . .
```

To display all software products installed:

---

swlist –l product
```
# Initializing...
# Contacting target "hp01"...
# Target: hp01:/
  ATOK                    B.11.31           ATOK (Japanese Input Method Server)
. . . . . . . .
```

To display all installed sub-products:

swlist –l subproduct
```
# Initializing...
# Contacting target "hp01"...
# Target: hp01:/
# ATOK                    B.11.31           ATOK (Japanese Input Method Server)
  ATOK.Runtime
. . . . . . . .
```

To display all installed filesets:

swlist –l fileset
```
# Initializing...
# Contacting target "hp01"...
# Target: hp01:/
# ATOK                    B.11.31           ATOK (Japanese Input Method Server)
  ATOK.ATOK-COM           B.11.31           ATOK Runtime
  ATOK.ATOK-RUN           B.11.31           ATOK Runtime Programs
. . . . . . . .
```

To run *swlist* in GUI or TUI mode, use –i option. If DISPLAY environment variable is properly set, it will start in graphical mode, otherwise, it will come up in textual mode.

swlist –i

```
 ===              SD List - View Software (hp01) (1)
File View Options Actions                                        Help
                  Press CTRL-K for keyboard help.
Target:  hp01:/


Top  (Bundles and Products)                        0 of 96 selected

  Name              Revision       Information

  B2491BA      ->   B.11.31        MirrorDisk/UX (Server)
  B3701AA      ->   C.04.62.000    HP GlancePlus/UX Pak for 11.31
  B3835DA      ->   C.03.03.01     HP Process Resource Manager
  B3929EA      ->   B.11.31        HP OnLineJFS (Server)
  B5736DA      ->   A.04.20.31     HA Monitors
  B6848BA      ->   1.4.gm.46.16   Ximian GNOME 1.4 GTK+ Libraries for
  Base-VXFS    ->   B.11.31        Base VxFS File System 4.1 Bundle fo
  Base-VXVM    ->   B.4.10.032     Base VERITAS Volume Manager Bundle
  BaseLVM      ->   B.11.31.0709.  Logical Volume Manager
  CIFS-CLIENT  ->   A.02.02.01     HP CIFS Client
  CIFS-SERVER  ->   A.02.03.02     HP CIFS Server
```

Figure 10-1 Listing Software

10.2.2   Installing Software

Software install is performed using the *swinstall* command, which can be run in either GUI or TUI mode depending on whether the DISPLAY environment variable is properly set. This command can also be run without getting into graphical or textual mode by supplying proper parameters at the command line. The third way of running it is via SMH.

The *swinstall* command requires the hostname and a full path to the location where the software to be installed resides. If codeword and customer ID are required, *swinstall* prompts for it. The command validates the input and performs a number of checks such as if the software is already installed, enough disk space available and whether dependencies are met. If no errors are encountered, it displays a message and seeks your input to proceed, among other choices. If all parameters are met, the software install continues after the OK button is pressed. The command generates messages as it proceeds and logs them. It updates and rebuilds the kernel, if required. When the installation is finished, a message is displayed on the screen. If the kernel is rebuilt, the server or partition reboots automatically after you press Enter to confirm, otherwise, you can simply exit out of the *swinstall* interface.

To start *swinstall* in GUI or TUI mode, simply run *swinstall*. A sample *swinstall* screen is shown in Figure 10-2.

   # **swinstall**

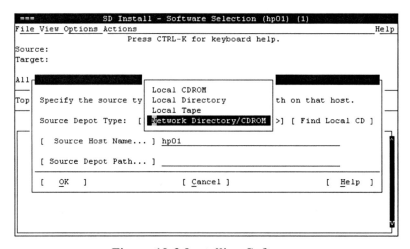

Figure 10-2 Installing Software

One of the main menu choices displayed is "Options". Choose "Change Options" from "Options". Modify any options if necessary before proceeding with software installation. Figure 10-3 displays available options.

Let us take a look at a few examples to understand various scenarios of software installation.

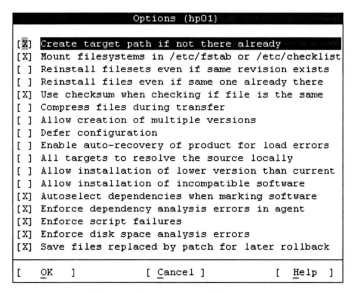

```
                     Options (hp01)

[X]  Create target path if not there already
[X]  Mount filesystems in /etc/fstab or /etc/checklist
[ ]  Reinstall filesets even if same revision exists
[ ]  Reinstall files even if same one already there
[X]  Use checksum when checking if file is the same
[ ]  Compress files during transfer
[ ]  Allow creation of multiple versions
[ ]  Defer configuration
[ ]  Enable auto-recovery of product for load errors
[ ]  All targets to resolve the source locally
[ ]  Allow installation of lower version than current
[ ]  Allow installation of incompatible software
[X]  Autoselect dependencies when marking software
[X]  Enforce dependency analysis errors in agent
[X]  Enforce script failures
[X]  Enforce disk space analysis errors
[X]  Save files replaced by patch for later rollback

[    OK    ]          [ Cancel ]           [  Help  ]
```

Figure 10-3 *swinstall* **Options**

Suppose there is a software called IGNITE located in the */var/depot* depot directory. To install this software with all default options, execute *swinstall* with –s switch:

swinstall –s /var/depot

This command will bring up GUI or TUI and display all available software in the specified depot. Highlight IGNITE and select "Install" from "Actions". An analysis will be done to check whether the software is already installed, enough disk space is available and so on. Click OK to proceed with installation after the analysis is finished.

To install the same software, assuming it resides on a remote machine *hp02* in */var/depot* directory, with default options:

swinstall –s hp02:/var/depot

To install IGNITE without invoking the graphical or textual interface:

swinstall –s /var/depot IGNITE
```
======= 03/13/08 12:20:40 EDT  BEGIN swinstall SESSION
    (non-interactive) (jobid=hp01-0010)
  * Session started for user "root@hp01".
  * Beginning Selection
  * Target connection succeeded for "hp01:/".
  * Source connection succeeded for "hp01:/var/depot".
  * Source:          /var/depot
  * Targets:         hp01:/
  * Software selections:
      IGNITE,r=C.7.3.144,a=HP-UX_B.11.31_IA/PA,v=HP

. . . . . . . .
  * Selection succeeded.
```

Software Management

 * Beginning Analysis and Execution
 * Session selections have been saved in the file "/.sw/sessions/swinstall.last".
 * The analysis phase succeeded for "hp01:/".
 * The execution phase succeeded for "hp01:/".
 * Analysis and Execution succeeded.
NOTE: More information may be found in the agent logfile using the
  command "swjob -a log hp01-0010 @ hp01:/".
======= 03/13/08 12:22:04 EDT END swinstall SESSION (non-interactive)
 (jobid=hp01-0010)

Additional information can be found in the agent logfile using the command "swjob -a log hp01-0010 @hp01:/ "
after the *swinstall* task is finished.

There are numerous options available to *swinstall*. Refer to man pages for detailed information.

10.2.3 Verifying Installed Software

Verifying installed software checks all files and associated attributes against the information stored in IPD about the software to ensure that the software is installed successfully. The *swverify* command is used for this purpose. It reports any issues found.

To verify the IGNITE package, run *swverify* with –v option for verbosity:

 # swverify –v IGNITE
======= 03/13/08 12:35:22 EDT BEGIN swverify SESSION
 (non-interactive) (jobid=hp01-0012)
 * Session started for user "root@hp01".
 * Beginning Selection
 * Target connection succeeded for "hp01:/".
 * Software selections:
  IGNITE,r=C.7.3.144,a=HP-UX_B.11.31_IA/PA,v=HP
. . . .
 * Selection succeeded.
 * Beginning Analysis
 * Session selections have been saved in the file "/.sw/sessions/swverify.last".
 * The analysis phase succeeded for "hp01:/".
 * Verification succeeded.
NOTE: More information may be found in the agent logfile using the
  command "swjob -a log hp01-0012 @ hp01:/".
======= 03/13/08 12:35:32 EDT END swverify SESSION (non-interactive)
 (jobid=hp01-0012)

Additional information can be found in the agent logfile using the command "swjob -a log hp01-0012 @hp01:/"
after the *swverify* task is finished.

There are numerous options available with *swverify*. Refer to its man pages for more information.

10.2.4 Removing Software

The *swremove* command is used to remove installed software from the system. The command unconfigures the software before it proceeds with the removal. It is invoked in GUI or TUI mode depending on whether the DISPLAY environment variable is set.

Start *swremove* and highlight the software to remove from "Software Selection" window. See Figure 10-4. Go to Actions and select Remove. The command performs an analysis on the software and then proceeds with removing it.

swremove

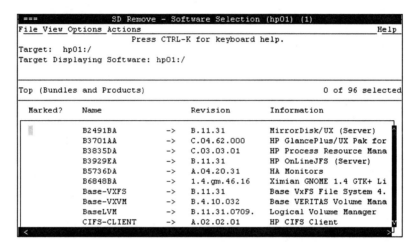

Figure 10-4 Removing Software

To remove IGNITE without invoking the graphical or textual interface:

swremove IGNITE
======= 03/13/08 12:39:00 EDT BEGIN swremove SESSION
    (non-interactive) (jobid=hp01-0013)
  * Session started for user "root@hp01".
  * Beginning Selection
  * Target connection succeeded for "hp01:/".
  * Software selections:
      IGNITE,r=C.7.3.144,a=HP-UX_B.11.31_IA/PA,v=HP
. . . .
  * Session selections have been saved in the file "/.sw/sessions/swremove.last".
  * The analysis phase succeeded for "hp01:/".
  * Analysis succeeded.
  * Beginning Execution
  * The execution phase succeeded for "hp01:/".
  * Execution succeeded.
NOTE: More information may be found in the agent logfile using the
    command "swjob -a log hp01-0013 @ hp01:/".
======= 03/13/08 12:39:08 EDT END swremove SESSION (non-interactive)
    (jobid=hp01-0013)

Additional information can be found in the agent logfile using the command "swjob -a log hp01-0013 @hp01:/" after the *swremove* task is finished.

There are numerous options available with *swremove*. Refer to its man pages for more information.

10.3   Software Depots

A depot is a location that holds software products in installable format. The location may be a directory, a CD/DVD drive or a tape drive. A directory depot is created to copy installable software in it, whereas a CD/DVD or tape depot is used for software distribution purposes.

The process of configuring a directory depot is to copy the software to the directory using the *swcopy* command. A directory depot sitting on a server offers several advantages:

- ✓ The server acts as a central software repository. You need to manage software only on one system.
- ✓ You can have as many depots on the server as you wish. Application depots, patch depots, etc. can be setup.
- ✓ When required software needs to be installed on a client machine, invoke *swinstall* on the client and perform a pull install of the software.
- ✓ Installation of one software can be done on multiple servers simultaneously.
- ✓ Having software in depots eliminates (or at least reduces) loading and unloading of CD/DVD and tape.

A tape depot is created using *swpackage* command. It can be accessed by only one user at a time.

10.3.1   Catalog Files

Catalog files hold depot description and software information located in depots. Catalog files are equivalent to IPD and are stored in the catalog directory that resides in the same directory as the depot software.

Catalog files are automatically updated when a modification to the depot is performed, and are removed when the depot is removed.

10.4   Managing Software Depots

Managing software depots involves copying software to a depot, registering a depot, unregistering a depot, listing depots, listing software in a depot, verifying depot contents, removing software from a depot and removing a depot. The following sub-sections elaborate depot management tasks.

10.4.1   Copying Software to a Depot

Copying software to a depot copies an entire installable image of the software to a depot for later installations. The *swcopy* command is used for this purpose. Note that there is a difference between copying software and installing it. Copying software duplicates an entire image of the software to a depot, while installing software puts files in different directory locations for execution purposes. Simply copying software to a directory using the *cp* command and then trying to install it does not work. The *swcopy* command maintains the software structure.

To start *swcopy* in GUI or TUI, issue the command at the prompt:

 # swcopy

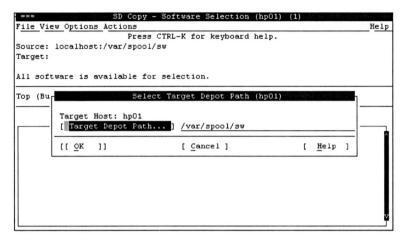

Figure 10-5 Copying Software to a Depot

A "Software Selection" window will pop up with a "Select Target Depot Path" dialog box superimposed. The "Target Depot Path" will display the default target depot, which is */var/spool/sw*. If you want the software to be copied to this location, click OK to proceed with analysis and copy process, otherwise specify an alternate location.

The following examples show various software copy tasks performed at the command line without invoking GUI or TUI.

Copy IGNITE software located on a local CD/DVD to a depot at */var/depot* on the local system. See Chapter 14 "File Systems" on how to mount a CD/DVD. Create the */dvdrom* directory if it does not already exist.

 # swcopy –s /dvdrom IGNITE @ /var/depot
```
======= 03/13/08 12:09:27 EDT  BEGIN swcopy SESSION (non-interactive)
    (jobid=hp01-0008)
  * Session started for user "root@hp01".
  * Beginning Selection
  * "hp01:/var/depot":  This target does not exist and will be
  created.
  * Source:          /dvdrom
  * Targets:         hp01:/var/depot
  * Software selections:
       IGNITE,r=C.7.3.144,a=HP-UX_B.11.31_IA/PA,v=HP
. . . . . . . .
  * Selection succeeded.
  * Beginning Analysis and Execution
  * Session selections have been saved in the file "/.sw/sessions/swcopy.last".
  * The analysis phase succeeded for "hp01:/var/depot".
  * The execution phase succeeded for "hp01:/var/depot".
```

* Analysis and Execution succeeded.
NOTE: More information may be found in the agent logfile using the
        command "swjob -a log hp01-0008 @ hp01:/var/depot".
======= 03/13/08 12:11:35 EDT END swcopy SESSION (non-interactive)
        (jobid=hp01-0008)

Additional information can be found in the agent logfile using the command "swjob -a log hp01-0008 @hp01:/var/depot" after the *swcopy* task is finished.

To copy IGNITE software from a local depot */var/depot* to another local depot */var/depot1*:

 # swcopy –s /var/depot IGNITE @ /var/depot1
======= 03/13/08 12:44:10 EDT BEGIN swcopy SESSION (non-interactive)
        (jobid=hp01-0014)
    * Session started for user "root@hp01".
    * Beginning Selection
    * "hp01:/var/depot1": This target does not exist and will be created.
    * Source connection succeeded for "hp01:/var/depot".
    * Source: /var/depot
    * Targets: hp01:/var/depot1
    * Software selections:
        IGNITE,r=C.7.3.144,a=HP-UX_B.11.31_IA/PA,v=HP
. . . .
    * Selection succeeded.
    * Beginning Analysis and Execution
    * Session selections have been saved in the file "/.sw/sessions/swcopy.last".
    * The analysis phase succeeded for "hp01:/var/depot1".
    * The execution phase succeeded for "hp01:/var/depot1".
    * Analysis and Execution succeeded.
NOTE: More information may be found in the agent logfile using the
        command "swjob -a log hp01-0014 @ hp01:/var/depot1".
======= 03/13/08 12:44:19 EDT END swcopy SESSION (non-interactive)
        (jobid=hp01-0014)

To copy all software on a local CD/DVD to a depot at */var/depot2* on the local system:

 # swcopy –s /dvdrom '*' @ /var/depot2

To copy all software on a local CD/DVD to a depot at */var/depot1* on *hp02* server:

 # swcopy –s /dvdrom '*' @ hp02:/var/depot1

To copy all software from a tape drive at */dev/rtape/tape1_BEST* (or */dev/rmt/0m*) to */var/spool/sw* on the local system:

 # swcopy –s /dev/rtape/tape1_BEST *

10.4.2　Registering and Unregistering a Depot

A depot must be registered before it can be used. When the *swcopy* command is executed to copy software to a depot, it registers the depot automatically. Downloaded software must be registered prior to use. The *swreg* command performs registering and unregistering functions.

To register a software depot located at */var/depot3*, do either of the following:

> **# swreg –l depot /var/depot3**
> **# swreg –l depot @ /var/depot3**
> ======= 03/13/08 12:51:41 EDT BEGIN swreg SESSION (non-interactive)
>   * Session started for user "root@hp01".
>   * Beginning Selection
>   * Targets:　　　　hp01
>   * Objects:　　　　/var/depot3
>   * Selection succeeded.
> ======= 03/13/08 12:51:41 EDT END swreg SESSION (non-interactive)

To unregister the depot, do either of the following:

> **# swreg –ul depot /var/depot3**
> **# swreg –ul depot @ /var/depot3**
> ======= 03/13/08 12:52:50 EDT BEGIN swreg SESSION (non-interactive)
>   * Session started for user "root@hp01".
>   * Beginning Selection
>   * Targets:　　　　/var/depot3
>   * Selection succeeded.
> ======= 03/13/08 12:52:50 EDT END swreg SESSION (non-interactive)

10.4.3　Listing Depots

Listing depots displays what software depots are registered and available for use.

To list all depots currently registered on the local system:

> **# swlist –l depot**
> # Initializing...
> # Target "hp01" has the following depot(s):
> /var/depot
> /var/depot1

To list all depots registered on the remote system *hp02*:

> **# swlist –l depot @ hp02**
> # Initializing...
> # Target "hp01" has the following depot(s):
> /var/depot1
> /var/depot2

10.4.4 Listing Depot Contents

Listing depot contents displays what software are available in registered depots.

To list software residing in a depot on the local system:

```
# swlist –l product –d @ /var/depot
# Initializing...
# Contacting target "hp01"...
# Target:  hp01:/var/depot
  Ignite-UX    C.7.3.144      HP-UX System Installation Services
```

The output indicates that IGNITE is the only registered software in */var/depot*.

To list software in */var/depot* on the remote system *hp02*:

```
# swlist –l product –d @ hp02:/var/depot
```

To list software on local tape depot located at */dev/rtape/tape1_BEST* (or */dev/rmt/0m*):

```
# swlist –d @ /dev/rtape/tape1_BEST
```

10.4.5 Verifying Depot Contents

The *swverify* command is used to verify software in a depot. It verifies dependencies, reports missing files and checks file attributes including permissions, file type, size, checksum, modification time and major/minor number attributes.

To verify all software in */var/depot* depot on the local system:

```
# swverify –d \* @ /var/depot
======= 03/13/08 12:58:03 EDT  BEGIN swverify SESSION
     (non-interactive) (jobid=hp01-0015)
   * Session started for user "root@hp01".
   * Beginning Selection
   * Target connection succeeded for "hp01:/var/depot".
   * Software selections:
       IGNITE,r=C.7.3.144,a=HP-UX_B.11.31_IA/PA,v=HP
. . . . . . . .
   * Selection succeeded.
   * Beginning Analysis
   * Session selections have been saved in the file "/.sw/sessions/swverify.last".
   * The analysis phase succeeded for "hp01:/var/depot".
   * Verification succeeded.
NOTE:   More information may be found in the agent logfile using the
     command "swjob -a log hp01-0015 @ hp01:/var/depot".
======= 03/13/08 12:58:11 EDT  END swverify SESSION (non-interactive)
     (jobid=hp01-0015)
```

More information may be found in the agent logfile using the command "swjob -a log hp01-0015 @hp01:/var/depot" after the *swverify* task is finished.

10.4.6   Removing Software from a Depot

The *swremove* command is used to remove one or more software from a depot.

To remove IGNITE from the depot at */var/depot* on the local machine:

 # swremove –d IGNITE @ /var/depot
```
======= 03/13/08 13:00:07 EDT  BEGIN swremove SESSION
     (non-interactive) (jobid=hp01-0017)
   * Session started for user "root@hp01".
   * Beginning Selection
   * Target connection succeeded for "hp01:/var/depot".
   * Software selections:
       IGNITE,r=C.7.3.144,a=HP-UX_B.11.31_IA/PA,v=HP
. . . . . . . .
   * Selection succeeded.
   * Beginning Analysis
   * Session selections have been saved in the file "/.sw/sessions/swremove.last".
   * The analysis phase succeeded for "hp01:/var/depot".
   * Analysis succeeded.
   * Beginning Execution
   * The execution phase succeeded for "hp01:/var/depot".
   * Execution succeeded.
NOTE:   More information may be found in the agent logfile using the
     command "swjob -a log hp01-0017 @ hp01:/var/depot".
======= 03/13/08 13:00:09 EDT  END swremove SESSION (non-interactive)
     (jobid=hp01-0017)
```

More information may be found in the agent logfile using the command "swjob -a log hp01-0017 @hp01:/var/depot" after the *swremove* task is finished.

To remove App1 from the default depot on the local machine:

 # swremove –d App1

To remove all software from the default depot on the remote machine *hp02*:

 # swremove –d @ hp02

To remove IGNITE from the depot at */var/depot* on the remote machine *hp02*:

 # swremove –d IGNITE @ hp02:/var/depot

10.4.7 Removing a Depot

When all software in a depot are removed, the depot automatically gets unregistered and is considered removed although the directory where it resided still exists.

To remove all software located in */var/depot* depot and unregister it:

swremove –d * @ var/depot
======= 03/13/08 13:04:02 EDT BEGIN swremove SESSION
    (non-interactive) (jobid=hp01-0025)
  * Session started for user "root@hp01".
  * Beginning Selection
  * Target connection succeeded for "hp01:/var/depot1".
  * Software selections:
    IGNITE,r=C.7.3.144,a=HP-UX_B.11.31_IA/PA,v=HP

. . . .
  * Selection succeeded.
  * Beginning Analysis
  * Session selections have been saved in the file "/.sw/sessions/swremove.last".
  * The analysis phase succeeded for "hp01:/var/depot1".
  * Analysis succeeded.
  * Beginning Execution
  * The execution phase succeeded for "hp01:/var/depot1".
  * Execution succeeded.
NOTE: More information may be found in the agent logfile using the
    command "swjob -a log hp01-0025 @ hp01:/var/depot".
======= 03/13/08 13:04:04 EDT END swremove SESSION (non-interactive)
    (jobid=hp01-0025)

More information may be found in the agent logfile using the command "swjob -a log hp01-0025 @hp01:/var/depot" after the *swremove* task is finished.

To remove all software located on the remote machine *hp02* in */var/depot* depot and unregister it:

swremove –d * @ hp02:/var/depot

Summary

This chapter discussed software management in HP-UX. You learned concepts and components involved including Installed Product Database, dependencies, protection on some software, and catalog files. You performed tasks on software and software depots such as listing installed software, depots and depot contents; installing software from local media and depot; copying software to a depot; registering and unregistering depot software; verifying installed software and depot contents; removing an installed software and software from a depot; and removing a depot.

## 11

Patch Management

This chapter covers the following major topics:

- ✓ Why patches are necessary
- ✓ Understand HP-UX patch management and naming scheme
- ✓ Patch attributes – suppression, dependency, rating, critical and non-critical, status, state, category tag and ancestry
- ✓ List installed patches and patch bundles
- ✓ Acquire and install individual patches and patch bundles
- ✓ Install patches from CD/DVD and tape
- ✓ Verify patches and patch bundles
- ✓ Roll back (remove) and commit patches
- ✓ Patch assessment and security patch check tools
- ✓ HP-UX Software Assistant (SWA) tool

11.1　Understanding Patch Management

Patch management is carried out to reduce the risk of potential problems arising out of system crashes, panics, memory leaks, data corruption, application failures and security breaches. Some patches also deliver new functionality and features, enable new hardware and update firmware levels. Having proper patches installed ensures:

- ✓ Smooth system operation
- ✓ Optimum performance
- ✓ Enhanced system security
- ✓ Better reliability and higher availability
- ✓ Latest system enhancements and functionality
- ✓ Less patches to install if a problem is encountered
- ✓ Less time required to troubleshoot a problem

Patch management involves tasks such as acquiring, installing, updating, verifying, testing, listing, copying, committing and removing patches.

11.1.1　Patch Naming Convention

Each HP-UX patch has a unique patch identification string and fall under one of four categories:

- ✓ **Common patches** identified by CO. These are general HP-UX patches and do not usually require a system reboot after an installation.
- ✓ **Kernel patches** identified by KL. These patches modify and update HP-UX kernel and related structure and almost always require a system reboot after an installation.
- ✓ **Network patches** identified by NE. These patches relate to HP-UX network components and may or may not require a system reboot after an installation.
- ✓ **Subsystem patches** identified by SS. These patches relate to HP-UX subsystems other than general, kernel and networking, and may or may not require a system reboot after an installation.

HP-UX patches have the syntax: PHXX_#####, where P stands for Patch, H stands for HP-UX, XX corresponds to one of the four categories mentioned above and ##### is a unique four or five character numeric string. Usually, the higher this number is the more recently released the patch is.

Patches are installed and managed via the SD-UX commands that were covered in Chapter 10 "Software Management".

11.2　Patch Attributes

Before jumping into managing patches, you need to understand patch attributes, an understanding of which helps you while working with acquiring, downloading, installing and managing patches.

11.2.1 Patch Suppression

When a new patch is released, it replaces and supersedes any earlier patches distributed for the same reasons. The new patch fixes any bugs in the previous version of that patch or addresses any other issues reported in it. This is called *patch suppression*.

You can view patch details or associated readme file to view what patches a given patch has superseded. For patches already installed on the system, execute the following to display this information:

```
# swlist –l patch –x show_superseded_patches=true
# Initializing...
# Contacting target "hp01"...
# Target:  hp01:/
# ATOK                    B.11.31          ATOK (Japanese Input Method Server)
# ATOK.ATOK-COM           B.11.31          ATOK Runtime
# ATOK.ATOK-RUN           B.11.31          ATOK Runtime Programs
# Accounting              B.11.31          Accounting
. . . . . . . .
```

You may wish to run the *show_patches* utility that displays the output in a formatted way:

```
# show_patches
   Active                  Patch
   Patch                   Description
   ------------------      ----------------------------------------
. . . . . . . .
   PHCO_36555              idisk(1M) cumulative patch
   PHCO_36569              Firmware/software compatibility check
   PHKL_35900              evacd performance, kvaddr leak panic
   PHKL_35973              IDE/ATAPI cumulative patch
```

11.2.2 Patch Dependency

A patch that depends on one or more other patches in order to be installed or work appropriately is said to have dependency on those other patches.

HP-UX patches are cumulative. This means that a patch automatically satisfies all the dependencies that all of its superseded patches satisfy.

There are three common dependency types:

- ✓ **Patch Dependencies** – Patches required for proper operation.
- ✓ **Hardware Dependencies** – Patches for specific system hardware models.
- ✓ **Other Dependencies** – Various dependencies needed only under specific circumstances.

11.2.3 Patch Rating

Every patch has a quality rating between 1 and 3 (inclusive) indicated by corresponding number of asterisk (*) characters. This quality rating (a.k.a. star rating) is displayed beside the name of each patch in the ITRC patch database located at *http://www2.itrc.hp.com/service/patch/mainPage.do*. A patch gets the star rating of 1 at the time it is released. This implies that the patch is not well tested in the customer environment and there might be side effects of applying it on the system. As time passes, this rating may be augmented to 2 or 3 stars, indicating increased confidence in the patch.

11.2.4   Critical and Non-Critical Patches

HP-UX patches are either critical or non-critical. This attribute can be viewed under the "Critical" field on the patch details page or in the patch readme file.

A patch is considered critical if it provides a fix for a critical problem such as system panic and process abort. All other patches are considered non-critical.

11.2.5   Patch Status

Each patch has a status that identifies if the patch is for general use or special. Moreover, it tells if the patch has any warnings associated with it.

11.2.6   Patch State

An installed patch is in one of four states: applied, committed, superseded or committed / superseded. This represents the current state of the patch.

The *applied* state indicates that the patch is currently active on the system. The *committed* state indicates that the patch cannot be removed from the system since the files it replaced are no longer available. The *superseded* state states that the patch has been superseded by another installed patch. The *committed/superseded* state means the patch has been committed and superseded by another installed patch.

Do the following to determine current patch states of installed patches:

```
# swlist –l fileset –a patch_state *,c=patch
# Initializing...
# Contacting target "hp01"...
# Target: hp01:/
# PHCO_36032
  PHCO_36032.UX-CORE            applied
# PHCO_36038
  PHCO_36038.TRUEVM-MIN         applied
. . . . . . . .
```

11.2.7   Category Tag

A category tag associated with a given patch helps determine the patch category it falls under. Some of the category tags are *hardware enablement* (provides support for new hardware), *enhancement* (provides added feature), *special release* (developed for a specific situation), *critical* (fixes a critical issue) and *firmware* (provides firmware update).

The patch category for a patch can be determined by viewing the patch details page or the patch's readme file. For installed patches, you can view this information using *swlist*:

```
# swlist –l fileset –a category_tag *,c=patch
# Initializing...
# Contacting target "hp01"...
# Target:  hp01:/
# PHCO_36032                        patch      defect_repair  general_release
  PHCO_36032.UX-CORE              patch
# PHCO_36038                        patch      defect_repair  general_release
  PHCO_36038.TRUEVM-MIN          patch
. . . . . . . .
```

11.2.8   Patch Ancestry

The ancestor of a patch is the original software component that the patch modified. Ancestry impacts patch installation and removal. Run the following to determine ancestors of all installed patches:

```
# swlist –l fileset –a ancestor *,c=patch
# Initializing...
# Contacting target "hp01"...
# Target:  hp01:/
# PHCO_36032
  PHCO_36032.UX-CORE              OS-Core.UX-CORE,fr=B.11.31,v=HP
# PHCO_36038
  PHCO_36038.TRUEVM-MIN          EVM-EventMgr.TRUEVM-MIN,fr=B.11.31,v=HP
. . . . . . . .
```

11.3   Managing Patches

Patches are available individually and in bundle form. A patch bundle is a collection of patches. You can install specific patches to the system according to your needs or apply an entire bundle. Most administrators prefer applying patch bundles as opposed to applying individual patches for ease of management.

In the following sub-sections, you are going to see how patches are listed, acquired, installed, verified, rolled back and committed.

11.3.1   Listing Installed Patches

Listing installed patches displays all individual patches currently installed on the system. Use the *swlist* command to list them:

```
# swlist –l patch
# Initializing...
# Contacting target "hp01"...
# Target: hp01:/
# ATOK                B.11.31           ATOK (Japanese Input Method Server)
# ATOK.ATOK-COM       B.11.31           ATOK Runtime
# ATOK.ATOK-RUN       B.11.31           ATOK Runtime Programs
. . . . . . . .
```

Alternatively, you can use the *show_patches* command to display patches:

```
# show_patches
   Active                 Patch
   Patch                  Description
   ----------------       ---------------------------------------
   . . . . . . . .
   PHCO_36555             idisk(1M) cumulative patch
   PHCO_36569             Firmware/software compatibility check
   PHKL_35900             evacd performance, kvaddr leak panic
   PHKL_35973             IDE/ATAPI cumulative patch
```

11.3.2   Acquiring Individual Patches

Individual patches may be obtained from either of the following two sites:

- ✓ IT Resource Center (ITRC) website at *www.itrc.hp.com.*
- ✓ ITRC ftp site at *ftp://ftp.itrc.hp.com.*

Figure 11-1 shows the main ITRC web page. Obtaining patches from this site using the procedure mentioned below is recommended. It automatically selects dependent patches as well.

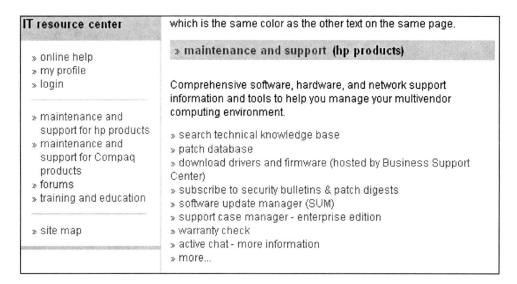

Figure 11-1 IT Resource Center Main Page

1. Go to *www.itrc.hp.com.*
2. Under "maintenance and support for hp products", click "find individual patches".
3. Go to "HP-UX".
4. Choose appropriate HP-UX OE level.
5. You have three search options to choose from:

    ✓ Select "Search by Patch IDs" and specify a patch ID if you already know it.

✓ Select "Search by Keyword" if you do not know the exact patch ID you are looking for and wish to search for the patch based on some matching description.
✓ Select "Browse Patch List" to list all available patches and choose the one you need.

6. Review patch information once you find the desired patch. Choose the one that is recommended by checking the box next to it.
7. Click the patch name to review details of it.
8. Click "add to selected patch list". If the patch has a warning associated with it, the patch warning page will appear.
9. You may see some more patches automatically added to the download list. These are automatically chosen and are required to satisfy dependencies. Download all of them.
10. Click "download selected".
11. Click "Expand to view additional download options".
12. Choose a desired format – zip, gzip or tar – and click "download". Use the tar format for this demonstration. You also have the option to download a script which will ftp the patches.
13. Click "download" to get patches.

To acquire individual patches from *ftp://ftp.itrc.hp.com*, follow the steps below. This method does not automatically select dependent patches.

1. Open up a browser window and type *ftp://ftp/itrc.hp.com*.
2. Click "hp-ux_patches".
3. Click "s700_800".
4. Click "11.X".
5. All available patches are listed here. Choose the one that you need and download it. Do not forget to download the corresponding text file.

You may download patches from *ftp://ftp.itrc.hp.com* by running the *ftp* command at the command line as well. Login as *anonymous* user and supply your email address as password. This method does not automatically select any dependent patches either.

11.3.3 Installing Individual Patches

Assume the downloaded patch is *hpux_11.31_04150209.tar* and was downloaded from ITRC. Follow the steps below to install it:

1. Move the patch to a directory where it can be unpacked:

   # **mkdir /var/depot/patches**
   # **mv hpux_11.31_04150209.tar /var/depot/patches**
   # **cd /var/depot/patches**

2. Untar the patch file:

   # **tar –xvf hpux_11.31_04150209.tar**

   Run "**unzip hpux_11.31_04150209.zip**" if the patch file was in zip format.
   Run "**gunzip hpux_11.31_04150209.tgz | tar xvf –**" if the patch file was in gzip format.

Some files will be generated by the untar operation. A readme file that contains details about the patch, a *create_depot_hpux.11.31* script and a file with *.depot* extension. The *.depot* file is the file that holds the actual patch software.

3. Execute the *create_depot_hpux.11.31* script. This script performs unshar function (using the *sh* command) on the patch and then *swcopy* and *swverify* operations. It creates a directory called *depot* where it swcopies the patch depot:

> # **./create_depot_hpux.11.31**
> DEPOT: /var/tmp/depot
> BUNDLE: BUNDLE
> TITLE: Patch Bundle
> UNSHAR: y
> PSF: depot.psf
> Expanding patch shar files...
> x - PHCO_36032.text
> x - PHCO_36032.depot [non-ascii]
> list of SD installable patches = PHCO_36032
> Copying PHCO_36032 into depot /var/tmp/depot
> ======== 04/15/08 08:03:19 EDT BEGIN swcopy SESSION (non-interactive)
>   (jobid=hp01-0014)
>   * Session started for user "root@hp01".
> . . . .
>   * Beginning Analysis
>   * Session selections have been saved in the file "/.sw/sessions/swverify.last".
>   * "hp01:/var/tmp/depot": There will be no attempt to mount
>   filesystems that appear in the filesystem table.
>   * Verification succeeded.
> NOTE: More information may be found in the agent logfile using the
>   command "swjob -a log hp01-0015 @ hp01:/var/tmp/depot".
> ======== 04/15/08 08:03:21 EDT END swverify SESSION (non-interactive)
>   (jobid=hp01-0015)

4. Install the patch with *swinstall*. The system will reboot automatically, if necessary:

> # **swinstall –s /depot/patches/depot**

Assume the downloaded patch, after unpacking, is *hpux_800_11.31.depot* and was downloaded using one of the ftp methods. Follow the steps below to install it:

1. Move this depot file to a directory where you want to register it:

> # **mkdir /depot/patch_depot**
> # **mv hpux_800_11.31.depot /depot/patch_depot**
> # **cd /depot/patch_depot**

2. Register the depot:

> # **swreg –l depot /depot/patch_depot/hpux_800_11.31.depot**

3. Install the patch with *swinstall*. The system will reboot automatically, if necessary:

    # **swinstall –s /depot/patch_depot/hpux_800_11.31.depot**

11.3.4   Listing Installed Patch Bundles

Listing installed patch bundles displays all patch bundles currently installed on the system. Use the *swlist* command to list them. The following output only shows the patch bundles installed.

    # **swlist**
    BUNDLE   B.2008.04.15   Patch Bundle
    FEATURE11i   B.11.31.0709.312   Feature Enablement Patches for HP-UX 11i v3, September 2007
    HWEnable11i B.11.31.0709.312   Hardware Enablement Patches for HP-UX 11i v3, Septemb 2007
    OnlineDiag   B.11.31.02.05   HPUX 11.31 Support Tools Bundle, Sep 2007
    QPKBASE   B.11.31.0709.312a Base Quality Pack Bundle for HP-UX 11i v3, September 2007

11.3.5   Acquiring Patch Bundles

Patch depots may be obtained from one of the following sources:

✓ IT Resource Center (ITRC) website at *www.itrc.hp.com*
✓ ITRC ftp site at *ftp://ftp.itrc.hp.com*
✓ Software depot at *software.hp.com*
✓ HP Support Plus DVD

You may download standard HP-UX patch bundles that provide recommended set of system patches. Table 11-1 lists standard bundles available for HP-UX 11i v3.

Patch Bundles for HP-UX 11i v3	Description
QPKBASE	Contains defect fixes for core OS.
QPKAPPS	Contains defect fixes for add-on applications.
FEATURE11i	Contains feature enablement patches and core defect fixes uncovered by new product features.
HWEnable11i	Contains hardware enablement patches.

Table 11-1 Standard Patch Bundles

Apply the first three bundles on new system installs. You should apply updated bundles periodically to keep the patch level current. If you are adding new hardware to the system for which support is not already present in the OE, you need to install Hardware Enablement patch bundle as well. In case you are unsure which bundles to load, installing all of them is not a bad idea.

Follow the procedure below to obtain patch bundles from *www.itrc.hp.com*:

1. Go to *www.itrc.hp.com*.
2. Under "maintenance and support for hp products", click "standard patch bundles – find patch bundles".
3. Go to "HP-UX patch bundles".
4. Click a release name for HP-UX 11.31.

5. Click a bundle to download and then "add to selected patch list".
6. Click "download selected" and then "Expand to view additional download options".
7. Choose one of the file formats – zip, gzip or tar.
8. Click "download" to get the bundle.

This method automatically selects and downloads dependent patches as well.

You can also acquire patch bundles from *ftp://ftp.itrc.hp.com*. With this method you will have to determine and download dependent patches manually.

1. Open up a browser window and type *ftp://ftp/itrc.hp.com*.
2. Go to "patch_bundles".
3. Go to "hp-ux". You will see several directories there. Hardware Enablement patches are located in the HWE directory, Quality patches in the QUALITYPACK directory, and Bundle11i and Feature11i in the SPECIAL directory.
4. Go to the desired directory and download the required bundle. Also download corresponding text file.

You may also download patch bundles by running the *ftp* command at the command line as well. Login as *anonymous* user and supply your email as password. This method does not automatically select any dependent patches either.

11.3.6 Installing Patch Bundles

Suppose the downloaded patch bundle name is *hpux_800_11.31.tar* and was downloaded from ITRC. Follow the steps below to install it:

1. Move the bundle file to the directory where you want it unpacked:

   # **mkdir /depot/patch_depot**
   # **mv hpux_800_11.31.tar /depot/patch_depot**
   # **cd /depot/patch_depot**

2. Untar the depot file:

   # **tar –xvf hpux_800_11.31.tar**

   Run "**unzip hpux_800_11.31.zip**" if the patch file was in zip format.
   Run "**gunzip hpux_800_11.31.tgz | tar xvf –**" if the patch file was in gzip format.

   Some files will be generated by the untar operation. A readme file that contains details about the bundle, a *create_depot_hpux.11.31* script and a file with *.depot* extension. The *.depot* file is the file that holds the actual patch bundle software.

3. Execute the *create_depot_hpux.11.31* script. This script performs unshar function (using the *sh* command) on all the patches included in the bundle and then *swcopy* and *swverify* operations. It creates a directory called *depot* where it copies the depot contents.

```
# ./create_depot_hpux.11.31
DEPOT: /softdepot/depot
BUNDLE: BUNDLE
TITLE: Patch Bundle
UNSHAR: y
PSF: depot.psf
Expanding patch shar files...
x - PHCO_36032.text
x - PHCO_36032.depot [non-ascii]
. . . . . . . .
======= 04/10/08 12:09:11 EDT  END swverify SESSION (non-interactive)
     (jobid=hp02-0154)
```

Install the bundle using *swinstall*. The system will reboot automatically, if necessary.

 # swinstall –s /depot/patch_depot/depot

Suppose the downloaded patch bundle, after unpacking, is *hpux_800_11.31.depot* and was downloaded using one of the ftp methods. Follow the steps below to install it:

1. Move the depot file to the directory where you wish to register it:

    # mkdir /depot/patch_depot
    # mv hpux_800_11.31.depot /depot/patch_depot
    # cd /depot/patch_depot

2. Register the depot:

    # swreg –l depot /depot/patch_depot/hpux_800_11.31.depot

3. Install the bundle with *swinstall*. The system will reboot automatically, if necessary:

    # swinstall –s /depot/patch_depot/hpux_800_11.31.depot

11.3.7   Installing Patches from DVD

To install patches located on a DVD, you need to mount the DVD and then register the desired depot using *swreg*. The following example assumes that the DVD is mounted on */dvdrom*:

 # swreg –l depot /dvdrom
 # swinstall –s /dvdrom

It is a good idea to *swcopy* all bundles from a DVD to a directory depot so you do not have to mount, unmount and remount the DVD repeatedly.

11.3.8   Installing Patches from Tape

The following example assumes that the device file for tape is */dev/rtape/tape1_BEST* (or */dev/rmt/0m*):

 # swinstall –s /dev/rtape/tape1_BEST

It is a good idea to *swcopy* all bundles from a tape to a directory depot so you do not have to load and unload the tape repeatedly.

11.3.9   Verifying a Patch and Patch Bundle

After completing the installation of a patch or patch bundle, you may wish to verify if it is loaded successfully. Use the *swverify* command for this purpose.

To verify an individual patch, specify its name with *swverify*:

 # swverify PHCO_36032
```
======= 04/15/08 08:29:31 EDT  BEGIN swverify SESSION
    (non-interactive) (jobid=hp01-0017)
  * Session started for user "root@hp01".
  * Beginning Selection
  * Target connection succeeded for "hp01:/".
  * Software selections:
      PHCO_36032.UX-CORE,l=/,r=1.0,a=HP-UX_B.11.31_IA/PA,v=HP,fr=1.0,fa=HP-
UX_B.11.31_IA/PA
    * Selection succeeded.
    * Beginning Analysis
    * Session selections have been saved in the file "/.sw/sessions/swverify.last".
    * The analysis phase succeeded for "hp01:/".
    * Verification succeeded.
NOTE:    More information may be found in the agent logfile using the
    command "swjob -a log hp01-0017 @ hp01:/".
======= 04/15/08 08:29:34 EDT  END swverify SESSION (non-interactive)
    (jobid=hp01-0017)
```

To verify a patch bundle, specify its name with *swverify*:

 # swverify BUNDLE
```
======= 04/15/08 08:43:04 EDT  BEGIN swverify SESSION
    (non-interactive) (jobid=hp01-0020)
  * Session started for user "root@hp01".
  * Beginning Selection
  * Target connection succeeded for "hp01:/".
  * Software selections:
      BUNDLE,r=B.2008.04.15,a=HP-UX_B.11.00_32/64,v=HP
      PHCO_36032.UX-CORE,l=/,r=1.0,a=HP-UX_B.11.31_IA/PA,v=HP,fr=1.0,fa=HP-
UX_B.11.31_IA/PA
```

* Selection succeeded.
 * Beginning Analysis
 * Session selections have been saved in the file "/.sw/sessions/swverify.last".
 * The analysis phase succeeded for "hp01:/".
 * Verification succeeded.
NOTE: More information may be found in the agent logfile using the
    command "swjob -a log hp01-0020 @ hp01:/".
======= 04/15/08 08:43:07 EDT END swverify SESSION (non-interactive)
    (jobid=hp01-0020)

Also, you can run the *check_patches* command anytime, or after the patches have been installed, to determine if there are any issues with them. This command creates a report and stores it in */tmp/check_patches.report* file for review.

> # **check_patches**
> Obtaining information on installed patches
> Checking for invalid patches
> Checking object module checksums for active patch fileset   68 of   68
> Checking patch filesets for active patch   43 of   43
> Checking state for patch fileset   68 of   68
> Checking patch_state for patch fileset   68 of   68
> Running swverify on all patch filesets, this may take several minutes
> RESULT: No problems found, review /tmp/check_patches.report for details.

11.3.10   Rolling Back (Removing) a Patch

In the event that an installed patch is not wanted or did not solve the problem for which it was installed, the patch can be safely removed and the system can be restored to its pre-patched state. This process is known as *patch rollback*. By default, the files being replaced with a patch install are saved, unless you specifically tell *swinstall* not to save them. Patch rollback is only possible if the replaced files were saved.

The *swremove* command is used to rollback a patch. Basically, it removes the specified patch and restores the original files. To rollback/remove PHCO_36250, do the following:

> # **swremove PHCO_360250**
> ======= 04/15/08 08:47:56 EDT BEGIN swremove SESSION
>   (non-interactive) (jobid=hp01-0023)
> * Session started for user "root@hp01".
> * Beginning Selection
> * Target connection succeeded for "hp01:/".
> * Software selections:
> . . . .
> * Selection succeeded.
> * Beginning Analysis
> * Session selections have been saved in the file "/.sw/sessions/swremove.last".
> * The analysis phase succeeded for "hp01:/".
> * Analysis succeeded.
> * Beginning Execution

```
      * The execution phase succeeded for "hp01:/".
      * Execution succeeded.
NOTE:    More information may be found in the agent logfile using the
      command "swjob -a log hp01-0023 @ hp01:/".
======= 04/15/08 08:48:05 EDT  END swremove SESSION (non-interactive)
      (jobid=hp01-0023)
```

11.3.11   Committing a Patch

By default, as you know, when a patch is installed, all files it replaces are saved. If you ever want to remove the saved files to claim disk space, you will need to commit the patch. After a patch is committed, you cannot roll it back.

Execute the *swmodify* command to commit a patch. To commit PHCO_36569, do the following:

> **# swmodify –x patch_commit=true PHCO_36569**

To commit all superseded patches and remove files associated with them, use the *cleanup* command. With –c option, you can specify the number of times the patches (to be committed) have been superseded. The command saves log information in */var/adm/cleanup.log* file.

```
# cleanup –c 1
### Cleanup program started at 04/15/08  08:50:10
Commit patches superseded at least 1 time(s) on 'hp01'.
Obtaining superseded patch information...done.
No non-committed patches superseded at least 1 time(s) are present.
All information has been logged to /var/adm/cleanup.log.
### Cleanup program completed at 04/15/08  08:50:10
```

The *cleanup* utility can also be used to remove superseded patches from a patch depot. Execute the following on */depot/patch_depot* patch depot:

> **# cleanup –d /depot/patch_depot**

11.4   The Patch Assessment Tool

The *patch assessment tool* allows you to create custom patch bundle for the system. The tool helps analyze and select missing patches. Follow steps below to use this tool:

1. Go to *http://itrc.hp.com*.
2. Under "maintenance and support for hp products", click "patch database".
3. Click "run a patch assessment".
4. Click "upload new system information".
5. Download the *swainv* script.
6. Add execute permission to the *swainv* script.
7. Execute *swainv* on the system where you wish to perform the assessment. This script will collect current patch information and puts it in a file called *inventory.xml*:

```
# ./swainv.txt
Copyright (c) Hewlett-Packard 2005-2006.  All rights reserved.
  ./swainv.txt revision: 3.47
This script lists the patches, products, bundles, and filesets found in a system or depot and packages
the information in a file for transfer to the ITRC or the Response Center.
    * Listing Filesets
    * Listing Products
    * Listing Bundles
    * Inventory written to ./inventory.xml
# ll inventory.xml
-rw-r--r--  1 root      sys         616474 Apr 15 08:55 inventory.xml
```

8. Click "browse" and select the *inventory.xml* file.
9. Click "submit" to upload the file.
10. You will see three options on the next screen – create a new assessment profile, import an exported assessment profile or choose hprecommended. Many administrators prefer to use "hprecommended" profile. If you wish to create a new assessment profile, click "create a new assessment profile" and fill out the form. If you have previously created a profile and is sitting on the system, click "import an exported assessment profile" and upload the profile. Choose "hprecommended" for this demonstration.
11. Click "display candidate patches". This will generate the patch assessment result and display patches recommended for the system.
12. Review listed patches and place a check mark beside the ones you need and click "add to selected patch list". Alternatively, you can click "select all" and then "add to selected patch list" to choose all patches.
13. Additional patches needed to satisfy dependencies for the selected patches appear on the next page automatically.
14. Click "download selected".
15. Choose a file format – zip, gzip or tar – and click "download" to download all patches as a single bundle in the specified format.

Follow the patch bundle installation method discussed earlier to install this bundle.

11.5   The Security Patch Check Tool

The *security patch check* tool allows you to check the system against a catalog file containing a list of all recommended and required patches that the system should have in order for it to operate securely. This tool generates a report listing missing patches and actions to take. You need to download this tool from *software.hp.com* → "Security and manageability" and install it using *swinstall* as explained earlier in this and the previous chapter.

Execute the following to automatically download the security catalog from ITRC and compare security related patches on the system against a list of patches provided in the security catalog. This command assumes that you have internet connectivitiy in place.

    # /opt/sec_mgmt/spc/bin/security_patch_check –d –r

Alternatively, follow the steps below to update patches on the system if it does not have direct access to the internet:

1. Download the security catalog from *ftp://ftp.itrc.hp.com/export/patches/security_catalog2.gz*.
2. Move *security_catalog2.gz* file into */tmp*.
3. Uncompress the catalog file:

    # **gunzip /tmp/security_catalog2.gz**

4. Run the *security_patch_check* command to check what security patches are missing on the system:

    # **/opt/sec_mgmt/spc/bin/security_patch_check –d –c /tmp/security_catalog2**
    . . . .
    *** BEGINNING OF SECURITY PATCH CHECK REPORT ***
    Report generated by: /opt/sec_mgmt/spc/bin/security_patch_check.pl, run as root
    Analyzed localhost (HP-UX 11.31) from hp01
    Security catalog: /tmp/security_catalog2
    Security catalog created on: Tue Apr 15 01:32:18 2008
    Time of analysis: Tue Apr 15 01:53:20 2008
    List of recommended actions for most secure system:
    . . . .
    *** END OF REPORT ***
    NOTE: Security bulletins can be found ordered by Document ID at
    http://www.itrc.hp.com/service/cki/secBullArchive.do

A report similar to the above will be generated and recommended actions will be provided. Follow the recommendations to obtain patches and apply them on the system to bring it up to the latest security patch level.

11.6   HP-UX Software Assistant (SWA)

The HP-UX *software assistant* product is a software upgrade to patch assessment and security patch check tools. SWA offers the functionalities of both tools into one for ease of analyzing systems, generating reports and creating depots.

SWA performs a number of checks on the system or a depot for patch warnings, critical defects, security bulletins and missing patches. SWA downloads any recommended patches or patch bundles for security vulnerabilities identified in the analysis performed and creates a depot for installation.

SWA can be integrated with HP SIM for central management.

11.6.1   SWA Commands

Table 11-2 lists and explains key SWA administration commands.

Command	Description
swa	Analyzes a system or depot and generates reports for recommended actions.
swa-report	Reports software and security issues, vulnerabilities and resolutions. May also be run as "*swa report*".

Command	Description
swa-get	Downloads patches in a depot format to resolve issues identified by *swa-report*. May also be run as "*swa get*".
swa-step	Executes *swa* step by step. May also be run as "*swa step*".
swa-clean	Removes any files created by *swa* command. May also be run as "*swa clean*".

Table 11-2 SWA Commands

11.6.2   Downloading and Installing SWA

If not already installed on the system, you can download HP-UX SWA from *http://software.hp.com* → "Security and manageability", move it to */var/tmp* directory and install using the *swinstall* command:

 # swinstall –s /var/tmp/SwAssistant_C.01.04_HP-UX_11iv2+v3_IA_PA.depot

11.6.3   Using SWA

If your HP-UX system has access to the internet, execute the following command to automatically download the security catalog from ITRC and compare patches on the system against a list of patches in the security catalog:

 # swa report

Follow the steps below to update patches on the system if the system does not have access to the internet:

1. Download the security catalog from *https://ftp.itrc.hp.com/wpsl/bin/doc.pl/screen=wpslDownloadPatch/swa_catalog.xml.gz?PatchName=/export/patches/swa_catalog.xml.gz.*
2. Move the catalog file *swa_catalog.xml.gz* into */tmp*.
3. Uncompress it:

   # gunzip /tmp/swa_catalog.xml.gz

4. Run the *swa* command to generate a report against the catalog file:

   # swa report –x catalog=/tmp/swa_catalog.xml
   ```
   ======= 04/15/08 09:29:48 EDT  BEGIN Report on Issues and New Software (user=root)
       (jobid=hp01)
     * Gathering Inventory
     * Using existing inventory for host "hp01"
     * Getting Catalog of Recommended Actions and Software
     * Using existing local catalog file
     * Performing Analysis
     * Generating Reports
   NOTE:   See HTML-formatted report "/.swa/report/swa_report.html"
               Software Assistant Actions Summary Report
   ```

ASSESSMENT PROFILE
Catalog Information
  Catalog File: /tmp/swa_catalog.xml
  Catalog Date: 15 April 2008 06:02:16 EDT
Inventory Source
  Name: hp01
  OS: HP-UX B.11.31
  Model: 9000/800/rp7410
  Inventory File: /.swa/cache/swa_inventory_2686927786.xml
  Inventory Date: 15 April 2008 09:13:06 EDT
Analysis Information
  Analysis File: /.swa/cache/swa_analysis.xml
  Analysis Date: 15 April 2008 09:30:01 EDT
  Ignore File(s): /.swa/ignore
  Issues Ignored: 0
  Selected Analyzers
    QPK: latest Quality Pack patch bundle
    SEC: security bulletins
    PCW: patches with critical warnings

RECOMMENDED ACTIONS
Patch Bundles
  The following bundles are recommended by HP. The patches delivered in these patch bundles
may include fixes for patches not listed in this report. If you will not install the patch bundle(s)
listed here, please re-run the analysis without the "QPK" analyzer and generate a new report to
obtain a full list of patches.

  Bundle   Revision   Description
  ------   --------   -----------
  QPK1131   B.11.31.0803.318a Quality Pack Depot for 11i v3, March 2008
    With bundle QPKBASE revision B.11.31.0803.318a
    With bundle QPKBASE revision B.11.31.0803.318a

Patches
  See detail or html report for more links to patch details such as special installation instructions,
patch quality rating, patch reboot, and other dependencies.

  Patch ID   Date   Description
  --------   ----   -----------
  PHNE_36281 2008-02-25 cumulative ARPA Transport patch
  PHNE_36449 2007-06-08 rpc.yppasswdd patch
  PHNE_36574 2008-02-25 STREAMS Cumulative Patch
  PHSS_36871 2007-08-21 HP System Management Homepage A.2.2.6.2
  PHSS_37226 2008-01-08 X Font Server Patch

Manual Actions
  See detail or html report for more information on each action.
  The following Detection Confidence (DC) levels are used:
    D - Detection confidence is "definite" and based on specific revisions of installed software.

R - Detection confidence is "relevant" and based on installed software
but can not determine if action has been taken.
U - Detection confidence is "unknown" and based only on operating system version.

```
Issue    DC Date      Description
-----    -- ----      -----------
02156r4  D  2008-01-07 For Tbird, install revision 2.0.0.9 or subsequent
02235r1  D  2007-08-07 For HPOvLcore, install revision 3.10.040 or subsequent
02249r3  D  2008-02-11 For Ignite-UX, install revision C.7.3.148 or subsequent
02249r3  D  2008-02-11 For DRD, install revision A.3.0.0 or subsequent
02251r3  D  2007-11-26 For NameService, install revision C.9.3.2.1.0 or subsequent
02262r1  D  2007-10-02 For hpuxwsAPACHE, restart Apache
02262r1  D  2007-10-02 For hpuxwsAPACHE, install revision B.2.0.59.00 or subsequent
02277r1  D  2007-10-15 For openssl, install revision A.00.09.08g.001 or subsequent
02284r4  D  2007-12-19 For Jdk14, install revision 1.4.2.17.00 or subsequent
02284r4  D  2007-12-19 For Jpi14, install revision 1.4.2.17.00 or subsequent
02284r4  D  2007-12-19 For Jre14, install revision 1.4.2.17.00 or subsequent
02284r4  D  2007-12-19 For Jdk15, install revision 1.5.0.11 or subsequent
02284r4  D  2007-12-19 For Jre15, install revision 1.5.0.11 or subsequent
02316r1  D  2008-03-08 For CIFS-Server, install revision A.02.03.03 or subsequent
02309r1  U  2008-02-06 Upgrade Select Identity software if in use.
02317r1  U  2008-04-01 Upgrade Select Identity software if in use.
```

SEE ALSO
swa "issue", "detail", and "html" reports, swa-report(1m).
* Gathering Inventory succeeded with 1 warning.
======== 04/15/08 09:30:05 EDT END Report on Issues and New Software succeeded with 1
warning. (user=root) (jobid=hp01)
NOTE: More information may be found in the Software Assistant logfile "/var/opt/swa/swa.log".

A report is generated and saved in *$HOME/.swa/report/swa_report.html* file.

5. Re-run the *swa* command to download the identified patches into the specified directory:

 # swa get –t /var/depot
```
======== 04/15/08 09:53:28 EDT  BEGIN Get New Software From HP (user=root) (jobid=hp01)
* Analyzing Required Disk Space
* System Information
Name: hp01
OS: HP-UX 11.31
Model: 9000/800/rp7410
Inventory File: /.swa/cache/swa_inventory_2686927786.xml
Inventory Date: 15 April 2008 09:13:06 EDT
* Analysis Information
Analysis File: //.swa/cache/swa_analysis.xml
Analysis Date: 15 April 2008 09:50:36 EDT
Catalog: /tmp/swa_catalog.xml
Catalog Date: 15 April 2008 06:02:16 EDT
Ignore File: /.swa/ignore
```

     * Selected Analyzers
      QPK - latest quality pack bundle
      SEC - security bulletins
      PCW - patches with critical warnings
     * Software Cache
      /var/opt/swa/cache
     * Target Depot
      /var/depot
     * Downloading Software from HP to Local Cache
NOTE: Estimated total download size: 58141066 bytes.
     * Downloading PHNE_36449 (1 of 6)
     * Download complete: 107kB
     * Downloading PHSS_37226 (2 of 6)
     * Download complete: 415kB

. . . .
======= 04/15/08 09:55:42 EDT END Get New Software From HP failed with 6 errors.
    (user=root) (jobid=hp01)
NOTE: More information may be found in the Software Assistant logfile "/var/opt/swa/swa.log".

6.   Follow the procedure to install patches using *swinstall* as explained earlier in this chapter.

Summary

Patches are installed on a system to fix existing problems and reduce the risk of potential problems. Patches may also bring new functionality to your system. Enabling new hardware and update system firmware are also typically done via patches. You built in this chapter an understanding of standard HP patch naming convention. You understood patch attributes such as suppression, dependency, ratings, state, status, category tags, ancestry, and critical and non-critical.

You saw how individual patches and patch bundles could be downloaded using different methods and applied to a system. You also saw how to list, verify, roll back and commit patches.

Finally, you looked at patch assessment and security patch check tools. The former enabled you to create custom patch bundle for your system and the latter used for analyzing whether required security patches were installed on your system. You were introduced to software assistant intended to replace both patch assessment and security patch check tools. You looked at how to use it.

## 12

Users and Groups

This chapter covers the following major topics:

- ✓ Understand /etc/passwd and /etc/group user authentication files
- ✓ Verify /etc/passwd and /etc/group file consistency
- ✓ Lock /etc/passwd file while editing
- ✓ Administer user accounts including creating, modifying, disabling, enabling and deleting them
- ✓ Display successful and unsuccessful user login attempts history
- ✓ Display currently logged in users
- ✓ Display and set user limits
- ✓ Administer group accounts including creating, modifying and deleting them
- ✓ Assign a user membership to multiple groups
- ✓ User login process & initialization files

12.1 Why Create Users and Groups

In order for an authorized person to gain access to the system, a unique *username* (a.k.a. *login name*) must be assigned and a user account must be created on the system. This user is assigned membership to one or more groups. Members of the same group have the same access rights on files and directories. Other users and members of other groups may or may not be given access to those files.

User account information is stored in two files – */etc/passwd* and */etc/group*. These files are updated when a user account is created, modified or removed. The same files are referenced when a user attempts to login to the system and hence referred to as user authentication files. The following sub-sections discuss the files in detail.

12.1.1 User Authentication – The /etc/passwd File

The */etc/passwd* file contains vital user login information. Each line entry in the file contains information about one user account. There are seven fields per line entry separated by the colon (:) character. A sample entry from */etc/passwd* file is displayed in Figure 12-1.

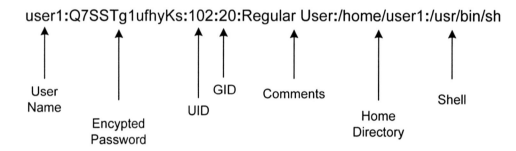

Figure 12-1 User Authentication File – /etc/passwd

Here is what is stored in each field:

- ✓ The first field contains a login name that a user uses to login to the system. It should not exceed eight characters in length and must start with a letter. Usernames up to 255 characters are supported.
- ✓ The second field contains 13 alphanumeric characters. These characters hold a user password in encrypted form. If this field is empty, it indicates that a password has not been assigned.
- ✓ The third field holds a unique number between 0 and approximately 2 billion. This number is known as *User ID* (UID). User ID 0 is reserved for the *root* user, UIDs between 1 and 99 are typically reserved for system accounts and UIDs 100 and up are used for all other users.
- ✓ The fourth field holds a number referred to as *Group ID* (GID). This number corresponds with a group entry in the */etc/group* file. The GID defined here represents a user's primary group.
- ✓ The fifth field optionally contains general comments about a user that may include the user's name, phone number and location. This data may be viewed using commands such as *finger*.

✓ The sixth field defines absolute path to the user home directory. A *home* directory is the location where a user is placed after logging in to a system, and is typically used to store a user's personal files.
✓ The last field contains absolute path of the shell file that the user will be using as his primary shell after logging in. Common shells are POSIX (*/sbin/sh* or */usr/bin/sh*), Korn (*/usr/bin/ksh*) and C (*/usr/bin/csh*).

A sample */etc/passwd* file is shown below:

```
# cat /etc/passwd
root:/af/4dEOdgkpY:0:3::/:/sbin/sh
daemon:*:1:5::/:/sbin/sh
bin:*:2:2::/usr/bin:/sbin/sh
sys:*:3:3::/:
adm:*:4:4::/var/adm:/sbin/sh
uucp:*:5:3::/var/spool/uucppublic:/usr/lbin/uucp/uucico
lp:*:9:7::/var/spool/lp:/sbin/sh
nuucp:*:11:11::/var/spool/uucppublic:/usr/lbin/uucp/uucico
hpdb:*:27:1:ALLBASE:/:/sbin/sh
nobody:*:-2:-2::/:
www:*:30:1::/:
smbnull:*:101:101:DO NOT USE OR DELETE - needed by Samba:/var/opt/samba/nologin:/bin/false
ids:*:102:102:HP-UX Host IDS Administrator:/opt/ids/home:/sbin/sh
hpsmdb:*:103:20::/home/hpsmdb:/sbin/sh
sshd:*:104:103:sshd privsep:/var/empty:/bin/false
tftp:*:105:104:Trivial FTP user:/home/tftp:/usr/bin/false
sfmdb:*:106:20::/home/sfmdb:/sbin/sh
iwww:*:107:1::/home/iwww:/sbin/sh
owww:*:108:1::/home/owww:/sbin/sh
hpsmh:*:109:106:System Management Homepage:/var/opt/hpsmh:/sbin/sh
```

The above accounts are standard, and created automatically during HP-UX installation.

 Permissions on */etc/passwd* should be 444 and the file must be owned by the *root* user.

12.1.2   User Authentication – The /etc/group File

The */etc/group* file contains group information. Each row in the file contains one group entry. Each user is assigned at least one group, which is referred to as the user's primary group. There are four fields per line entry and are separated by the colon (:) character. A sample entry from */etc/group* file is exhibited in Figure 12-2.

Here is what is stored in each field:

✓ The first field contains a unique group name. It should not be more than eight characters in length and must start with an alphabet. Group names up to 255 characters are supported.
✓ The second field is not typically used and is left blank. It may, however, contain an encrypted group-level password (copied and pasted from */etc/passwd* file). You may implement this on

---

a group if you want non-members to be able to change their group membership to this group using the *newgrp* command. The non-members will have to enter the correct password to accomplish this.

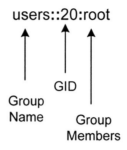

Figure 12-2 User Authentication File – /etc/group

✓ The third field defines the GID, which is placed in the GID field of the */etc/passwd* file. Normally, groups are created with GIDs starting at 100. Several users can be members of one single group. Similarly, one user can be a member of several groups.

✓ The last field holds usernames that belong to the group. Note that a user's primary group is defined in the */etc/passwd* file, and not here.

A sample */etc/group* file is shown below:

```
# cat /etc/group
root::0:root
other::1:root,hpdb
bin::2:root,bin
sys::3:root,uucp
adm::4:root,adm
daemon::5:root,daemon
mail::6:root
lp::7:root,lp
tty::10:
nuucp::11:nuucp
users::20:root
nogroup:*:-2:
smbnull::101:
ids::102:
sshd::103:
tftp::104:
hpsmc::105:
hpsmh::106:
```

All these group accounts are standard and created automatically during HP-UX installation.

 Permissions on the */etc/group* file should be 444 and the file must be owned by the *bin* user.

12.1.3   Verifying /etc/passwd and /etc/group File Consistency

Sometimes inconsistencies occur in */etc/passwd* and */etc/group* files. To check if the information in */etc/passwd* is valid and not inconsistent, use the *pwck* command. This command checks and validates each field in each row, and reports any inconsistencies.

To verify if the information in */etc/group* is valid and not inconsistent, use the *grpck* command. This command checks and validates each field in each row, and reports whether a user belonging to a group is missing from the */etc/passwd* file.

12.1.4   Locking /etc/passwd File

Although not recommended, periodically it is imperative to modify the */etc/passwd* file by hand using the vi editor. However, if another user attempts to change his password while */etc/passwd* is being edited, the end result is a successful password modification for the user and the */etc/passwd* file is updated to reflect the change. Unfortunately, this change is lost when the file is saved.

To prevent such an unwanted situation from happening, use the *vipw* command to edit */etc/passwd*. This command copies */etc/passwd* to a temporary file called */etc/ptmp* and disables write access to */etc/passwd*. When another user attempts to change his password while you are editing the file, he is denied permission. When you quit *vipw*, some automatic checks are performed on */etc/ptmp* to validate contents. If no errors are encountered, this file is moved back to */etc/passwd*, otherwise, */etc/passwd* remains unchanged. The other user should now be able to change his password.

12.2   Managing User Accounts and Passwords

Managing user accounts and passwords involve creating, assigning passwords to, modifying, disabling, enabling and deleting user accounts. You can use commands or SMH to manage them.

12.2.1   Creating a User Account

Use the *useradd* command to create a user account. This command adds entries to the */etc/passwd* file and optionally to the */etc/group* file. It creates a home directory for the user and copies default user initialization files from the */etc/skel* skeleton directory into the user's home directory. There are several options available to the *useradd* command. Table 12-1 explains most of them.

Option	Description
–u	Indicates a unique user ID. If this option is not specified, the next available UID from */etc/passwd* file is used.
–o	Means that the new user can share the UID with an existing user. When two users share a UID, both get identical rights on each other's files. This should only be done in specific situations.
–g	Specifies the primary group. If this option is not used, the default group ID (20 for *users* group) is assigned.
–G	Specifies membership to up to 20 supplementary groups. If this option is not specified, no supplementary groups are added.
–d	Defines absolute path to the user home directory.
–m	Creates home directory if it does not already exist.
–s	Defines absolute path to the shell file.
–c	Defines useful comments or remarks.

Option	Description
–k	Specifies location of the skeleton directory (default is */etc/skel*), which contains user initialization template files. These files are copied to the user's home directory when it is created. Four files are available in this directory by default: *.profile* (for POSIX and Korn shell users) *.login* and *.cshrc* (for C shell users) *.exrc* (shell startup configuration script) You may customize these files and add more files to this directory so every new user gets all of them. Existing user home directories will not be affected by this change.
–f	Denotes maximum days of user inactivity before the user account is declared invalid.
–e	Specifies a date after which this account is automatically disabled.
login	Specifies a login name to be assigned to the new user account.

Table 12-1 *useradd* Command Options

Let us take a look at a few examples to understand the behavior of the command.

To create an account for user *aghori* with home directory */home/aghori*, shell */usr/bin/sh*, UID 111 and membership of *users* group, do the following. Also make certain that the default initialization scripts from the skeleton directory are copied.

 # useradd –u 111 –g users –m –d /home/aghori –k /etc/skel –s /usr/bin/sh aghori

Create an initial password for *aghori* with the *passwd* command:

 # passwd aghori
Changing password for aghori
New password:
Re-enter new password:
Passwd successfully changed

The user account is created and now you can use it to login to the system.

A password protects a user account from unauthorized access into the system. It is the user's responsibility to change his password periodically. The following password setting requirements should be kept in mind:

✓ Must be six to eight characters in length.
✓ Must start with a letter.
✓ Must contain at least one lowercase letter and one numeric or special character.
✓ Must differ from the login username.
✓ Must differ from the previous password by at least three characters.
✓ Can contain spaces and periods.

These requirements do not apply to *root* user password. In fact, *root* can have any or no password.

To modify a user's password, issue the *passwd* command. The following demonstrates how user *aghori* can change his password from the command line:

1. Enter the *passwd* command and press Enter.
2. Type the current password and press Enter.
3. Type a new password and press Enter.
4. Re-type the new password to verify and press Enter.

The *root* user has the privilege to change the password of any user on the system including its own. Also, when *root* changes a password, it is not prompted to enter the current user password.

To create an account for user *bghori* with all defaults, do the following. The default values for this user will be *users* (primary group), */home/bghori* (home directory), */sbin/sh* (shell) and no comments. Initialization files will be copied from */etc/skel* as well.

useradd bghori

To verify:

grep bghori /etc/passwd
bghori:*:112:20::/home/bghori:/sbin/sh

Create an initial password for this user with the *passwd* command.

In this example, you have used user defaults. These defaults are defined in the */etc/default/useradd* file. You can either view the file contents with the *cat* command or do the following to view them:

useradd –D
GROUPID 20
BASEDIR /home
SKEL   /etc/skel
SHELL   /sbin/sh
INACTIVE -1
EXPIRE
COMMENT
CHOWN_HOMEDIR no
CREAT_HOMEDIR no
ALLOW_DUP_UIDS no

You may modify these defaults. For example, do the following to change default base directory to */usr/home* so new user home directories are created in there:

useradd –D –b /usr/home

This modification is reflected in the */etc/default/useradd* file.

Let us use SMH to create a user account.

☞ Go to SMH → Accounts for Users and Groups → Local Users. Press a to add a user. A blank form will pop up as illustrated in Figure 12-3.

```
             SMH->Accounts for Users and Groups->Local Users->Add User
---------------------------------------------------------------------------
* Required Field

*Login Name                :  ▌_____

User ID                    :   (X) Next Available ID
                               ( ) Specify ID

Primary Group              :  users_____
[ Change Primary Group ]

Home Directory             :  default_____
(default : /home/{login-name})

Create Home Directory      : Yes ->

Start-Up Program Options   :   (X) Select Start-Up Program
                               ( ) Specify Start-Up Program
Start-Up Program           : /sbin/sh ->

Comments                   :  _____
                               (Real Name, Location, Phone, Home Phone)

Password Aging Options     : No Restrictions (Normal Behavior) ->

Account Status             :   (X) Enabled
                               ( ) Disabled

[ Add ] [ Preview ] [ Cancel ] [ Help ]
```

Figure 12-3 SMH – User Add

You need to input user information such as login name, UID, home directory, primary group name, shell, password options, etc. In "Password Aging Options", there are four sub-options. You need to choose one of them. Table 12-2 describes each of these options.

Password Aging Option	Description
No restrictions	You assign a password and communicate to the user. The user may change it later. This is the default option.
Force password change at next login	You assign an initial password and communicate to the user. The user must change it at the first login attempt.
Allow only superuser to change password	You assign a password and communicate to the user. Whenever the user wants his password changed, only you, as a system administrator, can change it.
Enable password aging	You assign a password and communicate to the user. With this option, you need to set additional parameters such as minimum time required between password changes. Refer to Chapter 36 "HP-UX Security" for details.

Table 12-2 SMH – User Add Password Aging Options

Press OK when the form is filled out. This will create a user account based on the data provided.

Alternatively, you can use the *ugweb* command to go directly to SMH → Accounts for Users and Groups.

12.2.2 Creating Multiple User Accounts in One Go

You can simultaneously add multiple user accounts with similar requirements. You need to create a template in SMH (or via *ugweb*). This template can then be used to add multiple accounts.

☞Go to SMH → Accounts for Users and Groups → Templates. Press a to add user template. See Figure 12-4. Supply a template title and description. Most other fields are the same as on the "Add User" form. You have two options – "first available" and "prompt for it" – for UID generation if you do not wish to specify one for each new individual user. You may also go to "Password Aging Options" to modify any password aging options. Press Add when you are done.

```
          SMH->Accounts for Users and Groups->User Templates->Add Template
--------------------------------------------------------------------------------
* Required Field

*Template Name       (Max Chars: 16)  :  |_____

Template Description  (Max Chars: 50)  :   _____

UID Generation Method                  :  (X) First Available
                                          ( ) Prompt for it

Primary Group Name                     :  users_____
[ Change Primary Group ]

Home Directory                         :  /home_____

Create Home Directory                  :  (X) Yes
                                          ( ) No

Start-Up Program Options               :  (X) Select Start-Up Program
                                          ( ) Specify Start-Up Program
Start-Up Program                       : /sbin/sh ->

Comment Settings                       :  (X) Prompt For It
                                          ( ) None

Account Status                         :  (X) Enable
                                          ( ) Disable

Account Password                       :  (X) Prompt for It
                                          ( ) Null

Account Aging Options                  : No Restrictions (Normal Behavior)  ->

Password Aging Options                 : No Restrictions (Normal Behavior)  ->

Security Options                       : Use System-Wide values for Security Attributes

[ Add ] [ Cancel ] [ Help ]
```

Figure 12-4 SMH – User Creation Template

To use the template to create several user accounts, do the following:

Go to SMH → Accounts for Users and Groups → Templates. Highlight the template you want to use and press s to "Apply/Select" it. The selected template will take effect right away and be used for all new user adds until you discard it from SMH → Accounts for Users and Groups → Templates by pressing d to "Discard Active User Template".

12.2.3   Modifying a User Account

You can modify a user account with the *usermod* command. Majority of the options that this command accepts are identical to that of *useradd* command's, except with –F, -i and –l options. These options are used to force the changes, inherit an existing home directory, and specify a new login name for the user, respectively.

Let us look at a couple of examples.

To modify user *aghori*'s login name to *aghori1*, home directory to */home/aghori1*, login shell to */usr/bin/csh*:

> **# usermod –m –d /home/aghori1 –s /usr/bin/csh –l aghori1 aghori**

To verify:

> **# grep aghori /etc/passwd**
> aghori1:fEncR9gI/GKQE:111:20::/home/aghori1:/usr/bin/csh

To modify user *bghori*'s UID and primary group using SMH (or *ugweb* command):

Go to SMH → Accounts for Users and Groups → Local Users. Highlight user *bghori* from the list and press m for "Modify User". Make appropriate changes and press Modify to alter it.

12.2.4   Checking Status of a User Account

Status of a user account such as account locks and any other abnormal conditions can be checked using the *userstat* command. This command prints nothing if the status is normal. The following command is run on user *aghori1*:

> **# userstat –u aghori1**

If you wish to check the status of all users listed in the */etc/passwd* file, use –a option with *userstat*.

12.2.5   Deactivating and Reactivating a User Account

Deactivating a user account locks the user account and the user will be unable to login to the system. Execute the *passwd* command for this purpose, which will replace the encrypted password field with an asterisk (*) character:

> **# passwd –l aghori1**
> **# grep aghori1 /etc/passwd**
> aghori1:*:111:20::/home/aghori1:/usr/bin/csh

Unless the *root* user runs the *passwd* command again with –d option and supply a new password to the user account, the account will remain locked.

To lock a user account through SMH (or *ugweb* command), follow the steps:

☞ Go to SMH → Accounts for Users and Groups → Local Users. Highlight the user you want to deactivate and press d to "disable" it.

To enable the user account through SMH (or *ugweb* command), follow the steps:

☞ Go to SMH → Accounts for Users and Groups → Local Users. Highlight the user you want to activate and press e to "enable" it.

12.2.6   Deleting a User Account

Removing a user account removes the user from the system. Execute the *userdel* command for this purpose. For example, the following will delete user *bghori* including the home directory:

   # userdel –r bghori

Do not specify the –r option if you do not want to remove user *bghori*'s home directory.

To remove a user account through SMH (or *ugweb* command), follow the steps:

☞ Go to SMH → Accounts for Users and Groups → Local Users. Highlight the user you wish to remove and press r to "remove" it.

12.2.7   Displaying Successful User Login Attempts History

The *last* command reports on successful user login attempts history and system reboots by reading the */var/adm/wtmps* file. This file keeps a record of all login and logout activities including the login time, duration a user stays logged in and the tty where the user session takes place. Consider the following examples.

To list all login and logout activities, type the *last* command without any arguments:

```
# last
root        pts/0          Tue  Apr 15 08:00        still logged in
root        console        Mon Apr 14 08:57 - 11:08(02:11)
reboot      system boot    Mon Apr 14 08:54        still logged in
reboot      system boot    Mon Apr 14 08:26 - 08:54(00:28)
root        pts/0          Mon Apr 14 07:59 - 08:21(00:22)
user1       console        Thu  Apr 10 11:41 - 14:19(02:37)
reboot      system boot    Thu  Apr 10 09:32 - 08:26(3+22:54)
WTMPS_FILE begins at Tue Apr  8 11:52:27
```

To list only system reboot information:

```
# last reboot
reboot       system boot     Mon Apr 14 08:54          still logged in
reboot       system boot     Mon  Apr 14 08:26 - 08:54(00:28)
reboot       system boot     Thu   Apr 10 09:32 - 08:26(3+22:54)
WTMPS_FILE  begins at Tue Apr  8 11:52:27
```

12.2.8   Displaying Unsuccessful User Login Attempts History

The *lastb* command reports on unsuccessful user login attempts history by reading the */var/adm/btmps* file. This file keeps a record of all unsuccessful login attempt activities including login name, time and the tty where the attempt is made. Consider the following example:

```
# lastb
user1        ssh:notty       Tue  Apr 15 14:21
user1        ssh:notty       Tue  Apr 15 14:21
root         console         Wed Apr  9 09:51
BTMPS_FILE  begins at Wed Apr  9 09:51:22
```

12.2.9   Displaying Currently Logged In Users

The *who* command looks into the */etc/utmps* file, which keeps a record of all currently logged in users, and lists them on the screen.

```
# who
root         pts/0           Apr 9 09:57
root         pts/1           Apr 9 11:54
```

12.2.10   Displaying and Setting User Limits

ulimit is used to display and set user process resource limits. When executed with –a option, it reports default limits for a user. Limits are categorized as either *soft* or *hard*. With the *ulimit* command, you can change the soft limits up to the maximum set by hard limits. The hard limits can be set only by *root*.

```
# ulimit –a
time(seconds)        unlimited
file(blocks)         unlimited
data(kbytes)         2015464
stack(kbytes)        8192
memory(kbytes)       unlimited
coredump(blocks)     4194303
```

To change the maximum file size, say from unlimited to 1KB, that a user can create:

```
# ulimit –f 1
```

Now try to create a file larger than 1KB in size. The system will not allow you to do that.

12.3　Managing Group Accounts

Managing group accounts involve creating, modifying and deleting groups. You can use commands or SMH to manage them.

12.3.1　Creating a Group Account

Use the *groupadd* command to add a new group account. There are only two options that this command supports: –g and –o. With –g, it assigns the specified GID to the group and with –o, it allows assigning a duplicate GID to the group.

To create a new group called *dba* with GID 111:

   # **groupadd –g 111 dba**

To verify:

   # **grep dba /etc/group**
   dba::111:

When more than one group share a GID, group members get identical rights on one another's files. This should be done only in specific situations.

Let us use SMH (or *ugweb* command) to create a group called *sysadmin*. Follow the steps:

☞ Go to SMH → Accounts for Users and Groups → Groups. Press a to "Add Group". Enter required information and press Add. Consult Figure 12-5.

```
                SMH->Accounts for Users and Groups->Groups->Add Group
-----------------------------------------------------------------------
* Required Field

*Group Name                        :  ▓_____

Group ID                           :   (X) Next Available ID
                                       ( ) Specify ID

Users with this Group as Secondary Group:   [ ] root
                                            [ ] daemon
                                            [ ] bin
                                            [ ] sys
                                       \/[ ] adm

[ Add ] [ Preview ] [ Cancel ] [ Help ]
```

Figure 12-5 SMH – Group Add

12.3.2　Modifying a Group Account

You can modify a group account with the *groupmod* command. Table 12-3 lists and explains key options that this command accepts.

Option	Description
–a	Assigns users specified with the –l option supplementary group membership of this group.
–d	Deletes users specified with the –l option from the supplementary group membership of this group.
–g	Specifies a new GID to be assigned to the group.
–l	Supplies usernames for –a, –m and –d options.
–m	Modifies the supplementary group membership of this group to users specified with the –l option.
–n	Specifies a new group name.
–o	Allows a duplicate GID.
group	Specifies the group name to be modified.

Table 12-3 *usermod* Command Options

To modify group *dba* to *dba1* and GID to 211:

   # **groupmod –g 211 –n dba1 dba**

To verify:

   # **grep dba /etc/group**
   dba1::211:

To do the same change using SMH (or *ugweb* command):

☞ Go to SMH → Accounts for Users and Groups → Groups. Highlight group *dba* from the list and press m for "Modify Group". Make appropriate changes and press Modify.

12.3.3   Deleting a Group Account

To delete a group account from the system use the *groupdel* command. For example, to delete group *dba1*, perform the following:

   # **groupdel dba1**

To do the same action using SMH (or *ugweb* command):

☞ Go to SMH → Accounts for Users and Groups → Groups. Highlight the group *dba1* from the list and press r for "Delete/Remove Group".

12.3.4   Assigning Multiple Group Memberships

A user can be a member of up to 20 groups at a time. One of the groups is primary and defined in the GID field for the user in the */etc/passwd* file. The primary group is also the default group for the user. All other groups are secondary (or supplementary) and the user is listed in the fourth field of each of the secondary groups in the */etc/group* file.

A user can alter his primary group membership temporarily by using the *newgrp* command. The *id* command can be used by the user anytime to view his primary and secondary group memberships. For example, if you are logged in as *aghori1* with UID 111, primary group *users* with GID 20, and you are also a member of *dba1* and *other* groups:

```
$ id
uid=111(aghori1) gid=20(users) groups=1(other),211(dba1)
$ newgrp dba1
$ id
uid=111(aghori1) gid=211(dba1) groups=20(users),1(other)
```

The *id* command above shows identification information including associated UID and GIDs. After running *newgrp*, the primary group is changed to *dba1*, which is reflected in the second output of the *id* command.

This change is temporary. You have two options to revert to the original primary group setting: log off and log back in or simply run the *newgrp* command without any options or arguments.

```
$ newgrp
$ id
uid=111(aghori1) gid=20(users) groups=1(other),211(dba1)
```

To permanently change the primary group membership, you need to modify the */etc/passwd* file.

12.4   User Login Process & Initialization Files

The user login process starts when you attempt to login to the system at the login prompt. The default login prompt displayed when you are at the system console is similar to:

```
GenericSysName [HP Release B.11.31] (see /etc/issue)
console login:
```

This login prompt message is stored in the */etc/issue* file. You can modify the text in the file to suit your needs.

The default login prompt displayed when you *telnet* into the system, *hp01* for example, is similar to:

```
HP-UX hp01 B.11.31 U 9000/800 (ta)
login:
```

When you type in a username, the system prompts for password. You enter a password. The system attempts to match the username with an entry in the */etc/passwd* file. If it finds a match, it begins to validate the password entered by comparing it with the corresponding encrypted password entry for the user in the */etc/passwd* file. If the password is validated, the system lets you in. If either the username or the password is incorrect or invalid, you are denied access into the system.

Upon successful user authentication, the contents of two files are displayed on the screen. These files are */etc/copyright* and */etc/motd*.

The *etc/copyright* file displays copyright information and the */etc/motd* (message of the day) file, if exists, displays its contents. You can put informational or warning messages in */etc/motd*. Sample */etc/copyright* file is displayed below:

cat /etc/copyright
(c)Copyright 1983-2006 Hewlett-Packard Development Company, L.P.
(c)Copyright 1979, 1980, 1983, 1985-1993 The Regents of the Univ. of California
(c)Copyright 1980, 1984, 1986 Novell, Inc.
. . . .

12.4.1   Initialization Files

In Chapter 05 "The Shells" you used local and environment variables. You modified default command prompt and added useful information to it. You created shortcuts using aliases. In other words you modified your default shell environment to customize according to your needs. The changes you made were lost when you logged off the system. What if you wanted to make those changes permanent so each time you logged in they were there for you?

Modifications to the default shell environment can be stored in text files called *initialization* files, which are executed after you are authenticated by the system and before getting the command prompt. There are two types of initialization files: system-wide and per-user.

The *system-wide* initialization files define general environment variables required by all or most users of the system. These files are maintained by the system administrator and can be modified to define any additional environment variables and customization needed by all system users. By default, these files define environment variables such as PATH, MANPATH, TZ and TERM by sourcing */etc/PATH*, */etc/MANPATH*, */etc/TIMEZONE* and */usr/share/lib/terminfo/** files, respectively. Sample */etc/PATH*, */etc/MANPATH* and */etc/TIMEZONE* files are shown below:

cat /etc/PATH
/usr/bin:/usr/ccs/bin:/usr/contrib/bin:/usr/contrib/Q4/bin:/opt/perl/bin:/opt/ipf/bin:/opt/nettladm/bin:/opt/fc
ms/bin:/opt/wbem/bin:/opt/wbem/sbin:/opt/rdma/bin:/opt/ssh/bin:/opt/mx/bin:/opt/graphics/common/bin:/
opt/atok/bin:/usr/bin/X11:/usr/contrib/bin/X11:/opt/sec_mgmt/bastille/bin:/opt/drd/bin:/opt/dsau/bin:/opt/d
sau/sbin:/opt/resmon/bin:/opt/firefox:/opt/gnome/bin:/opt/perf/bin:/opt/ignite/bin:/usr/contrib/kwdb/bin:/o
pt/mozilla:/var/opt/netscape/server7/shared/bin:/var/opt/netscape/server7/bin:/opt/perl_32/bin:/opt/perl_64
/bin:/opt/prm/bin:/usr/sbin/diag/contrib:/opt/sfm/bin:/opt/swm/bin:/opt/sec_mgmt/spc/bin:/opt/java1.4/jre/
bin:/opt/spb/bin:/opt/swa/bin:/opt/hpsmh/bin

cat /etc/MANPATH
/usr/share/man/%L:/usr/share/man:/usr/contrib/man/%L:/usr/contrib/man:/usr/local/man/%L:/usr/local/ma
n:/opt/ldapux/share/man/%L:/opt/ldapux/share/man:/opt/ipf/man:/opt/ldapux/ypldapd/man:/opt/samba/cfs
m_man:/opt/cifsclient/share/man:/opt/rdma/share/man:/opt/openssl/man:/opt/openssl/prngd/man:/opt/wbe
m/share/man:/opt/hpsmdb/pgsql/man:/opt/ssh/share/man:/opt/mx/share/man/%L:/opt/mx/share/man:/opt/g
raphics/common/man:/opt/amgr/man:/opt/amgr/man/%L:/opt/sec_mgmt/share/man:/usr/dt/share/man:/opt/
drd/share/man/%L:/opt/drd/share/man:/opt/dsau/man:/opt/resmon/share/man/%L:/opt/resmon/share/man:/
opt/gnome/man:/opt/perf/man/%L:/opt/perf/man:/opt/ignite/share/man/%L:/opt/ignite/share/man:/usr/cont
rib/kwdb/share/man:/opt/prm/man/%L:/opt/prm/man:/opt/sfmdb/pgsql/man:/opt/sfm/share/man:/opt/swm/
share/man/%L:/opt/swm/share/man:/opt/sec_mgmt/share/man/%L:/opt/spb/share/man:/opt/swa/share/man
/%L:/opt/swa/share/man

 # cat /etc/TIMEZONE
TZ=EST5EDT
export TZ

The *per-user* initialization files override or modify system defaults set by system-wide initialization files. These files may be customized by individual users to suit their needs.

You may create additional per-user initialization files in your home directory to define additional environment variables or set additional shell properties.

Table 12-4 lists default initialization files for the POSIX, Korn and C shells.

Shell	System-Wide	Per-User	When new shell is invoked
POSIX	*/etc/profile*	*$HOME/.profile*	
Korn	*/etc/profile*	*$HOME/.profile*	
C	*/etc/csh.login*	*$HOME/.login* *$HOME/.cshrc*	*$HOME/.cshrc*

Table 12-4 Shell Initialization Files

Table 12-4 shows that */etc/profile* is the system-wide initialization file for the POSIX and Korn shell users and */etc/csh.login* is for the C shell users. Excerpts from the two files are shown below:

 # cat /etc/profile
. . . .
Ignore HUP, INT, QUIT now.
    trap "" 1 2 3
# Set the default paths - Do NOT modify these.
# Modify the variables through /etc/PATH and /etc/MANPATH
PATH=/usr/bin:/usr/ccs/bin:/usr/contrib/bin:/usr/contrib/Q4/bin:/opt/perl/bin
    MANPATH=/usr/share/man:/usr/contrib/man:/usr/local/man

. . . .
 # cat /etc/csh.login
. . . .
    set path=(/usr/bin /usr/ccs/bin /usr/contrib/bin)
    if (-r /etc/PATH) then
        # Insure that $PATH includes /usr/bin . If /usr/bin is
        # present in /etc/PATH then $PATH is set to the contents
        # of /etc/PATH. Otherwise, add the contents of /etc/PATH
        # to the end of the default $PATH definition above.
        grep -q -e '^/usr/bin$' -e '^/usr/bin:' -e ':/usr/bin:'\
            -e ':/usr/bin$' /etc/PATH
        if ($status) then
            set path=($path `tr ":" " " </etc/PATH `)
        else
            set path=(`tr ":" " " </etc/PATH `)
        endif
    endif
. . . .

The per-user initialization file for the POSIX and Korn shell users is *.profile* and that for the C shell users are *.login* and *.cshrc*. Excerpts from the three files are shown below:

```
# cat $HOME/.profile
........
    if [ "$TERM" = "" ]
    then
            eval ` tset -s -Q -m ':?hp' `
    else
            eval ` tset -s -Q `
    fi
    stty erase "^H" kill "^U" intr "^C" eof "^D"
    stty hupcl ixon ixoff
    tabs
    echo
    echo "Value of TERM has been set to \"$TERM\". "
........
```

```
# cat $HOME/.login
........
stty erase "^H" kill "^U" intr "^C" eof "^D" susp "^Z" hupcl ixon ixoff tostop
tabs
# Set up shell environment:
set noclobber
set history=20
```

```
# cat $HOME/.cshrc
........
    set path=( $path )
# Set up C shell environment:
    if ( $?prompt ) then         # shell is interactive.
        set history=20           # previous commands to remember.
        set savehist=20          # number to save across sessions.
........
```

Summary

In this chapter you started off with building an understanding of */etc/passwd* and */etc/group* files. You looked at what the files contain, the syntax and how to verify their consistency. You looked at the way to lock the *passwd* file while editing so no other user can gain write access to it until you release the lock.

You studied user management including creating, modifying, disabling, enabling and deleting them. You learned about a few simple tools that allowed you to view history of successful and unsuccessful user login attempts, display currently logged in users, and view and display user limits. Likewise, you studied group management including creating, modifying and deleting group accounts, and assigning multiple group memberships to a user.

Finally, you learned what happened when a user entered a valid username and correct password, contents of which files were displayed, what initialization files were involved and so on.

## 13

Logical Volume Manager

This chapter covers the following major topics:

- ✓ LVM concepts, components and structure
- ✓ Manage disks including creating a physical volume, creating and displaying a volume group, creating and displaying a logical volume, extending a volume group, extending a logical volume, adjusting a physical volume size in a volume group, reducing a logical volume, removing a logical volume, reducing and removing a volume group, backing up and recovering LVM configuration, and converting legacy DSFs to persistent in a volume group
- ✓ LVM mirroring concepts and requirements
- ✓ Manage mirroring of boot and non-boot volume groups including creating, extending, reducing, synchronizing, splitting and merging mirrored logical volumes
- ✓ Mirroring and allocation policies
- ✓ Whole disk solution

13.1   Disk Partitioning Solutions

Data is stored on disk drives that are logically divided into partitions. A partition can exist on an entire disk or it can span multiple disks. Each partition may contain a file system, a raw data space, a swap space or a dump space.

A file system holds files and directories, a raw data space is used by databases and other applications, a swap space supplements physical memory on a system and a dump space stores memory image after a system crashes.

HP-UX offers three solutions for creating and managing disk partitions. These are referred to as the *Logical Volume Manager* (LVM) solution, the *Veritas Volume Manager* (VxVM) solution and the *whole disk* solution. All three can be used concurrently on a system, but cannot co-exist on the same physical disk.

In this chapter, LVM is covered at length and whole disk is briefly discussed, as it is not commonly used anymore. A discussion on VxVM is beyond the scope of this book.

13.2   The Logical Volume Manager (LVM) Solution

The LVM solution is widely used on HP-UX systems to manage disk storage. LVM enables you to accumulate spaces taken from one or more disks (called *physical volumes*) to form a large logical container (called *volume group*), which can then be divided into partitions (called *logical volumes*). Figure 13-1 demonstrates LVM components.

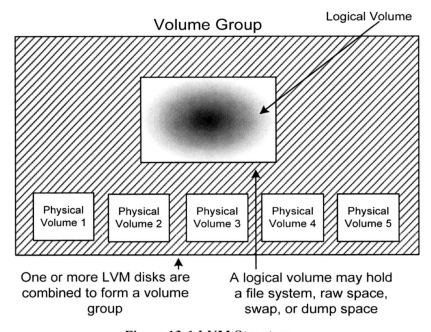

Figure 13-1 LVM Structure

13.2.1   LVM Features and Benefits

LVM offers the following features and benefits:

- ✓ Supports RAID 0, RAID 1 and RAID 0+1. RAID stands for *Redundant Array of Independent Disks*
- ✓ Supports online resizing of logical volumes
- ✓ Supports persistent DSFs
- ✓ Supports multipathing and load balancing
- ✓ Supports up to 3 copies of a logical volume (1 standard and 2 mirrored)

13.2.2   LVM Concepts and Components

LVM structure is made up of three key virtual objects called physical volume, volume group and logical volume. The concept and components are explained below.

Physical Volume

When a disk is brought under LVM control, it is known as a *physical volume* (PV). This process initializes the disk and creates LVM data structures on it. A disk must first be initialized before it can be used in a volume group.

A disk has block and character DSFs associated with it. When it is converted into a physical volume, it continues to use the same device naming convention that it used outside the LVM control. A block DSF such as */dev/disk/disk2* has a corresponding character DSF */dev/rdisk/disk2*. Notice an "r" in the character DSF that makes the difference.

Volume Group

A *volume group* (VG) is created when at least one physical volume is added to it. The maximum number of physical volumes supported in a volume group is 25, but the default is 16. The space from all physical volumes in a volume group is summed up to form a large pool of storage, which is then used to build one or more logical volumes. The default naming convention for volume groups is *vg00*, *vg01*, *vg02* and so on. You may, however, use any naming scheme you wish. For example, a volume group can be called *vgora102*, *vgtuxedo*, *vgsap* and so on.

Each volume group has a sub-directory under */dev* that corresponds to the volume group's name and contains a *group* device file for the volume group and device files for all logical volumes within that volume group. For example, */dev/vg01* is the sub-directory for *vg01*, */dev/vg02* is the sub-directory for *vg02* and so on. The following shows the group device file for the *vg00* volume group:

```
# ll /dev/vg00 | grep group
crw-r-----  1 root    sys      64 0x000000 Dec 16 07:01  group
```

On every system that uses LVM solution for disk management, the *vg00* volume group is special. This volume group contains the boot disk(s) and logical volumes that contain the entire HP-UX OE software. This volume group is also referred to as the *root volume group*.

By default, you can create as many as 256 volume groups in the system with each containing different application software.

Physical Extent

When a volume group is created, the physical volume added to it is divided into several smaller logical pieces known as *physical extents* (PEs). An extent is the smallest allocatable unit of space in LVM. The default PE size is 4MB, which can be set between 1MB and 256MB at volume group creation. This means a 4GB disk would contain approximately 1000 PEs. All physical volumes in a volume group must use the same PE size. You cannot have some physical volumes set to one PE size and the rest using different.

The following command displays physical extent size used in *vg00* volume group:

```
# vgdisplay vg00
--- Volume groups ---
VG Name                  /dev/vg00
VG Write Access          read/write
VG Status                available
Max LV                   255
Cur LV                   8
Open LV                  8
Max PV                   16
Cur PV                   1
Act PV                   1
Max PE per PV            2500
VGDA                     2
PE Size (Mbytes)         4
Total PE                 2169
Alloc PE                 2169
Free PE                  0
Total PVG                0
Total Spare PVs          0
Total Spare PVs in use   0
VG Version               1.0.0
```

Logical Volume

A volume group contains a pool of space taken from one or more physical volumes added to it. This volume group space is divided into one or more logical volumes.

A logical volume can be increased or decreased in size and can use space taken from several physical volumes inside the volume group. The minimum number of logical volumes that can be created in a volume group is 0 and the maximum 255 (which is also the default).

The default naming convention for logical volumes is *lvol1, lvol2, lvol3* and so on. You may, however, use any naming scheme you wish. For example, a logical volume can be called *system*, *undo*, *table* and so on. The following demonstrates device files for logical volumes in the *vg00* volume group. Notice that each logical volume has a block and a corresponding character DSF.

```
# ll /dev/vg00
brw-r-----   1   root   sys   64   0x000001   Dec 19 10:10   lvol1
brw-r-----   1   root   sys   64   0x000002   Dec 16 07:01   lvol2
brw-r-----   1   root   sys   64   0x000003   Dec 16 07:01   lvol3
```

brw-r-----	1	root	sys	64	0x000004	Dec 16 07:01	lvol4
brw-r-----	1	root	sys	64	0x000005	Dec 16 07:01	lvol5
brw-r-----	1	root	sys	64	0x000006	Dec 16 07:01	lvol6
brw-r-----	1	root	sys	64	0x000007	Dec 16 07:01	lvol7
brw-r-----	1	root	sys	64	0x000008	Dec 16 07:01	lvol8
crw-r-----	1	root	sys	64	0x000001	Dec 16 07:01	rlvol1
crw-r-----	1	root	sys	64	0x000002	Dec 16 07:01	rlvol2
crw-r-----	1	root	sys	64	0x000003	Dec 16 07:01	rlvol3
crw-r-----	1	root	sys	64	0x000004	Dec 16 07:01	rlvol4
crw-r-----	1	root	sys	64	0x000005	Dec 16 07:01	rlvol5
crw-r-----	1	root	sys	64	0x000006	Dec 16 07:01	rlvol6
crw-r-----	1	root	sys	64	0x000007	Dec 16 07:01	rlvol7
crw-r-----	1	root	sys	64	0x000008	Dec 16 07:01	rlvol8

Logical Extent

A logical volume is made up of extents called *logical extents* (LEs). Logical extents point to physical extents. The larger a logical volume size is, the more LEs it would contain.

The PE and LE sizes are usually kept the same within a volume group. A logical extent, however, can be smaller or larger than a physical extent. The default size for an LE is 4MB. The following command displays information about */dev/vg00/lvol1* logical volume. The output does not indicate the LE size, however, you can divide the LV Size by the Current LE count to get the LE size (which comes to 4MB in this example).

 # lvdisplay /dev/vg00/lvol1

--- Logical volumes ---	
LV Name	/dev/vg00/lvol1
VG Name	/dev/vg00
LV Permission	read/write
LV Status	available/syncd
Mirror copies	0
Consistency Recovery	MWC
Schedule	parallel
LV Size (Mbytes)	**300**
Current LE	**75**
Allocated PE	75
Stripes	0
Stripe Size (Kbytes)	0
Bad block	off
Allocation	strict
IO Timeout (Seconds)	default

13.2.3   LVM Major and Minor Numbers

Block and character DSFs are created for each logical volume in the volume group directory which the logical volume belongs to. These DSFs have major and minor numbers associated with them. The standard major number used by LVM is 64. The minor numbers may be assigned as follows:

```
0x000000, 0x000001, 0x000002 . . . . . . . .
0x010000, 0x010001, 0x010002 . . . . . . . .
0x020000, 0x020001, 0x020002 . . . . . . . .
```

The 0x in the minor number indicates that the number is in hexadecimal, the next two digits are unique to the *group* file of a volume group and hence to the volume group itself, and the last two digits represent a unique logical volume device file number within the volume group. 00 represents the *group* file, 01 represents the first LV, 02 represents the second LV and so on.

For example:

0x000000 represents the *group* file for the first volume group.
0x000001 represents the first logical volume device file for the first volume group.
0x000002 represents the second logical volume device file for the first volume group.
. . . .
0x010000 represents the *group* file for the second volume group.
0x010001 represents the first logical volume device file for the second volume group.
0x010002 represents the second logical volume device file for the second volume group.
. . . .

The following depicts LVM major and minor numbers for *vg00*. Notice that both block and character DSFs for a logical volume have identical minor number.

 # ll /dev/vg00

crw-r-----	1	root	sys	64	0x000000	Dec 16 07:01	group
brw-r-----	1	root	sys	64	0x000001	Dec 19 10:10	lvol1
brw-r-----	1	root	sys	64	0x000002	Dec 16 07:01	lvol2
. . . .							
crw-r-----	1	root	sys	64	0x000001	Dec 16 07:01	rlvol1
crw-r-----	1	root	sys	64	0x000002	Dec 16 07:01	rlvol2
. . . .							

13.2.4   LVM and Mass Storage Stack

LVM supports both legacy and persistent DSFs. A volume group can have physical volumes defined using legacy DSFs, persistent DSFs, or a combination of both. As an 11i v3 administrator, it is suggested that you use persistent DSFs going forward and migrate volume groups currently using legacy view to agile view using LVM commands such as *vgdsf*, *vgscan* and *vgimport*.

13.2.5   LVM Data Structure

LVM reserves some area at the beginning of a disk when the disk is initialized to become a physical volume. Additional structural components are added when the physical volume is included in a volume group and logical volumes are created. The following data structure components are essential:

PVRA (*Physical Volume Reserved Area*) – holds LVM information specific to the entire volume group of which the physical volume is part. It also holds a copy of VGRA.

VGRA (*Volume Group Reserved Area*) – contains both VGSA and VGDA. It also maintains a mapping for LEs and PEs. This area is created by the *vgcreate* command.

VGSA (*Volume Group Status Area*) – contains quorum information for the volume group.

VGDA (*Volume Group Descriptor Area*) – contains information that the device driver needs to configure the volume group for LVM.

BDRA (*Boot Disk Reserved Area*) – is created only on a bootable disk when the disk is initialized using the *pvcreate* command with –B option.

BBRA (*Bad Block Relocation Area*) – contains information specific to the recovery of any bad block generated on the physical volume. It is created at the time a logical volume is formed. In 11i v3, enabling or disabling bad block relocation does not have any effect. This feature is deprecated and will be removed from a future HP-UX release.

The remaining disk space of a PV is divided into PEs for file system, raw partition or swap usage.

13.3 Managing Disks Using LVM

Managing disks using LVM involves several tasks such as identifying available disk devices, creating a physical volume, creating and displaying a volume group, creating and displaying a logical volume, extending a volume group, extending a logical volume, reducing a logical volume, removing a logical volume, reducing a volume group, removing a volume group and backing up and recovering LVM configuration.

13.3.1 Identifying Available Disk Devices

Before starting to work with LVM, you need to figure out what disks are available on the system. Execute the *ioscan* command to identify disks and DSFs, and then use the *diskinfo* command to determine disk sizes. Here is how you can do it:

```
# ioscan –fNnkCdisk
```

Class	I	H/W Path	Driver	S/W State	H/W Type	Description
disk	2	64000/0xfa00/0x0 /dev/disk/disk2	esdisk /dev/rdisk/disk2	CLAIMED	DEVICE	HP 36.4GMAP3367NC
disk	3	64000/0xfa00/0x1 /dev/disk/disk3	esdisk /dev/rdisk/disk3	CLAIMED	DEVICE	HP DVD-ROM 305
disk	5	64000/0xfa00/0x6 /dev/disk/disk5	esdisk /dev/rdisk/disk5	CLAIMED	DEVICE	HP 36.4GST336753LC
disk	22	64000/0xfa00/0x9 /dev/disk/disk22	esdisk /dev/rdisk/disk22	CLAIMED	DEVICE	ABC ABC350WDR5
disk	23	64000/0xfa00/0xa /dev/disk/disk23	esdisk /dev/rdisk/disk23	CLAIMED	DEVICE	ABC ABC350WDR5
disk	24	64000/0xfa00/0xb /dev/disk/disk24	esdisk /dev/rdisk/disk24	CLAIMED	DEVICE	ABC ABC350WDR5
disk	25	64000/0xfa00/0xc /dev/disk/disk25	esdisk /dev/rdisk/disk25	CLAIMED	DEVICE	ABC ABC350WDR5

The *ioscan* output shows that there are six hard drives and one DVD drive in the system. You can also view them using SMH (or *fsweb* command) as follows:

☞Go to SMH → Disks and File Systems → Disks. SMH also displays disk sizes and usage information. Highlight a disk and press Enter to see details of it. For example, here is the information on */dev/disk/disk2*.

```
            HP-UX System Management Homepage (Text User Interface)
                  SMH->Disks and File Systems->Disks->Details
----------------------------------------------------------------------------------
Detail View of Disk:  64000/0xfa00/0x0
----------------------------------------------------------------------------------

LUN H/W Path                      64000/0xfa00/0x0
Persistent Device File            /dev/disk/disk2
Legacy Device File(s)             /dev/dsk/c0t6d0;
Legacy H/W Path(s)                0/0/0/3/0.6.0;
Device Health                     online
Device Identifier
Alias
World Wide ID                     0x00000e11006b94c3
Size                              33.9188 GB
Block Size (bytes)                512
Capacity (blocks)                 71132960
Use                               LVM
VG Name                           vg00
Device Type                       direct access
Instance Number                   2
Total Path Count                  1
Device Class                      disk
Driver                            esdisk
State                             ONLINE
Vendor                            HP 36.4G
Product                           MAS3367NC
Serial Number                     KT002892   0328
Firmware Revision                 HPC3
SCSI Protocol Revision            3


------------------------------------------------------------------------------
x-Exit smh    v-View/Clear Statistics  s-LUN Attributes   p-Physical Volume
ESC-Back    m-Mark disk as used     l-LUN Paths        Ctrl o-Other Actions
```

One of these hard drives is in use as HP-UX boot disk. Do a *setboot* command and find out which one it is:

```
# setboot
Primary bootpath            : 0/0/0/3/0.0x6.0x0 (/dev/rdisk/disk2)
HA Alternate bootpath       : 0/0/0/0/0 (No dsf found)
Alternate bootpath          : 0/0/0/0/0 (No dsf found)
Autoboot is ON (enabled)
Autosearch is ON (enabled)
```

The *setboot* command notifies that the primary boot disk is installed at hardware address 0/0/0/3/0.0x6.0x0, which corresponds to */dev/rdisk/disk2*. Leaving this disk out, you have five disks – *disk5, disk22, disk23, disk24* and *disk25* – available to play with. Issue the *diskinfo* command with –b option on the DSFs to determine the disk sizes. The sizes will be displayed in KBs.

```
# diskinfo –b /dev/rdisk/disk5
35566480
# diskinfo –b /dev/rdisk/disk22
10485760
# diskinfo –b /dev/rdisk/disk23
10485760
# diskinfo –b /dev/rdisk/disk24
10485760
# diskinfo –b /dev/rdisk/disk25
10485760
```

And the boot disk is of the following size:

```
# diskinfo –b /dev/rdisk/disk2
35566480
```

So you have 2 x 36GB and 4 x 10GB disks of which 5 (1 x 36GB and 4 x 10GB) are available to work with.

13.3.2 Creating a Physical Volume

A disk must be initialized with the *pvcreate* command before it can be used in LVM. After initialization the disk is added to a volume group as a physical volume to create logical volumes.

Occasionally, a utility called *mediainit* is run to format a disk and verify its integrity before bringing it under LVM control. This command wipes out everything from the disk. Run it on the raw DSF if required:

```
# mediainit /dev/rdisk/disk22
```

Now, execute *pvcreate* to reserve space for LVM data structures and create other necessary structures. The command must be run on the raw DSF such as */dev/rdisk/disk22*:

```
# pvcreate /dev/rdisk/disk22
Physical volume "/dev/rdisk/disk22" has been successfully created.
```

If the disk was used previously in another volume group, specify the –f option with the command to force create structures on it:

```
# pvcreate –f /dev/rdisk/disk22
Physical volume "/dev/rdisk/disk22" has been successfully created.
```

13.3.3 Creating and Displaying a Volume Group

The next step is to create a volume group. Creating a volume group requires that you first setup a directory and a *group* file. Follow the steps below to create a volume group *vg01*:

mkdir /dev/vg01
cd /dev/vg01
mknod group c 64 0x010000
ll
crw-rw-rw- 1 root   sys   64 0x010000 Dec 25 09:01 group

In the above sequence of activities, a *vg01* directory under */dev* is created that houses the volume group control device file *group*. The *mknod* command creates the *group* file as a character DSF with major number 64 and minor number 0x010000 assigned to it.

Now, create *vg01* volume group using the *vgcreate* command and add the physical volume */dev/disk/disk22* to it:

vgcreate vg01 /dev/disk/disk22
Increased the number of physical extents per physical volume to 2559.
Volume group "/dev/vg01" has been successfully created.
Volume Group configuration for /dev/vg01 has been saved in /etc/lvmconf/vg01.conf

There are options available with *vgcreate* that you can use if you need to modify certain properties of the volume group. Some of these options are described in Table 13-1.

Option	Description
–e	Limits the maximum number of PEs that can be created on a physical volume . The default is 1016, and the maximum supported is 65535.
–l	Limits the maximum number of LVs that can be created in a volume group (default is 255).
–p	Limits the maximum number of PVs that can be added to a volume group. The default is 16, and the maximum supported is 255.
–s	Assigns the PE size, in MBs, to be used in a volume group. The default is 4MB, and the maximum supported is 256.

Table 13-1 *vgcreate* Command Options

To view what *vgcreate* has done, execute the *vgdisplay* command. Run this command with and without the –v option. With –v, it reports details.

vgdisplay –v vg01
--- Volume groups ---
VG Name   /dev/vg01
VG Write Access   read/write
VG Status   available
Max LV   255
Cur LV   0
Open LV   0
Max PV   16

Cur PV	1
Act PV	1
Max PE per PV	2559
VGDA	2
PE Size (Mbytes)	4
Total PE	2559
Alloc PE	0
Free PE	2559
Total PVG	0
Total Spare PVs	0
Total Spare PVs in use	0
VG Version	1.0.0
--- Physical volumes ---	
PV Name	/dev/disk/disk22
PV Status	available
Total PE	2559
Free PE	2559
Autoswitch	On
Proactive Polling	On

The *vgdisplay* command confirms that there is one physical volume in the volume group with 2559 PEs, each with a size of 4MB. Currently, none of the PEs are allocated and no logical volume exists. The last portion from the output under "Physical volumes" displays information about the physical volume.

You can view detailed information about a physical volume using the *pvdisplay* command. Run this command with and without the –v option on */dev/disk/disk22*:

pvdisplay /dev/disk/disk22

--- Physical volumes ---	
PV Name	/dev/disk/disk22
VG Name	/dev/vg01
PV Status	available
Allocatable	yes
VGDA	2
Cur LV	0
PE Size (Mbytes)	4
Total PE	2559
Free PE	2559
Allocated PE	0
Stale PE	0
IO Timeout (Seconds)	default
Autoswitch	On
Proactive Polling	On

You can use SMH (or *fsweb* command) to create a volume group. Follow the steps below:

☞ Go to SMH → Disks and File Systems → Volume Groups. Press c for "Create Volume Group". Fill out the form with required information and press "Create VG". See Figure 13-2.

```
                          Disks and File Systems Administration
                   SMH->Disks and File Systems->Volume Groups->Create New
-----------------------------------------------------------------------------
Complete the form below to create a new volume group.
* Required Field

VG Name*    :  ▌_____

Configure Physical Volumes

[ Select Unused Disk...* ]


WARNING: Care should be taken to assure any selected disks are really
not in use before using the following option as the data on ALL disks
selected will be destroyed:
  [ ] Force physical volume creation (no checks performed before initialization)

Optional Attributes

Physical Extent Size (MB)(default 4)    : 4 ->
Max Logical Volumes (1-255; default 255) :  255_____
Max Physical Volumes (1-255; default 16) :  16_____
Max Physical Extents (1-65535; default 0):  0_____
  [X] Automatically Backup Configuration (default checked)
  [X] Allow Extensibility (default checked)

[ Create VG ] [ Preview ] [ Cancel ] [ Help ]
```

Figure 13-2 SMH – Volume Group Creation

13.3.4   Creating and Displaying a Logical Volume

At this point, you have a pool of storage space available within *vg01* that you can use to construct logical volumes. Create a logical volume with all default values using the *lvcreate* command:

 # lvcreate vg01
Logical volume "/dev/vg01/lvol1" has been successfully created with character device "/dev/vg01/rlvol1".
Volume Group configuration for /dev/vg01 has been saved in /etc/lvmconf/vg01.conf

Several defaults have been used. Table 13-2 shows options that you can use with the command.

Option	Description
–L	Specifies the logical volume size in MBs (default is 0MB).
–l	Specifies the logical volume size in LEs (default is 0).
–n	Specifies logical volume name (default is *lvol1*, *lvol2*, *lvol3* and so on).

Table 13-2 *lvcreate* Command Options

Run the *vgdisplay* command to see what *lvcreate* has performed:

 # vgdisplay –v vg01
--- Volume groups ---
VG Name   /dev/vg01
VG Write Access   read/write
VG Status   available
Max LV   255
Cur LV   1
Open LV   1
Max PV   16

Cur PV	1
Act PV	1
Max PE per PV	2559
VGDA	2
PE Size (Mbytes)	4
Total PE	2559
Alloc PE	0
Free PE	2559
Total PVG	0
Total Spare PVs	0
Total Spare PVs in use	0
VG Version	1.0.0
--- Logical volumes ---	
LV Name	/dev/vg01/lvol1
LV Status	available/syncd
LV Size (Mbytes)	0
Current LE	0
Allocated PE	0
Used PV	0
--- Physical volumes ---	
PV Name	/dev/disk/disk22
PV Status	available
Total PE	2559
Free PE	2559
Autoswitch	On
Proactive Polling	On

Notice the change in the *vgdisplay* output before and after the creation of the logical volume. The logical volume constructed above has used all the defaults. It is created with 0 bytes in size using the default naming convention.

Allocate 1000MB to *lvol1*:

> # **lvextend –L 1000 /dev/vg01/lvol1**
> Logical volume "/dev/vg01/lvol1" has been successfully extended.
> Volume Group configuration for /dev/vg01 has been saved in /etc/lvmconf/vg01.conf

The size can be specified in LEs too. Since the default LE size is 4MB, the 1000MB *lvol1* requires 250 LEs. The following command does exactly what the above has accomplished:

> # **lvextend –l 250 /dev/vg01/lvol1**
> Logical volume "/dev/vg01/lvol1" has been successfully extended.
> Volume Group configuration for /dev/vg01 has been saved in /etc/lvmconf/vg01.conf

This way a logical volume is setup in two steps. In step one, it was created and in step two, it was given the required space.

The following example does both in a single attempt. It creates a logical volume *lvol2* and allocates space to it. You can use either of the following. Both will produce identical results.

lvcreate –L 2000 vg01
lvcreate –l 500 vg01

Use the *vgdisplay* or the *lvdisplay* command in verbose mode and check the *lvol2* information.

Another example below creates a 3150MB *lvdata1* logical volume in *vg01*:

lvcreate –L 3150 –n lvdata1 vg01
Warning: rounding up logical volume size to extent boundary at size "3152" MB.
Logical volume "/dev/vg01/lvdata1" has been successfully created with
character device "/dev/vg01/rlvdata1".
Logical volume "/dev/vg01/lvdata1" has been successfully extended.
Volume Group configuration for /dev/vg01 has been saved in /etc/lvmconf/vg01.conf

The *lvcreate* command ensures that the size specified with the –L option is a multiple of the LE size. If not, it rounds it up to the nearest higher multiple (3152 in this example).

Display the *lvdata1* logical volume information with the *lvdisplay* command:

lvdisplay /dev/vg01/lvdata1
--- Logical volumes ---

LV Name	/dev/vg01/lvdata1
VG Name	/dev/vg01
LV Permission	read/write
LV Status	available/syncd
Mirror copies	0
Consistency Recovery	MWC
Schedule	parallel
LV Size (Mbytes)	**3152**
Current LE	788
Allocated PE	788
Stripes	0
Stripe Size (Kbytes)	0
Bad block	on
Allocation	strict
IO Timeout (Seconds)	default

Also try *vgdisplay* with –v option to check the logical volume information.

SMH (or *fsweb* command) can be used for this purpose. Follow the steps below:

☞ Go to SMH → Disks and File Systems → Logical Volumes. Press c for "Create LV". See Figure 13-3. Fill out the form with required information and press Create.

```
                        Disks and File Systems Administration
                SMH->Disks and File Systems->Logical Volumes->Create LV
----------------------------------------------------------------------------
Create a new logical volume on a selected volume group
* Required Field

     VG Name            Free Size        Free Extents  # PVs  # LVs
  (X) /dev/vg00         8.51562   GB       8720          1      8
  ( ) /dev/vg01         3.98828   GB       4084          1      3

* LV Name:      _____
(must be a simple file name, not a path name)

* Size:      _____
Size in Units: GB ->

Configure General Options
Access Permission:    (X) read/write
                      ( ) read-only

Allocation Policy: strict ->

IO Timeout(seconds):   0_____

  [X] Automatically backup configuration

  [X] Make logical volume available

Configure Mirroring
  [ ] Enable Mirroring




Extent Allocation Options
Note: When mirroring, selection applies to the original and not the mirror copies
  (X) Let LVM Choose Physical Volumes for Extent Allocation
  ( ) Specify Physical Volume(s) for Allocation

Selected
None


[ Create ]  [ Preview ]  [ Cancel ]  [ Help ]
```

Figure 13-3 SMH – Logical Volume Creation

At this stage, you may want to view the contents of the */etc/lvmtab* (lvm table) file, which maintains a list of all volume groups defined on the system together with what physical volumes each of them contains. You must use the *strings* command to view this file.

strings /etc/lvmtab
/dev/vg00
/dev/disk/disk2
/dev/vg01
/dev/disk/disk22

As you can see, there are two volume groups with each containing a single physical volume. This file is created when the first disk on the system is pvcreated.

13.3.5   Extending a Volume Group

Extending a volume group adds one or more physical volumes to it. Currently, *vg01* includes one physical volume. The following example adds to it another disk */dev/disk/disk23*. Run *pvcreate* and then *vgextend* to achieve this:

```
# pvcreate /dev/rdisk/disk23
# vgextend vg01 /dev/disk/disk23
Volume group "vg01" has been successfully extended.
Volume Group configuration for /dev/vg01 has been saved in /etc/lvmconf/vg01.conf
```

Do a *vgdisplay* with –v to see the updated *vg01* volume group information.

13.3.6   Extending a Logical Volume

Extending a logical volume increases the logical volume in size. Currently, three logical volumes – *lvol1, lvol2* and *lvdata1* – with sizes 1000MB, 2000MB and 3152MB, respectively, exist. The following example extends *lvol1* to 3500MB using the *lvextend* command. You can specify the size in either MBs or LEs. Both of the following will generate identical result:

```
# lvextend –L 3500 /dev/vg01/lvol1
# lvextend –l 875 /dev/vg01/lvol1
```

The *lvextend* command took the additional space from the free storage pool in the volume group. This is referred to as RAID 0 where the storage spaces are concatenated for use within a single logical volume container.

13.3.7   Adjusting the Size of a Physical Volume in a Volume Group

Several configuration settings of a volume group may be modified using the *vgmodify* command. One of the examples where this command provides help is when the size of a physical volume is changed at the LUN level and you need to reflect the new size in the volume group.

The following example assumes that the LUN size for *disk23* has been increased from 10GB to 15GB. Run the *vgmodify* command to expand the physical volume:

```
# vgmodify –v vg01 /dev/rdisk/disk23
```

Run *vgdisplay* on *vg01* with –v option to view the new size.

13.3.8   Reducing a Logical Volume

Reducing a logical volume decreases the logical volume in size. Currently, *lvol1* is 3500MB. The following example reduces it to 500MB using the *lvreduce* command. You can specify the size in either MBs or LEs. Both of the following will do exactly the same:

```
# lvreduce –L 500 /dev/vg01/lvol1
# lvreduce –l 125 /dev/vg01/lvol1
When a logical volume is reduced useful data might get lost;
do you really want the command to proceed (y/n) : y
Logical volume "/dev/vg01/lvol1" has been successfully reduced.
Volume Group configuration for /dev/vg01 has been saved in /etc/lvmconf/vg01.conf
```

There are risk involved when reducing the size of a logical volume, critical data may be lost. Always perform a backup of data in the logical volume before reducing its size. See Chapter 18 "Backup and Restore" for details on how to perform backups.

13.3.9 Removing a Logical Volume

Removing a logical volume is a destructive task. Make sure that you perform a backup of any data in the target logical volume prior to deleting it. You will need to unmount the file system (if there is one) in the logical volume. See Chapter 14 "File Systems" on how to unmount a file system. If the logical volume is being used as a device swap, swapping must be disabled in it. See Chapter 15 "Swap Space" on how to disable swap.

Use the *lvremove* command to remove *lvol1*:

> # **lvremove /dev/vg01/lvol1**
> The logical volume "/dev/vg01/lvol1" is not empty;
> do you really want to delete the logical volume (y/n) : **y**
> Logical volume "/dev/vg01/lvol1" has been successfully removed.
> Volume Group configuration for /dev/vg01 has been saved in /etc/lvmconf/vg01.conf

The command gives a warning message. Proceed with caution.

13.3.10 Reducing a Volume Group

Reducing a volume group removes one or more physical volumes out of it. Currently, *vg01* includes two physical volumes: */dev/disk/disk22* and */dev/disk/disk23*. Use *vgreduce* to remove */dev/disk/disk23* from it. The physical volume must not be in use.

> # **vgreduce vg01 /dev/disk/disk23**
> Volume group "vg01" has been successfully reduced.
> Volume Group configuration for /dev/vg01 has been saved in /etc/lvmconf/vg01.conf

Issue *vgdisplay* with –v option to see the updated *vg01* volume group configuration information.

13.3.11 Backing Up and Restoring Volume Group Configuration

LVM structural information for each volume group is stored automatically in the */etc/lvmconf* directory when the volume group is created. The file name where the information is stored corresponds to the volume group's name. Later, any modifications performed using LVM commands such as *vgextend, vgreduce, lvcreate, lvextend, lvreduce, lvremove, lvsplit, lvmerge, lvchange, lvlnboot, lvrmboot, pvmove* and *pvchange* that alter the volume group's structure, an LVM utility called *vgcfgbackup* is executed automatically. This utility saves a copy of the volume group configuration file and updates it to reflect the new information.

Presently, you have *vg00* and *vg01* volume groups. When you do an *ll* on the */etc/lvmconf* directory, you will see something similar to the following:

```
# ll /etc/lvmconf
total 336
----------  1  root    sys          0  Apr  8  09:08  lvm_lock
-rw-------  1  root    bin         24  Apr 15  15:57  pv_lock
-rw-------  1  root    bin      45056  Apr 15  15:46  vg00.conf
-rw-------  1  root    sys      45056  Apr  8  08:59  vg00.conf.old
-rw-------  1  root    bin      29696  Apr 15  15:58  vg01.conf
-rw-------  1  root    bin      29696  Apr 15  15:58  vg01.conf.old
```

You can run *vgcfgbackup* manually if you wish to. The following example command backs up *vg01* configuration (assuming the volume group exists):

```
# vgcfgbackup vg01
Volume Group configuration for /dev/vg01 has been saved in /etc/lvmconf/vg01.conf
```

The saved information can be used to restore corrupted or lost LVM structures of the volume group. The *vgcfgbackup* command partners with the *vgcfgrestore* command, which restores a volume group's configuration if needed. The following example demonstrates how *vg01* configuration can be restored to the */dev/disk/disk22* physical volume:

```
# vgcfgrestore –n vg01 /dev/rdisk/disk22
Volume Group configuration has been restored to /dev/rdisk/disk22
```

13.3.12   Recovering lost or Corrupted LVM Configuration

LVM information about physical volumes and which volume groups they belong to is added to the */etc/lvmtab* file when volume groups are created. This file is updated each time a volume group is extended, reduced or removed. If this file is lost or becomes corrupted or inconsistent, you can use the *vgscan* command to force a rescan of all physical volumes the system has access to and rebuild the file with correct information. Without any options the command adds missing volume group and physical volume entries. By default, legacy DSFs are used for physical volumes with one exception. For volume groups using persistent DSFs for their physical volumes when the volume groups were activated, *vgscan* populates the file using persistent DSFs for those physical volumes.

```
# vgscan
```

Several options are available with this command. Table 13-3 elaborates some of them.

Option	Description
–a	Scans all paths of multipathed physical volumes.
–B	Populates */etc/lvmtab* with both persistent and legacy DSFs.
–f	Replaces any existing entries for the specified volume group with updated entries.
–N	Populates */etc/lvmtab* with persistent DSFs, with one exception. For volume groups using legacy DSFs for their physical volumes when the volume groups were activated, *vgscan* populates the file using legacy DSFs for those physical volumes.

Table 13-3 *vgscan* Command Options

13.3.13 Converting Volume Group Configuration from Legacy to Persistent DSFs

To convert a volume group configuration to use persistent DSFs for all physical volumes, run the command *vgdsf* on the volume group. For example, do the following to convert *vg01*:

vgdsf –c vg01
Converting legacy DSFs to persistent DSFs in VG vg01
Persistent DSF /dev/disk/disk23 added to VG vg01
Legacy DSF /dev/dsk/c8t0d1 removed from VG vg01
Volume Group configuration for /dev/vg01 has been saved in /etc/lvmconf/vg01.conf

Run the *vgdisplay* command on the volume group with –v option to validate the change.

The conversion is only required if a volume group is using legacy DSFs and you want it to switch to persistent DSFs.

13.3.14 Renaming a Volume Group

To rename a volume group, you need to export the volume group with the *vgexport* command and re-import it using the *vgimport* command. *vgexport* removes the information of the volume group and associated logical volumes from the system. It does not wipe out any data from them, but preserves it across the rename process.

To rename *vg01* volume group to *vg01ora*, unmount all of its mounted file systems and run the following pair of commands to deactivate and export it:

vgchange –a n vg01
Volume group "vg01" has been successfully changed.
vgexport –sv –m /tmp/vg01.map vg01
vgexport: Volume group "vg01" has been successfully removed.

With –s and –m options, *vgexport* creates a map file to capture information for all logical volumes the volume group contains and the VGID of the volume group.

Next, you need to create a directory and *group* file for the new *vg01ora* volume group:

mkdir /dev/vg01ora
cd /dev/vg01ora
mknod group c 64 0x020000

Now import *vg01* as *vg01ora* and activate it:

vgimport –sv –m /tmp/vg01.map vg01ora
Beginning the import process on Volume Group "vg01ora".
Logical volume "/dev/vg01ora/lvol1" has been successfully created with lv number 1.
Logical volume "/dev/vg01ora/lvol2" has been successfully created with lv number 2.
vgimport: Volume group "/dev/vg01ora" has been successfully created.
Warning: A backup of this volume group may not exist on this machine.
Please remember to take a backup using the vgcfgbackup command after activating the volume group.

```
# vgchange –a y vg01ora
Activated volume group
Volume group "vg01ora" has been successfully changed.
```

Do not forget to create a backup of this volume group using the *vgcfgbackup* command:

```
# vgcfgbackup vg01ora
Volume Group configuration for /dev/vg01ora has been saved in /etc/lvmconf/vg01ora.conf
```

Do a *vgdisplay* on *vg01ora* and you should be able to see the exact same information that *vg01* had.

13.3.15   Removing a Volume Group

There are two options for removing a volume group: one, remove all logical volumes from the volume group and then remove it; and two, use the command *vgexport* and blow away the volume group including all logical volumes within it. Examples of both are given below.

Currently, you have *lvol2* and *lvdata1* logical volumes in *vg01ora*. Use *lvremove* and delete both logical volumes. Next, use the *vgremove* command to remove *vg01ora*:

```
# vgremove vg01ora
Volume group "vg01ora" has been successfully removed.
```

The other method requires that you run the following two commands. Note that *vg01ora* must not be in use. The *vgchange* command with "–a n" option deactivates *vg01ora* and *vgexport* blows it away. This method does not require you to delete logical volumes prior to removing the volume group.

```
# vgchange –a n vg01ora
Volume group "vg01ora" has been successfully changed.
# vgexport vg01ora
vgexport: Volume group "vg01ora" has been successfully removed.
```

Remember to proceed with caution whenever you perform reduce and remove operations.

13.4   LVM Mirroring

LVM supports replication of data on up to two additional physical volumes for high availability purposes. This is known as *mirroring* (or RAID 1). With mirroring configuration, if one of the physical volumes fails, there is no service interruption and users continue to access data on the remaining physical volume(s). LVM mirroring is performed at the logical volume level, which may contain a file system, a raw database partition or a device swap. One important point to note here is that mirroring does not protect against data loss or corruption; it only protects against disk failures.

13.4.1   Requirements for Mirroring

In order to perform LVM mirroring, you need to ensure that the following requirements are met:

✓ The system must have HP-UX MirrorDisk/UX software installed. MirrorDisk/UX is part of HP-UX 11i v3 VSE-OE, HA-OE and DC-OE.

✓ It is important to have a minimum of two separate physical volumes each of which connected to a separate physical controller card. If this requirement is not met, you can still do the mirroring but will not get the benefits of it.

✓ A logical volume must be available for mirroring or create one for this purpose.

✓ The target logical volume must be the same size or larger than the source logical volume.

13.4.2   Mirroring the Boot Volume Group on 9000

In this sub-section, you are going to create a two-way mirror of all the logical volumes that reside in the boot volume group *vg00* on a 9000 server. A two-way mirror refers to using two physical volumes and a three-way mirror refers to using three physical volumes.

This sub-section contains references to shutting down and booting up the system, modifying boot paths, and some pre-boot tasks. Refer to Chapter 16 "HP-UX Shutdown and Startup" for details.

From previous sections, you know that *vg00* resides on *disk2* and contains eight logical volumes – *lvol1* through *lvol8*. For the purpose of this demonstration, let us use *disk5*, which is available, resides on a separate physical controller card and is of the same size as *disk2*. Here are the steps:

1. Bring *disk5* under LVM control. Run *pvcreate* with –B option to create BDRA on it:

    # **pvcreate –fB /dev/rdisk/disk5**

2. Extend *vg00* with *vgextend* command to include the physical volume:

    # **vgextend vg00 /dev/disk/disk5**

3. Copy boot utilities to BDRA of *disk5* with the *mkboot* command:

    # **mkboot /dev/rdisk/disk5**

4. Copy AUTO file to boot LIF area. Enclose contents within quotes. The AUTO file is read at boot time to determine the HP-UX kernel file name and directory location. The –lq options force the boot process to ignore quorum checking and boot the system or partition even if the other physical volume(s) included in the mirrored configuration is defective:

    # **mkboot –a "hpux –lq(;0)/stand/vmunix" /dev/rdisk/disk5**

5. Mirror all eight logical volumes. The –m option with the *lvextend* command specifies the number of mirrors that you want (the maximum number of mirrors supported by LVM is 2). Each logical volume will be replicated to *disk5*. The output from the first instance of the *lvextend* command is displayed. It will be very similar for the remaining logical volumes. Depending on the size of a logical volume, it may take long to synchronize mirrors.

lvextend −m 1 /dev/vg00/lvol1 /dev/disk/disk5
The newly allocated mirrors are now being synchronized. This operation will
take some time. Please wait ....
Logical volume "/dev/vg00/lvol1" has been successfully extended.
Volume Group configuration for /dev/vg00 has been saved in /etc/lvmconf/vg00.conf
lvextend −m 1 /dev/vg00/lvol2 /dev/disk/disk5

. . . .
lvextend −m 1 /dev/vg00/lvol7 /dev/disk/disk5
lvextend −m 1 /dev/vg00/lvol8 /dev/disk/disk5

Run *vgdisplay* in verbose mode to view the updated configuration of the volume group.
Notice, the number of Allocated PEs is twice as many as the number of Current LEs and the
number of Used PVs is changed to 2. This means each LV resides on a different PV and
occupies an exact number of PEs on each PV. The available/syncd status confirms that both
mirrors are in sync.

```
# vgdisplay −v vg00
. . . . . . . .
    --- Logical volumes ---
    LV Name              /dev/vg00/lvol1
    LV Status            available/syncd
    LV Size (Mbytes)     1000
    Current LE           125
    Allocated PE         250
    Used PV              2
. . . . . . . .
    LV Name              /dev/vg00/lvol8
    LV Status            available/syncd
    LV Size (Mbytes)     4000
    Current LE           500
    Allocated PE         1000
    Used PV              2
    --- Physical volumes ---
    PV Name              /dev/disk/disk2
    PV Status            available
    Total PE             4341
    Free PE              1090
    Autoswitch           On
    Proactive Polling    On
    PV Name              /dev/disk/disk5
    PV Status            available
    Total PE             4341
    Free PE              1090
    Autoswitch           On
    Proactive Polling    On
```

Let us issue the *lvdisplay* command on one of the mirrored logical volumes such as
/dev/vg00/lvol1 and see how PEs are allocated on the two physical volumes:

```
# lvdisplay –v /dev/vg00/lvol1
--- Logical volumes ---
LV Name                  /dev/vg00/lvol1
VG Name                  /dev/vg00
LV Permission            read/write
LV Status                available/syncd
Mirror copies            1
Consistency Recovery     MWC
Schedule                 parallel
LV Size (Mbytes)         1000
Current LE               125
Allocated PE             250
Stripes                  0
Stripe Size (Kbytes)     0
Bad block                off
Allocation               strict/contiguous
IO Timeout (Seconds)     default
   --- Distribution of logical volume ---
   PV Name            LE on PV  PE on PV
   /dev/disk/disk2      125       125
   /dev/disk/disk5      125       125
   --- Logical extents ---
   LE     PV1               PE1    Status 1  PV2              PE2     Status 2
   00000  /dev/disk/disk2   00000  current   /dev/disk/disk5  00000   current
   00001  /dev/disk/disk2   00001  current   /dev/disk/disk5  00001   current
   00002  /dev/disk/disk2   00002  current   /dev/disk/disk5  00002   current
   00003  /dev/disk/disk2   00003  current   /dev/disk/disk5  00003   current
. . . . . . . .
```

6. Run the *lvlnboot* command to update *vg00* configuration information. With –b, –r, –s and –d options, it re-establishes the location of boot, root, swap and dump logical volumes. With –R option, the command recovers any missing links to logical volumes within *vg00* volume group and updates BDRA on all bootable physical volumes.

```
# lvlnboot –b /dev/vg00/lvol1
# lvlnboot –r /dev/vg00/lvol3
# lvlnboot –s /dev/vg00/lvol2
# lvlnboot –d /dev/vg00/lvol2
# lvlnboot –R
Volume Group configuration for /dev/vg00 has been saved in /etc/lvmconf/vg00.conf
```

7. Edit */stand/bootconf* file and make certain that it contains the following two lines. This tells HP-UX that there are two boot devices.

```
# cat /stand/bootconf
l /dev/disk/disk2
l /dev/disk/disk5
```

8. All the mirrored logical volumes are set to have *Mirror Write Cache* (MWC) enabled. MWC forces logical volumes to synchronize quickly by synching only the stale (out of sync) physical extents. This feature is very useful when the system or a logical volume crashes and recovery of the stale extents takes place. The synchronization and re-synchronization processes are time consuming and generate plenty of I/O activities on the mirrored disks. The only logical volume you do not need to have this feature enabled is the primary swap area. Although it does not cause any harm to leave MWC enabled on *lvol2*, disabling it improves overall system recovery time after a system crash. Use the *lvdisplay* command to view the setting of *consistency recovery* for */dev/vg00/lvol2*:

```
# lvdisplay /dev/vg00/lvol2
--- Logical volumes ---
LV Name                  /dev/vg00/lvol2
VG Name                  /dev/vg00
LV Permission            read/write
LV Status                available/syncd
Mirror copies            1
Consistency Recovery     MWC
Schedule                 parallel
LV Size (Mbytes)         8000
Current LE               1000
Allocated PE             2000
Stripes                  0
Stripe Size (Kbytes)     0
Bad block                off
Allocation               strict/contiguous
IO Timeout (Seconds)     default
```

In order to disable MWC on the primary swap logical volume, you need to close (stop) it. The only way to close the primary swap volume and disable MWC on it is to shut down the system or partition and go to the LVM maintenance mode.

```
# shutdown –ry now
. . . . . . . .
Processor is booting from first available device.
To discontinue, press any key within 10 seconds.

Boot terminated.
        Main Menu: Enter command or menu > bo pri
        Interact with IPL (Y, N, or Cancel) ?> y
. . . . . . . .
```

```
ISL> hpux –lm
```

9. Activate *vg00* in LVM maintenance mode. The –a option with y as an argument activates the volume group and –s option stops synchronization on all logical volumes:

```
# vgchange –a y –s vg00
```
Activated volume group
Volume group "/dev/vg00" has been successfully changed.

10. Execute the *lvchange* command to disable MWC on *lvol2*. The "–M n" option turns MWC off and "–c n" ensures deactivation of mirror consistency recoveries for this logical volume at subsequent *vg00* activations:

```
# lvchange –M n –c n /dev/vg00/lvol2
```
Logical volume "/dev/vg00/lvol2" has been successfully changed.
Volume Group configuration for /dev/vg00 has been saved in /etc/lvmconf/vg00.conf

Run *lvdisplay* command on *lvol2* to verify the change:

```
# lvdisplay /dev/vg00/lvol2
```
--- Logical volumes ---

LV Name	/dev/vg00/lvol2
VG Name	/dev/vg00
LV Permission	read/write
LV Status	available/syncd
Mirror copies	1
Consistency Recovery	**NONE**
Schedule	parallel
LV Size (Mbytes)	8000
Current LE	1000
Allocated PE	2000
Stripes	0
Stripe Size (Kbytes)	0
Bad block	off
Allocation	strict/contiguous
IO Timeout (Seconds)	default

11. Reboot the system to normal mode:

```
# reboot
```

12. Configure the mirrored boot disk as an alternate boot device. This ensures that the system will boot from this disk if the primary boot disk is not available. Issue the *setboot* command and use the hardware address of the mirrored boot disk. You can use the *ioscan* command to determine its hardware address.

```
# setboot –a 0/0/4/0/0.0x0.0x0
```

13. Verify to ensure that the primary and alternate boot paths are set properly. Use the *lvlnboot* and *setboot* commands:

```
# lvlnboot −v
Boot Definitions for Volume Group /dev/vg00:
Physical Volumes belonging in Root Volume Group:
    /dev/disk/disk2 -- Boot Disk
    /dev/disk/disk5 -- Boot Disk
Boot: lvol1 on:        /dev/disk/disk2
                       /dev/disk/disk5
Root: lvol3 on:        /dev/disk/disk2
                       /dev/disk/disk5
Swap: lvol2 on:        /dev/disk/disk2
                       /dev/disk/disk5
Dump: lvol2 on:        /dev/disk/disk2, 0
# setboot
Primary bootpath : 0/0/0/3/0.0x6.0x0 (/dev/rdisk/disk2)
HA Alternate bootpath : 0/0/0/0/0 (No dsf found)
Alternate bootpath : 0/0/4/0/0.0x0.0x0 (/dev/rdisk/disk5)
Autoboot is ON (enabled)
Autosearch is ON (enabled)
```

14. Update the AUTO file on the primary boot disk to specify ignoring quorum check at boot time in case the alternate boot disk is unavailable:

    # **mkboot −a "hpux −lq(;0)/stand/vmunix" /dev/rdisk/disk2**

    Verify that the correct label has been applied to the AUTO file:

    # **lifcp /dev/rdisk/disk2:AUTO −**
    hpux −lq(;0)/stand/vmunix

    The system will always attempt to boot with the primary boot disk and then the alternate if primary is unavailable.

This completes *vg00* mirroring configuration and verification on a 9000 server.

13.4.3   Mirroring the Boot Volume Group on Integrity

In this sub-section, you are going to create a two-way mirror of all the logical volumes that reside in the boot volume group *vg00* on an Integrity server. Note that most steps are identical to that you performed on 9000 in the previous sub-section.

This sub-section contains references to shutting down and booting up the system, modifying boot paths, and some pre-boot tasks. Refer to Chapter 16 "HP-UX Shutdown and Startup" for details.

Let us assume that *vg00* resides on *disk2* and contains eight logical volumes – *lvol1* through *lvol8*, and a spare disk *disk5* is available.

1. Create a file such as *part_desc* under */tmp* and add the following partition information to it. The first entry specifies number of partitions to be created on *disk5* and the remaining entries list names and sizes of the partitions:

    # **vi /tmp/part_desc**
    3
    EFI   500MB
    HPUX   100%
    HPSP   400MB

2. Run the *idisk* command to create partition information as identified in the */tmp/part_desc* file:

    # **idisk –wf /tmp/part_desc /dev/rdisk/disk5**
    idisk version: 1.44
    ********************* WARNING **********************
    If you continue you may destroy all data on this disk.
    Do you wish to continue(yes/no)? **yes**
    EFI Primary Header:
         Signature   = EFI PART
         Revision   = 0x10000
         HeaderSize   = 0x5c
    . . . .
    Legacy MBR (MBR Signatures in little endian):
      MBR Signature = 0x520d9677
    Protective MBR

3. Run the *idisk* command again to verify:

    # **idisk /dev/rdisk/disk5**
    idisk version: 1.44
    EFI Primary Header:
         Signature   = EFI PART
         Revision   = 0x10000
         HeaderSize   = 0x5c
         HeaderCRC32   = 0x9899c61
         MyLbaLo   = 0x1
         MyLbaHi   = 0x0
    . . . .

4. Execute the *insf* command to create the device files for the three partitions:

    # **insf –e**

5. Do an *ll* on the */dev/rdisk* and */dev/disk* directories and grep for *disk5*. You should be able to see the character and block DSFs:

```
# ll /dev/rdisk | grep disk5
crw-r-----  1 bin    sys    3 0x000008 May 14 12:43  disk5_p1
crw-r-----  1 bin    sys    3 0x000009 May 14 12:03  disk5_p2
crw-r-----  1 bin    sys    3 0x00000a May 14 12:03  disk5_p3
# ll /dev/rdisk | grep disk5
brw-r-----  1 bin    sys    3 0x000008 May 14 12:43  disk5_p1
brw-r-----  1 bin    sys    3 0x000009 May 14 12:03  disk5_p2
brw-r-----  1 bin    sys    3 0x00000a May 14 12:03  disk5_p3
```

6. Bring *disk5* under LVM control. Run *pvcreate* on it. Do not forget to specify the –B option:

   # **pvcreate –fB /dev/rdisk/disk5**

7. Copy EFI utilities to *disk5* with the *mkboot* command:

   # **mkboot –e –l /dev/rdisk/disk5**

8. Copy AUTO file to the EFI partition. This is a two-step procedure. First, copy AUTO file contents from the existing boot disk partition *disk2_p1* to a file such as */tmp/auto_file* and second, copy them to the boot partition *disk5_p1* on *disk5*:

   # **efi_cp –d /dev/rdisk/disk2_p1 –u /efi/hpux/auto /tmp/auto_file**
   # **efi_cp –d /dev/rdisk/disk5_p1 /tmp/auto_file /efi/hpux/auto**

9. Run *vgextend* to extend *vg00* to include the physical volume partition:

   # **vgextend vg00 /dev/disk/disk5_p2**

10. Follow steps 5 through 8 from previous sub-section "Mirroring the Boot Volume Group on 9000". For step 8, use the following to boot to LVM maintenance mode. Other information in that step will apply as is:

    HPUX> **boot –lm vmunix**

11. Follow steps 9 through 13 as described in "Mirroring the Boot Volume Group on 9000".

12. Update the AUTO file in the EFI partition on each boot disk and specify to ignore quorum check at boot time in case one of them is unavailable:

    # **vi /tmp/auto_file**
    boot vmunix –lq
    # **efi_cp –d /dev/disk/disk2_p1 /tmp/auto_file /efi/hpux/auto**
    # **efi_cp –d /dev/disk/disk5_p1 /tmp/auto_file /efi/hpux/auto**

    The system will always attempt to boot with the primary boot disk and then the alternate if primary is unavailable.

This completes *vg00* mirroring configuration and verification on an Integrity server.

13.4.4   Mirroring a Non-Boot Volume Group on 9000 and Integrity

Mirroring a non-boot volume group is a straight forward process. In this sub-section, you are going to create a two-way mirror of all the LVs that reside in a non-boot volume group such as *vg02*.

Assume that *vg02* volume group exists on *disk22* physical volume and contains *lvol1* and *lvol2* logical volumes. Also assume that a spare disk *disk23* is available, connected to a separate physical controller card and is no less than the size of *disk22*. Here is the procedure to mirror both logical volumes within *vg02*:

1. Bring *disk23* under LVM control with *pvcreate*:

    # **pvcreate –f /dev/rdisk/disk23**

2. Extend *vg02* with the *vgextend* command to add the physical volume to it:

    # **vgextend vg01 /dev/disk/disk23**

3. Mirror the two logical volumes:

    # **lvextend –m 1 /dev/vg01/lvol1 /dev/disk/disk23**
    # **lvextend –m 1 /dev/vg01/lvol2 /dev/disk/disk23**

    Use the *vgdisplay* and *lvdisplay* commands to verify.

This completes the mirroring procedure for a non-boot volume group on 9000 and Integrity servers.

13.5   Mirroring and Allocation Policies

From a mirroring standpoint, LVM offers certain policies to better control which specific physical volume(s) can be used to allocate physical extents. These policies are referred to as *allocation policies,* and are listed and explained below:

- ✓ Strict Allocation Policy
- ✓ PVG-Strict Allocation Policy
- ✓ Distributed Allocation Policy

13.5.1   Strict Allocation Policy

By default, when a logical volume is created, *strict allocation policy* is enforced on it. If this logical volume is mirrored later, it will not allow the physical volume it resides on to have a mirror of itself on that physical volume. In other words, the mirror of the logical volume must be created on a separate physical volume. If strict allocation policy is not enforced, both mirrors will be able to reside on the same physical volume. Although, the latter configuration is supported, it should be avoided as it defeats the purpose of mirroring.

Let us create another volume group *vg03* containing *disk24* with *lvol1* logical volume of size 2000MB:

```
# pvcreate –f /dev/rdisk/disk24
# mkdir /dev/vg03
# cd /dev/vg03
# mknod group c 64 0x02000
# vgcreate vg03
# lvcreate –L 2000 vg03
```

To validate if strict policy is enforced on the logical volume, do an *lvdisplay* on it and check the value of "Allocation":

```
# lvdisplay /dev/vg03/lvol1
. . . . . . . .
Allocation              strict
IO Timeout (Seconds)    default
```

Now, let us try to mirror this logical volume using the *lvextend* command and see what happens:

```
# lvextend –m 1 /dev/vg03/lvol1
lvextend: Not enough free physical extents available.
Logical volume "/dev/vg03/lvol1" could not be extended.
Failure possibly caused by strict allocation policy
```

This is what you are going to see if you try to mirror a logical volume on the same physical volume with strict allocation policy enabled.

Let us now create a mirrored logical volume *lvol2* with strict allocation policy disabled (–s n). You will notice that the system will allow both the logical volume and its mirror to share the *disk24* physical volume.

```
# lvcreate –L 1000 –m 1 –s n vg03
Logical volume "/dev/vg03/lvol2" has been successfully created with character device "/dev/vg03/rlvol2".
Logical volume "/dev/vg03/lvol2" has been successfully extended.
Volume Group configuration for /dev/vg03 has been saved in /etc/lvmconf/vg03.conf
```

Use the *lvdisplay* command to view what *lvcreate* has done. The output indicates that both copies of the logical volume reside on the same physical volume:

```
# lvdisplay –v /dev/vg03/lvol2
--- Logical volumes ---
LV Name                 /dev/vg03/lvol2
VG Name                 /dev/vg03
LV Permission           read/write
LV Status               available/syncd
Mirror copies           1
. . . . . . . .
Allocation              non-strict
IO Timeout (Seconds)    default
   --- Distribution of logical volume ---
   PV Name          LE on PV          PE on PV
```

/dev/disk/disk24	250		500			

--- Logical extents ---

LE	PV1	PE1	Status 1	PV2	PE2	Status 2
00000	/dev/disk/disk24	00500	current	/dev/disk/disk24	00750	current
00001	/dev/disk/disk24	00501	current	/dev/disk/disk24	00751	current
00002	/dev/disk/disk24	00502	current	/dev/disk/disk24	00752	current

. . . .

Let us *pvcreate* another disk *disk25*, vgextend it into *vg03* and create a logical volume *lvol3* with strict allocation enabled:

pvcreate /dev/rdisk/disk25
Physical volume "/dev/rdisk/disk25" has been successfully created.
vgextend vg03 /dev/disk/disk25
Volume group "vg03" has been successfully extended.
Volume Group configuration for /dev/vg03 has been saved in /etc/lvmconf/vg03.conf
lvcreate –L 2000 –m 1 vg03
Logical volume "/dev/vg03/lvol3" has been successfully created with
character device "/dev/vg03/rlvol3".
Logical volume "/dev/vg03/lvol3" has been successfully extended.
Volume Group configuration for /dev/vg03 has been saved in /etc/lvmconf/vg03.conf

Use *lvdisplay* to view the properties of */dev/vg03/lvol3*. The output indicates that each copy of the logical volume is on a separate physical volume:

lvdisplay –v /dev/vg03/lvol3
--- Logical volumes ---

LV Name	/dev/vg03/lvol3
VG Name	/dev/vg03
LV Permission	read/write
LV Status	available/syncd
Mirror copies	1

. . . .

Allocation	**strict**
IO Timeout (Seconds) default	

  --- Distribution of logical volume ---

PV Name	LE on PV	PE on PV
/dev/disk/disk24	**500**	**500**
/dev/disk/disk25	**500**	**500**

  --- Logical extents ---

LE	PV1	PE1	Status 1	PV2	PE2	Status 2
00000	/dev/disk/disk24	01000	current	/dev/disk/disk25	00000	current
00001	/dev/disk/disk24	01001	current	/dev/disk/disk25	00001	current
00002	/dev/disk/disk24	01002	current	/dev/disk/disk25	00002	current
00003	/dev/disk/disk24	01003	current	/dev/disk/disk25	00003	current
00004	/dev/disk/disk24	01004	current	/dev/disk/disk25	00004	current

. . . .

13.5.2   PVG-Strict Allocation Policy

The *Physical Volume Group* (PVG) *strict allocation policy* is preferred when working with a large number of physical volumes within a single volume group.

PVG is a group of physical volumes defined within a volume group. When you plan to setup a two-way mirror, for instance, for a number of logical volumes, you can create two PVGs (PVG0 and PVG1) in the volume group. See Figure 13-4. Suppose there is a group of 3 physical volumes (4GB each) connected to c2 controller card and another group of 3 physical volumes (4GB each) connected to c3 controller card. All 6 of them reside within a single volume group *vgweb*. You need to define the PVGs in the */etc/lvmpvg* file. This file does not exist by default, but can be created manually. When using the PVG-strict policy, one copy of the logical volume resides in PVG0 and the other in PVG1. This way an automatic separation of mirrors takes place.

The following demonstrates how you can have the two PVGs defined in */etc/lvmpvg* for *vgweb* volume group with physical volumes – *disk10*, *disk11*, *disk12*, *disk30*, *disk31* and *disk32* – connected to c2 and c3 controllers:

```
# vi /etc/lvmpvg
VG     /dev/vgweb
PVG    PVG0
/dev/disk/disk10
/dev/disk/disk11
/dev/disk/disk12
PVG    PVG1
/dev/disk/disk30
/dev/disk/disk31
/dev/disk/disk32
```

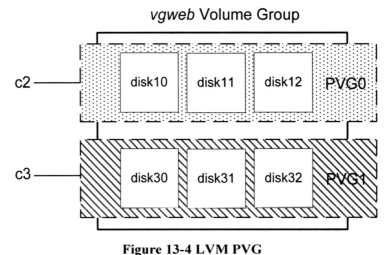

Figure 13-4 LVM PVG

Here is the *vgdisplay* output of *vgweb* after defining PVGs in */etc/lvmpvg* file:

```
# vgdisplay –v vgweb
. . . . . . . .
Cur LV               0
Open LV              0
```

Max PV	16
Cur PV	6
Act PV	6
Max PE per PV	1023
VGDA	12
PE Size (Mbytes)	4
Total PE	6138
Alloc PE	0
Free PE	6138
Total PVG	**2**
Total Spare PVs	0
Total Spare PVs in use	0

--- Physical volumes ---

PV Name	/dev/disk/disk10
PV Status	available
Total PE	1023
Free PE	1023
Autoswitch	On
PV Name	/dev/disk/disk11
PV Status	available
Total PE	1023
Free PE	1023
Autoswitch	On
PV Name	/dev/disk/disk12
PV Status	available
Total PE	1023
Free PE	1023
Autoswitch	On
PV Name	/dev/disk/disk30
PV Status	available
Total PE	1023
Free PE	1023
Autoswitch	On
PV Name	/dev/disk/disk31
PV Status	available
Total PE	1023
Free PE	1023
Autoswitch	On
PV Name	/dev/disk/disk32
PV Status	available
Total PE	1023
Free PE	1023
Autoswitch	On

--- Physical volume groups ---

PVG Name	**PVG0**
PV Name	**/dev/disk/disk10**
PV Name	**/dev/disk/disk11**
PV Name	**/dev/disk/disk12**
PVG Name	**PVG1**

PV Name	/dev/disk/disk30
PV Name	/dev/disk/disk31
PV Name	/dev/disk/disk32

Let us create a mirrored logical volume *lvol1* of size 2000MB in *vgweb*. The "–s g" option forces the *lvcreate* command to use the PVG-strict policy.

lvcreate –L 2000 –m 1 –s g vgweb
Logical volume "/dev/vgweb/lvol1" has been successfully created with
character device "/dev/vgweb/rlvol1".
Logical volume "/dev/vgweb/lvol1" has been successfully extended.
Volume Group configuration for /dev/vgweb has been saved in /etc/lvmconf/vgweb.conf

Use *lvdisplay* to view the properties of *lvol1*. The output indicates that each copy of the logical volume is on a separate physical volume in different PVGs.

lvdisplay –v /dev/vgweb/lvol1
--- Logical volumes ---

LV Name	/dev/vgweb/lvol1
VG Name	/dev/vgweb
LV Permission	read/write
LV Status	available/syncd
Mirror copies	1
Consistency Recovery	MWC
Schedule	parallel
LV Size (Mbytes)	2000
Current LE	500
Allocated PE	1000
Stripes	0
Stripe Size (Kbytes)	0
Bad block	on
Allocation	**PVG-strict**
IO Timeout (Seconds)	default

--- Distribution of logical volume ---

PV Name	LE on PV	PE on PV
/dev/disk/disk10	**500**	**500**
/dev/disk/disk30	**500**	**500**

--- Logical extents ---

LE	PV1	PE1	Status 1	PV2	PE2	Status 2
00000	/dev/disk/disk10	00000	current	/dev/disk/disk30	00000	current
00001	/dev/disk/disk10	00001	current	/dev/disk/disk30	00001	current
00002	/dev/disk/disk10	00002	current	/dev/disk/disk30	00002	current
00003	/dev/disk/disk10	00003	current	/dev/disk/disk30	00003	current

. . . .

13.5.3   Distributed Allocation Policy

With *distributed allocation policy*, physical extents are allocated in a round-robin fashion on a series of available physical volumes within a PVG. These physical extents are then mirrored on the physical volumes that reside in the other PVG in the round-robin fashion. This means that the first free PE is allocated from the first available PV, the second free PE is allocated from the second available PV, the third free PE is allocated from the third available PV and so on. This policy only works with PVG-strict and is disabled by default. The default behavior uses all free physical extents from the first available physical volume before starting to allocate from the next physical volume. This type of mirroring setup is referred to as RAID 0+1. The *etc/lvmpvg* file is referenced to obtain the list of available physical volumes within each PVG.

Let us create a mirrored logical volume *lvol2* of size 2000MB in *vgweb*. The "–s g" option forces *lvcreate* to use physical extents from both PVGs and "–D y" option enables the distributed allocation policy on the logical volume.

> # **lvcreate –L 2000 –m 1 –D y –s g vgweb**
> Logical volume "/dev/vgweb/lvol2" has been successfully created with
> character device "/dev/vgweb/rlvol2".
> Logical volume "/dev/vgweb/lvol2" has been successfully extended.
> Volume Group configuration for /dev/vgweb has been saved in /etc/lvmconf/vgweb.conf

Use the *lvdisplay* command to view the properties of */dev/vgweblvol2*. Notice that the allocation policy used is PVG-strict/distributed. The output also indicates that physical extents are taken in round-robin fashion from each of the three physical volumes in the PVGs.

> # **lvdisplay –v /dev/vgweb/lvol2**
> --- Logical volumes ---
> LV Name   /dev/vgweb/lvol2
> VG Name   /dev/vgweb
> LV Permission   read/write
> LV Status   available/syncd
> Mirror copies   1
> Consistency Recovery   MWC
> Schedule   parallel
> LV Size (Mbytes)   2000
> Current LE   500
> Allocated PE   1000
> Stripes   0
> Stripe Size (Kbytes)   0
> Bad block   on
> **Allocation**   **PVG-strict/distributed**
> IO Timeout (Seconds)   default

| --- Distribution of logical volume --- | | |
PV Name	LE on PV	PE on PV
/dev/dsk/disk10	**167**	**167**
/dev/dsk/disk11	**167**	**167**
/dev/dsk/disk12	**166**	**166**
/dev/dsk/disk30	**167**	**167**
/dev/dsk/disk31	**167**	**167**
/dev/dsk/disk32	**166**	**166**

> --- Logical extents ---
> LE   PV1   PE1   Status 1 PV2   PE2   Status 2
> 00000 /dev/disk/disk10 00500 current /dev/disk/disk30 00500 current

```
00001 /dev/disk/disk11    00000 current /dev/disk/disk31    00000 current
00002 /dev/disk/disk12    00000 current /dev/disk/disk32    00000 current
00003 /dev/disk/disk10    00501 current /dev/disk/disk30    00501 current
00004 /dev/disk/disk11    00001 current /dev/disk/disk31    00001 current
00005 /dev/disk/disk12    00001 current /dev/disk/disk32    00001 current
. . . . . . . .
```

13.6   Managing Mirrors

Managing logical volume mirrors involve several tasks such as extending and reducing their sizes, splitting and merging them, and synchronizing if they are out of sync. These tasks are explained in the following sub-sections.

13.6.1   Extending Mirrors

Extending a mirrored logical volume increases the logical volume in size. Let us extend */dev/vgweb/lvol1* logical volume from 2000MB to 4000MB with the *lvextend* command. Specify the size in either MBs or LEs.

> # **lvextend –L 4000 /dev/vgweb/lvol1**

Although the size is increased by 2000MB, the number of PEs allocated is twice as many as the number of LEs. In mirrored configuration, LVM takes the exact number of PEs from each physical volume. For instance, 2000MB is equal to 500 PEs per physical volume totaling 1000 PEs on both. This calculation is based on the assumption that the PE size is 4MB.

Run *vgdisplay* in verbose mode on *vgweb* and check for the number of allocated PEs, current LEs and used PVs to validate.

13.6.2   Reducing Mirrors

Reducing a mirrored logical volume decreases the logical volume in size. Let us reduce */dev/vgweb/lvol1* logical volume from 4000MB to 1000MB with the *lvreduce* command. Specify the size in either MBs or LEs.

> # **lvreduce –L 1000 /dev/vgweb/lvol1**
> Warning: The Logical Volume has a file system larger than the reduced size.
> Reducing the Logical Volume will cause file system corruption.
> When a logical volume is reduced useful data might get lost;
> do you really want the command to proceed (y/n) : **y**
> Logical volume "/dev/vgweb/lvol1" has been successfully reduced.
> Volume Group configuration for /dev/vgweb has been saved in /etc/lvmconf/vgweb.conf

Run *vgdisplay* in verbose mode on *vgweb* and check for the number of allocated PEs, current LEs and used PVs to validate.

13.6.3   Splitting Mirrors

Splitting a two-way mirrored logical volume creates two logical volumes out of it, one stays as the primary logical volume and the other becomes a detached or secondary copy of it. You will need to decide what you will want to do with the detached copy. You may perform an online backup of it, remove it if not needed and so on.

Here are examples on how to split mirrors.

To split */dev/vgweb/lvol1* and assign the default suffix "b" to the secondary copy, use the *lvsplit* command:

lvsplit /dev/vgweb/lvol1
Logical volume "/dev/vgweb/lvol1b" has been successfully created with character device "/dev/vgweb/rlvol1b".
Logical volume "/dev/vgweb/lvol1" has been successfully split.
Volume Group configuration for /dev/vgweb has been saved in /etc/lvmconf/vgweb.conf

To split */dev/vgweb/lvol2* and assign the suffix "mir" to the secondary copy, use the *lvsplit* command:

lvsplit –s mir /dev/vgweb/lvol2
Logical volume "/dev/vgweb/lvol2mir" has been successfully created with character device "/dev/vgweb/rlvol2mir".
Logical volume "/dev/vgweb/lvol2" has been successfully split.
Volume Group configuration for /dev/vgweb has been saved in /etc/lvmconf/vgweb.conf

13.6.4   Merging Mirrors

If you split the mirrors temporarily, you can merge the secondary copy with the primary at a later time. Merging mirrors synchronizes the detached copy with the primary.

Here are examples on how to merge the two secondary copies */dev/vgweb/lvol1b* and */dev/vgweb/lvol2mir* to their respective primary copies. Use the *lvmerge* command:

lvmerge /dev/vgweb/lvol1b /dev/vgweb/lvol1
Logical volume "/dev/vgweb/lvol1b" has been successfully merged with logical volume "/dev/vgweb/lvol1".
Logical volume "/dev/vgweb/lvol1b" has been successfully removed.
Volume Group configuration for /dev/vgweb has been saved in /etc/lvmconf/vgweb.conf
lvmerge /dev/vgweb/lvol2mir /dev/vgweb/lvol2
Logical volume "/dev/vgweb/lvol2mir" has been successfully merged with logical volume "/dev/vgweb/lvol2".
Logical volume "/dev/vgweb/lvol2mir" has been successfully removed.
Volume Group configuration for /dev/vgweb has been saved in /etc/lvmconf/vgweb.conf

13.6.5   Synchronizing Stale Mirrors

Mirrored logical volumes in a volume group are automatically synchronized when the volume group is activated. This is the default behavior. Sometimes, logical volumes get out of sync because of intermittent problems with one of the mirrored disks. The *vgdisplay* command shows their status as available/stale.

LVM offers two commands – *lvsync* and *vgsync* – to synchronize stale mirrors. The *lvsync* command synchronizes a single logical volume while *vgsync* synchronizes all stale logical volumes within the volume group. For example:

To synchronize */dev/vgweb/lvol1*, run *lvsync*:

> # **lvsync /dev/vgweb/lvol1**
> Resynchronized logical volume "/dev/vgweb/lvol1".

To synchronize all logical volumes within *vgweb*, run *vgsync*:

> # **vgsync vgweb**
> Resynchronized logical volume "/dev/vgweb/lvol1".
> Resynchronized logical volume "/dev/vgweb/lvol2".
> Resynchronized volume group "vgweb".

13.7   The Whole Disk Solution

The *whole disk* solution is no longer used by a vast majority of system administrators due to limitations. Major disadvantages with this solution are:

✓ Cannot create a partition larger than the size of a single physical disk.
✓ Cannot have more than one file system per physical disk.
✓ Cannot increase or decrease the size of a file system on the fly.

Using this solution, a disk can be partitioned in one of the following five ways only:

✓ An entire disk is used for a single file system only.
✓ An entire disk is used for a single swap partition only.
✓ An entire disk is used for a single raw partition only.
✓ An entire disk can have one file system and one swap space only.
✓ An entire disk can have the root file system (along with boot area) and one swap space only.

These limitations make the whole disk solution impractical for today's data storage requirements.

Summary

In this chapter you looked at features and benefits associated with LVM. You learned concepts, components and structure of LVM in detail.

Next, you learned how to manage LVM disks including listing available disks, finding their sizes, converting them into physical volumes, creating, displaying, extending, reducing and removing volume groups, and creating, extending, reducing, removing and displaying logical volumes. You looked at how to backup LVM configuration information and restore it when needed.

Finally, in the sections that followed, you studied requirements for mirroring. You performed mirroring of boot and non-boot volume groups that covered creating, extending, reducing, synchronizing, splitting and merging mirrored logical volumes. You looked at various allocation policies that you might want to use when mirroring logical volumes. At the end of the chapter a brief introduction was given on whole disk management method.

## 14

File Systems

This chapter covers the following major topics:

- ✓ File system concepts
- ✓ Supported file system types in HP-UX
- ✓ Structure and components of High-Performance File System (HFS)
- ✓ Structure and components of Journaled File System (VxFS)
- ✓ Manage file systems including creating, mounting, viewing, extending, reducing, tuning, defragmenting, unmounting and removing them
- ✓ Mount file systems automatically at system reboots
- ✓ Check and repair HFS and VxFS file system structures
- ✓ Mount and unmount CDFS and LOFS file systems
- ✓ Use tools such as bdf, df, du and quot to monitor file system space utilization
- ✓ Encrypted volume and file system (EVFS) concepts, features and components
- ✓ Manage EVFS volumes including configuring, enabling, disabling, opening, closing and removing them
- ✓ Generate, display, modify and delete keys

14.1   File System Concepts

A *file system* is a logical container that holds files and directories. Each file system is created in a separate logical volume. A typical HP-UX machine usually has numerous file systems. The following list shows file systems that *vg00* volume group normally contains and are created by default at the time HP-UX is installed.

vg00 Logical Volume	File System Type	Mount Point
/dev/vg00/lvol1	VxFS	*/stand*
/dev/vg00/lvol3	VxFS	*/*
/dev/vg00/lvol4	VxFS	*/home*
/dev/vg00/lvol5	VxFS	*/opt*
/dev/vg00/lvol6	VxFS	*/tmp*
/dev/vg00/lvol7	VxFS	*/usr*
/dev/vg00/lvol8	VxFS	*/var*

As you can see each file system is constructed in a separate logical volume and holds a unique type of information. / (root) and */stand* are special file systems without which the system cannot boot. All file systems are of type VxFS. You may create as many file systems with different types as the system permits.

Storing similar data in separate file systems versus storing all data in a single file system offers advantages such as:

✓ You can make a file system accessible or inaccessible to users independent of other file systems. This hides or unhides information contained within that file system.
✓ You can perform file system repair activities on individual file systems.
✓ You can optimize or tune each file system independently.
✓ You can grow or shrink a file system independently.

14.2   File System Types

There are several different types of supported file systems. Some of the key ones are:

✓ High-Performance File System (HFS)
✓ Veritas File System (VxFS) [a.k.a. Journaled File System (JFS)]
✓ CD/DVD File System (CDFS)
✓ Loopback File System (LOFS)
✓ Network File System (NFS)
✓ Auto File System (AutoFS)
✓ Common Internet File System (CIFS)
✓ Cache File System (CacheFS)

The *fstyp* command displays a list of all supported file system types:

```
# fstyp –l
hfs
nfs
cdfs
DevFS
ffs
lofs
procfs
vxfs
nfs3
nfs4
autofs
cachefs
cfsm
cifs
pipefs
dnlc_neg_fs
```

This chapter covers HFS, VxFS, CDFS and LOFS file system types. NFS is covered in Chapter 28 "Network File System (NFS)", AutoFS in Chapter 29 "AutoFS" and CIFS is covered in Chapter 30 "Common Internet File System".

The CacheFS file system is used to enhance access to a slow file system, usually located on a CD or DVD medium by caching its contents in physical memory. A discussion on CacheFS is beyond the scope of this book.

The following sub-sections provide in-depth information on HFS and JFS file systems. A discussion on CDFS and LOFS follows them.

14.2.1   The High-Performance File System (HFS)

HFS (also called *Unix File System* – UFS) has been supported on HP-UX for a long period of time, but is deprecated in HP-UX 11i v3 and will be removed from a future HP-UX release. HFS is designed to work on hard disk devices.

The HFS structure is built in a logical volume when an HFS file system is created in it, and is divided into two sets. One set that consists of not too many blocks, holds file system metadata information. The other set that consists of majority of file system blocks, holds actual data.

The metadata contains file system structural information including superblock, cylinder group blocks and inode table. It also contains pointers that point to specific location in the other set where actual user files are stored. See Figure 14-1.

HFS Superblock

When a file system is built, the first 8KB area is reserved for storing critical file system information. This area is referred to as the *superblock* and contains the following data about the file system:

✓   Type of the file system
✓   Size of the file system

- ✓ Number of data blocks in the file system
- ✓ Number of cylinder groups in the file system
- ✓ Data block and fragment sizes used in the file system
- ✓ File system status

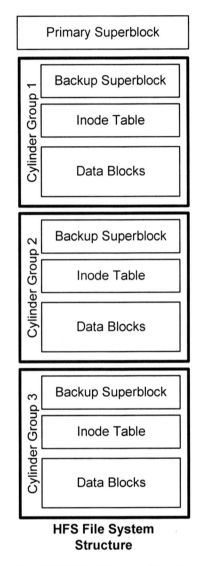

**HFS File System
Structure**

Figure 14-1 HFS File System Structure

Since the superblock holds vital information, a copy of it is automatically stored in each cylinder group within the file system, as well as in the */var/adm/sbtab* file. The superblock at the beginning of the file system is referred to as the *primary superblock* and all others as *backup superblocks*.

HFS Cylinder Groups

A file system is further divided into *cylinder groups* for better performance and manageability. The larger an HFS file system is, the more cylinder groups it will have. Each cylinder group contains a copy of the primary superblock and a portion of a file system's inodes and data blocks to be used within that cylinder group. Each cylinder group maintains its portion of inodes and data blocks.

HFS Inodes

Each file in HP-UX has an associated *index node* number, which contains information about the file. This information includes the file type, permissions on it, ownership and group membership, its size, last access/modification time, as well as pointers to data blocks that store the file contents. By default, a fixed number of inodes are generated in each cylinder group when a file system is constructed, and are allocated to files as they are created. A different number can be specified at the time of file system construction.

Inodes are maintained in *inode table* that contains information about the usage and allocation of each inode in the file system. Within a file system, each inode number is unique. If a file system runs out of inodes, you cannot create any more files in it.

HFS Data Blocks

When a file system is formed, several *data blocks* are constructed in it. These data blocks are used to store file contents. The larger a file is, the more data blocks it requires to store its contents. HFS allows a file to use scattered data blocks in a file system.

The default HFS block size is 8KB, which can be customized to a value between 4KB and 64KB at the time of file system creation.

HFS Fragments

Each HFS data block is sub-divided into *fragments*. A fragment is the smallest unit of space allocated to a file. A file system's fragment size is defined at file system creation time and cannot be altered later. The default fragment size is 1KB.

14.2.2   The Journaled File System (JFS)

The *Journaled File System* is the HP-UX implementation of the popular *Veritas File System* (VxFS), which is an extent-based journaling file system that offers several benefits over conventional HFS file system type. Some of the key advantages are:

- ✓ Superior reliability
- ✓ Fast file system recovery after a system crash
- ✓ Online file system resizing
- ✓ Online backup
- ✓ Online reorganization and defragmentation

This file system type has also been supported on HP-UX for a long period of time and is designed to work on hard disk devices.

The JFS structure is built in a logical volume when a JFS file system is created in it, and is divided into two sets. One set that consists of not too many blocks, holds file system metadata information. The other set that consists of majority of file system blocks, holds actual data.

The metadata contains file system structural information including superblock, allocation units and inode table. It also contains pointers that point to specific location in the other set where actual user files are stored. See Figure 14-1.

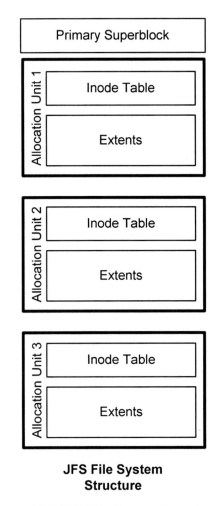

JFS File System Structure

Figure 14-2 JFS File System Structure

JFS Superblock

Like HFS, VxFS has a *superblock* at the beginning of a file system that describes the file system type, size, number of data blocks and allocation units, data block size, fragment size and file system status information.

Unlike HFS, VxFS does not keep information of its backup superblock locations in a file, rather, it finds them automatically whenever it requires.

JFS Intent Log

The journaled file system keeps track of file system structural updates in *intent log*. Each metadata update is written in its entirety to the intent log after it is complete. When the system reboots after a crash, it looks in the intent log of each JFS file system and recovers the file system rapidly using the updated structural information stored in the intent log.

JFS Allocation Units

A VxFS file system is further divided into *allocation units* for enhanced performance and manageability. The larger a VxFS file system is, the more allocation units it will have. Each allocation unit contains and maintains a portion of the file system inodes and data blocks. JFS allocation units are conceptually similar to HFS cylinder groups.

JFS Inodes

Like HFS, each file has an associated *index node* number, which contains information about the file such as the file type, permissions, ownership, group membership, size, access time and pointers to data blocks that store the file contents. When a file system is created, several inodes are generated in each allocation unit. These inodes are allocated to files as they are created. Unlike HFS, when VxFS runs out of inodes, it dynamically creates additional inodes as long as there are free data blocks available in the file system. Each inode number is unique within the file system.

JFS Blocks and Extents

In JFS, a file requires one or more blocks to store its contents. A *block* is the smallest unit of disk space that can be allocated. The default JFS block size is 1KB, which can be modified at the time the file system is created.

When you make a file, JFS allocates an *extent* to it. An extent is a contiguous group of blocks in a file system. As the file grows, JFS tries to increase the size of the extent if contiguous space is available. If contiguous space is not available, JFS uses another extent elsewhere in the file system and moves the file contents there. In order to optimize performance, JFS tries to allocate the next extent in the same allocation unit. Since file blocks are arranged contiguously in a JFS file system, JFS can read large amounts of data into memory with a single I/O operation.

14.3   Managing HFS and JFS File Systems

Managing file systems involves creating a file system, mounting it to make it accessible, extending its size, reducing its size, unmounting it to make it inaccessible, and removing it. The following sub-sections explain how to perform these operations.

14.3.1   Creating a File System

In Chapter 13, you learned about LVM and how to create logical volumes. In order for a logical volume to be able to store files and directories, it needs to be initialized as a file system, otherwise it can only be used as a raw partition or swap.

The command used to make HFS and VxFS file systems is *newfs*, which is the front-end to the *mkfs* command. In other words, *newfs* runs *mkfs* behind the scenes.

Let us assume that there are two logical volumes *lvol1* and *lvol2* in *vg01* volume group available with sizes 1GB and 2GB. Let us initialize them with the *newfs* command using different options.

To create an HFS file system in */dev/vg01/rlvol1* with all default HFS characteristics:

 # newfs –F hfs /dev/vg01/rlvol1
mkfs (hfs): Warning - 2139032776 sector(s) in the last cylinder are not allocated.
mkfs (hfs): /dev/vg01/rlvol1 - 1024000 sectors in 1642 cylinders of 16 tracks, 39 sectors
1048.6Mb in 103 cyl groups (16 c/g, 10.22Mb/g, 1600 i/g)
Super block backups (for fsck -b) at:
    16, 10040, 20064, 30088, 40112, 50136, 60160, 70184, 80208, 90232,
. . . .

To create a JFS file system in */dev/vg01/rlvol2* with all default VxFS characteristics:

 # newfs –F vxfs /dev/vg01/rlvol2
    version 6 layout
    2048000 sectors, 2048000 blocks of size 1024, log size 16384 blocks
    largefiles supported

There is no need to specify "–F vxfs" option when you create a JFS file system. The command looks into the */etc/default/fs* file for the variable LOCAL. By default, this variable is set to "vxfs".

The *newfs* command supports various options, some of which are listed in Table 14-1 and used in examples below.

Option	Description
–o largefiles	Enables you to create files of sizes up to 128GB in the file system. This is default.
–b	Specifies the block size.
–m	Minimum amount of free space, as a percent of the total file system size, to be maintained in the file system (HFS only).

Table 14-1 *newfs* Command Options

The following example demonstrates how to create an HFS file system in */dev/vg01/rlvol1* with largefiles support and 15% minimum free space to maintain:

 # newfs –F hfs –o largefiles –m 15 /dev/vg01/rlvol1
mkfs (hfs): Warning - 2139032792 sector(s) in the last cylinder are not allocated.
mkfs (hfs): /dev/vg01/rlvol1 - 1024000 sectors in 1642 cylinders of 16 tracks, 39 sectors
1048.6Mb in 103 cyl groups (16 c/g, 10.22Mb/g, 1600 i/g)
Super block backups (for fsck -b) at:
    16, 10040, 20064, 30088, 40112, 50136, 60160, 70184, 80208, 90232,
. . . .

Instead of using *newfs*, you may use its variants to create HFS or VxFS file system. The variants are */sbin/fs/hfs/newfs* for HFS and */sbin/fs/vxfs/newfs* for VxFS. There is no need to use the –F option with them. Here is how you would create the */dev/vg01/rlvol1* and */dev/vg01/rlvol2* file systems using these commands:

 # /sbin/fs/hfs/newfs /dev/vg01/rlvol1
 # /sbin/fs/vxfs/newfs /dev/vg01/rlvol2

Notice that the results of these commands and those of *newfs* with –F option are identical.

14.3.2   Mounting a File System

After a file system is constructed, it must be made accessible by connecting it to the root of the directory hierarchy. A directory needs to be created for this purpose, which will be referred to as the *mount point*. Next, use the *mount* command to mount the file system on the mount point.

Currently, there are two file systems */dev/vg01/lvol1* and */dev/vg01/lvol2* from the previous subsection. Here is the procedure to mount them using appropriate options.

To mount */dev/vg01/lvol1* HFS file system on */data1*, use any of the two *mount* commands:

> # **mkdir /data1**
> # **mount –F hfs /dev/vg01/lvol1 /data1**
> # **/sbin/fs/hfs/mount /dev/vg01/lvol1 /data1**

To mount */dev/vg01/lvol2* JFS file system on */data2*, use any of the two *mount* commands:

> # **mkdir /data2**
> # **mount –F vxfs /dev/vg01/lvol2 /data2**
> # **/sbin/fs/vxfs/mount /dev/vg01/lvol2 /data2**

Note that "–F hfs" and "–F vxfs" are optional. There is no need to specify them when you use the *mount* command. The reason being that the *mount* command detects the file system type and automatically mounts an HFS file system as HFS and a JFS file system as JFS.

When a file system is mounted, an entry is added to the mount table located in the */etc/mnttab* file. Here are the file contents after mounting the two file systems:

> # **cat /etc/mnttab**
> /dev/vg00/lvol3 /   vxfs ioerror=nodisable,log,dev=40000003 0 1 1208356058
> /dev/vg00/lvol1 /stand vxfs ioerror=nodisable,log,dev=40000001 0 0 1208356072
> /dev/vg00/lvol8 /var   vxfs ioerror=mwdisable,delaylog,dev=40000008 0 0 1208356089
> /dev/vg00/lvol7 /usr   vxfs ioerror=mwdisable,delaylog,dev=40000007 0 0 1208356089
> /dev/vg00/lvol6 /tmp   vxfs ioerror=mwdisable,delaylog,dev=40000006 0 0 1208356089
> /dev/vg00/lvol5 /opt   vxfs ioerror=mwdisable,delaylog,dev=40000005 0 0 1208356090
> /dev/vg00/lvol4 /home vxfs ioerror=mwdisable,delaylog,dev=40000004 0 0 1208356090
> -hosts   /net   autofs ignore,indirect,nosuid,soft,nobrowse,dev=4000002 0 0 1208356148
> **/dev/vg01/lvol2 /data2 vxfs ioerror=mwdisable,delaylog,dev=40010002 0 0 1208357340**
> **/dev/vg01/lvol1 /data1 hfs defaults,dev=40010001 0 0 1208357345**

14.3.3   Viewing Mounted File Systems

There are several tools available to list mounted file systems; two tools – *bdf* and *mount* – are more common and both read the */etc/mnttab* file to display the information.

Run the *bdf* command to view mounted file systems. Notice that *lvol1* and *lvol2* file systems are mounted on */data1* and */data2*:

bdf

Filesystem	kbytes	used	avail	%used	Mounted on
/dev/vg00/lvol3	1024000	856632	166104	84%	/
/dev/vg00/lvol1	990968	53464	838400	6%	/stand
/dev/vg00/lvol8	4096000	853576	3217144	21%	/var
/dev/vg00/lvol7	4096000	2295632	1786368	56%	/usr
/dev/vg00/lvol6	516096	20200	492088	4%	/tmp
/dev/vg00/lvol5	7168000	4551936	2595976	64%	/opt
/dev/vg00/lvol4	516096	5888	506224	1%	/home
/dev/vg01/lvol2	**2048000**	**17587**	**1903520**	**1%**	**/data2**
/dev/vg01/lvol1	**1001729**	**9**	**901547**	**0%**	**/data1**

Run the *mount* command with and without –v option to view mounted file systems:

mount –v

/dev/vg00/lvol3 on / type vxfs ioerror=nodisable,log,dev=40000003 on Wed Apr 16 10:27:38 2008
/dev/vg00/lvol1 on /stand type vxfs ioerror=nodisable,log,dev=40000001 on Wed Apr 16 10:27:52 2008
/dev/vg00/lvol8 on /var type vxfs ioerror=mwdisable,delaylog,dev=40000008 on Wed Apr 16 10:28:09 2008
/dev/vg00/lvol7 on /usr type vxfs ioerror=mwdisable,delaylog,dev=40000007 on Wed Apr 16 10:28:09 2008
/dev/vg00/lvol6 on /tmp type vxfs ioerror=mwdisable,delaylog,dev=40000006 on Wed Apr 16 10:28:09 2008
/dev/vg00/lvol5 on /opt type vxfs ioerror=mwdisable,delaylog,dev=40000005 on Wed Apr 16 10:28:10 2008
/dev/vg00/lvol4 on /home type vxfs ioerror=mwdisable,delaylog,dev=40000004 on Wed Apr 16 10:28:10 2008
-hosts on /net type autofs ignore,indirect,nosuid,soft,nobrowse,dev=4000002 on Wed Apr 16 10:29:08 2008
/dev/vg01/lvol2 on /data2 type vxfs ioerror=mwdisable,delaylog,dev=40010002 on Wed Apr 16 10:49:00 2008
/dev/vg01/lvol1 on /data1 type hfs defaults,dev=40010001 on Wed Apr 16 10:49:05 2008

14.3.4 Creating, Mounting and Viewing a File System Using SMH

SMH (or *fsweb* command) may be used to add file systems. Follow the steps below:

☞ Go to SMH → Disks and File Systems → File Systems. Press v to add a VxFS file system or h to add an HFS file system. Fill out the form with required information. Press "Select Unused LV" to choose the logical volume to create a new file system in. The "Mount now and save configuration in /etc/fstab" will mount the file system and add an entry for it to the */etc/fstab* file so that the file system is automatically mounted at each system reboot. Choose any other options and press "Add VxFS" to create file system structures in the specified logical volume. Figure 14-3 shows the form to create a VxFS type file system.

```
                    HP-UX System Management Homepage (Text User Interface)
                    SMH->Disks and File Systems->File Systems->New VxFS File System
--------------------------------------------------------------------------------
Mount Point * (specify an absolute path):  █_____

[ Select Unused Disk... ] [ Select Unused LV... ]
No disk or LV has been selected

Configure File System Attributes
Add File System Method:   (X) Create new file system on device (newfs)
                          ( ) Add existing file system on device (mount)
VxFS Version (leave blank to use default):  __
  [X] Enable large files(largefiles/nolargefiles)
  [ ] Run file system consistency check (fsck)

[ Advanced VxFS Options >> ]




Configure Mount Options
Mount Method:   (X) Mount now and save configuration in /etc/fstab
                ( ) Only mount(do not store any configuration /etc/fstab
                ( ) Save configuration in /etc/fstab

  [ ] Mount read-only(ro/rw)

  [X] Enable suid(suid/nosuid)

  [ ] Enable quota(quota/noquota)

  [X] Enable synchronous write logging(datainlog/nodatainlog)

Intent Logging Policy: delaylog          ->

[ Advanced VxFS Mount Options >> ]




[ Add VxFS ] [ Preview ] [ Cancel ] [ Help ]
```

Figure 14-3 SMH – File System Add

14.3.5   Extending a File System

Extending a file system adds more space to it. Both HFS and VxFS file systems can be extended. The first step is to grow the logical volume that contains the file system using the procedure outlined in Chapter 13 "Logical Volume Manager". Next, follow the steps below for HFS and VxFS file system expansion.

To add space to the HFS file system */dev/vg01/rlvol1* mounted on */data1*, unmount the file system and extend it with the *extendfs* command. When done, remount it and use *bdf* to verify.

umount /data1
extendfs −F hfs /dev/vg01/rlvol1
     max number of sectors extendible is 512000.
extend file system /dev/vg01/rlvol1 to have 512000 sectors more.
Warning: 288 sector(s) in last cylinder unallocated
extended super-block backups (for fsck -b#) at:
 1028648, 1038672, 1048696, 1058720, 1068744, 1078768, 1088792, 1098816, 1108840, 1118224,
. . . .
mount −F hfs /dev/vg01/lvol1 /data1

To add space to the VxFS file system */dev/vg01/rlvol2* mounted on */data2*, follow the procedure outlined above (use −F vxfs instead) for HFS file system. Alternatively, use the *fsadm* command to extend the size online, provided the OnlineJFS product is installed. Run the following to grow the size to 2.5GB assuming that OnlineJFS is loaded:

> **# fsadm −F vxfs −b 2560000 /data2**
> vxfs fsadm: V-3-23585: /dev/vg01/rlvol2 is currently 2048000 sectors - size will be increased

The −b option specifies the total number of blocks to be allocated to */data2*. The value 2560000 comes by multiplying 2500MB with 1024. Confirm the new size with the *bdf* command.

14.3.6   Reducing a File System

There are times when you need to reduce the size of a file system. It is possible to reduce a JFS file system size online, provided OnlineJFS product is installed. However, an HFS file system cannot be reduced online. The only way to shrink it is to back it up, reduce the logical volume it resides in, run *newfs* on the logical volume, mount the file system and restore the data in it.

To decrease */data2* from 2.5GB to 2GB, reduce the file system and then the logical volume:

> **# fsadm −F vxfs −b 2048000 /data2**
> vxfs fsadm: V-3-23586: /dev/vg01/rlvol2 is currently 2560000 sectors - size will be reduced
> **# lvreduce −L 2000 /dev/vg01/lvol2**
> When a logical volume is reduced useful data might get lost;
> do you really want the command to proceed (y/n) : y
> Logical volume "/dev/vg01/lvol2" has been successfully reduced.
> Volume Group configuration for /dev/vg01 has been saved in /etc/lvmconf/vg01.conf

Observe extreme caution when reducing a file system size. Any data on the blocks being removed will be lost. It is highly recommended to do a backup prior to performing this action.

14.3.7   Tuning a JFS File System

When mounting a JFS file system, you have the choice to supply options with the *mount* command. There is a command called *vxtunefs* that provides the ability to display and tune I/O parameters of a mounted JFS file system. This command can be used to display or tune parameters that:

- ✓ Describe I/O properties of the underlying device
- ✓ Indicate when to treat an I/O as direct I/O
- ✓ Control the extent allocation policy

To display existing parameters for the */home* file system, for instance, do the following:

> **# vxtunefs /home**
> Filesystem i/o parameters for /home
> read_pref_io = 65536
> read_nstream = 1
> . . . .

Any of these parameters can be tuned with the *vxtunefs* command. See its man pages on usage.

14.3.8   Defragmenting a JFS File System

Over the period of time, files are created and removed in a file system. Also, files are edited and their sizes are increased or decreased. Similar functions are performed at the directory level too. These operations result in file system fragmentation causing portions of files to reside in extents and blocks physically away from one another. Fragmentation affects data read and write performance in the file system.

HP-UX allows you to defragment a JFS file system online using the *fsadm* command. In fact, it is not a bad idea to run defragmentation once in a while automatically via *cron*.

To defragment extents (–e option) and directory entries (–d option) in a JFS file system, */var* for example, do the following:

 # fsadm –F vxfs –ed /var

This command may take several minutes to finish.

14.3.9   Unmounting a File System

Unmounting a file system makes the file system inaccessible to users by disconnecting it from the directory structure. The procedure to unmount both HFS and JFS file systems is the same. Use the *umount* command to unmount both file systems constructed earlier:

 # umount /data1
 # umount /data2

The *umount* command scans the */etc/mnttab* file and determine the logical volume device file associated with the mount point to unmount it.

Occasionally, you get the "Device busy" message when attempting to unmount a file system:

 # umount /data1
umount: cannot unmount /data1 : Device busy

This message indicates that the specified file system is currently busy. A process or a user might be using it or a file in that file system is open.

To determine who or what processes are using the file system, use the *fuser* command:

 # fuser –cu /data1
/data1:   26458c(root)   11411c(root)

The –c option tells the process ID and –u gives the username who owns the process ID.

You can kill all the processes using the file system by running the *fuser* command with –k option:

 # fuser –ck /data1
/data1:   26458c   11411c

Now you should be able to unmount */data1*.

Alternatively, you can use the –f switch with the *umount* command to forcibly kill all processes using the file system and unmount it.

At times, it becomes crucial to unmount all mounted file systems, other than */var*, */usr* and */* that cannot be unmounted. Issue the *umount* command with –a option or the *umountall* command:

```
# umount –a
# umountall
umountall: umount : has failed.
umountall: diagnostics from umount
umount: cannot unmount /dev/vg00/lvol3 : Device busy
umount: return error 1.
umountall: umount : has failed.
umountall: diagnostics from umount
umount: cannot unmount /dev/vg00/lvol7 : Device busy
umount: return error 1.
umountall: umount : has failed.
umountall: diagnostics from umount
umount: cannot unmount /dev/vg00/lvol8 : Device busy
umount: return error 1.
```

14.3.10 Mounting a File System at System Boot

So far, you have mounted file systems from the command line or using SMH. If the system reboots, no file systems will be remounted automatically, and will need to be mounted manually. To automate mounting of a file system across system reboots, file system entries must be placed in the */etc/fstab* file.

When the system comes up, the */sbin/init.d/localmount* script is called that executes the *mountall* command, which attempts to mount all file systems listed in the */etc/fstab* file. This file needs to be manually updated to add or remove a file system entry.

Another advantage is that the file system can be mounted by specifying only its mount point or the associated device file. There is no need to type in the full command.

The default */etc/fstab* file contains entries only for file systems that make up the root volume group, as shown below:

```
# cat /etc/fstab
# System /etc/fstab file.  Static information about the file systems
# See fstab(4) and sam(1M) for further details on configuring devices.
/dev/vg00/lvol3      /        vxfs    delaylog      0      1
/dev/vg00/lvol1      /stand   vxfs    delaylog      0      1
/dev/vg00/lvol4      /home    vxfs    delaylog      0      2
/dev/vg00/lvol5      /opt     vxfs    delaylog      0      2
/dev/vg00/lvol6      /tmp     vxfs    delaylog      0      2
/dev/vg00/lvol7      /usr     vxfs    delaylog      0      2
/dev/vg00/lvol8      /var     vxfs    delaylog      0      2
```

Notice that there are six fields per line entry:

- ✓ The first field defines the block device for the logical volume where the file system resides.
- ✓ The second field defines the mount point.
- ✓ The third field specifies the type of file system such as vxfs, hfs, cdfs, nfs, swap and swapfs.
- ✓ The fourth field specifies any options to use when mounting the file system. Available options are: defaults, ro, nosuid, quota, delaylog, etc. The "defaults" option includes rw, suid, largefiles and noquota. Some options such as delaylog are used only with JFS file systems.
- ✓ The fifth field is always "0"; it is reserved for future use.
- ✓ The last field indicates the sequence number in which to run the *fsck* (file system check and repair) utility on the file system. It is 1 for / and */stand,* and 2 for others, by default.

Add the */data1* and */data2* file system entries to */etc/fstab* using vi. The updated file will look like:

cat /etc/fstab

System /etc/fstab file. Static information about the file systems
See fstab(4) and sam(1M) for further details on configuring devices.

/dev/vg00/lvol3	/	vxfs	delaylog	0	1
/dev/vg00/lvol1	/stand	vxfs	defaults	0	1
/dev/vg00/lvol4	/home	vxfs	delaylog	0	2
/dev/vg00/lvol5	/opt	vxfs	delaylog	0	2
/dev/vg00/lvol6	/tmp	vxfs	delaylog	0	2
/dev/vg00/lvol7	/usr	vxfs	delaylog	0	2
/dev/vg00/lvol8	/var	vxfs	delaylog	0	2
/dev/vg01/lvol1	/data1	hfs	defaults	0	2
/dev/vg01/lvol2	/data2	vxfs	delaylog	0	2

After making the entries, if you wish to mount all file systems listed in the file but not currently mounted, use one of the following:

mount –a
mountall

To mount only */data1*, do one of the following:

mount /data1
mount /dev/vg01/lvol1

Remember, the *mount* and *mountall* commands look into the */etc/fstab* file to mount file systems.

14.3.11   Removing a File System

Removing a file system is a destructive operation. It wipes out all data from the file system. To remove a file system, simply unmount it and remove the logical volume that holds it. The procedure is same for both HFS and JFS file systems. Use the *lvremove* command to remove *lvol1* from *vg01*. Type y for confirmation, when prompted.

---

lvremove /dev/vg01/lvol1
The logical volume "/dev/vg01/lvol1" is not empty;
do you really want to delete the logical volume (y/n) : **y**
Logical volume "/dev/vg01/lvol1" has been successfully removed.
Volume Group configuration for /dev/vg01 has been saved in /etc/lvmconf/vg01.conf

To remove a file system using SMH (or *fsweb* command), follow the steps below:

☞ Go to SMH → Disks and File Systems → File Systems. Highlight the file system, press Enter to Select it and then u to unmount/remove it.

14.4   Repairing a Damaged File System

The structure of a file system could be damaged when an abnormal system shutdown or crash occurs. To maintain file system integrity, a utility called *fsck* is used. This utility is executed automatically at system reboot following an abnormal shutdown or crash. It checks file system structures and corrects any inconsistencies found. The utility can also be executed manually on a file system from the command line.

14.4.1   Repairing a Damaged HFS File System

fsck performs multiple checks on an HFS file system and reports any inconsistencies found. It also attempts to fix them. If an inconsistency cannot be resolved, it prompts for intervention. You run *fsck* manually and try to fix the inconsistencies. The command prompts for a "yes" or "no" reply. It may take several minutes to check and repair an HFS file system. The following example runs *fsck* on a mounted (use –f option) HFS file system. There is no need to use the –f option if the command is run on an unmounted file system. Specify appropriate device file for the logical volume:

fsck –F hfs –f /dev/vg01/rlvol1
** /dev/vg01/rlvol1
** Last Mounted on /data1
** Phase 1 - Check Blocks and Sizes
** Phase 2 - Check Pathnames
** Phase 3 - Check Connectivity
** Phase 4 - Check Reference Counts
** Phase 5 - Check Cyl groups
2 files, 0 icont, 9 used, 1001720 free (8 frags, 125214 blocks)
***** MARKING FILE SYSTEM CLEAN *****
***** FILE SYSTEM WAS MODIFIED *****

If the primary superblock is missing or corrupted, check the */var/adm/sbtab* file and use one of the backup superblock locations to repair the primary. For example, do the following to restore the primary superblock using an alternate location at block number 16:

fsck –F hfs –b 16 /dev/vg01/rlvol1
Alternate super block location: 16
fsck: /dev/vg01/rlvol1: mounted file system
continue (y/n)? y
** /dev/vg01/rlvol1

```
** Last Mounted on
** Phase 1 - Check Blocks and Sizes
** Phase 2 - Check Pathnames
** Phase 3 - Check Connectivity
** Phase 4 - Check Reference Counts
** Phase 5 - Check Cyl groups
2 files, 0 icont, 9 used, 1001720 free (8 frags, 125214 blocks)
***** FILE SYSTEM WAS MODIFIED *****
```

While checking a file system, *fsck* may encounter a file with a missing name. It moves the file to the *lost+found* directory located in that file system. This file is known as an *orphan* file and is renamed to correspond to its inode number. You need to figure out the actual name of the file. Use the *file* command to determine the file's type. If it is a text file, use *cat* or *more* to view contents, otherwise, use the *strings* command to view legible contents in it. You can move the file to its correct directory location if you determine the whereabouts of it.

14.4.2   Repairing a Damaged JFS File System

Issue the *fsck* command on a VxFS file system the way you ran it on the HFS file system, however, there is no need to specify the file system type. The *fsck* command looks into the */etc/default/fs* file where vxfs is pre-defined as the default file system type. On a VxFS file system, *fsck* simply replays the intent log and completes any pending transactions. It takes only a few seconds for the command to check and fix a VxFS file system. A VxFS file system must be unmounted to run *fsck* on it. Specify an appropriate device file for the logical volume:

> # **fsck /dev/vg01/rlvol2**
> file system is clean - log replay is not required

You can force *fsck* to do a full check of all file system structures by supplying to the command "–o full" option or simply use "–o nolog" option to prevent an intent log replay:

> # **fsck –o full /dev/vg01/rlvol2**
> log replay in progress
> pass0 - checking structural files
> pass1 - checking inode sanity and blocks
> pass2 - checking directory linkage
> pass3 - checking reference counts
> pass4 - checking resource maps
> OK to clear log? (ynq)y
> flush fileset headers? (ynq)y
> set state to CLEAN? (ynq)y

14.5   Managing CDFS and LOFS File Systems

Other than VxFS and HFS file systems, you may need to manage CDFS and LOFS file systems as well. Managing them usually involves mounting and unmounting them.

14.5.1   Mounting and Unmounting a CDFS File System

Software on CDs and DVDs are available in read-only mode. A CD or DVD contains CDFS file system structure. To mount it, determine its block DSF using the *ioscan* command:

 # ioscan –fNnkCdisk | DVD
disk   3 64000/0xfa00/0x1 esdisk CLAIMED   DEVICE   HP   DVD-ROM 305
            /dev/disk/disk3   /dev/rdisk/disk3

The output indicates that there is a DVD drive at */dev/disk/disk3*.

Load a CD or DVD in the drive. Create a mount point such as */dvdrom*:

 # mkdir /dvdrom

Mount the CD/DVD in read-only mode:

 # mount –F cdfs –o ro /dev/disk/disk3 /dvdrom

–F specifies file system type and –o instructs the command to mount the CD/DVD as read-only.

Now the CD/DVD contents are available for use from the */dvdrom* directory.

At times, you need to use the "cdcase" or the "rr" option when mounting a CD/DVD, otherwise, all file names under */dvdrom* are displayed in uppercase letters, which is not a desirable condition since HP-UX is case-sensitive and normally works with lowercase letters. Do the following to use the two options:

 # mount –F cdfs –o cdcase –o ro /dev/disk/disk3 /dvdrom
 # mount –F cdfs –o rr –o ro /dev/disk/disk3 /dvdrom

To unmount a CD/DVD file system, issue the *umount* command and supply either the mount point or the associated device file as an argument. If mount point is supplied, the command gets the device file name from the */etc/mnttab* file:

 # umount /dvdrom
 # umount /dev/disk/disk3

14.5.2   Mounting and Unmounting a LOFS File System

The *Loopback File System* (LOFS) is a virtual file system that provides an alternate path to access an existing directory or file system. The existing directory or file system can be local or remote, and of any type (in case of a file system). If there are any local or remote file systems mounted under that directory or file system, they will become available as part of the mount as well. For example, let us mount */usr* as a loopback file system on */lofs* directory:

 # mkdir /lofs
 # mount –F lofs /usr /lofs

This makes all files and sub-directories beneath */usr* to become accessible via paths */usr* and */lofs*.

14.6   Monitoring File System Space Utilization

File system monitoring involves checking used and available file system space and inodes. It also includes watching space occupied by individual users. Several tools such as *bdf*, *df*, *du* and *quot* are available to view this information. These tools are discussed in the following sub-sections.

14.6.1   Using bdf

bdf displays information about file system utilization. Run this command without any options and you would see output similar to the following. It is assumed that both *lvol1* and *vol2* in *vg01* still exist and are mounted.

```
# bdf
```

Filesystem	kbytes	used	avail	%used	Mounted on
/dev/vg00/lvol3	1024000	856696	166040	84%	/
/dev/vg00/lvol8	4096000	853824	3216896	21%	/var
/dev/vg00/lvol7	4096000	2295656	1786344	56%	/usr
/dev/vg00/lvol6	516096	20200	492088	4%	/tmp
/dev/vg00/lvol5	7168000	4552024	2595888	64%	/opt
/dev/vg00/lvol1	990968	53464	838400	6%	/stand
/dev/vg00/lvol4	516096	5888	506224	1%	/home
/dev/vg01/lvol1	1001729	9	901547	0%	/data1
/usr	4096000	2295656	1786344	56%	/lofs
/dev/vg01/lvol2	2048000	17587	1903520	1%	/data2

There are six fields in the output. A description of each is given in Table 14-2.

Field	Description
File system	Block device file for the logical volume that contains the file system.
Kbytes	Total amount of disk space allocated to the file system.
Used	Amount of used file system space.
Avail	Amount of file system space available for use.
%Used	Percentage amount of used file system space.
Mounted on	Mount point.

Table 14-2 *bdf* Command Output Description

Try running *bdf* with –i option. It adds three columns to the output, providing information on inode utilization as well.

```
# bdf –i
```

Filesystem	kbytes	used	avail	%used	iused	ifree	%iuse	Mounted on
/dev/vg00/lvol3	1024000	856696	166040	84%	3448	5224	40%	/
/dev/vg00/lvol8	4096000	853824	3216896	21%	20591	101297	17%	/var
/dev/vg00/lvol7	4096000	2295656	1786344	56%	38184	56248	40%	/usr
/dev/vg00/lvol6	516096	20200	492088	4%	35	15485	0%	/tmp
/dev/vg00/lvol5	7168000	4551992	2595920	64%	66705	81743	45%	/opt
/dev/vg00/lvol1	990968	53464	838400	6%	196	158012	0%	/stand
/dev/vg00/lvol4	516096	5888	506224	1%	28	15940	0%	/home

/dev/vg01/lvol1	1001729	9 901547 0%	4 164796 0%	/data1
/usr	4096000	2295656 1786344 56%	38184 56248 40%	/lofs
/dev/vg01/lvol2	2048000	17587 1903520 1%	4 507600 0%	/data2

The *bdf* command with –t option displays utilization of only the specified file system type:

```
# bdf –t hfs
```

Filesystem	kbytes	used	avail	%used	Mounted on
/dev/vg01/lvol1	1001729	9	901547	0%	/data1

```
# bdf –t vxfs
```

Filesystem	kbytes	used	avail	%used	Mounted on
/dev/vg00/lvol1	990968	53464	838400	6%	/stand
/dev/vg00/lvol3	1024000	856696	166040	84%	/
/dev/vg00/lvol8	4096000	853928	3216792	21%	/var
/dev/vg00/lvol7	4096000	2295656	1786344	56%	/usr
/dev/vg00/lvol6	516096	20200	492088	4%	/tmp
/dev/vg00/lvol5	7168000	4552024	2595888	64%	/opt
/dev/vg00/lvol4	516096	5888	506224	1%	/home
/dev/vg01/lvol2	2048000	17587	1903520	1%	/data2

14.6.2   Using df

df reports on available file system blocks and inodes. It lists each file system with its corresponding logical volume device file, free blocks (in 512 byte size) and free inodes.

```
# df
```

/data2	(/dev/vg01/lvol2	):	3807040 blocks	507600 i-nodes
/lofs	(/usr	):	3572688 blocks	56248 i-nodes
/data1	(/dev/vg01/lvol1	):	1803094 blocks	164796 i-nodes
/home	(/dev/vg00/lvol4	):	1012448 blocks	15940 i-nodes
/stand	(/dev/vg00/lvol1	):	1676800 blocks	158012 i-nodes
/opt	(/dev/vg00/lvol5	):	5191920 blocks	81745 i-nodes
/tmp	(/dev/vg00/lvol6	):	984176 blocks	15485 i-nodes
/usr	(/dev/vg00/lvol7	):	3572688 blocks	56248 i-nodes
/var	(/dev/vg00/lvol8	):	6433680 blocks	101297 i-nodes
/	(/dev/vg00/lvol3	):	332080 blocks	5224 i-nodes

Try this command with –k option to see results in 1KB block size:

```
# df –k
```

/data2	(/dev/vg01/lvol2	) : 1921107 total allocated Kb
		1903520 free allocated Kb
		17587 used allocated Kb
		1 % allocation used
/lof	(/usr	) : 4082000 total allocated Kb
		1786344 free allocated Kb
		2295656 used allocated Kb
		57 % allocation used
/data1	(/dev/vg01/lvol1	) : 901556 total allocated Kb

```
                        901547 free allocated Kb
                           9 used allocated Kb
                           1 % allocation used
/home       (/dev/vg00/lvol4    ) :  512112 total allocated Kb
                      506224 free allocated Kb
                        5888 used allocated Kb
                           2 % allocation used
/stand      (/dev/vg00/lvol1    ) :  891864 total allocated Kb
                      838400 free allocated Kb
                       53464 used allocated Kb
                           6 % allocation used
/opt        (/dev/vg00/lvol5    ) : 7147912 total allocated Kb
                     2595920 free allocated Kb
                     4551992 used allocated Kb
                          64 % allocation used
/tmp        (/dev/vg00/lvol6    ) :  512288 total allocated Kb
                      492088 free allocated Kb
                       20200 used allocated Kb
                           4 % allocation used
/usr        (/dev/vg00/lvol7    ) : 4082000 total allocated Kb
                     1786344 free allocated Kb
                     2295656 used allocated Kb
                          57 % allocation used
/var        (/dev/vg00/lvol8    ) : 4070720 total allocated Kb
                     3216864 free allocated Kb
                      853856 used allocated Kb
                          21 % allocation used
/           (/dev/vg00/lvol3    ) : 1022736 total allocated Kb
                      166040 free allocated Kb
                      856696 used allocated Kb
                          84 % allocation used
```

Try running *df* with "–F hfs" and "–F vxfs" options.

14.6.3   Using du

du calculates amount of disk space a file, directory or file system is currently using.

 # du –k /stand
```
    64 /stand/lost+found
    24 /stand/krs
    16 /stand/current/bootfs/stand/current/krs
   248 /stand/current/bootfs/stand/current/mod
   272 /stand/current/bootfs/stand/current
   280 /stand/current/bootfs/stand
   288 /stand/current/bootfs
 17464 /stand/current/mod
   112 /stand/current/krs
 50656 /stand/current
```

```
    896 /stand/last_install/mod
    112 /stand/last_install/krs
     16 /stand/last_install/bootfs/stand/current/krs
    248 /stand/last_install/bootfs/stand/current/mod
    272 /stand/last_install/bootfs/stand/current
    280 /stand/last_install/bootfs/stand
    288 /stand/last_install/bootfs
   1320 /stand/last_install
    896 /stand/backup/mod
    112 /stand/backup/krs
     16 /stand/backup/bootfs/stand/current/krs
    248 /stand/backup/bootfs/stand/current/mod
    272 /stand/backup/bootfs/stand/current
    280 /stand/backup/bootfs/stand
    288 /stand/backup/bootfs
   1320 /stand/backup
  53464 /stand
```

The –k option displays the output in KBs. The –s option shows only the total count. Try running the command again with –sk options.

14.6.4   Using quot

quot gives information on file system space usage by individual users.

```
# quot /var
/dev/vg00/rlvol8 (/var):
421541  root
105109  hpsmdb
104204  sfmdb
 96190  bin
 28353  cimsrvr
  8334  adm
   370  daemon
   146  hpsmh
. . . . . . . .
```

The *quot* command picks up the file system type from */etc/default/fs* file. For an HFS file system, you must specify "–F hfs" with the command.

This command reports on all file systems with –a option, number of files owned by individual users with –f option, and provides verbose information with –v option. Try these options with *quot*.

14.7   Encrypted Volume and File System (EVFS)

Encrypted Volume and File System (EVFS) is a virtual device driver that uses encryption techniques to safeguard data that resides in a logical volume from unauthorized users. The other major use of EVFS is to create encrypted backup media. After a logical volume is constructed, the next step is to create an EVFS volume in it, which is used as a virtual device. File system structures are then created in the EVFS volume. In other words, EVFS is a virtual layer sandwiched between a logical volume and the file system structures (or raw partition). Any data written to the volume will now be encrypted. Similarly, any data read from the volume will be decrypted.

An EVFS volume has several encryption attributes associated with it which are stored in the volume itself. These attributes include encryption keys, and are collectively referred to as *Encryption Meta Data* (EMD).

EVFS has limitations. It does not currently support data encryption in */, /stand* and */usr* file systems, and in swap and dump devices.

EVFS uses a *symmetric encryption key* algorithm called *volume encryption key* algorithm, to generate user keys (public and private key pair) for data encryption. The public key must be decrypted with the private key to retrieve the volume encryption key. 128-bit, 192-bit and 256-bit symmetric key algorithms based on *Advanced Encryption Standard* (AES) are supported. For user keys 1024-bit, 1536-bit and 2048-bit *Rivest Shamir Adleman* (RSA) key algorithms are supported.

14.7.1   Benefits

Software applications in an EVFS volume see nothing unusual. For them, encryption and decryption operations are transparent. For increased protection, each private key may be encrypted with a user-specified or a system-generated passphrase that contains system-specific information. The passphrase may be stored in either the EMD or a file. If stored in the EMD, it enables EVFS to retrieve a user's private key without being prompted for the passphrase. If stored in a file, the passphrase can be retrieved to execute EVFS commands automatically at system boot.

14.7.2   EVFS Keys Recommendations

Certain recommendations should be followed when working with EVFS keys. These are:

- ✓ Generate at least one user key pair for the EVFS volume owner
- ✓ Generate separate key pair for each EVFS volume
- ✓ Generate at least one recovery key pair per EVFS volume
- ✓ Generate a passphrase file
- ✓ Generate and configure an authorized user key pair

14.7.3   EVFS User Keys

EVFS *user keys* are generated to add protection to an EVFS volume. Each user key pair has an owner and a key name. There are three types of user keys: EVFS volume owner key, recovery key and authorized user key.

An EVFS *volume owner key* is the key specified when creating an EVFS volume. The user who owns it is called *volume owner*. The volume owner has administrative rights to perform management operations such as enabling and disabling EVFS for the volume and adding key records to the EMD.

A *recovery key* is the key used to change the volume owner key in case it is lost.

An *authorized user* key allows a user to perform management operations on an EVFS volume that are otherwise performed by the owner, with the exception that the user is unable to change the volume owner, add keys to the volume and destroy the EMD.

14.7.4　Commands and Files

Table 14-3 lists and explains EVFS administration commands.

Command	Description
evfsadm	Manages EVFS tasks such as starting and stopping EVFS, and creating EVFS volume device files.
evfspkey	Creates, stores and administers user keys and passphrases.
evfsvol	Performs EVFS volume tasks such as creating and enabling EVFS volumes, displaying EVFS volume information and adding user keys to EVFS volumes.

Table 14-3 EVFS Commands

Table 14-4 lists and explains EVFS configuration, startup and shutdown files.

File	Description
/etc/evfs/evfs.conf	Main EVFS configuration file for setting attributes such as: data_cipher to specify the default data encryption algorithm. 128-bit (default), 192-bit and 256-bit AES algorithms are supported. emd_backup to specify the directory location where EMD backup copies are stored. Default is */etc/evfs/emd*.
/etc/evfs/emd	Default directory location to store EMD backup copies.
/etc/evfs/pkey	Directory location to store user keys and passphrases. A sub-directory for each user who owns user keys is created here. The sub-directory name is the same as the username. For example, the default user keys for *user1* would be: */etc/evfs/pkey/user1/user1.pub* (public key) */etc/evfs/pkey/user1/user1.priv* (private key) */etc/evfs/pkey/user1/user1.pass.nnn* (passphrase), where nnn is a number based on system-specific data.
/etc/rc.config.d/evfs	Startup / shutdown configuration file.
/sbin/init.d/evfs_local	Starts (and stops) EVFS volumes that have keys stored on the root disk of the local system.
/sbin/init.d/evfs_local2	Starts (and stops) EVFS volumes that have keys stored on a non-root disk of the local system.
/sbin/init.d/evfs_remote	Starts (and stops) EVFS volumes that have keys stored on an NFS-mounted file system.
/etc/evfs/evfstab	Lists EVFS volumes to be enabled at system boot based on the boot_local, boot_local2 and boot_remote options. The syntax for each line entry in the file is: v /dev/vg01/lvol1 /dev/evfs/vg01/lvol1 user1.user1key boot_local

Table 14-4 EVFS Files

14.7.5   Configuring EVFS

Configuring EVFS on a volume requires performing a series of tasks. These tasks are highlighted below:

1. If not already installed, go to *www.software.hp.com* → Security and manageability → HP-UX 11i Encrypted Volume and File System → Receive for Free. Fill out the form and download the software.
2. Store the depot file in a directory such as */var/tmp*.
3. Install the software using the *swinstall* command:

    # swinstall –s /var/tmp/EVFS_A.01.00.02_HP-UX_B.11.31_IA+PA.depot

4. Verify the installation with the *swverify* command:

    # swverify EVFS
    . . . .
            EVFS,r=A.01.00.02,a=HP-UX_B.11.31_IA/PA,v=HP
    . . . .
        * The analysis phase succeeded for "hp01:/".
        * Verification succeeded.
    . . . .

5. A user account and a group account by the name *evfs* are automatically created as part of the install. This user account will be used to control EVFS functionality.

    # grep evfs /etc/passwd
    evfs:x:108:106:EVFS pseudo-user -- Do not delete or use -- Needed by HP-UX
    EVFS:/home/evfs:/sbin/false

    # grep evfs /etc/group
    evfs::106:

6. Edit the */etc/evfs/evfs.conf* file if you wish to customize any EVFS parameters. The default contents are:

    evfsconf_vers = 1.0
    pub_key = /usr/lib/evfs/pa20_64/libevfs_pkey.sl[pkeydir:/etc/evfs/pkey,onfail:continue]
    priv_key = /usr/lib/evfs/pa20_64/libevfs_pkey.sl[pkeydir:/etc/evfs/pkey,onfail:continue]
    pass_key = /usr/lib/evfs/pa20_64/libevfs_pkey.sl[pkeydir:/etc/evfs/pkey,onfail:continue]
    keywrap = evfs-pbe1 # evfs-pbe2
    pbe = /usr/lib/evfs/pa20_64/libevfs_pbe.sl
    passwrap = evfs-pbe1 #evfs-pbe2
    passx = /usr/lib/evfs/pa20_64/libevfs_pbe.sl
    emd_backup = /etc/evfs/emd/
    keygen = rsa-1536
    evfs_user = evfs
    emd_envelopes = 1024
    emd_digest = sha1

```
data_cipher = aes-128-cbc #aes-192-cbc or aes-256-cbc
trace_file = /var/evfs/trace/evfstrace.log
trace_size = 100 #MBytes
kernel_encryption_mode = distributed
```

If you want normal users to be able to create EVFS keys, either provide *root* privileges to the users to be able to write to the */etc/evfs/pkey* directory or configure EVFS to use an alternate directory location called *fallback* directory for them to store their keys. The fallback directory location will need to be defined in the */etc/evfs/evfs.conf* file. Default settings for the public key, private key and the passphrase are highlighted in the output above. Table 14-5 lists and explains each field in the pub_key, priv_key and pass_key line entries.

Field	Description
pub_key	Specifies user public keys.
priv_key	Specifies user private keys.
pass_key	Specifies passphrases.
pkey_dir	Specifies an alternate directory location to store user keys. Default is */etc/evfs/pkey*.
onfail	Specifies "continue" to continue if an attempt to read from or write to the pkey_dir fails.

Table 14-5 Key Fields

7. Edit */etc/rc.config.d/evfs* file and set the EVFS_ENABLED parameter to 1 to ensure that EVFS starts automatically at each system reboot:

    ```
    EVFS_ENABLED=1
    ```

8. Start EVFS using any of the following:

    ```
    # evfsadm start
    # /sbin/init.d/evfs.local start
    EVFS subsystem started.
    ```

9. Create key pairs for the volume owner (*root* in this case) using the *evfspkey* command. Use *rk100* as the key name. Without –k option, the username will be used as the key name. Specify at least eight characters for the passphrase.

    ```
    # evfspkey keygen –k rk100
    Enter passphrase:
    Re-enter passphrase:
    Public/Private key pair "root.rk100" has been successfully generated
    ```

    If you wish to generate keys for an authorized user, say *user1*, with an automatically generated passphrase (–s option), do the following:

    ```
    # evfspkey keygen –s –u user1 –k uk100
    Public/Private key pair "user1.uk100" has been successfully generated
    ```

10. Create recovery keys (–r option). The following prompts for a passphrase and stores it in the current directory in a file called *evfs.priv*:

```
# evfspkey keygen –r
Enter recovery passphrase:
Re-enter recovery passphrase:
Public/Private key pair "evfs.evfs" has been successfully generated
```

The contents of the *evfs.priv* are shown below:

```
# cat evfs.priv
----- BEGIN EVFS ENCRYPTED PRIVATE KEY -----
version      evfs-pkey-1.0
keyid        evfs.evfs
keycipher    rsa-1536
keywrap      evfs-pbe1,f30610c5f25ac3b9,3000
keyval
U6UEqDe1Qc3rrPDgCW2ZgnQqHVwqEjJ7Gij4SdcVtr2OtSxexNp/I4P/lBSbzLmNpJxAoGMie5
OTn3d/RS4ss3MyLAaWM6zBSG4RPRqszNBUGBgf5oJO0ivMuGC/a9BbhNr1iJPyFZj6Q5IlHgL
7k8Z3+lvVIHvKhZe+wMVFIJctKde80lPO//RTAqY8J1D9lmeBe+xhjMaNIt6pLOd3aRU9kQjgqX
EOl15FUigxnExAoOZhTdY68U0MhD4Gul2hqZlQxofm1CJri8FnE3yvtMq8FSIHbqsMUiuE6Bzo
o9VJFLZaKkJYln0YzIpQyMFjN242LKyQiTGMGmj5pZ4GodO7Q9SDO8jdXV2wZ1hYrhyipz0
qpzBvRuP+75VD7ChJ4nlD7UAysyUZ8IKExkX02pDvrNYnVqsa5fjWaE0XBGeUUs+STl5y/1Y
CFKb/GQ8SC+srbOV2kufS+Gilgzt4CIf3Bzty2xdAHmilTddY9T0sxmKt7dE1xzqg87xOmrv92hcI
fDXreDx5uGCin1LTkmy0GpbMWQ+e4wd9o+NwA7kE
----- END EVFS ENCRYPTED PRIVATE KEY -----
```

11. Create a logical volume *lvol_evfs1* of size 500MB in *vg00* volume group using the *lvcreate* command:

```
# lvcreate –L 500 –n lvol_evfs1 vg00
Warning: rounding up logical volume size to extent boundary at size "504" MB.
Logical volume "/dev/vg00/lvol_evfs1" has been successfully created with
character device "/dev/vg00/rlvol_evfs1".
Logical volume "/dev/vg00/lvol_evfs1" has been successfully extended.
Volume Group configuration for /dev/vg00 has been saved in /etc/lvmconf/vg00.conf
```

12. Map the logical volume to EVFS using the *evfsadm* command. This will create EVFS volume device files in the */dev/evfs* directory.

```
# evfsadm map /dev/vg00/lvol_evfs1
Volume "/dev/vg00/lvol_evfs1" has been successfully mapped to EVFS volume
"/dev/evfs/vg00/lvol_evfs1"
```

13. Create EMD on the EVFS volume and specify the owner keys using the *evfsvol* command:

```
# evfsvol create –k rk100 /dev/evfs/vg00/lvol_evfs1
Enter owner passphrase:
Encrypted volume "/dev/evfs/vg00/lvol_evfs1" has been successfully created
```

The *evfsvol* command sources the */etc/evfs/evfs.conf* file when creating or updating EMD.

14. (optional) Add the recovery and authorized user keys to the EVFS volume. Enter the owner paraphrase for the recover key.

> # **evfsvol add −r /dev/evfs/vg00/lvol_evfs1**
> Enter owner passphrase:
> Key "evfs.evfs" has been successfully added to EVFS volume "/dev/evfs/vg00/lvol_evfs1"
> # **evfsvol add −u user1 −k user1 /dev/evfs/vg00/lvol_evfs1**
> Enter owner passphrase:
> Key "user1.user1" has been successfully added to EVFS volume "/dev/evfs/vg00/lvol_evfs1"

15. Enable encryption and decryption on the EVFS volume:

> # **evfsvol enable −k rk100 /dev/evfs/vg00/lvol_evfs1**
> Enter user passphrase:
> Encrypted volume "/dev/evfs/vg00/lvol_evfs1" has been successfully enabled

16. Create file system structures on the EVFS volume:

> # **newfs −F vxfs /dev/evfs/vg00/rlvol_evfs1**
>   version 6 layout
>   515576 sectors, 515576 blocks of size 1024, log size 1024 blocks
>   largefiles supported

17. Create a mount point such as */var/evfs1*:

> # **mkdir /var/evfs1**

18. Mount the file system:

> # **mount −F vxfs /dev/evfs/vg00/lvol_evfs1 /var/evfs1**

19. Add an entry to the */etc/fstab* file:

> **/dev/evfs/vg00/lvol_evfs1 /var/evfs1 vxfs delaylog 0 2**

20. Check the statistics:

> # **evfsadm stat −a**
> ----- EVFS statistics -----
> Total EVFS Volumes: 1
> EVFS Subsystem Status: up
> Active Encryption Threads: 3
>
> ----- EVFS Volume Name -----|--- State ---|---------------- Queues ---------------|
>   orr   owr   odr   oer
> /dev/evfs/vg00/lvol_evfs1 enabled   0   0   0   0

```
----- EVFS Volume Name -----|--- State ---|--------------- Counters --------------|
                                           bpr    bpw    bpd    bpe
/dev/evfs/vg00/lvol_evfs1     enabled      413    737    349    1849


----- EVFS Volume Name -----|--- State ---|--------------- Rates ---------------|
                                           kbpsr  kbpsw  dkbps  ekbps
/dev/evfs/vg00/lvol_evfs1     enabled      31     5      174    154
```

The output shows blocks read (bpr), written (bpw), decrypted (bpd) and encrypted (bpe).

```
# evfsvol display /dev/evfs/vg00/lvol_evfs1
EVFS Volume Name:            /dev/evfs/vg00/lvol_evfs1
Mapped Volume Name:          /dev/vg00/lvol_evfs1
EVFS Volume State:           enabled
EMD Size (Kbytes):           520
Max User Envelopes:          1024
Data Encryption Cipher:      aes-128-cbc
Digest:                      sha1
Owner Key ID:                root.rk100
Recovery Agent Key IDs:      evfs.evfs
Total Recovery Agent Keys:   1
User Key IDs:                user1.user1
Total User Keys:             1
```

The above displays information about the EVFS volume.

This completes the configuration and verification process for EVFS.

14.8   Administering EVFS Volumes and Encryption Keys

Several administrative tasks can be performed on EVFS volumes and encryption keys. Some of the common tasks are discussed in the following sub-sections.

14.8.1   Starting and Stopping EVFS Subsystem

To start the EVFS subsystem, perform one of the following:

```
# evfsadm start
# /sbin/init.d/evfs start
EVFS subsystem started
```

To stop the EVFS subsystem, stop all applications that are using EVFS volumes, unmount the file systems in the EVFS volumes, disable the EVFS volumes and run the following:

```
# evfsadm stop
# /sbin/init.d/evfs stop
EVFS subsystem stopped
```

14.8.2 Enabling and Disabling an EVFS Volume

To enable an EVFS volume, perform the following:

> **# evfsvol enable –k rk100 /dev/evfs/vg00/lvol_evfs1**
> Enter user passphrase:
> Encrypted volume "/dev/evfs/vg00/lvol_evfs1" has been successfully enabled

To disable an EVFS volume, stop all applications that are using the EVFS volume, unmount the file system in the EVFS volume and run the following:

> **# evfsvol disable –k rk100 /dev/evfs/vg00/lvol_evfs1**
> Enter user passphrase:
> Encrypted volume "/dev/evfs/vg00/lvol_evfs1" has been successfully disabled

14.8.3 Opening and Closing an EVFS Volume for Raw Access

To open an EVFS volume for raw access, run the following commands. The first command will disable the EVFS volume if it is enabled and the second will open raw access to it.

> **# evfsvol disable –k rk100 /dev/evfs/vg00/lvol_evfs1**
> **# evfsvol raw /dev/evfs/vg00/lvol_evfs1**
> Are you sure you want to enable raw access to "/dev/evfs/vg00/lvol_evfs1"?
> Raw access returns encrypted data to the user.
> Answer [yes/no]:**yes**
> Successfully enabled raw access to EVFS volume "/dev/evfs/vg00/lvol_evfs1"

To close an EVFS volume for raw access, perform the following:

> **# evfsvol close /dev/evfs/vg00/lvol_evfs1**
> Successfully closed raw access to EVFS volume "/dev/evfs/vg00/lvol_evfs1"

14.8.4 Changing Owner Keys for an EVFS Volume

To assign a different owner such as *user2* to an EVFS volume, run the following:

> **# evfsvol assign –u user2 /dev/evfs/vg00/lvol_evfs1**

14.8.5 Deleting Keys from an EVFS Volume

To delete a key record pair from the EMD for an EVFS volume for *user1*, perform the following:

> **# evfsvol delete –u user1 /dev/evfs/vg00/lvol_evfs1**
> Enter owner passphrase:
> Key ID "user1.user1" has been successfully removed from EVFS volume "/dev/evfs/vg00/lvol_evfs1"

You can use the –r option to delete recovery keys as well.

14.8.6 Creating or Changing Passphrase for a Key

To modify the passphrase for a private key, do the following:

```
# evfspkey passgen –u user1
Enter new passphrase:
Re-enter new passphrase:
Passphrase for key "user1.user1" has been succesfully generated
```

To modify the passphrase for a recovery key, do the following:

```
# evfspkey passgen –r evfs.pass
Enter current/old recovery passphrase:
Enter new recovery passphrase:
Re-enter new recovery passphrase:
Passphrase for key "evfs.evfs" has been succesfully generated
```

14.8.7   Removing a Volume from EVFS Subsystem

To completely remove a logical volume from the EVFS subsystem, follow the steps below:

1. Stop applications using the logical volume.
2. Unmount the file system.
3. Disable encryption and decryption:

    ```
    # evfsvol disable –k rk100 /dev/evfs/vg00/lvol_evfs1
    Enter user passphrase:
    Encrypted volume "/dev/evfs/vg00/lvol_evfs1" has been successfully disabled
    ```

4. Destroy the EMD:

    ```
    # evfsvol destroy –f /dev/evfs/vg00/lvol_evfs1
    Encrypted volume "/dev/evfs/vg00/lvol_evfs1" has been successfully destroyed
    ```

5. Unmap EVFS volume device files:

    ```
    # evfsadm unmap /dev/evfs/vg00/lvol_evfs1
    EVFS volume "/dev/evfs/vg00/lvol_evfs1" has been successfully unmapped
    ```

6. Update */etc/fstab* and */etc/evfs/evfstab* files and remove any entries for the volume.

14.8.8   Verifying EMD Integrity

To verify the integrity of EMD of a volume, disable the volume and run the following:

```
# evfsvol check –a
Encrypted volume "/dev/evfs/vg00/lvol_evfs1" status OK
```

14.8.9   Displaying User Keys

To display keys for a specific user such as *root*, do the following:

```
# evfspkey lookup –u root –k rk100
Key ID: root.rk100
Key Cipher: rsa-1536
Public Key Fingerprint: 9fb3d6cb7f6e26be0ea96e84d84d39f200fe71aa
Private Key Keywrap: evfs-pbe1
Private Key Fingerprint: 8ec1c5211caab97a22e442b60723ea1ed5d4845a
Passphrase Keywrap: n/a
Passphrase Fingerprint: n/a
```

Summary

In this chapter you learned about file systems. You learned concepts and types of file systems supported in HP-UX. You looked in detail at the structure and components of both HFS and JFS file systems.

The chapter then talked about managing file systems, which involved creating, mounting, viewing, extending, reducing, tuning, defragmenting, unmounting and removing them using both command line and GUI tools. You saw how file systems were defined to get automatically mounted at system reboots.

You were explained how to check and repair HFS and VxFS file system structures after a system crash, and manually. You looked at mounting and unmounting CDFS and LOFS file systems.

You learned about file system monitoring tools such as *bdf*, *df*, *du* and *quot* to monitor file system space utilization.

Finally, a detailed discussion was presented on EVFS file systems. You learned EVFS concepts, features and components and EVFS management tasks such as configuring, enabling, disabling, opening, closing and removing EVFS volumes, and generating, displaying, modifying and deleing keys.

15

Swap Space

This chapter covers the following major topics:

- ✓ Physical memory and how it is used
- ✓ What is swap and how demand paging works
- ✓ Device and file system swap
- ✓ Primary and secondary swap
- ✓ What is pseudo swap?
- ✓ Create and enable device and file system swap spaces
- ✓ View swap utilization
- ✓ Priority and best practices
- ✓ Swap space kernel parameters

15.1 Understanding Swap

Physical memory installed in the system is a finite temporary storage resource used for loading HP-UX kernel and data structures, as well as running user programs. The system automatically reserves a portion of memory, called *reserved* memory, for the kernel and data structures at system startup. The remaining physical memory, referred to as *available* memory, is used by the system for two purposes. Some of it is locked by HP-UX subsystems and user processes, and called *lockable* memory. Data located in the lockable memory cannot be paged out (moved to alternate location). The lockable memory typically holds frequently accessed programs for performance improvement reasons. The remaining available memory is used for *demand paging* purposes. Figure 15-1 shows how physical memory is divided into available and reserved memory areas.

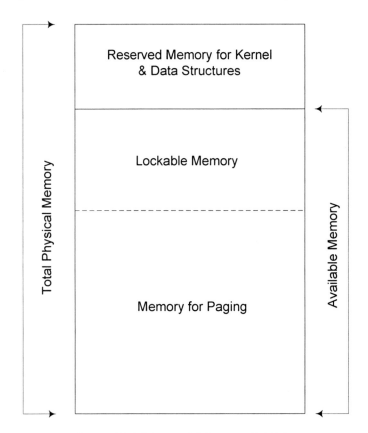

Figure 15-1 Physical Memory Division

The amount of physical, lockable and available memory is displayed when the system boots up. The information may be viewed later by running the *dmesg* command or looking into the system log file */var/adm/syslog/syslog.log*.

A sample *dmesg* command output below displays that the total physical memory in the system is 8GB with ~6GB lockable and ~7GB available:

```
# dmesg
Memory Information:
    physical page size = 4096 bytes, logical page size = 4096 bytes
    Physical: 8380416 Kbytes, lockable: 6105044 Kbytes, available: 6946632 Kbytes
```

The output also displays the size of physical page, which is, by default, 4KB. When paging occurs, this is the smallest unit of memory content that is paged out or paged in.

15.1.1   Swap Space and Demand Paging

Swap space is a region on a physical disk used for demand paging purposes. When a program or process is started, it requires space in the memory to run and be processed. Although many programs can run concurrently, but the physical memory cannot hold all of them at the same time. The kernel maintains a threshold called *lotsfree,* and it monitors free physical memory. As long as this threshold is not surpassed, no paging occurs. When the amount of free physical memory falls below lotsfree, a daemon called *vhand* comes into action and starts moving selected idle pages of data from physical memory to the swap space to make room to accommodate other programs. This is referred to as *page out.* Since system CPU performs process execution in a round-robin fashion, when the time comes for the paged out data to be executed, the CPU looks for that data in the physical memory and *page fault* occurs. The pages are then moved back into the physical memory from the swap space. The moving back into the physical memory of paged out data is referred to as *page in,* and the entire process of paging data out and in is known as *demand paging.*

HP-UX systems with less physical memory but high memory requirements can become so busy doing paging out and in that they do not have enough time to carry out other useful tasks causing system performance to degrade. When this occurs, the system appears to be frozen. The excessive amount of paging that causes the system performance to go down is called *thrashing.*

When thrashing begins, or when the free physical memory falls below another threshold, called *desfree,* the *swapper* process becomes activated, which deactivates idle processes and prevents new processes from initiating. Once the *swapper* process discovers that available physical memory has climbed above the *minfree* threshold level and thrashing has stopped, it reactivates the deactivated processes and allows new processes to spawn.

15.1.2   Device and File System Swap

There are two types of swap space: device swap and file system swap.

The swap space created and enabled in a logical volume is called *device swap*, whereas, a *file system swap* is the portion in a mounted file system allocated and enabled for paging purposes.

When file system swap is enabled, a directory called *paging* is created at the root of that file system. Under the *paging* directory, files are created for each individual swap chunk used in file system paging. By default, a swap chunk is 2MB in size.

A file system swap can be defined and enabled dynamically. It may be defined to use a fixed or any amount of file system area. Remember, once a file system has been enabled for swapping, it is not possible to unmount that file system. You must reboot the machine with the swap space line entry commented out, if defined, in the */etc/fstab* file.

15.1.3   Primary and Secondary Swap

The *primary* swap is the device swap created during HP-UX installation and becomes available each time the system boots up. It usually exists in *vg00* volume group with OS file systems, and shares the same physical disk.

The primary swap location is defined on the boot disk in BDRA. You can change this location using the *lvlnboot* command with –s option. Refer to *lvlnboot* man pages.

In addition to the primary swap, one or more *secondary* swap spaces may be defined based on application requirements. It is recommended to always use device swap for improved performance, and create it on a physical disk with no other swap area.

If you must use a file system swap, always define it as a secondary swap.

Secondary swap spaces can be enabled automatically at boot time if an entry is defined in the */etc/fstab* file. They may also be added manually on a running system.

15.1.4   Pseudo Swap

Pseudo swap is the portion of physical memory used for swapping purposes. It is used by the kernel as an additional swap space. By default, pseudo swap is enabled at system boot. Pseudo swap is beneficial on systems with large amounts of physical memory. There is no need to create the same size (or larger) device swap as the amount of physical memory. HP-UX allocates 3/4 of the physical memory as pseudo swap, which is used by the kernel to spawn new processes as needed.

For example, on a system with 8GB of physical memory and 8GB of device swap with pseudo swap enabled, the total amount of swap available to the system would be 14GB (8 + (8 x 0.75)). This includes 8GB of configured device swap and 6GB of pseudo swap.

One key point to note about pseudo swap is that it is not used for demand paging purposes; it is only used by the system to reserve swap space for new processes.

15.2   Managing Swap

Managing swap involves viewing swap areas, creating device and file system swap areas and enabling them. The following sub-sections describe these operations.

15.2.1   Viewing Swap Areas

Available swap spaces can be viewed using the *swapinfo* command. This command also displays their utilization. For example, run this command and it will display the current swap areas:

```
# swapinfo
            Kb        Kb       Kb    PCT  START/       Kb
TYPE     AVAIL      USED     FREE   USED  LIMIT  RESERVE   PRI  NAME
dev     8192000        0  8192000    0%      0        -     1  /dev/vg00/lvol2
reserve       -   462092  -462092
memory  7970816  1212768  6758048   15%
```

The output provides a snapshot of available swap spaces and their utilization. It indicates that there is only one swap space area currently configured on the system, which is primary device swap in

/dev/vg00/lvol2 logical volume. There are several columns in the output. Table 15-1 lists and describes them.

Column Title	Description
TYPE	Shows the type of memory/swap: "dev" for device swap, "localfs" for file system swap, "reserve" for reserved paging space and "memory" for memory-based paging space (a.k.a. pseudo swap).
Kb AVAIL	Amount of swap space in KBs.
Kb USED	Swap space used in KBs.
Kb FREE	Free swap space in KBs.
PCT USED	Swap space used in percentage.
START / LIMIT	For device swap, this value is set to 0 to represent entire logical volume. For file system swap, START represents the starting block for the swap and LIMIT represents the maximum amount of space that can be used for paging.
Kb RESERVE	For device swap, this value is always –. For file system swap, this value is the amount, in KBs, of swap space that cannot be used as swap.
PRI	Defines the order in which to use a swap space.
NAME	For device swap, this represents block device file. For file system swap, this indicates name of the paging directory.

Table 15-1 *swapinfo* **Output Explanation**

Options available with *swapinfo* are given in Table 15-2.

Option	Description
–a	Displays all swap areas. This is default.
–t	Shows total at the bottom.
–m	Displays information in MBs instead of (default) KBs.
–d	Shows information on device swap only.
–f	Shows information on file system swap only.
–q	Shows available KBs only.
–s	Displays setting of the primary swap for next reboot.

Table 15-2 *swapinfo* **Command Options**

Try each of these options and see results. For example, when you run *swapinfo* with –atm options, it will display information as follows:

swapinfo –atm

TYPE	Mb AVAIL	Mb USED	Mb FREE	PCT USED	START/ LIMIT	Mb RESERVE	PRI	NAME
dev	8000	0	8000	0%	0	-	1	/dev/vg00/lvol2
reserve	-	451	-451					
memory	7784	1185	6599	15%				
total	15784	1636	14148	10%	-	0	-	

15.2.2   Creating and Enabling a Device Swap

To create and enable a device swap called *swaplvol* of size 500MB in *vg01* volume group, perform the following two steps. The first command creates the logical volume and the second enables swapping in it.

> **# lvcreate –L 500 –n swaplvol vg01**
> Logical volume "/dev/vg01/swaplvol" has been successfully created with
> character device "/dev/vg01/rswaplvol".
> Logical volume "/dev/vg01/swaplvol" has been successfully extended.
> Volume Group configuration for /dev/vg01 has been saved in /etc/lvmconf/vg01.conf
> **# swapon /dev/vg01/swaplvol**

Run the *swapinfo* command to verify that the new device swap is created and enabled:

> **# swapinfo | grep swaplvol**
> dev   512000   0   512000   0%   0   -   1   /dev/vg01/swaplvol
> **# swapinfo –m | grep swaplvol**
> dev   500   0   500   0%   0   -   1   /dev/vg01/swaplvol

Some common options available with the *swapon* command related to the device swap are listed in Table 15-3.

Option	Description
–a	Enables all device and file system swap spaces defined in *etc/fstab*.
–f	Enables force swapping on a logical volume that contains file system structures. Be careful when using this option; it destroys all file system structures as well as data from the specified logical volume.
–p	Defines the sequence in which to use a swap space.
–s	Sets or unsets the specified device to be used as primary swap at next and subsequent system reboots.
–t	Specifies the swap space type. It would be "dev" for device swap and "local" for local swap areas.
Device	Block device file for the logical volume.

Table 15-3 *swapon* Options for Device Swap

SMH (GUI) can be used to create and enable a device swap. Follow the sequence below:

☞Go to SMH → Disks and File Systems → Paging Space → Add Paging Space on Device. Select an unused disk or an unused logical volume to create paging space on. Specify the priority and other parameters and click "Add Paging Space". See Figure 15-2.

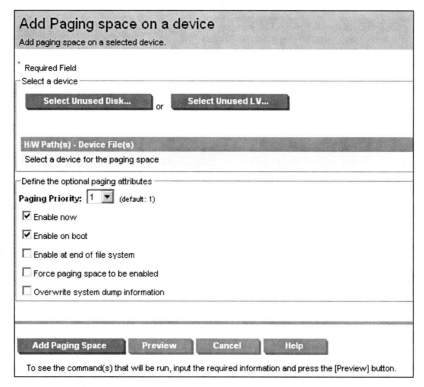

Figure 15-2 SMH GUI – Add Device Swap

15.2.3 Creating and Enabling a File System Swap

To create and enable a file system swap in */data2* file system, for example, and limit it to use not more than 100MB of its space, run *swapon* with –l option:

> # **swapon –l 100m /data2**

Run *swapinfo* to verify that the file system swap is enabled:

> # **swapinfo | grep swaplvol**
> localfs   102400   0   102400   0%   100   0   1   /data2/paging
> # **swapinfo –m | grep data2**
> localfs   100   0   100   0%   100   0   1   /data2/paging

Some common options available with the *swapon* command related to the file system swap are listed in Table 15-4.

Option	Description
–a	Enables all device and file system swap spaces defined in the */etc/fstab* file.
–m	Denotes the minimum amount of paging space in KBs, MBs or blocks that you want the paging system to initially reserve.

Option	Description
–l	Specifies the maximum limit in KBs, MBs or blocks that the swap system can use (default is unlimited).
–r	Specifies total space to be reserved strictly for file system usage. This space will not be used for paging.
–p	Defines the priority in which to use a swap space.
–t	Specifies the swap space type. It would be "fs" for file system swap and "local" for local swap areas.
directory	The file system mount point.

Table 15-4 *swapon* Options for File System Swap

To use SMH (GUI) to create and enable a file system swap, follow the sequence:

☞ Go to SMH → Disks and File Systems → Paging Space → Add Paging Space to File System. Select an unused disk or an unused logical volume to create paging space on. Choose a file system to create the swap space in, set minimum, maximum and reserved paging sizes (if you wish to), and define priority. Fill out any other information as shown in Figure 15-3. Click "Add Paging Space" when done.

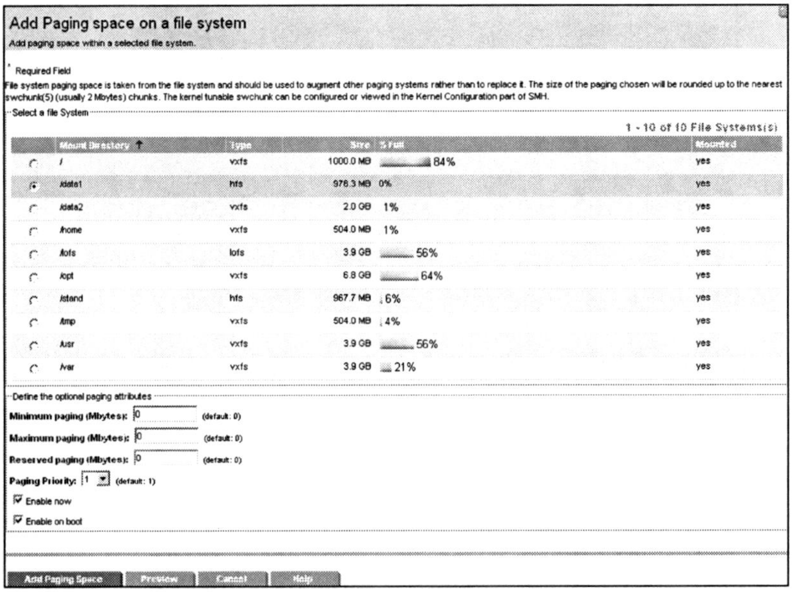

Figure 15-3 SMH GUI – Add File System Swap

15.2.4   Enabling Swap Space at System Boot

In order to make all swap spaces activated when the system reboots, you need to define them in the */etc/fstab* file. During the boot process, the */sbin/init.d/swap_start* script is executed, which runs the *swapon* command with –at options. The –at options instruct the command to activate all local swap spaces listed in */etc/fstab*.

Here is how the *swaplvol* (device) and */data2* (file system) swap entries will look like in the */etc/fstab* file:

```
# cat /etc/fstab
. . . . . . . .
/dev/vg01/swaplvol    .        swap      pri=1          0     0
/dev/vg01/lvol2      /data2    swapfs    defaults       0     0
```

The syntax of *etc/fstab* and description of fields were explained in Chapter 14 "File Systems". Only the third field is different, which defines the type of swap. Use "swap" for the device swap and "swapfs" for the file system swap. If you do not wish to use the "defaults" option for the file system swap, refer to Table 15-4 earlier in this chapter for options available to set priority, limit, minimum space, etc.

To manually enable all swap spaces listed in the */etc/fstab* file, do the following:

```
# swapon –a
```

15.3   Priority and Best Practices

Swap space is assigned a priority between 0 and 10, with 0 being the highest and 1 being the default. The HP-UX kernel uses a higher priority swap area before using a lower priority one. If two swap regions have identical priority, the kernel utilizes them alternately. If multiple devices have the same priority, swap space is allocated from the devices in a round-robin fashion. Thus, to interleave swap requests among a number of device swap regions, a common priority should be assigned to them. Similarly, if multiple file system swap areas have an identical priority, requests for swap are interleaved among them.

To alter priority of the file system swap created earlier, use *swapon* and verify it with *swapinfo*:

```
# swapon –p 2 /data2/paging
# swapinfo –m | grep data2
localfs   100    0   100   0%   100    0   2  /data2/paging
```

If both device and file system swap regions carry an identical priority, the device swap will be given preference over the file system swap.

Some best practices should be followed when choosing what type of swap space to configure and, what priorities to set. The following list of best practices is related to swap space management and should be adhered to for better and improved swap performance:

- ✓ Do not configure more than one swap space on a single physical disk.
- ✓ Favor faster devices over slower devices.
- ✓ Two smaller, same size device swap spaces on two different physical disks are better than one large swap space on one single physical disk.
- ✓ Assign an identical priority to all device swap areas to enable them to be used in a round-robin fashion.
- ✓ Avoid using file system swap as much as possible. Use it only if there is absolutely no physical disk space left for building an additional device swap.
- ✓ Choose less utilized file systems over busier file systems if you have to ue them for swap.

15.4 Related Kernel Tunables

Some key kernel tunables related to swap are listed in Table 15-5.

Tunable	Description
nswapdev	Defines maximum number of devices that can be enabled simultaneously for swap. Minimum is 1, maximum is 1024 and the default is 32.
nswapfs	Defines maximum number of file systems that can be simultaneously enabled for swap. Minimum is 0, maximum is 1024 and the default is 32.
swchunk	Defines swap chunk size. Minimum is 2048, maximum is 65536 and the default is 2048. HP-UX uses chunks from swap space one by one for paging purposes.

Table 15-5 Swap Kernel Parameters

Summary

You learned in this chapter concepts of swapping and paging. You saw how physical memory was divided to be shared and how paging worked on demand. Device and file system swap, primary and secondary swap regions, and pseudo swap were discussed along with associated advantages and disadvantages.

You looked at managing swap space areas that covered creating, enabling and viewing both device and file system swap. You saw how configured swap areas could be enabled manually and at each system reboot.

Finally, swap priority, best practices and a few key kernel tunables related to swap were covered.

## 16

HP-UX Shutdown and Startup

This chapter covers the following major topics:

- ✓ Explain run control levels and determine current and previous run levels
- ✓ Tools to shutdown and change run control levels
- ✓ Interact with PDC and BCH on an HP 9000 server to view and modify autoboot, autosearch and AUTO file; and view and modify primary, HA alternate and alternate boot device paths
- ✓ Interact with BCH and secondary boot loader on an HP 9000 server to boot it normally and into various maintenance states
- ✓ Interact with EFI and Boot Manager on an HP Integrity server to view and modify autoboot, boot delay period and AUTO file; and view and modify primary, HA alternate and alternate boot device paths
- ✓ Interact with EFI and Boot Manager on an HP Integrity server to boot it normally and into various maintenance states
- ✓ Describe HP-UX kernel and initialization phases on HP 9000 and Integrity servers
- ✓ Discuss system startup scripts and associated configuration files

16.1   Shutting Down the HP-UX Server

HP-UX servers need to be shutdown periodically for maintenance such as adding or removing hardware components. Sometimes, software is installed or patches are applied that affect kernel configuration and a reboot is required prior to the new configuration taking effect. There may be other situations when a reboot of the server becomes necessary.

HP-UX changes run levels when a system shutdown or startup occurs. The following sub-sections discuss system run control levels and how to manipulate them.

16.1.1   Run Control Levels

System *run control* (rc) levels are pre-defined and determines the current state of the system. HP-UX supports eight rc levels of which six are currently implemented. Not all of these are commonly used though. The default rc level is 3. Table 16-1 describes various run levels.

Run Level	Description
0	HP-UX is down and the system is halted.
s	Single user state with critical file systems mounted. The system can be accessed only at the system console.
S	Single user state with critical file systems mounted. The terminal where this run level is invoked becomes the logical console.
1	Single user state with all file systems mounted and a few critical processes running.
2	Multi-user state. All services running except NFS server processes.
3	Multi-user state. All services including NFS server processes running. This is the default rc level for HP-UX.
4	GUI presentation managers and some other system processes started.
5 and 6	Not implemented. Users may define their own.

Table 16-1 System Run Levels

16.1.2   Checking Current and Previous Run Control Levels

To check the current and previous rc levels of the system, use the *who* command with –r option:

 # who –r

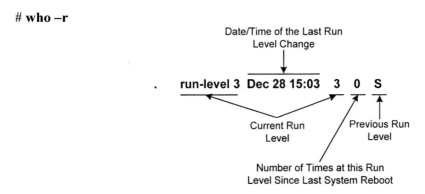

Figure 16-1 Current and Previous System rc Levels

The output of this command, as shown in Figure 16-1, indicates that the system is currently running at run level 3 and its last run level was S. The output also displays the date and time of the last system run level change.

16.1.3 Changing Run Control Levels

Run control levels are also referred to as *init* levels because the system uses the *init* command to alter levels. The *shutdown* and the *reboot* commands are also widely used to change system run levels. Refer to Figure 16-2 that displays various run levels and commands to switch from one run level to another.

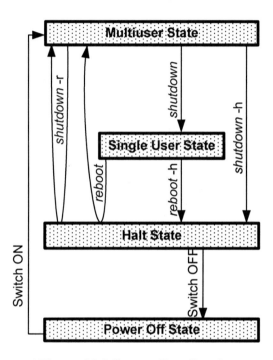

Figure 16-2 System Run Levels

The *init* Command

The *init* command is employed to change run levels. If the system is currently in run level 3 and you want to switch to run level 2, issue the command as follows:

   # **init 2**

This command gracefully stops all services and daemons that should not be running in rc level 2, and does not affect any other processes and services.

Similarly, by initiating *init* 1 from run level 2, most system services and daemons can be stopped and the system is transitioned to single user state.

To stop all system services normally and go to system halt state, do the following:

   # **init 0**

The *shutdown* Command

The *shutdown* command is more commonly used than the *init* command. It stops all services, processes and daemons in a sequential and consistent fashion as does the *init* command. It broadcasts a message to all logged in users and waits for one minute, by default, for users to log off, after which time it begins stopping services, processes and daemons. It unmounts file systems and proceeds as per the options specified at the command line.

The following examples show options and arguments that can be supplied with *shutdown*:

# **shutdown**	(broadcasts a message, waits for one minute, prompts you to confirm the shutdown and then takes the system to single user mode).
# **shutdown –hy 300**	(broadcasts a message, waits for 5 minutes and then takes the system to the halt state).
# **shutdown –ry 300**	(broadcasts a message, waits for 5 minutes, stops all services gracefully, shuts down the system and automatically reboots it to the default run control level).
# **shutdown –ry 0**	(broadcasts a message, begins stopping immediately all services gracefully, shuts down the system and automatically reboots it to the default run control level).
# **shutdown –ry now**	(same as "shutdown –ry 0").
# **shutdown –Ry now**	(On hardware partitionable servers, this command broadcasts a message, begins stopping immediately all services gracefully, shuts down the system to a ready-to-reconfigure state and automatically reboots it (if possible) to the default run control level).
# **shutdown –RHy 0**	(On hardware partitionable servers, this command broadcasts a message, begins stopping immediately all services gracefully and shuts down the system to a ready-to-reconfigure state).

When the *shutdown* command is initiated to halt the system, you would see messages similar to the following on the system console:

```
SHUTDOWN PROGRAM
04/14/08 08:46:18 EDT
Broadcast Message from root (console) Mon Apr 14 08:46:18...
SYSTEM BEING BROUGHT DOWN NOW ! ! !
/sbin/auto_parms: DHCP access is disabled (see /etc/auto_parms.log)

   System shutdown in progress
   _____
   Stopping Control Daemon ......................................... N/A
   Stopping OVTrcSrv... .............................................. OK
   Stop CDE login server ................................................ OK
   Stop NDDB Comm Server ......................................... N/A
   Stop kwdbd ................................................................. N/A
   Stopping HP-UX Apache-based Web Server ............. OK
   Stopping HP-UX Tomcat-based Servlet Engine. ........ N/A
. . . . . . . .
sync'ing disks (0 buffers to flush):
 0 fcache pages still dirty
```

```
0 buffers not flushed
0 buffers still dirty
Calling function a5b550 for Shutdown State 5 type 0x1
Calling function 5d6508 for Shutdown State 5 type 0x1
Closing open logical volumes...
Done

System has halted
OK to turn off power or reset system
UNLESS "WAIT for UPS to turn off power" message was printed above
```

By default, only *root* can execute the *shutdown* command. If you wish to delegate the system shutdown responsibility to other users of the system as well, you will need to add entries for the users in the */etc/shutdown.allow* file. This file controls which users can shutdown the system. For example, the following two entries in the file would enable *user1* and *user2* to bring *hp01* down:

```
hp01   user1
hp01   user2
```

The *shutdown* command actually calls the *init* command behind the scenes to perform run level changes. You may use the *init* command instead. The only two features not available with *init* compared to *shutdown* are that *init* does not broadcast a message and does not wait for a specified period of time. It starts the run level change process immediately.

When the system is shutdown or rebooted, a time stamp, along with who performed the action, is logged to the */etc/shutdownlog* file. This log file can also be accessed via */var/adm/shutdownlog* file, which has a symbolic link to */etc/shutdownlog*. Some sample entries from this file are shown below:

```
# cat /etc/shutdownlog
09:06      Wed Apr  9, 2008.      Reboot: (by hp01!root)
09:27      Thu  Apr 10, 2008.     Reboot: (by hp01!root)
08:21      Mon Apr 14, 2008.      Reboot:
16:39      Tue  Apr 15, 2008.     Reboot:
16:39      Tue  Apr 15, 2008.     Reboot: (by hp01!root)
20:49      Tue  Apr 15, 2008.     Reboot:
10:23      Wed Apr 16, 2008.      Reboot: (by hp01!root)
```

The *reboot* Command

The *reboot* command calls the *kill* command with –9 signal to terminate all running processes. This makes the system go down rapidly, however, it introduces the risk of damaging application files and file system structures. It is not recommended to invoke this command from any multi-user run level. The *reboot* command may be used if the system is in single user state or, for some reasons, you wish to bring it down quickly.

The following examples show options and arguments that can be supplied with *reboot*:

```
# reboot                    (kills all processes, restarts the system and brings it back to the
                            default run level).
```

# **reboot –h**	(shuts the system down and puts it in the halt state).
# **reboot –s**	(syncs file systems before shutting down and rebooting).
# **reboot –n**	(does not sync file systems before shutting down and rebooting).
# **reboot –t +10**	(same as "reboot", but waits for 10 minutes).
# **reboot –m message**	(broadcasts the specified message, kills all processes, restarts the system and brings it back to the default run level).
# **reboot –R**	(On hardware partitionable servers, this command begins stopping all services immediately, shuts down the system to a ready-to-reconfigure state and automatically reboots it (if possible) to the default run control level).
# **reboot –RH**	(On hardware partitionable servers, this command begins stopping all services immediately and shuts down the system to a ready-to-reconfigure state).

When the *reboot* command is initiated to halt the system, you would see messages similar to the following on the system console:

 # reboot –h
Shutdown at 15:04 (in 0 minutes)
　　*** FINAL System shutdown message from root@hp01 ***
System going down IMMEDIATELY
System shutdown time has arrived
Apr 16 15:04:17 /usr/sbin/envd[1728]: terminated by signal 15
Apr 16 15:04:17 rpcbind: rpcbind terminating on signal.
　　* The kernel registry database has been saved to disk.

sync'ing disks (0 buffers to flush):
 0 fcache pages still dirty
 0 buffers not flushed
 0 buffers still dirty
Calling function a5b550 for Shutdown State 5 type 0x1
Calling function 5d6508 for Shutdown State 5 type 0x1
Closing open logical volumes...
Done

The *reboot* command writes to the */etc/shutdownlog* file the same way as the *shutdown* command.

16.2　Booting the HP 9000 Server

When the HP 9000 system is powered on or reset, it goes through the *boot* process until the login prompt is displayed. A step-by-step boot process for a standalone server is presented below:

✓　Power on external devices.
✓　Power on the server.
✓　System firmware, called *Processor Dependent Code* (PDC), is initiated, which runs *Power On Self Test* (POST) on the system hardware components such as processor, memory and I/O, and initializes them.
✓　PDC looks into *stable storage* to get hardware addresses for system console display and boot devices. The stable storage is a small non-volatile area in PDC that contains hardware paths

of the system console and boot devices. It also stores the values of the Autoboot and Autosearch flags. The two flags determine if the system is to be booted automatically and from which boot device.

✓ PDC initializes the system console display and the boot device.
✓ PDC locates the HP-UX kernel in the boot device.
✓ PDC loads *Initial System Loader* (ISL) into memory from the LIF area located on the boot device. The LIF area, also called *boot area*, is a small portion on the boot disk reserved to keep boot utilities needed to find and load the kernel. The files here are in a special format called *Logical Interchange Format* (LIF). The LIF area contains the ISL, the AUTO file and the *Secondary Boot Loader* program called *hpux*, among others. The ISL includes utilities to display AUTO file contents, modify hardware paths for console, primary boot disk and alternate boot disk, and set Autoboot and Autosearch flags. Help on ISL commands is available by issuing the *help* command.

You can use the "lifls –l /dev/disk/disk2" at the command prompt to view a list of all commands available in the LIF area.

lifls –l /dev/disk/disk2
volume ISL10 data size 7984 directory size 8 07/01/10 17:13:32

filename	type	start	size	implement	created
ISL	-12800	584	242	0	07/01/10 17:13:32
AUTO	-12289	832	1	0	07/01/10 17:13:32
HPUX	-12928	840	1024	0	07/01/10 17:13:32
PAD	-12290	1864	1468	0	07/01/10 17:13:33
LABEL	BIN	3336	8	0	08/04/08 08:59:00

✓ PDC transfers the control to the ISL.
✓ ISL calls the secondary boot loader and loads it into memory.
✓ The secondary boot loader uses the contents in the AUTO file to locate the kernel file to boot.
✓ The secondary boot loader loads the kernel into memory and initializes it. The default kernel is located in the */stand* file system on the boot disk and is called *vmunix*.
✓ The kernel starts the *swapper* daemon.
✓ The kernel calls the *init* command and transfers the control over to it to initiate the system initialization process.
✓ The *init* command references the */etc/inittab* file to determine the default run level to boot to.
✓ The *init* command calls */sbin/rc* script, which calls all startup scripts needed to bring the system to the default run level.
✓ Finally, *init* presents the login prompt.

A complete system boot up process from powering it up to displaying the login prompt on an rp7410 server looks similar to the following:

Firmware Version   17.008
Duplex Console IO Dependent Code (IODC) revision 1

   (c) Copyright 1995-2002, Hewlett-Packard Company, All rights reserved

```
-----------------------------------------------------------------

       Cab/  Cell  ------------- Processor ------------  Cache  Size
  Cell Slot  State  #   Speed        State              Inst   Data
  ---- ----  ------------ ---  ----------  --------------------  ------  ------
   0   0/0   Active  0  750  MHz  Active              768 KB  1.5 MB
                     1  750  MHz  Idle                768 KB  1.5 MB
                     2  750  MHz  Idle                768 KB  1.5 MB
                     3  750  MHz  Idle                768 KB  1.5 MB


    Primary Boot Path:  0/0/0/3/0.6
       Boot Actions:  Boot from this path.
                      If unsuccessful, go to next path.
    HA Alternate Boot Path:  0/0/0/0/0.0
       Boot Actions:  Skip this path.
                      Go to next path.
  Alternate Boot Path:  0/0/4/0/0.0
       Boot Actions:  Skip this path.
                      Go to BCH.
       Console Path:  0/0/0/0/1.0
Attempting to boot using the primary path.
----------------------------------------------------------

 To discontinue, press any key within 10 seconds.
10 seconds expired.

. . . . . . . .
ISL booting  hpux

Boot
: disk(0/0/0/3/0.6.0.0.0.0.0;0)/stand/vmunix
17227776 + 5660704 + 21885968 start 0x1409e8
DoCalllist done

. . . . . . . .
Memory Class Setup
-------------------------------------------------------------------

Class    Physmem        Lockmem         Swapmem
-------------------------------------------------------------------

System :  7784 MB        7784 MB         7784 MB
Kernel :  7783 MB        7783 MB         7783 MB
User   :  7399 MB        6559 MB         6585 MB

-------------------------------------------------------------------
Starting ktracer 0 1
Installing Socket Protocol families AF_INET and AF_INET6
Lowfat driver is the master here
Kernel EVM initialized
sec_init(): kernel RPC authentication/security initialization.
secgss_init():  kernel RPCSEC_GSS security initialization.
rpc_init(): kernel RPC initialization.
rpcmod_install(): kernel RPC STREAMS module "rpcmod" installation. ...(driver_install)
NOTICE: nfs_client_pv3_install(): nfs3 File system was registered at index 10.
```

NOTICE: nfs_client_pv4_install(): nfs4 File system was registered at index 11.
NOTICE: cachefsc_install: cachefs File system was registered at index 13.
td: claimed Tachyon XL2 Fibre Channel Mass Storage card at 0/0/10/0/0
. . . .
td: claimed Tachyon XL2 Fibre Channel Mass Storage card at 0/0/12/0/0

   System Console is on the Built-In Serial Interface
igelan4: INITIALIZING HP A6794-60001 PCI 1000Base-T at hardware path 0/0/8/0/0/4/0
AF_INET socket/streams output daemon running, pid 38
afinet_prelink: module installed
Starting the STREAMS daemons-phase 1
LVM: Root VG activated
   Swap device table: (start & size given in 512-byte blocks)
    entry 0 - major is 64, minor is 0x2; start = 0, size = 16384000
livedump: Current architecture is not supported.
Checking root file system.
file system is clean - log replay is not required
Root check done.
NOTICE: return ramfs memory for BTL: [FREE] top 0x0000001188300000, pages 3749

Create STCP device files
Starting the STREAMS daemons-phase 2
   $Revision: vmunix: B.11.31_LR FLAVOR=perf
Memory Information:
   physical page size = 4096 bytes, logical page size = 4096 bytes
   Physical: 8380416 Kbytes, lockable: 6105044 Kbytes, available: 6951452 Kbytes

/sbin/ioinitrc:
/sbin/krs_sysinit:
   * The module 'rng' has been loaded.
   * The module 'rtp' has been loaded.
   * The module 'rtcp' has been loaded.
   * The module 'nsamod' has been loaded.
   * The module 'ipf' has been loaded.

insf: Installing special files for pseudo driver framebuf

/sbin/bcheckrc:
Checking for LVM volume groups and Activating (if any exist)
Volume group "/dev/vg00" is already active on this system.
Resynchronized volume group /dev/vg00
Checking hfs file systems
/sbin/fsclean: /dev/vg00/lvol1 (mounted) ok
HFS file systems are OK, not running fsck
Checking vxfs file systems
vxfs fsck: V-3-20913: /dev/vg00/lvol3:sanity check: root file system OK (mounted read/write)
vxfs fsck: V-3-20915: /dev/vg00/lvol4:sanity check: /dev/vg00/lvol4 OK
vxfs fsck: V-3-20915: /dev/vg00/lvol5:sanity check: /dev/vg00/lvol5 OK
vxfs fsck: V-3-20915: /dev/vg00/lvol6:sanity check: /dev/vg00/lvol6 OK

```
vxfs fsck: V-3-20915: /dev/vg00/lvol7:sanity check: /dev/vg00/lvol7 OK
vxfs fsck: V-3-20915: /dev/vg00/lvol8:sanity check: /dev/vg00/lvol8 OK
Cleaning /etc/ptmp...
. . . . . . . .
/sbin/auto_parms: DHCP access is disabled (see /etc/auto_parms.log)

    HP-UX Start-up in progress
    _____

    Configure system crash dumps ................................ OK
    Removing old vxvm files ...................................... OK
    VxVM INFO V-5-2-3360 VxVM device node check ............. OK
    VxVM INFO V-5-2-3362 VxVM general startup .................. OK
    VxVM INFO V-5-2-3366 VxVM reconfiguration recovery ... OK
    Mount file systems ................................................. OK
    Setting hostname ................................................... OK
    Start containment subsystem configuration ............................ OK

. . . . . . . .
The system is ready.

GenericSysName [HP Release B.11.31] (see /etc/issue)
Console Login:
```

16.2.1   Processor Dependent Code and Boot Console Handler

The system firmware is called the *Processor Dependent Code* (PDC). When the system is powered on, the PDC runs POST on hardware components and initializes them. It displays a message on the console, prompting to press any key to discontinue the autoboot process. It waits for an input for 10 seconds, by default. If a key is pressed within that time duration, the PDC loads a menu driven program called the *Boot Console Handler* (BCH). The BCH interface is shown below:

```
Processor is booting from first available device.
To discontinue, press any key within 10 seconds.
Boot terminated.
------- Main Menu ---------------------------------------------------------------------------
        Command                              Description
        ---------------                      ----------------

        BOot [PRI|ALT|<path>]                Boot from specified path
        PAth [PRI|ALT|CON|KEY] [<path>]      Display or modify a path
        SEArch [DIsplay|IPL] [<path>]        Search for boot devices
        COnfiguration [<command>]            Access Configuration menu/commands
        INformation [<command>]              Access Information menu/commands
        SERvice [<command>]                  Access Service menu/commands
        Display                              Redisplay the current menu
        HElp [<menu>|<command>]              Display help for menu or command
        RESET                                Restart the system

-------
Main Menu: Enter command >
```

A number of tasks such as searching for alternate boot devices, performing a manual boot from a non-default boot device or kernel, viewing or altering configuration can be performed from the PDC main menu. Rather than typing an entire command, just type the first two to three letters (displayed in uppercase letters) and press `Enter`.

16.2.2 Viewing and Modifying Autoboot and Autosearch Flags

The settings of the two flags determine system's boot behavior. *Autoboot* flag setting indicates automatic system booting and *autosearch* determines a boot source.

The following explains the impact of the settings of the two flags on the system boot process:

- ✓ Set both flags ON if you wish the system to be able to automatically search for boot sources and boot from a primary, HA alternate or an alternate boot source, whichever is available in that sequence.
- ✓ Set autosearch ON and autoboot OFF if you wish the system to be able to automatically search for boot sources and list them, but not boot from any of them automatically.
- ✓ Set autoboot ON and autosearch OFF if you wish the system to be able to automatically boot from the primary boot source, but not attempt to boot or list other boot sources if primary is unavailable.
- ✓ Set both flags OFF if you wish to manually supply a boot device path and interact with BCH each time the system restarts.

The values of the autoboot and autosearch flags can be viewed at the ISL prompt or the HP-UX command prompt, but can be modified only at the command prompt.

To view the values at the ISL prompt:

ISL > **display**
    Autoboot is ON (enabled)
    Autosearch is OFF (disabled)

To view and modify the values at the command prompt:

setboot
Autoboot is ON (enabled)
Autosearch is ON (enabled)
setboot –b on   (enables autoboot)
setboot –b off   (disables autoboot)
setboot –s on   (enables autosearch)
setboot –s off   (disables autosearch)

16.2.3 Viewing and Setting Primary, HA Alternate and Alternate Boot Paths

There are three possible boot sources – *primary*, *high-availability alternate* (HA alternate) and *alternate* – that can be defined on the system. The primary boot source is the boot disk that normally boots the system. In case the primary becomes unavailable, the system automatically boots via the HA alternate boot disk. The HA alternate boot disk is usually a mirror of the primary. If none of them is available, the system attempts to boot from an alternate source, which could be a

DVD, a tape or a LAN interface. The primary, HA alternate and alternate boot paths, as well as path to the system console can be viewed at the BCH menu, the ISL prompt or the command prompt, but can be modified at the BCH or command prompt only.

To view and set the values at the BCH prompt:

Main Menu: Enter Command > **pa**   (view paths)
Main Menu: Enter Command > **pa pri 0/0/0/3/0.6**   (set primary boot path)
Main Menu: Enter Command > **pa haa 0/0/0/0/0/0.0** (set HA alternate boot path)
Main Menu: Enter Command > **pa alt 0/0/4/0/0/0.0** (set alternate boot path)

To view the values at the ISL prompt:

ISL > **display**
    Primary boot path is 0/0/0/3/0.6.0.0.0.0.0
    Primary boot path is (hex) 0/0/0/3/0.6.0.0.0.0.0
    Alternate boot path is 0/0/4/0/0.0.0.0.0.0.0
    Alternate boot path is (hex) 0/0/4/0/0.0.0.0.0.0.0
    System console path is 0/0/0/0/0/0/0/0.0.0.0.0.0.0
    System console path is (hex) 0/0/0/0/0/0/0/0.0.0.0.0.0.0

To view and set the values at the command prompt:

setboot   (view paths)
Primary bootpath : 0/0/0/3/0.0x6.0x0 (/dev/rdisk/disk2)
HA Alternate bootpath : 0/0/0/0/0 (No dsf found)
Alternate bootpath : 0/0/4/0/0.0x0.0x0 (/dev/rdisk/disk5)
setboot –p 0/0/0/3/0.0x6.0x0   (set primary boot path)
setboot –h 0/0/0/0/0   (set HA alternate boot path)
setboot –a 0/0/4/0/0.0x0.0x0   (set alternate boot path)

16.2.4   Booting from Primary, HA Alternate and Alternate Boot Devices

The following examples demonstrate how to boot the system using the three sources:

From the primary boot disk:

Main Menu: Enter command or menu > **boot**

From the HA alternate boot disk:

Main Menu: Enter command or menu > **boot haa**

From the alternate boot device:

Main Menu: Enter command or menu > **boot alt**

16.2.5 Booting from an Undefined Boot Device

To boot the system from a device other than the three boot sources mentioned above, run the *search* command at the BCH prompt to find all possible boot devices:

```
Main Menu: Enter command > sea
Searching for potential boot device(s)
This may take several minutes.
To discontinue search, press any key (termination may not be immediate).
                                         IODC
    Path#  Device Path (dec)             Device Type             Rev
    -------  --------------------        ----------------------------   ----
    P0     0/0/0/3/0.6                   Random access media     3
    P1     0/0/4/0/0.0                   Random access media     3
    P2     0/0/8/0/0/1/0.4               Random access media     3
    P3     0/0/8/0/0/1/0.2               Sequential access media  3
           0/0/10/0/0.0.0.0.0.0.0        Fibre Channel Protocol  6
           0/0/12/0/0.0.0.0.0.0.0        Fibre Channel Protocol  6
Main Menu: Enter command >
```

The output indicates that there are four possible boot devices. The first two (P0 and P1) are hard drives, the third (P2) is the DVD drive and the fourth (P3) is the tape drive. The last two are the fibre channel cards. If you know the device path to the boot device you wish to boot from, specify it with the *boot* command. For example, if the boot device path is 0/0/0/3/0.6, do either of the two:

```
Main Menu: Enter command or menu > boot 0/0/0/3/0.6
Main Menu: Enter command or menu > boot p0
```

16.2.6 Booting to Single User State

At times, it is necessary to boot the system to single user mode in order to perform maintenance tasks. After the *boot* command is executed at the BCH prompt, you need to answer "y" to the question "Interact with ISL (Y, N or Cancel ?>" to be placed at the ISL prompt.

Type *hpux* and supply −is options to go to the single user state using the default kernel file */stand/vmunix*. The −i (init) option specifies to boot to the single user (−s) state.

```
ISL> hpux −is
Boot
: disk(0/0/0/3/0.6.0.0.0.0.0;0)/stand/vmunix
17227776 + 5660704 + 21885968 start 0x1409e8
. . . . . . . .
INIT: Overriding default level with level 's'
INIT: SINGLE USER MODE
INIT: Running /sbin/sh
#
```

16.2.7 Booting to LVM Maintenance State

Sometimes LVM structures develop problems due to misconfiguration or abnormal system shutdown. In such a situation, it is best to boot the system to LVM maintenance state in order to fix the problems and bring the system back up normally.

To boot to LVM maintenance state, you need to answer "yes" to the question "Interact with ISL (Y, N or Cancel?>" after the *boot* command is executed at the BCH prompt, as explained above.

Type *hpux* and supply –lm options to boot to LVM maintenance state using the default kernel file */stand/vmunix*. The –l (LVM) option forces *hpux* secondary boot loader to take the system to the maintenance (–m) state.

> ISL> **hpux –lm**
> Boot
> : disk(0/0/0/3/0.6.0.0.0.0.0;0)/stand/vmunix
> 17227776 + 5660704 + 21885968 start 0x1409e8
>
> . . . .
> INIT: Overriding default level with level 's'
> INIT: SINGLE USER MODE
> INIT: Running /sbin/sh
> #

Reboot the system with –n option when you are finished with the maintenance work:

> # **reboot –n**

16.2.8 Booting without Quorum Checking

With LVM mirrored boot disk configuration, both disks are required to be present for the system to boot up normally. In the event one of the disks malfunctions, the system can still be booted up by ignoring the presence of the other disk using the –lq options at the ISL prompt.

> ISL> **hpux –lq**
> Boot
> : disk(0/0/0/3/0.6.0.0.0.0.0;0)/stand/vmunix
> 17227776 + 5660704 + 21885968 start 0x1409e8
>
> . . . .
> INIT: Overriding default level with level 's'
> INIT: SINGLE USER MODE
> INIT: Running /sbin/sh
> #

16.2.9 Viewing and Modifying AUTO File Contents

The AUTO file is located in the LIF area and it contains the command string used to load the secondary boot loader *hpux*. You can view and modify the string at either the ISL prompt or the command prompt. One of the reasons to make this change would be to specify the default kernel file location and ignore the quorum checking after mirroring is configured, as explained in Chapter 13 "Logical Volume Manager".

To set the string at the ISL prompt:

ISL > hpux set autofile "hpux –lq(;0)/stand/vmunix"
Set autofile
: disk(0/0/0/3/0.6.0.0.0.0.0;0x800000)
AUTO file now contains (hpux -lq(;0)/stand/vmunix)

To view and verify the file's contents at the ISL prompt, use the *lsautofl* command:

ISL > lsautofl
Auto-execute file contains:
hpux –lq(;0)/stand/vmunix

To set the string at the command prompt, use the *mkboot* command:

 # mkboot –a "hpux –lq(;0)/stand/vmunix" /dev/rdisk/disk2

To view and verify the file's contents at the command prompt, use the *lifcp* command:

 # lifcp /dev/rdisk/disk2:AUTO –
hpux -lq(;0)/stand/vmunix

16.2.10   Booting an Alternate Kernel

Sometimes, it is imperative to boot the system from a non-default kernel file. One possible reason, you have modified the kernel and rebooted the system, however, the system does not boot up and is unable to load the kernel.

To boot from a non-default kernel file such as */stand/backup/vmunix,* located on the ALT boot disk at 0/0/4/0/0.0 hardware address, go to the ISL prompt and type:

ISL> hpux (0/0/4/0/0.0;0)/stand/backup/vmunix

If the kernel file is located on the primary boot disk:

ISL> hpux /stand/backup/vmunix

Run the *hpux* command as follows if you wish to list the contents of the */stand* or */stand/backup* directory where kernel files are stored:

```
ISL > hpux ll /stand
total 64832
dr-xr-xr-x  7 bin   bin     1024   Apr 16 19:47   ./
dr-xr-xr-x  7 bin   bin     1024   Apr 16 19:47   ../
drwxr-xr-x  5 root  sys     1024   Apr 14 12:19   backup/
-rw-r--r--  1 root  sys       19   Apr  8 12:59   bootconf
lrwxr-xr-x  1 root  root      14   Apr 16 19:52   bootfs -> current/bootfs
drwxr-xr-x  5 root  sys     1024   Apr  8 14:26   current/
-rw-r--r--  1 root  sys    15184   Apr 16 19:52   ext_ioconfig
```

-rw-r--r--	1 root	sys	6092	Apr 16 19:52	ioconfig
drwxr-xr-x	2 root	sys	1024	Apr 16 19:47	krs/
drwxr-xr-x	5 root	sys	1024	Apr 8 15:21	last_install/
drwxr-xr-x	2 root	root	65536	Apr 8 12:58	lost+found/
lrwxr-xr-x	1 root	root	8192	Apr 16 19:52	nextboot
-rw-------	1 root	root	40	Apr 16 19:52	rootconf
lrwxr-xr-x	1 root	roo	15	Apr 16 19:52	system -> nextboot/system
-rw-r--r--	1 root	sys	4429	Apr 10 13:33	system.prev
-rwxr-xr-x	4 root	sys	32940544	Apr 8 14:21	vmunix

ISL > **hpux ll /stand/backup**

total 64116

-rw-r--r--	1 root	sys	147	Apr 16 11:59	README
drwxr-xr-x	1 root	root	96	Apr 16 11:59	bootfs/
drwxr-xr-x	2 root	sys	1024	Apr 16 11:59	krs/
drwxr-xr-x	2 root	sys	8192	Aug 16 11:59	mod/
-rwxr-xr-x	1 root	roo	5048	Apr 16 11:59	system
-rwxr-xr-x	4 root	sys	30210326	Apr 16 11:59	vmunix

Choose the kernel you want to boot and specify it with the *hpux* command at the ISL prompt.

16.3   Booting the HP Integrity Server

The Integrity server goes through the system boot process similar to the 9000 server boot process with some differences. The differences are discussed in the next sub-section. Here is the step-by-step boot process for the Integrity server:

- ✓ Power on external devices.
- ✓ Power on the server.
- ✓ The system firmware runs *Power On Self Test* (POST) on the system hardware components such as processor, memory and I/O, and initializes them.
- ✓ The system locates hardware path to the boot device from the non-volatile area in memory.
- ✓ The boot disk has an EFI partition from where the *boot manager* is automatically launched, which initiates the loading of HP-UX boot loader program called *hpux.efi*.
- ✓ The *hpux.efi* boot loader uses the contents in the AUTO file to locate the kernel file to boot.
- ✓ The *hpux.efi* boot loader loads the kernel into memory and initializes it. The default kernel is located in the */stand* file system on the boot disk and is called *vmunix*.
- ✓ The kernel starts the *swapper* daemon.
- ✓ The kernel calls the *init* command and transfers the control over to it to initiate the system initialization process.
- ✓ The *init* command references the */etc/inittab* file to determine the default run level to boot to.
- ✓ The *init* command calls */sbin/rc* script, which calls all startup scripts needed to bring the system to the default run level.
- ✓ Finally, *init* presents the login prompt.

16.3.1   Extensible Firmware Interface and Boot Manager

The Integrity system uses *Extensible Firmware Interface* (EFI), which makes the pre-boot level different from the 9000 servers. EFI is a hardware and operating system independent interface that contains boot utilities similar to those found on the PA-RISC based systems. EFI lives between HP-

UX and the system firmware, allowing HP-UX to boot without the knowledge of the underlying hardware and firmware. The two main components of EFI are the *boot manager* and the *shell*. A bootable disk in the Integrity system contains either an EFI operating system loader or an *EFI partition*. The EFI partition is a small, special area that contains EFI utilities for pre-boot administration tasks. Among such utilities is the boot manager and the EFI shell. Figure 16-3 shows the EFI boot manager and Figure 16-4 shows the EFI shell interfaces.

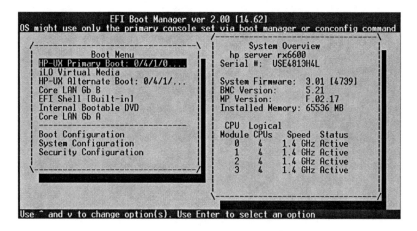

Figure 16-3 EFI Boot Manager

```
Shell> ?
List of classes of commands:

boot          -- Booting options and disk-related commands
configuration -- Changing and retrieving system information
device        -- Getting device, driver, and handle information
memory        -- Memory related commands
shell         -- Basic shell navigation and customization
scripts       -- EFI shell-script commands

Use 'help <class>' for a list of commands in that class
Use 'help <command>' for full documentation of a command
Use 'help -a' to display list of all commands.

Shell> _
```

Figure 16-4 EFI Shell

The EFI shell is invoked by choosing the "EFI Shell [Build-in]" option in the boot manager.

From the boot manager and the EFI shell, you can perform several tasks such as booting HP-UX with primary, alternate or DVD device, searching for alternate boot devices, performing a boot from a non-default kernel or boot device, modifying the boot entry, boot order and autoboot configuration, and resetting the system.

16.3.2 Booting Manually versus Automatically

The system automatically boots up if the autoboot parameter is set to ON and the AUTO file with a proper string defined, is present in the EFI partition on the boot device.

Sometimes, you need to boot the system manually to interact with the boot manager. To do so, hit any key before autoboot delay period expires. The following lists steps to use the EFI shell to boot the system manually:

1. Highlight "EFI Shell [Built-in]" from the boot manager main menu and press Enter to get to the EFI shell.
2. Use the *map* command to list file systems that are known and mapped. Select a file system to use by entering its mapped name (fs0, fs1, etc.) followed by the colon character and press Enter. The prompt will change to reflect the selected file system.

> Shell> **map**
> Device mapping table
> fs0:Acpi(HWP0002,PNP0A03,0)/Pci(2|1)/Usb(0, 0)/DVDROM(Entry0)
> fs1:Acpi(HWP0002,PNP0A03,400)/Pci(1|0)/Scsi(Pun5,Lun0)/HD(Part1,Sig03699A00-B066-11DB-8002-D6217B60E588)
> fs2: Acpi(HWP0002,PNP0A03,400)/Pci(1|0)/Scsi(Pun5,Lun0)/HD(Part3,Sig03699A64-B066-11DB-8004-D6217B60E588)
> fs3:Acpi(HWP0002,PNP0A03,400)/Pci(1|0)/Sas(Addr500000E0140986D2,Lun0)/HD(Part1,SigE4635232-F8B7-11DB-8002-D6217B60E588)
> . . . .
> Shell> **fs1:**

3. Enter *hpux* at the prompt to launch the *hpux.efi* loader. The loader is located in *\EFI\HPUX*.

> fs1:\> **hpux**

4. The *hpux.efi* loader executes the *boot* command using the AUTO file contents located in the *\EFI\HPUX* directory on the EFI partition of the selected boot device. The AUTO file typically contains "*boot vmunix*". If you wish to manually boot the system, interrupt the boot process within the timeout period provided by the loader to get to the HPUX> prompt. You may need to interrupt the boot process at this time to boot an alternate kernel, boot to single user mode, boot to LVM maintenance mode and so on.

16.3.3   Viewing and Modifying Autoboot and Boot Delay Period

You can enable or disable automatic booting of the system and modify the delay time.

The value of autoboot flag can be set from the EFI Shell or at the command prompt.

From the EFI shell, use the *autoboot* command:

> Shell> **autoboot on**   (enables autoboot)
> Shell> **autoboot off**   (disables autoboot)

At the command prompt, use the *setboot* command:

> # **setboot –b on**   (enables autoboot)
> # **setboot –b off**   (disables autoboot)

The default automatic boot delay is set to 10 seconds. This value can be modified from the boot manager or the EFI shell. The number specified is in seconds.

From the boot manager:

Go to Boot Configuration → AutoBoot Configuration → Set AutoBoot Timeout. Specify a number.

From the EFI shell:

Shell> **autoboot 20**   (Changes to 20 seconds)

16.3.4   Viewing and Setting Primary, HA Alternate and Alternate Boot Paths

The primary, HA alternate and alternate boot paths can be viewed and modified from the boot manager or at the command prompt.

From the boot manager:

Go to Boot Configuration. The "Edit OS Boot Order" lists the boot order and the "Add Boot Entry", "Edit Boot Entry" and "Remove Boot Entry" allow you to add, modify and remove entries for primary, HA alternate and alternate boot devices.

At the command prompt:

setboot   (view paths)
Primary bootpath : 0/0/0/3/0.0x6.0x0 (/dev/rdisk/disk2)
HA Alternate bootpath : 0/0/0/0/0 (No dsf found)
Alternate bootpath : 0/0/4/0/0.0x0.0x0 (/dev/rdisk/disk5)
setboot –p 0/0/0/3/0.0x6.0x0   (set primary boot path)
setboot –h 0/0/0/0/0   (set HA alternate boot path)
setboot –a 0/0/4/0/0.0x0.0x0   (set alternate boot path)

16.3.5   Booting from an Alternate Boot Device

If an alternate boot device is listed in the boot menu, select it and press the Enter key, otherwise, go to the boot manager and follow the procedure below to choose another boot device:

1. Run the EFI shell.
2. Enter *map* command to list available boot devices. Look for entries that begin with *fs#* (where # is 0, 1, 2 and so on).
3. Select the desired entry and press Enter.
4. Enter *hpux* to run the boot loader, which uses the AUTO file to determine the kernel to boot.

16.3.6   Booting to Single User State

From the EFI shell, boot to single-user state by stopping the boot process at the *hpux.efi* interface and entering the *boot* command with proper switches. Here is the procedure:

1. Run the EFI shell.

2. Enter *map* to list available boot devices. Look for entries that begin with *fs#* (where # is 0, 1, 2 and so on).
3. Select the desired entry and press Enter.
4. Run the *hpux* command to invoke the *\EFI\HPUX\HPUX.EFI* loader.
5. Boot to the HPUX> prompt by hitting any key within 10 seconds.
6. At the *hpux.efi* interface, enter the following to boot the */stand/vmunix* kernel to single-user state:

```
HPUX> boot –is
> System Memory = 4063 MB
loading section 0
................................................. (complete)
loading section 1
........ (complete)
loading symbol table
loading System Directory(boot.sys) to MFS
....
loading MFSFILES Directory(bootfs) to MFS
......
Launching /stand/vmunix
SIZE: Text:25953K + Data:3715K + BSS:3637K = Total:33306K

Console is on a Serial Device
Booting kernel...
```

16.3.7   Booting to LVM Maintenance State

The procedure for booting HP-UX to LVM maintenance state is similar to that of booting it to single user state, except that you specify appropriate boot options. Do the following:

```
HPUX> boot –lm
```

16.3.8   Viewing and Modifying AUTO File Contents

The AUTO file is located in *\EFI\HPUX\AUTO* on the boot device. The contents of this file can be modified from the EFI shell, *hpux.efi* prompt or at the command prompt.

From the EFI shell:

1. Use the *map* command to list all available devices.
2. Choose the desired device by selecting its *fs#*.
3. Change to *\EFI\HPUX* directory using the *cd* command.
4. Run the *ls* command to list all boot loader files there.
5. View AUTO file contents with the *cat* command:

```
fs0:\EFI\HPUX> cat AUTO
FILE: fs0:\EFI\HPUX\AUTO, Size 12
boot vmunix
```

6. Use the *edit* command to modify the entry:

    fs0:\EFI\HPUX> **edit AUTO**

From the HPUX secondary boot loader prompt:

1. Access the *hpux.efi* loader for the boot device that contains the AUTO file to be configured.
2. At the *hpux.efi* boot loader prompt, enter the *showauto* command to display current contents of the AUTO file:

    HPUX> **showauto**
    \EFI\HPUX\AUTO => boot vmunix –lq

3. Enter the *setauto* command to delete or modify the AUTO file:

    HPUX> **setauto –d**   (deletes the AUTO file)
    HPUX> **setauto "boot vmunix –lq"**   (modifies the contents to "boot vmunix –lq)

At the command prompt:

1. Copy the AUTO file from the EFI partition:

    # **efi_cp –d /dev/rdisk/disk2s1 –u /EFI/HPUX/AUTO AUTO**

2. Edit the file and modify the contents.
3. Copy the updated AUTO file back to the EFI partition:

    # **efi_cp –d /dev/rdisk/disk2s1 AUTO /EFI/HPUX/AUTO**

16.3.9   Booting an Alternate Kernel

The default kernel file is *vmunix* and is located in the */stand* directory on the boot device. The AUTO file in the EFI partition contains the entry "*boot vmunix*", which references this kernel.

If you need to boot using an alternate kernel such as */stand/backup/vmunix*, follow the procedure given below:

1. Go to the boot manager and then to the EFI shell.
2. Enter the *map* command to list available boot devices.
3. Determine the entry that maps to the device containing the kernel file you want to boot from and enter the *fs#* at the shell prompt.
4. Enter the command *hpux* at the shell prompt and stop the autoboot sequence by pressing any key.
5. At the boot loader prompt, enter the command *boot* and specify an alternate kernel file name to boot from:

    HPUX> **boot /stand/backup/vmunix**

16.4 Preventing Security Breaches During System Boot

Security breaches can happen during system boot. An unauthorized person can interrupt the boot process to gain single-user access into the system. By default, *root* is allowed to enter into the single-user mode without being prompted for a password.

The person may change or remove files that might leave the system unbootable. To prevent such a situation, create or edit */etc/default/security* file and ensure that the following two variables are set to force the *root* user to enter a password to gain single-user access.

```
BOOT_AUTH=1
BOOT_USERS=root
```

If you wish to allow any other users to be able to gain single-user access, you will need to add that user's name to the BOOT_USERS variable. For example, if *user1* requires this access as well, modify the variable as shown below:

```
BOOT_USERS=root,user1
```

16.5 Initializing HP-UX

HP-UX initialization phase begins when the *boot* command is executed with correct boot device and kernel file specified. The initialization phase is similar for both 9000 and Integrity systems, and includes everything, from loading the kernel to screen login prompt.

16.5.1 Kernel Initialization

The HP-UX kernel is loaded into the memory and initialized. The kernel starts the *swapper* daemon and runs the */sbin/pre_init_rc* script. This script checks the root file system and executes *fsck* on it, if required.

16.5.2 The init Process

The kernel calls the */sbin/init* command and transfers the control over to it to initiate the system initialization process. The *init* command looks into the */etc/inittab* file to determine the default run control level for the system to boot to.

A sample */etc/inittab* file is shown below. The first line in the file defines the default run control level, which is 3.

```
# cat /etc/inittab
init:3:initdefault:
ioin::sysinit:/sbin/ioinitrc >/dev/console 2>&1
tape::sysinit:/sbin/mtinit > /dev/console 2>&1
muxi::sysinit:/sbin/dasetup   </dev/console >/dev/console 2>&1 # mux init
stty::sysinit:/sbin/stty 9600 clocal icanon echo opost onlcr ixon icrnl ignpar </dev/systty
fs01::wait:/sbin/fs/fsdaemon -k > /dev/null 2>&1  # kill fsdaemon

. . . . . . . .
```

As you can see, there are four fields per line separated by the colon character. The fields are:

- ✓ The first field defines a unique identification string containing 1–4 characters for each line item.
- ✓ The second field identifies run levels at which the entry is executed. If the field is empty, the entry is valid for all run levels.
- ✓ The third field determines an action. There are many possible actions, some of which are:

> **initdefault** – this action determines the default run level for the system. The *init* command reads this line and boots the system to the specified run level.
> **sysinit** – this action executes the specified process before *init* tries to access the system console display.
> **bootwait** – this action takes place during the system boot process only.
> **wait** – when an entry with this action is being executed, other entries at the same run level wait for its completion before their turn comes.
> **respawn** – restarts the specified process as soon as it dies. If the process is running, no action is taken.

- ✓ The fourth field defines the fully qualified pathname to the process or command that is to be executed.

16.5.3   Building Hardware Device Tree

The next command that *init* calls from the */etc/inittab* file is */sbin/ioinitrc*. This command executes the */sbin/ioinit* command, which maintains an up to date hardware device information database in the */etc/ioconfig* file. At system boot, *ioinit* tests consistency between hardware available at that time against what is already listed in the */etc/ioconfig* file from the previous reboot. If a new device has been added to the system, the *insf* command is issued, which creates device files for the new device and adds an entry for it to the file. Similarly, if a device has been removed from the system, the corresponding entry is removed from the file. A copy of */etc/ioconfig* file is also stored in the */stand* file system.

16.5.4   Checking and Activating Volume Groups

After the hardware information is updated, the */sbin/bcheckrc* command is executed. This command performs several actions including checking and activating LVM volume groups by calling the */sbin/lvmrc* command and checking, cleaning and mounting all local file systems listed in the */etc/fstab* file.

16.5.5   Starting Up Services

Next, the *init* command calls the */sbin/rc* script, which starts up all HP-UX services configured to run in the default run level.

The */sbin/rc* script locates the services to be started in the sequencer directories */sbin/rc#.d*, gets configuration information from the startup configuration files located in the */etc/rc.config.d* directory and starts up services from the initialization directory */sbin/init.d*.

Here is a list of the sequencer directories:

```
# ll –d /sbin/rc* | grep d
dr-xr-xr-x   2  bin   bin      8192   Apr  8  09:10  /sbin/rc0.d
dr-xr-xr-x   2  bin   bin      8192   Apr 14  08:20  /sbin/rc1.d
dr-xr-xr-x   2  bin   bin      8192   Apr 14  09:01  /sbin/rc2.d
dr-xr-xr-x   2  bin   bin      8192   Apr  8  11:32  /sbin/rc3.d
dr-xr-xr-x   2  bin   bin        96   Apr  8  09:07  /sbin/rc4.d
```

The following shows contents of the *rc0.d* directory. Notice that all scripts here are mere soft links to startup scripts located in the */sbin/init.d* directory.

```
# ll /sbin/rc0.d
lrwxr-xr-x   1  bin   bin      18   Apr 8  09:07  K400utmpd -> /sbin/init.d/utmpd
lrwxr-xr-x   1  bin   bin      21   Apr 8  09:07  K460livedump -> /sbin/init.d/livedump
lrwxr-xr-x   1  bin   bin      19   Apr 8  09:07  K480syncer -> /sbin/init.d/syncer
lrwxr-xr-x   1  bin   bin      20   Apr 8  09:07  K800killall -> /sbin/init.d/killall
lrwxr-xr-x   1  bin   bin      21   Apr 8  09:07  K810fsdaemon -> /sbin/init.d/fsdaemon
lrwxr-xr-x   1  bin   bin      16   Apr 8  09:07  K850kcshutdown -> /sbin/kcshutdown
lrwxr-xr-x   1  bin   bin      23   Apr 8  09:07  K900localmount -> /sbin/init.d/localmount
. . . . . . . .
```

The following lists contents of the *rc3.d* directory. Notice again that all scripts here are soft links to startup scripts in the */sbin/init*.d directory.

```
# ll /sbin/rc3.d
lrwxr-xr-x   1  bin   bin      23   Apr 8  09:18  S100nfs.server -> /sbin/init.d/nfs.server
lrwxr-xr-x   1  root  sys      21   Apr 8  11:32  S110idsagent -> /sbin/init.d/idsagent
lrwxr-xr-x   1  bin   bin      19   Apr 8  09:46  S200tps.rc -> /sbin/init.d/tps.rc
lrwxr-xr-x   1  bin   bin      24   Apr 8  09:14  S823hpws_apache -> /sbin/init.d/hpws_apache
lrwxr-xr-x   1  bin   bin      24   Apr 8  09:15  S823hpws_tomcat -> /sbin/init.d/hpws_tomcat
. . . . . . . .
```

The sequencer directories are *rc0.d, rc1.d, rc2.d, rc3.d* and *rc4.d*. The *rc4.d* directory is empty. There are two types of scripts located in the sequencer directories: *start* and *kill*. The names of the start scripts begin with an uppercase S and that for the kill scripts with an uppercase K. These scripts are symbolically linked to actual startup/shutdown scripts located in the */sbin/init.d* directory. Each startup/shutdown script contains start and stop functions corresponding to starting and stopping a service. Similarly, each startup/shutdown script contains "start_msg" and "stop_msg" functions. When a service is started, the start function of the script is executed and the message defined in the "start_msg" function is displayed. Likewise, when a service is stopped, the stop function of the script is executed and the message defined in the "stop_msg" function is displayed. The contents of one of the scripts, */sbin/init.d/lp*, is shown below as an example:

```
# cat /sbin/init.d/lp
. . . . . . . .
case $1 in
start_msg)
      echo "Start print spooler"
      ;;
stop_msg)
```

```
        echo "Stop print spooler"
        ;;

'start')
        if [ -f /etc/rc.config.d/lp ] ; then
            . /etc/rc.config.d/lp
        else
            echo "ERROR: /etc/rc.config.d/lp defaults file MISSING"
        fi

        if [ "$LP" -eq 1 -a -s /var/spool/lp/pstatus ]; then
            ps -ef | grep lpsched | grep -iv grep > /dev/null 2>&1
            if [ $? = 0 ]
            then
              /usr/sbin/lpshut > /dev/null 2>&1
            set_return
            fi
            rm -f /var/spool/lp/SCHEDLOCK
            /usr/sbin/lpsched && echo line printer scheduler started
            set_return
        else
            rval=2
        fi
        ;;

'stop')
        if [ -s /var/spool/lp/pstatus ]; then
            if /usr/sbin/lpshut > /dev/null 2>&1; then
                echo line printer scheduler stopped
            else
                set_return
            fi
        fi
        ;;

*)
        echo "usage: $0 {start|stop}"
        ;;
esac

exit $rval
```

All scripts located in the *rc0.d* directory are kill scripts; *rc1.d* and *rc2.d* contain both start and kill scripts; and *rc3.d* contains only start scripts.

When the system comes up, S scripts are executed one after the other in ascending numerical sequence from the *rc1.d*, *rc2.d* and *rc3.d* directories. In the same way, when the system goes down, K scripts are executed one after the other in descending numerical sequence from the *rc2.d*, *rc1.d* and *rc0.d* directories.

The following lists configuration files for the startup/shutdown scripts placed in the */etc/rc.config.d* configuration directory:

```
# ll /etc/rc.config.d
total 1536
-r--r--r--    1 bin    bin      225 Feb 15 2007  LANG
-r--r--r--    1 root   sys      158 Jun  8 2007  Nds-adm7
-r--r--r--    1 root   sys      151 Jun  8 2007  Nds-ds7
-r--r--r--    1 bin    bin      848 Jan 12 2007  Rpcd
. . . . . . . .
```

Each of these configuration files has a variable value set to 1 or 0, 1 means to start the service at system boot and 0 means otherwise. A sample startup configuration file for the print services is shown below:

```
# cat /etc/rc.config.d/lp
. . . . . . . .
LP=1
```

If you are ever required to replace a misconfigured, corrupted or lost startup configuration file in the */etc/rc.config.d* directory with the original file added at the time of system installation, it can be obtained from the */usr/newconfig/etc/rc.config.d* directory.

The following listing from the */sbin/init.d* directory shows actual startup/shutdown scripts:

```
# ll /sbin/init.d
total 2864
-r-xr-xr-x    1 bin    bin     4500   Jul 23 2007  CreateUsbSf
-r-xr-xr-x    1 root   sys     1616   Jun  8 2007  Nds-adm7
-r-xr-xr-x    1 root   sys     2685   Jun  8 2007  Nds-ds7
-rwxr-xr-x    1 root   root    4361   Apr  8 09:33  OVCtrl
-rwxr-xr-x    1 root   root    1004   Apr  8 09:33  OVTrcSrv
-r-xr-xr-x    1 bin    bin     3757   Feb 15 2007  OspfMib
-r-xr-xr-x    1 bin    bin     3621   Jan 12 2007  Rpcd
. . . . . . . .
```

16.5.6 Starting and Stopping Services Manually

Any of the services from the */sbin/init.d* directory can be started or stopped manually. For example, to stop the printing service daemon, *lpsched*, do the following:

```
# /sbin/init.d/lp stop
line printer scheduler stopped
```

To start it:

```
# /sbin/init.d/lp start
scheduler is running
```

16.5.7   System Startup Log File

Log information for each service startup status at system boot is captured in the */etc/rc.log* file. This file can also be referenced via the */var/adm/rc.log* file, which is a soft link to it. Here is a excerpt from the file:

 # cat /etc/rc.log
Old /etc/rc.log moved to /etc/rc.log.old

```
*************************************************
HP-UX Start-up in progress
Thu Apr 17 07:28:19 EDT 2008
*************************************************
Configure system crash dumps
Output from "/sbin/rc1.d/S080crashconf start":
----------------------------
crashconf: concurrent mode not supported on this platform
EXIT CODE: 0
Removing old vxvm files
Output from "/sbin/rc1.d/S090sw_clean_vxvm start":
----------------------------
VxVM INFO V-5-2-3360 VxVM device node check
Output from "/sbin/rc1.d/S091vxvm-nodes-check start":
----------------------------
VxVM INFO V-5-2-3362 VxVM general startup
Output from "/sbin/rc1.d/S092vxvm-startup start":
----------------------------
VxVM INFO V-5-2-3366 VxVM reconfiguration recovery
Output from "/sbin/rc1.d/S093vxvm-reconfig start":
----------------------------
Mount file systems
Output from "/sbin/rc1.d/S100localmount start":
. . . . . . . .
*************************************************
HP-UX run-level transition completed
Thu Apr 17 07:29:57 EDT 2008
*************************************************
```

Summary

In this chapter you learned how to shutdown an HP-UX system using various available tools. You saw different run levels that a system could run at.

You learned system startup that covered pre-boot administration tasks, and kernel and system initialization. Pre-boot administration tasks included interacting with BCH and EFI, setting automatic/manual system boot attributes, setting autosearch attribute for bootable devices, setting and modifying boot device paths and so on. These tasks were presented for both HP 9000 and Integrity servers.

The following section talked about kernel and system initialization where you studied various commands and scripts that were executed to bring up system services. You were introduced to sequencer directories, startup configuration files and actual system startup scripts that were run to bring a system to a fully functional state.

## 17

Kernel Management

This chapter covers the following major topics:

- ✓ Static and dynamic kernel modules and tunables
- ✓ Kernel administration interfaces – kcweb, SMH and commands
- ✓ Manage kernel configurations with kcweb and SMH
- ✓ Manage running and saved kernel configurations using kconfig command
- ✓ Manage kernel modules and tunables using kcmodule and kctune commands
- ✓ View kernel logs
- ✓ Boot a saved configuration, via override tunables and to tunable maintenance mode

17.1   Introduction

The default kernel configuration when HP-UX is initially loaded is usually sufficient to install and run many applications, however, the kernel requires a reconfiguration when its settings are modified. HP-UX allows you to generate and store several custom kernel configurations. Each custom configuration may include varying kernel settings. At any given time, only one configuration can be activated, which is referred to as the *currently running* kernel configuration, all others are referred to as the *saved* kernel configurations. HP-UX allows switching between configurations without a system reboot in many cases.

The default kernel configuration includes several software and hardware subsystems such as LVM, CD/DVD and networking. Support for these subsystems is added to the kernel in the form of modules so that the functionalities they offer can be employed. A new module may be added to a kernel configuration as and when required. Similarly, if the functionality is no longer required, the module may be removed. The associated kernel configuration is updated as part of both processes.

To control the behavior of the modules, and the kernel in general, several tunable parameters are set. These parameters define a baseline for the kernel functionality. Some of these parameters are required to be modified when certain applications or database software needs to be loaded and used on the system. This allows the applications or the database software to be installed smoothly and function properly.

17.2   Kernel Components

The HP-UX kernel is made up of two major components: *modules* and *tunable parameters*. Some of the modules and tunable parameters are static, while others dynamic.

17.2.1   Static and Dynamic Modules

The kernel is composed of a number of modules. Each module contains software that adds a functionality to the system. Modules can be added or removed using commands or SMH.

Modules can be *static* or *dynamic*. A static module requires a kernel rebuild and a system reboot to make it effective. On the contrary, a dynamic (a.k.a. *Dynamically Loadable Kernel Module –* DLKM) module can be added to or removed from the kernel while the system is up and running; there is no need to bounce the server. A dynamic module is automatically loaded into the memory when needed and gets unloaded when no longer required.

17.2.2   Static and Dynamic Tunables

There are several tunable parameters defined in the kernel, the values of which affect the overall behavior of the system. The sizes of many kernel tables are determined by these tunables. Tunables manage the allocation of system resources, overall system performance, etc. Tunable values can be altered using commands or SMH.

Tunable parameters can be static or dynamic. After modifying the value of a static kernel parameter, the kernel needs to be rebuilt and the server must be rebooted for the new value to take effect. A dynamic (a.k.a. *Dynamically Tunable Kernel Parameter –* DTKP) tunable parameter, in contrast, does not require a server reboot after its value is altered. The value takes effect as soon as it is changed.

17.3 Kernel Administration Interfaces

The kernel configuration can be performed using commands or SMH. This section elaborates performing these tasks using both interfaces.

17.3.1 Directory Structure

The HP-UX kernel, its backup and all other configuration information is stored in a separate file system that is mounted on the */stand* directory. Do an *ll* on the directory to list the contents:

```
# ll /stand
total 241440
drwxr-xr-x   5 root   sys         8192   Aug 26 02:31   backup
-rw-r--r--   1 root   sys           46   May 15 12:22   bootconf
lrwxr-xr-x   1 root   root          14   Sep  8 18:04   bootfs -> current/bootfs
drwx------   5 root   sys         8192   Sep  8 18:04   current
-rw-r--r--   1 root   sys       384392   Sep  8 18:04   ext_ioconfig
-rw-r--r--   1 root   sys        58768   Sep  8 18:04   ioconfig
drwxr-xr-x   2 root   sys           96   Sep  8 18:06   krs
drwxr-xr-x   5 root   sys         8192   May 14 09:58   last_install
drwxr-xr-x   2 root   root          96   May 13 16:33   lost+found
drwx------   5 root   sys         8192   Sep  9 07:04   nextboot
-rw-------   1 root   root          40   Sep  8 18:04   rootconf
lrwxr-xr-x   1 root   root          15   Sep  8 18:04   system -> nextboot/system
-rwxr-xr-x   4 root   sys    123113368   Aug 25 22:32   vmunix
```

Key files and sub-directories are described in Table 17-1.

Files / Sub-directories	Description
backup	Contains the last kernel configuration before any modifications.
bootconf	Contains the DSF for the boot device.
bootfs	Contains current kernel registry services (krs) and module information.
current	Contains the current kernel and related configuration.
ext_ioconfig	Contains additional agile entries.
ioconfig	Contains system I/O configuration information.
krs	Contains *kernel registry services* information.
last_install	Contains previous kernel and related configuration.
nextboot	Contains the kernel configuration that will become active at the next system boot.
rootconf	Contains the root file system information.
system	Kernel configuration file.
vmunix	The current HP-UX kernel. A copy is saved in the *current* sub-directory also.

Table 17-1 HP-UX Kernel Key Files and Sub-directories

17.3.2 Configuration Interfaces

Kernel configuration may be performed using commands or SMH. Several commands are available, which are described in Table 17-2.

Command	Description
kcalarm	Manages kernel tunable alarms. This command allows you to: ✓ List and remove tunable alarms. ✓ Add tunable alarms to be generated when usage exceeds a pre-defined threshold. ✓ Disable or enable alarms.
kclog	Manages the kernel configuration log file */var/adm/kc.log*. By default, all kernel configuration activities are logged to this file.
kcmodule	Manages kernel modules and subsystems. This command allows you to: ✓ List and remove modules. ✓ Add a module to the configuration in default state. ✓ Add a module to the configuration statically bound into the kernel executable. ✓ Add a module to the configuration dynamically loaded now and at each system boot. ✓ Add a module to the configuration to be auto-loaded at first use. ✓ Remove a module from a configuration. ✓ Apply changes to a saved or current configuration.
kconfig	Manages kernel configurations. This command allows you to: ✓ List, load, copy, rename or delete a saved configuration. ✓ Display changes being held for the next system boot. ✓ Force kernel configuration changes being held for the next system boot. ✓ Discard kernel configuration changes being held for the next system boot. ✓ Create a saved configuration from the running configuration.
kcpath	Displays the location of the currently running kernel configuration or the specified saved configuration.
kctune	Manages kernel tunable parameters. This command allows you to: ✓ Display and modify tunable parameters in the current or a saved configuration. ✓ List tunable parameters in the current or a saved configuration. ✓ Apply changes to the current or a saved configuration.
kcusage	Queries the usage of kernel resources that are controlled by kernel tunable parameters.
kcweb	A kernel configuration and management tool that can be invoked from within SMH or from the command prompt. It supports both graphical and textual interfaces.
mk_kernel	Builds a new kernel based on the contents of the *system* file. This command is deprecated and will be removed in a future HP-UX release. Use *kconfig* instead.

Table 17-2 Kernel Management Commands

Of the commands listed in Table 17-2, three of them *kconfig*, *kcmodule* and *kctune* support several common options listed and explained in Table 17-3.

Option	Description
–a	Displays all information.
–b	Specifies whether to update the automatic backup configuration before a requested change takes place.
–c	Specifies a saved configuration to administer. Default is current configuration. With *kconfig*, this option saves a copy of the saved configuration by the specified name.
–C	Includes a comment in the *kclog* file.
–d	Displays item description. With *kconfig*, this option deletes the specified saved configuration.
–D	Displays items for which a change is held for the next system boot (difference).
–h	Holds the requested change for the next system boot, even if it could be applied instantly. Without this option, the changes are applied immediately to the currently running configuration if possible.
–S	Displays items set to non-default.
–v	Verbose.

Table 17-3 *kconfig/kcmodule/kctune* Command Options

Additional options that the *kconfig* command supports are listed and described in Table 17-4.

Option	Description
–e	Exports a system file from the current or a saved configuration.
–f	Forces the command to proceed with the change.
–H	Discards all changes being held for the next system boot.
–i	Imports a system file to the current or a saved configuration.
–l	Loads a saved configuration.
–n	Marks a saved configuration for use at the next system boot.
–r	Renames a saved configuration.
–s	Saves a copy of the running configuration.
–t	Sets a title of a saved configuration.
–w	Lists a saved configuration marked for use at the next system boot. Also lists the source of the currently running configuration.

Table 17-4 Additional *kconfig* Command Options

17.4   Managing Kernel Configurations Using kcweb

kcweb (kernel configuration web) is a kernel configuration and management tool. It runs in both graphical and textual modes, and may be invoked from within SMH or at the command prompt. It allows you to query and change the states of kernel modules in the currently running configuration, determine which modules are currently running, view details about a specific module, modify the state of a module and perform several tasks on kernel tunable parameters including listing and modifying their values. The *kcweb* tool automatically saves the running kernel configuration before a change is applied to it, and maintains a log of all configuration changes.

To invoke *kcweb* from the command prompt either type *kcweb* or go to SMH → Kernel Configuration. See Figure 17-1 for the text interface.

---

kcweb

```
                        SMH->Kernel Configuration
----------------------------------------------------------------------
    t - Tunables        View or modify kernel tunables

    m - Modules         View or modify kernel modules and drivers

    a - Alarms          View or modify alarms for kernel tunables

    l - Log Viewer      View the changes made to kernel tunables or modules

    u - Usage           View usage of kernel tunables




----------------------------------------------------------------------
x-Exit smh    ENTER-Select    ESC-Back    1-Help
```

Figure 17-1 *kcweb* – Text Interface

This is the main *kcweb* screen. There are five menu items. Here is an explanation of them:

✓ Select "Tunables" and press Enter (or press t) to view or modify kernel tunables. A list of all tunables is displayed along with their current values, modified values being held for the next system boot, the default values, their usage and the modules they are associated with. The list also indicates if the tunable is static or dynamic. To display detailed information about a specific tunable, highlight the tunable and press Enter. To display all tunables in pending state, press p, or press d to display all dynamic tunables. See Figure 17-2.

```
                     SMH->Kernel Configuration->Tunables (All)
----------------------------------------------------------------------------
Tunable              Tuning       Current  Next Boot  Default  Usage  Module
                     Capability   Value    Value      Value
============================================================================
NSTREVENT            Static       50       50         50       -      hpstreams
NSTRPUSH             Static       16       16         16       -      hpstreams
NSTRSCHED            Static       0        0          0        -      hpstreams
STRCTLSZ             Static       1024     1024       1024     -      hpstreams
STRMSGSZ             Static       0        0          0        -      hpstreams
acctresume           Static       4        4          4        -      pm_acct
acctsuspend          Static       2        2          2        -      pm_acct
aio_iosize_max       Dynamic      0        0          0        -      aio
aio_listio_max       Dynamic      256      256        256      -      aio
aio_max_ops          Dynamic      2048     2048       2048     -      aio
aio_monitor_run_sec  Dynamic      30       30         30       -      aio
aio_physmem_pct      Dynamic      10       10         10       -      aio
aio_prio_delta_max   Dynamic      20       20         20       -      aio
aio_proc_max         Dynamic      0        0          0        -      aio
aio_proc_thread_pct  Dynamic      70       70         70       -      aio
aio_proc_threads     Dynamic      1024     1024       1024     -      aio
----------------------------------------------------------------------------
x-Exit smh     ESC-Back     p-Pending   1-Help           3-Tunable Manpage
ENTER-Details  m-Modify     d-Dynamic   2-kctune Manpage  /-Search
```

Figure 17-2 *kcweb* TUI – Kernel Tunables Administration

To modify the value of a tunable, highlight the parameter and press m. Figure 17-3 shows the screen that will pop up when m is pressed on aio_listio_max tunable.

```
                 Kernel Configuration->Tunables (All)->Modify
--------------------------------------------------------------------------
Tunable               aio_iosize_max
Description           Maximum size (in bytes) of any single AIO I/O
Module                aio
Current Value         0 [Default]
Value at Next Boot    0
Value at Last Boot    0
Default Value         0
Constraints           aio_iosize_max >= 0
                      aio_iosize_max <= 268435456
Can Change            Immediately or at Next Boot



NOTE:   If the new Value is specified as Default, the next boot value
        will be default value for the tunable as reccomended by HP.
        However, if the tunable is being autotuned then the value assigned
        will be determined dynamically by kernel during run-time.



New setting[Expression/Value]:  1_____

New setting (evaluated):  1_____
[ Recalculate ]


Do you want to hold the change until next reboot ?:    (X) Yes
                                                       ( ) No

Back up the current configuration before applying change:   (X) Yes
                                                            ( ) No

Reason for change : _____
[ Modify ] [ Preview ] [ Cancel ]
```

Figure 17-3 *kcweb* **TUI – Kernel Tunable Modification**

✓ Select "Modules" and press Enter (or press m) to view or modify kernel modules and drivers. A list of all modules is displayed along with their current states, modified states being held for the next system boot and time stamps. The list also indicates if the module is dynamic and modifiable. To display detailed information about a specific module, highlight the module and press Enter. To display all modules in pending state or modules that are required by the system, press p and r, respectively. See Figure 17-4.

```
                      SMH->Kernel Configuration->Modules (All)
--------------------------------------------------------------------------
Module              Dynamic   Modifiable  Current   NextBoot   Time Stamp
                                          State     State
==========================================================================
DeviceFileSystem    no        yes         unused    unused     Mon Jul 23 20:55:51 2007
DlkmDrv             no        no          static    static     Thu Feb 15 16:31:10 2007
KeyboardMUX         no        yes         unused    unused     Mon Jul 23 20:55:51 2007
LegacyDeviceDriver  no        yes         unused    unused     Mon Jul 23 20:55:51 2007
MouseMUX            no        yes         unused    unused     Mon Jul 23 20:55:51 2007
OOCdio              no        yes         unused    unused     Mon Jul 23 20:55:51 2007
OocCore             no        yes         unused    unused     Mon Jul 23 20:55:51 2007
OocSrvcs            no        yes         unused    unused     Mon Jul 23 20:55:51 2007
PCItoPCI            no        yes         static    static     Tue May 22 06:06:22 2007
UsbBootKeyboard     no        yes         unused    unused     Mon Jul 23 20:55:51 2007
UsbBootMouse        no        yes         unused    unused     Mon Jul 23 20:55:50 2007
UsbBulkOnlyMS       no        yes         unused    unused     Mon Jul 23 20:55:50 2007
UsbCore             no        yes         unused    unused     Mon Jul 23 20:55:50 2007
UsbEhci             no        yes         unused    unused     Mon Jul 23 20:55:50 2007
UsbHid              no        yes         unused    unused     Mon Jul 23 20:55:50 2007
UsbIomega           no        yes         unused    unused     Mon Jul 23 20:55:50 2007
--------------------------------------------------------------------------
x-Exit smh       ESC-Back     r-Required   1-Help              /-Search
ENTER-Details    p-Pending    m-Modify     2-kcmodule Manpage
```

Figure 17-4 *kcweb* **TUI – Kernel Modules Administration**

To modify the value of a module, highlight the module and press m. Figure 17-5 shows the screen that will pop up when m is pressed on UsbHid module.

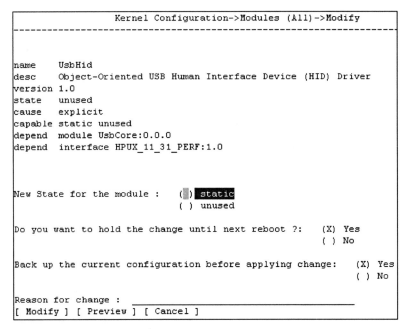

Figure 17-5 *kcweb* **TUI – Kernel Module Modification**

✓ Select "Alarms" and press Enter (or press a) to view or modify alarms for kernel tunables.
✓ Select "Log Viewer" and press Enter (or press l) to view the changes made to kernel tunables or modules.
✓ Select "Usage" and press Enter (or press u) to view usage and values of kernel tunables. To enable usage monitoring, press s.

```
                  SMH->Kernel Configuration->Usage
                       Usage Monitoring is Off
-------------------------------------------------------------------
Tunable                   Current Usage         Current Setting
===================================================================
filecache_max             175960064             4081057792
maxdsiz                   33550336              2063835136
maxdsiz_64bit             1720320               4294967296
maxfiles_lim              85                    4096
maxssiz                   2146304               8388608
maxssiz_64bit             98304                 268435456
maxtsiz                   2789376               100663296
maxtsiz_64bit             716800                1073741824
maxuprc                   3                     256
max_thread_proc           31                    3000
msgmni                    2                     512
msgtql                    0                     1024
nflocks                   27                    4096
ninode                    856                   8192
nkthread                  396                   8416
nproc                     148                   4200
<------------------------------------------------------> SCROLL
x-Exit smh      ESC-Back               1-Help          /-Search
ENTER-Details   s-Start Usage Monitoring   2-kcusage Manpage
```

Figure 17-6 *kcweb* **TUI – Kernel Tunable Usage Administration**

The graphical equivalent of the text interface for tunables and modules administration is shown in Figures 17-7 and 17-8.

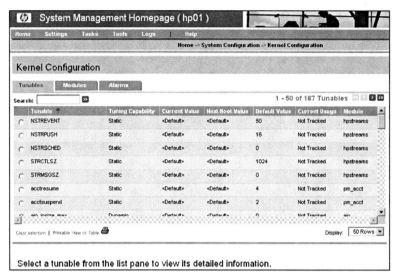

Figure 17-7 *kcweb* **GUI – Kernel Tunables Administration**

Figure 17-8 *kcweb* **GUI – Kernel Modules Administration**

17.5   Managing Kernel Configurations Using Commands

The kernel configuration and management can be performed using the *kconfig*, *kcmodule*, *kctune* and *kclog* commands. This section elaborates the use of these commands and demonstrates how to manage running and saved configurations, modules and tunable parameters, and view the kernel log.

17.5.1   Managing the Currently Running Configuration

To display all changes to the currently running kernel configuration that are being held for the next system boot, do the following. This example assumes that the UsbHid module and the aio_listio_max tunable parameter were modified using *kcweb* earlier in this chapter.

```
# kconfig –D
Module                  State    Cause
UsbHid  (now)           static   best
      (next boot)       static   explicit
Tunable                 Value    Expression      Changes
aio_listio_max  (now)   256      Default         Immed
          (next boot)   1000     1000
```

The above is similar to running both *kcmodule –D* and *kctune –D*.

To display all configuration settings that are set to non-default values:

```
# kconfig –S
Module                  State    Cause    Notes
PCItoPCI                static   best
UsbBulkOnlyMS           static   best
UsbEhci                 static   best
UsbHid        (now)     static   best
          (next boot)   static   explicit
UsbMiniBus              static   best
UsbOhci                 static   best
acpi_node               static   best
asio0                   static   best
asyncdsk                static   best
autofs                  static   best
btlan                   loaded   best     loadable, unloadable
c8xx                    loaded   best     loadable, unloadable
cachefs                 static   best
cdfs                    loaded   auto     auto-loadable, unloadable
. . . . . . . .
```

The above is similar to running both *kcmodule –S* and *kctune –S*.

The commands above display information about each module in four columns: "Module", "State", "Cause" and "Notes". Table 17-5 lists and describes the four columns.

Column	Description
Module	Name of the module.
State	State of the module. States include "auto" (gets dynamically loaded into the kernel when accessed), "best" (the best state for this module), "loaded" (dynamically loaded into the kernel), "static" (statically bound in the kernel, requires a system reboot to take effect if modified) and "unused" (not in use).

Column	Description
Cause	Tells how the module got into the current state. Causes include "auto" (automatically loaded into the kernel when accessed), "best" (the best possible state for this module), "depend" (inherits this state from a module that depends on it), "explicit" (the administrator puts the module in this state) and "required" (marked as a required module).
Notes	Comments about the module. This could be "auto-loadable" (supports the auto state), "loadable" (dynamically change the state to loaded) and "unloadable" (dynamically change the state to unused).

Table 17-5 Command Output Explanation

To discard all pending changes being held for the next system boot:

 # kconfig –H
       * All changes being held for next boot have been discarded.

At this point if you run the *kconfig* command with –D option again, you will see the following output:

 # kconfig –D
NOTE: There are no module state changes being held for next boot.
NOTE: There are no tunable changes being held for next boot.

17.5.2   Managing Saved Configurations

Run the *kconfig* command without any options to display all saved configurations:

 # kconfig
Configuration   Title
backup   Automatic Backup
last_install   Created by last OS install

The output indicates that there are two saved configurations called "backup" and "last_install".

Run the *kconfig* command in verbose mode to display details about the two saved configurations:

 # kconfig –v
Configuration backup
Title   Automatic Backup
Created   Sun Sep 14 07:15:44 2008 by ag786
              by saving the running configuration
Kernel Path   /stand/backup/vmunix

Configuration last_install
Title   Created by last OS install
Created   Wed May 14 09:58:56 2008 by root
              by saving the running configuration
Modified   Wed May 14 09:58:57 2008 by root
Kernel Path   /stand/last_install/vmunix

Run the *kconfig* command with –a option to display saved configurations with settings of each module and tunable:

```
# kconfig –a
Module          DeviceFileSystem  (1.0)
Description     Device File System (DevFS)
Timestamp       Mon Jul 23 20:55:51 2007 [46A54E17]
State           unused
Capable         static unused
Depends On      module OocCore:0.0.0
                interface HPUX_11_31_PERF:1.0
. . . . . . . .
```

To save the currently running configuration as SC_1 with comments "This is config #1":

 # kconfig –C "This is config #1" –s SC_1
     * The currently running configuration has been saved as 'SC_1'.

To assign the title "Updated Configuration" to the saved configuration SC_1:

 # kconfig –t SC_1 "Updated Configuration"
     * The title of the configuration 'SC_1' has been set to "Updated Configuration".

To copy the saved configuration SC_1 as SC_2:

 # kconfig –c SC_1 SC_2
     * The configuration 'SC_1' has been copied to 'SC_2'.

To load the saved configuration SC_1:

 # kconfig –l SC_1
     * The automatic 'backup' configuration has been updated.
     * The requested changes have been applied to the currently running configuration.
     * The configuration 'SC_1' has been loaded and is now in use.

To display which saved configuration is marked for use at the next system boot:

 # kconfig –w
     * The currently running configuration was created on Tue Apr 22
     07:14:11 2008 by root as a copy of 'SC_1'.
     * It was last saved on Tue Apr 22 07:15:41 2008 by root.

To rename the saved configuration SC_1 as SC_3:

 # kconfig –r SC_1 SC_3
     * The configuration 'SC_1' has been renamed to 'SC_3'.

To delete the saved configuration SC_3:

 # kconfig –d SC_3
WARNING: It is not possible to recover a deleted configuration.
  ==> Delete the configuration 'SC_3'? y
    * The configuration 'SC_3' has been deleted.

17.5.3   Managing Configurations Using system Files

Each saved kernel configuration, as well as the currently running kernel configuration, has its own configuration file called the *system* file, which contains all required settings for that kernel configuration. The system file is a text file and can be modified as per the requirements and applied to the HP-UX system when needed. The system file for the currently running kernel configuration is located in the */stand/current* directory, whereas, for each saved configuration, it is located in that configuration's sub-directory under */stand*.

The following demonstrates a few tasks related to the system file. It is assumed that you are located in the */stand/temp_files* directory while performing the following tasks.

To export (generate) the currently running kernel configuration information into *system_current* file:

 # kconfig –e system_current
    * The currently running configuration has been exported to '/stand/temp_files/system_current'.

To export (generate) the saved kernel configuration information from SC_2 into the *system_SC_2* file:

 # kconfig –e SC_2 system_SC_2
    * The configuration 'SC_2' has been exported to '/stand/temp_files/system_SC_2'.

Make any required modifications to the *system_current* and *system_SC_2* files (see the next two sub-sections on how to modify the *system* file) and use the following to import them.

To import (apply) *system_current* to the currently running configuration, now if possible:

 # kconfig –i system_current
  ==> Update the automatic 'backup' configuration first? y
    * The automatic 'backup' configuration has been updated.
    * Future operations will update the backup without prompting.
    * The requested changes have been applied to the currently running configuration.
    * The system file '/stand/temp_files/system_current' has been
    imported. The changes have been applied to the currently running system.

To import (apply) *system_current* to the currently running configuration and hold for the next system boot:

 # kconfig –h –i system_current
WARNING: The configuration has been changed since the system file was exported.
  ==> Overwrite it anyway? y
    * The system file '/stand/temp_files/system_current' has been
    imported. The changes will take effect at next boot.

To import (apply) *system_SC_2* to the saved configuration SC_2:

> **# kconfig –i SC_2 system_SC_2**
>> * The configuration 'SC_2' has been imported from '/stand/temp_files/system_SC_2'.

To import (apply) *system_current* to the currently running configuration, now if possible, using the *mk_kernel* command:

> **# mk_kernel –o /stand/vmunix –s system_current**
>> * The automatic 'backup' configuration has been updated.
>> * The requested changes have been applied to the currently running configuration.
>> * The system file '/stand/temp_files/system_current' has been
>> imported. The changes have been applied to the currently running system.

To import (apply) *system_SC_2* to the saved configuration SC_2 using the *mk_kernel* command:

> **# mk_kernel –o /stand/SC_2/vmunix –s system_SC_2**
>> * The configuration 'SC_2' has been imported from '/stand/temp_files/system_SC_2'.

17.5.4   Managing Modules in Current and Saved Configurations

The *kcmodule* command can be used for querying and modifying kernel modules. The following examples show the usage.

To list all modules from the running configuration along with their current states and the states they will have at the next system boot:

```
# kcmodule
Module                State    Cause        Notes
DeviceFileSystem      static   depend
KeyboardMUX           static   depend
LegacyDeviceDriver    static   depend
MouseMUX              static   depend
OOCdio                static   depend
OocCore               static   depend
OocSrvcs              static   depend
PCItoPCI              static   best
UsbBootKeyboard       static   depend
UsbBootMouse          unused
UsbBulkOnlyMS         static   best
UsbCore               static   depend
UsbEhci               static   best
UsbHid                static   best
. . . . . . . .
```

Refer to Table 17-5 for a description of the columns in the above command output.

To list a specific module such as "cdfs" from the running configuration along with its current state and the state it will have at the next system boot:

 # kcmodule cdfs

Module	State	Cause	Notes
cdfs	loaded	explicit	auto-loadable, unloadable

To list "cdfs" from the running configuration along with its description, current state and the state it will have at the next system boot:

 # kcmodule –d cdfs

Module	State	Cause	Notes	Description
cdfs	loaded	explicit	auto-loadable, unloadable	CD File System

To view verbose information about "cdfs":

 # kcmodule –v cdfs

Module	cdfs (0.1)
Description	CD File System
Timestamp	Thu Feb 15 16:31:08 2007 [45D4D11C]
State	loaded (via autoload)
State at Next Boot	auto (as requested)
Capable	auto static loaded unused
Depends On	interface HPUX_11_31_PERF:1.0

To view more detailed information about "cdfs":

 # kcmodule –P ALL cdfs

name	cdfs
desc	CD File System
version 0.1	
timestamp	Thu Feb 15 16:31:08 2007 [45D4D11C]
state	loaded
cause	explicit
next_state	loaded
next_cause	explicit
capable	auto static loaded unused
depend	interface HPUX_11_31_PERF:1.0

To list all modules from the saved configuration SC_2 along with their current states and the states they will have at the next system boot:

 # kcmodule –c SC_2

Module	State	Cause	Notes
DeviceFileSystem	static	depend	
KeyboardMUX	static	depend	
LegacyDeviceDriver	static	depend	
MouseMUX	static	depend	
OOCdio	static	depend	
OocCore	static	depend	
OocSrvcs	static	depend	
PCItoPCI	static	best	

```
UsbBootKeyboard    static    depend
UsbBootMouse       unused
UsbBulkOnlyMS      static    best
UsbCore            static    depend
UsbEhci            static    best
UsbHid             static    best
UsbIomega          static    depend
UsbMiniBus         static    best
UsbOhci            static    best
acdd               unused              loadable, unloadable
. . . . . . . .
```

To list all modules from all configurations that have state changes being held for the next system boot:

 # kcmodule –D
NOTE: There are no module state changes being held for next boot.

To list all modules that have been explicitly defined:

 # kcmodule –S

Module	State	Cause	Notes
PCItoPCI	static	best	
asio0	static	best	
asyncdsk	static	best	
autofs	static	best	
btlan	loaded	best	loadable, unloadable
c8xx	loaded	best	loadable, unloadable
cachefs	static	best	
cdfs	loaded	auto	auto-loadable, unloadable
cell	static	best	
cfsm	auto	explicit	auto-loadable, unloadable
cfsmdr	auto	explicit	auto-loadable, unloadable

. . . .

To load a dynamic module "cdfs":

 # kcmodule cdfs=loaded
   * The automatic 'backup' configuration has been updated.
   * The requested changes have been applied to the currently running configuration.

Module		State	Cause	Notes
cdfs	(before)	loaded	auto	auto-loadable, unloadable
	(now)	loaded	explicit	

To unload the dynamic module "cdfs":

kcmodule cdfs=unused

```
    * The automatic 'backup' configuration has been updated.
    * The requested changes have been applied to the currently running configuration.
Module          State    Cause   Notes
cdfs  (before)  loaded   explicit auto-loadable, unloadable
      (now)     unused
```

To load the dynamic module "cdfs" at the next system reboot:

kcmodule –h cdfs=loaded

```
    * The requested changes have been saved, and will take effect at next boot.
Module              State    Cause   Notes
cdfs  (now)         unused           auto-loadable, unloadable
      (next boot)   loaded   explicit
```

To modify the *system_current* file and mark the module "cdfs" not to be loaded at the next system boot:

kcmodule –h cdfs=unused

```
    * The requested changes have been saved, and will take effect at next boot.
Module              State    Cause   Notes
cdfs      (now)     loaded   auto    auto-loadable, unloadable
      (next boot)   unused
```

To modify the *system_SC_2* file and mark the module "cdfs" not to be loaded when this configuration is activated:

kcmodule –c SC_2 cdfs=unused

```
    * The requested changes have been applied to the configuration 'SC_2'.
Module          State    Cause   Notes
cdfs  (before)  loaded   explicit auto-loadable, unloadable
      (now)     unused
```

17.5.5   Managing Tunables in Current and Saved Configurations

The *kctune* command can be used for querying and modifying kernel tunables. The following examples show the usage.

To query and display all kernel tunables from the running configuration along with their current values, and expressions used to calculate the values, execute the following. The output will also display any value changes being held for the next system boot.

kctune

```
Tunable          Value   Expression      Changes
NSTREVENT        50      Default
NSTRPUSH         16      Default
NSTRSCHED        0       Default
STRCTLSZ         1024    Default

. . . . . . . .
```

To query a specific tunable such as "shmmni" from the running configuration along with its current value and expression that is used to calculate the value:

 # kctune shmmni

Tunable	Value	Expression	Changes
shmmni	400	Default	Immed

To query a specific tunable "shmmni" from the running configuration along with its description, current value and the value it will have at the next system boot:

 # kctune –d shmmni

Tunable	Value	Expression	Changes	Description
shmmni	400	2*200	Immed	Maximum number of shared memory segments on the system

To query "shmmni" and display detailed information about it:

 # kctune –v shmmni

Tunable	shmmni
Description	Maximum number of shared memory segments on the system
Module	vm_asi
Current Value	400 [Default]
Value at Next Boot	400 [Default]
Value at Last Boot	400
Default Value	400
Constraints	shmmni >= 3
	shmmni <= 32768
	shmmni >= shmseg
Can Change	Immediately or at Next Boot

To view more detailed information about "shmmni":

 # kctune –P ALL shmmni

name	shmmni
module	vm_asi
desc	Maximum number of shared memory segments on the system
defvalue	400
bootvalue	400
current	400
next_boot	400
expr	2*200
next_expr	2*200
min	3
max	32768
dynamic	y
canauto	n
default	n
auto_default	n
next_default	n
signed	n

```
flags           0x2c3
constraint      shmmni >= 3
constraint      shmmni <= 32768
constraint      shmmni >= shmseg
```

To list all tunables from the saved configuration SC_2 along with their current values:

 # kctune –c SC_2

Tunable	Value	Expression
NSTREVENT	50	Default
NSTRPUSH	16	Default
NSTRSCHED	0	Default
STRCTLSZ	1024	Default
STRMSGSZ	0	Default
acctresume	4	Default
acctsuspend	2	Default

. . . .

To list tunables that have value changes being held for the next system boot:

 # kctune –D
NOTE: There are no tunable changes being held for next boot.

To list tunables that have been explicitly defined:

 # kctune –S

Tunable	Value	Expression	Changes
filecache_max	5226574315	8%	Imm (auto disabled)
filecache_min	3266608947	5%	Imm (auto disabled)
lcpu_attr	0	0	Imm (auto disabled)
max_thread_proc	3000	3000	Immed
maxdsiz_64bit	17179869184	17179869184	Immed
maxfiles	4096	4096	
maxssiz	134217728	134217728	Immed
maxssiz_64bit	1073741824	1073741824	Immed

. . . .

To modify the value of "shmmni" to 600 at the next system boot:

 # kctune –h shmmni=600
     * The requested changes have been saved, and will take effect at next boot.

Tunable	Value	Expression	Changes
shmmni (now)	400	Default	Immed
(next boot)	600	600	

To modify the value of "shmmni" to 700 and make the change take effect right away:

 # kctune shmmni=700

   * The automatic 'backup' configuration has been updated.

   * The requested changes have been applied to the currently running configuration.

WARNING: The previous change of the tunable 'shmmni' to '600', which was

    being held for next boot, has been discarded.

Tunable		Value	Expression	Changes
shmmni	(before)	400	Default	Immed
	(now)	700	700	

To modify the value of "shmmni" based on a formula:

 # kctune 'shmmni=4*200'

   * The automatic 'backup' configuration has been updated.

   * The requested changes have been applied to the currently running configuration.

Tunable		Value	Expression	Changes
shmmni	(before)	700	700	Immed
	(now)	800	4*200	

To modify the value of "shmmni" to default, execute any of the following:

 # kctune shmmni=

 # kctune shmmni=Default

   * The automatic 'backup' configuration has been updated.

   * The requested changes have been applied to the currently running configuration.

Tunable		Value	Expression	Changes
shmmni	(before)	800	4*200	Immed
	(now)	400	Default	

17.5.6　Viewing Kernel Logs

The *kclog* command can be used to view logs generated by the kernel configuration commands. Without any arguments, *kclog* displays the last transaction on a kernel configuration. A number such as 2, 3, 4 can be passed as an argument to display that number of transactions in reverse chronological order. The first example below displays the output of the command when run without an argument and the second example runs it with 2 as an argument:

 # kclog

```
=====================================================================
2008-04-22 07:44:59 EDT root:
kctune shmmni=
```

   * The automatic 'backup' configuration has been updated.

   * The requested changes have been applied to the currently running configuration.

Tunable		Value	Expression	Changes
shmmni	(before)	800	4*200	Immed
	(now)	400	Default	

 # kclog 2

```
=====================================================================
2008-04-22 07:44:17 EDT root:
```

```
kctune shmmni=4*200

       * The automatic 'backup' configuration has been updated.
       * The requested changes have been applied to the currently running configuration.
Tunable              Value   Expression        Changes
shmmni  (before)     700        700            Immed
        (now)        800     4*200

==============================================================
2008-04-22 07:44:59 EDT root:
kctune shmmni=

       * The automatic 'backup' configuration has been updated.
       * The requested changes have been applied to the currently running configuration.
Tunable              Value   Expression        Changes
shmmni  (before)     800     4*200             Immed
        (now)        400     Default
```

17.6   Booting Using Non-Default Configuration

In a situation where there are several kernel configurations, you can boot the system with any one of them as needed. The following demonstrates some examples.

17.6.1   Booting a Saved Configuration

To boot the saved configuration SC_2, interrupt the autoboot process and manually boot to the HPUX> (Integrity) or ISL> (PA-RISC) prompt, and type:

    HPUX> **boot SC_2**
    ISL> **hpux SC_2/vmunix**

The system will boot the SC_2 configuration, which will become the current configuration.

17.6.2   Booting via Override Tunables

To modify a tunable value such as "shmmni" to 1000 at boot time, interrupt the autoboot process and manually boot to the HPUX> (Integrity) or ISL> (PA-RISC) prompt, and type:

    HPUX> **boot shmmni=1000**
    ISL> **hpux shmmni=1000**

To modify a tunable value at boot time and use the saved configuration SC_2, interrupt the autoboot process and manually boot to the HPUX> (Integrity) or ISL> (PA-RISC) prompt, and type:

    HPUX> **boot SC_2 shmmni=1000**
    ISL> **hpux SC_2/vmunix shmmni=1000**

17.6.3   Booting to Tunable Maintenance Mode

To boot to tunable maintenance mode in case you wish to modify a tunable before booting the system to multiuser state, interrupt the autoboot process and manually boot to the HPUX> (Integrity) or ISL> (PA-RISC) prompt, and type:

HPUX> **boot –tm**
ISL> **hpux –tm**

Reboot the system to multiuser mode after making required modifications.

Summary

This chapter examined HP-UX kernel management tasks. You learned about static and dynamic kernel modules and tunable parameters.

You developed skills to create and manage kernel configurations. You studied *kcweb* tool that enabled you to perform kernel configuration tasks via text and graphical interfaces. You learned how to list, copy, rename, query, load and unload configurations, modules and tunables using commands.

Finally, you were presented with how to boot the system using non-default kernel configurations.

Backup and Restore

This chapter covers the following major topics:

- ✓ Reasons to perform backups
- ✓ Define backup, restore and recovery functions
- ✓ Backup types – full, incremental and differential
- ✓ Backup levels
- ✓ Backup schedule
- ✓ Restore from multi-level backups
- ✓ Understand and use different tools to perform backups
- ✓ Understand and use different tools to perform restores

18.1 Basics of Backup

Backing up system and data files is a vital function of system administration. To minimize the chance of a complete data loss, backups are performed and backup media is stored at an alternate, secure location geographically separated from the system. The alternate location may be another room, building, city or another site.

In order to save valuable system data on external media, a *backup strategy* needs to be developed. A backup strategy is based on several factors. The following sub-sections highlight backup and restore functions, and some critical backup strategy components.

18.1.1 Backup, Archive, Restore and Recovery Functions

Backup is a function of duplicating files and directories on a hard disk to an alternate media for extended storage, emergency and safety purposes. The alternate media could be a tape, a LUN in a storage system, a re-writeable optical disc or a hard drive on a remote system. Backups are typically meant to be recycled and over-written with updated data.

Archive is a function which is similar to backup, but the backed up data is intended to be kept for an extended period of time for historical purposes without being recycled or over-written. Archives may be made on tapes or write-once-read-many (WORM) discs. It is common in the IT industry to use the same alternate media for archiving purposes as is used for backups. Throughout this book the terms backup and archive are used interchangeably.

Restore is the opposite function of backup. Restore retrieves files or directories from the alternate media and places them back to where they are supposed to be on the hard disk.

A similar function called *recovery* recovers a crashed system to its previous normal state. It may require restoring lost data files from alternate media.

18.1.2 Types of Backup

There are three common types of backup performed. These are referred to as full, incremental and differential.

A *full* backup copies all selected files and directories and, therefore, it is self-contained. This type of backup normally takes more time to complete than other backup methods, and is usually scheduled to occur every week and once every month.

An *incremental* backup copies only those files that have been modified since their last full, incremental or differential backup was done. This type of backup usually takes the least amount of time to complete. An incremental backup is usually scheduled to happen on a daily basis.

A *differential* backup copies only those files that have been modified since they were last backed up as part of a full backup. This type of backup normally takes more time to finish than an incremental backup. A differential backup may be scheduled to occur on a daily basis in place of an incremental backup, or on a weekly basis in place of a full backup. In the latter situation, full backups are then scheduled to run once per month.

18.1.3   Levels of Backup

There are certain pre-defined backup levels that can be used for backups. In fact, employing these levels make backups full, incremental or differential. These levels are relative to one another. There are 10 supported levels as listed in Table 18-1.

Backup Level	Description
0	Corresponds to a full backup of selected files and directories. This is the default level.
1	Corresponds to an incremental or differential backup since the last level 0 backup occurred.
2	Represents an incremental backup since the last level 1 backup was performed and corresponds to a differential backup since the last level 0 backup occurred.
3	Represents an incremental backup since the last level 2 backup was performed and corresponds to a differential backup since the last level 0 backup occurred.
4	Represents an incremental backup since the last level 3 backup was performed and corresponds to a differential backup since the last level 0 backup occurred.
5 – 9	Follow the same rule as above for all subsequent backup levels.

Table 18-1 Backup Levels

18.1.4   Sample Backup Schedule

The following example explores setting up a backup schedule for a file system */opt/oracle* with the following scheduling requirements:

- ✓ A monthly full backup on the first Sunday of each month.
- ✓ A weekly differential backup on each Sunday, other than the first Sunday of each month.
- ✓ A daily incremental backup, except on Sundays, to backup all files and directories that have changed since their last incremental or differential backup, whichever is more recent.

To develop a backup schedule to meet the above requirements, you can use level 0 to represent the full backup, level 1 to correspond to differential backups and level 2 to represent incremental backups. The following displays the schedule for five weeks to accomplish above requirements:

Date: 1 2 3 4 5 6 7 8 9 10 11 12 13 14 15 16 17 18 19 20 21 22 23 24 25 26 27 28 29 30 1 2 3 4 5 6
Day: s m t w t f s s m t w t   f   s   s   m   t w   t   f   s   s   m   t   w   t   f   s   s m t w t f s s
Level: 0 2 2 2 2 2 2 1 2   2 2   2   2   2   1   2   2   2   2   2 2   1   2   2   2   2   2   2 1 2 2 2 2 2 2 0

18.1.5   Restore Procedure for the Sample Backup

From restore perspective, if the data becomes corrupted on Wednesday the 18th before the Wednesday backup is commenced, you will need to perform restores in the following sequence to get the data back to the Tuesday the 17th state:

- ✓ Restore the full backup from Sunday the 1st.
- ✓ Restore the differential backup from Sunday the 15th.
- ✓ Restore the incremental backup from Monday the 16th.
- ✓ Restore the incremental backup from Tuesday the 17th.

This will bring the data in *opt/oracle* file system to the state where it was on Tuesday the 17th.

18.2 Managing Backups and Restores

There are many tools available in HP-UX that can be utilized to do backups and restores of files and directories. These tools include *pax, fbackup/frecover, dump/restore, vxdump/vxrestore, tar, cpio, ftio* and *dd*. The following sub-sections discuss them in detail.

18.2.1 Performing Backups Using pax

The *pax* (portable archive exchange) command archives, lists and extracts files to and from disk or tape. This command is very powerful and is compatible with *cpio* and *tar* commands in that it can list and restore archives created using them. The *pax* command supports both legacy and persistent tape DSFs.

Certain switches used with *pax* are summarized in Table 18-2.

Switch	Definition
–a	Appends to an archive.
–f	Specifies backup destination.
–r	Reads an archive.
–v	Verbose output.
–w	Writes to the specified location.
–x	Specifies cpio, pax or tar format.

Table 18-2 *pax* Command Options

The *pax* command has four modes of operation – write, list, read and copy – and are summarized in Table 18-3.

Switch	Definition
write	Writes to the destination using –w option.
list	Lists backup contents without using –r or –w options.
read	Extracts backup contents using –r option.
copy	Copies to alternate destination using both –r and –w options.

Table 18-3 *pax* Command Operating Modes

The following examples explain how *pax* works.

To write the contents of */etc* directory to the tape device at */dev/rtape/tape1_BEST*:

```
# pax –vwf /dev/rtape/tape1_BEST /etc
/etc/
/etc/fstab
/etc/opt/
/etc/opt/swm/
/etc/opt/swm/swm.conf.template
/etc/opt/swm/swm.conf
. . . . . . . .
```

To list contents of the tape device at */dev/rtape/tape1_BEST*:

 # pax –vf /dev/rtape/tape1_BEST

```
USTAR format archive
dr-xr-xr-x    0  bin   bin              Apr 23 07:37   /etc/
-rw-r--r--    0  root  sys         412  Apr 22 14:35   /etc/fstab
dr-xr-xr-x    0  bin   bin              Apr 22 16:26   /etc/opt/
dr-xr-xr-x    0  bin   bin              Apr 22 16:21   /etc/opt/swm/
-r--r--r--    0  bin   bin       40350  Jun 11 2007    /etc/opt/swm/swm.conf.template
. . . . . . . .
```

To read (extract) */etc* directory from the tape device:

 # pax –vrf /dev/rtape/tape1_BEST

```
USTAR format archive
/etc/
/etc/fstab
/etc/opt/
/etc/opt/swm/
/etc/opt/swm/swm.conf.template
. . . . . . . .
```

To copy the */etc* directory into */var/tmp*:

 # pax –vrw /etc /var/tmp/etc

```
/var/tmp/etc/etc
/var/tmp/etc/etc/fstab
/var/tmp/etc/etc/opt
. . . . . . . .
```

18.2.2   Performing Backups Using fbackup

The *fbackup* command is the HP-UX-specific native tool for performing full, incremental and differential backups. This command is deprecated in 11i v3 and will not be available in a future HP-UX release to create archives.

Some essential options *fbackup* supports are listed in Table 18-4.

Option	Description
–f	Specifies the device to be used for backup. There is no default tape device for *fbackup*.
[0 – 9]	Defines full, incremental and differential backups.
–u	Updates */var/adm/fbackupfiles/dates* file at successful completion of a backup. Information written includes start and end backup time stamps, level of backup and name of the graph file used. The */var/adm/fbackupfiles* directory must be available prior to using this option.
–i	Specifies files and directories to be backed up.
–e	Specifies files and directories to be excluded.

Option	Description
–g	Specifies the name of a *graph* file that contains a list of files and directories to be included in or excluded from a backup. A graph file can be used instead of –i and –e options at the command line. Each line in a graph file begins with either an "i" for include or an "e" for exclude, followed by a file or directory name.
–I	Specifies the name of a file to write index information to.
–v	Displays verbose information.

Table 18-4 *fbackup* Command Options

Let us look at a few examples to understand the working of *fbackup*.

To perform a level 0 backup of */home* directory to the tape device at */dev/rtape/tape1_BEST*, and write an index of the files being backed up to */tmp/index.home*:

```
# fbackup –f /dev/rtape/tape1_BEST –i /home –I /tmp/index.home
fbackup(1004): session begins on Thu Apr 17 08:45:09 2008
fbackup(3024): writing volume 1 to the output file /dev/rtape/tape1_BEST
fbackup(3055): total file blocks read for backup: 83
fbackup(3056): total blocks written to output file /dev/rtape/tape1_BEST: 216
```

To perform a level 0 backup of the root directory to the tape device at */dev/rtape/tape1_BEST* on the first Sunday of a month based on the *graph* file contents (include /, exclude */var/adm/crash* and */tmp*), write an entry to */var/adm/fbackupfiles/dates* file and generate an index of the files in */tmp/index.full*:

```
i /
e /var/adm/crash
e /tmp
```

```
# fbackup –f /dev/rtape/tape1_BEST –u0g graph –I /tmp/index.full
```

To perform an incremental backup of the files and directories the next six days (Monday to Saturday) based on the contents in the graph file mentioned above, update the */var/adm/fbackupfiles/dates* file and create an index file */tmp/index.incremental*:

```
# fbackup –f /dev/rtape/tape1_BEST –u2g graph –I /tmp/index.incremental
```

To perform a differential backup of the files and directories on the following Sunday based on the contents in the graph file mentioned above, update the */var/adm/fbackupfiles/dates* file, use tape drive at */dev/rtape/tape2_BEST* and create an index file */tmp/index.differential*:

```
# fbackup –f /dev/rtape/tape2_BEST –u1g graph –I /tmp/index.differential
```

To do the same level 0 backup (from above) over the network on another machine's tape device at */dev/rtape/tape2_BEST*. Suppose the remote machine is *hp02* and you are on *hp01*. The index file */tmp/index.full* will be created on *hp01*.

fbackup –f hp02:/dev/rtape/tape2_BEST –u0g graph –I /tmp/index.full

18.2.3   Performing Restores Using frecover

The *frecover* command is the HP-UX-specific native tool for performing restores done using *fbackup*. This command is deprecated in HP-UX 11i v3 and will not be available in a future HP-UX release.

Some essential options *frecover* supports are listed in Table 18-5.

Option	Description
–f	Specifies the device to be used for restore. The default is */dev/rtape/tape1_BEST* (or */dev/rmt/0m*).
–g	Specifies the name of a *graph* file that contains a list of files and directories to be included in or excluded from a restore. A graph file can be used instead of –i and –e options at the command line. Each line in a graph file begins with either an "i" for include or an "e" for exclude, followed by a file or directory name.
–r	Restores an entire backup. This is default.
–x	Restores selected files and directories only.
–v	Displays verbose information.
–F	Ignores leading directories from the path names of files being restored. This will allow */usr/bin/cat* to be restored in */root* directory as */root/cat*.
–I	Specifies the name of a file to write index information to.

Table 18-5 *frecover* Command Options

Let us look at a few examples to understand the working of *frecover*.

To restore all files from the default tape device */dev/rtape/tape1_BEST* and display details:

frecover –rv

To extract only */home* from a full backup using tape device at */dev/rtape/tape2_BEST*:

frecover –f /dev/rtape/tape2_BEST –i /home –xv

To do the same restore (from above) over the network from another machine's tape device at */dev/rtape/tape2_BEST*. Suppose the remote machine is *hp02* and you are on *hp01*.

frecover –f hp02:/dev/rtape/tape2_BEST –rv

18.2.4   Performing Backups/Restores Using dump/restore

These tools function similar to the way *fbackup* and *frecover* work, but with three major differences. One, these tools work at the file system level and not on individual files and directories, two, they can backup and restore only an HFS file system, and three, they do not support persistent DSFs for tape devices. Both tools support multi-level backups, store time stamp information in */var/adm/dumpdates* file and use various levels of backups described earlier in the chapter.

Let us look at a couple of examples.

To pa level 0 backup of the *data1* file system to the default tape device at */dev/rtape/tape1_BEST* and update the */var/adm/dumpdates* file (create this file before running the *dump* command):

 # dump 0u /data1
  DUMP: Date of this level 0 dump: Thu Apr 17 08:57:54 2008
  DUMP: Date of last level 0 dump: the epoch
  DUMP: Dumping /dev/vg01/rlvol1 (/data1) to /dev/rtape/tape1_BEST
  DUMP: This is an HP long file name filesystem
  DUMP: mapping (Pass I) [regular files]
  DUMP: mapping (Pass II) [directories]
  DUMP: estimated 58029 tape blocks on 1.49 tape(s).
  DUMP: dumping (Pass III) [directories]
  DUMP: dumping (Pass IV) [regular files]
  DUMP: DUMP: 58612 tape blocks on 1 tape(s)
  DUMP: DUMP: /dev/vg01/rlvol1 has 0 inodes with unsaved optional acl entries
  DUMP: DUMP IS DONE
  DUMP: Date of completion of this level 0 dump: Thu Apr 17 08:59:03 2008

The */var/adm/dumpdates* file will contain the following information after the backup is complete:

  /dev/vg01/rlvol1   0   Thu Apr 17 08:57:54 2008

To restore the above:

 # restore r

Use the same syntax to backup to or restore from a tape device connected to a remote system as was demonstrated with *fbackup* and *frecover*. Many options used with *dump*/*restore* are similar to that of *fbackup*/*frecover*. Refer to man pages on usage.

18.2.5   Performing Backups/Restores Using vxdump/vxrestore

These tools work identically as *dump* and *restore*, but backs up and restores only JFS file systems. The two commands also support persistent DSFs. Here are a couple of examples.

To perform a level 0 backup of the */home* file system to a tape device at */dev/rtape/tape2_BEST*, and update the */var/adm/dumpdates* file:

 # vxdump 0uf /dev/rtape/tape2_BEST /home
  vxfs vxdump: Date of this level 0 dump: Thu Apr 17 09:10:21 2008
  vxfs vxdump: Date of last level 0 dump: the epoch
  vxfs vxdump: Dumping /dev/vg00/rlvol4 (/home) to /dev/rtape/tape2_BEST
  vxfs vxdump: mapping (Pass I) [regular files]
  vxfs vxdump: mapping (Pass II) [directories]
  vxfs vxdump: estimated 1456 blocks (728KB).
  vxfs vxdump: dumping (Pass III) [directories]
  vxfs vxdump: dumping (Pass IV) [regular files]
  vxfs vxdump: vxdump: 970 tape blocks on 1 volumes(s)

vxfs vxdump: level 0 dump on Thu Apr 17 09:11:03 2008
vxfs vxdump: Closing /dev/rtape/tape2_BEST
vxfs vxdump: vxdump is done

To restore the above from the same tape device:

vxrestore r /dev/rtape/tape2_BEST

Use the same syntax to backup to and restore from a tape device connected to a remote system as was demonstrated with *fbackup* and *frecover* previously. Check man pages of *vxdump* and *vxrestore* on usage.

18.2.6   Using tar

The *tar* (tape archive) command archives, lists and extracts files to and from a single file called a *tar* file. A tar file can be created as a regular file on disk or tape. This command supports both legacy and persistent tape DSFs.

Certain switches used with *tar* are summarized in Table 18-6.

Switch	Definition
c	Creates a backup.
t	Lists backup contents.
x	Extracts from a backup.
f	Specifies backup destination.
v	Verbose mode.

Table 18-6 *tar* Command Options

A few examples follow to explain how *tar* works.

To create an archive on default tape device at */dev/rtape/tape1_BEST* of the */home* directory:

tar cv /home
a /home/user1/.profile 3 blocks
a /home/user1/file20 1 blocks
a /home/user1/file2 link to /home/user1/file20
. . . .

To create a single archive file called */tmp/files.tar* containing files – *file1*, *file2*, *file3* and *file4*:

tar cvf /tmp/files.tar file1 file2 file3 file4

To view the contents of tape in the default tape device:

tar tv
x /home/user1/.profile, 1089 bytes, 3 tape blocks
x /home/user1/file20, 101 bytes, 1 tape blocks
x /home/user1/file2 linked to /home/user1/file20
. . . .

To view the contents of the archive file *files.tar*:

tar tvf /tmp/files.tar

To restore */home* directory from the default tape device:

tar xv

To extract files from */tmp/files.tar*:

tar xvf /tmp/files.tar

18.2.7   Using cpio

The *cpio* (copy in/out) command archives, lists and extracts files to and from a tape or single file. This command supports both legacy and persistent tape DSFs.

Certain options available with *cpio* are summarized in Table 18-7. The *cpio* command requires that o, i or p option be specified.

Option	Description
o	Creates a backup.
i	Extracts from a backup.
c	Reads or writes header information in ASCII format.
t	Lists backup contents.
v	Verbose mode.
p	Reads from backup to get pathnames.
a	Resets access times of files after they are copied.

Table 18-7 *cpio* Command Options

Here are a few examples to understand the usage.

To archive current directory contents and copy them to the */dev/rtape/tape1_BEST* tape device:

find . | cpio –ocv > /dev/rtape/tape2_BEST
(Using tape drive with immediate report mode enabled (reel #1).)

.
lost+found
ids
user1
user1/.profile
user1/file20
user1/file2
. . . .

To archive only those files in the current directory that have changed within the last week, and copy them to a file called */tmp/mod.cpio*:

find . –mtime –7 | cpio –ocv > /tmp/mod.cpio

To list the two archive files created:

> # **cpio –itvc < /dev/rtape/tape1_BEST**
> # **cpio –itvc < /tmp/mod.cpio**

To restore files from */tmp/mod.cpio:*

> # **cpio –ivc < /tmp/mod.cpio**

18.2.8   Using ftio

The *ftio* (faster tape in/out) command archives, lists and extracts files to and from a tape device. This command is similar in operation to the *cpio* command, but is used only with tape drives. *ftio* is deprecated in HP-UX 11i v3 and will no longer be available in a future HP-UX release to create archives.

Here are a few examples to understand the usage.

To archive current directory contents and copy them to the */dev/rtape/tape1_BEST* tape device:

> # **find . | ftio –ocv > /dev/rtape/tape2_BEST**

To list the archive:

> # **cpio –itvc < /dev/rtape/tape1_BEST**

To restore the archive:

> # **cpio –ivc < /dev/rtape/tape1_BEST**

18.2.9   Using dd

The *dd* command performs a bit for bit duplication. This command is useful in some limited situations and is technically not a backup command. Here is how it works.

To duplicate everything that resides under */dev/vg00/lvol1* to */dev/vg01/lvol1:*

> # **dd if=/dev/vg00/lvol1 of=/dev/vg01/lvol1**
> 112373+0 records in
> 112372+0 records out

where:

> "if" stands for input file and "of" for output file.

The destination *lvol1* in *vg01* must be either of the same size as *lvol1* in *vg00* or larger. View man pages of *dd* on detailed usage.

Summary

In this chapter you looked at reasons to perform backups of your system and data files. You learned definitions of backup, restore and recovery functions. You saw backup types such as full, incremental and differential that were based on backup levels you defined when configuring or running a backup.

You looked at various tools such as *pax*, *fbackup/frestore*, *dump/restore*, *vxdump/vxrestore*, *tar*, *cpio*, *ftio* and *dd*. You used these tools to perform data backups and restores.

## 19

Print Services

This chapter covers the following major topics:

- ✓ Print spooler concepts and directory tree
- ✓ Local and remote printing daemons
- ✓ Types of printer configurations – local, remote and network
- ✓ Why define printer classes
- ✓ Configure local, remote and network printers
- ✓ Administer printers – configure default print destination, enable and disable a printer, allow and disallow users to submit print requests, check printer status, modify a printer priority, modify a printer's fence level and remove a printer
- ✓ Administer print requests – submit, list, modify, move and cancel a print request

19.1 Understanding Print Spooler

The HP-UX *Line Printer* (LP) spooler subsystem is a set of utilities to:

- ✓ Configure, modify and remove printers
- ✓ Manage user print requests

The print spooler subsystem is based on client/server architecture where a print client sends a file to a print server for printing. The print client is typically the *lp* command that submits a file to the print server. The print server is the print scheduler daemon called *lpsched*.

When a print request comes in from a local system user, *lpsched* takes care of it until it is printed on the specified printer. This daemon is automatically started at boot time by */sbin/rc2.d/S720lp* script, or when the system enters run level 2.

When a print request comes in over the network from a remote system user, a master internet services daemon called *inetd* intercepts it. This daemon consults its configuration file */etc/inetd.conf* and starts the remote print daemon called *rlpdaemon*, and hooks the client request up with it. This daemon accepts or rejects the incoming remote print request. If the print request is accepted, it is passed to the *lpsched* daemon, which gets the print request printed, otherwise, the request is rejected.

19.1.1 Print Spooler Directory Hierarchy

The print spooler directory hierarchy comprises of two types of files: *static* and *dynamic*. Static files reside in */etc* and */usr* directories and include configuration files, commands, interface scripts, model scripts, etc. Dynamic files reside in */var* directory and include status files, log files and so on. The dynamic directory structure also holds print requests temporarily in a printer spool directory before they are sent to a printer for printing.

Table 19-1 lists and explains some key print subsystem directories.

Directory	Purpose
Static Files	
/etc/lp	Parent directory for all printer-related configuration.
/etc/lp/class	Contains information that tells which printers belong to which printer classes.
/etc/lp/interface	Contains one file per configured printer that includes interface program to be used for the printer.
/etc/lp/member	Contains one file per configured printer that includes printer port/device file information.
/usr/lib/lp/model	Contains scripts for various printer models. Copied to */etc/lp/interface* and renamed to match the printer name at the time of printer setup.
/usr/lib/lp/fonts	Contains printer fonts.
/usr/bin	Contains user-specific print commands such as *lp*, *lpalt, lpstat, cancel, enable* and *disable*.

Directory	Purpose
/usr/sbin	Contains superuser-specific print administration commands such as *lpadmin, lpsched, lpshut, lpana, lpmove, lpfence, accept* and *reject*.
Dynamic Files	
/var/spool/lp	Parent directory for LP spooler. Information about printer status, print requests, etc. is located here.
/var/spool/lp/request	Print requests are temporarily held here before being sent to a printer for printing.
/var/adm/lp	Contains print spooler log files.

Table 19-1 Print Spooler Directory Hierarchy

19.1.2   Starting and Stopping Print Spooler Daemon

The *lpsched* daemon is started by the *lpsched* command and stopped by the *lpshut* command. The daemon is started automatically at system boot, or when the system changes to run level 2.

If you wish to manually start the daemon, do one of the following:

```
# /sbin/init.d/lp start
scheduler is running
line printer scheduler started
# lpsched
scheduler is running
```

Similarly, to stop the daemon manually, you can do either of the following:

```
# /sbin/init.d/lp stop
line printer scheduler stopped
# lpshut
scheduler stopped
```

To do the above using SMH, follow the steps below:

☞ Go to SMH → Printers and Plotters → Printers and Plotters→ Actions → Stop (or Start) Print Spooler.

Sometimes you try to start or stop the scheduler daemon, but it does not come up or go down. For the startup problem, check if */var/spool/lp/SCHEDLOCK* file exists. If it does, remove it and retry starting the scheduler. For the stop problem, terminate the *lpsched* process with the *kill* command and then retry stopping it.

19.2   Types of Printer Configuration

Printers are normally configured in three ways, referred to as local, remote and network printer setups. Figure 19-1 illustrates four systems (*hp01, hp02, hp03* and *hp04*) and one printer (*prn2*) connected to the network. There is another printer (*prn1*) shown, which is connected directly to *hp01*.

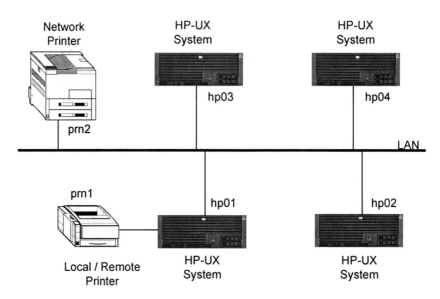

Figure 19-1 Types of Printer Setups

19.2.1   Local Printer

A printer attached physically to a system's parallel or serial port, and accessed by users of that system only is called a *local* printer. In Figure 19-1, *prn1* is a local printer to users on *hp01* system.

When a print request is submitted by a user on *hp01* using the *lp* command to print to *prn1*, the request goes to the print scheduler daemon *lpsched* and a unique print request ID is generated, and assigned to it. The *lpsched* daemon uses the interface program defined for the printer, spools the request in */var/spool/lp/request* directory and finally forwards the request to *prn1* for printing.

19.2.2   Remote Printer

A local printer acts as a *remote* printer to users on remote systems. In Figure 19-1, *prn1* acts as a remote printer to *hp02*, *hp03* and *hp04* users. The system that has the local printer connected, must have a daemon called *rlpdaemon,* enabled through *inetd* in order for it to receive and process remote print requests. In Figure 19-1, *hp01* must have this daemon enabled.

When a print request is submitted by a user on *hp03*, for example, using the *lp* command to print to the remote printer *prn1*, the request goes directly to the *inetd* daemon running on *hp01*, which examines its configuration file */etc/inetd.conf* to determine if the remote printing daemon service, *rlpdaemon*, is enabled. If it is, *inetd* starts the *rlpdaemon* and establishes a connection between the client print request and this daemon. The *rlpdaemon* daemon then forwards the request to the local *lpsched* daemon and a unique print request ID is generated and assigned to the print request. The *lpsched* daemon on *hp01* uses the interface program defined for the printer, spools the request in */var/spool/lp/request* directory and, finally, forwards the print request to *prn1* for printing.

19.2.3   Network Printer

A *network* printer has a network card installed, is physically connected to a network port and has its own hostname and IP address. It is configured on the system after which it becomes accessible to users. A software program called *JetDirect HP Printer Installer* (hppi) is typically used on HP-UX to configure a network printer.

In Figure 19-1, *prn2* is a network printer and is accessible to users of all four systems.

19.3   Configuring Printers

Configuring a local, remote or a network printer requires some attributes as listed in Table 19-2. Note, not all attributes are required for each type of printer setup.

Attribute	Description	Which Setup Needs It
Printer name	A unique name with up to 250 alphanumeric characters.	Local, remote, network
Printer model/interface	Each printer has an interface model script defined that enables the print spooler to access special features of the printer. These scripts are located in */usr/lib/lp/model*.	Local, network
Printer class	A group of similar printers combined to form a single print destination for increased availability and better utilization. When a print request is sent to a class of printers, the first available printer in the class prints it. A class name can include up to 250 alphanumeric characters.	Local, network
IP Address	A unique IP address of the printer.	Network
Default request priority	Default priority level. Any print request submitted to a printer uses this priority level, unless it is explicitly set to a different value using –p option with the *lp* command. Priorities range between 0 and 7, with 0 being the lowest.	Local, remote, network
Default destination	All print requests sent by the *lp* command without –d option are sent to the default printer, unless LPDEST variable is set in user's shell environment.	Local, remote, network
Remote system name	Remote system name where a printer is physically connected.	Remote
Remote printer name	Printer name on the remote machine.	Remote
BSD system	Choose if both print client and print server run HP-UX.	Remote
Remote cancel model	Interface program to cancel print requests on a remote system. Use "rcmodel" for remote printers.	Remote
Remote status model	Interface program to obtain status of print requests on a remote system. Use "rsmodel" for remote printers.	Remote
Allow anyone to cancel	Say yes if you wish users to cancel other users' print requests. Say "no" if you wish otherwise.	Remote

Table 19-2 Printer Configuration Attributes

19.3.1   Configuring a Local Printer

Let us configure a local printer *prn1* on *hp01*, with "laserjet" printer model, default priority, default fence level and */dev/lp* as the device file. Use the *lpadmin* command:

> **# lpadmin –pprn1 –v/dev/lp –mlaserjet**

Create a printer class *prn_class* on *hp01* and define and add to it another local printer *prn3,* with "laserjet" printer model, default priority, default fence level and */dev/lp* as the device file. Use the *lpadmin* command:

> **# lpadmin –pprn3 –v/dev/lp –cprn_class –mlaserjet**

Now add *prn1* to *prn_class*:

> **# lpadmin –pprn1 –cprn_class**

To do the above using SMH, follow the steps below:

☞Go to SMH → Printers and Plotters → Printers and Plotters → Actions → Add Local Printer/Plotter. See Figure 19-2. SMH presents a list of types of local printers to choose from, including parallel and serial. SMH scans for appropriate available devices. Highlight the device file to use and press OK. SMH will then display a form. Fill out the form using attributes listed in Table 19-2, and press OK when done.

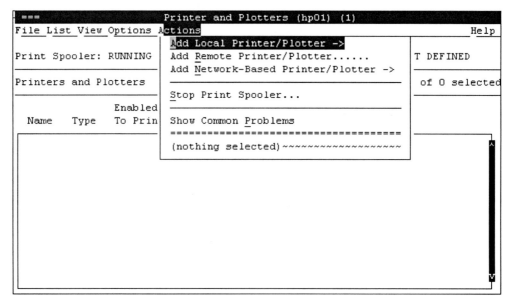

Figure 19-2 SMH – Add Local Printer

19.3.2   Configuring a Remote Printer

A remote printer is a printer that has already been configured on another system as a local printer. A remote printer is only defined on remote machines that wish to access that printer.

To add access to *prn1* on *hp01* from another HP-UX system *hp02*, run the following on *hp02*. Assign the printer a name, *prn1* for example (same as on *hp01*), and specify remote model, remote cancel model and remote printer status access model.

> # **lpadmin –pprn1 –v/dev/null –mrmodel –ocmrcmodel –osmrsmodel –ormhp01 \
> –orpprn1 –v/dev/null**

Next, edit the *etc/inetd.conf* file on *hp01* and ensure that the following line entry is not commented. If it is, uncomment it and execute *inetd* with –c option.

> printer   stream   tcp   nowait   root   /usr/sbin/rlpdaemon   rlpdaemon -i

To do the above using SMH, follow the steps below:

☞ Go to SMH → Printers and Plotters → Printers and Plotters → Actions → Add Remote Printer/Plotter. SMH presents you with a form as shown in Figure 19-3. Fill out the form with attributes outlined in Table 19-2 and hit the OK button.

```
┌─────────────────────────────────────────────────────────────┐
│          Add Remote Printer/Plotter (hp01)                   │
├─────────────────────────────────────────────────────────────┤
│                                                              │
│          Printer Name:  ▓_____                     │
│                                                              │
│    Remote System Name:     _____                   │
│                                                              │
│    Remote Printer Name:    _____                   │
│                                                              │
│  [ ] Remote Printer is on a BSD System                       │
│                                                              │
│  [ Remote Cancel Model... ] rcmodel_____            │
│                                                              │
│  [ Remote Status Model... ] rsmodel_____            │
│                                                              │
│  Default Request Priority:  [ 0  ->]                         │
│                                                              │
│  [ ] Allow Anyone to Cancel a Request                        │
│                                                              │
│  [ ] Make This Printer the Default Destination               │
├─────────────────────────────────────────────────────────────┤
│  [   OK   ]          [ Cancel ]          [  Help  ]          │
└─────────────────────────────────────────────────────────────┘
```

Figure 19-3 SMH – Add Remote Printer

19.3.3 Configuring a Network Printer

To configure a network printer on HP-UX, JetDirect HP Printer Installer (hppi) software must be loaded on the system. A hostname and an IP address are required, in addition to other attributes listed in Table 19-2. Use the *hppi* command to define *prn2* network printer:

/opt/hpnp/bin/hppi

```
*****************************************************************
*****]       ****
**** ]       ****    JetDirect Printer Installer for UNIX
**** ]]]]] ]]]]] ****    Version E.10.34
**** ]  ]]  ] ****
**** ]  ] ]]]]] ****   M A I N    M E N U
*****     ]   ****
******    ]   ****    User: (root)   OS: (HP-UX B.11.31)
      I N V E N T
*****************************************************************
1) Spooler Administration (super-user only)
2) JetDirect Configuration (super-user only)
  - TCP/IP configurable parameters
3) Diagnostics:
  - diagnose printing problems
        ?) Help       q) Quit
```

Select option #1 to go to Spooler Administration:

```
Please enter a selection (q - quit): 1
*****************************************************************
*****]       ****
**** ]       ****    JetDirect Printer Installer for UNIX
**** ]]]]] ]]]]] ****    Version E.10.34
**** ]  ]]  ] ****
**** ]  ] ]]]]] ****    Spooler Administration
*****     ]   ****
******    ]   ****    User: (root)   OS: (HP-UX B.11.31)
      I N V E N T
*****************************************************************
Spooler:
    1) Add printer to local spooler
    2) Delete printer from local spooler
    3) Modify existing spooler queue(s)
    4) Install New Model Script
    5) Remove Model Script

        ?) Help       q) Quit
```

Select option #1 to add printer to local spooler. You will be prompted to enter hostname or IP address of the printer. If you specify a hostname, ensure the hostname is already defined in the */etc/hosts* file. Next, a list of printer models appears. Choose the one that fits your needs.

Finally, you will be presented with a list of suggested parameter values. If you are satisfied, press 0 to complete the procedure.

> The following is a list of suggested parameter values for this queue. You
> may change any settings by selecting the corresponding non-zero numbers.
> The values will be used to configure this queue when '0' is selected.
> To abort the operation, press 'q'.
> Configurable Parameters: Current Settings
> ----------------------------------   --------------------
> 1) Lp destination (queue) name: [prn2_1]
> 2) Status Log   [(No Log)]
> 3) Queue Class   [(Not assigned)]
> 4) Default Queue   [NO]
> 5) Additional printer configuration...
> Select an item for change, or '0' to configure (q - quit): **0**
> Ready to shut down the spooler and configure the new print queue.
> The spooler will be running again after the configuration is done.
> WARNING: If there are jobs currently being printed, and the page count is enabled (i.e. when True End-
> of-Job is turned on), this shutdown and rerun of the spooler may result in incorrect page count.
> OK to continue? (y/n/q, default=y) **y**
>
> ......
> Finished adding "prn2" to the spooler.

 The *lpsched* daemon is stopped and restarted to complete the network printer add process.

To do a network printer setup using SMH, follow the steps below:

☞ Go to SMH → Printers and Plotters → Printers and Plotters → Actions → Add Network-Based Printer/Plotter → Add Printer/Plotter Connected to HP JetDirect. SMH will now execute the */opt/hpnp/bin/hppi* command. Supply the required information.

19.4   Administering Printers

Printer administration includes tasks such as setting default print destination, enabling and disabling a printer, making a printer accept or reject print requests, checking printer status, setting printer priority, modifying printer fence level and removing a printer. The following sub-sections examines these tasks.

19.4.1   Setting Default Print Destination

A printer, or a printer class, can be defined as the default print destination for all user print requests. Here is how to do it.

To make *prn1* the default printer, use the –d option with the *lpadmin* command:

lpadmin –dprn1

To make *prn_class* the default print destination, use the –d option with the *lpadmin* command:

lpadmin –dprn_class

To view current default print destination setting:

lpadmin –d

To set default print destination using SMH, follow the steps below:

☞ Go to SMH → Printers and Plotters → Printers and Plotters. A list of existing printers will be displayed. Highlight a printer and go to Actions → Set as System Default Destination. Press OK to complete the task.

19.4.2   Enabling and Disabling a Printer

A printer must be activated before it can print. The *enable* command activates the specified printer and enables it to print requests. The *disable* command deactivates the specified printer and disables it from printing requests.

To enable *prn1*:

enable prn1
printer "prn1" now enabled

To disable *prn1*:

disable prn1
printer "prn1" now disabled

To disable *prn1* and specify a reason for disabling it, use the –r option with *disable*. The reason will be displayed on the user terminal when he tries to submit a print request.

disable –r "prn1 is down for maintenance for 1 hour" prn1

To do the above using SMH, follow the steps below:

☞ Go to SMH → Printers and Plotters → Printers and Plotters. A list of existing printers will be displayed. Highlight a printer and go to Actions → Enable (or Disable).

19.4.3   Accepting and Rejecting Print Requests

A printer must be accepting requests in its queue before it can actually print them. The *accept* command allows user print requests to be queued for printing. The *reject* command denies queuing user print requests.

To accept user print requests in *prn1* or *prn_class* queue:

accept prn1
destination "prn1" now accepting requests
accept prn_class
destination "prn_class" now accepting requests

To reject user print requests from being queued in *prn1* and *prn_class*:

> # **reject –r "prn1 is down for 15 minutes for toner replacement" prn1**
> destination "prn1" will no longer accept requests
> # **reject prn_class**
> destination "prn_class" will no longer accept requests

The –r option allows you to specify some text to explain a reason for rejecting user requests. This text will be displayed on user terminals when they send print requests to *prn1*.

To do the above using SMH, follow the steps below:

☞ Go to SMH → Printers and Plotters → Printers and Plotters. A list of existing printers and printer classes will be displayed. Highlight a printer or printer class and go to Actions → Accept (or Reject) Requests.

19.4.4 Checking Printer Status

To check the status of printers and user print requests, use the *lpstat* command. Several options are available with this command, some of them are listed in Table 19-3.

Option	Description
–a	Displays accept/reject status.
–d	Displays default destination printer or printer class.
–o	Displays queued print requests only.
–p	Displays enable/disable status.
–r	Displays scheduler status.
–s	Displays summary information.
–t	Displays detailed information about all configured printers and all queued requests.
–v	Displays printer device file.

Table 19-3 *lpstat* Command Options

> # **lpstat –t**
> scheduler is running
> system default destination: prn1
> device for prn1: /dev/lp
> prn1 accepting requests since Feb 3 13:10
> printer prn1 enabled since Feb 3 16:16 -
> fence priority : 0

19.4.5 Setting Printer Priority

Priorities can be set on printers and user print requests. Printer priority is defined when a printer is setup, and can be altered later. If a priority is not specified when issuing the *lp* command, the print request is sent with the printer's default priority, which is 0.

To change the priority of *prn1* to 5, use the *lpadmin* command:

```
# lpadmin –pprn1 –g5
```

19.4.6   Setting Printer Fence Level

A printer's fence level defines the minimum required priority for a submitted print request to be able to print. The fence level is configured with the *lpfence* command or SMH. A print request, with a priority lower than the printer's fence level, will sit in the printer's queue forever until either the print request's priority is raised or the printer's fence level is lowered.

To increase the fence level of *prn1* to 5, run the *lpfence* command:

```
# lpfence prn1 5
```

To reset it to default:

```
# lpfence prn1 0
```

The *lpfence* command requires *root* privileges to be executed. Ordinary users can use the *lpalt* command instead.

To modify fence level using SMH, follow the steps below:

☞ Go to SMH → Printers and Plotters → Printers and Plotters. A list of existing printers will be displayed. Highlight a printer and go to Actions → Modify Fence Priority. Specify a new fence priority and hit OK.

19.4.7   Removing a Printer

To remove a printer such as *prn1*, use the *lpadmin* command with –x option. Make sure to execute the *reject* and *disable* commands on the printer prior to removing it. Follow the steps below:

```
# reject prn1
# disable prn1
# lpadmin –xprn1
```

To do the above using SMH, follow the steps below:

☞ Go to SMH → Printers and Plotters → Printers and Plotters. A list of existing printers will be displayed. Highlight a printer to be removed and go to Actions → Remove.

19.5   Administering Print Requests

Administering print requests involves submitting, listing, modifying, moving and canceling a print request. The following sub-sections describe these tasks.

19.5.1   Submitting a Print Request

To submit a print request to a printer or printer class, use the *lp* command. This command supports several options, some of which are captured in Table 19-4.

Option	Description
−c	Copies the specified file to the spool directory and then sends it to a printer or printer class for printing.
−d	Sends a print request to the specified destination printer.
−m	Notifies the user by sending a mail when a print request submitted by that user is finished printing.
−n	Defines number of copies to print.
−p	Denotes a priority for the print request.
−t	Specifies a title to be printed on the first page. By default, username is printed.
−w	Writes a message to the user's terminal when the print request is finished. If the user is logged off, a mail will be sent to him.

Table 19-4 *lp* Command Options

Let us take a look at some examples.

To print */etc/group* file on the default printer *prn1*:

> **# lp /etc/group**
> request id is prn1-0

The output indicates that prn1-0 is the first print request submitted to this printer.

To print */etc/passwd* file on a non-default printer *prn2*:

> **# lp −dprn2 /etc/passwd**
> request id is prn2-0

To submit */etc/passwd* file to *prn_class*:

> **# lp −dprn_class /etc/passwd**
> request id is prn_class-0

All print requests are queued in their destination printer's spool directory in priority order. A print request with a higher priority gets printed before a lower priority print request is printed. If two requests have an identical priority, they will be printed in the order they were submitted. For example:

To send */etc/group* to *prn2* and *prn_class* at priority 5:

> **# lp −p5 −dprn2 /etc/group**
> **# lp −p5 −dprn_class /etc/group**

To raise the priority of a submitted print request such as prn2−2 or prn_class−2 to 5, use the *lpalt* command:

> **# lpalt prn2−2 −p5**
> **# lpalt prn_class−2 −p5**

19.5.2 Listing a Print Request

To list all print requests submitted to all defined printer queues on the system, use the *lpstat* command with –o option:

    # **lpstat –o**

To do the above using SMH, follow the steps below:

☞Go to SMH → Printers and Plotters → Print Requests. A list of existing print requests will be displayed.

19.5.3 Modifying a Print Request

A print request can be modified after submission for printing. The *lpalt* command is used for this purpose. The following raises the priority of the queued print requests prn2-0 and prn_class-0 to 6:

    # **lpalt prn2–0 –p6**
    # **lpalt prn_class–0 –p6**

19.5.4 Moving a Print Request

Submitted print requests can be moved from one printer queue to another using either *lpmove* or *lpalt* command. For example:

To move all print requests from *prn1* to *prn2*:

    # **lpmove prn1 prn2**

To move only prn1-0 from *prn1* to *prn2*, use either of the following:

    # **lpalt prn1–0 prn2**
    # **lpmove prn1–0 prn2**

19.5.5 Canceling a Print Request

To cancel a single print request, use the *cancel* command:

    # **cancel prn2–0**
    # **cancel prn_class–0**

To cancel all print requests queued on *prn2* and *prn_class*, use the *cancel* command:

    # **cancel –e prn2**
    # **cancel –e prn_class**

To do the above using SMH, follow the steps below:

☞Go to SMH → Printers and Plotters → Print Requests. A list of existing print requests will be displayed. Highlight the one you wish to cancel and go to Actions → Cancel Request.

Summary

You learned inside-out of printing in HP-UX in this chapter. You developed a good understanding of print spooler, the directory structure where files related to print spooling were stored, and daemons that enabled you to print to printers. You looked at local, remote and network printer definitions, and reasons behind combining printers into classes. You setup local, remote and network printers and defined default printer and printer class. You looked at starting and stopping the print scheduler daemon automatically and manually.

You studied print spooler administration that involved activating and deactivating a printer, allowing and disallowing users to submit print requests, verifying if a printer is working, modifying a printer priority and fence level, and removing a printer from the system.

Finally, you learned how to submit print requests to a printer or printer class; list, cancel and modify submitted print requests; and move submitted print requests to another printer or printer class.

## 20

Job Scheduling and System Logging

This chapter covers the following major topics:

- ✓ What is job scheduling?
- ✓ Start and stop the cron daemon
- ✓ Allow and disallow users to schedule jobs
- ✓ Log cron activities
- ✓ Schedule, list and remove at jobs
- ✓ Schedule, list and remove jobs using crontab command
- ✓ What is system logging?
- ✓ Types of messages and level of criticality
- ✓ Where to send messages
- ✓ Syslog and syslog configuration file

20.1 What is Job Scheduling?

Job scheduling is a feature that allows a user to schedule a command to be executed at the specified time in future. The execution of the command could be one time in future or at regular intervals based on a pre-determined time schedule.

Usually, one-time execution is scheduled for an activity that is to be performed at times of low system usage. One example of such an activity is running a lengthy shell program.

In contrast, recurring activities could include performing backups, creating system recovery archives, trimming log files and removing unwanted files from the system.

20.1.1 Starting and Stopping the cron Daemon

All scheduled jobs are controlled by the cron daemon. This daemon is started when the system boots up and enters run level 2. At run level 2, a script called */sbin/rc2.d/S730cron,* which is symbolically linked to the actual startup script */sbin/init.d/cron*, executes the start function (defined in the script) based on the setting of a variable CRON in the */etc/rc.config.d/cron* file. If the variable is set to 1, the daemon is started.

To start or stop the *cron* daemon manually, do the following:

```
# /sbin/init.d/cron start
cron started
# /sbin/init.d/cron stop
cron stopped
```

When the system changes run level to 1, or when it shuts down, a script called */sbin/rc1.d/K270,* which is symbolically linked to */sbin/init.d/cron*, executes the stop function (defined in the script) to terminate the daemon.

20.1.2 Controlling User Access

Which users can or cannot submit an *at* or *cron* job is controlled through files located in the */var/adm/cron* directory. For *at* job control, the *at.allow* and *at.deny* files are used. For *cron* job control, the *cron.allow* and *cron.deny* files are used.

The syntax of all four files is identical. You only need to list usernames who need to be permitted or denied access to these tools. Each file takes one username per line.

Table 20-1 shows various combinations and the impact on user access.

at.allow / cron.allow	at.deny / cron.deny	Impact
Exists, and contains user entries	Does not matter if exists or not	All users listed in *.allow files are permitted.
Exists, but empty	Does not matter if exists or not	No users are permitted.
Does not exist	Exists, and contains user entries	All users, other than those listed in *.deny files, are permitted.
Does not exist	Exists, but empty	All users are permitted.

HP Certified Systems Administrator 11i v3

at.allow / cron.allow	at.deny / cron.deny	Impact
Does not exist	Does not exist	No user, other than *root,* is permitted.

Table 20-1 Controlling User Access

By default, the **.allow* files exist and **.deny* files do not.

The following message will appear on the screen if you attempt to execute the *at* command, but are not authorized:

```
you are not authorized to use at.  Sorry.
```

The following message will appear on the screen if you attempt to execute the *crontab* command, but are not authorized:

```
crontab: you are not authorized to use cron.  Sorry.
```

20.1.3   cron Log File

All activities involving the *cron* daemon are logged in the */var/adm/cron/log* file. Information such as owner, start time and end time is captured. The file also keeps track of when the *cron* daemon started, PID associated with it, spooled *at* and *cron* jobs, etc. Sample entries from the log file are shown below:

```
# cat /var/adm/cron/log
! *** cron started ***   pid = 11314 Thu Apr 17 11:28:23 EDT 2008
> CMD:   sleep 15;/etc/opt/resmon/lbin/mon_EMSHAProvider_state.sh
> root 11322 c Thu Apr 17 11:29:00 EDT 2008
< root 11322 c Thu Apr 17 11:29:16 EDT 2008
```

20.2 Job Scheduling Using at

The *at* command is used to schedule a one-time execution of a program. All submitted jobs are spooled in the */var/spool/cron/atjobs* directory.

20.2.1   Scheduling an at Job

To understand scheduling an *at* job, consider the following examples.

To schedule an *at* job to run the *find* command tonight at 11pm to look for all core files in the system and remove them:

```
# at 11pm find / –name core –exec rm {} \;
Ctrl+d
Warning: commands will be executed using /usr/bin/sh
job 1208533079.a at Fri Apr 17 23:00:00 2008
```

You have to press Ctrl+d to submit an *at* job. An ID is assigned along with a time stamp when Ctrl+d is pressed. The job ID is a long integer value followed by ".a". The integer value is a number, in seconds, calculated from the epoch time, January 01, 1970, to the job execution time. A file is created in the */var/spool/cron/atjobs* directory with the same name as the job ID. This file includes all variable settings that are to be used when the job is actually executed. These variables establish the user's shell environment so that the job is properly carried out. This file also includes the name of the command or script to be executed.

There are multiple ways of specifying an execution time with the *at* command. Some examples are:

at 11am	(executes the task at next 11am)
at 23:00	(another way of specifying 11pm tonight)
at 17:30 tomorrow	(executes the task at 5:30 pm next day)
at now + 5 days	(executes the task at this time after 5 days)

 When year is not mentioned, the current year is assumed; when no date is mentioned, today's date is assumed.

If you wish to run a series of commands or scripts that reside in a file, supply the file's name as input to the *at* command using the –f option. Here is how you would do it:

> # **at –f file1 now + 5 days**

In the above example, the contents of *file1* will be executed at the current time after 5 days.

The *at* command can also be used to schedule several jobs to run concurrently by setting the MULTI_JOB_SUPPORT variable to 1 in the */etc/default/cron* file.

20.2.2   Listing and Removing at Jobs

Use the *at* command to list and remove *at* jobs.

To list the current spooled *at* jobs, use the –l option. This option lists all job IDs and their execution time.

> # **at –l**
> user = root   1139284800.a   Thu Apr 17 11:38 2008

Alternatively, you can do an *ll* on the spool directory to view a list of spooled jobs:

> # **ll /var/spool/cron/atjobs**
> total 16
> -r-Sr-Sr-- 1 root   sys   2497 Apr 17 11:38 1208533079.a

To remove a spooled *at* job, use the –r option and specify a job ID to be removed:

> # **at –r 1208533079.a**

20.3   Job Scheduling Using crontab

Using the *crontab* command is the other method for scheduling tasks to be executed in future. Unlike *at*, *crontab* executes jobs on a regular basis and at specified time defined in the crontab file.

Crontab files for users are located in the */var/spool/cron/crontabs* directory. Each user, who is allowed, and has scheduled a cron job, has a file by his login name in this directory. The *cron* daemon scans entries in these files to determine job execution times. The daemon runs the commands or scripts at the specified time and puts a log entry into the */var/adm/cron/log* file.

The *crontab* command is used to edit, list and remove crontab files.

20.3.1   Syntax of the crontab File

Each line in the crontab file that contains an entry for a scheduled job comprises of 6 fields. These fields must be in the precise sequence in order for the *cron* daemon to interpret them correctly. See Figure 20-1 for syntax of the crontab file.

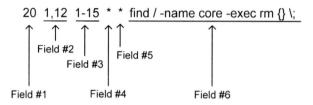

Figure 20-1 Syntax of the crontab File

A description of each field is given in Table 20-2.

Field #	Field Content	Description
1	Minute of the hour	Valid values are from 0 (represents exact hour) to 59. This field can have one specific value (see Field #1 for usage), multiple comma-separated values (see Field #2 for usage), a range of values (see Field #3 for usage) or the * character that represents every minute of the hour (see Field #4 and #5).
2	Hour of the day	Valid values are from 0 (represents midnight) to 23. Values are defined exactly the way they are defined for Field #1, except that the * character represents every hour of the day.
3	Date of the month	Valid values are from 1 to 31. Values are defined exactly the way they are defined for Field #1, except that the * character represents every day of the month.
4	Month of the year	Valid values are from 1 to 12, with 1 represents January, 2 represents February and so on. Values are defined exactly the way they are defined for Field #1, except that the * character represents every month of the year.
5	Day of the week	Valid values are from 0 to 6, with 0 represents Sunday, 1 represents Monday and so on. Values are defined exactly the way they are defined for Field #1, except that the * character represents every day of the week.
6	Command to execute	Specifies the full path name of the command or script to be executed.

Table 20-2 crontab File Description

20.3.2   Scheduling a cron Job

To schedule a *cron* job, execute the *crontab* command with –e option:

> **$ crontab –e**

This opens up for editing the crontab file for the user who has executed this command based on permissions defined for that user in the *cron.allow* or the *cron.deny* file. Note that *root* can modify the contents of any other user's crontab file. For example, to open up the crontab file for *user1* as *root*, do the following:

> **# crontab –e user1**

The name of the crontab file for a user matches the user's login name. For example, crontab file for *root* is called *root*, crontab file for *user1* is called *user1* and so on.

> You do not have to be in the */var/spool/cron/crontabs* directory to open your crontab file. In fact, you can be anywhere in the directory structure.

Let us put the following entry in the *root* user's crontab file:

> **# crontab –e**
> 20 1,12 1-15 * * find / -name core –exec rm {} \;

This entry tells the *cron* daemon to execute the *find* command at 1:20 am and 12:20 pm every day from the 1st of the month to the 15th.

20.3.3   Listing and Removing cron Jobs

Use the *crontab* command to list and remove cron jobs. See the examples below to understand the usage.

To list contents of the crontab file for *user1*, use –l option and run it as *user1*:

> **$ crontab –l**

To list contents of the crontab file for *user1* as *root*:

> **# crontab –l user1**

To remove an entry from a user crontab file, use –e option to open the file in the vi editor and remove the desired entry.

To remove a crontab file completely, use –r option. This will remove the crontab file for the user who has executed the command.

> **# crontab –r**

To remove *user1*'s crontab file as *root*:

crontab –r user1

20.4 System Logging

System logging is performed to keep track of messages generated by various sources such as kernel, daemons and commands. A daemon called *syslogd* is responsible for all logging activities. It is started at system boot by the */sbin/rc2.d/S220syslogd* script, which is symbolically linked to the actual startup script */sbin/init.d/syslogd*, when the system enters run level 2. The daemon reads its configuration file */etc/syslog.conf* when coming up.

This daemon can be started or stopped manually. Here is how:

/sbin/init.d/syslogd start
System message logger started
/sbin/init.d/syslogd stop
syslogd stopped

A process ID is assigned to the *syslogd* daemon and stored in the */var/run/syslogd.pid* file.

20.4.1 The System Log Configuration File

The system log configuration file is located in the */etc* directory and is called *syslog.conf*. The contents of the default *syslog.conf* file are shown below:

cat /etc/syslog.conf

```
. . . . . . . .
mail.debug              /var/adm/syslog/mail.log
*.info;mail.none        /var/adm/syslog/syslog.log
*.alert                 /dev/console
*.alert                 root
*.emerg                 *
```

Notice that each line entry consists of two fields. The field on the left is called *selector* and the field on the right is referred to as *action*. The selector field is further divided into two sub-fields, which are separated by the period character. The left sub-field, called *facility*, represents various system process categories that can generate messages. Multiple facilities can be defined, with each facility separated from the other by the semicolon character. The right sub-field, called *level*, represents severity associated with the message. The action field determines where to send the message.

Some of the facilities are kern, user, mail, daemon and cron. The * character represents all of them.

In the same way, there are multiple severity levels such as emergency (emerg), critical (crit), error (err), warning (warn) and none. The * character represents all of them.

Some sample entries are listed and explained below:

1. mail.debug   /var/adm/syslog/mail.log
2. *.info;mail.none   /var/adm/syslog/syslog.log
3. *.alert   /dev/console
4. *.alert   root
5. *.emerg   *

6.	cron.err	user1,user2,user3
7.	kern.err	@hp02

In the first line entry, facility is "mail", level is "debug" and the action field is */var/adm/syslog/mail.log*. This line entry tells the *syslogd* daemon to log all debug messages generated by the mail subsystem to the */var/adm/syslog/mail.log* file.

In the second line entry, two facilities are defined. The first facility tells the *syslogd* daemon to capture all informational messages generated by any service on the system and log them to *syslog.log* file. The second facility tells the daemon not to capture any messages generated by the mail subsystem to the *syslog.log* file.

The third and the fourth line entries tell the daemon to capture all alerts, and display them on the system console as well as on the terminals where the *root* user is logged in.

The fifth line indicates that the *syslogd* daemon will display all emergency messages on the terminals of all logged in users.

The sixth line tells the *syslogd* daemon to display error messages generated by the *cron* daemon on the terminals of *user1*, *user2* and *user3*.

The last line entry tells the *syslogd* daemon to forward all kernel error messages to the *syslogd* daemon running on another system *hp02* to handle them.

20.4.2   The System Log File

The default system log file is located in the */var/adm/syslog* directory and is called *syslog.log*. This is a plain text file and can be viewed with *cat, more, pg, view, head* or *tail* command. This file may be viewed in real time using the *tail* command with –f option. The *syslog.log* file captures time stamp, hostname, daemon or command executed, PID of the process and other related information.

The following shows sample entries from the *syslog.log* file:

```
# cat /var/adm/syslog/syslog.log
Apr 17 07:28:48 hp01 syslogd: restart
Apr 17 07:28:48 hp01 vmunix: Module btlan is put into ramfs:load time: driver_install, state: loaded
Apr 17 07:28:48 hp01 vmunix: Module procsm is put into ramfs:load time: driver_install, state: loaded
Apr 17 07:28:48 hp01 vmunix: Module c8xx is put into ramfs:load time: driver_install, state: loaded
Apr 17 07:28:48 hp01 vmunix: Module cdfs is put into ramfs:load time: driver_install, state: auto
Apr 17 07:28:48 hp01 vmunix: Module cfsmdr is put into ramfs:load time: driver_install, state: auto
```

Summary

You learned two system administration areas in this chapter. First, you learned how to schedule commands and scripts to run automatically at pre-determined time in future. This included two tools: *at* and *crontab*. Both shared a common daemon called *cron*. Normal users could automate their own tasks, if they were permitted. You looked at ways to permit and prohibit users to use the tools. Furthermore, you were presented with examples that listed and removed spooled jobs.

Second, you looked at system activity logging functionality of HP-UX. You understood contents of the */etc/syslog.conf* configuration file. You looked at the */var/adm/syslog/syslog.log* file where all system activities were logged based on the configuration defined in */etc/syslog.conf*.

Performance Monitoring

This chapter covers the following major topics:

- ✓ Performance bottleneck areas
- ✓ Performance monitoring tools such as uptime, w, sar, top, glance, swapinfo, vmstat, iostat, ps, time, timex and ipcs
- ✓ Monitor CPU, memory, swap, disk, process and network adapter performance

21.1 Performance Monitoring

As a system administrator, it is one of your responsibilities to ensure the systems you manage are operating at optimum performance levels and there are no bottlenecks affecting performance. If there are performance issues, you need to address them appropriately.

Performance monitoring is the process of acquiring performance data from system components such as CPU, memory, swap, disk, processes and network adapters. This data is analyzed and results generated are utilized to understand trends as they develop, prevent unsatisfactory performance and optimize system resources. Performance data helps locate bottlenecks and identify under- and over-utilized resources. After data analysis, arrangements can be made to carry out necessary changes to component(s) affecting performance.

The system may perform slowly or sluggishly for numerous reasons, and you need to determine the cause of the problem. There are several tools available to obtain performance data, the following topics cover these tools in detail.

You need to focus on three performance-related areas to effectively monitor a system. These areas are *throughput, response time* and *resource utilization*. Throughput is the amount of work done within certain time limits. It is normally measured in *Transactions Per Second* (TPS) or *Million Instructions Per Second* (MIPS). Response time is the wait time for the completion of a task. Resource utilization tells how much resources of the system are being used to conduct a task.

21.1.1 Performance Monitoring Tools

There are numerous tools available for performance monitoring of system components. Many of them are available natively in HP-UX. Table 21-1 lists and describes them.

Tool	Description
uptime/w	Shows CPU load averages.
sar	Reports on CPU, virtual memory, disk and network activities.
top	Displays CPU, memory, swap, disk, processes and network activities.
glance (or gpm)	Reports on CPU, memory, swap, disk, processes and network utilization in both text and graphics modes. This tool comes standard with HP-UX VSE-OE, HA-OE and DC-OE.
swapinfo	Shows memory and swap usage.
vmstat	Reports on virtual memory statistics.
iostat	Reports I/O activities.
ps	Displays detailed process activities.
ipcs	Displays information about active IPC facilities such as semaphores, message queues and shared memory segments.
time/timex	Measures elapsed time, in seconds, for the specified command and displays actual time spent, time spent in user space and time spent in the system.
nwmgr/netstat/lanadmin	Displays network adapter activities.

Tool	Description
Performance Manager / Performance Agent	A client/server software tool primarily used for performance monitoring and trending. The server portion is called *performance manager* and the client portion is known as *performance agent*. Performance agent comes standard with VSE-OE, HA-OE and DC-OE. The server portion is separately purchasable.

Table 21-1 Performance Monitoring Tools

21.1.2   Monitoring CPU Performance

To monitor CPU performance, use the *uptime, sar*, *top* and *glance* commands.

The *uptime* command produces a rough, quick estimate of system load, in addition to displaying the length of time the system has been up for:

 # uptime
11:45am up 4:18, 2 users, load average: 0.02, 0.02, 0.02

The load average displays a rough estimate of CPU utilization over the past 1, 5 and 15 minutes. The higher the load average numbers are, the heavier the system utilization is. Normally, a load average of 3 or less is considered good. The *w* command also shows the same estimates in the first line of its output.

The *sar* command automates gathering of system activity data. It collects performance data from all major system components. Some essential options to the *sar* command are listed in Table 21-2.

Option	Action
A	Reports on overall system performance.
b	Monitors buffer activities.
d	Monitors disk activities.
k	Checks kernel memory allocation.
o	Specifies the output file.
q	Monitors queue length.
r	Checks unused memory.
u	Reports on CPU utilization.
w	Checks swapping activities.

Table 21-2 *sar* Command Options

Use the –u option with the *sar* command to display CPU activities. The following runs the command every 5 seconds for 5 times:

```
# sar –u 5 5
HP-UX  hp01  B.11.31  U  9000/800   04/17/08
11:46:40   %usr   %sys   %wio   %idle
11:46:45    3      0      0      97
11:46:50    0      0      0      99
11:46:55    0      0      0      100
11:47:00    0      0      0      100
11:47:05    0      0      0      99
Average     1      0      0      99
```

The output is displayed in five columns. The first column shows the five second sampling time. The second and the third columns demonstrate percentages of time the CPU spends to execute the user and system processes, respectively. The fourth column lists the wait time for I/O operations to complete. If this value is too high, check disk, network adapter and NFS I/O operations. The last column shows idle CPU time. If this value is too low, it indicates that the CPU is heavily used.

The *top* command exhibits quantity of CPUs installed in the system and their utilization. The following *top* command output shows the main window:

```
# top
System: hp01                                          Thu Apr 17 11:47:42 2008
Load averages: 0.01, 0.01, 0.02
163 processes: 112 sleeping, 51 running
Cpu states:
CPU  LOAD  USER  NICE   SYS   IDLE   BLOCK  SWAIT  INTR  SSYS
0    0.02  0.2%  0.0%   0.4%  99.4%  0.0%   0.0%   0.0%  0.0%
1    0.01  0.0%  0.0%   0.2%  99.8%  0.0%   0.0%   0.0%  0.0%
2    0.00  0.0%  0.0%   0.2%  99.8%  0.0%   0.0%   0.0%  0.0%
3    0.01  0.0%  0.0%   0.0%  100.0% 0.0%   0.0%   0.0%  0.0%

---  ----  ----- -----  ----- -----  -----  -----  ----- -----
avg  0.01  0.0%  0.0%   0.2%  99.8%  0.0%   0.0%   0.0%  0.0%


System Page Size: 4Kbytes
Memory: 1017920K (903568K) real, 2347872K (2174996K) virtual, 5066448K free  Page# 1/1


CPU TTY PID  USERNAME PRI NI  SIZE   RES   STATE TIME %WCPU %CPU COMMAND
1   ?   7581 root     152 20  968M   486M  run   10:08 2.32  2.31 mxdomainmgr
2   ?     61 root     191 20  8316K  8316K run   1:18  1.17  1.17 vxfsd
3   ?   2106 root     152 20  311M   79136K run   1:05  0.80  0.80 mxdtf
2   ?   1612 cimsrvr  152 20 42668K 10920K run   1:44  0.59  0.59 cimservermain
3   ?   8002 root     152 20  375M  99172K run   0:17  0.44  0.44 mxinventory
2   ?   8003 root     152 20  383M  81712K run   0:20  0.41  0.41 mxinventory
. . . . . . . .
```

The *glance* command starts the HP GlancePlus software in text mode. This tool displays quantity of CPUs installed in the system and their utilization. The output of the command looks similar to the following:

glance

B3692A Glance C.04.60.000   11:48:15   hp01 9000/800   Current Avg High

---

					Current	Avg	High
CPU Util	SA			|	3%	3%	3%
Disk Util	FVV			|	5%	5%	5%
Mem Util	S	SU	U	|	39%	39%	39%
Swap Util	U	UR	R	|	19%	19%	19%

PROCESS LIST   Users= 2

Process Name	PID	User Name	CPU % (400% max)	Thrd Cnt	Disk IOrate	Memory RSS/VSS		Block On
glance	11782	root	11.8	1	21.4	436kb	464kb	SLEEP
vxfsd	61	root	0.0	28	11.4	8.1mb	8.1mb	SLEEP
midaemon	1821	root	0.0	4	0.0	41.0mb	41.8mb	SLEEP
mxdtf	2106	root	0.0	32	0.0	79.9mb	280.9mb	SLEEP
mxdomainmgr	7581	root	0.0	159	0.0	478.3mb	923.2mb	SLEEP

C - cum/interval toggle   Page 1 of 1

ProcList CPU Rpt Mem Rpt Disk Rpt   NextKeys SlctProc Help Exit

To run HP GlancePlus in graphical mode, use the *gpm* command. See Figure 21-1. The figure shows graphical representation of CPU, memory, disk and network utilization.

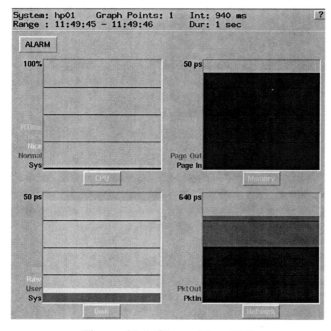

Figure 21-1 GlancePlus GUI

21.1.3   Monitoring Physical Memory and Swap Performance

To monitor physical memory and swap consumption, use the *swapinfo*, *top* and *glance* commands. The *vmstat* and *sar* commands may also be used to monitor swap.

The *swapinfo* command reports on physical memory and swap as follows:

```
# swapinfo –atm
              Mb      Mb      Mb    PCT   START/      Mb
TYPE        AVAIL   USED   FREE   USED   LIMIT   RESERVE    PRI    NAME
dev          8000      0    8000    0%       0       -       1     /dev/vg00/lvol2
dev           500      0     500    0%       0       -       1     /dev/vg01/swaplvol
localfs       100      0     100    0%     100       0       1     /data2/paging
reserve         -    451    -451
memory       7784   1185    6599   15%
total       16384   1636   14148   10%       -       0       -
```

The above output depicts information about all swap spaces and their utilization. It also shows physical memory usage. The first three rows show the amount of device and file systerm swap, and their usage. The fourth row indicates the amount of swap space on reserve, which might be required by running processes. The fifth row shows the physical memory utilization, and the last row displays the sum of all. A very high value (80% plus) would most likely mean that the system needs more physical memory.

The *top* and *glance* (or *gpm*) commands show amount and utilization of physical memory and swap space. See the output of the *top* and *glance* commands in sub-section "Monitoring CPU Performance" earlier in this chapter.

The *vmstat* command displays virtual memory statistics:

```
# vmstat
  procs       memory              page                faults              cpu
  r b w     avm   free     re   at  pi po  fr de sr    in    sy    cs     us sy id
  1 0 0   13660  1721    233  103   3   0   0  0  6   108  1443  1191     6  4 90
```

The following tells *vmstat* to run every 15 seconds for 10 times:

```
# vmstat 15 10
```

The *vmstat* command outputs several columns of information with the main header across the top and sub-heading underneath. The output is divided into two sections: a VM section and a CPU section. The VM section covers information on memory, page and faults. The CPU section covers information on procs and CPU. Table 21-3 describes each field.

Main Heading	Sub-Heading	Description
procs	r	Processes waiting to be processed by CPU.
procs	b	Kernel threads blocked while waiting for I/O.
procs	w	Swapped out idle processes.
memory	avm	Free, unreserved, active virtual memory space.
memory	free	Free memory.
page	re	Pages reclaimed. The higher this number is, the more the shortage of physical memory is.
page	at	Address translation.
page	pi	Paged in from swap.

Main Heading	Sub-Heading	Description
page	po	Paged out to swap.
page	fr	Freed pages.
page	de	Anticipated short-term memory shortfall.
page	sr	Scan rate. This number is reported as a total number of pages scanned.
faults	in	Interrupts per second.
faults	sy	System calls per second.
faults	cs	Context switches per second.
cpu	us	CPU time taken by users.
cpu	sy	CPU time taken by the system (kernel).
cpu	id	CPU idle time.

Table 21-3 *vmstat* Command Output Description

The *sar* command also displays virtual memory statistics. The following runs the command every 5 seconds for 5 times:

```
# sar –w 5 5
HP-UX hp01 B.11.31 U 9000/800    04/17/08
13:53:03    swpin/s bswin/s   swpot/s bswot/s   pswch/s
13:53:08    0.00    0.0       0.00    0.0       144
13:53:13    0.00    0.0       0.00    0.0       140
13:53:18    0.00    0.0       0.00    0.0       172
13:53:23    0.00    0.0       0.00    0.0       159
13:53:28    0.00    0.0       0.00    0.0       145
Average     0.00    0.0       0.00    0.0       152
```

21.1.4   Monitoring Disk Performance

Use the *iostat*, *sar* and *glance* commands to check disk load I/O activities.

The *iostat* command is used to monitor and gather disk performance data. Use the command during peak hours and observe I/O requests being directed at disk devices.

```
# iostat
device    bps    sps    msps
disk2     66     7.3    1.0
disk5     30     2.9    1.0
disk23    0      0.0    1.0
```

The *iostat* command generated several columns of information that are described in Table 21-4.

Column	Description
bps	Kilobytes transferred per second.
sps	Number of disk seeks per second.
msps	Milliseconds per average disk seek.
device	Disk device name.

Table 21-4 *iostat* Command Output Description

The presence of high values for a device in the output, indicates heavy disk utilization. The device may have an extensively-used swap on it. You need to determine the root cause.

The following runs *iostat* every 5 seconds for 5 times:

iostat 5 5

Run *iostat* with –L option to report statistics using lunpath:

iostat –L

lunpath	bps	sps	msps
disk2_lunpath0	66	7.3	1.0
disk5_lunpath3	30	2.9	1.0
disk23_lunpath9	0	0.0	1.0

Use the *sar* command with –d option for 5 times at every 5th second to display disk activities:

sar –d 5 5

HP-UX hp01 B.11.31 U 9000/800   04/17/08

13:54:35	device	%busy	avque	r+w/s	blks/s	avwait	avserv
13:54:40	disk2	3.41	0.50	5	144	0.00	14.67
	disk5	2.00	0.50	3	48	0.00	13.11
	disk23	0.60	0.50	0	0	0.01	39.18
13:54:45	disk2	3.19	0.50	6	82	0.00	13.26
	disk5	1.80	0.50	3	40	0.00	10.52
13:54:50	disk2	1.60	0.50	3	41	0.00	13.11
	disk5	1.60	0.50	2	34	0.00	16.84
13:54:55	disk2	1.60	0.50	2	46	0.00	16.01
	disk5	1.00	0.50	1	30	0.00	9.04
13:55:00	disk2	1.60	0.50	2	22	0.00	14.23
	disk5	0.80	0.50	1	13	0.00	7.45
Average	disk2	2.28	0.50	4	67	0.00	14.07
Average	disk5	1.44	0.50	2	33	0.00	12.20
Average	disk23	0.12	0.50	0	0	0.01	39.18

The *glance* (or *gpm*) command displays overall disk utilization. See the output of the *glance* command in sub-section "Monitoring CPU Performance" earlier in this chapter.

21.1.5   Monitoring System Processes

You can view process statistics using the *ps*, *top* and the *glance* commands, and active IPC facilities' status using the *ipcs* command. In addition, *time* and *timex* commands are available that measure time spent on a given process or command.

The *ps* command displays detailed information about processes running on the system. There are several options available to it, but normally –e, –f and –l are used. These options provide a complete picture of all running processes.

```
# ps –elf
 F   S UID PID PPID C PRI NI  ADDR      SZ     WCHAN  STIME  TTY TIME COMD
1003 S  root   0   0   0 127 20    15634f8    0     13ac184 07:27:31 ?  0:09 swapper
 141 R  root   1   0   0 152 20 10801542c0 262          -  07:27:15 ?  0:03 init
1003 S  root  14   0   0 152 20 10802b0d00   0  108034e080 07:27:15 ?  0:00 net_str_cached
. . . . . . . .
```

The *top* and the *glance* (or *gpm*) commands show a list of all processes currently running on the system along with relevant details. See the output of *top* in section "Monitoring CPU Performance" earlier. The thread list is shown by *gpm* as demonstrated in Figure 21-2.

```
System: hp01     Last Update: 14:01:51    Int: 1 sec     T  ?

Thread List: All 623 Selected                       Users: 4

              Process                            Phys
     TID      Name              PID     CPU %   IO Rt
        0     swapper             0      0.0     0.0
        5     init                1      0.0     0.0
      211     init                1      0.0     0.0
       47     net_str_cached     14      0.0     0.0
       46     net_str_cached     13      0.0     0.0
       45     net_str_cached     12      0.0     0.0
       44     ibd                11      0.0     0.0
       28     escsid             10      0.0     0.0
       29     escsid             10      0.0     0.0
       30     escsid             10      0.0     0.0
       31     escsid             10      0.0     0.0
       32     escsid             10      0.0     0.0
       33     escsid             10      0.0     0.0
       34     escsid             10      0.0     0.0
       35     escsid             10      0.0     0.0
       36     escsid             10      0.0     0.0
       37     escsid             10      0.0     0.0
       38     escsid             10      0.0     0.0
       39     escsid             10      0.0     0.0
       40     escsid             10      0.0     0.0
       41     escsid             10      0.0     0.0
       42     escsid             10      0.0     0.0
       43     escsid             10      0.0     0.0
       27     ttisr               9      0.0     0.0
```

Figure 21-2 *gpm* Thread List

The *time* command reports, in seconds, on the elapsed time during the execution of a command, time in the system and execution time of itself:

```
# time find / –name core
real    0m19.90s
user    0m0.56s
sys     0m7.43s
```

The *timex* command reports, in seconds, on the elapsed time, user time and system execution time. For example, run SMH and measure the time. Exit SMH to see the numbers.

```
# timex smh
real      17.85
user       0.22
sys        0.23
```

The above output indicates that SMH was run for total 17.85 seconds.

 Both *time* and *timex* commands produce similar outputs.

The *ipcs* command displays status information about active IPC facilities. With no options specified, the command displays active message queues, shared memory segments and semaphores.

```
# ipcs
IPC  status from /dev/kmem as of Thu Apr 17 14:03:20 2008
T     ID    KEY            MODE         OWNER    GROUP
Message Queues:
q     0    0x3c1c0711  -Rrw--w--w-    root      root
q     1    0x3e1c0711  --rw-r--r--    root      root
Shared Memory:
m     0    0x411c0161  --rw-rw-rw-    root      root
m     1    0x4e0c0002  --rw-rw-rw-    root      root
m     2    0x41202774  --rw-rw-rw-    root      root
m     3    0x00a5c581  --rw-------    sfmdb     users
m     4    0x411c0eac  --rw-------    root      root
m     5    0x02fb07f1  --rw-------    hpsmdb    users
Semaphores:
s     0    0x4f1c0496  --ra-------    root      root
s     1    0x411c0161  --ra-ra-ra-    root      root
s     2    0x4e0c0002  --ra-ra-ra-    root      root
s     3    0x41202774  --ra-ra-ra-    root      root
. . . . . . . .
```

21.1.6   Monitoring Network Performance

To monitor network adapter activities, use the *lanadmin*, *netstat* or *nwmgr* commands. See Chapter 25 "Network Connectivity Troubleshooting" for a detailed understanding of these tools.

21.2   Fixing a Performance Problem

When the root cause of a system bottleneck is identified, perform necessary modifications to the area or areas affecting the performance. If multiple areas are required to be modified, implement the fixes one at a time.

It is highly recommended that proactive monitoring of systems be performed on a regular basis to capture any bottlenecks before system performance is impacted.

Summary

In this chapter you learned about performance bottleneck areas and tools to monitor performance. You looked at common performance bottleneck areas including CPU, memory, swap, disk, process and LAN adapters. You used performance monitoring tools such as *uptime*, *w*, *sar*, *top*, *glance*, *swapinfo*, *vmstat*, *iostat*, *ps*, *time*, *timex* and *ipcs* and how to use them to measure performance.

## 22

Shell Scripting

This chapter covers the following major topics:

- ✓ What is shell scripting?
- ✓ Write scripts to display basic system information, set local and environment variables, use values of pre-defined environment variables, parse command outputs to variables, and understand usage of command line arguments and the role the shift command plays
- ✓ Execute and debug scripts
- ✓ Write interactive scripts
- ✓ Write scripts to create logical constructs using if-then-fi, if-then-else-fi, if-then-elif-fi and case structures
- ✓ Write scripts to create looping constructs using for-do-done, while-do-done and until-do-done structures
- ✓ Understand exit codes and test conditions
- ✓ Control loops using break, continue and sleep commands
- ✓ Ignore signals using the trap command

22.1   Shell Scripting

Shell scripts (a.k.a. *shell programs* or simply *scripts*) are text files that contain UNIX commands and control structures to automate long, repetitive tasks. Commands are interpreted and run by the shell one at a time in the order they are listed in the script. Control structures are utilized for creating and managing logical and looping constructs. Comments are also usually included in shell scripts to add general information about the script such as author name, creation date, last modification date and purpose of the script.

Although shell scripting is typically part of UNIX fundamentals, which was covered in the first few chapters of this book, it is purposely included here after discussing all system administration topics. The reason is to provide better and useful example scripts that employ the system administration knowledge you have gained.

Throughout this chapter, the approach will be to write scripts and examine them line-by-line. The chapter will begin with simple scripts and move forward to more complicated ones. As with any other programming languages, the scripting skill will develop overtime as you write, read and understand more and more scripts.

Scripts covered in this chapter are written for the POSIX shell */usr/bin/sh*. They can be used in Korn shell without any modifications, but not all of them can be run in C shell.

Shell scripting enables you to create programs for various purposes including automation of system and network administration tasks such as manipulating physical volumes, volume groups, logical volumes and file systems, monitoring file system utilization, trimming log files, performing tape and network recovery archives, doing system backups, removing core, temporary and unnecessary files, automating software and patch management, generating reports, and managing user accounts.

The shell reads the contents of a script line by line when it is run. Each line is executed as if it is typed and executed at the command prompt. If the script encounters an error, the error message is displayed on the screen. There is nothing that can be placed in a script, but cannot run at the command prompt.

Scripts do not need to be compiled as many other programming languages do.

22.2   Creating Shell Scripts

Use the vi editor to create example shell scripts presented in this chapter. This gives you an opportunity to practice the editor. The *cat* command with –n option is used to display the contents of the scripts. It is recommended to store these scripts in the */usr/local/bin* directory, and add the directory to the PATH. Following example scripts are created in */usr/local/bin* directory with an assumption that the directory path is defined in the PATH variable.

22.2.1 Displaying Basic System Information

Let us create the first script called *sys_info.sh* and then examine it. Change directory into */usr/local/bin* and use the vi editor to construct the script. Type in what you see below, but do not include the line numbers:

 # cat –n sys_info.sh
```
1   #!/usr/bin/sh
2   # The name of this script is sys_info.sh.
3   # The author of this script is Asghar Ghori.
4   # The script is created on February 24, 2006.
5   # This script is last modified by Asghar Ghori on April 17, 2008.
6   # This script should be located in /usr/local/bin directory.
7   # The purpose of this script is to explain construct of a simple shell program.
8   echo "Display Basic System Information"
9   echo "-------------------------------------------"
10  echo
11  echo "The hardware model of this machine is:"
12  /usr/bin/model
13  echo "This machine is running the following version of HP-UX:"
14  /usr/bin/uname –r
```

 To view line numbers associated with each line entry while in the vi editor, type (:set nu).

In this script, comments and commands are used.

The first line indicates the shell the script will use to run. This line must start with the "#!" character combination followed by the full pathname to the shell file.

The next six lines contain comments to include the script name, author name, creation time, the last modification time, default location to store and purpose. The # sign indicates that anything written to the right of this character is for informational purposes and will not be executed when the script is run. Note that line 1 uses this character too followed by the ! mark; this combination has a special meaning to the shell, which specifies the location of the shell file. Do not get confused between the two usages.

Line number 8 has the first command of the script. The *echo* command prints on the screen whatever follows it. In this case, you will see "Display Basic System Information" printed.

Line number 9 underlines the "Display Basic System Information" heading.

Line number 10 has the *echo* command followed by nothing. This means an empty line will be inserted in the output.

Line number 11 prints on the screen "The hardware model of this machine is:".

Line number 12 executes the *model* command. This command displays the hardware model of the machine you are on.

Line number 13 prints on the screen "This machine is running the following version of HP-UX:".

Line number 14 executes the *uname* command with –r option. This command returns the HP-UX version being used.

22.2.2   Executing a Script

When you have a script constructed, it is usually not executable since the umask value is typically set to 022, which allows only rw permissions to the owner and r permission to group members and public on new files. You will need to run the script as follows while you are in */usr/local/bin*:

    # sh ./sys_info.sh

Alternatively, give the owner of the file execute permission:

    # chmod +x sys_info.sh

Now you can run the script using either its relative path or fully qualified path:

    # ./sys_info.sh   or   **# /usr/local/bin/sys_info.sh**

If the */usr/local/bin* directory is not set in the PATH variable, define it in either */etc/profile* or */etc/PATH* file so whoever logs on to the system has this path set. The following shows how to set the path at the command prompt:

    # PATH=$PATH:/usr/local/bin
    # export PATH

Let us run *sys_info.sh* and see what the output will look like:

    # sys_info.sh
    Display Basic System Information

    The hardware model of this machine is:
    9000/800/rp7410
    This machine is running the following version of HP-UX:
    B.11.31

22.2.3   Debugging a Shell Script

If you would like to use the basic debugging technique when you see that a script is not functioning the way it should be, you may want to append –x to "#!/usr/bin/sh" in the first line of the script to look like "#!/usr/bin/sh –x". Alternatively, you can execute the script as follows:

    # sh –x /usr/local/bin/sys_info.sh
    + echo Display Basic System Information
    Display Basic System Information
    + echo --

    + echo

```
+ echo The hardware model of this machine is:
The hardware model of this machine is:
+ /usr/bin/model
9000/800/rp7410
+ echo This machine is running the following version of HP-UX:
This machine is running the following version of HP-UX:
+ /usr/bin/uname -r
B.11.31
```

With the + sign, the actual line from the script will be echoed to the screen followed in the next line by what it would produce in the output.

22.2.4   Using Local Variables

You have dealt with variables previously and seen how to use them. To recap, there are two types of variables: *local* (or *private*) and *global* (or *environment*). They are defined and used in scripts and at the command line in the exact same manner. A local variable defined in a script disappears once the script execution is finished, whereas a global variable persists even after the execution finishes.

In the second script called *loc_var.sh,* a local variable is defined and its value displayed. After the script execution is complete, check the value of the variable again.

```
# cat –n loc_var.sh
1    #!/usr/bin/sh
2    # The name of this script is loc_var.sh.
3    # The author of this script is Asghar Ghori.
4    # The script is created on February 24, 2006.
5    # This script is last modified by Asghar Ghori on April 17, 2008.
6    # This script should be located in /usr/local/bin directory.
7    # The purpose of this script is to explain how a local variable is defined and used in a
8    # shell program.
9    echo  "Setting a Local Variable".
10   echo  "--------------------------------"
11   echo
12   SYS_NAME=hp01
13   echo  "The hostname of this system is $SYS_NAME".
```

When this script is run, the output will be:

```
# loc_var.sh
Setting a Local Variable.
--------------------------------

The hostname of this system is hp01.
```

Now since it was a local variable and the script was run in a sub-shell, the variable disappeared after the script execution completed. Here is what you will see if you try to *echo* on the variable:

```
# echo $SYS_NAME
sh: SYS_NAME: Parameter not set
```

22.2.5   Using Pre-Defined Environment Variables

In the next script called *pre_env.sh*, values of two pre-defined environment variables SHELL and
LOGNAME are displayed:

```
# cat –n pre_env.sh
1    #!/usr/bin/sh
2    # The name of this script is pre_env.sh.
3    # The author of this script is Asghar Ghori.
4    # The script is created on February 24, 2006.
5    # This script is last modified by Asghar Ghori on April 17, 2008.
6    # This script should be located in /usr/local/bin directory.
7    # The purpose of this script is to explain how a pre-defined environment variable is used
8    # in a shell program.
9    echo "The location of my shell command is:"
10   echo $SHELL
11   echo "You are logged in as $LOGNAME".
```

The output will be:

```
# pre_env.sh
The location of my shell command is:
/sbin/sh
You are logged in as root.
```

22.2.6   Setting New Environment Variables

In the next script *new_env.sh*, two environment variables SYS_NAME and OS_NAME are set
during script execution. Once the script is done, you will see that the two variables still exist.

```
# cat –n new_env.sh
1    #!/usr/bin/sh
2    # The name of this script is new_env.sh.
3    # The author of this script is Asghar Ghori.
4    # The script is created on February 24, 2006.
5    # This script is last modified by Asghar Ghori on April 17, 2008.
6    # This script should be located in /usr/local/bin directory.
7    # The purpose of this script is to explain how environment variables are defined and
8    # used in a shell program.
9    echo "Setting New Environment Variables".
10   echo "----------------------------------------------"
11   echo
12   SYS_NAME=hp01
13   OS_NAME="HP-UX 11i v3"
14   export SYS_NAME OS_NAME
15   echo "The hostname of this system is $SYS_NAME".
```

16   echo "This system is running $OS_NAME software".

The output will be:

 # new_env.sh
Setting New Environment Variables.

The hostname of this system is hp01.
This system is running HP-UX 11i v3 software.

The *export* command makes the specified variables environment variables. Even though the script was run in a sub-shell, both environment variables retained their values. Do an *echo* on them o check the values:

$ echo $SYS_NAME
hp01
$ echo $OS_NAME
HP-UX 11i v3

22.2.7   Parsing Command Output

Shell scripts allow you to run a command and capture its output into a variable. For example, the following script called *cmdout.sh* is a modified version of the *new_env.sh* script. You must enclose the *hostname* and *uname* commands in forward quotes.

 # cat –n cmdout.sh
1   #!/usr/bin/sh
2   # The name of this script is cmdout.sh.
3   # The author of this script is Asghar Ghori.
4   # The script is created on February 24, 2006.
5   # This script is last modified by Asghar Ghori on April 17, 2008.
6   # This script should be located in /usr/local/bin directory.
7   # The purpose of this script is to display how a command output is captured and stored
8   # in a variable.
9   echo "Parsing Command Output".
10   echo "----------------------------------"
11   echo
12   SYS_NAME=`/usr/bin/hostname`
13   OS_VER=`/usr/bin/uname  –r`
14   export SYS_NAME OS_VER
15   echo "The hostname of this system is $SYS_NAME".
16   echo "This system is running $OS_VER of HP-UX software".

The output will be:

```
# new_env.sh
Parsing Command Output.
------------------------------------

The hostname of this system is hp01.
This system is running B.11.31 of HP-UX software.
```

22.2.8   Using Command Line Arguments

Command line arguments (also called *positional parameters*) are the arguments specified at the command line with a command or script when it is executed. The locations at the command line of the arguments as well as the command or script itself, are stored in corresponding variables. These variables are special shell variables. Figure 22-1 and Table 22-1 help you understand them.

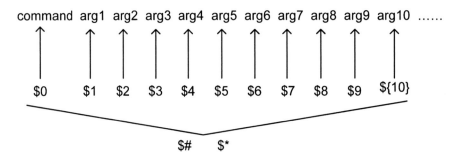

Figure 22-1 Command Line Arguments

Variable	Description
$0	Represents the command or script.
$1 to $9	Represents arguments 1 through 9.
${10} ……	Represents arguments 10 and further.
$#	Represents total number of arguments.
$*	Represents all arguments.
$$	Represents the PID of a running script.

Table 22-1 Command Line Arguments Description

The script *com_line_arg.sh* shows the command line arguments supplied, a count of them, value of the first argument and the process ID of the script itself:

```
# cat –n com_line_arg.sh
1    #!/usr/bin/sh
2    # The name of this script is com_line_arg.sh.
3    # The author of this script is Asghar Ghori.
4    # The script is created on February 24, 2006.
5    # This script is last modified by Asghar Ghori on April 17, 2008.
6    # This script should be located in /usr/local/bin directory.
7    # The purpose of this script is to explain the usage of command line arguments.
8    echo "There are $# arguments supplied at the command line".
9    echo "The arguments supplied are: $*"
```

```
10   echo "The first argument is: $1"
11   echo "The Process ID of the script is: $$"
```

When this script is executed with four arguments toronto, chicago, london and tokyo, the result will be:

 # com_line_arg.sh toronto chicago london tokyo
There are 4 arguments supplied at the command line.
The arguments supplied are: toronto chicago london tokyo
The first argument is: toronto
The Process ID of the script is: 2422

22.2.9   Shifting Command Line Arguments

The *shift* command is used to move command line arguments one position to the left. The first argument is lost. *com_line_arg_shift.sh* script below uses the *shift* command:

 # cat –n com_line_arg_shift.sh
```
1    #! /usr/bin/sh
2    # The name of this script is com_line_arg_shift.sh.
3    # The author of this script is Asghar Ghori.
4    # The script is created on February 24, 2006.
5    # This script is last modified by Asghar Ghori on April 17, 2008.
6    # This script should be located in /usr/local/bin directory.
7    # The purpose of this script is to show you impact of the shift command on command line
8    # arguments.
9    echo "There are $# arguments specified at the command line".
10   echo "The arguments supplied are: $*"
11   echo "The first argument is: $1"
12   echo "The Process ID of the script is: $$"
13   shift
14   echo "The new first argument after the first shift is: $1"
15   shift
16   echo "The new first argument after the second shift is: $1"
```

Let us execute *com_line_arg_shift.sh* with four arguments toronto, chicago, london and tokyo. Notice that after each shift, a new value is assigned to $1.

 # com_line_arg_shift.sh toronto chicago london tokyo
There are 4 arguments specified at the command line.
The arguments supplied are: toronto chicago london tokyo
The first argument is: toronto
The Process ID of the script is: 2430
The new first argument after the first shift is: chicago
The new first argument after the second shift is: london

Multiple shifts in one attempt may be performed by supplying a number to the *shift* command as an argument. For example, "*shift* 2" will carry out two shifts, "*shift* 3" will do three shifts and so on.

22.2.10 Writing an Interactive Script

Interactive shell scripts are written where you want the script to prompt for input and continue execution based on the input provided. The input is stored into a variable. The *read* command is used for reading the input, and is usually preceded by the *echo* command to display a message telling what is expected as input.

inter_read.sh lists files and prompts to enter a file name to be removed. Note a \c in the eleventh line. This is an example of *escape sequence*. It tells the *echo* command not to send carriage return and line feed after displaying "Enter name of file you want to remove:". When you enter a file name, you will be typing it on the same line right beside the colon character. Try running this script with and without \c. Also, a pre-defined environment variable called PWD is used in the script. This will display your location in the directory tree.

cat –n inter_read.sh
```
1    #! /usr/bin/sh
2    # The name of this script is inter_read.sh.
3    # The author of this script is Asghar Ghori.
4    # The script is created on February 24, 2006.
5    # This script is last modified by Asghar Ghori on April 17, 2008.
6    # This script should be located in /usr/local/bin directory.
7    # The purpose of this script is to show you an example of how an interactive script works.
8    echo  "Here is a list of all files in $PWD directory:"
9    /usr/bin/ls –l
10   echo
11   echo  "Enter name of file you want to remove: \c"
12   read  FILE
13   echo  "Type 'y' to remove it, 'n' if you do not want to:"
14   /usr/bin/rm –i $FILE
15   echo  "The file is removed".
```

Let us assume that you are in */var/adm/syslog* directory when this script is run. Here is what the *inter_read.sh* script will do:

inter_read.sh
```
Here is a list of all files in /var/adm/syslog directory:
total 176
-rw-r--r--  1 root    root       29349 Apr 17 11:41 OLDsyslog.log
-rw-r--r--  1 root    sys          621 Apr 17 14:11 a
-r--------  1 root    root       36318 Apr 17 13:38 mail.log
-rw-r--r--  1 root    sys         1041 Apr 17 13:38 syslog.log

Enter name of file you want to remove:
Type 'y' to remove it, 'n' if you do not want to:
<filename>: ? (y/n)
The file is removed.
```

There are some other escape sequences such as \t for tab, \n for new line, \a for beep, \f for form feed, \r for carriage return and \b for backspace that can be used in shell scripts to increase readability. Try using a few of them in *inter_read.sh* script.

Another example of an interactive script is given below. Script *userc.sh* prompts to input required user information. Each value entered is stored in a separate variable and finally the *useradd* command is executed to create an account based on the input provided, followed by the *passwd* command to set an initial password.

 # cat –n userc.sh

```
1    #! /usr/bin/sh
2    # The name of this script is userc.sh.
3    # The author of this script is Asghar Ghori.
4    # The script is created on February 24, 2006.
5    # This script is last modified by Asghar Ghori on April 17, 2008.
6    # This script should be located in /usr/local/bin directory.
7    # The purpose of this script is to show you how a user can be created using an interactive script.
8    echo "This simple program creates user accounts based on input provided."
9    echo "Enter required information."
10   echo "---------------------------------"
11   echo
12   echo "Enter username:\c"
13   read  USER
14   echo "Enter user ID:\c"
15   read  UID
16   echo "Enter primary group name or group ID:\c"
17   read  GID
18   echo "Enter shell:\c"
19   read  SH
20   echo "Enter home directory for the user:\c"
21   read  HD
22   echo "Enter comments:\c"
23   read  COMMENT
24   /usr/sbin/useradd –u $UID –g $GID –s $SH –m –d $HD –c $COMMENT $USER
25   /usr/bin/passwd  $USER
```

Ensure that username and UID are unique and comments are included in quotes, otherwise the script will fail.

Try logging in as this user to verify. Also do a *tail* on */etc/passwd* to check for an entry.

22.3 Logical Constructs

In shell scripting there are times when a decision whether to perform an action needs to be made. In other words, a test condition (or logic) is defined in a script and based on the true or false status of the condition, the script decides what to do next.

The shell offers two logical constructs: the *if-then-fi* construct and the *case* construct. The if-then-fi construct has a few variations, which will also be covered in this chapter.

Before looking at example scripts and see how logical constructs are used, let us discuss *exit codes* and *test* conditions. These will be employed in the example scripts.

22.3.1 Exit Codes

Exit codes refer to the value returned when a program or script finishes execution. This value is based on the outcome of the program. If the program ran successfully, you will get a zero exit code, otherwise, a non-zero exit code will be received.

You may use the terms "zero status code", "zero exit code", "successful script completion" or "true value", interchangeably. Similarly, you may use the terms "non-zero status code", "failed script completion" or "false value", interchangeably. These values or codes are also referred to as *return codes,* and are stored in a special shell variable called ?. Let us look at the following two examples to understand exit codes:

```
# ls
file1 file2 file3 file4 file5 file6
# echo $?
0

# man
Usage: man [-M path] [-T macro-package] [ section ] name ...
or: man -k keyword ...
or: man -f file ...
# echo  $?
1
```

In the first example, the *ls* command ran successfully and it produced desired results, hence a zero return code. In the second example, the *man* command did not run successfully since it required an argument, therefore a non-zero return code. To display the value stored in the special variable ?, the *echo* command was used as shown in both examples above.

Within a script you may wish to define exit codes at different locations. This would help debug by letting you know where exactly the script quit.

22.3.2 Test Conditions

Test conditions can be set on numeric values, string values or files using the *test* command. You may instead enclose a test condition inside the square brackets [] without using the *test* command explicitly. This is exhibited in logical construct examples later.

Table 22-2 shows various testing condition operations that you can perform.

Operation on Numeric Value	Meaning
integer1 –eq integer2	Integer1 is equal to integer2.
integer1 –ne integer2	Integer1 is not equal to integer2.
integer1 –lt integer2	Integer1 is less than integer2.
integer1 –gt integer2	Integer1 is greater than integer2.
integer1 –le integer2	Integer1 is less than or equal to integer2.

integer1 −ge integer2	Integer1 is greater than or equal to integer2.
Operation on String Value	**Meaning**
string1−string2	Checks if the two strings are identical.
string1! −string2	Checks if the two strings are not identical.
−l string or −z string	Checks if string length is zero.
−n string	Checks if string length is non-zero.
string	Same as "−n string".
Operation on File	**Meaning**
−b file	Checks if file exists and is a block device file.
−c file	Checks if file exists and is a character device file.
−d file	Checks if file is a directory.
−e file	Checks if file exists.
−f file	Checks if file exists and is a normal file.
−g file	Checks if file exists and has setgid bit on it.
−L file	Checks if file exists and is a symbolic link.
−r file	Checks if file exists and is readable.
−s file	Checks if file exists and is non-zero in length.
−u file	Checks if file exists and has setuid bit set on it.
−w file	Checks if file exists and is writable.
−x file	Checks if file exists and is executable.
file1 −nt file2	Checks if file1 is newer than file2.
file1 −ot file2	Checks if file1 is older than file2.
Logic Operator	**Meaning**
!	Opposite result of expression.
−a	AND operator.
−o	OR operator.

Table 22-2 Testing Conditions

Having described exit codes and various test condition operations, let us take a look at a few scripts and see how some of these can be utilized.

22.3.3   The if-then-fi Construct

The if-then-fi construct checks a condition for true or false. If the condition is true, an action is performed, otherwise, it gets you out of the if statement. The if statement ends with a fi. The syntax of this construct is:

```
if
        condition
then
        action
fi
```

It has been demonstrated earlier how to check the number of arguments specified at the command line. A shell script can be writted to determine that number and print an error message if there are none specified. The *if_then_fi.sh* does that.

 # cat –n if_then_fi.sh

```
1    #!/usr/bin/sh
2    # The name of this script is if_then_fi.sh.
3    # The author of this script is Asghar Ghori.
4    # The script is created on February 24, 2006.
5    # This script is last modified by Asghar Ghori on April 17, 2008.
6    # This script should be located in /usr/local/bin directory.
7    # The purpose of this script is to explain the usage of if-then-fi logical construct.
8    if
9            [ $# –ne 2 ]     # You can also use it as "test $# –ne 2" in explicit mode.
10   then
11           echo "Error: Invalid number of arguments supplied."
12           echo "Usage: $0 source_file destination_file."
13   exit 2
14   fi
15   echo "Script terminated."
```

This script will display the following message on the screen if executed without specifying exactly two arguments at the command line:

```
Error: Invalid number of arguments supplied.
Usage: if_then_fi.sh source_file destination_file
```

If you check the return code, a value of 2 will appear. This value reflects the exit code defined in the action.

 # echo $?
```
2
```

Conversely, if you supply two arguments, the return code will be 0 and the message will be:

```
Script terminated.
```

 # echo $?
```
0
```

22.3.4   The if-then-else-fi Construct

This construct is used when you want to execute one or the other action, depending on the result of a test. The general syntax of the structure is:

```
if
        condition
then
        action1
else
        action2
fi
```

If the result of the condition is true, action1 is executed, otherwise action2.

The following script called *if_then_else_fi.sh* accepts an integer value as an argument and tells if it is positive or negative. If no argument is provided, it will display the script usage.

 # cat –n if_then_else_fi.sh
```
1    #!/usr/bin/sh
2    # The name of this script is if_then_else_fi.sh.
3    # The author of this script is Asghar Ghori.
4    # The script is created on February 24, 2006.
5    # This script is last modified by Asghar Ghori on April 17, 2008.
6    # This script should be located in /usr/local/bin directory.
7    # The purpose of this script is to explain the usage of if-then-else-fi logical construct.
8    if
9            [ $1 –gt 0 ]                 # You can also use it as "test  $1  –ge  0" in explicit mode.
10   then
11           echo  "$1 is a positive integer value".
12   else
13           echo  "$1 is a negative integer value".
14   fi
```

Run this script one time with a positive integer value and the next time with a negative value:

 # if_then_else_fi.sh 10
10 is a positive integer value.

 # if_then_else_fi.sh –10
-10 is a negative integer value.

22.3.5   The if-then-elif-fi Construct

This construct defines multiple conditions; whichever is met, an action associated with it is executed. The general syntax of the structure is:

```
if
            condition1
then
            action1
elif
            condition2
then
            action2
…………
…………
else
            action(n)
fi
```

The following script called *if_then_elif_fi.sh* is an enhanced version of *if_then_else_fi.sh* script. It accepts an integer value as an argument and tells if it is positive, negative or zero. If a non-integer value or no command line argument is supplied, the script will complain about it.

cat –n if_then_elif_fi.sh

```
1   #!/usr/bin/sh
2   # The name of this script is if_then_elif_fi.sh.
3   # The author of this script is Asghar Ghori.
4   # The script is created on February 24, 2006.
4   # This script is last modified by Asghar Ghori on April 17, 2008.
6   # This script should be located in /usr/local/bin directory.
7   # The purpose of this script is to explain you the usage of if-then-elif-fi logical construct.
8   if
9           [ $1 –gt  0 ]
10  then
11          echo "$1 is a positive integer value".
12          exit  1
13  elif
14          [ $1 –eq  0 ]
15  then
16          echo "$1 is zero integer value".
17          exit  2
18  elif
19          [ $1 –lt  0 ]
20  then
21          echo "$1 is a negative integer value".
22          exit  3
23  else
24          echo "$1 is not an integer value. Please supply an integer".
25          exit  4
26  fi
```

Run this script one time with a positive value, the second time with 0, the third time with a negative value and the fourth time with a non-integer value. Each time you run it, check the value of exit code to see where the script actually exits out.

if_then_elif_fi.sh 10
10 is a positive integer value.
echo $?
1

if_then_elif_fi.sh 0
0 is zero integer value.
echo $?
2

if_then_elif_fi.sh –10
-10 is a negative integer value.

22.3.6   The case Construct

The case construct compares a value against listed patterns. If a match is made, the commands associated with that pattern are executed and $? is assigned a 0 value.

Wildcard characters such as *, ? and [] can be used in patterns. The pipe character can be used for logical OR operation. If you make an invalid choice, the last part of the case construct (followed by *)) is executed.

The general syntax of the case construct is given below:

```
case VAR in
        pattern1)
        command(s)
        ;;
        pattern2)
        command(s)
        ;;
......
......
        patternX)
        command(s)
        ;;
        *)
        command(s)
        ;;
esac
```

VAR is a variable whose value is checked against each pattern listed in the case statement. Note the two semicolon ;; characters. When the value of VAR matches a pattern, commands corresponding to that pattern are executed up to the next occurrence of the ;; characters. The) character marks the end of a pattern. If VAR matches none of the patterns, commands after *) are executed. The case statement ends with an "esac".

The following example script called *case_menu.sh* is a menu-driven program and uses case construct:

cat –n case_menu.sh

```
1    #!/usr/bin/sh
2    # The name of this script is case_menu.sh.
3    # The author of this script is Asghar Ghori.
4    # The script is created on February 24, 2006.
```

```
5    # This script is last modified by Asghar Ghori on April 17, 2008.
6    # This script should be located in /usr/local/bin directory.
7    # The purpose of this script is to explain you the usage of the logical case construct.
8    /usr/bin/clear
9    echo
10   echo "                    Menu "
11   echo "    ------------------------------------------------------"
12   echo "    [1] Display System's Current Date and Time".
13   echo "    [2] Display Boot Paths and Autoboot/Autosearch Settings".
14   echo "    [3] Run ioscan with –fNnk options to list all disks".
15   echo "    [4] Run SMH".
16   echo "    ==================================="
17   echo
18   echo "Enter Your Choice [1-4] \c: "
19   read VAR
20   case $VAR in
21        1) echo "Current System Date and Time is `/usr/bin/date`"
22        echo
23        ;;
24        2) /usr/sbin/setboot
25        echo
26        ;;
27        3) /usr/sbin/ioscan –fNnkCdisk
28        echo
29        ;;
30        4) /usr/sbin/smh
31        echo
32        ;;
33        *) echo "You have selected an invalid choice".
34        echo
35        ;;
36   esac
```

This script will clear the screen and display a menu with four choices. Option 1 will execute the *date* command, option 2 the *setboot* command, option 3 the *ioscan* command, option 4 the *smh* command, and entering any other character will display the message "You have selected an invalid choice" and the script will terminate.

22.4 Looping Constructs

In shell scripting there are times when you need to perform a task on a number of given values, or until a specified condition becomes true or false. For example, if you wish to *pvcreate* a number of physical disk DSFs, you can either run the command on each DSF one at a time, or employ a loop to do it in one go. Likewise, based on a defined condition, you may want a program to continue to run until the condition becomes either true or false.

There are three constructs that implement looping: the for-do-done construct, the while-do-done construct and the until-do-done construct.

The *for-do-done* construct performs an operation on a list of given elements until the list is exhausted. The *while-do-done* construct performs an operation repeatedly based on a specified condition until the condition becomes false. The *until-do-done* construct does the opposite of what the while-do-done construct does. It performs an operation repeatedly based on a specified condition until the condition becomes true.

22.4.1   Test Conditions

The *let* command is used in looping constructs to check a condition every time a repetition is made. It compares the value stored in a variable against a defined value. Each time a loop does an iteration, the value in the variable is altered. You can enclose the test condition within (( )) or double quotes " ", instead of using the *let* command explicitly. This is exhibited in looping construct examples.

Table 22-3 lists operators that can be used with the *let* command.

Operator	Description
–	Unary minus.
!	Unary negation (same value but with a negative sign).
+	Addition.
–	Subtraction.
*	Multiplication.
/	Integer division.
%	Remainder.
<	Less than.
<=	Less than or equal to.
>	Greater than.
>=	Greater than or equal to.
=	Assignment.
==	Comparison for equality.
!=	Comparison for non-equality.

Table 22-3 *let* Operators

Having described various test condition operators, let us take a look at a few scripts and see how some of these can be utilized.

22.4.2   The for-do-done Loop

The for-do-done loop is executed on a list of elements until all the elements are exhausted. Each element is assigned to a variable one after the other to be processed in the loop. The syntax of the for-do-done loop is:

```
for  VAR  in  list
do
        command block
done
```

The *for_do_done.sh* script below initializes a variable COUNT to 0. An array of items are supplied to a variable ALPHABET. The for-do-done loop reads the ALPHABET value one after the other, assigns it to another variable LETTER, and displays it on the screen. The *expr* command is an arithmetic processor and it simply increments the COUNT by 1 at each iteration of the loop.

cat –n for_do_done.sh

```
1    #!/usr/bin/sh
2    # The name of this script is for_do_done.sh.
3    # The author of this script is Asghar Ghori.
4    # The script is created on February 24, 2006.
5    # This script is last modified by Asghar Ghori on April 17, 2008.
6    # This script should be located in /usr/local/bin directory.
7    # The purpose of this script is to explain you the usage of the for-do-done looping construct.
8    COUNT=0
9    ALPHABET="A B C D E F G H I J K L M N O P Q R S T U V W X Y Z"
10   for  LETTER  in  $ALPHABET
11   do
12           COUNT=`/usr/bin/expr  $COUNT + 1`
13           echo "Letter $COUNT is [$LETTER]"
14   done
```

The output of the script will be:

for_do_done.sh

```
Letter 1 is [A]
Letter 2 is [B]
Letter 3 is [C]
Letter 4 is [D]
. . . . . . . .
Letter 24 is [X]
Letter 25 is [Y]
Letter 26 is [Z]
```

The following for-do-done loop example script called *pvcreate_many.sh* defines a variable called j and contains a list of disk drives to be pvcreated. The script will take the disk name from the list one by one and execute the *pvcreate* command on it.

cat –n pvcreate_many.sh

```
1    #!/usr/bin/sh
2    # The name of this script is pvcreate_many.sh.
3    # The author of this script is Asghar Ghori.
4    # The script is created on February 24, 2006.
5    # This script is last modified by Asghar Ghori on April 17, 2008.
6    # This script should be located in /usr/local/bin directory.
7    # The purpose of this script is to perform LVM pvcreate operation on a number of physical
8    # disk devices.
9    for  j  in  disk5  disk22  disk23  disk24  disk25
10   do
11           echo "Creating LVM Structures on $j".
```

```
12          /usr/sbin/pvcreate  /dev/rdisk/$j
13    done
```

The execution of the script will produce the following output:

 # pvcreate_many.sh

Creating LVM Structures on disk5.
Physical volume "/dev/rdisk/disk5" has been successfully created.
Creating LVM Structures on disk22.
Physical volume "/dev/rdisk/disk22" has been successfully created.
Creating LVM Structures on disk23.
Physical volume "/dev/rdisk/disk23" has been successfully created.
Creating LVM Structures on disk24.
Physical volume "/dev/rdisk/disk24" has been successfully created.
Creating LVM Structures on disk25.
Physical volume "/dev/rdisk/disk25" has been successfully created.

Another example is given below. This script called *create_user.sh* can be used to create several user accounts. As each account is created, the value of $? is checked. If the value is 0, a message saying the account is created successfully will be displayed, otherwise the script will terminate. In case of a successful user creation, the *passwd* command will be invoked to assign a password to the user.

 # cat –n create_user.sh
```
1     #!/usr/bin/sh
2     # The name of this script is create_user.sh.
3     # The author of this script is Asghar Ghori.
4     # The script is created on February 24, 2006.
5     # This script is last modified by Asghar Ghori on April 17, 2008.
6     # This script should be located in /usr/local/bin directory.
7     # The purpose of this script is to create multiple user accounts in one go.
8     for USER in user10 user11 user12 user13 user14
9     do
10            echo "Creating account for user $USER".
11            /usr/sbin/useradd –m –d /home/$USER –s /usr/bin/sh $USER
12            if [ $? = 0 ]
13                    then
14                            echo "$USER is created successfully."
15                    else
16                            echo "Failed to create user account $USER".
17                            exit
18            fi
19    /usr/bin/passwd $USER
20    done
```

22.4.3   The while-do-done Loop

The while-do-done loop checks for a condition and goes on executing a block of commands until the specified condition becomes false. The general syntax of the loop is:

```
while
        condition
do
        command block
done
```

The condition is usually an expression containing a *test* or *let* command in either implicit or explicit mode, but they are normally used in implicit mode.

Let us look at the *while_do_done.sh* script below. This is an enhanced version of *case_menu.sh* that was created earlier in this chapter. The entire case statement is defined as a block of commands within the while-do-done loop here. When you choose one of the options listed, the command associated with that option is executed. Once the command is finished executing, you will be prompted to press a key to go back to the menu. The loop will continue until you choose option 5 to terminate.

 # cat –n while_do_done.sh

```
1    #!/usr/bin/sh
2    # The name of this script is while_do_done.sh.
3    # The author of this script is Asghar Ghori.
4    # The script is created on February 24, 2006.
5    # This script is last modified by Asghar Ghori on April 17, 2008.
6    # This script should be located in /usr/local/bin directory.
7    # The purpose of this script is to show you an example of how a menu driven program can
8    # be included in a while loop so it continues to run until a specific option from the menu is
9    # chosen to exit out.
10   while  true
11   do
12           /usr/bin/clear
13           echo "                    Menu "
14           echo "   -------------------------------------------------------"
15           echo "   [1] Display System's Current Date and Time".
16           echo "   [2] Display Boot Paths and Autoboot/Autosearch Settings".
17           echo "   [3] Run ioscan with –fNnk options to list all disks".
18           echo "   [4] Run SMH".
19           echo "   [5] Exit".
20           echo "   ===================================="
21           echo
22           echo "Enter Your Choice [1-5] \c: "
23           read  VAR
24           case $VAR  in
25                   1) echo  "Current System Date and Time is `/usr/bin/date`"
26                       echo
27                       echo  "Press any key to go back to the Menu......"
28                       read
29                       ;;
30                   2) /usr/sbin/setboot
31                       echo
32                       echo  "Press any key to go back to the Menu......"
```

```
33                    read
34                    ;;
35                    3) /usr/sbin/ioscan  −fNnkCdisk
36                    echo  "Press any key to go back to the Menu......"
37                    read
38                    ;;
39                    4) /usr/sbin/smh
40                    echo  "Press any key to go back to the Menu......"
41                    read
42                    ;;
43                    5) echo  "Exiting ........."
44                    exit  0
45                    ;;
46                    *) echo  "You have selected an invalid choice".
47                    echo  "Please make a valid choice".
48                    echo  "Press any key to go back to the Menu......"
49                    read
50                    ;;
51          esac
52   done
```

22.4.4   The until-do-done Loop

The until-do-done loop repeats execution of a block of commands until the specified condition becomes true. The only difference between this and the while-do-done loop is that this loop tests condition for false. The general syntax is:

```
until
            condition
do
            command block
done
```

The next script called *until_do_done.sh* does exactly what the *while_do_done.sh* script did. The only difference between the two is that "until false" is defined as opposed to "while true".

 # cat −n until_do_done.sh

```
1    #!/usr/bin/sh
2    # The name of this script is until_do_done.sh.
3    # The author of this script is Asghar Ghori.
4    # The script is created on February 24, 2006.
5    # This script is last modified by Asghar Ghori on April 17, 2008.
6    # This script should be located in /usr/local/bin directory.
7    # The purpose of this script is to show you an example of how a menu driven program can
8    # be included in an until loop so it continues to run until a specific option from the menu is
9    # chosen to exit out.
10   until  false
11   do
12            /usr/bin/clear
```

```
13          echo "                    Menu "
14          echo "    -----------------------------------------------------------"
15          echo "    [1] Display System's Current Date and Time".
16          echo "    [2] Display Boot Paths and Autoboot/Autosearch Settings".
17          echo "    [3] Run ioscan with –fNnk options to list all disks".
18          echo "    [4] Run SMH".
19          echo "    [5] Exit".
20          echo "    ===================================="
21          echo
22          echo "Enter Your Choice [1-5] \c: "
23          read  VAR
24          case $VAR in
25                  1) echo  "Current System Date and Time is `/usr/bin/date`"
26                  echo
27                  echo  "Press any key to go back to the Menu......"
28                  read
29                  ;;
30                  2) /usr/sbin/setboot
31                  echo
32                  echo  "Press any key to go back to the Menu......"
33                  read
34                  ;;
35                  3) /usr/sbin/ioscan  –fNnkCdisk
36                  echo  "Press any key to go back to the Menu......"
37                  read
38                  ;;
39                  4) /usr/sbin/smh
40                  echo  "Press any key to go back to the Menu......"
41                  read
42                  ;;
43                  5) echo  "Exiting ........."
44                  exit  0
45                  ;;
46                  *) echo  "You have selected an invalid choice".
47                  echo  "Please make a valid choice".
48                  echo  "Press any key to go back to the Menu......"
49                  read
50                  ;;
51          esac
52   done
```

22.4.5   Controlling Loop Behavior

There are three commands that may be used to control the behavior of a loop. These commands are *break*, *continue* and *sleep*.

The *break* Command

The *break* command discontinues the execution of a loop immediately and transfers the control to the command following the done keyword.

The *continue* Command

The *continue* command skips execution of the remaining part of the loop and transfers the control back to the beginning of the loop for next iteration.

The *sleep* Command

The *sleep* command suspends the execution of a loop for a time period. It takes the value in seconds. The default is one second.

The next script *file_remove.sh* is a simple text file removal program. It displays a list of files in the current directory and prompts you to enter a text file name to be deleted. If the name entered is a directory, a block DSF, a character DSF or a soft link, the execution of the while-do-done loop will break (the *break* command) and the control will be transferred to the command that immediately follows the done keyword (which is *echo* in *file_remove.sh* script).

If the name supplied is a text file, the script will execute the *rm* command with –i option asking whether to remove the file. If you reply "y", the file will be deleted and the control of the loop will be given back to the start of the loop.

The *sleep* command is supplied with an argument 5. This will force the loop to wait for 5 seconds before running *ls* –F.

The \t escape sequence is used to insert a tab before the text "Here are $PWD Contents:" for better readability.

The last line of the script contains the *exit* command with 0 as an argument. Right after the program is finished, execute *echo* command with $? to verify whether the script ran successfully.

Notice that the colon (:) character is used with the *while* command in the script. This is another way of specifying "true" with while.

```
# cat –n file_remove.sh
1    #!/usr/bin/sh
2    # The name of this script is file_remove.sh.
3    # The author of this script is Asghar Ghori.
4    # The script is created on February 24, 2006.
5    # This script is last modified by Asghar Ghori on April 17, 2008.
6    # This script should be located in /usr/local/bin directory.
7    # The purpose of this script is to explain the usage of the break, continue and sleep
8    # commands in looping constructs.
9    PWD=`/usr/bin/pwd`
10   while  :
11   do
12           echo
13           echo  "\t Here are $PWD Contents:"
14           echo  "\t -------------------------------------------"
15           echo
```

```
16          sleep 5
17          /usr/bin/ls −F
18          echo
19          echo "Enter name of text file you want to remove: \c"
20          read FILE
21          if [ −d $FILE ]
22                  then
23                              echo "This is a directory, not a text file. Enter a text file name."
24                              break
25          elif [ −L $FILE ]
26                  then
27                              echo "This is a symbolic link, not a text file. Enter a text file name."
28                              break
29          elif [ −c $FILE ]
30                  then
31                              echo "This is a character DSF, not a text file. Enter a text file name."
32                              break
33          elif [ −b $FILE ]
34                  then
35                              echo "This is a block DSF, not a text file. Enter a text file name."
36                              break
37          elif [ −p $FILE ]
38                  then
39                              echo "This is a named pipe, not a text file. Enter a text file name."
40                              break
41          elif [ −f $FILE ]
42                  then
43                              echo "Type y to remove $FILE, n if you do not want to:\c"
44                              /usr/bin/rm −i $FILE
45                              echo "The file is removed."
46                              continue
47              fi
48      done
49      echo
50      echo "Good Bye. See you later."
51      exit 0
```

Try running this script and supply a directory name, a block/character DSF, a symbolic file name and a regular text file name, and see the results.

22.4.6   Ignoring Signals

A shell script is terminated when a user interrupts it by pressing the Ctrl+c sequence or by executing the *kill* or *pkill* command with −1, −2, −3, −9 or −15 signal. If you want these signals to be ignored while a script is running, you can make use of the *trap* command. The *trap* command catches a specified signal and ignores it. For example, in *ignore_signals.sh* script, signals 1, 2, 3 and 15 are ignored when the script runs. These signals represent hangup, interrupt, quit and terminate, respectively.

```
1    #!/usr/bin/sh
2    # The name of this script is ignore_signals.sh.
3    # The author of this script is Asghar Ghori.
4    # The script is created on February 24, 2006.
5    # This script is last modified by Asghar Ghori on April 17, 2008.
6    # This script should be located in /usr/local/bin directory.
7    # The purpose of this script is to see how the trap command can be used in scripts to ignore
8    # signals.
9    trap '' 1 2 3 15
10   until false
11   do
12           /usr/bin/clear
13           echo "                    Menu "
14           echo "    ----------------------------------------------------------"
15           echo "    [1] Display System's Current Date and Time".
16           echo "    [2] Display Boot Paths and Autoboot/Autosearch Settings".
17           echo "    [3] Run ioscan with –fNnk options to list all disks".
18           echo "    [4] Run SMH".
19           echo "    [5] Exit".
20           echo "    ===================================="
21           echo
22           echo "Enter Your Choice [1-5] \c: "
23           read  VAR
24           case $VAR  in
25                   1) echo  "Current System Date and Time is `/usr/bin/date`"
26                   echo
27                   echo  "Press any key to go back to the Menu......"
28                   read
29                   ;;
30                   2) /usr/sbin/setboot
31                   echo
32                   echo  "Press any key to go back to the Menu......"
33                   read
34                   ;;
35                   3) /usr/sbin/ioscan  –fNnkCdisk
36                   echo
37                   echo  "Press any key to go back to the Menu......"
38                   read
39                   ;;
40                   4) /usr/sbin/smh
41                   echo  "Press any key to go back to the Menu......"
42                   read
43                   ;;
44                   5) echo  "Exiting ........."
45                   exit  0
46                   ;;
47                   *) echo  "You have selected an invalid choice".
48                   echo  "Please make a valid choice".
```

```
49                    echo  "Press any key to go back to the Menu......"
50                    read
51                    ;;
52           esac
53   done
```

Run this script and try to terminate it by sending signals 1, 2, 3 and 15 using the *kill* or *pkill* command. You will notice that the script will continue to run until you choose option 5 from the menu or send signal –9 from another terminal window.

The *trap* command is normally used in scripts to perform some sort of cleanup or rollback function prior to ending a program after the program encounters a hangup, quit, kill or terminate signal.

Summary

Shell scripting allows you to enclose one or more long and repetitive set of tasks into files called scripts, and run them when needed to accomplish desired results. This saves you a lot of typing. In this chapter you started off with an introduction to shell scripting. You were introduced to the components of a shell script. You wrote simple scripts to gather basic system information, define and manipulate local and environment variables, use and move command line arguments and prompt for user input. You looked at requirements to run scripts and how to debug them.

You then moved on to more sophisticated and complicated scripts. You wrote and analyzed logical constructs based on the if-then-fi, if-then-else-fi, if-then-elif-fi and case structures. You understood the purpose of exit codes and test conditions.

Finally, you learned how to create scripts that used for-do-done, while-do-done and until-do-done looping constructs. You understood the use of the *break, continue* and *sleep* commands within these loops. At the end you looked at an example that explained the usage of the *trap* command to ignore signals.

## 23

Basic Networking

This chapter covers the following major topics:

- ✓ What is a Network?
- ✓ Network topologies – bus, star, ring and hybrid
- ✓ Network access methods – CSMA/CD, token passing, FDDI, ATM, HIPPI and Hyperfabric
- ✓ LAN cables
- ✓ Introduction to OSI Reference Networking Model
- ✓ The seven layers of the OSI Model
- ✓ Basic network terminology – gateway, protocol, port, socket, router, switch, bridge, repeater and hub
- ✓ Understand packet encapsulation and de-encapsulation
- ✓ What is peer to peer networking?
- ✓ Introduction to the TCP/IP protocol stack and the TCP/IP layers
- ✓ Understand and use MAC addresses, ARP and RARP
- ✓ Understand and define a system's hostname
- ✓ Understand IP addresses, network classes and IP multiplexing
- ✓ Divide a network into multiple, smaller sub-networks and the role of subnet mask

23.1   What is a Network?

A *network* is formed when two or more computers are interconnected to share resources and information. The computers may be connected via wired or wireless means. You need a cable, connectors, network ports and the software that support the connectivity to connect two computers. To interconnect several computers so that they can talk to one another, you need an interconnect device such as a hub, switch, router or a gateway, in addition to cables and connectors. A network also typically has other shared devices such as printers, plotters, disk storage and tape libraries. Among these, printers are the most common. Throughout this and subsequent chapters the term *node* is used to refer to shared networked devices including computers and printers. Figure 23-1 illustrates five nodes – four computers and one printer.

There are two types of networks – *Local Area Network* (LAN) and *Wide Area Network* (WAN).

A LAN is composed of nodes usually located at a single physical location such as a building or campus. Figure 23-1 illustrates a typical LAN.

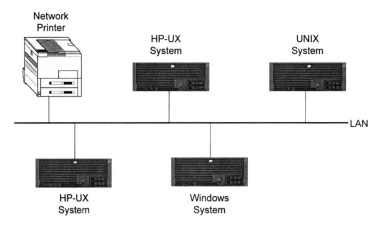

Figure 23-1 Local Area Network

LANs typically use *Ethernet* protocol to transfer data from one node to another. Ethernet was developed in the late 1970s and is presently the global standard for data transmission in today's computer networks. Some of the reasons for its popularity include support for a variety of cable types, topologies, affordability, scalability and native support within almost all network operating systems out there. The data transmission speed on an Ethernet LAN ranges from 10Mbps (*megabits per second*) to 1Gbps (*gigabits per second*).

A WAN is composed of individual nodes or entire LANs that may be located geographically apart in different cities, countries or continents. Devices such as routers and gateways are employed to form a WAN using phone lines, satellites, wireless and other means. Figure 23-2 shows a typical WAN.

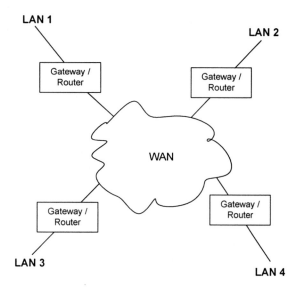

Figure 23-2 Wide Area Network

23.2 Network Topologies

A *network topology* refers to how nodes, interconnect devices and physical media are coupled together. There are three common types of physical topologies: *bus*, *star* and *ring*. The fourth type is a combination of bus and star, and is known as *hybrid*.

The following sub-sections discuss these topologies.

23.2.1 Bus Topology

The bus topology consists of a main backbone cable with a terminator connector at either end. All nodes are attached to the backbone. This type of topology is relatively inexpensive and easy to implement. Figure 23-1 shows a bus topology network diagram with a line across representing a backbone cable.

The primary disadvantage with this topology is that a break in the backbone cable or fault in one of the terminators might shut the entire network down.

23.2.2 Star Topology

The star topology uses an interconnect device called *switch* (or *hub*), with each node connected directly to it. Data packets must pass through this device to reach their destination. This topology is widely used in Ethernet networks. Figure 23-3 illustrates a star topology based network diagram.

Star topology networks are easier to deploy and manage, and are highly scalable. Nodes can be attached or detached without any disruption to the function of the network. If there is a broken cable, only the node using it is affected, however, if an interconnect device is down, all nodes connected to it become inaccessible.

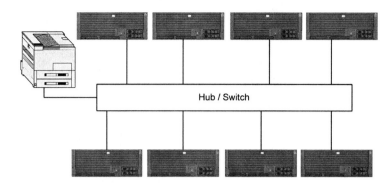

Figure 23-3 Star Topology

23.2.3 Ring Topology

The ring topology is a wiring scheme that allows information to pass from one node to another in a circle or ring. Nodes are joined in the shape of a closed loop so that each node is joined directly to two other nodes, one on either side of it. Figure 23-4 shows a ring topology network diagram.

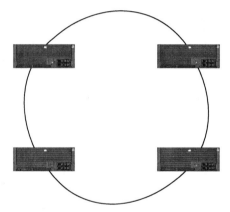

Figure 23-4 Ring Topology

The disadvantage with the ring topology is that if one of the cables in the ring breaks, all nodes in the ring become unreachable. This type of topology is more difficult to configure and wire than other topologies. The token ring protocol uses this topology on token ring networks.

23.2.4 Hybrid Topology

Corporate networks are generally formed using a combination of bus and star topologies. Interconnect devices are installed on different floors of a building or in different buildings and campuses using the bus topology scheme. The star topology is employed to join individual nodes to the interconnect devices.

23.3 Network Access Methods

Network access refers to the technique to send data over a physical medium. When a node wants to send a data packet to another node, it first needs to know if another node on the network is currently using the medium. There are two methods commonly employed for network access: *Carrier Sense Multiple Access with Collision Detection* (CSMA/CD) and *Token Passing*. CSMA/CD is used on Ethernet networks and token passing on IBM's token ring networks.

23.3.1 CSMA/CD

When data transfer occurs between two nodes, the Ethernet protocol tries to determine whether the network medium is being used by another node. In case the medium is in use, the Ethernet protocol waits until the medium is freed up. If, by chance, two nodes detect that the medium is free, both try to transmit their data packets simultaneously. This results in a collision situation. With Ethernet, each node that sends data over the medium also continuously checks for collision occurrences. If a collision is detected, other nodes are forced to wait and retry later at random time instances.

23.3.2 Token Passing

Token passing is a technique in which a node that wants to send data over the medium must capture a data frame called *token*. The token travels on the ring constantly from node to node in a defined sequence. If a node wants to transmit data, it has to await and get the token. As soon as it gets the token, it attaches its data to the token and passes the token to the next node in the series. Each node along the way determines if the attached data is intended for it. If the destination address does not match the node address, the token is passed to the next node until it reaches the correct destination node. The receiving node detaches the data, frees up the token and passes it on to the next node.

One of the nodes on the token ring network monitors the token activity so that if the token is lost, it generates a new one. If the destination node dies and no node is able to receive data attached to the token, this node detaches the data and mark the token free.

23.3.3 Other Network Access Methods

HP-UX natively support other physical medium technologies including *Fiber Distributed Data Interface* (FDDI), *Asynchronous Transfer Mode* (ATM), *High Performance Parallel Interface* (HIPPI) and *Hyperfabric*.

FDDI uses fiber cables in a dual ring topology that provides redundancy. ATM uses switching techniques. HIPPI and Hyperfabric allow high-speed point-to-point and node-to-node data communication links, respectively.

23.4 LAN Cables

Cables are run to connect nodes to permit data transmission among them. Ethernet and token ring are two physical medium protocols commonly employed in computer networks.

Ethernet LANs primarily use two types of cables: *Twisted Pair* (*Shielded Twisted Pair* – STP and *Unshielded Twisted Pair* – UTP) and *fiber*. The Ethernet naming convention is based on the type of cable, supported maximum speed and allowable maximum distance. For example, 10Base-T, 100Base-T and 1000Base-T use UTP cables and are employed in star topology networks. They support maximum 10Mbps, 100Mbps and 1Gbps speeds at distances of up to 100 meters per segment. All three cable types mentioned use copper wires.

Ethernet is also supported on fiber cables at 1Gbps and on much longer distances. Ethernet standard for fibre is called 1000Base-FX and is used with 1000BaseSX card types.

Token ring networks usually use STP cables and support up to 1000Mbps data transfer rate.

Cables are categorized based on their electrical characteristics. Category 5 (or Cat 5) and Category 5e (or Cat 5 enhanced) copper cables are widely used today. These cables are good to support data transmissions at up to 100Mbps speed, but also used on 1000Mbps networks. Cat 6 has been available for 1000Mbps data transmissions and is preferred over Cat 5 and Cat 5e.

23.5   Introduction to OSI Reference Model

The *Open Systems Interconnection* (OSI) is a reference networking model developed in the early 1980s by the *International Organization for Standardization* (universally abbreviated as ISO) to provide guidelines to networking product manufacturers. These guidelines has enabled them to develop products that can communicate with each other's software and hardware network products in a heterogeneous computing environment. The OSI reference model is defined and divided for ease in seven layers (Figure 23-5), with each layer performing a unique function independent of other layers.

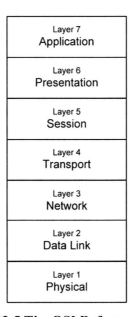

Figure 23-5 The OSI Reference Model

Each layer in the model interacts directly with two layers, one above it and one below it, except the top and the bottom layers. Functionality provided by the seven layers can be divided into three categories: application (such as FTP or telnet), set of transport/network protocols (such as TCP and IP) and related software and hardware (such as cables).

The function of the seven layers can be segregated into two groups. One group, containing the upper three layers (5 to 7), relates to user applications such as formatting of data. The other group, containing the lower four layers (1 to 4), add transport information such as address of the destination node.

Each layer of the OSI reference model is explained in the following sub-sections.

23.5.1   Layer 7: The Application Layer

The *application* layer is where a user or program requests initiation of some kind of service on a remote node. Utilities and programs that work at this layer include *ftp, telnet, rlogin, remsh, rcp*, SNMP, SMTP, HTTP, TFTP, NFS, DHCP, secure shell and X windows. On the remote node, server daemons for these services (*ftpd, telnetd, rlogind* and so on) respond by providing the requested services. In other words, client and server programs for *ftp, telnet, http* etc. work at this layer.

Gateway

A device called *gateway* works at this layer. Actually, it works in such a way that it covers all seven layers. A gateway links two networks that run completely different protocols, viz., TCP/IP and NetBEUI, or TCP/IP and IPX/SPX, and enables them to talk to each other.

Protocol

A *protocol* is a set of rules governing the exchange of data between two nodes. These rules include how data is formatted, coded and controlled. The rules also provide error handling, speed matching and data packet sequencing. In other words, a protocol is a common language that all nodes on the network speak and understand. Some common protocols are TCP, IP, ICMP, Ethernet, NetBEUI and AppleTalk. Protocols are defined in the */etc/protocols* file. A sample */etc/protocols* file is shown below:

```
# cat /etc/protocols
. . . . . . . .
ip        0     IP       # internet protocol, pseudo protocol number
icmp      1     ICMP     # internet control message protocol
igmp      2     IGMP     # internet group management protocol
ggp       3     GGP      # gateway-gateway protocol
tcp       6     TCP      # transmission control protocol
egp       8     EGP      # exterior gateway protocol
pup       12    PUP      # PARC universal packet protocol
udp       17    UDP      # user datagram protocol
. . . . . . . .
```

The first column lists a protocol's official name, the second column shows the protocol number and the third column identifies any associated aliases.

23.5.2   Layer 6: The Presentation Layer

The *presentation* layer converts incoming data from the application layer into a format understandable by the remote machine where this message is destined. The layer manages the presentation of the data to be independent of the node hardware architecture.

23.5.3   Layer 5: The Session Layer

The *session* layer sets up, synchronizes, sequences and terminates communication session established between a client program at the source node and corresponding server program at the

---

destination node. This layer deals with session and connection coordination between source and destination nodes.

23.5.4   Layer 4: The Transport Layer

The *transport* layer manages end-to-end data transfer reliability. It makes sure that data from the source to destination arrives error-free. It retransmits the data if it does not reach the destination error-free. The protocols that work at this layer are *Transmission Control Protocol* (TCP) and *User Datagram Protocol* (UDP).

TCP

TCP is reliable, connection-oriented, point-to-point, but slow. When a stream of packets is sent to the destination node using TCP, the destination node checks for errors and packet sequencing upon its arrival. Each packet contains information such as IP addresses for both source and destination nodes, source and destination port numbers, the data, a sequence number and checksum fields. The TCP protocol at the source node establishes a point-to-point connection with the peer TCP protocol at the destination. When the packet is received by the receiving TCP, an acknowledgement is sent back. If the packet contains an error or is lost in transit, the destination node requests the source node to resend the packet. This ensures guaranteed data delivery and makes TCP reliable. Due to acknowledgment and handshaking, some overhead signals are added to TCP, making it slow. TCP is analogous to a telephone communication session between two parties.

TCP Window

It is important to mention the concept of *TCP window* here that affects data packet transmission performance and, therefore, contribute to overall network performance. As you know, TCP at the destination node, acknowledges all data packets as it receives them. The source node does not send more data packets than what the TCP window on the destination node can hold, until the source node gets an acknowledgment back from the destination node. Upon receiving an acknowledgment, the source node sends another stream of packets that the TCP window on the destination node can hold. The default TCP window size is 64KB. If this value is increased, the source node is able to transmit more data packets to the destination. This results in less number of acknowledgment signals going back, which contributes to improving overall network performance.

UDP

UDP is unreliable, connectionless, multi-point and faster than TCP. If a packet is lost or contains errors upon arrival at the destination node, the source node is unaware of it. The destination node does not send an acknowledgement back to the source node. UDP is normally used for broadcast purposes. There are no overhead signals involved, which makes UDP faster than TCP. UDP is analogous to a radio broadcast, where there is no connection between parties.

TCP vs. UDP

Differences between TCP and UDP are summarized in Table 23-1.

TCP	UDP
Reliable	Unreliable
Connection-oriented	Connectionless
Point-to-point	Multipoint

TCP	UDP
Slow	Fast
Sequenced	Unsequenced
Acknowledgement	No acknowledgement
Uses TCP window for flow control	N/A

Table 23-1 TCP vs UDP

Ports and Sockets

Both TCP and UDP use ports and sockets for data transmission between a client and its associated server program. A port is either well-known or private. A well-known port is pre-defined for a specific application to be used by that application only. It is standardized across all network operating systems including HP-UX. Well-known ports are defined in the */etc/services* file, an excerpt of which is shown below:

```
# cat /etc/services
. . . . . . . .
# The form for each entry is:
# <official service name> <port number/protocol name> <aliases>
#
ftp         21/tcp                      # File Transfer Protocol (Control)
telnet      23/tcp                      # Virtual Terminal Protocol
smtp        25/tcp                      # Simple Mail Transfer Protocol
time        37/tcp     timeserver       # Time
time        37/udp     timeserver       #
rlp         39/udp     resource         # Resource Location Protocol
whois       43/tcp     nicname          # Who Is
domain      53/tcp     nameserver       # Domain Name Service
domain      53/udp     nameserver       #
bootps      67/udp                      # Bootstrap Protocol Server
. . . . . . . .
```

The first column lists the official name of a network service, the second column contains associated well-known port number and the transport layer protocol the service uses, and the third column identifies any associated aliases.

Some common services and the ports they listen on are: *telnet* on port 23, *ftp* on 21, *sendmail* on 25, *http* on 80 and *ntp* on 123. Well-known ports range between 0 and 1023, inclusive.

A private port, on the other hand, is a random number generated when a client application attempts to establish a communication session with its server process. Private port numbers usually range between 1024 and 65535, inclusive.

When a *telnet* request is initiated on *hp01* (source node with IP address 192.168.1.201) to get into *hp02* (destination node with IP address 192.168.1.202), a private port number (4352 for example) is generated and appended to the IP address of *hp01* to form a source-side socket. This socket information is included in data packets carrying the *telnet* request to *hp02*. Similarly, the IP address of *hp02* is appended by the well-known *telnet* port number from the */etc/services* file to form a destination-side socket. This socket information too is added to data packets. Here is what the two sockets will look like:

| Source node (*hp01*) | : 192.168.1.201.4352 (IP address + private port number) |
| Destination node (*hp02*) | : 192.168.1.202.23 (IP address + well-known port number) |

A combination of the two sockets distinctively identifies this *telnet* communication session among several other possible *telnet* sessions established at that time.

23.5.5   Layer 3: The Network Layer

The *network* layer routes and forwards data packets to the right destination using the right network path. This layer manages data addressing and delivery functions. Protocols that work at this level are Internet Protocol (IP), Address Resolution Protocol (ARP), Reverse Address Resolution Protocol (RARP), Internet Control Message Protocol (ICMP), Serial Line Internet Protocol (SLIP), Point to Point Protocol (PPP), BootP, etc.

Router

A *router* is a device that works at the network layer, routing data packets from one network to another. The source and destination networks may be located thousands of miles apart. A router is widely employed on corporate networks and the internet.

23.5.6   Layer 2: The Data Link Layer

The *data link* layer manages the delivery of data packets beyond the physical network. This layer does packet framing and provides error detection functionality. Protocols available at this layer include Ethernet, IEEE 802.3, fast Ethernet, gigabit Ethernet, token ring, IEEE 802.5 and Fibre Distributed Data Interchange (FDDI).

Switch and Bridge

Network devices – switches and bridges – work at the data link layer.

A *switch* looks at the MAC address contained within each incoming packet and determines the output port to forward the packet to. Once it has that information, it switches the packet to the port and the packet ultimately reaches the destination node. A switch offers dedicated bandwidth to data flow.

A *bridge* is used to join LANs provided they use a common protocol (for example, Ethernet-Ethernet or token ring-token ring). A bridge examines MAC address contained within each data packet. If a match is found on the local network, the packet is passed to it, otherwise, the packet is forwarded to the destination on the other LAN.

23.5.7   Layer 1: The Physical Layer

The *physical* layer transmits data packets through the network. It describes network hardware characteristics including electrical, mechanical, optical and functional specifications to ensure compatibility between communicating nodes. Protocols available at this layer include 10Base-T, 100Base-T and 1000Base-T.

Repeater and Hub

Network devices – repeaters and hubs – work at this layer. Also falling under this layer are cables, connectors and LAN interfaces.

A *repeater* is a network device that takes data signals as input, filters out unwanted noise, amplifies the signals and regenerates them to cover extended distances.

A *hub* is a network device that receives data from one or more directions and forwards it to one or more directions. The bandwidth of a hub is shared among connected, active nodes. For example, the speed per port on a 100Mbps 12-port hub is 100/12, which is approximately equal to 8Mbps. This means each node is able to communicate at 8Mbps. This calculation is based on the assumption that all ports on the hub have nodes hooked up and being used.

23.5.8   Summary of OSI Layers

Table 23-2 summarizes OSI layer functions.

OSI Layer	Description
Application (7)	Users and programs request initiation of some kind of service on a remote system. Protocols/applications used at this layer include telnet, ftp, rlogin, rcp, remsh, SMTP, SNMP, NFS, HTTP, DNS, TFTP, DHCP and X Windows.
Presentation (6)	Manages presentation of data to be independent of computer hardware architecture.
Session (5)	Establishes, synchronizes, sequences and terminates communication session setup between source and destination nodes.
Transport (4)	Manages end-to-end data transfer reliability. Protocols used at this layer are TCP and UDP.
Network (3)	Manages data addressing and delivery functions. Protocols used at this layer include IP, ARP, RARP, ICMP, SLIP, PPP and BootP.
Data Link (2)	Performs packet framing and provides error detection functionality. Protocols used at this layer include Ethernet, IEEE 802.3, fast Ethernet, gigabit Ethernet, token ring, IEEE 802.5 and FDDI.
Physical (1)	Describes network hardware characteristics including electrical, mechanical, optical and functional specifications.

Table 23-2 OSI Layer Functions

23.5.9   Encapsulation and De-encapsulation

Data transmission from source node to destination node takes place in the form of packets. When a message is created at the application layer, subsequent layers add header information to the message as it passes down toward the physical layer. Headers contain layer-specific information. When the message along with header information, reaches the physical layer, it is referred to as a *packet*. The process of forming a packet through the seven layers is called *encapsulation*.

The packet is transmitted as a stream of 1s and 0s through the medium to the destination node where the physical layer receives the data stream and a reverse process begins. Headers are detached at each subsequent layer as the message passes up toward the application layer. This reverse process is referred to as *de-encapsulation*. Figure 23-6 illustrates encapsulation and de-encapsulation processes.

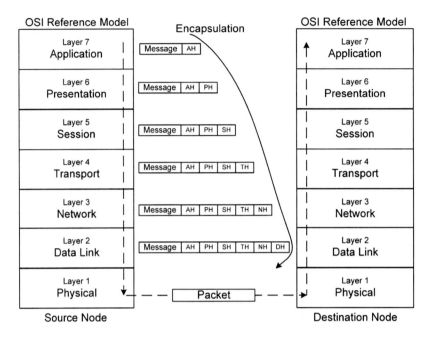

Figure 23-6 Encapsulation and De-encapsulation

23.5.10   Peer-to-Peer Model

Each layer on the source node acts as a peer layer to its corresponding layer on the destination node, making the OSI model *peer-to-peer*. Header information attached at the application layer can only be read, understood and removed by the application layer on the receiving side. Similarly, header attached at the session layer can only be read, understood and removed by the session layer on the receiving node, and so on for the other layers.

23.6   Introduction to TCP/IP

The *Transmission Control Protocol / Internet Protocol* (TCP/IP) is a suite of protocols developed by the US Department of Defense in 1969. Today, it is the global standard of information exchange. Although, there are scores of protocols within the TCP/IP suite, the name is derived from the two key protocols: Transmission Control Protocol (TCP) and Internet Protocol (IP).

TCP/IP uses the client/server model of communication in which a client program on a source node requests a service and the server program on the destination node responds. TCP/IP communication is primarily point-to-point, meaning each communication is between two nodes.

23.6.1   TCP/IP Layers

TCP/IP is layered similar to the OSI model. It is, in fact, based on the OSI reference model. Some vendors have defined the TCP/IP suite in four layers, while others in five. Figure 23-7 shows the suite in four layers, and compares it with the OSI reference model.

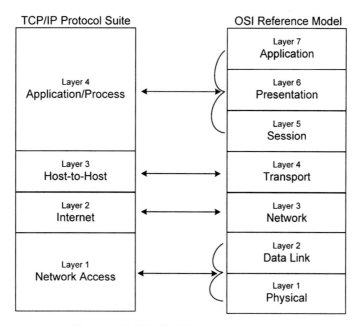

Figure 23-7 TCP/IP Protocol Suite

The figure illustrates the TCP/IP protocol stack on the left hand side. It is compared with the OSI reference model. Notice that the bottom four layers are the same, only the names are dissimilar. The difference lies at the top three layers where TCP/IP merges the application, presentation and session layer functionalities into one layer, collectively referred to as the *application* layer. For a detailed understanding of each layer and how they interact, refer to the earlier sub-section "Introduction to OSI Reference Model".

23.6.2   MAC Address

Medium Access Control (MAC) is a unique 48-bit address used to identify the correct destination node for data packets transmitted from a source node. The data packets include MAC addresses for both the source and the destination nodes. A network protocol called *Address Resolution Protocol* (ARP), maps the MAC address to the destination node's IP address.

MAC address is also referred to as *station* address, *physical* address, *link level* address, *Ethernet* address and *hardware* address.

Use the *nwmgr* or *lanscan* command to list all LAN interfaces available on the system along with associated MAC (station) addresses:

 # nwmgr

Name/ ClassInstance	Interface State	Station Address	Sub- system	Interface Type	Related Interface
==========	=======	=============	=====	=======	======
lan0	UP	0x00306E469D5C	either	10/100Base-TX 4 Port	
lan1	UP	0x00306E469D5D	either	10/100Base-TX 4 Port	
lan2	UP	0x00306E469D5E	either	10/100Base-TX 4 Port	
lan3	UP	0x00306E469D5F	either	10/100Base-TX 4 Port	

lan4		UP	0x00306EA7AC2D	either	1000Base-T
lan5		UP	0x00306E2DCCD4	iether	10/100Base-TX 4 Port
lan6		UP	0x00306E2DCCD5	iether	10/100Base-TX 4 Port
lan7		UP	0x00306E2DCCD6	iether	10/100Base-TX 4 Port
lan8		UP	0x00306E2DCCD7	iether	10/100Base-TX 4 Port

lanscan

Hardware Path	Station Address	Crd In#	Hdw State	Net-Interface NamePPA	NM ID	MAC Type	HP-DLPI Support	DLPI Mjr#
0/0/6/0/0/4/0	0x00306E469D5C	0	UP	lan0 snap0	1	ETHER	Yes	119
0/0/6/0/0/5/0	0x00306E469D5D	1	UP	lan1 snap1	2	ETHER	Yes	119
0/0/6/0/0/6/0	0x00306E469D5E	2	UP	lan2 snap2	3	ETHER	Yes	119
0/0/6/0/0/7/0	0x00306E469D5F	3	UP	lan3 snap3	4	ETHER	Yes	119
0/0/8/0/0/4/0	0x00306EA7AC2D	4	UP	lan4 snap4	5	ETHER	Yes	119
0/0/14/0/0/4/0	0x00306E2DCCD4	5	UP	lan5 snap5	6	ETHER	Yes	119
0/0/14/0/0/5/0	0x00306E2DCCD5	6	UP	lan6 snap6	7	ETHER	Yes	119
0/0/14/0/0/6/0	0x00306E2DCCD6	7	UP	lan7 snap7	8	ETHER	Yes	119
0/0/14/0/0/7/0	0x00306E2DCCD7	8	UP	lan8 snap8	9	ETHER	Yes	119

The station addresses shown in the output are in hexadecimal.

You can also use the *lanadmin* command to determine the hardware address of a LAN interface. Run the command as follows to find the MAC address for *lan4*:

```
# lanadmin –a 4
Station Address     =  0x00306ea7ac2d
```

To view MAC addresses using SMH, follow the links:

☞ Go to SMH → Networking and Communications → Network Interfaces Configuration → Network Interface Cards. Highlight a card and press Enter to view the MAC address.

Alternatively, you can run the *ncweb* command, which is equivalent to SMH → Networking and Communications, to display MAC addresses.

23.6.3   Address Resolution Protocol (ARP)

As you know that IP and MAC addresses work hand in hand with each other and a combination of both is critical to identifying the correct destination node. A protocol called *Address Resolution Protocol* (ARP) is used to enable IP and MAC addresses to work together. ARP determines the MAC address of the destination node when its IP address is already known.

ARP broadcasts messages over the network requesting each alive node to reply with its MAC and IP addresses. The addresses received are cached locally by the node in a special memory area called *ARP Cache*. To view all cached IP and MAC addresses, run the *arp* command with –a option:

```
# arp –a
192.168.1.1 (192.168.1.1)     at 0:40:f4:e3:ce:64  ether
sun05       (192.168.1.80)  at 8:0:20:a4:76:ab   ether
hp02        (192.168.1.202) at 0:60:b0:b6:ca:e3  ether
```

Entries in the ARP cache are normally kept for 10 minutes and then removed. These entries can be added to or removed/modified using the *arp* command.

To remove an entry from the ARP cache for the host *hp02*:

> # **arp –d hp02**

To determine the MAC address for *hp02* from *hp03*, issue the *arp* command on *hp03*:

> # **arp hp02**
> hp02   (192.168.1.202) at 0:60:b0:b6:ca:e3 ether

The *arp* command proves useful when you suspect duplicate IP addresses on the network. Check its output for any duplicate entries.

23.6.4   Reverse Address Resolution Protocol (RARP)

The reverse of ARP is possible with the *Reverse Address Resolution Protocol* (RARP). This protocol gets the IP address of a remote node if you already know the MAC address of it. RARP is typically used by DHCP, network printers, old diskless HP-UX workstations and X terminals, as they know MAC addresses, but not IP addresses.

23.6.5   Hostname

A *hostname* is a unique alphanumeric name assigned to a node. It is normally allotted based on the purpose and primary use of the node, although any naming standard can be followed in accordance with corporate IT naming convention policy. For example, the hostname "hpdbp001" in a multi-vendor environment can be assigned to the first HP-UX production database server and *sndbd003* can be given to the third SUN Solaris development database server.

The hostname is defined in the startup configuration file */etc/rc.config.d/netconf* via the HOSTNAME variable. It can be set or modified using the *set_parms* command:

> # **set_parms hostname**
> For the system to operate correctly, you must assign it a unique system name or "hostname". The hostname can be a simple name (example: widget) or an Internet fully-qualified domain name (example: widget.region.mycorp.com).
> A simple name, or each dot (.) separated component of a domain name, must:
>   * Start with an uppercase or lowercase letter.
>   * End with a letter or digit.
>   * Contain only letters, digits, underscore (_), or dash (-). The underscore (_) is not recommended.
>   * Contain no more than 63 characters per component.
>   * Contain no more than 255 total characters.
>   * Each dot (.) separated component of a domain name, can start with a digit.
> NOTE: The first or only component of a hostname should contain no more than 8 characters and the full hostname should contain no more than 63 characters for maximum compatibility with HP-UX software.
>
> The current hostname is hp01.
> _____
> Enter the system name, then press [Enter] or just press [Enter] to retain the current host name (hp01):

23.6.6   IP Address

IP stands for *Internet Protocol* and represents a unique 32-bit software address that every single node on the network must have in order to communicate with other nodes. Every data packet sent out from a source node contains the destination node's IP address to determine the correct recipient of the packet and the route to be taken to reach that destination. MAC and IP addresses work together to identify the correct LAN interface.

An IP address consists of four 8-bit octets separated by the period character. Each octet can have values between 0 and 255 (00000000 to 11111111) inclusive, based on 2^8 (2x2x2x2x2x2x2x2=256) formula. An IP address can be determined in both binary and decimal notations. Given an IP address in binary, you can convert it into decimal, and vice versa. For instance, an address 192.168.1.202 is shown below in both notations:

11000000.10101000.00000001.11001010	(binary notation)
128+64 128+32+8 1 128+64+8+2	
192 . 168 . 1 . 202	(decimal notation)

Each bit in an octet has a weight based on its position in the octet. Figure 23-8 depicts that as either 0 or 1.

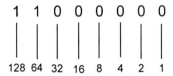

Figure 23-8 Binary to Decimal Conversion

The two left-most bits in the first octet of the IP address given above are 1. Based on the formula, they add up to 192. The second octet has the 1st, 3rd and the 5th left-most bits set to 1, which sum up to 168; and so on for the last two octets.

To view IP addresses assigned to LAN interfaces, use the *netstat* or *ifconfig* commands:

```
# netstat –in
Name      Mtu      Network      Address        Ipkts    Ierrs   Opkts    Oerrs   Coll
lo0       32808    127.0.0.0    127.0.0.1      290644   0       290644   0       0
lan4      1500     192.168.1.0  192.168.1.201  758505   0       101016   0       523
# ifconfig lan4
lan4: flags=1843<UP,BROADCAST,RUNNING,MULTICAST,CKO>
     inet 192.168.1.201 netmask ffffff00 broadcast 192.168.1.255
```

You can also use SMH (or *ncweb* command) to view IP addresses. Follow the links below:

☞Go to SMH → Networking and Communications → Network Interfaces Configuration → Network Interface Cards.

The explosive growth of the internet, the presence of an extremely large number of nodes and an ever increasing demand for additional addresses, the conventional IP address space, which is 2^{32}

(four octets) and provides approximately 4.3 billion addresses, is almost used up. To meet the future demand, a new version of IP address space has been introduced and is now available. This new version is referred to as *IPv6* (IP version 6). IPv6 addresses are 128-bit and provide 2^{128} (16 octets) additional addresses. Also, IPv6 provides simplified packet header format, better routing capabilities, enhanced security controls and many other new and enhanced features as compared to the conventional IP address space.

23.6.7   Network Classes

Each IP address is divided into two portions: a *network* portion and a *node* portion. The *network* portion identifies the correct destination network and the *node* portion identifies the correct destination node on that network.

Based on how many bits are allocated to the network portion, there are five useable IP address classes: A, B, C, D and E. Classes A, B and C are widely used, while classes D and E are dedicated for multicast networks and scientific purposes respectively. The following provides an explanation of classes A, B and C.

Class A

Class A IP addresses are used for networks with an extremely large number of nodes. The first octet defines the network address and the rest are allocated to nodes. Figure 23-9 displays the division of bits in a class A IP address.

Figure 23-9 Class A Address

The total number of useable network addresses in class A can be up to $2^{8-1} - 2$ (126) and the total number of useable node addresses can be up to $2^{24} - 2$ (16,777,214). Two is subtracted in both calculations because addresses with all 0s in the first octet and all 1s in the last octet are reserved. Also, one network bit is subtracted from 8 to get 2^7 network numbers since 0 is always reserved. The network address range for class A networks is between 0 and 127 (00000000 to 01111111). See the example below that also shows reserved addresses:

```
00001010.01111001.00110011.11010001        (binary notation)
   10    .  121  .  51  .  209              (decimal notation)

10.121.51.0           (network address)
10.121.51.255         (broadcast address)
```

0 and 255 in the decimal notation are network and broadcast addresses and are always reserved. Class A IP addresses always begin with 0 as shown in the binary notation.

Class B

Class B IP addresses are used for mid-sized networks. The first two octets define the network address and the remaining are allocated to nodes. See Figure 23-10.

Network bits		Network bits		Host bits		Host bits

Figure 23-10 Class B Address

The total number of useable network addresses in class B can be up to 2^{16-2} (16,384) and the total number of useable node addresses can be up to $2^{16} - 2$ (65,534). The first two bits in class B network addresses are reserved and, therefore, not used in calculation. The network address range for class B networks is between 128 and 191 (**10**000000 to **10**111111). See the example below that also shows reserved addresses:

10100001.01111001.00110011.11010001   (binary notation)
   161   .   121   .   51   .   209   (decimal notation)

161.121.51.**0**   (network address)
161.121.51.**255**   (broadcast address)

Class B IP addresses always begin with 10 as shown in the binary notation.

Class C

Class C IP addresses are used for small networks with not more than 254 nodes. The first three octets define the network address and the fourth is allocated to nodes. Refer to Figure 23-11.

Network bits		Network bits		Network bits		Host bits

Figure 23-11 Class C Address

The total number of useable network addresses in class C can be up to 2^{24-3} (2,097,152) and the total number of useable node addresses can be up to $2^{8} - 2$ (254). The first three bits in the network address are reserved and, therefore, not used in calculation. The network address range for class C networks is between 192 and 223 (**110**00000 to **110**11111). See the example below that also shows reserved addresses:

11010111.01111001.00110011.11010001   (binary notation)
   215   .   121   .   51   .   209   (decimal notation)

215.121.51.**0**   (network address)
215.121.51.**255**   (broadcast address)

Class C IP addresses always begin with 110 as shown in the binary notation.

Class D ranges from 224 to 239 and class E from 240 to 255.

23.6.8   Subnetting

Subnetting is a method by which a large network address space can be divided into several smaller and more manageable logical sub-networks, commonly referred to as *subnets*. Subnetting usually results in reduced network traffic, improved network performance, and de-centralized and easier administration, among other benefits.

Subnetting does not touch the network bits, it makes use of the node bits only.

The following should be kept in mind when working with subnetting:

✓ Subnetting does not increase the number of IP addresses in a network. In fact, it reduces the number of useable IP addresses.
✓ All nodes in a given subnet must have the same subnet mask.
✓ Each subnet acts as a separate network and requires a router to talk to other subnets.
✓ The first and the last IP addresses in a subnet (similar to a network) are reserved. The first address points to the subnet itself and the last is the broadcast address.

Subnetting employs using required number of node bits. For example, if you wish to divide a class C network address of 192.168.12.0 with default netmask of 255.255.255.0 into 6 useable subnets each with 30 useable node IP addresses, you need 3 left-most node bits (highlighted) from the right-most octet (node octet), as shown below:

192 . 168 . 12 . 0
11000000.10101000.00001100.**000**00000

Here is the formula to calculate useable subnets. 2 subnet bits give $2^2 - 2 = 2$ subnets, 3 subnet bits give $2^3 - 2 = 6$ subnets, 4 subnet bits give $2^4 - 2 = 14$ subnets, 5 subnet bits give $2^5 - 2 = 30$ subnets, 6 subnet bits give $2^6 - 2 = 62$ subnets, 7 subnet bits give $2^7 - 2 = 126$ subnets and so on. This formula is applicable to determine number of useable subnets created out of a class A, B or C network address.

Similarly, use the same formula to determine number of useable node addresses. 2 node bits give $2^2 - 2 = 2$ IP addresses, 3 node bits give $2^3 - 2 = 6$ IP addresses, 4 node bits give $2^4 - 2 = 14$ IP addresses, 5 node bits give $2^5 - 2 = 30$ IP addresses, 6 node bits give $2^6 - 2 = 62$ IP addresses, 7 node bits give $2^7 - 2 = 126$ IP addresses and so on. This formula is applicable to determine number of useable node addresses created out of a class A, B or C network address.

As an example, suppose there are 3 subnet bits available to work with. These bits would generate eight combinations – 000, 001, 010, 011, 100, 101, 110 and 111. The first and the last set of values (000 and 111) are reserved for network and broadcast addresses. This leaves the remaining 6 combinations useable. Table 23-3 lists the combinations along with subnet IP, range of useable IP addresses available within the subnet that can be assigned to nodes and broadcast subnet addresses.

Subnet Bits	Subnet IP	First Useable IP	Last Useable IP	Broadcast Subnet IP
000	Reserved for subnet address			
001	192.168.12.32	192.168.12.33	192.168.12.62	192.168.12.63
010	192.168.12.64	192.168.12.65	192.168.12.94	192.168.12.95
011	192.168.12.96	192.168.12.97	192.168.12.126	192.168.12.127
100	192.168.12.128	192.168.12.129	192.168.12.158	192.168.12.159
101	192.168.12.160	192.168.12.161	192.168.12.190	192.168.12.191
110	192.168.12.192	192.168.12.193	192.168.12.222	192.168.12.223
111	Reserved for subnet broadcast address			

Table 23-3 Subnetting

23.6.9   Subnet Mask

After a network address is subnetted, you need to determine something called *subnet mask* or *netmask*. The subnet mask is the network portion plus the subnet bits. In other words, the subnet mask segregates the network bits from the node bits. It is used by routers to identify the start and end of the network/subnet portion and the start and end of the node portion of a given IP address.

The subnet mask, like an IP address, can be represented in either decimal or binary notation. The 1s in the subnet mask identify the subnet bits and 0s identify the node bits. The default subnet masks for class A, B and C networks are 255.0.0.0, 255.255.0.0 and 255.255.255.0, respectively.

To determine the subnet mask of the class C address 192.168.12.0 in the example earlier, set all network and subnet bits to 1 and all node bits to 0. This means the first 3 octets in the network portion plus the first 3 left-most bits in the node portion are set to 1 and the remaining 5 right-most node bits to 0.

> 11111111.11111111.11111111.**111**00000
> 255 . 255 . 255 . 224

This gives the netmask of 255.255.255.224. In class A networks, there are 22 valid netmasks. Consult Table 23-4.

Subnet Mask	# of Subnet Bits	Useable Subnets	Nodes per Subnet
255.128.0.0	1	1	8,388,606
255.192.0.0	2	2	4,194,302
255.224.0.0	3	6	2,097,150
255.240.0.0	4	14	1,048,574
255.248.0.0	5	30	524,286
255.252.0.0	6	62	262,142
255.254.0.0	7	126	131,070
255.255.0.0	8	254	65,534
255.255.128.0	9	510	32,766
255.255.192.0	10	1,022	16,382
255.255.224.0	11	2,046	8,190
255.255.240.0	12	4,094	4,094
255.255.248.0	13	8,190	2,046
255.255.252.0	14	16,382	1,022
255.255.254.0	15	32,766	510
255.255.255.0	16	65,534	254
255.255.255.128	17	131,070	126
255.255.255.192	18	262,142	62
255.255.255.224	19	524,286	30
255.255.255.240	20	1,048,574	14
255.255.255.248	21	2,097,150	6
255.255.255.252	22	4,194,302	2

Table 23-4 Subnet Masks for Class C

In class B networks, there are 14 valid netmasks. Consult Table 23-5.

Subnet Mask	# of Subnet Bits	Useable Subnets	Nodes per Subnet
255.255.128.0	1	1	32,766
255.255.192.0	2	2	16,382
255.255.224.0	3	6	8,190
255.255.240.0	4	14	4,094
255.255.248.0	5	30	2,046
255.255.252.0	6	62	1,022
255.255.254.0	7	126	510
255.255.255.0	8	254	254
255.255.255.128	9	510	126
255.255.255.192	10	1,022	62
255.255.255.224	11	2,046	30
255.255.255.240	12	4,094	14
255.255.255.248	13	8,190	6
255.255.255.252	14	16,382	2

Table 23-5 Subnet Masks for Class B

In class C networks, there are 6 valid netmasks. Consult Table 23-6.

Subnet Mask	# of Subnet Bits	Useable Subnets	Nodes per Subnet
255.255.255.128	1	1	126
255.255.255.192	2	2	62
255.255.255.224	3	6	30
255.255.255.240	4	14	14
255.255.255.248	5	30	6
255.255.255.252	6	62	2

Table 23-6 Subnet Masks for Class C

To determine the subnet IP for a given IP address such as 192.168.12.72 with netmask 255.255.255.224, write the IP address in binary format. Then write the subnet mask in binary format with all network and subnet bits set to 1 and all node bits set to 0. Now perform the logical AND operation. For each matching 1 you get 1, otherwise 0. The following highlights ANDed bits:

```
11000000.10101000.00001100.01001000     (IP address)
11111111.11111111.11111111.11100000     (subnet mask)
================================
11000000.10101000.00001100.01000000     (subnet IP in binary format)
   192  .  168  .  12  .  64             (subnet IP in decimal format)
```

This calculation enables you to determine subnet IP from a given IP address and subnet mask.

23.6.10 IP Multiplexing

A single physical LAN interface can have multiple IP addresses assigned to create multiple logical interfaces. Each IP address can then be assigned to a unique hostname. Binding multiple IP addresses to a single physical LAN interface is referred to as *IP multiplexing*.

IP multiplexing enables a single system with single LAN interface to be seen as multiple systems, with each one of them having its own IP address and unique hostname. This functionality allows several applications to run on one system, but appears to users as if they are running on separate, physical systems.

Each logical interface uses a unique logical instance number. For instance, the first logical interface on *lan1* would be *lan1:1*, the second would be *lan1:2* and so on. In this naming convention, "lan" refers to the network interface card, digit "1" represents the *Physical Point of Attachment* (PPA), which is a numerical index for the physical interface within its class, and ":1" and ":2" represent logical instances corresponding to logical interfaces for the specified physical interface. The default is 0. The interface name *lan1* is the same as *lan1:0*.

The first logical instance such as *lan1:0* is known as the *initial* interface, which must be configured before any subsequent logical interfaces such as *lan1:1*, *lan1:2* and *lan1:3* can be configured. Logical interfaces do not need to be assigned in sequence; in fact, *lan1:3* can be configured even if *lan1:1* and *lan1:2* do not exist.

Summary

In this chapter you were introduced to basics of networking. The chapter started off with providing an understanding of network, types of network and various common network topologies and access methods being employed in the industry.

The next section covered the OSI reference networking model in detail. You learned about the layers of the model, how packets were encapsulated and de-encapsulated and the peer-to-peer nature of the model. You looked at a few other sub-topics including key transport protocols, concepts of ports and sockets, and definitions of devices such as gateways, routers, switches, repeaters and hubs.

The TCP/IP protocol stack and concepts related to it were discussed in detail. Topics such as TCP/IP layers, MAC address, ARP, RARP, hostname, IP address, network classes and IP multiplexing provided you good understanding of the basics of TCP/IP. Finally, you were explained what the concepts of subnetting and subnet mask were, how to divide a network address into multiple sub-networks, and the role subnet mask played. At the end, you looked at some basic information on virtual private network that allowed secure transmission of confidential data over public network infrastructure.

## 24

LAN Interface Administration and Routing

This chapter covers the following major topics:

- ✓ Configure a LAN interface and assign a single IP address
- ✓ Configure a LAN interface and assign multiple IP addresses
- ✓ Enable a LAN interface to activate at each system reboot
- ✓ The role of the /etc/hosts file
- ✓ What is routing?
- ✓ Add, delete and display routes
- ✓ Establish default routes and flush routing table
- ✓ Activate DHCP client functionality

24.1 LAN Interface Administration

In order for the system to communicate with other nodes on the network, one of its LAN interfaces must be configured with a unique IP address, hostname and other required network parameters. The following sub-sections provide procedures on how to configure a LAN interface.

24.1.1 Configuring a LAN Interface

To successfully configure a LAN interface, follow the steps below:

1. Ensure HP-UX networking software, which includes TCP/IP, is installed. Execute the *swlist* command to verify the presence of the software:

   # swlist –l product | grep –i networking
   Networking   B.11.31   HP-UX_Lanlink_Product

   If the software is not loaded, use the *swinstall* command to install it.

2. Verify if proper software drivers are loaded in the kernel for the LAN cards to operate properly. The drivers for most LAN cards are automatically installed and configured when HP-UX is initially installed. Use the *ioscan* command to check:

   # ioscan –fnkC lan

Class	I	H/W Path	Driver	S/W State	H/W Type	Description
lan	0	0/0/6/0/0/4/0	btlan	CLAIMED	INTERFACE	HP A5506B PCI 10/100Base-TX 4 Port
lan	1	0/0/6/0/0/5/0	btlan	CLAIMED	INTERFACE	HP A5506B PCI 10/100Base-TX 4 Port
lan	2	0/0/6/0/0/6/0	btlan	CLAIMED	INTERFACE	HP A5506B PCI 10/100Base-TX 4 Port
lan	3	0/0/6/0/0/7/0	btlan	CLAIMED	INTERFACE	HP A5506B PCI 10/100Base-TX 4 Port
lan	4	0/0/8/0/0/4/0	igelan	CLAIMED	INTERFACE	HP A6794-60001 PCI 1000Base-T
lan	5	0/0/14/0/0/4/0	btlan	CLAIMED	INTERFACE	HP A5506B PCI 10/100Base-TX 4 Port
lan	6	0/0/14/0/0/5/0	btlan	CLAIMED	INTERFACE	HP A5506B PCI 10/100Base-TX 4 Port
lan	7	0/0/14/0/0/6/0	btlan	CLAIMED	INTERFACE	HP A5506B PCI 10/100Base-TX 4 Port
lan	8	0/0/14/0/0/7/0	btlan	CLAIMED	INTERFACE	HP A5506B PCI 10/100Base-TX 4 Port

   The output shows the S/W State of all LAN interfaces as "CLAIMED", which indicates that their driver is installed and the LAN interfaces are bound to it. In case the state is "UNCLAIMED", it would indicate the absence of a proper driver. In that situation, you will have to take steps to load an appropriate driver, regenerate the kernel and reboot the machine.

   You can also use the *lsdev* command to list the LAN driver configured in the system:

   # lsdev –C lan

Character	Block	Driver	Class
44	-1	kwdb	lan

3. Identify a LAN interface to be used. The *ioscan* command as displayed in the previous step can be used. Alternatively, you can use the *nwmgr* and *lanscan* commands:

```
# nwmgr
```

Name/ ClassInstance	Interface State	Station Address	Sub- system	Interface Type	Related Interface
==========	=======	============	=====	=======	======
lan0	UP	0x00306E469D5C	either	10/100Base-TX 4 Port	
lan1	UP	0x00306E469D5D	either	10/100Base-TX 4 Port	
lan2	UP	0x00306E469D5E	either	10/100Base-TX 4 Port	
lan3	UP	0x00306E469D5F	either	10/100Base-TX 4 Port	
lan4	UP	0x00306EA7AC2D	either	1000Base-T	
lan5	UP	0x00306E2DCCD4	iether	10/100Base-TX 4 Port	
lan6	UP	0x00306E2DCCD5	iether	10/100Base-TX 4 Port	
lan7	UP	0x00306E2DCCD6	iether	10/100Base-TX 4 Port	
lan8	UP	0x00306E2DCCD7	iether	10/100Base-TX 4 Port	

```
# lanscan
```

Hardware Path	Station Address	Crd In#	Hdw State	Net-Interface NamePPA	NM ID	MAC Type	HP-DLPI Support	DLPI Mjr#
0/0/6/0/0/4/0	0x00306E469D5C	0	UP	lan0 snap0	1	ETHER	Yes	119
0/0/6/0/0/5/0	0x00306E469D5D	1	UP	lan1 snap1	2	ETHER	Yes	119
0/0/6/0/0/6/0	0x00306E469D5E	2	UP	lan2 snap2	3	ETHER	Yes	119
0/0/6/0/0/7/0	0x00306E469D5F	3	UP	lan3 snap3	4	ETHER	Yes	119
0/0/8/0/0/4/0	0x00306EA7AC2D	4	UP	lan4 snap4	5	ETHER	Yes	119
0/0/14/0/0/4/0	0x00306E2DCCD4	5	UP	lan5 snap5	6	ETHER	Yes	119
0/0/14/0/0/5/0	0x00306E2DCCD5	6	UP	lan6 snap6	7	ETHER	Yes	119
0/0/14/0/0/6/0	0x00306E2DCCD6	7	UP	lan7 snap7	8	ETHER	Yes	119
0/0/14/0/0/7/0	0x00306E2DCCD7	8	UP	lan8 snap8	9	ETHER	Yes	119

The output indicates that there are nine LAN interfaces available on this system.

4. Assign IP address and other network parameters to the LAN interface using the *ifconfig* command. For example, use *lan1* and assign it 193.11.211.2 with default netmask 255.255.255.0 and broadcast address 193.11.211.255:

   # ifconfig lan1 inet 193.11.211.2 netmask 255.255.255.0 broadcast 193.11.211.255 up

   You can also achieve the above by running the *ifconfig* command as follows:

   # ifconfig lan1 193.11.211.2 netmask 255.255.255.0

   The *ifconfig* command is used to assign IP, subnet mask, broadcast and local loopback addresses to an interface. It can also be used to activate or deactivate it. This command is executed automatically at system boot via the */sbin/init.d/net* startup script. The keywords "inet", "broadcast" and "up" are default. The keyword "netmask" must be specified, otherwise the interface will be configured as point-to-point. The point-to-point setup is only required if there is a need to configure direct TCP/IP link between two systems.

5. Run the *ifconfig* and *netstat* commands to verify the new IP assignment:

   # ifconfig lan1
   lan1: flags=843<**UP**,BROADCAST,**RUNNING**,MULTICAST>
        inet **193.11.211.2** netmask **ffffff00** broadcast **193.11.211.255**

The output demonstrates that the IP address 193.11.211.2 is assigned to *lan1* with netmask 255.255.255.0 and broadcast address 193.11.211.255. It also confirms that the interface is in up and running state.

```
# netstat –in
```

Name	Mtu	Network	Address	Ipkts	Ierrs	Opkts	Oerrs	Coll
lan1	1500	193.11.211.0	193.11.211.2	0	0	0	0	0
lo0	32808	127.0.0.0	127.0.0.1	855663	0	855663	0	0
lan4	1500	192.168.1.0	192.168.1.201	2313215	0	240677	0	728

24.1.2   Configuring IP Multiplexing

If there is a plan to run multiple applications on a single system, you can have multiple IP addresses and hostnames assigned to a single physical LAN interface (assuming there is only one in the system). Users of each application will be given a unique hostname and IP address for access. The *ifconfig* command below assigns three IP addresses to *lan1* with default netmask:

```
# ifconfig lan1:1 193.12.211.2
# ifconfig lan1:2 193.13.211.2
# ifconfig lan1:3 193.14.211.2
```

Run the *netstat* or *ifconfig* command to check the results:

```
# netstat –in
```

Name	Mtu	Network	Address	Ipkts	Ierrs	Opkts	Oerrs	Coll
lan1:1	1500	193.12.211.0	193.12.211.2	0	0	0	0	0
lan1	1500	193.11.211.0	193.11.211.2	0	0	0	0	0
lo0	32808	127.0.0.0	127.0.0.1	856153	0	856153	0	0
lan1:3	1500	193.14.211.0	193.14.211.2	0	0	0	0	0
lan1:2	1500	193.13.211.0	193.13.211.2	0	0	0	0	0
lan4	1500	192.168.1.0	192.168.1.201	2315042	0	241125	0	733

```
# ifconfig lan1:1
lan1:1: flags=843<UP,BROADCAST,RUNNING,MULTICAST>
      inet 193.12.211.2 netmask ffffff00 broadcast 193.12.211.255
# ifconfig lan1:2
lan1:2: flags=843<UP,BROADCAST,RUNNING,MULTICAST>
      inet 193.13.211.2 netmask ffffff00 broadcast 193.13.211.255
# ifconfig lan1:3
lan1:3: flags=843<UP,BROADCAST,RUNNING,MULTICAST>
      inet 193.14.211.2 netmask ffffff00 broadcast 193.14.211.255
```

24.1.3   Setting a LAN Interface to Activate at System Boot

The LAN interface configuration performed in previous sub-sections will not survive at the next system reboot. To preserve the settings across system reboots and get them assigned automatically to the LAN interface, you need to edit the */etc/rc.config.d/netconf* startup network configuration file and add entries there. This file is the source for */sbin/init.d/net* startup script, which is executed at boot time when the system enters run level 2. This script reads the configuration file and executes *ifconfig* on all LAN interface entries that it finds in the file.

Here is what you will need to add to the *etc/rc.config.d/netconf* file for the four IP addresses assigned earlier:

```
INTERFACE_NAME[1]=lan1
IP_ADDRESS[1]=193.11.211.2
SUBNET_MASK[1]=255.255.255.0
BROADCAST_ADDRESS[1]=""
INTERFACE_STATE[1]=up

INTERFACE_NAME[2]=lan1:1
IP_ADDRESS[2]=193.12.211.2
SUBNET_MASK[2]=255.255.255.0
BROADCAST_ADDRESS[2]=""
INTERFACE_STATE[2]=up

INTERFACE_NAME[3]=lan1:2
IP_ADDRESS[3]=193.13.211.2
SUBNET_MASK[3]=255.255.255.0
BROADCAST_ADDRESS[3]=""
INTERFACE_STATE[3]=up

INTERFACE_NAME[4]=lan1:3
IP_ADDRESS[4]=193.14.211.2
SUBNET_MASK[4]=255.255.255.0
BROADCAST_ADDRESS[4]=""
INTERFACE_STATE[4]=up
```

The */sbin/init.d/net* script can be run manually to activate the entries (if not already activated):

 # /sbin/init.d/net start

Use the *netstat* command with –in switches to verify the settings:

 # netstat –in

With SMH (or *ncweb* command), you can perform the above tasks. Follow the links below:

☞ Go to SMH → Networking and Communications → Network Interfaces Configuration → Network Interface Cards. Highlight a LAN interface such as *lan2* from the list and press the Enter key to view details. Press p to modify IP attributes:

```
Details of Interface: lan2
----------------------------------------------------------------------------
Group Name            NIC Attributes
MAC Address           0x00306E469D5E
MTU                   1500
Probable State Cause  PCI Error
```

```
Link Information
---------------------
Link State          Down
Speed               Autonegotiation : On

IPv4 Attributes
-------------------
IPv4 Address        -
IPv4 Status         Not Configured
Subnet Mask         -
Broadcast Address   -
Alias               -
Comments            -

IPv6 Attributes
------------------
IPv6 Address        -
IPv6 Status         Not Configured
Prefix Length       -
Alias               -
Comments            -

----------------------------------------------------------------------
x-Exit smh    h-Help          p-View/Modify IP Attributes
Esc-Back      v-Add VLAN      a-View/Modify NIC Attributes
```

24.1.4 Defining an IP Address and Hostname in the /etc/hosts File

You need to choose hostnames to be assigned to each individual IP address. For example, the four IP addresses configured earlier require unique hostnames such as *server1*, *server2*, *server3* and *server4*. These entries will need to be added to the */etc/hosts* file as shown below:

```
193.11.211.2  server1  db01    # first logical server
193.12.211.2  server2  db02    # second logical server
193.13.211.2  server3  db03    # third logical server
193.14.211.2  server4  db04    # fourth logical server
```

The */etc/hosts* file is typically used if you need to access systems on a local network only. This file must be maintained locally on each system.

Each line in the file contains an IP address in the first column followed by an official (or *canonical*) hostname in the second column. You may also define one or more aliases per entry (*db01*, *db02*, *db03* and *db04* in the above example). The official hostname and one or more aliases allow you to have multiple hostnames assigned to a single IP address. This enables the system to be accessed using any of the hostnames.

Since */etc/hosts* is maintained locally, it must be updated manually on each system to maintain consistency whenever an update is required.

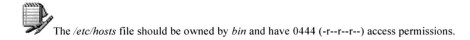

The */etc/hosts* file should be owned by *bin* and have 0444 (-r--r--r--) access permissions.

You can use SMH (or *ncweb* command) to edit the */etc/hosts* file. Follow the steps below:

☞Go to SMH → Networking and Communications → Network Services Configuration → Hosts → Local Hosts File. Go to Actions and choose Add, Modify or Remove.

24.2   Routing

Routing refers to the process of choosing a path over which to send a data packet. To perform the routing function, a routing device is needed. The routing device can be a specialized and sophisticated hardware device called router or it can be an HP-UX system with more than one network interface. An HP-UX system can perform the routing function, but it will not be as sophisticated. The following sub-sections discuss the basics of routing.

24.2.1   Routing Concepts

When nodes on two separate networks (or subnets) communicate with each other, proper route(s) must be setup. For instance, if a node on network A sends a data packet to a node on network B, one or more routing devices get involved to route the packet to the correct destination network. The two networks can be located in the same data center or thousands of miles apart. Once the data packet reaches a router, the router selects the next router along the path toward the destination node. The packet passes from router to router until it reaches the router that can deliver the packet directly to the destination node. Each router along the path is referred to as a *hop*.

One of the three rules is followed when a node sends out a packet:

✓ If both the source and the destination nodes are on the same network (or subnet), the packet is sent directly to the destination node since the destination node is on the same network.
✓ If the source and the destination nodes are on two different networks, all defined routes are tried one after the other. If a proper route is found, the packet is forwarded to it, which then forwards the packet to the destination node.
✓ If the source and the destination nodes are on two different networks but no routes are defined, the packet is forwarded to the *default router* (or *default gateway*), which tries to find an appropriate route to the destination. If found, the packet is delivered to the destination node.

There are two types of routes: *static* and *dynamic*.

A static route is fixed and does not get changed over time or across system reboots. It is defined in the */etc/rc.config.d/netconf* file.

A dynamic route, on the other hand, changes constantly. Some of the common dynamic routing protocols are *Routing Information Protocol* (RIP), *Open Shortest Path First* (OSPF), *Exterior Gateway Protocol* (EGP) and *Border Gateway Protocol* (BGP). HP-UX supports all of them.

Routing protocols are classified into two major groups – *distance vector* protocols and *link state* protocols – based on the mechanism they use to determine the best route between the source and destination.

Distance vector protocols choose a routing path that has the least number of routers (or hops). RIP uses this routing mechanism.

Link state protocols use additional factors such as link bandwidth and reliability to determine the best route. OSPF belongs to this group of protocols.

24.2.2 Routing Table

The *routing table* maintains information about available routes and their status. It is maintained by the kernel in memory. The routing table can be viewed with the *netstat* command using –r option:

 # netstat –r
Routing tables

Destination	Gateway	Flags	Refs	Interface	Pmtu
localhost	localhost	UH	0	lo0	32808
hp01	hp01	UH	0	lan4	32808
193.11.211.2	193.11.211.2	UH	0	lan1	32808
193.13.211.2	193.13.211.2	UH	0	lan1:2	32808
193.12.211.2	193.12.211.2	UH	0	lan1:1	32808
193.14.211.2	193.14.211.2	UH	0	lan1:3	32808
192.168.1.0	hp01	U	2	lan4	1500
193.11.211.0	193.11.211.2	U	5	lan1	1500
193.12.211.0	193.12.211.2	U	5	lan1:1	1500
193.13.211.0	193.13.211.2	U	5	lan1:2	1500
193.14.211.0	193.14.211.2	U	5	lan1:3	1500
loopback	localhost	U	0	lo0	32808
default	192.168.1.1	UG	0	lan4	1500

With –n option, the *netstat* command displays the output in numerical format:

 # netstat –rn
Routing tables

Destination	Gateway	Flags	Refs	Interface	Pmtu
127.0.0.1	127.0.0.1	UH	0	lo0	32808
192.168.1.201	192.168.1.201	UH	0	lan4	32808
193.11.211.2	193.11.211.2	UH	0	lan1	32808
193.13.211.2	193.13.211.2	UH	0	lan1:2	32808
193.12.211.2	193.12.211.2	UH	0	lan1:1	32808
193.14.211.2	193.14.211.2	UH	0	lan1:3	32808
192.168.1.0	192.168.1.201	U	2	lan4	1500
193.11.211.0	193.11.211.2	U	5	lan1	1500
193.12.211.0	193.12.211.2	U	5	lan1:1	1500
193.13.211.0	193.13.211.2	U	5	lan1:2	1500
193.14.211.0	193.14.211.2	U	5	lan1:3	1500
127.0.0.0	127.0.0.1	U	0	lo0	32808
default	192.168.1.1	UG	0	lan4	1500

The output has six columns and are explained in Table 24-1.

Column	Description
Destination	Destination route to a host or network.
Gateway	Packets are routed to the destination through this address.
Flags	Displays route type. Following are various flags: U – route is up and it is a network route. H – route is a host route. UH – route is up and it is a host route. G – route is through a gateway. D – route is created dynamically. M – gateway route has been modified. ? – gateway route is unknown.
Refs	Displays current route usage.
Interface	LAN interface used by the route.
Pmtu	*Path Maximum Transfer Unit*. Default for Ethernet is 1500 and that for loopback is 4136.

Table 24-1 *netstat* Command Output Description

24.3   Managing Routes

Managing routes involves adding a route, modifying a route, deleting a route and flushing the routing table. The *route* command or SMH can be used to perform these tasks. Alternatively, the */etc/rc.config.d/netconf* file can be edited directly to add, modify or delete a route entry. Entries added with the *route* command are lost when the system is rebooted, whereas entries added via SMH or by editing the */etc/rc.config.d/netconf* file are permanent and available across system reboots. SMH automatically updates the */etc/rc.config.d/netconf* file to reflect the add, modify and delete operations.

24.3.1   Adding a Route

A route can be set to a network or host. Following provides procedures for both.

Adding a Route to a Network

To add a route to a network such as 192.168.2 with default class C netmask and gateway 192.168.1.1:

> # **route add net 192.168.2.0 netmask 255.255.255.0 192.168.1.1 1**

To make the route permanent, edit the */etc/rc.config.d/netconf* file and add the following entry to it. The */sbin/init.d/net* script executes the *route* command at each system reboot and sources this file.

```
ROUTE_DESTINATION[0]="net 192.168.2.0"
ROUTE_MASK[0]="255.255.255.0"
ROUTE_GATEWAY[0]=192.168.1.1
ROUTE_COUNT[0]=1
ROUTE_ARGS[0]=""
```

After placing the entry, you may manually set the route by running the following. Note that this will also execute other entries defined in the */etc/rc.config.d/netconf* file. It is assumed that the *route* command above was not already run.

> # **/sbin/init.d/net start**

Use the *netstat* command with –rn switches to verify the settings:

> # **netstat –rn**

Adding a Route to a Host

To add a route to a host such as 192.168.3.31 with default class C netmask and gateway 192.168.1.1:

> # **route add host 192.168.3.31 netmask 255.255.255.0 192.168.1.1 1**

To make the route permanent, edit the */etc/rc.config.d/netconf* file and add the following entry to it. The */sbin/init.d/net* script executes the *route* command at each system reboot and sources this file.

> ROUTE_DESTINATION[1]="192.168.3.31"
> ROUTE_MASK[1]="255.255.255.0"
> ROUTE_GATEWAY[1]=192.168.1.1
> ROUTE_COUNT[1]=1
> ROUTE_ARGS[1]=""

After placing the entry, you may manually set the route by running the following. Note that this will also execute other entries defined in the */etc/rc.config.d/netconf* file. It is assumed that the *route* command above was not already run.

> # **/sbin/init.d/net start**

Use the *netstat* command with –rn switches to verify the settings:

> # **netstat –rn**

To add a route using SMH (or *ncweb* command), follow the steps below:

☞Go to SMH → Networking and Communications → Network Services Configuration → Routes → Actions → Add Route. Fill out the form. See Figure 24-1.

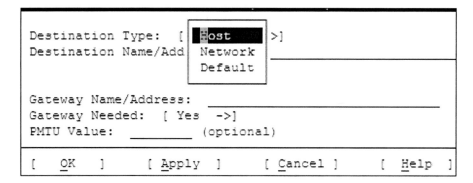

Figure 24-1 SMH – Add Route

24.3.2   Modifying a Route

To modify a route, use SMH (or *ncweb* command) as follows:

☞Go to SMH → Networking and Communications → Network Services Configuration →
Routes. Highlight a route and go to Actions → Modify Route.

24.3.3   Deleting a Route

To delete the two routes added in previous sub-sections:

> # **route delete net 192.168.2.0 192.168.1.1**
> delete net 192.168.2.0: gateway 192.168.1.1
> # **route delete host 192.168.3.31 192.168.1.1**
> delete host 192.168.3.31: gateway 192.168.1.1

Run the *netstat* command to confirm.

To delete a route using SMH (or *ncweb* command), follow the steps below:

☞Go to SMH → Networking and Communications → Network Services Configuration →
Routes. Highlight a route and go to Actions → Remove Route.

24.3.4   Flushing Routing Table

To flush the entire routing table, run the *route* command with –f option:

> # **route –f**

This will remove all routing entries from the routing table. At this point, you may re-execute the
/sbin/init.d/net script or define routes manually.

24.3.5   Setting the Default Route

Most nodes define the nearest dedicated router as the default route in their routing table to reach
other networks. The default route is used if there is no other route present in the routing table for the

---

destination. Only one default route can be defined on a system. Issue the *route* command as follows to define the default route through 192.168.1.1:

 # route add default 192.168.1.1 1

Alternatively, the *set_parms* command can be used for this purpose. Use the command with caution. It prompts to keep or modify several other network parameters too.

 # set_parms initial

To configure the default route using SMH (or *ncweb* command), follow the steps below:

☞Go to SMH → Networking and Communications → Network Services Configuration → Routes → Actions → Add Route.

The default route can be defined in the */etc/rc.config.d/netconf* file by hand. For instance, see the following sample entries:

```
ROUTE_DESTINATION[2]=default
ROUTE_GATEWAY[2]=192.168.1.1
ROUTE_COUNT[2]=1
```

24.4 Enabling DHCP Client Service

Dynamic Host Configuration Protocol (DHCP) enables a system that acts as a *DHCP server,* to provide IP address and other network parameters including subnet mask, default route, DNS/NIS/NTP server IP to other systems automatically. These other systems are called *DHCP clients.*

When an HP-UX system with DHCP client functionality enabled boots up, it broadcasts a message on the network requesting an available DHCP server to provide an IP address and network parameter information. An available DHCP server responds and sends the requested information back to the client, which the client uses to set it up. The IP address is leased to the DHCP client for a specific amount of time.

DHCP client functionality can be enabled by inserting an entry in the */etc/rc.config.d/netconf* file, running the *set_parms* command or using SMH.

The following two step procedure shows how to enable DHCP client functionality for *lan4*. The first step edits the *netconf* file and adds an entry. The second step executes the */sbin/init.d/net* startup script manually to re-execute entries in the file.

```
# vi /etc/rc.config.d/netconf
DHCP_ENABLE[4]=1
# /sbin/init.d/net start
```

To enable the functionality using the *set_parms* command, do the following. Use this tool with caution. It prompts to keep or modify several other network parameters.

 # set_parms initial

To enable the functionality using SMH (or *ncweb* command), follow the links:

☞Go to SMH → Networking and Communications → Network Interfaces Configuration →
Network Interface Cards. Highlight a LAN interface and press Enter. Press p to "View/Modify IP
Attributes" and select "Enable DHCP client", as shown below:

```
Interface Name              : lan4
Hardware Path               : 0/0/8/0/0/4/0

Encapsulation Type          : Ethernet ->

  [X] IPv4 Attributes (Select to enable)

IPV4                        :  (X)  Enable  IPv4
                               ( )  Disable IPv4

* IPv4 Address              : 192.168.1.201_____
Subnet Mask                 : 255.255.255.0_____
Broadcast Address           : 192.168.1.255_____
Comments                    : _____
Enable DHCP client          :  [ ]

[ Modules ]
[ IPv4 Alias ]

  [ ]  IPv6 Attributes (Select to enable)

IPv6 Configuration          : Auto Configuration  ->

IPV6                        :  (X)  Enable  IPv6
                               ( )  Disable IPv6

* IPv6 Address              : _____
Prefix Length               :
Comments                    : _____
Enable DHCPv6 client        :  [ ]

Disable Forwarding of Packets by this interface         :  [ ]
Disable Processing of Received Router Advertisements     :  [ ]

[ Modules ]
[ IPv6 Alias ]

Configuration Options       :  [X]  Current
                               [X]  Saved

[ Modify ] [ Cancel ] [ Preview ] [ Help ]
```

Summary

In this chapter you learned how to assign network parameters to a LAN interface including assigning it a single IP address and multiple IP addresses. You looked at how to edit the network startup configuration file so the entries become activated whenever a system reboot occurs. You then defined IP addresses and hostnames in */etc/hosts* database.

The next major topic in the chapter was on routing. You studied routing concepts and how it worked. You understood the concept of default route. You used examples to add, delete and display routes. You saw how to zero out routing table entries by using the *route* command.

The last topic explained briefly Dynamic Host Configuration Protocol and how it worked. You used ways of activating DHCP client functionality.

Network Connectivity Troubleshooting

This chapter covers the following major topics:

✓ Understand network connectivity troubleshooting concepts
✓ Perform network connectivity troubleshooting using tools such as ioscan, lanscan, linkloop, lanadmin, nwmgr, ping, netstat, traceroute, ndd and nettl

25.1   Network Connectivity Troubleshooting

Network problems usually involve physical connectivity or incorrect configuration issues. Physical connectivity issues may include LAN card not seated properly in the slot, cable plugged into wrong LAN interface, a broken cable, bad or loose connectors at cable ends, cable length too long, router, switch or hub not functioning or malfunctioning and so on.

Configuration issues may involve LAN card software driver not installed, duplicate IP addresses on the network, wrong IP address assignment, incorrect subnet mask, incorrect routing table entries, IP address and other network parameters lost at system boot, LAN interface not in UP state and so on.

In the following sub-sections various network troubleshooting tools are presented that aid in troubleshooting physical connectivity issues. These tools come standard with HP-UX and include *ioscan, lanscan, linkloop, lanadmin, nwmgr, ping, netstat, traceroute, ndd* and *nettl*. For problems related to incorrect configuration, check network assignments in key configuration files such as */etc/hosts* and */etc/rc.config.d/netconf*. Refer to Chapter 23 "Basic Networking" and Chapter 24 "LAN Interface Administration and Routing" for in-depth coverage on network parameter settings.

25.1.1   Using ioscan

The *ioscan* command is a powerful tool. It looks into the running kernel or scans the entire system and displays useful information about I/O devices and their status. From network connectivity troubleshooting perspective, this command helps to determine if a LAN card has the proper software driver installed, configured and bound.

 # ioscan –fnkC lan

Class	I	H/W Path	Driver	S/W State	H/W Type	Description
lan	0	0/0/6/0/0/4/0	btlan	CLAIMED	INTERFACE	HP A5506B PCI 10/100Base-TX 4 Port
lan	1	0/0/6/0/0/5/0	btlan	CLAIMED	INTERFACE	HP A5506B PCI 10/100Base-TX 4 Port
lan	2	0/0/6/0/0/6/0	btlan	CLAIMED	INTERFACE	HP A5506B PCI 10/100Base-TX 4 Port
lan	3	0/0/6/0/0/7/0	btlan	CLAIMED	INTERFACE	HP A5506B PCI 10/100Base-TX 4 Port
lan	4	0/0/8/0/0/4/0	igelan	CLAIMED	INTERFACE	HP A6794-60001 PCI 1000Base-T
lan	5	0/0/14/0/0/4/0	btlan	CLAIMED	INTERFACE	HP A5506B PCI 10/100Base-TX 4 Port
lan	6	0/0/14/0/0/5/0	btlan	CLAIMED	INTERFACE	HP A5506B PCI 10/100Base-TX 4 Port
lan	7	0/0/14/0/0/6/0	btlan	CLAIMED	INTERFACE	HP A5506B PCI 10/100Base-TX 4 Port
lan	8	0/0/14/0/0/7/0	btlan	CLAIMED	INTERFACE	HP A5506B PCI 10/100Base-TX 4 Port

Check under the column "S/W State" for the CLAIMED or UNCLAIMED state. A CLAIMED state indicates that a software driver is properly loaded, configured and the LAN card is bound to it. An UNCLAIMED state means that a software driver needs to be installed for the associated LAN card. In the *ioscan* output above, all LAN interfaces are in the CLAIMED state.

There are several options available with *ioscan*. Some of them are described in Table 25-1.

Option	Description
–C	Displays information about devices belonging to the specified class.
–d	Displays information about devices controlled by the specified software driver.
–f	Displays full information including module's class, instance number, hardware path, driver, software state, hardware type and a brief description.
–H	Displays information about devices attached at the specified hardware path.
–I	Displays information about devices at the specified instance number.
–k	Reads information from the running kernel data structures. If this option is not specified, the command scans the entire system for I/O.
–N	Displays DSFs in persistent format.
–n	Displays DSFs in legacy format.
–u	Displays information about devices that have CLAIMED state and an assigned instance number.

Table 25-1 *ioscan* Command Options

Try running the command with options listed in Table 25-1 and compare results.

Refer to Chapter 07 "System Administration and HP-UX Server Hardware" for detailed information on output produced by running the *ioscan* command.

25.1.2   Using lanscan

Once it is determined that a proper software driver is installed and configured for the LAN card, you need to determine the MAC address of the LAN interface being troubleshot. Run the *lanscan* command to obtain this information:

lanscan

Hardware Path	Station Address	Crd In#	Hdw State	Net-Interface NamePPA	NM ID	MAC Type	HP-DLPI Support	DLPI Mjr#
0/0/6/0/0/4/0	0x00306E469D5C	0	UP	lan0 snap0	1	ETHER	Yes	119
0/0/6/0/0/5/0	0x00306E469D5D	1	UP	lan1 snap1	2	ETHER	Yes	119
0/0/6/0/0/6/0	0x00306E469D5E	2	UP	lan2 snap2	3	ETHER	Yes	119
0/0/6/0/0/7/0	0x00306E469D5F	3	UP	lan3 snap3	4	ETHER	Yes	119
0/0/8/0/0/4/0	0x00306EA7AC2D	4	UP	lan4 snap4	5	ETHER	Yes	119
0/0/14/0/0/4/0	0x00306E2DCCD4	5	UP	lan5 snap5	6	ETHER	Yes	119
0/0/14/0/0/5/0	0x00306E2DCCD5	6	UP	lan6 snap6	7	ETHER	Yes	119
0/0/14/0/0/6/0	0x00306E2DCCD6	7	UP	lan7 snap7	8	ETHER	Yes	119
0/0/14/0/0/7/0	0x00306E2DCCD7	8	UP	lan8 snap8	9	ETHER	Yes	119

A short description of each column is given in Table 25-2.

Column	Description
Hardware Path	Displays each LAN interface's physical path.
Station Address	Displays each LAN interface's MAC address.
Card Instance #	Displays each LAN interface's instance number (a.k.a. PPA).
Hardware State	Displays UP or DOWN status.
Net Interface Name PPA	Displays each LAN interface's name followed by the interface's PPA.

Column	Description
NM ID	Displays a unique *Network Management ID* used by the *lanadmin* command and other network management tools.
MAC Type	Displays each LAN interface's access method. Default is ETHER for Ethernet.
HP-DLPI Support	Displays if the LAN interface supports *Data Link Provider Interface* (DLPI). Used by the *linkloop* and *lanadmin* commands.
Major Number	Displays the associated major number for DLPI.

Table 25-2 *lanscan* Command Output Description

There are several options available with the *lanscan* command. Some of them are described in Table 25-3. Try running the command with these options and compare results.

Option	Description
–a	Displays MAC addresses.
–i	Displays interface names.
–m	Displays MAC types.
–n	Displays network management IDs.
–p	Displays PPAs.
–v	Displays detailed information.

Table 25-3 *lanscan* Command Options

The *lanscan* command is deprecated in HP-UX 11i v3 and will no longer be available in a future HP-UX release. A new command *nwmgr* should be used instead.

25.1.3 Using linkloop

This command tests physical connectivity between LAN interfaces installed in two different systems that are physically connected via a cable or an interconnect device, and reports whether the connectivity is OK. This command works at the physical layer and does not require TCP/IP parameters configured.

To test physical connectivity between *hp01* and *hp02*, assuming both are physically connected and using *lan4*, run the *linkloop* command on *hp01* and specify the MAC address of *lan4* of *hp02* (use *lanscan* or *nwmgr* to get the MAC address):

```
# linkloop  0x00306E469D5C
Link connectivity to LAN station: 0x00306E469D5C
-- OK
```

There are several options available with the *linkloop* command. Some of them are described in Table 25-4. Try running the command with these options and compare results.

Option	Description
–i	Specifies the PPA. Default is the first available.
–n	Specifies the number of data frames to be sent to destination.
–s	Defines the size of data frame.
–t	Specifies time, in seconds, to wait for a reply before aborting.

Option	Description
−v	Displays detailed information.

Table 25-4 *linkloop* Command Options

The *linkloop* command is deprecated in HP-UX 11i v3 and will no longer be available in a future HP-UX release. A new command *nwmgr* should be used instead.

25.1.4   Using lanadmin

The *lanadmin* command is a menu-driven utility for displaying a LAN interface's statistics, and changing characteristics. This command can be useful in troubleshooting LAN interface related issues. It does the following:

- ✓ Displays or changes the MAC address.
- ✓ Displays or changes the *Maximum Transmission Unit* (MTU) size.
- ✓ Displays or changes the speed.
- ✓ Displays statistics including inbound/outbound traffic, errors, etc.
- ✓ Resets a LAN interface and executes self-test on it.

The following menu pops up when the *lanadmin* command is invoked:

lanadmin

```
        LOCAL AREA NETWORK ONLINE ADMINISTRATION, Version 1.0
                  Fri, Apr 18,2008  09:23:49
           Copyright 1994 Hewlett Packard Company.
                   All rights are reserved.

Test Selection mode.
    lan       = LAN Interface Administration
    menu     = Display this menu
    quit      = Terminate the Administration
    terse     = Do not display command menu
    verbose  = Display command menu
Enter command:
```

The only sub-command to work with here is "lan". Others are self-explanatory. Enter "lan" and the following sub-menu will appear:

```
LAN Interface test mode. LAN Interface PPA Number = 0
    clear    = Clear statistics registers
    display  = Display LAN Interface status and statistics registers
    end      = End LAN Interface Administration, return to Test Selection
    menu     = Display this menu
    ppa      = PPA Number of the LAN Interface
    quit     = Terminate the Administration, return to shell
    reset    = Reset LAN Interface to execute its selftest
    specific = Go to Driver specific menu
Enter command:
```

Here, several choices are available for the LAN interface. For example, "clear" clears statistics registers, "display" displays status and statistics, "end" returns to the main menu, "menu" re-displays this menu, "ppa" allows to choose a LAN interface's instance number to test, "quit" returns to the command prompt, "reset" resets the LAN interface and runs self-test on it, and "specific" takes to the driver-specific sub-menu.

To view statistics, for example, choose the "display" sub-command:

```
            LAN INTERFACE STATUS DISPLAY
              Fri, Apr 18,2008  09:24:37

     PPA Number                    = 4
     Description                   = lan4 HP PCI Core I/O 1000Base-T Release B.11.31.0709.01
     Type (value)                  = ethernet-csmacd(6)
     MTU Size                      = 1500
     Speed                         = 100000000
     Station Address               = 0x306ea7ac2d
     Administration Status (value) = up(1)
     Operation Status (value)      = up(1)
     Last Change                   = 178
     Inbound Octets                = 845476121
     Inbound Unicast Packets       = 145490
     Inbound Non-Unicast Packets   = 4781298
     Inbound Discards              = 0
     Inbound Errors                = 0
     Inbound Unknown Protocols     = 2444646
     Outbound Octets               = 21271437
     Outbound Unicast Packets      = 141213
     Outbound Non-Unicast Packets  = 14203
     Outbound Discards             = 0
     Outbound Errors               = 0
     Outbound Queue Length         = 2
     Specific                      = 655367

     Ethernet-like Statistics Group
     Index                         = 5
     Alignment Errors              = 0
     FCS Errors                    = 0
     Single Collision Frames       = 781
     Multiple Collision Frames     = 73
     Deferred Transmissions        = 1126
     Late Collisions               = 986
     Excessive Collisions          = 0
     Internal MAC Transmit Errors  = 3
     Carrier Sense Errors          = 0
     Frames Too Long               = 0
     Internal MAC Receive Errors   = 0
```

The *lanadmin* command has several options available to do things without having to enter the menu. Some common options are listed in Table 25-5.

Option	Description
–a / –A	Displays / Changes the MAC address.
–m / –M	Displays / Changes the MTU size.
–s / –S	Displays / Changes the speed.
–x / –X	Displays / Changes the current configuration.

Table 25-5 *lanadmin* Command Options

Let us use these options in the following examples.

To display the MAC address of the LAN interface at PPA 1:

lanadmin –a 1
Station Address   = 0x00306e469d5d

To display the MTU size of the LAN interface at PPA 1:

lanadmin –m 1
MTU Size   = 1500

To display the speed of the LAN interface at PPA 1:

lanadmin –s 1
Speed   = 10000000

To display the current configuration of the LAN interface at PPA 1:

# **lanadmin –x 1**
Speed = 10 Half-Duplex.
Autonegotiation = On.

To change the current configuration of the LAN interface at PPA 1 to full-duplex and 100Mbps speed:

lanadmin –X 100fd 1
WARNING: an incorrect setting could cause serious network problems!!!

Driver is attempting to set the new speed
Reset will take approximately 11 seconds

With –X option, the following choices are available:

hd to change to half duplex.
fd to change to full duplex.
10hd to change to half duplex at 10 Mbps.
10fd to change to full duplex at 10 Mbps.

100hd to change to half duplex at 100 Mbps.
100fd to change to full duplex at 100 Mbps.
auto_on to enable automatic detection of speed and duplex mode.

The *lanadmin* command is deprecated in HP-UX 11i v3 and will no longer be available in a future HP-UX release. A new command *nwmgr* should be used instead.

25.1.5   Using nwmgr

Introduced in HP-UX 11i v3, the *nwmgr* (network manager) command is used for LAN interface management. Operations such as displaying interface information, resetting an interface, diagnosing link connectivity, creating and setting configuration parameters for a component and deleting components are supported. In a future HP-UX release, this command will replace *lanadmin*, *lanscan* and *linkloop* commands.

When run without any options, the *nwmgr* command displays information about LAN interfaces. This information includes the interface state and corresponding station address and type.

```
# nwmgr
```

Name/ ClassInstance	Interface State	Station Address	Sub- system	Interface Type	Related Interface
lan0	DOWN	0x00306E469D5C	btlan	100Base-TX	
lan1	DOWN	0x00306E469D5D	btlan	100Base-TX	
lan2	DOWN	0x00306E469D5E	btlan	100Base-TX	
lan3	DOWN	0x00306E469D5F	btlan	100Base-TX	
lan4	UP	0x00306EA7AC2D	igelan	1000Base-T	
lan5	DOWN	0x00306E2DCCD4	btlan	100Base-TX	
lan6	DOWN	0x00306E2DCCD5	btlan	100Base-TX	
lan7	DOWN	0x00306E2DCCD6	btlan	100Base-TX	
lan8	DOWN	0x00306E2DCCD7	btlan	100Base-TX	

To get detailed information about an interface such as *lan4*, use the –v option with the command and specify the interface name with –c option:

```
# nwmgr –v –c lan4
lan4:
   Interface State =UP
   MAC Address = 0x00306EA7AC2D
   Subsystem = igelan
   Interface Type = 1000Base-T
   Hardware Path = 0/0/8/0/0/4/0
   NMID = 5
   Feature Capabilities = Physical Interface
             IPV4 Recv CKO
             IPV4 Send CKO
             VLAN Tag Offload
             64Bit MIB Support
             IPV4 TCP Segmentation Offload
```

```
                    UDP Multifrag CKO
    Feature Settings = Physical Interface
                    VLAN Tag Offload
                    64Bit MIB Support
    MTU = 1500
    Speed = 100 Mbps Full Duplex (Autonegotiation : On)
```

Without –v, the output will be:

 # nwmgr –c lan4

Name/ ClassInstance	Interface State	Station Address	Sub- system	Interface Type	Related Interface
lan4	UP	0x00306EA7AC2D	igelan	1000Base-T	

25.1.6   Using ping

ping (packet internet groper) tests connectivity at the TCP/IP level when the physical connectivity is ok, and proper IP address and network assignments are in place. It sends out a series of 64-byte *Internet Control Message Protocol* (ICMP) test packets to a destination IP address and waits for a response.

```
# ping 192.168.1.202
PING hp02: 64 byte packets
64 bytes from 192.168.1.202: icmp_seq=0. time=2. ms
64 bytes from 192.168.1.202: icmp_seq=1. time=0. ms
64 bytes from 192.168.1.202: icmp_seq=2. time=0. ms
64 bytes from 192.168.1.202: icmp_seq=3. time=0. ms
64 bytes from 192.168.1.202: icmp_seq=4. time=0. ms
64 bytes from 192.168.1.202: icmp_seq=5. time=0. ms
64 bytes from 192.168.1.202: icmp_seq=6. time=0. ms
64 bytes from 192.168.1.202: icmp_seq=7. time=0. ms
Ctrl+c
----hp02 PING Statistics----
8 packets transmitted, 8 packets received, 0% packet loss
round-trip (ms)  min/avg/max = 0/0/2
```

You have to press Ctrl+c to terminate the command execution. At the bottom of the output under "hp02 PING Statistics", the number of packets transmitted, received and lost are shown. The packet loss should be 0% and the round trip time should not be high. You can ping the system's own IP, the loopback address (127.0.0.1), the default route, a node on the local network and a node through a router to check if the system is properly set to communicate to itself, nodes on local network and nodes beyond the local network.

Another item to notice in the output is that the first ICMP reply took longer to come back than the subsequent replies. This is based on the fact that the command broadcasts the destination interface's MAC address over the network using the *arp* command and the node with that MAC address replies. This process takes additional time and results in a longer reply time. It might not be the case always.

If *ping* fails in any of the situations, check if the LAN card is seated in the slot properly, its driver is installed and configured (use *ioscan*), LAN cable is secured appropriately, IP and subnet mask are set correctly (use *ifconfig* and *netstat*) and the default route is configured right (use *netstat*). Verify the entries in the */etc/hosts* and */etc/rc.config.d/netconf* files as well.

25.1.7   Using netstat

netstat (network statistics) reports network interface statistics including their status. When this command is executed with –i option, it displays the hostname and IP addresses, and incoming and outgoing packet information. Examine its output when you suspect an issue with one of the LAN interfaces. By default, this command resolves hostname to IP address, but if you like to see results in numerical format, add –n option.

 # netstat –i

Name	Mtu	Network	Address	Ipkts	Ierrs	Opkts	Oerrs	Coll
lan1:1	1500	193.12.211.0	193.12.211.2	0	0	0	0	0
lan1	1500	193.11.211.0	193.11.211.2	0	0	0	0	0
lo0	32808	127.0.0.0	127.0.0.1	856153	0	856153	0	0
lan1:3	1500	193.14.211.0	193.14.211.2	0	0	0	0	0
lan1:2	1500	193.13.211.0	193.13.211.2	0	0	0	0	0
lan4	1500	192.168.1.0	192.168.1.201	2315042	0	241125	0	733

The *netstat* command with –r option generates routing information:

 # netstat –r
Routing tables

Destination	Gateway	Flags	Refs	Interface	Pmtu
localhost	localhost	UH	0	lo0	32808
hp01	hp01	UH	0	lan4	32808
193.11.211.2	193.11.211.2	UH	0	lan1	32808
193.13.211.2	193.13.211.2	UH	0	lan1:2	32808
193.12.211.2	193.12.211.2	UH	0	lan1:1	32808
193.14.211.2	193.14.211.2	UH	0	lan1:3	32808
192.168.1.0	hp01	U	2	lan4	1500
193.11.211.0	193.11.211.2	U	5	lan1	1500
193.12.211.0	193.12.211.2	U	5	lan1:1	1500
193.13.211.0	193.13.211.2	U	5	lan1:2	1500
193.14.211.0	193.14.211.2	U	5	lan1:3	1500
loopback	localhost	U	0	lo0	32808
default	192.168.1.1	UG	0	lan4	1500

Above output in numerical format:

 # netstat –rn
Routing tables

Destination	Gateway	Flags	Refs	Interface	Pmtu
127.0.0.1	127.0.0.1	UH	0	lo0	32808
192.168.1.201	192.168.1.201	UH	0	lan4	32808
193.11.211.2	193.11.211.2	UH	0	lan1	32808

193.13.211.2	193.13.211.2	UH	0	lan1:2	32808
193.12.211.2	193.12.211.2	UH	0	lan1:1	32808
193.14.211.2	193.14.211.2	UH	0	lan1:3	32808
192.168.1.0	192.168.1.201	U	2	lan4	1500
193.11.211.0	193.11.211.2	U	5	lan1	1500
193.12.211.0	193.12.211.2	U	5	lan1:1	1500
193.13.211.0	193.13.211.2	U	5	lan1:2	1500
193.14.211.0	193.14.211.2	U	5	lan1:3	1500
127.0.0.0	127.0.0.1	U	0	lo0	32808
default	192.168.1.1	UG	0	lan4	1500

With –a option, this command displays status of socket connections:

 # netstat –a
Active Internet connections (including servers)

Proto	Recv-Q	Send-Q	Local Address	Foreign Address	(state)
tcp	0	0	*.discard	*.*	LISTEN
tcp	0	0	*.chargen	*.*	LISTEN
tcp	0	0	*.echo	*.*	LISTEN

. . . .

With –s option, it displays network activity statistics:

 # netstat –s
tcp:
      58907 packets sent
         45019 data packets (3013575 bytes)
         88 data packets (387 bytes) retransmitted
         13881 ack-only packets (7779 delayed)
         5 keepalive probes sent
         1 connection dropped by keepalive
      0 connect requests dropped due to full queue
      1 connect request dropped due to no listener
udp:
      0 incomplete headers
      0 bad checksums
ip:
      205656 total packets received
      0 bad IP headers
      0 fragments received
      0 packets not forwardable
icmp:
      30176 calls to generate an ICMP error message
      0 ICMP messages dropped
      address mask reply: 0
      15 responses sent

. . . .

From network connectivity troubleshooting perspective, use this command to check if proper routes and IP addresses are set, and if packets are going out and coming in.

25.1.8   Using traceroute

traceroute tests connectivity at the TCP/IP level between hosts. It sends out packets of data to the destination host and displays the route the packets take to reach it. As an example, issue the following on *hp01* to trace the route to *hp02*:

traceroute hp02
traceroute to hp02 (192.168.1.202), 30 hops max, 40 byte packets
 1 192.168.1.1 (192.168.1.1) 0.264 ms 0.197 ms 0.201 ms
 2 hp02 (192.168.1.202) 0.197 ms 0.163 ms 0.165 ms

The output indicates that the packets went out of the system via the default gateway (192.168.1.1) to reach *hp02*.

If *traceroute* fails, check if the IP and subnet mask are set correctly (use *ifconfig* and *netstat*) and the default route configured properly (use *netstat*). Verify the entries in the */etc/hosts* and */etc/rc.config.d/netconf* files.

25.1.9   Using ndd

ndd displays TCP/IP tunable parameter information and allows you to fine tune them. Its output can be used to troubleshoot a network problem. A list of supported *ndd* tunable parameters is displayed using the –h option:

ndd –h supported
SUPPORTED ndd tunable parameters on HP-UX:
IP:
   ip_def_ttl   - Controls the default TTL in the IP header
   ip_forward_directed_broadcasts   - Controls subnet broadcasts packets
   ip_forward_src_routed   - Controls forwarding of source routed packets
   ip_forwarding   - Controls how IP hosts forward packets
   ip_fragment_timeout   - Controls how long IP fragments are kept
   ip_icmp_return_data_bytes   - Maximum number of data bytes in ICMP
. . . .
TCP:
   tcp_conn_request_max   - Max number of outstanding connection request
   tcp_ignore_path_mtu   - Disable setting MSS from ICMP 'Frag Needed'
   tcp_ip_abort_cinterval   - R2 during connection establishment
   tcp_ip_abort_interval   - R2 for established connection
   tcp_ip_notify_cinterval   - R1 during connection establishment
   tcp_ip_notify_interval   - R1 for established connection
. . . .

A list of unsupported ndd parameters is displayed using the –h option:

ndd –h unsupported

UNSUPPORTED ndd tunable parameters on HP-UX:
This set of parameters are not supported by HP and modification of
these tunable parameters are not suggested nor recommended.
IP:

ip_bogus_sap	- Allow IP bind to a nonstandard/unused SAP
ip_check_subnet_addr	- Controls the subnet portion of a host address
ip_debug	- Controls the level of IP module debugging
ip_dl_snap_sap	- The SAP to use for SNAP encapsulation
ip_dl_sap	- Set the SAP when IP binds to a DLPI device
ip_encap_ttl	- Set the TTL for the encapsulated IP header

. . . .

TCP:

tcp_conn_grace_period	- Additional time for sending a SYN packet
tcp_debug	- Internal TCP debug option
tcp_deferred_ack_interval	-Timeout interval for deferred ACK
tcp_discon	- Terminate a TCP connection
tcp_discon_by_addr	- Terminate a TCP connection
tcp_dupack_fast_retransmit	- No. of ACKs needed to trigger a retransmit

. . . .

The *ndd* command displays or sets any of these parameter values. For example, to display the value of a parameter "ip_def_ttl":

ndd –h ip_def_ttl

ip_def_ttl:
Sets the default time to live (TTL) in the IP header.
[1,225] Default: 255

To change its value to 100:

ndd –set /dev/ip ip_def_ttl 100

Parameters for *ndd* can be set in the */etc/rc.config.d/nddconf* file so that they automatically get set at each system reboot. The default *nddconf* file is shown below:

cat /etc/rc.config.d/nddconf

. . . .
Example 5: Change the amount of time that ARP entries can stay in
ARP cache to 10 minutes.
TRANSPORT_NAME[4]=arp
NDD_NAME[4]=arp_cleanup_interval
NDD_VALUE[4]=600000

25.1.10   Using nettl

nettl (network tracing and logging) controls network tracing and logging activities. Tracing captures inbound and outbound packets going through the network, as well as loopback or header

---

information. Logging captures network activities such as connection establishment, errors and state changes.

To start *nettl* service, ensure that the variable NETTL is set to 1 in */etc/rc.config.d/nettl* file and then execute one of the following:

 # /sbin/init.d/nettl start   or # **nettl –st**
Initializing Network Tracing and Logging...
Done.

To stop *nettl*, do any the following:

 # /sbin/init.d/nettl stop   or # **nettl –sp**
nettl stopped

To check the status of logging and tracing, execute *nettl* as follows:

 # nettl –status
Logging Information:
Log Filename: /var/adm/nettl.LOG*
Max Log file size(Kbytes):   1000   Console Logging: On
User's ID: 0   Buffer Size: 8192
Messages Dropped: 0   Messages Queued: 0
Subsystem Name: Log Class:
NS_LS_LOGGING   ERROR DISASTER
NS_LS_NFT   ERROR DISASTER
NS_LS_LOOPBACK   ERROR DISASTER
NS_LS_NI   ERROR DISASTER
NS_LS_IPC   ERROR DISASTER
NS_LS_SOCKREGD   ERROR DISASTER
. . . .
Tracing Information:
Trace Filename:
Max Trace file size(Kbytes): 0
No Subsystems Active

Summary

You studied the basic network connectivity troubleshooting techniques in this chapter.

You were presented with various native HP-UX tools that helped you with troubleshooting. The tools included *ioscan, lanscan, linkloop, lanadmin, nwmgr, ping, netstat, traceroute, ndd* and *nettl*.

## 26

Internet Services and Sendmail

This chapter covers the following major topics:

- ✓ Introduction to Berkeley and ARPA internet services
- ✓ The role of internet services daemon
- ✓ The role of internet services daemon configuration and security files
- ✓ Enable internet services logging
- ✓ Establish user and host equivalency
- ✓ Use Berkeley services
- ✓ Enable and Disable ARPA services
- ✓ Use ARPA services
- ✓ Enable and use anonymous ftp
- ✓ Configure sendmail and verify functionality
- ✓ Update sendmail aliases database

26.1 The Internet Services

HP-UX *internet services* enable a system to be used as a provider of one or more services to remote client systems over the network. These services include allowing users on the remote machines to login, transfer files, send and receive emails, execute commands without logging in, getting list of logged in users, synchronize time and so on.

When services are used over the network, two pieces of software program – client and server – are involved. The client program requests for a service running on a remote system. The server program (or daemon) on the remote system serves or responds to the client request, establishing a client/server communication channel. At any given time, an HP-UX system can act as both a server and a client. It can provide services to other machines and may use their services as a client.

Server programs are started in one of two ways: via startup scripts located in sequencer directories or via the master server program daemon called *inetd*. A detailed discussion on the startup scripts and sequencer directories is covered in Chapter 16 "HP-UX Shutdown and Startup".

The *inetd* daemon itself is started by one of the startup scripts when the system boots up to run level 2. This daemon reads its configuration file */etc/inetd.conf* and sits in the memory. It listens on ports listed in the */etc/services* and */etc/rpc* files for services defined and enabled in its configuration file. It waits for a client request to come in requesting for one of the *inetd*-controlled services. When one such request arrives on a particular port, this daemon starts the server program corresponding to that port. It hooks the client and server pieces up, gets itself out of that communication and starts listening on that port again on behalf of that server program. Remember, every service uses a unique port number defined in either the */etc/services* or the */etc/rpc* file.

26.1.1 Berkeley and ARPA Services

There are two major categories of the internet services: one developed at the University of California at Berkeley and referred to as *Berkeley* services and the other developed for the US Department of Defense's *Advanced Research Project Agency* and referred to as *ARPA* services.

The Berkeley services include BIND (DNS), sendmail, *finger*, *rexec*, *rcp*, *rlogin*, *remsh*, *ruptime*, *rup* and *rwho*. They were primarily developed to run on the UNIX platform, however, most of them today are available on non-UNIX platforms too. The names of most Berkeley services begin with an "r" and, therefore, also referred to as "r" commands.

The ARPA services, on the other hand, include *ftp* and *telnet*, which can be used on both UNIX and non-UNIX platforms.

Table 26-1 lists and describes some commonly used internet services.

Service	Description
bootpd	Enables boot clients such as diskless systems, X stations, Ignite-UX clients and old network printers to boot by providing them network configuration information. This daemon is started by *inetd* and it uses port 67. The *bootpd* entry in the */etc/inetd.conf* file looks like: bootps dgram udp wait root /usr/lbin/bootpd bootpd

Service	Description
fingerd	Enables the *finger* command to display information about users on local and remote systems. The *fingerd* daemon is started by *inetd* and it uses port 79. The *fingerd* entry in the */etc/inetd.conf* file looks like: finger stream tcp nowait bin /usr/lbin/fingerd fingerd
ftpd	Enables file transfer with other UNIX and non-UNIX systems. The client program is *ftp*. The *ftpd* daemon is started by *inetd* and it uses port 21. The *ftpd* entry in the */etc/inetd.conf* file looks like: ftp stream tcp nowait root /usr/lbin/ftpd ftpd –l
gated	Dynamically determines which of the several available routes to use to transport data from one machine to another on large networks and the internet. Updates routing table dynamically and automatically based on the updated routing information it discovers over time. Its configuration file is */etc/gated.conf* and it is started by the */sbin/init.d/gated* script at system boot up if the GATED variable is set to 1 in */etc/rc.config.d/netconf*. A detailed discussion on *gated* is beyond the scope of this book.
named	Enables hostname-to-IP and IP-to-hostname resolution. The *named* daemon responds to commands such as *nslookup* and *nsquery*. It is started via a startup script. A detailed discussion is covered in Chapter 32 "Domain Name System".
remshd	Enables two services: file transfer via *rcp,* and command execution and remote login using *remsh* on to a remote system. This daemon is started by *inetd*. The *remshd* entry in the */etc/inetd.conf* file looks like: shell stream tcp nowait root /usr/lbin/remshd remshd
rexecd	Enables executing a command on a remote system. The daemon is started by *inetd*. The *rexecd* entry in the */etc/inetd.conf* file looks like: exec stream tcp nowait root /usr/lbin/rexecd rexecd
rlogind	Enables a user to login to a remote system using the *rlogin* command. This daemon is started by *inetd* and it uses port 513. The *rlogind* entry in the */etc/inetd.conf* file looks like: login stream tcp nowait root /usr/lbin/rlogind rlogind
rlpdaemon	Enables a print request to print on a remote printer. This daemon is started by *inetd*. A detailed discussion on printers is covered in Chapter 19 "Print Services".
rwhod	Enables *rup, ruptime* and *rwho* commands to display remote system information. This daemon is started by the */sbin/init.d/rwhod* script at system boot if the RWHOD variable is set to 1 in the */etc/rc.config.d/netdaemons* file.
sendmail	Sendmail is the most widely used mail transport and delivery program on large networks and the internet. It works with various client mail programs. It is started by the */sbin/init.d/sendmail* script at boot time if the SENDMAIL_SERVER variable is set to 1 in the */etc/rc.config.d/mailservs* file. It uses port 25.

Service	Description
telnetd	Enables a user to login to a remote machine. The client program is *telnet*. *telnetd* is started by *inetd* and it uses port 23. The *telnetd* entry in the */etc/inetd.conf* file looks like: telnet stream tcp nowait root /usr/lbin/telnetd telnetd
tftpd	Works with *bootpd* to enable diskless systems, X stations, Ignite-UX clients and old network printers to transfer files containing boot and other configuration data. The client program is *tftp*. *tftpd* is started by *inetd* and it uses port 69. The *tftpd* entry in the */etc/inetd.conf* file looks like: tftp dgram udp wait root /usr/lbin/tftpd tftpd
xntpd	Keeps the system clock in sync with a more reliable and accurate source of time. A detailed discussion is covered in Chapter 27 "Network Time Protocol (NTP)".

Table 26-1 Internet Services

26.1.2   The inetd Daemon and the /etc/inetd.conf File

The *inetd* daemon is the master server daemon for many internet services. This daemon is started automatically at system boot when the */sbin/init.d/inetd* script is executed. It listens for connection requests for the services listed in its configuration file */etc/inetd.conf* over the ports defined in the */etc/services* and */etc/rpc* files, and starts up an appropriate server process when a request arrives.

The contents of */etc/inetd.conf* look similar to the following:

 # cat /etc/inetd.conf

```
. . . . . . . .
#       ARPA/Berkeley services
ftp           stream   tcp      nowait   root /usr/lbin/ftpd ftpd -l
telnet        stream   tcp      nowait   root /usr/lbin/telnetd      telnetd
tftp          dgram    udp      wait     root /usr/lbin/tftpd        tftpd   /opt/ignite  /var/opt/ignite
#bootps       dgram    udp      wait     root /usr/lbin/bootpd       bootpd
#finger       stream   tcp      nowait   bin  /usr/lbin/fingerd      fingerd
login         stream   tcp      nowait   root /usr/lbin/rlogind      rlogind
shell         stream   tcp      nowait   root /usr/lbin/remshd       remshd
exec          stream   tcp      nowait   root /usr/lbin/rexecd       rexecd
. . . . . . . .
```

There are at least seven columns per line entry for each non-RPC and nine columns per line entry for each RPC service defined in the file. Table 26-2 lists and explains each column. Line entries that begin with the # character represent disabled services.

Column	Description
1	Service name as listed in the */etc/services* or */etc/rpc* file.
2	Socket type. "Stream" for TCP and "dgram" (datagram) for UDP.
3	Protocol used (TCP or UDP) as defined in the */etc/protocols* file.

Column	Description
4	"wait" is used with UDP and tells *inetd* not to start another instance (or thread) of the same process until this one finishes. "nowait" is used with TCP and tells *inetd* to go ahead and start another instance (or thread) of the same process if additional requests come in. For example, you can have multiple *telnetd* daemons running simultaneously serving multiple *telnet* requests.
5	Run the server program as this user.
6	Absolute path to the server process.
7	Name of the server process in case of a non-RPC service, and RPC program number in case of an RPC service.
8	Any options or arguments.
9	Name of the server process in case of an RPC service.

Table 26-2 /etc/inetd.conf File Contents

Line entries for some internet services are extracted from the */etc/services* file and displayed below. The output shows service name in the first column, port number and protocol it uses in the second column, associated alias in the third column and comments in the last column.

```
# cat /etc/services

. . . . . . . .
# <official service name>  <port number/protocol name>  <aliases>
ftp          21/tcp                             # File Transfer Protocol (Control)
telnet       23/tcp                             # Virtual Terminal Protocol
smtp         25/tcp                             # Simple Mail Transfer Protocol
time         37/tcp        timeserver           # Time
time         37/udp        timeserver           #
rlp          39/udp        resource             # Resource Location Protocol
. . . . . . . .
```

Line entries for some RPC-based services are extracted from the */etc/rpc* file and displayed below. The output shows service name in the first column followed by port number and associated aliases.

```
# cat /etc/rpc

. . . . . . . .
rpcbind     100000   portmap sunrpc rpcbind
rstatd      100001   rstat rup perfmeter
rusersd     100002   rusers
nfs         100003   nfsprog
ypserv      100004   ypprog
mountd      100005   mount showmount
ypbind      100007
. . . . . . . .
```

Whenever a modification is made to the */etc/inetd.conf* file, the *inetd* daemon must be restarted with the –c option for the modifications to take effect.

The */etc/inetd.conf* file should have *root* ownership and *other* group membership with 444 permissions.

26.1.3   Securing inetd

By default, when a user on a client machine requests for a service managed by *inetd* on a remote system, the user is served if the service is enabled in */etc/inetd.conf* file. This access can be controlled at the user, system or network level by inserting appropriate entries in *inetd*'s security file */var/adm/inetd.sec*.

The following shows typical */var/adm/inetd.sec* file contents, appended by three example entries:

```
# cat /var/adm/inetd.sec
. . . . . . . .
telnet       allow    193.11.211.*
finger       deny     hp05  hp06
ftp          deny     *
```

The first line allows *telnet* access from only those systems that are on the 193.11.211 network. The second line denies *finger* access from *hp05* and *hp06* systems. The third line denies everyone access to using *ftp* service.

This file should have *root* ownership and *other* group membership with 444 permissions. Use of this security control is optional.

 Only the services configured in */etc/inetd.conf* can be controlled via */var/adm/inetd.sec*.

The */var/adm/inetd.sec* file can be managed using SMH (or *ncweb* command) as well. Follow the links below:

☞ Go to SMH → Networking and Communications → Network Services Configuration → System Access → Internet Services. Highlight a service and go to Actions → Modify. Choose "Selected-Allowed" or "Selected-Denied" and specify the systems and networks to be allowed or denied access. See Figure 26-1.

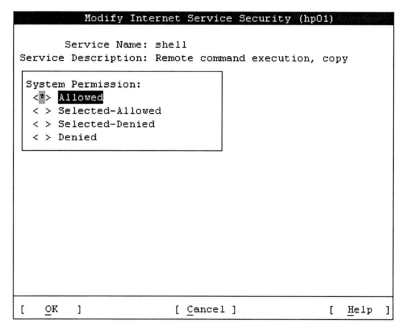

```
              Modify Internet Service Security (hp01)

              Service Name: shell
      Service Description: Remote command execution, copy

     ┌────────────────────────────────────────────────┐
     │ System Permission:                             │
     │  <*> Allowed                                   │
     │  < > Selected-Allowed                          │
     │  < > Selected-Denied                           │
     │  < > Denied                                    │
     └────────────────────────────────────────────────┘




   [   OK   ]                 [ Cancel ]                 [  Help  ]
```

Figure 26-1 SMH – Allow/Deny inetd-Controlled Services

26.1.4   Enabling inetd Connection Logging

The *inetd* daemon starts logging connection requests for all services listed in the */etc/inetd.conf* file through *syslogd* in */var/adm/syslog/syslog.log* file immediately if the –l option is specified with it at the command line. By default, the connection logging is disabled.

> # **inetd –l**

To make this change permanent so that every time the system reboots *inetd* connection logging is enabled, edit the */etc/rc.config.d/netdaemons* file and set the INETD_ARGS variable to 1:

> INETD_ARGS="–l"

From now on, whenever *inetd* is called either at system startup or manually through */sbin/init.d/inetd* script, it will log connection requests.

26.2   Using the Internet Services

The following sub-sections examine using selected Berkeley internet services. Prior to that, let us understand the concept of trust relationship, which is used by some services.

26.2.1   Establishing Trust Relationship

Making a system trusted on a remote machine means that any user from that system can run the *rlogin*, *rcp* or *remsh* command without being prompted for a password on the remote machine. This is called *host equivalency*. The equivalency information is stored in the */etc/hosts.equiv* file on the remote machine and includes hostnames of the systems whose users are to be allowed passwordless

---

entry into the remote machine for the three commands. Note that the same user must exist on both systems. This file does not support trusting *root* user account.

By default, the */etc/hosts.equiv* file does not exist. It must be created if needed.

To understand the concept, assume that the following entries are present in the */etc/hosts.equiv* file on *hp03*:

```
hp01
hp02     user1
+
-
```

Here is the explanation for the four entries:

✓ The first line entry allows all users from *hp01* passwordless access into *hp03*.
✓ The second line entry allows only *user1* from *hp02* passwordless access into *hp03*.
✓ The third line entry allows all users from all hosts passwordless access into *hp03*.
✓ The fourth line entry allows no users from any hosts passwordless access into *hp03*.

This file is created and maintained by *root*.

Unlike the */etc/hosts.equiv* file, a user on a system can create a *.rhosts* file in his home directory and allow a remote user by the same username to execute the three commands without furnishing a password. This is known as *user equivalency*. The *.rhosts* file may be created for any user including *root*.

By default, the *.rhosts* file does not exist in any user home directories. The syntax of this file is identical to that of the */etc/hosts.equiv* file.

To understand the concept, assume that the following entries are present in the *.rhosts* file for *user2* on *hp04*:

```
hp02
+
```

Here is the explanation for the two entries:

✓ The first line entry allows *user2* from only *hp02* system passwordless access into *hp04*.
✓ The second line entry allows *user2* from any system passwordless access into *hp04*.

Both host and user equivalency can be configured via SMH (or *ncweb* command). Follow the links below:

☞Go to SMH → Networking and Communications → Network Services Configuration → System Access → Remote Logins → Actions → Add. Fill out the form based on requirements and press the OK button. See Figure 26-2.

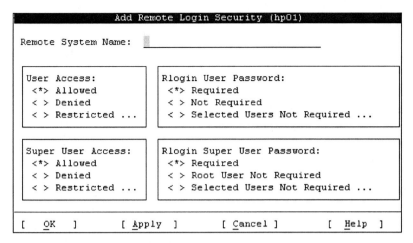

```
┌──────────────────────────────────────────────────────────────┐
│            Add Remote Login Security (hp01)                  │
│                                                              │
│ Remote System Name:  ▒ _____         │
│                                                              │
│  ┌──────────────────────┐  ┌──────────────────────────────┐ │
│  │ User Access:         │  │ Rlogin User Password:        │ │
│  │  <*> Allowed         │  │  <*> Required                │ │
│  │  < > Denied          │  │  < > Not Required            │ │
│  │  < > Restricted ...  │  │  < > Selected Users Not Required ... │ │
│  └──────────────────────┘  └──────────────────────────────┘ │
│                                                              │
│  ┌──────────────────────┐  ┌──────────────────────────────┐ │
│  │ Super User Access:   │  │ Rlogin Super User Password:  │ │
│  │  <*> Allowed         │  │  <*> Required                │ │
│  │  < > Denied          │  │  < > Root User Not Required  │ │
│  │  < > Restricted ...  │  │  < > Selected Users Not Required ... │ │
│  └──────────────────────┘  └──────────────────────────────┘ │
│                                                              │
│ [  OK  ]      [ Apply ]       [ Cancel ]       [ Help ]      │
└──────────────────────────────────────────────────────────────┘
```

Figure 26-2 SMH – Remote Access

26.2.2   Using Berkeley Services

Let us now look at the usage of some client programs such as *rlogin, rcp, remsh, rexec, rup,
ruptime, rwho* and *finger* included in the Berkeley internet services. The usage is explained using
examples. Ensure that none of these services are restricted in */var/adm/inetd.sec* file.

The following examples assume that *hp02* is trusted on *hp03* for *root*, and vice versa.

To use *rlogin* to enter from *hp02* into *hp03*, run the following on *hp02*. Make sure that the "login"
line entry in the */etc/inetd.conf* file is uncommented.

 # rlogin hp03
Last successful login: Fri Apr 18 08:14:57 EDT 2008 192.168.1.202
Last authentication failure: Thu Apr 17 16:06:40 EDT 2008

. . . .
#

To use *rcp* to copy *.dtprofile* from *root*'s home directory on *hp02* to its home directory on *hp03*, run
the following on *hp02*. Ensure that the "shell" line entry in the */etc/inetd.conf* file is uncommented.

 # rcp $HOME/.dtprofile hp03:$HOME

To use *rcp* to copy *.dtprofile* from *root*'s home directory on *hp02* to its home directory on *hp03*, run
the following on *hp03*. Make certain that the "shell" line entry in */etc/inetd.conf* is uncommented.

 # rcp hp02:$HOME/.dtprofile $HOME

The *remsh* command can be used to perform two functions: it can do the *rlogin* function and can
execute a command on a remote machine without logging on to it. The first example below lets *root*
login to *hp02* from *hp03*. The second example runs the *ls* command on the */etc* directory on *hp02*
from *hp03*. Make sure that the "shell" line entry in the */etc/inetd.conf* file is uncommented.

 # remsh hp02

---

remsh hp02 ls /etc

The following examples use neither */etc/hosts.equiv* nor *.rhosts* file. You must enter the correct password in order to get in.

The example below runs the *ls* command on the */etc* directory on *hp02* from *hp03*. Make sure that the "exec" line entry in the */etc/inetd.conf* file is uncommented.

```
# rexec hp02 ls /etc
Password (hp03:root):
```

The *rup* command broadcasts over the network, and all machines running the *rpc.rstatd* daemon responds with their brief status. Make certain that the "rpc.rstatd" line entry in the */etc/inetd.conf* file is uncommented.

```
# rup
hp02   up 13 days, 13:50,   load average: 0.50, 0.50, 0.50
hp03   up  3 days, 10 mins, load average: 2.32, 2.46, 2.50
```

The *ruptime* command broadcasts over the network, and all machines running the *rwhod* daemon responds with their brief status. Make sure that the "rwhod" line entry in the */etc/inetd.conf* file is uncommented.

```
# ruptime
hp02      up  13+13:45,   2 users,  load 0.50, 0.50, 0.50
hp03      up   3+00:02,   1 user,   load 2.53, 2.59, 2.51
```

The *rwho* command broadcasts over the network, and all machines running the *rwhod* daemon responds with a list of logged on users. Make certain that the "rwhod" line entry in the */etc/inetd.conf* file is uncommented.

```
# rwho
root     hp02:0    Apr  8 15:18
user1    hp02:1    Apr 17 21:32
root     hp03:0    Apr 17 21:35
```

The *finger* command broadcasts over the network, and all machines running the *fingerd* daemon responds with a list of logged on users. Make sure that the "finger" line entry in the */etc/inetd.conf* file is uncommented.

```
# finger @hp03
[hp02]
Login    Name    TTY  Idle    When        Bldg.    Phone
root     ???     *0   9d      Wed 15:18
root     ???     *1           Fri 21:32
```

These client programs cannot be used from SMH (or *ncweb* command), but can be enabled or disabled. Follow the links below:

☞Go to SMH → Networking and Communications → Network Services Configuration → System Access → Internet Services. Highlight a service and go to Actions → Modify. Select either "Allowed" or "Denied". This will update the */etc/inetd.conf* file and execute the *inetd* command with –c switch. Consult Figure 26-3.

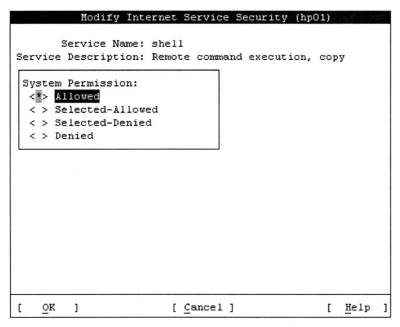

Figure 26-3 SMH – Internet Services Allow/Deny

26.2.3   Using ARPA Services

This sub-section is going to cover two ARPA services – *telnet* and *ftp*. The usage of both is explained using examples. Make sure that these services are not restricted in the */var/adm/inetd.sec* file. By default, both services are uncommented in the */etc/inetd.conf* file and are enabled.

Using *telnet*

The procedure to use *telnet* is such that the hostname or IP address of the remote system is specified with the command. *telnet* can be invoked from a Windows or UNIX system. For example, the following invokes a *telnet* session from the Windows prompt to enter *hp02* with IP address 192.168.1.202:

C:\> **telnet 192.168.1.202**
Trying 192.168.1.202...
Connected to hp02.
Escape character is '^]'.
HP-UX hp02 B.11.31 U 9000/800 (ta)
login:

When *telnet* contacts *hp02* on port 23, *inetd* spawns the *telnetd* daemon, which then takes over and establishes a communication session with *telnet*. A login prompt is displayed where a valid username and password is expected to be entered to login to *hp02*. Use the *exit* command or press `Ctrl+d` to exit.

Using *ftp*

The procedure to use *ftp* is such that the hostname or IP address of the remote machine is specified with the command. *ftp* can be invoked from a Windows or UNIX system. For example, the following invokes an *ftp* session from the Windows prompt to enter *hp02* with IP address 192.168.1.202:

> C:\> **ftp 192.168.1.202**
> Connected to 192.168.1.201.
> 220 hp01 FTP server (Revision 1.1 Version wuftpd-2.6.1 Fri Oct 6 07:58:07 GMT 006) ready.
> User (192.168.1.201:(none)): **root**
> 331 Password required for root.
> Password:
> 230 User root logged in.
> ftp>

As soon as *ftp* contacts *hp02* on port 21, *inetd* spawns the *ftpd* daemon, which then takes over and establishes a communication session with *ftp*. A login prompt is displayed where a valid username and password is expected to be entered to login to *hp02*. Use the *quit* or *bye* command to exit.

Available commands at the *ftp* prompt can be listed by typing a *?* at the ftp> prompt:

> ftp> **?**
> Commands may be abbreviated. Commands are:

!	debug	mdir	passive	site
$	dir	mget	put	size
account	disconnect	mkdir	pwd	status
append	form	mls	quit	struct
ascii	get	mode	quote	system
bell	glob	modtime	recv	sunique
binary	hash	mput	reget	tenex
bye	help	newer	rstatus	trace
case	idle	nmap	rhelp	type
cd	image	nlist	rename	user
cdup	lcd	ntrans	reset	umask

By default, everyone with a valid username and password is allowed to login using *ftp*. This open access can be controlled by creating a file */etc/ftpd/ftpusers* and listing names of users that need not be allowed to *ftp* in. Each user is listed one per line in the file. This file does not exist by default.

Enabling and Using Anonymous *ftp* Access

Anonymous *ftp* access into a system allows a user without knowing a valid username/password on the system to upload or download files to and from a public directory. The user types the *ftp* command to connect to the system and enters *anonymous* as the login name with any string of characters (preferably an email address) as the password. This access must be enabled before it can be used. Here is the procedure on how to enable it.

1. Add the following entry to the */etc/passwd* file:

   ftp:*:500:1:Anonymous FTP user:/home/ftp:/usr/bin/false

2. Create a home directory for *ftp* account in */home* with following permissions and ownership/membership:

   dr-xr-xr-x   6 root   other   96 Feb 17 10:55 ftp

3. Create *dist*, *etc*, *pub* and *usr* sub-directories under */home/ftp* and modify permissions and ownership as shown below:

   dr-xr-xr-x   2 root   other   96 Feb 17 10:55 dist
   dr-xr-xr-x   2 root   other   96 Feb 17 10:55 etc
   drwxrwxrwx   2 ftp   other   96 Feb 17 10:55 pub
   dr-xr-xr-x   4 root   other   96 Feb 17 10:55 usr

4. Copy */etc/passwd* and */etc/group* files to */home/ftp/etc* and modify permissions as shown below:

   -r--r--r--   2 root   other   223 Feb 17 10:55 group
   -r--r--r--   1 root   other   641 Feb 17 10:55 passwd

5. Create *bin* sub-directory under */home/ftp/usr*:

   dr-xr-xr-x   2 root   other   96 Feb 17 10:55 bin

6. Copy the *ls* command to */home/ftp/usr/bin* and modify permissions as shown below:

   ---x--x—x   1 root   other   286720 Nov 14 2000 ls

This sets up the anonymous *ftp* access and is ready to go.

SMH (or *ncweb* command) can be used instead for this purpose. Follow the links below to enable file uploads:

☞Go to SMH → Networking and Communications → Network Services Configuration → Network Services. Highlight "Anonymous FTP" and go to Actions → Enable. Both "Anon FTP Deposit" and "Anon FTP Retrieval" will be enabled. See Figure 26-4.

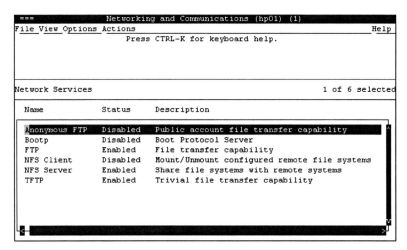

Figure 26-4 SMH – Anonymous FTP

The following runs *ftp* from the Windows prompt to enter *hp02* with IP address 192.168.1.202 to login as user *anonymous*:

C:\> **ftp 192.168.1.202**
Connected to 192.168.1.201.
220 hp01 FTP server (Revision 1.1 Version wuftpd-2.6.1 Fri Oct 6 07:58:07 GMT 2
006) ready.
User (192.168.1.201:(none)): **anonymous**
331 Guest login ok, send your complete e-mail address as password.
Password:
230 Guest login ok, access restrictions apply.
ftp>

ftp session and file transfer activities can be logged for auditing in the */var/adm/syslog/xferlog* file. Session activities include commands used, and successful and unsuccessful login attempts. File transfer activities include file transfer time, remote system name, name of the file transferred, its size and transfer mode (ASCII or binary) used.

To enable *ftp* session logging, specify the –L option and to enable incoming and outgoing file transfer activities, specify the –i and –o options with the *ftp* entry in the */etc/inetd.conf* file:

ftp stream tcp nowait root /usr/lbin/ftpd ftpd –L –i –o

Force *inetd* to reload updated configuration from */etc/inetd.conf*:

inetd –c

26.3   Configuring Basic Sendmail Functionality

Sendmail is the most widely used email routing and delivery application on the internet. In other words, it is the most widely used *Mail Transport Agent* (MTA) and *Mail Delivery Agent* (MDA). Since sendmail is used on the internet, it requires that the system be configured to use DNS for hostname resolution. The *etc/hosts* file may be employed if sendmail is to be used on the internal network only.

Sendmail works with a client mail program such as *mailx*, and routes mail messages using SMTP. It is started by the */sbin/init.d/sendmail* script at boot time if the SENDMAIL_SERVER variable is set to 1 in the */etc/rc.config.d/mailservs* file.

The following sub-sections explain how to setup and verify sendmail and update the *aliases* file.

26.3.1   Configuring Sendmail to be Used by Single System Users

Sendmail is ready to go by default when HP-UX is installed. The *sendmail* daemon is started automatically and users can send and receive mail. The default setup is restricted to users of that system only.

The following is done as part of HP-UX installation for sendmail configuration and automatic startup:

✓ The SENDMAIL_SERVER variable in */etc/rc.config.d/mailservs* is set to 1.
✓ The system's hostname is appended to the */etc/mail/sendmail.cw* file.
✓ Default */etc/mail/sendmail.cf* and */etc/mail/aliases* files are created.
✓ The sendmail startup script */sbin/init.d/sendmail* is executed that generates the aliases database file */etc/mail/aliases.db* from */etc/mail/aliases*, and starts the *sendmail* daemon.

If, for some reasons, sendmail setup is removed, follow the above steps to redo the configuration.

26.3.2   Configuring Sendmail in Client/Server Environment

You can configure one of the HP-UX systems as a sendmail server so that it receives and sends out mail messages for users on that system as well as on other systems on the network. The user mail is stored in the */var/mail* directory. This directory can be shared with client machines for user mail retrieval on those systems. Similarly, for sending mail out, the sendmail client forwards to the sendmail server any mail destined for local or over the internet delivery.

To configure *hp02* as both NFS and sendmail servers, do the following:

1. Ensure all mail users have accounts on the mail server, and that their UIDs and GIDs on the mail server are consistent with the ones on the client machines.
2. Edit */etc/rc.config.d/nfsconf* and set the NFS_SERVER variable to 1.
3. Add the following line to */etc/dfs/dfstab*:

   /var/mail

4. Edit */etc/rc.config.d/mailservs* and set the SENDMAIL_SERVER variable to 1.
5. Edit */etc/mail/sendmail.cw* file and add names of all client machines to the bottom.
6. Edit the sendmail configuration file */etc/mail/sendmail.cf* and append the following to the "Fw" keyword to look like:

   Fw/etc/mail/sendmail.cw

7. Execute the NFS server and sendmail startup scripts:

 # /sbin/init.d/nfs.server start
 # /sbin/init.d/sendmail start
/etc/mail/aliases: 7 aliases, longest 9 bytes, 88 bytes total

The next step will be to configure the client machines to forward and receive mail to and from *hp02*. Here is what you will need to perform on the client systems:

1. Edit */etc/rc.config.d/mailservs* and set the SENDMAIL_SERVER variable to 0 and SENDMAIL_SERVER_NAME variable to the hostname or IP address of the sendmail server:

   SENDMAIL_SERVER=0
   SENDMAIL_SERVER_NAME=hp02

2. Edit */etc/rc.config.d/nfsconf* and set the NFS_CLIENT variable to 1.
3. Add the following line to */etc/fstab*:

   hp02:/var/mail /var/mail nfs defaults 0 0

4. Start sendmail and NFS client functionalities:

   # /sbin/init.d/sendmail start
   # /sbin/init.d/nfs.client start

The client/server setup is complete and the client machines are ready to forward local mail to the sendmail server.

26.3.3   Verifying Sendmail Functionality

You can verify that sendmail has been configured properly by sending out a test mail.

To test local mail functionality, mail a message to a local user *user1* on the system:

   # date | mailx –s "Local Sendmail Test" user1

To test network mail functionality, mail a message to a remote user *user2* on *hp01*:

   # date | mailx –s "Remote Sendmail Test" user1%hp02@hp01

Outgoing mail messages are stored temporarily in the mail queue directory located in */var/spool/mqueue*. Use the *mailq* command to display the messages. Use –v for detailed output.

   # mailq –v

user1 can view his mail by running the *mailx* command on *hp01* as follows:

$ mailx
From root@hp01 Fri Apr 18 14:16:24 EDT 2008
Received: (from root@localhost)
        by hp01 (@(#)Sendmail version 8.13.3 - Revision 1.000 - 1st August,2006/8.13.3) id
m3IIGOPm010230
        for user1; Fri, 18 Apr 2008 14:16:24 -0400 (EDT)
Date: Fri, 18 Apr 2008 14:16:24 -0400 (EDT)
From: root@hp01
Message-Id: <200804181816.m3IIGOPm010230@hp01>
To: user1@hp01
Subject: Local sendmail Test
Mime-Version: 1.0
Content-Type: text/plain; charset=us-ascii
Content-Transfer-Encoding: 7bit

Fri Apr 18 14:16:24 EDT 2008
?

An entry for both mail messages will be logged in the */var/adm/syslog/mail.log* file.

26.3.4   Updating the Aliases File

When a new alias is added to the */etc/mail/aliases* database file, the *sendmail* daemon needs to be informed. The *newaliases* command is used for this purpose. Here is what is produced when this command is executed:

 # newaliases
/etc/mail/aliases: 8 aliases, longest 9 bytes, 107 bytes total

Summary

This chapter introduced you to the internet services and sendmail functionality.

You learned Berkeley and ARPA internet services and looked at how to activate/deactivate and use them. You understood the concept of trust relationship and how to setup user and host equivalency. You looked at how the internet services daemon worked and understood the contents of its configuration and security files.

Finally, you studied a little bit about sendmail. You were presented with step-by-step procedure on how to configure basic sendmail server and client functionality. You sent mail messages to local and network users and displayed the messages to verify client/server component functionality.

Network Time Protocol (NTP)

This chapter covers the following major topics:

- ✓ NTP concepts and components
- ✓ Configure an NTP server
- ✓ Configure an NTP peer
- ✓ Configure an NTP client
- ✓ Configure authentication
- ✓ Use ntpdate to update system clock
- ✓ Query NTP servers
- ✓ Trace NTP server roots
- ✓ Basic troubleshooting

27.1 NTP Concepts and Components

The *Network Time Protocol* (NTP) service maintains the clock on the system synchronized with a more accurate and reliable time source. Providing accurate and uniform time for systems on the network allows time-sensitive applications such as backup software, job scheduling tools and billing systems to perform correctly and precisely. NTP uses port 123 on the HP-UX system.

In order to understand NTP, a discussion of NTP components and roles is necessary. The following sub-sections explain them.

27.1.1 Time Source

A *time source* is a server that synchronizes its time with *Universal Coordinated Time* (UTC). Care should be taken when choosing a time source for a network. Preference should be given to a time server that is physically close to the system location and takes the least amount of time to send and receive NTP packets.

The most common time sources available are:

- ✓ A local system clock.
- ✓ An internet-based public time server.
- ✓ A radio clock.

Local System Clock

You can arrange for one of the HP-UX systems on the network to function as a provider of time for other machines. This requires the maintenance of correct time on this local server either manually or automatically via *cron*. Keep in mind, however, that since this server is using its own system clock, it has no way of synchronizing itself with a more reliable and accurate external time source. Therefore, using a local system that relies on its own clock as a time server is the least recommended option.

Internet-Based Public Time Server

Several public time servers that can be employed for the provision of correct time are available via the internet. One of the systems on the network must be connected to one or more such time servers. To make use of such a time source, a port in the firewall may need to be opened to allow for the flow of NTP traffic. Internet-based public time servers are typically operated by government organizations and universities. This option is more popular than using a local time server.

Several public time servers are available for access on the internet. Visit *www.ntp.org* to obtain a list.

Radio Clock

A radio clock is considered the most accurate source of time. Some popular radio clock methods include *Global Positioning System* (GPS), *National Institute of Science and Technology* (NIST) radio broadcasts in Americas and DCF77 radio broadcasts in Europe. Of these, GPS-based sources are the most accurate. In order to use them, some hardware must be added to one of the local systems on the network.

27.1.2 Stratum Levels

As you are aware that there are numerous time sources available to synchronize the system time with. These time sources are categorized into levels called *stratum levels* based on their reliability and accuracy. There are 15 stratum levels ranging from 1 to 15, with 1 being the most accurate. The radio clocks are at stratum 1 as they are the most accurate. Stratum 1 time sources, however, cannot be used on a network directly. Therefore, one of the machines on the network at stratum 2, for instance, needs to be configured to get time updates from a stratum 1 server. The stratum 2 server then acts as the primary source of time for secondary servers and/or clients on the network. It can also be configured to provide time to stratum 3 or lower-reliability time servers.

If a secondary server is also configured to get time from a stratum 1 server directly, it will act as a peer to the primary server.

27.1.3 NTP Roles

A role is a function that an HP-UX system performs from the NTP standpoint. A system can be configured to assume one or more of the following roles:

Primary NTP Server

A *primary NTP server* gets time from one of the time sources mentioned above and provides time to one or more secondary servers or clients, or both. It can also be configured to broadcast time to secondary servers and clients.

Secondary NTP Server

A *secondary NTP server* receives time from a primary server or from one of the time sources mentioned above. It can be used to provide time to a set of clients to offload the primary server or, as a redundant time server when the primary becomes unavailable. Having a secondary server is optional, but highly recommended. It can be configured to broadcast time to clients and peers.

NTP Peer

An *NTP peer* provides time to an NTP server and receives time from that server. They usually work at the same stratum level. Both primary and secondary servers can be peers of each other.

NTP Client

An *NTP client* receives time from either a primary or a secondary time server. A client can be configured in one of the following two ways:

- ✓ As a *polling* client that contacts a primary or secondary NTP server directly to get time updates to synchronize its system clock.
- ✓ As a *broadcast* client that listens to time broadcasts by a primary or secondary NTP server. A broadcast client binds itself with the NTP server that responds to its requests and synchronizes its clock with it. The NTP server must be configured in broadcast mode in order for the broadcast client to bind to it.

27.2   Configuring NTP

The following sub-sections provide step-by-step procedures on how to configure an NTP server, peer and client.

27.2.1   Configuring NTP Server and Peer

To configure an NTP server or peer (primary or secondary), follow the steps below:

1.   Select an appropriate time source.
2.   Add the time source information to the */etc/ntp.conf* configuration file:

For the local system clock, use the 127.127.1.1 reserved IP address. The fudge keyword defines the stratum level. Add the following two lines:

```
server      127.127.1.1
fudge       127.127.1.1      stratum  9
```

For an internet-based time server, specify either the fully qualified hostname or IP address of the server. For example, the entry for an IP address 11.59.99.3 will look like:

```
server      11.59.99.3
```

For a radio clock-based source of time, connect special hardware device to the system's serial port and add the following line to the file. The first three octets of the IP address (127.127.4) indicates that an external source of time is used. The last octet of the IP address (2) means that the radio clock hardware is connected to the second serial port of the system.

```
server      127.127.4.2
```

To setup a peer, specify the hostname or IP address of the NTP server with the keyword "peer". For example, enter the following to define that this machine is a peer of *hp03*:

```
peer        hp03
```

It is recommended to choose a minimum of two time servers physically located apart and accessed via different network routes for redundancy purposes. NTP automatically starts using the secondary server should the primary becomes unavailable. The servers can act as peers of each other if they are at the same stratum level.

3.   Edit the */etc/rc.config.d/netdaemons* file:

Set the variable NTPDATE_SERVER to the hostname of an NTP time server that is reachable (say 11.59.99.3). This will run the *ntpdate* command just before the NTP daemon is started at boot time and will bring the system clock very close to the NTP server clock. Setting this variable is not required, but recommended.

```
NTPDATE_SERVER=11.59.99.3
```

Set the XNTPD variable to 1 so the *xntpd* daemon starts automatically at each system reboot:

XNTPD=1

4. Start the daemon manually:

    # **/sbin/init.d/xntpd start**

An NTP server can be setup via SMH (or *ncweb* command) as well. Follow the links below:

☞ Go to SMH → Networking and communications → Network Services Configuration → Time → NTP Network Time Sources → Actions. Select an appropriate choice from "Add Remote Server or Peer", "Configure NTP Local Clock" or "Start or Stop NTP" as shown in Figure 27-1.

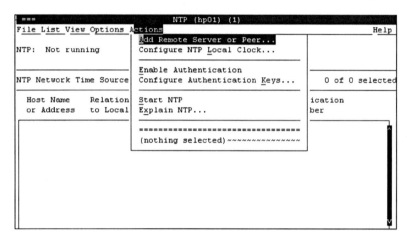

Figure 27-1 SMH – NTP Server Administration

27.2.2 Configuring an NTP Client

To configure an NTP client, follow the steps below:

1. Add the following lines to the */etc/ntp.conf* file:

    To setup a system as a polling client to synchronize time with NTP server *hp01*:

        server   hp01
        driftfile   /etc/ntp.drift

The *xntpd* daemon computes the clock frequency error in the local system every 64 seconds by default. It may take *xntpd* hours after it is started to compute a good estimate of the error. The current error value is stored in the */etc/ntp.drift* file (or any other file or directory location specified with the driftfile keyword). This allows *xntpd* to reinitialize itself to the estimate stored in the driftfile, saving time in recomputing a good frequency estimate. In short, the usage of driftfile helps *xntpd* track local system clock accuracy. A driftfile is not required, but recommended.

To setup the client as a broadcast client:

```
broadcastclient        yes
driftfile              /etc/ntp.drift
```

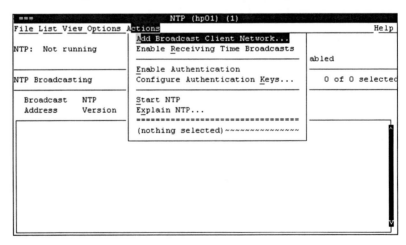To setup a broadcast client, define the broadcast network address in */etc/ntp.conf* on the NTP server and restart *xntpd*. An example entry would be "broadcast 11.69.99.255".

2.   Edit the */etc/rc.config.d/netdaemons* file:

Set the variable NTPDATE_SERVER to the hostname of one of the NTP time servers (*hp01* in this case). This will run the *ntpdate* command just before the NTP daemon is started at boot time and force the system clock to come very close to the NTP server's clock. Setting this variable is not required, but recommended.

        NTPDATE_SERVER=hp01

Set the XNTPD variable to 1 so the *xntpd* daemon starts automatically at each system reboot.

        XNTPD=1

3.   Start the daemon manually:

        # /sbin/init.d/xntpd start

SMH (or *ncweb* command) can be used to setup an NTP client. Follow the links below:

Go to SMH → Networking and Communications → Network Services Configuration → Time → NTP Broadcasting → Actions. Select an appropriate choice from "Add Broadcast Client Network", "Enable Receiving Time Broadcasts" or "Start or Stop NTP" as shown in Figure 27-2.

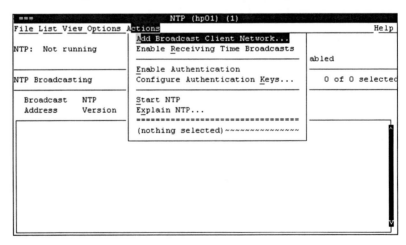

Figure 27-2 SMH – NTP Client Administration

27.2.3   Enabling Authentication

Enabling authentication on an NTP client helps protect against unauthorized access. It allows only those NTP servers that send messages encrypted with a configured key to be candidates with which a client system synchronizes.

The authentication key file */etc/ntp.keys* is configured on the NTP client. This file contains a list of keys and corresponding key numbers. Each key-key number combination is further defined by a key format, which determines the encryption method to be used.

To enable NTP authentication, include the following statement in the */etc/ntp.conf* file on an NTP client and restart the daemon:

    authenticate yes

You can enable NTP authentication using SMH (or *ncweb* command) as follows:

☞Go to SMH → Networking and Communications → Network Services Configuration → Time → NTP Network Time Sources → Actions → Enable Authentication. See Figures 27-1 and 27-2.

27.3   Managing NTP

Managing NTP involves updating system clock manually, querying NTP servers and tracing roots of an NTP server.

27.3.1   Updating System Clock Manually

You can run the *ntpdate* command anytime to bring the system clock close to the time on an NTP server. You can also schedule a cron job to execute this command periodically as an alternative to configuring the system as an NTP client. The *xntpd* daemon must not be running when *ntpdate* is executed. Run *ntpdate* manually and specify either the hostname such as *hp01.ntp.org* or IP address of the time server:

 # ntpdate hp01.ntp.org
7 Apr 18:21:12 ntpdate[4561]: adjust time server 19.33.42.222 offset 0.000023 sec

27.3.2   Querying NTP Servers

NTP servers may be queried for time synchronization and server association status using the *ntpq* command. This command sends out requests to and receives responses from NTP servers. The command may be run in interactive mode.

Run *ntpq* with –p option to print a list of NTP servers known to the system along with a summary of their states:

```
# ntpq –p
    remote         refid        st  t  when  poll  reach  delay   offset   disp
=================================================================================
*19.33.42.222  hp01.ntp.org   2   u   180  1024   377   28.95   -0.437   0.61
```

Each column from the output is explained in Table 27-1.

Column	Description
remote	Shows IP addresses or hostnames of all NTP servers and peers. Each IP/hostname may be preceded by one of the following characters: * Indicates the current source of synchronization. # Indicates the server selected for synchronization, but distance exceeds the maximum. o Displays the server selected for synchronization. + Indicates the system considered for synchronization. x Designated false ticker by the intersection algorithm. . Indicates the systems picked up from the end of the candidate list. - Indicates the system not considered for synchronization. Blank Indicates the server rejected because of high stratum level or failed sanity checks.
refid	Shows the current source of synchronization.
st	Shows stratum level of the server.
t	Shows available types: l=local (such as a GPS clock), u=unicast, m = multicast, b= broadcast and - = netaddr (usually 0).
when	Shows time, in seconds, since a response was received from the server.
poll	Shows the polling interval. Default is 64 seconds.
reach	Shows the number of successful attempts to reach the server. The value 001 indicates that the most recent probe was answered, 357 indicates that one probe was not answered and 377 indicates that all recent probes were answered.
delay	Shows how long, in milliseconds, it took for the reply packet to come back in response to the query sent to the server.
offset	Shows time difference, in milliseconds, between the server and the client clocks.
disp	Dispersion. Shows how much the "offset" measurement varies between samples. This is an error-bound estimate.

Table 27-1 *ntpq* Command Output Description

27.3.3   Tracing Roots of an NTP Server

The roots of a specified NTP server can be traced using the *ntptrace* command. For example, the following will locate the NTP server where *hp01.ntp.org* is getting time from:

ntptrace hp01.ntp.org
hp01.ntp.org: stratum 1, offset 0.000247, synch distance 0.00607, refid 'GPS'

The output indicates that *hp01.ntp.org* is at stratum 1 and using GPS. Try running *ntptrace* with –d and –v options to display debug and detailed information, respectively.

27.4   Troubleshooting Basic Issues

This section lists some common NTP-related error messages with an explanation and how to resolve them.

No Suitable Server for Synchronization Found

This message indicates that the NTP server is not responding for some reasons. Try stopping *xntpd* and running the *ntpdate* command with –d (debug) option to print information about the requests sent to the time server and the replies coming from it.

Startup Delay

This message indicates that there is a delay in the response from the server. What happens is that when *xntpd* is first started, it takes five poll cycles to bind itself with a server or peer. During this time *xntpd* does not respond to client requests. A server must be bound to a time server before it gives time to clients or peers.

Synchronization Lost

This message indicates that NTP has lost synchronization with the time server it was bound to and now it is in the process of choosing another to make time adjustments with. If a system makes such adjustments frequently, there might be congestion on the network. Use the *ntpq* command with –p option and examine dispersion statistics.

Time Difference Over 1000 Seconds

This message means that the difference in time is over 1000 seconds between the server and its peer or client, and, therefore, they have started to reject time updates coming from the NTP server. Try stopping *xntpd* and running *ntpdate* to get time from some other server or peer. Restart *xntpd*.

Summary

This chapter provided an introduction to Network Time Protocol and how to set it up. You learned concepts and components of it. You looked at configuring an NTP server, peer and client. You understood the rationale behind enabling authentication on NTP clients. You saw how to update the system clock manually, query NTP servers and trace roots of an NTP server.

Finally, you were presented with a few common error messages while working with NTP, along with an explanation and basic techniques to fix problems that potentially caused them.

28

Network File System (NFS)

This chapter covers the following major topics:

- ✓ Understand NFS concepts and benefits
- ✓ Understand NFS versions, security, daemons, commands, related files and startup scripts
- ✓ How NFS client and server interact with each other
- ✓ Configure NFS server and client
- ✓ Display shared and mounted NFS resources
- ✓ Unmount and unshare a resource
- ✓ Monitor NFS activities
- ✓ Basic troubleshooting

28.1   Understanding Network File System (NFS)

The *Network File System* (NFS) service is based on the client/server architecture whereby users on one system access files, directories and file systems (let us collectively call them *resources*) residing on a remote system as if they exist locally on their system. The remote machine that makes its resources available to be accessed over the network is called an *NFS server*, and the process of making them accessible is referred to as *sharing*. The resources shared by the NFS server can be accessed by one or more systems. These systems are called *NFS clients*, and the process of making the resources accessible on clients is referred to as *mounting*.

A system can function as both an NFS server and NFS client at the same time. When a directory or file system resource is shared, the entire directory structure beneath it becomes available for mounting on the client. A sub-directory or the parent directory of a shared resource cannot be re-shared if it exists in the same file system. Similarly, a resource mounted by an NFS client cannot be shared further by the client. A single shared file is mounted on a directory mount point.

NFS is built on top of *Remote Procedure Call* (RPC) and *eXternal Data Representation* (XDR) to allow a server and client to communicate. They provide a common "language" that both the server and client understand. This is standardized based on the fact that the NFS server and client may be running two completely different operating systems on different hardware platforms. RPC uses program numbers defined in the */etc/rpc* file.

The following data is extracted from the */etc/rpc* file. It shows official service names in the first column, followed by program numbers and associated alias names in subsequent columns:

```
# cat /etc/rpc
. . . . . . . .
rpcbind      100000  portmap  sunrpc  rpcbind
rstatd       100001  rstat  rup  perfmeter
rusersd      100002  rusers
nfs          100003  nfsprog
. . . . . . . .
```

28.1.1   Benefits

Some benefits associated with using NFS are listed below:

- ✓ Supports heterogeneous operating system platforms including all flavors of UNIX as well as Linux and Windows.
- ✓ Several client systems can access a single resource simultaneously.
- ✓ Enables sharing common application binaries and read-only information such as the *man* pages, instead of loading them on each single machine. This results in reduced overall disk storage cost and administration overhead.
- ✓ Gives users access to uniform data.
- ✓ Useful when many users exist on many systems with each user's home directory located on every single machine. In such a situation, create user home directories on a single machine under */home* for example, and share */home*. Now, whichever machine a user logs on to, his home directory becomes available there. The user will need to maintain only one home directory, and not a lot.

28.1.2   NFS Statelessness

NFS is *stateless* by design, meaning that the server does not keep track of what a client system is doing on the shared file system. If the client crashes and reboots, it reconnects to the server. You do not have to do anything on the NFS server. Similarly, if the NFS server crashes and is rebooted, the NFS client can continue accessing the NFS file system after the server is back up to normal. The only exception is that the client is unable to access the server for the period of time the server was down or unavailable. In this case too, there is nothing that needs to be done on the NFS server.

In the NFS model, the client keeps all information that it needs to mount a shared resource. After the client mounts a shared resource, the NFS server issues a file handle, which remains good even after the server is rebooted.

28.1.3   NFS Versions

When working with a mix of HP-UX versions newer and older than 11.0, ensure that proper NFS versions are specified in the configuration. The older versions supported NFS v1 and v2, 11i v1 and 11i v2 support NFS v2 and v3, and 11i v3 supports NFS v2, v3 and v4. The features and benefits introduced in NFS v3 were:

- ✓   Files of sizes up to 128GB (64 bit) are supported as compared to 2GB (32 bit) in v2.
- ✓   Uses TCP versus UDP in v2.
- ✓   Enhanced performance.
- ✓   AutoFS is supported versus Automounter in v2. AutoFS has better features than Automounter. See Chapter 29 "AutoFS" for details.

NFS v4 is an *Internet Engineering Task Force* (IETF) standard protocol that has added the following features and benefits to NFS v3:

- ✓   Enhanced security.
- ✓   Scalability.
- ✓   Better cross-platform interoperability.
- ✓   Works better through firewalls and on the internet.

NFS v3 is still the default protocol for NFS in 11i v3. However, NFS v4 can be enabled to take advantage of the benefits listed above.

28.1.4   NFS Security

NFS security is paramount in v4 to ensure that NFS operates securely in the WAN environment. In older versions, authentication was performed at the NFS client side. In contrast, an exchange of information takes place in v4 between the client and server for identification, authentication and authorization. Identification establishes identity of systems and users that will be accessing the shares, authentication confirms the identity and authorization controls what information systems and users will have access to. Exchange of information in transit between the client and server is encrypted to prevent eavesdropping and unauthorized access to private data.

28.1.5   NFS Daemons, Commands, Configuration Files and Scripts

When working with NFS, several daemons, commands, configuration files and scripts are involved. The tables given below list and explain them.

Table 28-1 describes NFS daemons.

Daemon	Description
rpc.mountd	Server-side daemon that responds to client requests to mount a resource and provide status of shared and mounted resources.
rpc.pcnfsd	Server-side daemon for PC-based operating systems.
nfsd	Server-side daemon that responds to client requests to access files.
rpcbind	Server- and client-side daemon responsible for forwarding incoming RPC requests to appropriate RPC daemons.
rpc.statd	Server- and client-side daemon. A client application may request this daemon to place a lock on the file being accessing to prevent other programs from modifying the file while in use.
rpc.lockd	Server- and client-side daemon that keeps an eye on the NFS client that has requested a lock on a file to make certain the client is up and running. If the client reboots unexpectedly, this daemon removes all locks placed on files so that other NFS clients may use them.

Table 28-1 NFS Daemons

Table 28-2 describes NFS commands.

Command	Description
share	Server-side command that: ✓ shares a resource specified at the command line ✓ displays shared resources listed in the */etc/dfs/sharetab* file
shareall	Server-side command that: ✓ shares resources listed in the */etc/dfs/dfstab* file ✓ displays shared resources listed in the */etc/dfs/sharetab* file
unshare	Server-side command that unshares a resource specified at the command line.
unshareall	Server-side command that unshares resources listed in */etc/dfs/sharetab*.
showmount	Server- and client-side command that: ✓ displays which resources are shared with which clients (consults */etc/dfs/sharetab* file on the NFS server) ✓ displays which clients have those resources mounted (consults */etc/rmtab* file on the NFS server)
mount	Client-side command that: ✓ mounts a resource specified at the command line or listed in the */etc/fstab* file followed by adding an entry to client's */etc/mnttab* file and server's */etc/rmtab* file via the *rpc.mountd* daemon ✓ displays mounted resources listed in the */etc/mnttab* file

Command	Description
mountall	Client-side command that mounts all resources listed in the */etc/fstab* file followed by adding entries to client's */etc/mnttab* file and server's */etc/rmtab* file via the *rpc.mountd* daemon.
umount	Client-side command that unmounts a single resource specified at the command line or listed in the */etc/mnttab* file followed by removing corresponding entry from this file and server's */etc/rmtab* file via the *rpc.mountd* daemon.
umountall	Client-side command that unmounts all resources listed in the */etc/mnttab* file followed by removing corresponding entries from this file and server's */etc/rmtab* file via the *rpc.mountd* daemon.
rpcinfo	Server-side command that checks whether NFS server daemons are registered with RPC.
nfsstat	Server- and client-side command that displays NFS and RPC statistics.

Table 28-2 NFS Commands

Table 28-3 describes NFS configuration and functional files.

File	Description
/etc/dfs/dfstab	Server-side file that contains a list of resources to be shared. This file has replaced */etc/exports* in 11i v3.
/etc/dfs/sharetab	Server-side file that contains a list of shared resources. This file is updated when a resource is shared or unshared, and is maintained by the *rpc.mountd* daemon. This file has replaced */etc/xtab* in 11i v3.
/etc/dfs/fstypes	Server-side file that contains the default file system type to be used for NFS. The default is "nfs".
/etc/rmtab	Server-side file that contains a list of shared resources that have been mounted by clients. This file is updated when a resource is mounted or unmounted, and is maintained by the *rpc.mountd* daemon.
/etc/fstab	Client-side file that contains a list of resources to be mounted at system reboots or manually using the *mount* or *mountall* commands.
/etc/mnttab	Client-side file that contains a list of mounted resources. The *mount*, *umount*, *mountall* and *umountall* commands update this file.
/etc/rc.config.d/nfsconf	Server- and client-side configuration file used by NFS startup scripts.
/etc/nfssec.conf	Server- and client-side configuration file that contains supported NFS security modes.
/etc/default/nfs	Server- and client-side configuration file used by various NFS commands and daemons for their default operation.
/etc/default/keyserv	Server- and client-side configuration file that contains default parameter values to set the use of default keys for nobody.

Table 28-3 NFS Configuration and Functional Files

Table 28-4 describes NFS startup and shutdown scripts.

Startup Scripts	Description
/sbin/init.d/nfs.core	Runs at run level 2 on both NFS server and client. Starts the *rpcbind* daemon. Looks into the */etc/rc.config.d/nfsconf* file for startup configuration information.
/sbin/init.d/nfs.server	Runs at run level 3 on the NFS server. Looks into the */etc/rc.config.d/nfsconf* file for startup configuration information.
/sbin/init.d/nfs.client	Runs at run level 2 on the NFS client. Looks into the */etc/rc.config.d/nfsconf* file for startup configuration information.
/sbin/init.d/lockmgr	Runs at run level 2 on both NFS server and client. Starts the *rpc.lockd* and *rpc.statd* daemons. Looks into the */etc/rc.config.d/nfsconf* file for startup configuration information.

Table 28-4 NFS Startup and Shutdown Scripts

28.1.6   How NFS Works?

The following outlines the process of sharing and mounting a resource. It is assumed that the startup configuration file */etc/rc.config.d/nfsconf* is properly configured.

- ✓ The */etc/dfs/dfstab* file contents are evaluated for any syntax problems and access issues.
- ✓ Each resource listed in this file is shared and an entry is put in the */etc/dfs/sharetab* file on the server. The *showmount* command looks into this file to display shared resource information.
- ✓ The client issues the *mount* command on the NFS client to request the NFS server to provide file handle for the requested resource.
- ✓ The request goes to the *rpc.mountd* daemon on the NFS server through the *rpcbind* daemon that runs on both the server and the client.
- ✓ The *rpc.mountd* daemon performs an access check to validate if the client is authorized to mount the resource.
- ✓ The *rpc.mountd* daemon sends the file handle for the requested resource to the client.
- ✓ The client mounts the resource if the correct *mount* command syntax is used. To automate the mount process, an entry for the resource can be added to the */etc/fstab* file, which ensures that the resource will get automatically mounted when the client reboots.
- ✓ The *mount* command tells the *rpc.mountd* daemon on the NFS server that the resource has been mounted successfully. Upon receiving the confirmation, the daemon puts an entry in the */etc/rmtab* file. The *showmount* command uses this file to display remotely mounted NFS resources. When the resource is unmounted on the client, the *umount* command sends a request to the *rpc.mountd* daemon to remove the entry from this file.
- ✓ The *mount* command also puts an entry in the */etc/mnttab* file for the mounted resource. The *mount*, *bdf* and *df* commands reference this file to display information about mounted resources. The *mount*, *umount*, *mountall* and *umountall* commands update this file whenever they are run successfully.
- ✓ Any file access request by the client on the mounted resource is now going to be handled by the server's *nfsd* daemon.
- ✓ The *rpc.lockd* and *rpc.statd* daemons are involved when the client requests the server to place a lock on a file.

28.2   Configuring NFS

This section discusses procedures on configuring NFS server and client.

28.2.1　Configuring an NFS Server

Let us look at the step-by-step procedure to configure *hp02* as an NFS server and share several resources. Prior to setting up an NFS environment ensure that UIDs and GIDs are consistent across all systems that will be configured and used as NFS servers and clients. Here is the procedure.

1. Edit */etc/dfs/dfstab* file and insert following entries one per line:

   ```
   share –F nfs –o ro /usr/share/man
   share –F nfs –o access=hp03:hp04 –d "Home directories" /home
   share –F nfs –o root=hp03:hp04 /var/mail
   share –F nfs –o anon=104 –d "Samba binaries" /opt/samba
   share –F nfs –o async /opt/perl_64
   share –F nfs –o anon=65535 /var/opt/samba
   ```

   Refer to Table 28-5 for option details.

   The "–F nfs" option can be omitted. The *share* command looks into the */etc/dfs/fstypes* file and picks up "nfs", which is the only supported network file system type.

2. Edit */etc/rc.config.d/nfsconf* file and set the NFS_CORE, NFS_SERVER and START_MOUNTD variables to 1. This ensures that NFS server functionality is started at each system reboot.

   ```
   NFS_CORE=1
   NFS_SERVER=1
   START_MOUNTD=1
   ```

3. Execute the following command to start NFS server processes and share the entries inserted in the */etc/dfs/dfstab* file:

   # /sbin/init.d/nfs.server start
   ```
   Starting NFS SERVER subsystem
   Reading in /etc/dfs/dfstab
   Starting up the mount daemon
      /usr/sbin/rpc.mountd
   Starting up the NFS server daemon
      /usr/sbin/nfsd
   Starting up nfsmapid daemon
   ```

   If the processes were already running, simply execute the following:

   # shareall

Note that you can run the *share* command and specify a resource to share it temporarily without making an entry in */etc/dfs/dfstab*. This resource will stay shared until it is manually unshared or the server is rebooted.

Common options that can be used when sharing or mounting a resource are described in Table 28-5. The server-side options are used when sharing resources and the client-side options are used when mounting the shares on NFS clients.

Option	Description
rw / ro (default=rw)	Server- and client-side options. "rw" (read/write) allows file modifications and "ro" (read only) prevents doing it.
access=client1:client2	Server-side option. Gives access to the specified clients.
root=client1:client2	Server-side option. Gives *root* access on the specified clients.
anon=UID	Server-side option. Anonymous users are assigned the specified UID. If UID 65535 is supplied, users without a valid UID are denied access. If this option is not used, the default UID of -2 is allocated, which belongs to user "nobody" and provides limited access to anonymous users.
async	Server-side option. NFS writes are made asynchronously (in parallel).
hard / soft (default=hard)	Client-side option. When an NFS client attempts to mount a resource using the "hard" option, the client keeps trying until either it succeeds or is interrupted with Ctrl+c or the *kill* command if "intr" option is also used. If the NFS server goes down, processes using the mounted resource hang until the server comes back up. Use "soft" to prevent NFS clients from being hung if the NFS server goes down. With this option, if an NFS client attempts to mount a resource for "retrans" times unsuccessfully, it displays an error message.
vers=n (default=3)	Client-side option. NFS version to be used.
suid / nosuid (default=suid)	Client-side option. "suid" enables users on an NFS client to execute a setuid-enabled program located on the NFS mounted resource with the same privileges as the owner of the program has on it. If the program has *root* ownership, it is executed with *root* privileges regardless of who runs it. "nosuid" prevents users from running setuid programs.
intr / nointr (default=intr)	Client-side option. Use "intr" (interruptible) if users do not wish to manually interrupt an NFS request. Use "nointr" for the opposite.
fg / bg (default=fg)	Client-side option. Use "fg" (foreground) for resources that must be available to the NFS client to boot or operate correctly. If a foreground mount fails, it is retried in the foreground until it succeeds or is interrupted. With "bg" option set, mount attempts are tried and retried in the background enabling an NFS client to continue to boot.
timeo=n (default=7)	Client-side option. Sets timeout, in tenths of a second, for NFS read and write requests. If an NFS request times out, this value is doubled and the request is attempted again for "retrans" times. When number of "retrans" attempts are made, a "soft" mount displays an error message, while a "hard" mount continues to retry.
retrans=n (default=5)	Client-side option. This many times an NFS client retransmits a read or write request after the first transmission times out. If the request does not succeed after *n* retransmissions, a "soft" mount displays an error message, while a "hard" mount continues to retry.

Option	Description
retry=n (default=1)	Client-side option. This many times a client tries to mount a resource after the first try fails. With "intr" option used, the mount attempt can be interrupted before *n* retries. If "nointr" option is used, the mount attempt must wait until *n* retries have been made, mount succeeds or the client is rebooted.
rsize=n (default=8k)	Client-side option. Size of each read request from client to server.
wsize=n (default=8k)	Client-side option. Size of each write request from client to server.

Table 28-5 *share* and *mount* Command Options

You can configure an NFS server using SMH (or *ncweb* command) as well. Follow the links below:

☞Go to SMH → Networking and Communications → Network Services Configuration → Networked File Systems → Share / Unshare File System. A list of currently shared resources will appear. See Figure 28-1.

```
-> Networking and Communications-> Networked File Systems-> Share/Unshare Filesy

NFS Server Enabled
--------------------------------------------------------------------------------
Local Directory         Currently Shared    Permanently Shared  Logging Enabled
--------------------------------------------------------------------------------
/usr/share/man          Yes                 Yes                 No
/home                   Yes                 Yes                 No
/var/mail               Yes                 Yes                 No
/opt/samba              Yes                 Yes                 No
/opt/perl_64            Yes                 Yes                 No
/var/opt/samba          Yes                 Yes                 No


--------------------------------------------------------------------------------
x-Exit smh              Enter-Show Details       Esc-Back
s-Share a File System   u-Unshare the File System  Ctrl o-Other Actions
```

Figure 28-1 SMH – List NFS-Shared Resources

To share a resource, press s and you will see the form as shown in Figure 28-2. Fill it out and press OK to share it. Under the "Share type", "Current" means share the resource temporarily, "Permanent" means add an entry for it in the */etc/dfs/dfstab* file and "Both Current and Permanent" means share the resource and add an entry for it in the file.

To unshare a resource, highlight it from the list and press u. A form will pop up as shown in Figure 28-3. Fill it out and press OK to unshare it. Under the "Unshare type", "Current" means unshare the resource temporarily, "Permanent" means remove its entry from the */etc/dfs/dfstab* file and "Both Current and Permanent" means unshare the resource and remove its entry from the file.

```
orking and Communications-> Networked File Systems-> Share/Unshare Filesystem->

-------------------------------------------------------------------SCROLL /
Local Directory Name*   :  ▓_____
Resource Name           :  _____
Description             :  _____
(Optional)


For unknown User ID     :  (X)  Use UID of user 'nobody'(default)
                           ( )  Disable Unknown UID Access
                           ( )  Specify UID for Unknown User


Enable Server Logging   :  (X)  No (default)
                           ( )  Yes


Specify Access Options  :  ( )  Secure Access
                           (X)  Standard Access
[ Configure ... ]


  [ ]  Allow Asynchronous writes
  [ ]  Ignore enabling the setuid/setgid mode bits(nosuid)
  [ ]  Prevent mounting subdirectories(nosub)
  [ ]  Move the Location of public file handle(public)
  Index Filename         :  _____


Share type              :  (X)  Current
                           ( )  Permanent
                           ( )  Both Current and Permanent


[ OK ] [ Cancel ] [ Preview ] [ Help ]
Absolute Path of directory to be shared
```

Figure 28-2 SMH – Share an NFS Resource

```
                    UNSHARING THE FILESYSTEM - CONFIRM

-------------------------------------------------------------------

Unshare the Filesystem: /usr/share/man
Current Share Status  : Current

Unshare type                    :  (X) Current
                                   ( ) Permanent
                                   ( ) Both Current and Permanent
[ OK ] [ Cancel ]



Unshare the filesystem permanently and/or currently
```

Figure 28-3 SMH – Unshare an NFS Resource

28.2.2   Configuring an NFS Client

Here is the procedure to configure an NFS client successfully.

1.   Execute the following command on the NFS server to determine available shared resources:

        # **showmount –e**
        export list for hp01:
        /usr/share/man (everyone)

```
/home          hp03,hp04
/var/mail      (everyone)
/opt/samba     (everyone)
/opt/perl_64   (everyone)
/var/opt/samba (everyone)
```

Alternatively, the *share* command without any options or a *cat* on the */etc/dfs/sharetab* file can be used:

share
```
-    /usr/share/man    ro              ""
-    /home             rw=hp03:hp04    "Home directories"
-    /var/mail         root=hp03:hp04  ""
-    /opt/samba        anon=104        "Samba binaries"
-    /opt/perl_64      async           ""
-    /var/opt/samba    anon=65535      ""
```

2. Edit */etc/rc.config.d/nfsconf* file and set NFS_CLIENT variable to 1 to ensure that NFS client functionality gets started each time the NFS client is rebooted:

    NFS_CLIENT=1

3. Run the NFS client startup script:

    # **/sbin/init.d/nfs.client start**
    ```
        Starting NFS CLIENT subsystem
        Starting up nfs4cbd daemon
         /usr/sbin/nfs4cbd
         Starting up nfsmapid daemon
        Mounting remote NFS file systems ...
        Mounting remote CacheFS file systems ...
    ```

4. Edit */etc/fstab* file and add the following lines for the resources. This is done to ensure the NFS resources get automatically mounted when this client reboots.

    ```
    hp02:/usr/share/man    /usr/share/man    nfs    ro        0  0
    hp02:/home             /home             nfs    defaults  0  0
    hp02:/var/mail         /var/mail         nfs    defaults  0  0
    hp02:/opt/samba        /opt/samba        nfs    defaults  0  0
    hp02:/opt/perl_64      /opt/perl_64      nfs    defaults  0  0
    hp02:/var/opt/samba    /var/opt/samba    nfs    defaults  0  0
    ```

5. Create required mount points if they do not already exist using the *mkdir* command.
6. Execute either the *mountall* command that attempts to mount all local and remote resources listed in the */etc/fstab* file or the *mount* command with "–aF nfs" options to mount only the remote resources:

    # **mountall**
    # **mount –aF nfs**

Alternatively, you can manually mount the resources in one of two ways. Repeat the first command below for each resource and specify correct options with –o switch. The second command gets additional information from the */etc/fstab* file:

> # **mount –F nfs –o ro hp02:/usr/share/man /usr/share/man**
> # **mount /usr/share/man**

A mount point should be empty when an attempt is made to mount a resource on it, otherwise, the contents of the mount point will be hidden. As well, the mount point must not be in use, otherwise, the mount attempt will fail.

You can configure an NFS client using SMH (or *fsweb* command) too. Follow the links below:

Go to SMH → Disks and File Systems → File Systems. Press n to add an NFS resource. Fill out the form and press "New Nfs". See Figure 28-4.

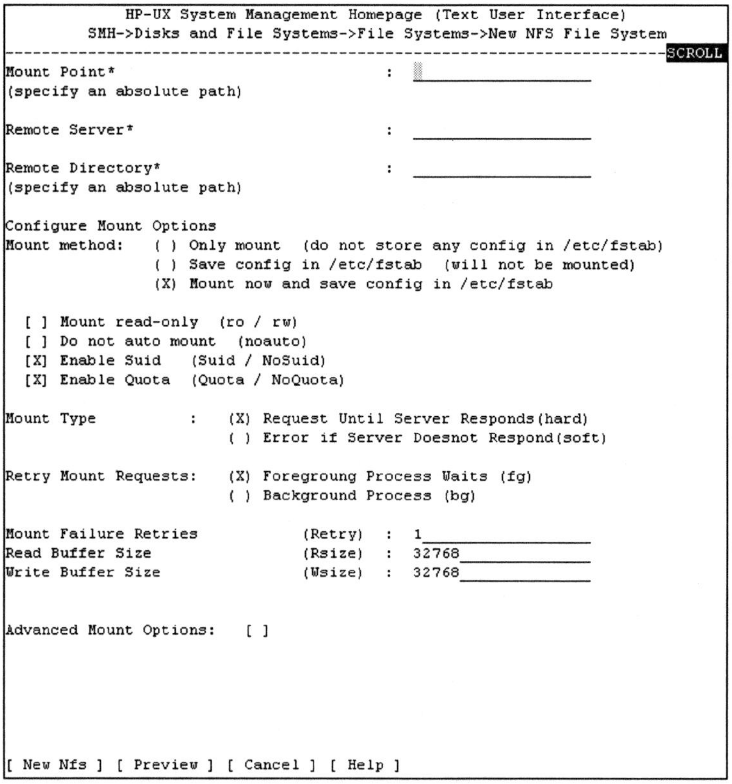

```
         HP-UX System Management Homepage (Text User Interface)
          SMH->Disks and File Systems->File Systems->New NFS File System
--------------------------------------------------------------------SCROLL
Mount Point*                           :
(specify an absolute path)

Remote Server*                         :  _____

Remote Directory*                      :  _____
(specify an absolute path)

Configure Mount Options
Mount method:   ( ) Only mount  (do not store any config in /etc/fstab)
                ( ) Save config in /etc/fstab  (will not be mounted)
                (X) Mount now and save config in /etc/fstab

   [ ] Mount read-only  (ro / rw)
   [ ] Do not auto mount  (noauto)
   [X] Enable Suid    (Suid / NoSuid)
   [X] Enable Quota  (Quota / NoQuota)

Mount Type        :  (X) Request Until Server Responds(hard)
                     ( ) Error if Server Doesnot Respond(soft)

Retry Mount Requests:  (X) Foregroung Process Waits (fg)
                       ( ) Background Process (bg)

Mount Failure Retries        (Retry) :  1_____
Read Buffer Size             (Rsize) :  32768_____
Write Buffer Size            (Wsize) :  32768_____


Advanced Mount Options:   [ ]




[ New Nfs ] [ Preview ] [ Cancel ] [ Help ]
```

Figure 28-4 SMH – Mount NFS Resource

28.3   Managing NFS

Managing NFS involves sharing, mounting, displaying, unsharing and unmounting resources. Some of these have been covered in the previous section; others are covered in the following sub-sections.

28.3.1   Viewing Shared and Mounted Resources

To verify the functionality of both the server and the client, *cd* into resource mount points and run the *ll* command. If both commands run successfully, it means the resource is shared and mounted. There are several commands such as *showmount*, *bdf* and *mount* that allow you to view what resources are shared by the server, available to a particular client for mounting, and mounted on a client. Let us look at some examples.

To view what resources are currently shared, execute any of the following on the NFS server:

> # **showmount –e**
> # **cat /etc/dfs/sharetab**

To view what resources are currently mounted by which NFS client, execute any of the following on the NFS server:

> # **showmount –a**
> hp03:/home
> hp03:/usr/share/man
> hp03:/opt/perl_64
> hp03:/opt/samba
> hp03:/var/mail
> hp03:/var/opt/samba
> # **cat /etc/rmtab**

To view what resources are currently mounted, execute any of the following on the NFS client:

> # **mount –v**
> # **bdf –t nfs**

File system	kbytes	used	avail	%used	Mounted on
hp02:/var/opt/samba	3006464	1665784	1330360	56%	/var/opt/samba
hp02:/var/mail	3006464	1665784	1330360	56%	/var/mail
hp02:/opt/samba	1785856	1241872	539752	70%	/opt/samba
hp02:/opt/perl_64	1785856	1241872	539752	70%	/opt/perl_64
hp02:/usr/share/man	1257472	905600	349352	72%	/export/man
hp02:/home	20480	3112	17296	15%	/export/home

> # **df –k**
> # **cat /etc/mnttab | grep –i nfs**

You can also view the shared and mounted resources using SMH. Follow the links in sections 28.2.1 and 28.2.2.

28.3.2   Unmounting a Resource

Follow the steps below to unmount a remote resource on an NFS client:

1. Make certain no users are accessing the resource (*/usr/share/man* for example). If a non-critical process is using the resource or a user is sitting in it, list their PIDs and usernames:

```
# fuser –cu /usr/share/man
/usr/share/man:    2805c(root)  26159c(root)
```

2. Kill any processes using the resource or wait until the processes terminate. To kill all processes using the resource, do the following:

```
# fuser –ck /usr/share/man
/usr/share/man:    2805c        26159c
```

3. Run the following to unmount the resource:

```
# umount /usr/share/man
```

   Alternatively, you can use the *umount* command to perform the function of both the *fuser* and the *umount* commands. With –f switch, the *umount* command forcibly kills all processes using the specified resource and unmounts it.

4. Edit */etc/fstab* and remove the associated resource entry if you wish to remove it for good.

28.3.3   Unsharing a Resource

After ensuring with the *showmount* command that the resource to be unshared is not mounted by any clients, do any of the following on the NFS server to unshare it:

```
# unshare /usr/share/man
```

If you unshare a mounted resource, the next time a user on that client requests access to the resource, NFS will return "NFS stale file handle" error message.

To unshare all resources listed in */etc/dfs/sharetab* file, use the *unshareall* command:

```
# unshareall
```

28.4   Monitoring NFS Activities

There is a tool called *nfsstat* that can be used to monitor NFS activities such as read and write. Options such as –c, –s and –r are available to capture client, server and RPC activities, respectively. With –m option, it displays all mounted resource activities.

Here is the output of this command. Without any options, it displays all information.

```
# nfsstat
Server rpc:
Connection oriented:
calls    badcalls  nullrecv  badlen   xdrcall  dupchecks dupreqs
49646  0         0         0        0        210       0
Connectionless oriented:
calls    badcalls  nullrecv  badlen   xdrcall  dupchecks dupreqs
```

```
0        0        0        0        0        0        0

Server nfs:
calls    badcalls
49646    0
Version 2: (0 calls)
null     getattr   setattr   root     lookup   readlink   read
0 0%     0 0%      0 0%      0 0%     0 0%     0 0%       0 0%
wrcache  write     create    remove   rename   link       symlink
0 0%     0 0%      0 0%      0 0%     0 0%     0 0%       0 0%
mkdir    rmdir     readdir   statfs
0 0%     0 0%      0 0%      0 0%
Version 3: (49646 calls)
. . . . . . . .
```

28.5 NFS Troubleshooting

When an issue in the functionality of NFS is encountered, you need to revisit NFS server and client configurations. A good understanding of how NFS works along with proper knowledge of individual files involved, daemons, commands, startup scripts and options used, help resolve most NFS-related problems quickly and with less pain. Since NFS uses the network, a stable and robust network infrastructure is necessary for its proper operation.

Some common error messages generated on NFS clients are explained below.

NFS Server Not Responding

Use *ping* on the NFS client to ensure the NFS server is up and reachable. If this command fails, the server might be down, is too busy or something wrong with the network.

Run the *rpcinfo* command on the client to ensure the server is running all required processes:

```
# rpcinfo –p hp02
program    vers    proto    port    service
100000     4       tcp      111     rpcbind
100000     3       tcp      111     rpcbind
100000     4       udp      111     rpcbind
100000     3       udp      111     rpcbind
100021     3       udp      4045    nlockmgr
100021     4       udp      4045    nlockmgr
100021     3       tcp      4045    nlockmgr
100021     4       tcp      4045    nlockmgr
. . . . . . . .
```

The following specifically checks if the *mountd* daemon is running:

```
# rpcinfo –u hp02 mountd
program 100005 version 3 ready and waiting
program 100005 version 4 ready and waiting
```

The *rpcinfo* command has –s and –m options available too for display purposes. Try running the command with these options and analyze the results.

Run the *nslookup* or *nsquery* command on both the server and the client to check that they "see" each other correctly. Refer to Chapter 32 "Domain Name System" on how to use these commands.

Stale File Handle

This message occurs when the server unshares a resource, but the client still has it mounted. To quickly resolve the issue, reshare the resource, and unmount and remount it on the client.

Too Many Levels of Remote in Path

This message occurs on the client when it attempts to mount a resource from a server that has that resource NFS-mounted from another server.

Access Denied

This error message is displayed on the client when it tries to mount a resource. Use the *showmount* command to check if the resource is really shared. Also check if the resource is shared with proper access options and the client's name is on it.

Permission Denied

When this message is generated, do the following:

✓ Check if the resource is not using read-only option in the client's */etc/fstab* file.
✓ Check if the resource is not using read-only option in the server's */etc/dfs/dfstab* file.
✓ Check */etc/passwd* on both the server and client to ensure a valid login exists and the UID of it is consistent.
✓ Check for the setuid bit in */etc/fstab* file.

Device Busy

If you get this message while attempting to mount a resource, check to see if the resource is not already mounted.

If you get this message while attempting to unmount a resource, check to see if no user or process is currently accessing it.

Summary

This chapter introduced you to one of the most common system administration tasks, the Network File System. You learned and understood concepts, benefits, versions, daemons, commands, related files and startup scripts pertaining to Network File System. You learned how NFS server and client interact with each other. You looked at procedures for configuring NFS server and client. You used commands that displayed shared and mounted NFS resources, unmounted and unshared resources, and captured and displayed NFS activity data.

Finally, common NFS error messages were presented along with a brief explanation on how to resolve them.

AutoFS

This chapter covers the following major topics:

- ✓ Understand AutoFS
- ✓ Features and benefits
- ✓ How AutoFS works
- ✓ AutoFS startup script and configuration file
- ✓ Configure AutoFS maps – master, special, direct and indirect maps
- ✓ Access an AutoFS resource from multiple NFS servers
- ✓ Mount user home directories

29.1   Understanding AutoFS

In Chapter 28 "Network File System (NFS)", you learned about NFS and how to mount an NFS shared resource on the client. This is the standard mount method. In this chapter, you are going to look at the AutoFS (*Auto File System*) facility that offers another method of mounting a resource.

AutoFS is the NFS client-side service that automatically mounts an NFS resource on an as-needed basis. When an activity occurs in the mount point with a command such as *ls* or *cd*, the configured NFS resource gets mounted. When the resource is no longer accessed for a pre-defined period of time, it automatically gets unmounted.

29.1.1   Features and Benefits

There are several features and benefits associated with AutoFS mount method compared with standard NFS mount method. These are described below:

- ✓ AutoFS requires that NFS resources be defined in text configuration files called *maps*, which are typically located in the */etc* directory. These maps may be managed centrally via NIS or LDAP. In contrast, the standard NFS mount information is defined in the */etc/fstab* file for each NFS resource that needs to be mounted automatically at each system reboot. Additionally, the */etc/fstab* file must be maintained separately on each NFS client system.
- ✓ AutoFS does not require *root* privileges to mount available NFS resources. In comparison, with the standard NFS mount method, only *root* can mount them.
- ✓ With AutoFS, the NFS client boot process never hangs if the NFS server is down or inaccessible. With the standard NFS mount, when a client system boots up and an NFS server listed in the */etc/fstab* file is unavailable, the client may hang until either the mount request times out or the NFS server becomes available.
- ✓ With AutoFS, a resource is unmounted automatically if it is not accessed for five minutes, by default. With the standard NFS mount method, a resource stays mounted until it is manually unmounted or the client system shuts down.
- ✓ AutoFS provides load balancing and high availability capabilities by automatically accessing a resource available from multiple, replicated NFS servers. In this case, whichever NFS server responds first, AutoFS mounts the resource from that server. This feature is unavailable with the standard NFS mount method.
- ✓ AutoFS supports wildcard characters and environment variables, whereas the standard NFS mount method does not.
- ✓ A special map is available with AutoFS that mounts all available NFS resources from a reachable NFS server when a user requests access to a resource on that server without explicitly defining each one of them. The standard mount method does not have any such features available.

AutoFS supports NFSv4, SecureNFS and IPv6.

29.1.2   How AutoFS Works?

AutoFS consists of the following components:

1. The *automount* command that loads AutoFS maps into memory.

---

2. The *automountd* daemon that mounts a resource automatically when accessed.
3. An AutoFS resource.

The *automount* command is invoked at system boot up. It reads the AutoFS master map and creates initial mount point entries in the */etc/mnttab* file, however, the resources are not actually mounted at this time. When a user activity occurs under one of the initial mount points, the *automountd* daemon contacts the *rpc.mountd* daemon on the NFS server and actually mounts the requested resource. If an automounted resource remains idle for a certain time period, *automountd* unmounts it.

The *automountd* daemon and the *automount* command are completely independent of each other, enabling you to modify AutoFS map contents without having to restart the daemon.

AutoFS uses RPC and its daemon is stateless and multi-threaded.

29.1.3 Starting and Stopping AutoFS

To start AutoFS functionality automatically on a client at every reboot, set the following variables in the */etc/rc.config.d/nfsconf* startup configuration file. These settings are also required if you start AutoFS manually.

```
NFS_CLIENT=1
AUTOFS=1
AUTOMOUNT_OPTIONS=""
AUTOMOUNTD_OPTIONS=""
```

The last two variables can be used to define additional options for the AutoFS daemon. Some common options are given in Table 29-1.

Option	Description
AUTOMOUNT_OPTIONS="–t 600"	Specifies, in seconds, the maximum idle time after which AutoFS automatically unmounts the resource.
AUTOMOUNT_OPTIONS="–v"	Displays a message on the screen when AutoFS configuration is altered.
AUTOMOUNTD_OPTIONS="–v"	Enables AutoFS logging.
AUTOMOUNTD_OPTIONS="–T"	Logs all AutoFS mount and unmount traces in */var/adm/automount.log* file.

Table 29-1 AutoFS Options

The timeout option can alternatively be defined in the */etc/default/autofs* file as follows:

```
AUTOMOUNT_TIMEOUT=600
```

Execute the NFS client startup script to bring both NFS client and AutoFS functionalities up. This script also mounts all NFS resources listed in the */etc/fstab* file.

 # /sbin/init.d/autofs start
    Starting NFS CLIENT subsystem
    Starting up nfs4cbd daemon

```
/usr/sbin/nfs4cbd
    Starting up nfsmapid daemon
    Mounting remote NFS file systems ...
    Mounting remote CacheFS file systems ...
```

Alternatively, you can manually start AutoFS functionality by executing the following two commands. The first command starts the *automountd* daemon and the second copies the AutoFS map contents into */etc/mnttab* so *automountd* knows which resources it is responsible for mounting.

 # automountd
 # automount −v

To bring both AutoFS and NFS client functionalities down, execute the same startup script again but with "stop" argument:

 # /sbin/init.d/autofs stop
killing nfs4cbd

29.2   The AutoFS Maps

As you know, AutoFS mounts NFS resources on-demand only. For this it needs to know the resources to mount, source NFS server names and any mount options to be used. All this information is defined in AutoFS map files.

There are four types of AutoFS maps: *master*, *special*, *direct* and *indirect*. The following sub-sections examine each one of them.

29.2.1   Defining the Master Map

The */etc/auto_master* file is the default *master* map, which contains special, direct and indirect map information, and is defined in the */etc/rc.config.d/nfsconf* file with the variable AUTO_MASTER. A sample */etc/auto_master* file is shown below that displays how the three map entries look like:

 # cat /etc/auto_master
/net −hosts −nosuid,soft,nobrowse
/− auto_direct
/home auto_indirect

The first entry is for a special map telling AutoFS to use −hosts special map whenever a user attempts to access anything under */net*.

The second entry is for a direct map telling AutoFS to look for information in */etc/auto_direct* file.

The last entry is for an indirect map telling AutoFS to refer to the */etc/auto_indirect* file for further information. The umbrella mount point */home* will precede all mount point entries listed in the */etc/auto_indirect* file.

The */etc/auto_master* file does not exist by default. This file is created automatically with a single line entry shown below when AutoFS is first started:

/net -hosts -nosuid,soft,nobrowse

Execute the *automount* command every time the */etc/auto_master* file is modified to make the changes effective.

29.2.2   Defining the Special Map

The –hosts *special* map allows all resources shared by all accessible NFS servers to get mounted under the */net* directory without explicitly mounting each one of them. Accessing */net/<NFS_server>* will cause AutoFS to automatically mount all resources available to the client from that NFS server. By default, an entry "/net –hosts –nosuid,soft,nobrowse" exists in the file for this type of map, and is enabled.

Run the *mount* command to view the special map entry in the mount table:

mount –v | grep autofs
-hosts on /net type autofs ignore,indirect,nosuid,soft,nobrowse,dev=4000002 on Thu Apr 17 07:29:042008

The *mount* command simply shows an entry for the special map, it does not show anything mounted under */net* even if you do an *ll* on the directory. However, if you try to access a specific NFS server (*hp02* for example, with */usr/share/man, /home, /var/mail, /opt/samba, /opt/perl_64* and */var/opt/samba* shared) under */net*, the *automountd* daemon mounts all resources available from that server:

ll /net/hp02

drwxr-xr-x	7	root	root	96	Feb 17 11:06	home
dr-xr-xr-x	2	root	root	4	Feb 22 10:42	opt
dr-xr-xr-x	2	root	root	4	Feb 22 10:42	usr
dr-xr-xr-x	2	root	root	4	Feb 22 10:42	var

The output does not indicate how many resources are mounted under */net/hp02*. Use the *mount* command to display that information:

mount –v
-hosts on /net type autofs ignore,indirect,nosuid,soft,nobrowse,dev=4000002 on Thu Apr 17 07:29:04 2008
hp02:/home on /net/hp02/home type nfs nosuid,soft,nobrowse,rsize=32768,wsize=32768,NFSv3 on Thu Apr 17 07:29:04 2008
hp02:/var/mail on /net/hp02/var/mail type nfs nosuid,soft,nobrowse,rsize=32768,wsize=32768,NFSv3 on Thu Apr 17 07:29:04 2008
hp02:/opt/perl_64 on /net/hp02/opt/perl_64 type nfs nosuid,soft,nobrowse,rsize=32768,wsize=32768,NFSv3 on Thu Apr 17 07:29:04 2008
hp02:/opt/samba on /net/hp02/opt/samba type nfs nosuid,soft,nobrowse,rsize=32768,wsize=32768,NFSv3 on Thu Apr 17 07:29:04 2008
hp02:/usr/share/man on /net/hp02/usr/share/man type nfs nosuid,soft,nobrowse,rsize=32768,wsize=32768,NFSv3 on Thu Apr 17 07:29:04 2008
hp02:/var/opt/samba on /net/hp02/var/opt/samba type nfs nosuid,soft,nobrowse,rsize=32768,wsize=32768,NFSv3 on Thu Apr 17 07:29:04 2008

The –hosts map is not recommended in an environment where there are many NFS servers sharing many resources because AutoFS mounts all available resources whether they are needed or not.

29.2.3 Defining a Direct Map

A *direct* map is used to mount resources automatically on any number of unrelated mount points. Some key points to note when working with direct maps are:

- ✓ Direct mounted resources are always visible to users.
- ✓ Local and direct mounted resources can co-exist under one parent directory.
- ✓ Each direct map entry adds an entry to the */etc/mnttab* file.
- ✓ When a user or program accesses a directory containing many direct mount points, all resources get mounted.

Let us use a direct map on a client to mount the six resources from NFS server *hp02*:

1. Edit */etc/auto_master* and add a direct map entry pointing to a file such as */etc/auto_direct*:

   /–   /etc/auto_direct

   Each direct map entry consists of three fields: the first field is always /–, which identifies the entry as a direct map entry, the second field is optional and specifies any mount options (not shown) and the third field points to the direct map file where actual NFS server resource and mount point information are stored.

2. Create */etc/auto_direct* file and input the following entries:

   ```
   /usr/share/man  –ro      hp02:/usr/share/man
   /home                    hp02:/home
   /var/mail                hp02:/var/mail
   /opt/samba      –ro      hp02:/opt/samba
   /opt/perl_64    –ro      hp02:/opt/perl_64
   /var/opt/samba           hp02:/var/opt/samba
   ```

3. Execute the *automount* command to make the changes take effect:

   # **automount –v**

Run the *automount* command each time an entry to a direct map is added or removed. There is no need to run it if the contents of an existing entry are modified.

Execute the *mount* command to check the mount status of the automounted resources. Note that the resource information is visible, but none of them is mounted.

```
# mount –v
auto_direct on /usr/share/man type autofs ignore,direct, on Thu Apr 17 07:29:04 2008
auto_direct on /home type autofs ignore,direct, on Thu Apr 17 07:29:04 2008
auto_direct on /var/mail type autofs ignore,direct, on Thu Apr 17 07:29:04 2008
auto_direct on /opt/samba type autofs ignore,direct, on Thu Apr 17 07:29:04 2008
auto_direct on /opt/perl_64 type autofs ignore,direct, on Thu Apr 17 07:29:04 2008
auto_direct on /var/opt/samba type autofs ignore,direct, on Thu Apr 17 07:29:04 2008
```

The first time a user accesses one of these mount points, AutoFS automatically mounts the resource associated with that mount point. Do an *ll* on all six resources and re-run the *mount* command:

ll /usr/share/man /home /var/mail /opt/samba /opt/perl_64 /var/opt/samba
mount –v

auto_direct on /usr/share/man type autofs ignore,direct, on Thu Apr 17 07:29:04 2008
auto_direct on /home type autofs ignore,direct, on Thu Apr 17 07:29:04 2008
auto_direct on /var/mail type autofs ignore,direct, on Thu Apr 17 07:29:04 2008
auto_direct on /opt/samba type autofs ignore,direct, on Thu Apr 17 07:29:04 2008
auto_direct on /opt/perl_64 type autofs ignore,direct, on Thu Apr 17 07:29:04 2008
auto_direct on /var/opt/samba type autofs ignore,direct, on Thu Apr 17 07:29:04 2008
hp02:/home on /home type nfs ro,rsize=32768,wsize=32768,NFSv3 on Thu Apr 17 07:29:04 2008
hp02:/var/mail on /var/mail type nfs rsize=32768,wsize=32768,NFSv3 on Thu Apr 17 07:29:04 2008
hp02:/opt/perl_64 on /opt/perl_64 type nfs ro,rsize=32768,wsize=32768,NFSv3 on Thu Apr 17 07:29:04 2008
hp02:/opt/samba on /opt/samba type nfs ro,rsize=32768,wsize=32768,NFSv3 on Thu Apr 17 07:29:04 2008
hp02:/var/opt/samba on /var/opt/samba type nfs rsize=32768,wsize=32768,NFSv3 on Thu Apr 17 07:29:04 2008
hp02:/usr/share/man on /usr/share/man type nfs ro,rsize=32768,wsize=32768,NFSv3 on Thu Apr 17 07:29:04 2008

29.2.4   Defining an Indirect Map

An *indirect* map is used to automatically mount resources under one common parent directory. Some key points to note when working with indirect maps are:

✓ Indirect mounted resources only become visible after being accessed.
✓ Local and indirect mounted resources cannot co-exist under the same parent directory.
✓ Each indirect map puts only one entry in the */etc/mnttab* file.
✓ There is no need to execute the *automount* command after adding, removing or modifying an indirect map entry.
✓ When a user or program accesses a directory containing many indirect mount points, only the directories that are already mounted appear.

Let us use an indirect map to mount the */opt/samba* and */opt/perl_64* resources from NFS server *hp02*:

1. Edit */etc/auto_master* and add the following indirect map entry. There is no default map file for an indirect map, however, you can use any name you want.

    /opt1   auto_indirect

2. Execute the *automount* command to make the changes take effect:

    # **automount –v**

3. Create */etc/auto_indirect* file. Each entry in this map has three fields: the first field identifies the relative pathname of a mount point directory, the second field is optional and specifies

any mount options and the third field identifies the resource to be mounted on the mount point identified in the first field.

```
samba          –ro      hp02:/opt/samba
perl           –ro      hp02:/opt/perl_64
```

Execute the *mount* command to check the mount status of the automounted resources:

mount –v
/etc/auto_indirect on /opt1 type autofs ignore,indirect

At this point */opt1* looks empty. The first time when a user accesses these resources, AutoFS creates necessary mount points and mounts associated resources. Do an *ll* on the two resources and then run the *mount* command:

ll /opt1/samba /opt1/perl
mount –v
/etc/auto_indirect on /opt1 type autofs ignore,indirect
auto_indirect on /opt1/samba type autofs ignore,direct, on Thu Apr 17 07:29:04 2008
auto_indirect on /opt1/perl type autofs ignore,direct, on Thu Apr 17 07:29:04 2008

29.2.5   Defining AutoFS Maps via SMH

You can define AutoFS maps using SMH (or *ncweb* command) also. Follow the links below:

Go to SMH → Networking and Communications → Network Services Configuration → Networked File Systems → Automounted Remote File Systems → Actions → Add Remote File System → Using the NFS Automounter. Fill out the form and hit the OK button. See Figure 29-1.

```
┌──────────────────────────────────────────────────────────────┐
│           Add Automounted Remote File System (hp01)           │
│ ┌──────────────────────────────────────────────────────────┐ │
│ │                                                          │ │
│ │   Local-Directory Name:  /_____      │ │
│ │                                                          │ │
│ │  Remote-Server Name/URL:    _____│ │
│ │                                                          │ │
│ │  Remote-Server Port(Only for NFS URL):  _____  (optional)│ │
│ │                                                          │ │
│ │  Remote-Directory Name:  /_____│ │
│ │                                                          │ │
│ │  [ Configure Multiple Servers... ]                       │ │
│ │                                                          │ │
│ │  Automounter-Map Type:  [ Indirect  ->]                  │ │
│ │                                                          │ │
│ │  [ Automounter-Map Name... ]  _____│ │
│ │                                                          │ │
│ │  [ Mount Options... ] Default Values Used                │ │
│ │ ┌──────────────────────────────────────────────────────┐│ │
│ │ │Add File System To:                                   ││ │
│ └─┴──────────────────────────────────────────────────────┴┘ │
│                                                              │
│ [   OK   ]      [ Apply ]      [ Cancel ]      [ Help ]      │
└──────────────────────────────────────────────────────────────┘
```

Figure 29-1 SMH – AutoFS Mount

29.3   Accessing Replicated Servers

AutoFS is able to mount a resource shared simultaneously by more than one NFS server. This means if one of the NFS servers becomes unavailable, the resource will get automatically mounted from another NFS server. The resource must be shared and mounted read-only to ensure data integrity. Either direct or indirect map may be used for this purpose.

For example, there are four NFS servers: *hp01*, *hp02*, *hp03* and *hp04* sharing an identical copy of */usr/share/man*. When a user tries to access the resource on an NFS client, the *automountd* daemon contacts all four servers concurrently and mounts the resource from the server that responds first. This functionality provides several advantages including quicker response time, minimized network traffic, load balancing and better availability.

The following shows an entry for such a setup in a direct map:

```
/usr/share/man          –ro        hp01,hp02,hp03,hp04:/usr/share/man
```

The following shows entries for such a setup in the */etc/auto_master* and */etc/auto_indirect* maps:

```
/usr/share    auto_indirect                                         # in auto_master
man           –ro                hp01,hp02,hp03,hp04:/usr/share/man  # in auto_indirect
```

29.4   Mounting User Home Directories

AutoFS allows using two special characters in indirect maps. These special characters are & and * and are used to replace references to NFS servers and mount points.

For example, with user home directories located under */home* shared by more than one NFS server, the *automountd* daemon will contact all available and reachable NFS servers concurrently when a user attempts to login on an NFS client system. The daemon will mount only that user's home directory rather than the entire */home*. The indirect map entry for this type of substitution will look like:

```
*      &:/home/&
```

With this simple entry in place, there is no need to update any AutoFS configuration if NFS servers with */home* shared are added or removed. Similarly, if user home directories are added or deleted, there will be no impact on AutoFS.

Summary

This chapter provided coverage on Auto File System. You learned concepts, features and benefits associated with it. You were presented with information that helped you understand how it worked. You looked at associated daemons, commands and startup configuration file.

You studied four types of AutoFS maps, their relationship and how to set them up. You looked at related advantages and disadvantages.

Finally, you learned how AutoFS could be setup to mount NFS resources from multiple, replicated NFS servers to increase availability. Similarly, you looked at how only needed user home directories could be mounted from whichever NFS server it resided on.

Common Internet File System (CIFS)

This chapter covers the following major topics:

- ✓ Describe HP CIFS product suite and its use
- ✓ Features of HP CIFS
- ✓ What is Samba and how to access it?
- ✓ Configure a CIFS server on HP-UX
- ✓ Access an HP-UX CIFS share on a Windows system
- ✓ Access a Windows CIFS share on an HP-UX system

30.1 Understanding HP CIFS

Common Internet File System (CIFS), originally called *Server Message Block* (SMB), is a networking protocol developed by Microsoft, IBM and Intel in late 1980s to enable Windows-based PCs to share file and print resources. This protocol has been used for this purpose in Windows operating systems as the primary native protocol. As time passed, the need to share the two types of resources with non-Windows systems arose. Operating system vendors started to develop and implement products based on the CIFS protocol to fulfill the sharing requirements in their operating system software. One such vendor was HP that introduced CIFS software product in HP-UX. HP CIFS is a client/server implementation of CIFS protocol on HP-UX. The product enabled heterogeneous operating systems including Windows and Linux, to share file and print resources with HP-UX, and vice versa. In the CIFS terminology, the system that offers its file and print resources for sharing is referred to as the *CIFS server* and the system that accesses the resources is called the *CIFS client*.

30.1.1 Features of HP CIFS

Some common features of HP CIFS product are:

- ✓ CIFS shared resources from an HP-UX server can be accessed on Windows-based CIFS clients as standard drive letters, and can be navigated via "Windows Explorer" or "Network Neighborhood".
- ✓ Windows-based shares can be mounted as CIFS resources on HP-UX.
- ✓ An HP-UX CIFS server can be configured as the *Primary Domain Controller* (PDC) in Windows environment.
- ✓ An HP-UX CIFS server can act as a print server for Windows-based CIFS clients.
- ✓ HP-UX and Windows domain usernames and passwords can be used on either platform for authentication.
- ✓ Linux and HP-UX can share their file and print resources via CIFS.

30.1.2 Introduction to Samba

The server component of HP CIFS is based on the freeware file and print software called *Samba*. Samba is an open source software, which may be freely acquired, modified and used. HP added enhancements to the Samba source code and implemented the product in HP-UX as part of HP CIFS product. Throughout this chapter, the terms CIFS server and Samba will be used interchangeably.

Samba can be configured and administered using a browser-based GUI called *Samba Web Administration Tool* (SWAT). To bring up SWAT, ensure that the following line is uncommented in the */etc/inetd.conf* file. If not, uncomment the line and execute "*inetd –c*" to make the change take effect.

```
swat        stream  tcp     nowait.400      root    /opt/samba/bin/swat         swat
```

Enter the following URL in a browser assuming that the hostname is *hp01*. The default port for SWAT is 901. Enter a UNIX username and password when prompted to login.

The main Samba screen comes up as shown in Figure 30-1. SWAT allows you to make local resources available to remote systems, access remote resources and view their status in addition to several other tasks that can be performed from this GUI.

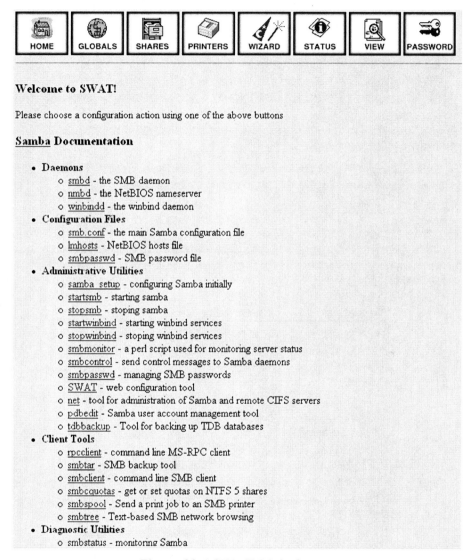

Figure 30-1 SWAT Main Screen

30.2   Configuring CIFS

This section covers configuring a CIFS server on HP-UX to share a resource and accessing the resource on a Windows CIFS client. It also describes how to mount a Windows share on HP-UX.

30.2.1   Configuring a CIFS Server on HP-UX

Here are the steps to configure a CIFS server on HP-UX to share */usr/share/man*, */home* and */var/mail* directories using the commands.

1. Verify that the HP CIFS software is loaded on the system:

    # swlist –l product | grep CIFS
CIFS-CFSM	A.02.03.02	HP CIFS File System Module
CIFS-Client	A.02.02.01	HP CIFS Client
CIFS-Development	A.02.03.02	HP CIFS Server Source Code Files
CIFS-Server	A.02.03.02	HP CIFS Server (Samba) File and Print Services

    If not, go to *software.hp.com* → Internet ready and networking. Download HP CIFS Server and install it using *swinstall*.

2. Edit */etc/rc.config.d/samba* file and set RUN_SAMBA variable to 1. This is to ensure that the functionality gets started automatically at each system reboot.

    RUN_SAMBA=1

3. Edit */etc/opt/samba/smb.conf* file and specify names of resources that needs to be shared. There are a number of parameters that can be set in this file, description of some of which is given in Table 30-1.

Parameter	Description
NetBIOS name	Name of the HP-UX CIFS server.
Workgroup	Name of Windows workgroup or domain.
Server string	Any description.
Hosts allow	IP address of the network or individual hosts to be allowed to access the shares.
Security	Security level.
Encrypt passwords	Whether to encrypt user passwords.
Comment	Any description.
Writeable	Write enabled or not.
Browseable	Users can browse files and directories.
Path	Absolute path to the share.
Default case	Upper or lowercase letters.

    Table 30-1 CIFS Configuration Parameters

4. Perform modifications to the *smb.conf* file to look like the following:

    ```
    [global]
            netbios name        = hp02
            workgroup           = localwg
            server string       = CIFS Server
            hosts allow         = 192.168.1
            security            = user
    ```

encrypt passwords	= yes
default case	= lower

[man]

comment	= UNIX manual pages
writeable	= no
browseable	= no
path	= /usr/share/man

[home]

comment	= User home directories
writeable	= yes
browseable	= yes

[mail]

comment	= Mail directory
path	= /var/mail
writeable	= yes
browseable	= no

5. Execute the *testparm* command to check for any syntax errors in the file:

 # /opt/samba/bin/testparm
```
Load smb config files from /etc/opt/samba/smb.conf
Processing section "[man]"
Processing section "[home]"
Processing section "[mail]"
Loaded services file OK.
Press enter to see a dump of your service definitions
[global]
    workgroup = LOCALWG
    realm = <REALM NAME, IN CAPS, FROM /ETC/KRB5.CONF ON THIS MACHINE>
    netbios name = HP02
    server string = CIFS Server
    log file = /var/opt/samba/log.%m
    max log size = 1000
    local master = No
    read only = No
    hosts allow = 192.168.1
    short preserve case = No
    dos filetime resolution = Yes
[homes]
    comment = Home Directories
    hosts allow =
    browseable = No
[tmp]
    comment = Temporary file space
    path = /tmp
    hosts allow =
[man]
    comment = UNIX manual pages
    path = /usr/share/man
```

```
        read only = Yes
        browseable = No
[home]
        comment = User home directories
        path = /tmp
[mail]
        comment = Mail directory
        path = /var/mail
        browseable = No
```

6. Create a CIFS password file */var/opt/samba/private/smbpasswd* to be used for authentication purposes to determine which users on the CIFS clients are allowed to access these resources. Note that user accounts must already be present in the */etc/passwd* file. Use the following procedure to add *user1*:

> # **touch /var/opt/samba/private/smbpasswd**
> # **chmod 600 /var/opt/samba/private/smbpasswd**
> # **chmod 500 /var/opt/samba/private**
> # **/opt/samba/bin/smbpasswd –a user1**
> New SMB password:
> Retype new SMB password:
> Added user user1.

7. Start the HP CIFS server daemons using one of the following:

> # **/sbin/init.d/samba start**
> # **/opt/samba/bin/startsmb**
> smbd & nmbd started successfully; process ids: smbd: 16039, nmbd: 16033.

8. Check the status of HP CIFS server:

> # **/opt/samba/bin/smbstatus**
> No path in service home - using /tmp
>
> Samba version 3.0.22 based HP CIFS Server A.02.03.02
> PID   Username   Group   Machine
> ---
> Service   pid   machine   Connected at
> ---
> No locked files

Instead of using the manual method or the GUI for configuring a CIFS server, you can use a menu-driven utility called *samba_setup*, which prompts for configuration parameters.

30.2.2   Accessing Shared CIFS Share on a Windows System

Verify that the Windows machine is a member of the same workgroup or domain as the CIFS server. Right click "My Computer", go to Properties, click "Computer Name" and you should be able to see the domain or workgroup name.

To access the share, use one of the following methods:

✓ Go to "My Network Places" and you should be able to see an icon "hp02" (the CIFS server name). Double click it and you will be prompted to enter a username and password. Enter *user1* and its SMB password, and all CIFS shares will become visible.

✓ Start the Windows Explorer. Go to Tools and choose Map Network Drive. Enter the following folder name and click OK:

\\hp02\user1

This will connect to the CIFS share and display the contents.

30.2.3   Accessing a Windows Share on HP-UX

Here are the steps to setup CIFS client functionality on *hp01*. This procedure assumes that a share called *data* is available from a Windows server *win-serv01* with IP address 192.168.1.220. It is also assumed that a user account *testuser* with password *test!123* exists on both *win-serv01* and *hp01*.

1. Verify that the HP CIFS software is loaded on the system:

   # swlist –l product | grep CIFS
   CIFS-CFSM   A.02.03.02   HP CIFS File System Module
   CIFS-Client   A.02.02.01   HP CIFS Client
   CIFS-Development   A.02.03.02   HP CIFS Server Source Code Files
   CIFS-Server   A.02.03.02   HP CIFS Server (Samba) File and Print Services

   If not, go to *software.hp.com* → Internet ready and networking. Download HP CIFS Client and install it using *swinstall*.

2. Edit the */etc/rc.config.d/cifsclient* file and set the variable RUN_CIFSCLIENT to 1:

   RUN_CIFSCLIENT=1

3. Define the Windows domain or workgroup in the */etc/opt/cifsclient/cifsclient.cfg* file:

   domain = "LOCALWG"

4. Start the CIFS client daemon using any of the following:

   # /sbin/init.d/cifsclient start
   # /opt/cifsclient/bin/cifsclient
   CIFS Client started; process id: 16341

5. Create a mount point such as */mntdata* on *hp01*:

   # mkdir /mntdata

6. Edit */etc/fstab* file and add an entry for the share so that it automatically gets mounted at each system reboot:

win-serv01:/data	/mntdata	cifs	defaults	0	0

7. Edit the */etc/hosts* file and insert an entry for *win-serv01*:

   192.168.1.220 win-serv01

8. Mount the share using the *mount* command:

   # **mount –aF cifs**

9. Logon to the CIFS share as user *testuser* using the *cifslogin* command:

   # **su – testuser**
   $ **cifslogin win-serv01 testuser –P test!123 –s**

   This command creates a password database file */var/opt/cifsclient/cifsclient.udb* for CIFS and add an entry for the user *testuser*.

10. Run the following to verify the share:

    # **cifslist**

Mounted Object	Mountpoint	State
\\win-serv01\data	/data	MS

Server	Local User	Remote User	Domain State
win-serv01	root	testuser	LS
win-serv01	testuser	testuser	LS

If you do not wish to automatically mount the CIFS share at each system reboot, do not add the entry to the */etc/fstab* file. You can use the following command as *testuser* to mount and logon to the share:

   # **su – testuser**
   $ **cifsmount //win-serv01/data /data –U testuser**

This command will prompt you to enter the password defined for *testuser* on *win-serv01*. After entering the correct password, the share will become available.

Summary

This chapter discussed HP CIFS. It provided an understanding of the CIFS protocol, the CIFS product suite and Samba. It explained how to configure a CIFS server on HP-UX, access an HP-UX CIFS share on a Windows system and access a Windows share on HP-UX.

## 31

Network Information Service (NIS)

This chapter covers the following major topics:

- ✓ NIS concepts and components – domain, maps, master server, slave server, client and daemons
- ✓ Configure master and slave NIS servers
- ✓ Configure an NIS client
- ✓ Configure /etc/nsswitch.conf file
- ✓ Verify NIS master, slave and client functionality
- ✓ Display and search NIS maps
- ✓ Modify NIS user password
- ✓ Update NIS maps on master and slave NIS servers
- ✓ Manually bind a client to alternate NIS server
- ✓ Use alternate passwd file
- ✓ Secure access to NIS servers

31.1 NIS Concepts and Components

Every networked HP-UX system requires some administrative work to be performed on it to stay current, and up and running. For example, if a user requires access to all networked HP-UX systems, an account is created on each individual machine for the user. Likewise, if a new system needs to be added to a network, the */etc/hosts* file is updated on all HP-UX systems on the network to include the hostname and IP address of the new system. As long as the number of users, systems and other system management requirements are low, administrative work can be done without much difficulty. However, when this number grows or requirements increase, system administration and updates to administrative files become tedious and time consuming.

Rather than managing user accounts, hostnames, etc. on each individual system, an HP-UX service called *Network Information Service* (NIS) may be used to maintain administrative files for these and several other services centrally on a single system. Other systems can then be configured to reference the central system to obtain user information, hostnames and so on. In an NIS environment, a new user account is setup on the central management system (and not on individual systems). This allows the user to login to any system on the network with user credentials authenticated by the central system.

Another key advantage with central management of administrative files is that the data remains consistent and uniform across all systems.

NIS was derived from *yellow pages* service developed by the British Telecom in the UK. Most NIS commands and daemon names precede "yp" (for yellow pages).

When working with NIS, certain components and roles are used. These are explained in the following sub-sections.

31.1.1 NIS Domain

An *NIS domain* is a set of NIS-managed systems sharing common NIS-converted administrative data files called *NIS maps*.

NIS maps are stored under a sub-directory beneath */var/yp* on an NIS server. The sub-directory is created when an NIS server is setup. The name of the sub-directory matches the name of the NIS domain.

 There is no relationship between NIS domain and DNS domain.

31.1.2 NIS Maps

There are numerous administrative files on the system, and most of them are located in the */etc* directory. These are text files which can be managed with a text editor or via system commands.

When a master NIS server is created, the information in these files is converted into a special NIS format and saved into new files under the domain directory beneath */var/yp*. These special files are called *NIS maps*.

By default, NIS manages thirteen administrative files: */etc/passwd*, */etc/group*, */etc/hosts*, */etc/ipnodes*, */etc/networks*, */etc/rpc*, */etc/services*, */etc/protocols*, */etc/netgroup*, */etc/mail/aliases*,

---

/etc/publickey, */etc/netid* and */etc/auto.master*. The names of these files are defined in the NIS configuration file called */var/yp/Makefile*. Do a more on the file and search for "^all" and you should be able to verify this information.

When an NIS server is setup, three types of map files are created under the */var/yp/<domainname>* directory, which can be listed with the *ll* command:

 # ll /var/yp/<domainname>

```
. . . . . . . .
-r--r--r--    1      root    sys      0     Feb 12 16:58    hosts.byaddr.dir
-r--r--r--    1      root    sys    1024    Feb 12 16:58    hosts.byaddr.pag
-r--r--r--    1      root    sys      0     Feb 12 16:58    hosts.byname.dir
-r--r--r--    1      root    sys    1024    Feb 12 16:58    hosts.byname.pag
-rw-r--r--    1      root    sys      0     Feb 12 16:58    hosts.time
. . . . . . . .
-r--r--r--    1      root    sys      0     Feb 12 16:58    passwd.byname.dir
-r--r--r--    1      root    sys    1024    Feb 12 16:58    passwd.byname.pag
-r--r--r--    1      root    sys      0     Feb 12 16:58    passwd.byuid.dir
-r--r--r--    1      root    sys    1024    Feb 12 16:58    passwd.byuid.pag
-rw-r--r--    1      root    sys      0     Feb 12 16:58    passwd.time
. . . . . . . .
```

Files with *.dir* extension contain indexing information for the *.pag* files provided *.pag* files are too big, files with *.pag* extension hold actual data and files with *.time* extension display time stamp for map creation or modification. Maps are indexed based on names and numbers. For example, "passwd" maps are indexed by username and by user ID, "group" maps are indexed by group name and group ID and so on for others.

31.1.3   NIS Server

There are two types of NIS server setups: *master NIS server* and *slave NIS server*.

A master NIS server is the system where the original (or master) administrative files are kept and maintained. These files are translated into NIS maps, which are stored under the NIS domain directory beneath */var/yp*. Any modifications to NIS maps must be made in the master administrative files on the master NIS server.

A slave NIS server is although not required for NIS functionality, however, having at least one on the network is highly recommended for redundancy and load balancing. Each slave server has an identical directory structure under */var/yp* containing a copy of NIS maps pulled from the master server.

31.1.4   NIS Client

An *NIS client* does not store a copy of master server's administrative files or NIS maps locally. It does have its own administrative files, but may not be referenced when the NIS client functionality is invoked, in which case it sends out a broadcast message on the network. Any server on the client's network that holds NIS maps for the client's domain responds. The NIS client forms binding with the first NIS server that responds. Subsequently, all client queries are replied to by that server.

31.1.5   NIS Daemons

When the NIS functionality on master and slave servers, and on clients is initiated, NIS daemons begin to run. Table 31-1 lists and explains the daemons.

Daemon	Runs On			Purpose
	Master	**Slave**	**Client**	
ypserv	Yes	Yes	–	Responds to client requests.
ypbind	Yes	Yes	Yes	Binds with a *ypserv* daemon to send and obtain requested information. Binding information is stored in the */var/yp/binding/<domainname>* file. This daemon dynamically binds itself to another NIS server should the one it was bound to fail.
rpcbind	Yes	Yes	–	Must be up and running prior to starting any RPC-based services including NIS and NFS.
rpc.yppasswdd	Yes	–	–	When a user password is changed on a client with the *yppasswd* or *passwd* command, *ypbind* sends the password change request to this daemon, which updates the */etc/passwd* file on the master server, regenerates "passwd" maps and pushes them out to slave servers.
rpc.ypupdated	Yes	–	–	Provides a secure mechanism to update NIS maps on the master server using configuration information located in the */var/yp/updaters* file.
ypxfrd	Yes	–	–	Responds to slave server's *ypxfr* command to pull maps.
keyserv	Yes	–	–	Stores private encryption keys of each logged in user.

Table 31-1 NIS Daemons

31.2   Configuring NIS

This section provides information on how to configure master and slave NIS servers, and clients.

31.2.1   Configuration Considerations

Keep the following design considerations in mind when setting up an NIS environment:

- ✓ A system cannot be the master server for more than one NIS domain.
- ✓ The master server for one domain may be configured to be used as a slave server for another domain.
- ✓ A system can be a slave server for multiple domains concurrently.
- ✓ Each system in an NIS environment including the master and any slave servers, is an NIS client as well.

✓ A client belongs to only one NIS domain.

✓ Each subnet in an NIS domain must include an NIS server. When the NIS client functionality is started, it broadcasts a message to search for a server to bind itself with. These broadcasts cannot pass through gateways and routers, therefore each subnet must have at least one slave NIS server. The master NIS server can exist on any subnet.

31.2.2 Configuring a Master NIS Server

To setup *hp02* to act as a master NIS server, perform the following steps:

1. Update administrative files on *hp02* to be brought under NIS control. For example, if you want */etc/passwd* file to be managed by NIS, consolidate all user entries from all systems that will be part of the NIS domain and append them to the */etc/passwd* file on *hp02*. Remove all duplicate entries and fix any inconsistencies.

2. Define a unique NIS domain name such as "nis_domain" using the *domainname* command:

    # **domainname nis_domain**

 Without any arguments, the *domainname* command displays the current NIS domain setting.

3. Edit */etc/rc.config.d/namesvrs* file and make the following modifications:

    Set the NIS_DOMAIN variable to the domain name:

    NIS_DOMAIN=nis_domain

    Set the NIS_MASTER_SERVER and NIS_CLIENT variables to 1 so the master server and client functionalities start automatically at each system reboot when the startup script */sbin/rc2.d/S410nis.server,* which is symbolically linked to the */sbin/init.d/nis.server* script, is executed:

    NIS_MASTER_SERVER=1
    NIS_CLIENT=1

4. Execute the *ypinit* command on *hp02* to create the master NIS server. This command calls the *makedbm* command in the background to generate NIS maps from the administrative files. Specify one or more system names (*hp03* in this demonstration) to be setup as slave NIS servers, followed by Ctrl+d.

    # **ypinit –m**
    You will be required to answer a few questions to install the Network Information Service.
    All questions will be asked at the beginning of this procedure.
    Do you want this procedure to quit on non-fatal errors? [y/n: n] **n**
    OK, but please remember to correct anything which fails.
    If you do not, some part of the system (perhaps the NIS itself) won't work.

    At this point, you must construct a list of the hosts which will be
    NIS servers for the "nis_domain" domain.

This machine, hp02, is in the list of Network Information Service servers.
Please provide the hostnames of the slave servers, one per line.
When you have no more names to add, enter a <ctrl+d> or a blank line.
    next host to add: **hp03**
    next host to add:
The current list of NIS servers looks like this:
hp02
hp03
Is this correct? [y/n: y] **y**

There will be no further questions. The remainder of the procedure should take 5 to 10 minutes.
Building the ypservers database... ypservers build complete.
Running make in /var/yp:
updated passwd
updated group
updated hosts

. . . .

hp02 has been set up as a master Network Information Service server without any errors.

If there are running slave NIS servers, run yppush(1M) now for any databases which have been
changed. If there are no running slaves, run ypinit on those hosts which are to be slave servers.

This command creates */var/yp/nis_domain* directory and runs *ypmake*. The *ypmake* command
looks into its configuration file */var/yp/Makefile* to get a list of administrative files to be
translated into NIS maps. As maps are created, they are saved in */var/yp/nis_domain*.

5. Start NIS by running the following two scripts. The first script starts *ypserv*, *rpc.yppasswdd*
    and *rpc.ypupdated* daemons from the */usr/lib/netsvc/yp* directory and *ypxfrd* daemon from the
    /usr/sbin directory. The second script starts *ypbind* and *keyserv* daemons from the
    /usr/lib/netsvc/yp and */usr/sbin* directories, respectively:

    # /sbin/init.d/nis.server start
       starting NIS SERVER networking
       starting up the rpcbind
          rpcbind already started, using pid: 669
          domainname nis_domain
       starting up the Network Information Service
          starting up the ypserv daemon
          /usr/lib/netsvc/yp/ypserv
          starting up the ypxfrd daemon
          /usr/sbin/ypxfrd
          starting up the rpc.yppasswdd daemon
          /usr/lib/netsvc/yp/rpc.yppasswdd /etc/passwd -m passwd PWFILE=/etc/passwd
          starting up the rpc.ypupdated daemon
          /usr/lib/netsvc/yp/rpc.ypupdated
          starting up the keyserv daemon
          /usr/sbin/keyserv
    # /sbin/init.d/nis.client start
       starting NIS CLIENT networking

```
starting up the rpcbind
    rpcbind already started, using pid: 669
    domainname nis_domain
starting up the Network Information Service
    starting up the ypbind daemon
    /usr/lib/netsvc/yp/ypbind
    Checking NIS binding.
    Bound to NIS server using domain nis_domain.
    starting up the keyserv daemon
    keyserv already started, using pid: 18410
```

The master NIS server is set and ready to go.

You can also setup the master NIS server using SMH (or *ncweb* command). Follow the links below:

Go to SMH → Networking and Communications → Network Services Configuration → NIS → Actions → Set Domain Name. Refer to Figure 31-1.

```
┌─────────────────────────────────────────────────┐
│            Set Domain Name (hp01)                │
├─────────────────────────────────────────────────┤
│                                                  │
│  Domain Name:    nis domain                      │
│                                                  │
├─────────────────────────────────────────────────┤
│  [   OK   ]        [ Cancel ]       [  Help  ]   │
└─────────────────────────────────────────────────┘
```

Figure 31-1 SMH – NIS Domain Name Setup

Go back to Actions. You will see the following choices:

- ✓ Set Domain Name
- ✓ Configure Master Server
- ✓ Configure Slave Server
- ✓ Enable Client
- ✓ Modify
- ✓ Remove

You can setup, modify or remove the master server, a slave server or a client.

31.2.3   Configuring a Slave NIS Server

To setup *hp03* to act as a slave NIS server, perform the following steps:

1. Set the NIS domain name "nis_domain" using the *domainname* command:

    # **domainname nis_domain**

2. Edit */etc/rc.config.d/namesvrs* file and make the following modifications:

    Set the NIS_DOMAIN variable to the domain name:

        NIS_DOMAIN=nis_domain

Set the NIS_SLAVE_SERVER and NIS_CLIENT variables to 1:

```
NIS_SLAVE_SERVER=1
NIS_CLIENT=1
```

3. Execute the following command to transfer all NIS maps from the master server into */var/yp/nis_domain* directory on the slave server *hp03*:

   # **ypinit –s hp02**
   You will be required to answer a few questions to install the Network Information Service.
   All questions will be asked at the beginning of this procedure.

   Do you want this procedure to quit on non-fatal errors? [y/n:] **n**
   OK, but please remember to correct anything which fails.
   If you do not, some part of the system (perhaps the NIS itself) won't work.

There will be no further questions asked. The remainder of the procedure will copy NIS map files over from *hp02*. If you see messages such as "no such map" during file transfer, ignore them.

```
Transferring group.bygid for domain nis_domain from hp02...
Transferring group.byname for domain nis_domain from hp02...
Transferring hosts.byaddr for domain nis_domain from hp02...
Transferring hosts.byname for domain nis_domain from hp02...
Transferring netgroup for domain nis_domain from hp02...
Transferring netgroup.byhost for domain nis_domain from hp02...
Transferring netgroup.byuser for domain nis_domain from hp02...
Transferring networks.byaddr for domain nis_domain from hp02...
Transferring networks.byname for domain nis_domain from hp02...
Transferring passwd.byname for domain nis_domain from hp02...
Transferring passwd.byuid for domain nis_domain from hp02...
. . . . . . . .
hp03 has been set up as a slave Network Information Service server without errors.
```

4. Start NIS by running the following two scripts:

   # **/sbin/init.d/nis.server start**
   # **/sbin/init.d/nis.client start**

A slave NIS server is set and ready to go.

You can setup a slave NIS server using SMH also. Refer to the previous sub-section "Configuring a Master NIS Server" for details.

31.2.4   Configuring an NIS Client

To setup an HP-UX machine to act as an NIS client, perform the following steps on that machine:

1. Set the NIS domain name "nis_domain" using the *domainname* command:

 # domainname nis_domain

2. Edit the */etc/rc.config.d/namesvrs* file and make the following modifications:

   Set the NIS_DOMAIN variable to the domain name:

   NIS_DOMAIN=nis_domain

   Set the NIS_CLIENT variable to 1 so NIS client functionality gets started at each system reboot when */sbin/rc2.d/S420nis.client* script, which is symbolically linked to */sbin/init.d/nis.client* script, is executed.

   NIS_CLIENT=1

3. Start NIS by running the following script:

   # /sbin/init.d/nis.client start

An NIS client is set and ready to go.

You can setup NIS client using SMH also. Refer to the sub-section "Configuring a Master NIS Server" for details.

31.2.5   Configuring /etc/nsswitch.conf File

In HP-UX, more than one source can be employed to get information. For example, user authentication information can be obtained from */etc/passwd* file, NIS or LDAP. Which of these sources to obtain information from and in what order, is determined by entries defined in the *name service switch* configuration file called *nsswitch.conf* located in the */etc* directory. An example entry below from the file consults the local */etc/passwd* file first and then an NIS server for user authentication:

   passwd: files   nis

By default, this file does not exist, however, there are several template files available in the */etc* directory. These templates include *nsswitch.compat*, *nsswitch.files*, *nsswitch.hp_defaults*, *nsswitch.ldap* and *nsswitch.nis*. Copy one of these files as *nsswitch.conf* and modify entries as per requirements. The following is an excerpt from */etc/nsswitch.nis*:

 # cat /etc/nsswitch.nis

passwd:	files	nis
group:	files	nis
hosts:	nis	[NOTFOUND=return] files
networks:	nis	[NOTFOUND=return] files
protocols:	nis	[NOTFOUND=return] files
rpc:	nis	[NOTFOUND=return] files
publickey:	nis	[NOTFOUND=return] files
netgroup:	nis	[NOTFOUND=return] files
automount:	files	nis

```
aliases:      files    nis
services:     files    nis
```

There are four keywords available to be used when more than one potential source is referenced in the */etc/nsswitch.conf* file. These keywords are listed in Table 31-2 with their meanings.

Keyword	Meaning
SUCCESS	Information found.
UNAVAIL	Source down or not responding.
NOTFOUND	Information not found.
TRYAGAIN	Source busy, try again later.

Table 31-2 Name Service Source Status

Based on the status code for a source, one of two actions, given in Table 31-3, take place.

Action	Meaning
continue	Try the next source listed.
return	Do not try the next source.

Table 31-3 Name Service Source Actions

As an example, if the "passwd" entry looks like the following, the search will terminate when the required user information is not found in NIS. The "files" source will be ignored.

```
passwd:       nis [NOTFOUND=return] files
```

Each keyword defined in Table 31-2 has a default action associated. If no keyword/action combination is specified, actions listed in Table 31-4 are assumed.

Keyword	Default Action
SUCCESS	return
UNAVAIL	continue
NOTFOUND	continue
TRYAGAIN	continue

Table 31-4 Name Service Source Default Actions

31.2.6   Testing NIS Master, Slave and Client Functionality

To test which NIS server a client is bound to, run the *ypwhich* command without any options. Note that every system in an NIS domain including master and slave servers, is an NIS client. With –m option, this command also displays what maps are available from that server:

```
# ypwhich
hp02
# ypwhich –m
. . . . . . . .
hosts.byaddr hp02
hosts.byname hp02
```

group.bygid hp02
group.byname hp02
passwd.byuid hp02
passwd.byname hp02
ypservers hp02

Use the *rpcinfo* command to list running NIS daemons:

rpcinfo

program	version	netid	address	service	owner
100000	3	ticots	hp02.rpc	rpcbind	superuser
100000	3	ticotsord	hp02.rpc	rpcbind	superuser
100000	3	ticlts	hp02.rpc	rpcbind	superuser
100000	3	tcp	0.0.0.0.0.111	rpcbind	superuser
100000	3	udp	0.0.0.0.0.111	rpcbind	superuser
100004	1	udp	0.0.0.0.3.105	ypserv	superuser
100004	1	tcp	0.0.0.0.3.106	ypserv	superuser
100069	1	udp	0.0.0.0.3.111	ypxfrd	superuser
100069	1	tcp	0.0.0.0.3.112	ypxfrd	superuser
100009	1	udp	0.0.0.0.3.254	yppasswdd	superuser
100028	1	tcp	0.0.0.0.3.121	ypupdated	superuser
100028	1	udp	0.0.0.0.3.122	ypupdated	superuser
100029	1	ticlts	hp02.keyserv	keyserv	superuser
100029	1	ticotsord	hp02.keyserv	keyserv	superuser
100029	1	ticots	hp02.keyserv	keyserv	superuser
100007	1	tcp	0.0.0.0.253.255	ypbind	sys
100007	1	udp	0.0.0.0.254.127	ypbind	sys

The output indicates that all NIS daemons: *rpcbind, ypserv, ypxfrd, yppasswdd, ypupdated, keyserv* and *ypbind* are registered and running.

To obtain user information on *user5* for instance, use the *nsquery* command and specify the type of source to be searched. You have two choices: passwd and group. The *nsquery* command consults the */etc/nsswitch.conf* file to determine potential sources for lookup. The last line in the output below indicates that the search has been terminated as the information is found:

nsquery passwd user5
Using "files nis" for the passwd policy.
Searching /etc/passwd for user5
User name: user5
User Id: 107
Group Id: 20
Gecos:
Home Directory: /home/user5
Shell: /sbin/sh
Switch configuration: Terminates Search

31.3　Managing NIS

Managing NIS involves tasks such as displaying and searching NIS maps, changing a user password, updating maps on master and slave servers, changing client binding and using alternate passwd file.

31.3.1　Displaying and Searching NIS Maps

The administrative data files are in plain ascii text. Translating them into NIS generates map files which contain data in non-text format. These map files require different set of commands to be viewed and searched.

To display "passwd" map contents, for instance, use the *ypcat* command. This command performs equivalent function to the *cat* command. There is no need to specify the location of the map. The *ypcat* command by default looks into the domain directory.

> # **ypcat passwd**
> root:/af/4dEOdgkpY:0:3::/:/usr/bin/sh
>
> . . . .
>
> user1:nui8KFHeIlhh6:103:20::/home/user1:/sbin/sh

To search for a string "users" in the "group" map, use the *ypmatch* command. This command performs equivalent function to the *grep* command. Again, there is no need to specify the map location.

> # **ypmatch users group**
> users::20:root

The *yppoll* command is another NIS command, which is used to display the time stamp of the creation of a map. The time displayed is calculated in seconds from the epoch time.

> # **yppoll passwd.byuid**
> Domain nis_domain is supported.
> Map passwd.byuid has order number 1139927840.
> The master server is hp02.

31.3.2　Changing a User Password

Once an NIS environment is established, use either the *yppasswd* or *passwd* command to change a user password. For example, to change *user1*'s password, do either of the following on the client:

> $ **yppasswd user1**
> Changing password for user1 on NIS server
> Old NIS password:
> New password:
> Re-enter new password:
> NIS(YP) passwd/attributes changed on hp02, the master NIS server.
> $ **passwd −r nis**
> Changing password for user1 on NIS server

Old NIS password:
New password:
Re-enter new password:
NIS(YP) passwd/attributes changed on hp02, the master NIS server.

Both commands contact the *rpc.yppasswdd* daemon on the master server, replace the existing encrypted passwd entry in the */etc/passwd* file on that server, regenerate NIS "passwd" maps from the updated */etc/passwd* file and push the "passwd" maps out to slave servers.

31.3.3   Updating NIS Maps on the Master Server

Administrative files change over time as they are updated. In an NIS environment, make sure that the updates are performed on the master server and pushed out to slave servers. For example, to add a new group, run the *groupadd* command on the master server and execute the *yppush* command from the */var/yp* directory to regenerate "group" maps and push them out to slave servers. The *yppush* command initiates the *ypxfr* command on the slave server, which pulls the specified maps from the master server.

 # ./ypmake group
For NIS domain nis_domain:
Building the group map(s)... group build complete.
   Pushing the group map(s): group.bygid.
  group.byname.

ypmake complete: no errors encountered.

Without any arguments, *ypmake* updates all maps and calls *yppush* to transfer maps to slave servers:

 # ./ypmake
For NIS domain nis_domain:
The passwd map(s) are up-to-date.
Building the group map(s)... group build complete.
   Pushing the group map(s): group.bygid.
  group.byname.
. . . .
The publickey map(s) are up-to-date.
Building the netid map(s)... netid build complete.
   Pushing the netid map(s): netid.byname.
The auto_master map(s) are up-to-date.
ypmake complete: no errors encountered.

The *make* command may be used instead of *ypmake*.

31.3.4   Updating NIS Maps on a Slave Server

There are three scripts – *ypxfr_1perday*, *ypxfr_2perday* and *ypxfr_1perhour* – in the */var/yp* directory on slave servers, which can be scheduled to run via cron to pull maps over. This ensures that no updates performed on the master server are missed.

Do the following as *root* on slave servers:

```
# crontab -e
0    0      *     *     *     /var/yp/ypxfr_1perday
0    0,12   *     *     *     /var/yp/ypxfr_2perday
0    *      *     *     *     /var/yp/ypxfr_1perhour
```

The *ypxfr_1perday* script will be executed at midnight each night, the *ypxfr_2perday* script at midnight and midday each day and the *ypxfr_1perhour* script will be executed each hour.

The *ypxfr_1perday* script pulls, by default, *group.bygid, group.byname, networks.byaddr, networks.byname, protocols.byname, protocols.bynumber, rpc.bynumber, services.byname* and *ypservers* maps.

The *ypxfr_2perday* script pulls, by default, *ethers.byaddr, ethers.byname, hosts.byaddr, hosts.byname, mail.aliases, netgroup, netgroup.byhost* and *netgroup.byuser* maps.

The *ypxfr_1perhour* script pulls, by default, *passwd.byname* and *passwd.byuid* maps.

You may consolidate them into a single script and then schedule the consolidated script to run via cron. Also, you can include or exclude any maps that need or need not be pulled.

31.3.5   Manually Binding a Client to Another NIS Server

In order for a client system to be able to reference NIS information, it must be bound to an NIS server. This binding is set automatically when either the client system reboots or you manually start the NIS functionality on it.

To manually alter the binding to another NIS server such as *hp03*, use the *ypset* command:

 # ypset hp03

Verify the change with the *ypwhich* command.

31.3.6   Using Alternate passwd File

The */etc/passwd* file stores information about user accounts including *root*. When user authentication takes place via NIS, passwords travel over the network and introduce security concerns especially for the *root* account. To safeguard *root*, exclude it from NIS control by using an alternate passwd file when configuring NIS. In an existing NIS environment, this can be achieved by rebuilding the "passwd" maps. Do the following on the master server:

1. Copy */etc/passwd* as */etc/passwd.nis*.
2. Edit */etc/passwd.nis* and remove users who should not be authenticated via NIS, including *root, bin, uucp* and *listen*. The system user accounts typically have UIDs less than 100.
3. Edit */var/yp/Makefile* and replace the value of the variable PWFILE from *PWFILE=$(DIR)/passwd* to *PWFILE=$(DIR)/passwd.nis*.
4. Edit */etc/rc.config.d/namesvrs* and do the following:

    Replace YPPASSWDD_OPTIONS="/etc/passwd –m passwd PWFILE=/etc/passwd" with
    YPPASSWDD_OPTIONS="/etc/passwd.nis –m passwd PWFILE=/etc/passwd.nis"

---

5. Execute the *ypmake* command (or the *make* command) from the */var/yp* directory to regenerate the "passwd" maps and push them out to slave servers:

> **# ./ypmake passwd**
> For NIS domain nis_domain:
> Building the passwd map(s)... passwd build complete.
>   Pushing the passwd map(s): passwd.byname.
>   passwd.byuid.
>
> ypmake complete: no errors encountered.

From now on, append to the */etc/passwd.nis* file new user account entries that need to be part of NIS and run either *ypmake* or *make*.

31.4   Securing Access to NIS Servers

By default, with *root* privileges, a user on a system outside of an NIS domain and located on any subnet, can make the system part of the NIS domain. To avoid this to happen, limit NIS domain access by specific systems and specific networks only. Perform the following on both master and slave servers to implement the control:

1. Create */var/yp/securenets* file.
2. Specify netmask and IP address of the system or network to be allowed access. The example entries below restrict all machines other than the ones on the 192.168.1 network and a particular machine with IP address 192.168.2.201:

> 255.255.255.0   192.168.1.0
> 255.255.255.255   192.168.2.201

3. Bounce NIS server daemons on both master and slave servers:

> **# /sbin/init.d/nis.server stop**
> **# /sbin/init.d/nis.server start**

This procedure can also be used to prevent one or more existing NIS client systems from requesting information from NIS servers. Similarly, the procedure is also valid to restrict one or more slave servers from transferring maps over.

Summary

In this chapter you learned about NIS. You looked at its concepts and components – domain, maps, master server, slave server, client and daemons. You performed configuration of master and slave NIS servers. You setup an NIS client including configuring the name service switch file.

You were presented with procedures on how to test the functionality of NIS master and slave servers, and client. You displayed NIS map contents and searched them for text using special commands. You saw how a user password was modified in an NIS environment. You looked at procedures to update NIS maps on both master and slave servers, manually bind a client to an alternate NIS server and use alternate passwd file.

The last section explained to you reasons behind securing NIS servers and how to implement that security feature.

## 32

Domain Name System (DNS)

This chapter covers the following major topics:

- ✓ What is name resolution?
- ✓ Various name resolution approaches
- ✓ DNS concepts, features and components – name space, domain, zone, zone files, master DNS server, slave DNS server, caching-only DNS server, DNS client and BIND versions
- ✓ How DNS works
- ✓ Configure master DNS server
- ✓ Understand DNS boot and zone files
- ✓ Configure slave and caching-only DNS servers
- ✓ Configure DNS client – the name service switch and resolver files
- ✓ Verify DNS functionality using nsquery, nslookup and dig
- ✓ Update master, slave and caching-only DNS servers
- ✓ Use rndc utility

32.1 Understanding Name Resolution

Name resolution is a technique for determining the IP address of a system by providing its hostname. In other words, name resolution is a way of mapping a hostname with its IP address. Name resolution is used on the internet and on corporate networks. When you enter the address of a website in a browser window, you actually specify the hostname of a remote machine that exists somewhere in the world. You do not know its exact location, but you do know its hostname. There is a complex web of hundreds of thousands of routers configured on the internet. These routers maintain information about other routers closer to them. When you hit the Enter key after entering a website name, the hostname (the website name) is passed to a DNS server, which tries to get the IP address associated with the website's hostname. Once it gets the IP address, the request to access the website is forwarded to the web server from one router to another, until the request reaches the destination system. Determining IP address by providing a hostname is referred to as *name resolution* (a.k.a. *name lookup* or *DNS lookup*), determining hostname by providing an IP address is referred to as *reverse name resolution* (a.k.a. *reverse name lookup* or *reverse DNS lookup*) and the service employed to perform name resolution is called *Domain Name System* (DNS). DNS is commonly recognized by the name *Berkeley Internet Name Domain* (BIND) in the UNIX world. BIND is an implementation of DNS on the UNIX platform, and was developed at the University of California, Berkeley. The two terms are used interchangeably throughout this chapter.

32.1.1 Name Resolution Approaches

There are three methods available in HP-UX for hostname resolution. These are explained below.

The */etc/hosts* File

The */etc/hosts* file is typically used when there are not too many systems on the network. This file is maintained locally on each system.

Each line in the */etc/hosts* file contains an IP address in the first column, followed by an official (or *canonical*) hostname in the second column. You may also define one or more aliases per entry. Aliases are nicknames. The official hostname and one or more aliases allow you to assign multiple hostnames to a single IP address. This way the same system can be accessed using any of these names. A few sample entries below from */etc/hosts* file display *hp01, hp02, hp03, hp04* and *hp05* systems with IP addresses 192.168.1.201, 192.168.1.202, 192.168.1.203, 192.168.1.204 and 192.168.1.205, and aliases *h1, h2, h3, h4* and *h5*, respectively.

```
192.168.1.201    hp01    h1    # Production database server
192.168.1.202    hp02    h2    # Development web server
192.168.1.203    hp03    h3    # Production application server
192.168.1.204    hp04    h4    # Production application server
192.168.1.205    hp05    h5    # Production backup server
```

Since the */etc/hosts* file is maintained locally, it must be updated manually on each system to maintain consistency whenever a system is added or removed.

Network Information Service

An NIS server can serve only the systems on its local network. NIS clients send out broadcasts to locate and bind to NIS servers. Each NIS server is able to respond to hostname queries on its local network.

NIS is not used for hostname resolution because of limitations and security issues.

Domain Name System

DNS is the de facto standard for name resolution used on the internet and on corporate networks.

Systems using DNS send name resolution requests to a DNS server instead of */etc/hosts* file or NIS.

The remainder of this chapter furnishes detailed information on DNS and how to set it up.

32.2 DNS Concepts and Components

This sections explains DNS concepts, identifies components, describes roles and explains how it works.

32.2.1 DNS Name Space and Domains

The DNS *name space* is a hierarchical organization of all the domains on the internet. The root of the name space is represented by the dot character. The hierarchy right below the root, is divided into top-level (first-level) domains such as com, gov, edu, mil, net, org, biz, tv, info and two-character country-specific domains such as ca, uk and au. A DNS *domain* is a collection of one or more systems. Sub-domains fall under domains. For example, the com domain consists of second-level sub-domains such as hp, ibm and sun. Sub-domains can then be further divided into multiple, smaller third-level sub-domains, each of which may contain one or several systems. For example, *hp.com* may contain a sub-domain represented as *ca.hp.com*. Within a domain, any number of sub-domains can be defined.

Figure 32-1 exhibits the hierarchical structure of the DNS name space. It also shows domain levels.

At the deepest level of the hierarchy are the *leaves* (systems) of the name space. For example, a system *hp01* in *ca.hp.com* will be represented as *hp01.ca.hp.com*. If the dot character is appended to this name to look like *hp01.ca.hp.com.*, it will be referred to as the *Fully Qualified Domain Name* (FQDN) for *hp01*.

A system in the DNS name space may be a computer, a router, a switch, a network printer, or any other device with an IP address.

The hierarchical structure of DNS enables the division of a domain into multiple sub-domains with management responsibility of each sub-domain delegated to different groups of administrators. This type of configuration allows each sub-domain to have its own DNS server with full "authority" on the information that the sub-domain contains. This distributed management approach simplifies overall DNS administration in large environments.

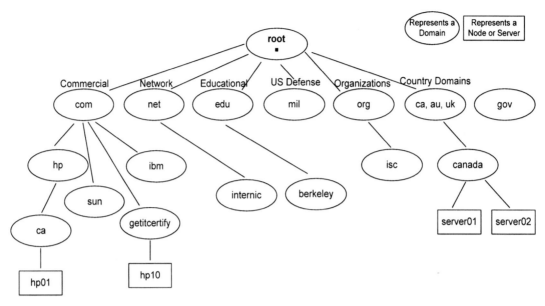

Figure 32-1 DNS Hierarchy

To run a server directly facing the internet, you must get a domain name registered for it. Contact one of the accredited domain registrars licensed by the *Internet Corporation for Assigned Names and Numbers* (ICANN). Visit *www.icann.com* to obtain a list of licensed registrars or simply contact an ISP to get a domain registered.

32.2.2 DNS Zones and Zone Files

Every DNS server maintains complete information about the portion of the DNS name space it is responsible for. This information includes a complete set of authoritative data files. The portion of the name space for which a DNS server has a complete set of authoritative data files is known as the server's *zone* and the set of authoritative data files is known as *zone files, zone databases* or simply *databases*.

32.2.3 DNS Roles

A role is a function that a system performs from DNS standpoint. A system is typically configured to function as one of the three types of DNS servers, or as a client.

Master DNS Server

A *master DNS server* has the authority for its domain (or sub-domain) and contains that domain's data. Each domain must have one master server, which may delegate responsibility of one or more sub-domains to other DNS servers, referred to as slave and caching-only DNS servers. When a system is added to or removed from a domain, zone files on the master server must be updated.

Slave DNS Server

A *slave DNS server* also has the authority for its domain and stores that domain's zone files, however, the zone files are copied from the master server. When updates are made to zone files on the master server, the slave server gets the updated zone files automatically. This type of DNS server is normally setup for redundancy purposes in case the master server fails, and for sharing master server's load. It is highly recommended to have at least one slave server per domain to supplement the master.

Caching-Only DNS Server

A *caching-only DNS server* has no authority for any domains. It gets data from the master or slave server and caches it locally in its memory. Like a slave server, a caching-only server is normally used for redundancy and load-sharing purposes. The replies to queries from a caching-only server are normally quicker than the replies from either a master or a slave server. This is because a caching-only server keeps data in memory rather than on disk. This type of DNS server is typically used by ISPs where hundreds of thousands of queries for name resolution arrive every minute.

DNS Client

A *DNS client* normally has two files configured that are used to resolve hostname queries by referencing information defined in them.

32.2.4   BIND Versions

The latest version of BIND software is 9.3.2 at the time of writing this chapter, and comes standard with HP-UX 11i v3. Note that BIND is an implementation of DNS on UNIX systems. You can download the latest version available for HP-UX from *software.hp.com* → Internet ready and networking, as exhibited in Figure 32-2.

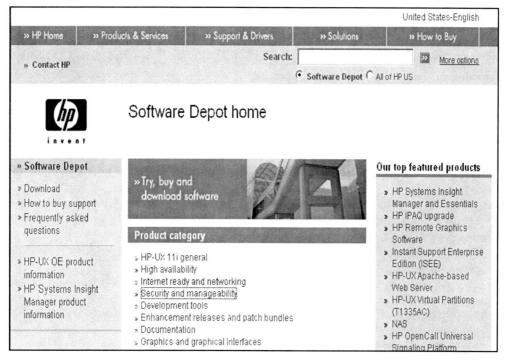

Figure 32-2 *software.hp.com* **Main Page**

To check the version of BIND, use the *what* command:

 # what /usr/sbin/named

/usr/sbin/named:
    $Revision: 92453-07 linker linker crt0.o B.11.16.01 030415 $
    named **9.3.2** $Revision: 0.0
    Copyright (C) 2004, 2005 Internet Systems Consortium, Inc.
    $Revision: B.11.31_LR

The third line indicates that the BIND version is 9.3.2.

32.2.5   BIND 9.3.2 New Features

BIND 9.3.2 supports the following new features:

- ✓ Implementation of DNS Security (DNSSEC).
- ✓ Support for IP6.ARPA reverse lookup domain.
- ✓ New method of listing master servers.
- ✓ New options in the Options statement in the */etc/named.data* file.
- ✓ New options to configure the ordering of records, restrict the character set of domain names, and enable and disable *Incremental Zone Transfer* (IXFR).
- ✓ Transition support for IPv4 and IPv6.
- ✓ Enhanced *rndc* command.
- ✓ New option in the zone statement.
- ✓ New command options.

32.2.6   How DNS Works

The following highlights what occurs when a user on *server01.canada.ca* initiates access to *hp10.getitcertify.com* using the *telnet* command:

- ✓ The *telnet* command calls the gethostbyname routine to get the IP address of *hp10.getitcertify.com*.
- ✓ The gethostbyname routine looks into the */etc/nsswitch.conf* file to check available name resolution methods.
- ✓ If DNS is selected, the gethostbyname routine invokes the DNS resolver to query DNS servers.
- ✓ If *server01.canada.ca* is a DNS server itself, the query is forwarded to it. If not, the resolver looks into the */etc/resolv.conf* file to get the IP address of the DNS server that serves the *canada.ca* domain.
- ✓ The query is sent to the DNS server, but it is unable to provide an answer since it has information about systems in its local domain *canada.ca* only.
- ✓ The DNS server queries a root DNS server, which typically stores information about DNS servers one or two levels below it.
- ✓ The root DNS server forwards the query to *.com* domain, which passes the query to the DNS server serving the *getitcertify.com* domain.
- ✓ The DNS server for *getitcertify.com* returns the authoritative address of *hp10.getitcertify.com* to the DNS server of *canada.ca* domain.

✓ The DNS server for *canada.ca* passes the requested IP address to the resolver, which passes it to gethostbyname routine to return to the *telnet* command.

32.3 Configuring DNS

Let us look at the step-by-step procedures on configuring a master, slave and a caching-only server, and a DNS client.

32.3.1 Configuring a Master DNS Server

To configure *hp01* to act as the master DNS server for domain *getitcertify.com*, perform the following steps:

1. Get *getitcertify.com* domain name registered.
2. Update the */etc/hosts* file on *hp01* with canonical hostnames, and aliases as needed, of all systems on the network. For example, *hp01*, *hp02*, *hp03*, *hp04* and *hp05* are five systems with official hostnames (after appending the domain name) *hp01.getitcertify.com*, *hp02.getitcertify.com*, *hp03.getitcertify.com*, *hp04.getitcertify.com* and *hp05.getitcertify.com*. The */etc/hosts* file will look like:

192.168.1.201	hp01.getitcertify.com	hp01	# Production database server
192.168.1.202	hp02.getitcertify.com	hp02	# Development web server
192.168.1.203	hp03.getitcertify.com	hp03	# Production application server
192.168.1.204	hp04.getitcertify.com	hp04	# Production application server
192.168.1.205	hp05.getitcertify.com	hp05	# Production backup server

    Note that the aliases *h1*, *h2*, *h3*, *h4* and *h5* defined previously have been removed.

3. Create */etc/dns* directory to store DNS zone files:

    # **mkdir /etc/dns**

4. Change directory to */etc/dns* and run the *hosts_to_named* command. This command scans the */etc/hosts* file and generates several files such as *named.conf, db.127.0.0, db.domain* and *db.net*. The zone files *db.domain* and *db.net* are created one per each domain and network, specified with –d and –n options, respectively. The –z option creates zone files for the slave DNS server that will be configured in the next sub-section. The –b option specifies the location of the BIND boot configuration file.

    # **cd /etc/dns**
    # **hosts_to_named –d getitcertify.com –n 192.168.1 –z 192.168.1.202 **
    –b /etc/named.conf
    Translating */etc/hosts* to lowercase ...
    Collecting network data ...
        192.168.1
    Creating list of multi-homed hosts ...
    Creating "A" data (name to address mapping) for net 192.168.1 ...
    Creating "PTR" data (address to name mapping) for net 192.168.1 ...
    Creating "MX" (mail exchanger) data ...

```
Building default named.conf file ...
Building default db.cache file ...
WARNING: db.cache must be filled in with the name(s) and address(es) of the rootserver(s)
Building default conf.sec.save for secondary servers ...
Building default conf.sec for secondary servers ...
Building default conf.cacheonly for caching only servers ...
done
```

Alternatively, a param file such as *param.dns* can be created with the vi editor and passed as an argument to the *hosts_to_named* command. Include all options and parameters in the file that were supplied at the command line above.

vi param.dns

```
–d  getitcertify.com        # Name of the domain.
–n  192.168.1               # IP address of the network.
–z  192.168.1.202           # IP address of the slave DNS server.
–b  /etc/named.conf         # location of the DNS boot file.
```
hosts_to_named –f param.dns

5. Download the *db.cache* file from *ftp://ftp.internic.net/domain* and copy it to the */etc/dns* directory. Overwrite existing *db.cache* in that directory. This file contains an updated list of root name servers.
6. Edit */etc/rc.config.d/namesvrs_dns* file and set the variable NAMED to 1:

    NAMED=1

7. Start the BIND server daemon:

    ### # /sbin/init.d/named start

Here is a list of the boot and zone database files created by running the *hosts_to_named* command:

ll /etc/dns

```
total 14
-rw-rw-rw-   1      root     sys     644     Feb 28 18:32     conf.cacheonly
-rw-rw-rw-   1      root     sys     439     Feb 28 18:32     conf.sec
-rw-rw-rw-   1      root     sys     439     Feb 28 18:32     conf.sec.save
-rw-rw-rw-   1      root     sys     251     Feb 28 18:31     db.127.0.0
-rw-rw-rw-   1      root     sys     399     Feb 28 18:31     db.192.168.1
-rw-rw-rw-   1      root     sys     972     Feb 28 18:32     db.getitcertify
```

SMH (or *ncweb* command) can also be used to configure a master DNS server. Follow the links below:

☞ Go to SMH → Networking and Communications → Network Services Configuration → DNS (BIND) → DNS Local Name Server → Actions → Add Master/Slave Information. Fill out the form and click "Start the DNS Name Server" from the Actions menu to run the *named* daemon. See Figure 32-3.

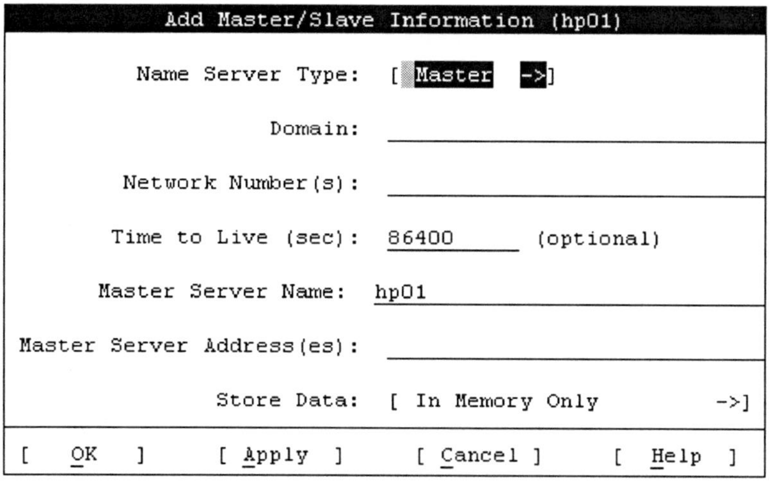

```
┌─────────────────────────────────────────────────────────────────┐
│            Add Master/Slave Information (hp01)                   │
│                                                                  │
│        Name Server Type:  [ Master   ->]                        │
│                                                                  │
│                 Domain:  _____            │
│                                                                  │
│       Network Number(s):  _____           │
│                                                                  │
│       Time to Live (sec):  86400_____  (optional)             │
│                                                                  │
│      Master Server Name:  hp01_____           │
│                                                                  │
│  Master Server Address(es):  _____            │
│                                                                  │
│             Store Data:  [ In Memory Only        ->]            │
├─────────────────────────────────────────────────────────────────┤
│  [   OK   ]     [ Apply ]     [ Cancel ]     [  Help  ]          │
└─────────────────────────────────────────────────────────────────┘
```

Figure 32-3 SMH – DNS Server Configuration

32.3.2   Understanding DNS Boot and Zone Files

The *hosts_to_named* command generates boot and zone files. The syntax of these files is similar. Table 32-1 describes the files.

File	Description
Boot Files	
/etc/named.conf	Used on the master server.
/etc/dns/conf.sec	Used as */etc/named.conf* on a slave server that does not save zone files locally. This type of slave server only works if the master server is up and running.
/etc/dns/conf.sec.save	Used as */etc/named.conf* on a slave server that saves zone files locally. This type of slave server does not require the presence of the master server.
/etc/dns/conf.cacheonly	Used as */etc/named.conf* on a caching-only server.
Zone Files	
db.getitcertify	Contains hostname to IP address mappings.
db.192.168.1	Contains IP address to hostname mappings.
db.127.0.0	Contains mapping for loopback addresses.
db.cache	Contains root name server database.

Table 32-1 DNS Boot and Zone Files

Let us look at the boot and zone files and see what kind of information they store.

The */etc/named.conf* Boot File

This file is read each time the DNS server daemon *named* is started or restarted either at boot time or manually after the system is up. It provides the master server with the location of zone databases for all domains that this server serves. In our case the contents of this file will look like:

```
# cat /etc/named.conf
. . . . . . . .
zone "0.0.127.IN-ADDR.ARPA" {
    type master;
    file "db.127.0.0";
};
zone "getitcertify.com" {
    type master;
    file "db.getitcertify";
};
zone "1.168.192.IN-ADDR.ARPA" {
    type master;
    file "db.192.168.1";
};
zone "." {
    type hint;
    file "db.cache";
};
```

Comments begin with // or can be contained within /* and */. Options can be defined at both the global and individual levels. The keyword "Options" defines global options. Individual options are defined with each zone statement, which includes the characteristics of a zone such as the location of its database files. Options defined at the individual level override the global options.

The "type" zone statement option defines the zone type and has the following valid choices:

- ✓ "master" designates the master DNS server as authoritative for the specified zone.
- ✓ "slave" designates the specified server as a slave DNS server for the specified zone. Also defines the master server's IP address.
- ✓ "hint" points to root DNS servers for resolving queries.

The /etc/dns/conf.sec and /etc/dns/conf.sec.save Boot Files

One of these files (see Table 32-1 on difference between the two) is copied over to a slave DNS server and renamed as /etc/named.conf. The contents of the two files are almost identical to that of the /etc/named.conf file for the master server with some exceptions.

```
# cat /etc/dns/conf.sec
. . . . . . . .
//
// type      domain          source file
//
zone "0.0.127.IN-ADDR.ARPA" {
    type master;
    file "db.127.0.0";
};
zone "getitcertify.com" {
    type slave;
    masters {
        192.168.1.202;
```

```
        };
    };
    zone "1.168.192.IN-ADDR.ARPA" {
        type slave;
        masters {
            192.168.1.202;
        };
    };
    zone "." {
        type hint;
        file "db.cache";
    };
```
 # cat /etc/dns/conf.sec.save
```
. . . . . . . .
//
// type      domain            source file
//
zone "0.0.127.IN-ADDR.ARPA" {
    type master;
    file "db.127.0.0";
};
zone "getitcertify.com" {
    type slave;
    file "db.getitcertify";
    masters {
        192.168.1.202;
    };
};
zone "1.168.192.IN-ADDR.ARPA" {
    type slave;
    file "db.192.168.1";
    masters {
        192.168.1.202;
    };
};
zone "." {
    type hint;
    file "db.cache";
};
```

The */etc/dns/conf.cacheonly* Boot File

This file is copied over to a caching-only DNS server and renamed as */etc/named.conf*. The contents of this file includes information on *db.127.0.0* and *db.cache* databases only.

 # cat /etc/dns/conf.cacheonly

```
. . . . . . . .
// type       domain              source file
//
zone "0.0.127.IN-ADDR.ARPA" {
    type master;
    file "db.127.0.0";
};
zone "." {
    type hint;
    file "db.cache";
};
```

The *db.getitcertify* Zone File

This is the domain database file that resides on the master server. This file contains address record for each system in the zone.

 # cat /etc/dns/db.getitcertify

```
@       IN    SOA    hp01.getitcertify.com.  root.hp01.getitcertify.com. (
                        1              ; Serial
                        10800          ; Refresh every 3 hours
                        3600           ; Retry every hour
                        604800         ; Expire after a week
                        86400 )        ; Minimum ttl of 1 day
        IN    NS     hp01.getitcertify.com.

localhost   IN    A               127.0.0.1
hp01        IN    A               192.168.1.201
hp01        IN    CNAME           hp01.getitcertify.com.
hp02        IN    A               192.168.1.202
hp02        IN    CNAME           hp02.getitcertify.com.
hp03        IN    A               192.168.1.203
hp03        IN    CNAME           hp03.getitcertify.com.
hp04        IN    A               192.168.1.204
hp04        IN    CNAME           hp04.getitcertify.com.
hp05        IN    A               192.168.1.205
hp05        IN    CNAME           hp05.getitcertify.com.
hp01        IN    MX      10      hp01.getitcertify.com.
hp02        IN    MX      10      hp02.getitcertify.com.
hp03        IN    MX      10      hp03.getitcertify.com.
hp04        IN    MX      10      hp04.getitcertify.com.
hp05        IN    MX      10      hp05.getitcertify.com.
```

There are several entries in this file and are known as *resource records*. Table 32-2 explains them.

Record	Description
SOA	*Start Of Authority*. Designates start of a domain. It indicates the DNS server (*hp01.getitcertify.com*) authoritative for the domain, the address (*root.hp01.getitcertify.com*) of the user responsible for the DNS server and the following values: Serial: Denotes the zone file version. It is incremented each time the files are refreshed. Slave servers look at this number and compare with theirs. If the number is higher on the master, a transfer of the updated files takes place. Refresh: Indicates, in seconds, how often a slave server refreshes itself with the master. Retry: Indicates, in seconds, how often a slave server retries to get updates from the master after the previous refresh attempt fails. Expire: Indicates, in seconds, the duration a slave server can use the zone data before the data is considered expired. Minimum ttl: Indicates, in seconds, the minimum amount of time (t*ime to live*) to keep an entry.
NS	*Name Server*. Lists DNS servers, and domains they have authority for.
A	*Address*. Assigns IP address to the corresponding system.
CNAME	*Canonical Name*. Official hostname of a system.
MX	*Mail eXchanger*. Specifies a weighted list of systems to try when sendmailing to a destination on the internet. MX data points to one or more alternate systems that accept emails for the target system if it is down or unreachable.

Table 32-2 Resource Records Description

The *db.192.168.1* Zone File

This database contains a *pointer* (PTR) for every host in the zone. It enables DNS to map IP addresses to their corresponding hostnames for reverse lookup.

 # cat /etc/dns/db.192.168.1

```
@     IN    SOA    hp01.getitcertify.com.  root.hp01.getitcertify.com. (
                          1                 ; Serial
                          10800             ; Refresh every 3 hours
                          3600              ; Retry every hour
                          604800            ; Expire after a week
                          86400 )           ; Minimum ttl of 1 day
      IN    NS     hp01.getitcertify.com.
201   IN    PTR    hp01.getitcertify.com.
202   IN    PTR    hp02.getitcertify.com.
203   IN    PTR    hp03.getitcertify.com.
204   IN    PTR    hp04.getitcertify.com.
205   IN    PTR    hp05.getitcertify.com.
```

The *db.127.0.0* Zone File

Each DNS server is authoritative of the network 127.0.0 and has the zone file *db.127.0.0*. This file includes the resource record that maps 127.0.0.1 to the name of the loopback (localhost) address. In other words, this file contains a pointer to the localhost.

```
# cat /etc/dns/db.127.0.0
@    IN    SOA    hp01.getitcertify.com.  root.hp01.getitcertify.com. (
                        1                ; Serial
                        10800            ; Refresh every 3 hours
                        3600             ; Retry every hour
                        604800           ; Expire after a week
                        86400 )          ; Minimum ttl of 1 day
      IN    NS     hp01.getitcertify.com.
1     IN    PTR    localhost.
```

The *db.cache* Zone File

The *db.cache* file lists servers for the root domain. A DNS server queries a root server if it is unable to resolve a hostname query from its local maps or cache.

Although the *hosts_to_named* command creates this file, but it is recommended to download a copy from *ftp://ftp.internic.net/domain*. Following is an excerpt from this file:

```
.                 3600000  IN NS   A.ROOT-SERVERS.NET.
A.ROOT-SERVERS.NET.     3600000    A      198.41.0.4
;
; formerly NS1.ISI.EDU
;
.                 3600000    NS   B.ROOT-SERVERS.NET.
B.ROOT-SERVERS.NET.     3600000    A      192.228.79.201
;
; formerly C.PSI.NET
;
.                 3600000    NS   C.ROOT-SERVERS.NET.
C.ROOT-SERVERS.NET.     3600000    A      192.33.4.12
. . . . . . . .
```

32.3.3   Configuring a Slave DNS Server

To configure *hp02* to act as a slave DNS server for domain *getitcertify.com*, perform the following:

1. Copy *conf.sec.save* file from the master server over into the */etc* directory, and rename the file as */etc/named.conf*.
2. Create */etc/dns* directory to store DNS zone files and *cd* into it:

    ```
    # mkdir /etc/dns
    # cd /etc/dns
    ```

3. Copy the */etc/dns/db.cache* and */etc/dns/db.127.0.0* files over from the master server.
4. Edit */etc/rc.config.d/namesvrs_dns* file and set the variable NAMED to 1:

   NAMED=1

5. Start the BIND service daemon:

   # /sbin/init.d/named start

To setup a slave DNS server using SMH (or *ncweb* command), follow the links below:

☞Go to SMH → Networking and Communications → Network Services Configuration → DNS (BIND) → DNS Local Name Server → Actions → Add Master/Slave Information. Fill out the form and click "Start the DNS Name Server" from the Actions menu to run the *named* daemon. See Figure 32-3 earlier.

32.3.4   Configuring a Caching-Only DNS Server

To configure *hp03* to act as a caching-only DNS server for domain *getitcertify.com*, perform the following:

1. Copy */etc/dns/conf.cacheonly* file from the master server over into the */etc* directory, and rename the file as */etc/named.conf*.
2. Create the */etc/dns* directory to store DNS zone files and *cd* into it:

   # mkdir /etc/dns
   # cd /etc/dns

3. Copy the */etc/dns/db.cache* and */etc/dns/db.127.0.0* files over from the master server.
4. Edit */etc/rc.config.d/namesvrs_dns* file and set the variable NAMED to 1:

   NAMED=1

5. Start the BIND server daemon:

   # /sbin/init.d/named start

To setup a caching-only DNS server using SMH (or *ncweb* command), follow the links below:

☞Go to SMH → Networking and Communications → Network Services Configuration → DNS (BIND) → DNS Local Name Server → Actions → Configure Caching-Only Server. Fill out the form and click "Start the DNS Name Server" from the Actions menu to run the *named* daemon. See Figure 32-3 earlier.

32.3.5   Configuring a DNS Client

To setup an HP-UX machine to act as a DNS client, you need to configure */etc/nsswitch.conf* and */etc/resolv.conf* files.

The */etc/nsswitch.conf* File

Refer to section "Configuring */etc/nsswitch.conf* File" in Chapter 31 "Network Information Service (NIS)" on an explanation of this file.

The */etc/resolv.conf* File

This is the DNS resolver file where you can define three keywords, as described in Table 32-3.

Keyword	Description
domain	Specifies the default domain name. It tells the gethostbyname and gethostbyaddr routines to search the specified domain for incoming name lookup queries. This keyword is defined when there are more than one domains. For a single domain environment, this keyword is not needed.
search	Specifies up to six domain names with the first one must be the local domain. The resolver appends these domain names one at a time in the order they are listed to the hostname specified when constructing queries destined for a DNS server.
nameserver	Specifies up to three DNS server IP addresses to be used for name resolution queries one at a time in the order they are listed. If none specified, the local DNS server is used.

Table 32-3 The */etc/resolv.conf* File Description

In our case, the DNS client will have the following entries in the */etc/nsswitch.conf* and */etc/resolv.conf* files:

/etc/nsswitch.conf file:	hosts: dns	files
/etc/resolv.conf file:	search	getitcertify.com
	nameserver	192.168.1.201 # IP address of the master DNS server
	nameserver	192.168.1.202 # IP address of the slave DNS server

To setup a DNS client using SMH (or *ncweb* command), follow the links below:

☞ Go to SMH → Networking and Communications → Network Services Configuration → DNS (BIND) → DNS Resolver → Actions. You will see "Specify Name Servers" and "Set Default Domain" choices. Fill out the form to complete the client configuration.

32.4   Managing DNS

Managing DNS involves verifying DNS functionality and updating master, slave and caching-only DNS servers.

32.4.1   Verifying DNS Functionality

HP-UX provides three utilities – *nsquery, nslookup* and *dig* – to test the DNS functionality. These utilities are explained below.

Using *nsquery*

To obtain IP address of a system such as *hp05*, use the *nsquery* (name server query) command and specify the type of source to be searched. This command consults the */etc/nsswitch.conf* file to determine sources for lookup. The last line of the output tells that the search is terminated since the information is found.

```
# nsquery  hosts  hp05
Using "dns" for the hosts policy.
Searching dns for hp05
Hostname: hp05.getitcertify.com
Aliases:
Address: 192.168.1.205
Switch configuration: Terminates Search
```

Using *nslookup*

To obtain IP address of a system such as *hp05*, use the *nslookup* (name server lookup) command:

```
# nslookup  hp05
Name Server: hp01.getitcertify.com
Address:  192.168.1.201
Trying DNS
Name:   hp05.getitcertify.com
Address:  192.168.1.205
```

The *nslookup* command can be run in interactive mode as well:

```
# nslookup
>
```

At the > prompt, you can run the *server* command to force *nslookup* to use an alternate DNS server. For example, to resolve hostnames using the slave DNS server *hp02* instead of the master, do the following:

```
> server  hp02
```

Type a system name to lookup:

```
> hp05
Name Server: getitcertify.com
Addresses: 192.168.1.202
Name: hp05.getitcertify.com
Address: 192.168.1.205
```

Type *exit* to quit *nslookup*.

Using *dig*

dig (domain information groper) is a DNS lookup utility and also used for troubleshooting DNS issues. This command looks into the */etc/resolv.conf* to determine DNS server information.

To obtain IP address of a system such as *hp05*, use the *dig* command:

```
# dig hp05
; <<>> DiG 9.1.1 <<>> hp05
;; global options: printcmd
;; Got answer:
;; ->>HEADER<<- opcode: QUERY, status: NOERROR, id: 39720
;; flags: qr aa rd ra; QUERY: 1, ANSWER: 1, AUTHORITY: 1, ADDITIONAL: 1

;; QUESTION SECTION:
;hp05.getitcertify.com.              IN       A

;; ANSWER SECTION:
hp05.getitcertify.com.       16000   IN       A         192.168.1.205

;; AUTHORITY SECTION:
getitcertify.com.            16000   IN       NS        hp01.getitcertify.com.

;; ADDITIONAL SECTION:
hp01.getitcertify.com.       16000   IN       A         192.168.1.201

;; Query time: 1 msec
;; SERVER: 192.168.1.201#53(192.168.1.201)
;; WHEN: Sat Mar 31 22:27:39 2007
;; MSG SIZE  rcvd: 83
```

32.4.2   Updating Master, Slave and Caching-Only DNS Servers

To update zone files on the master server, make required modifications to the */etc/hosts* file, run the *hosts_to_named* command as discussed earlier and restart the *named* daemon with the *sig_named* command as follows:

```
# sig_named restart
Name server is running and its process id is 5007.
Name server restarted
```

The slave and caching-only servers update their zone files automatically from the master server based on the SOA records in their database files. Refer to Table 32-2 for detailed information.

```
@     IN    SOA    hp01.getitcertify.com.  root.hp01.getitcertify.com. (
                        1                 ; Serial
                        10800             ; Refresh every 3 hours
                        3600              ; Retry every hour
                        604800            ; Expire after a week
                        86400 )           ; Minimum ttl of 1 day
```

32.4.3   Using rndc Utility

The *rndc* command is the name server control utility that is used to control the operation of a name server. This utility consults its configuration file */etc/rndc.conf* and determines appropriate course of action. Certain sub-commands are listed and explained in Table 32-4.

Sub-command	Description
reload	Reloads configuration file and zones.
refresh	Refreshes the name server's database.
retransfer	Retransfers a single zone.
freeze	Freezes updates to a dynamic zone.
thaw	Unfreezes updates to a dynamic zone and reloads it.
reconfig	Reloads configuration files and new zones.
stop	Saves pending updates and stops the server.
halt	Stops the server without saving pending updates.
flush	Flushes the server cache.
status	Displays server status.

Table 32-4 *rndc* Sub-Commands

Summary

This chapter introduced you to name resolution and DNS. You learned name resolution concepts, how name resolution and reverse of it worked and what name resolution methods were available.

You studied DNS features, and components including name space, domain, zone, zone files, master server, slave server, caching-only server and client.

On the implementation side, you were presented with step-by-step procedure on how to setup master, slave and caching-only DNS servers. You looked at the contents of the boot and zone files. You looked at files involved in DNS client setup.

The last couple of sections explained to you how to verify the functionality of DNS and update maps on master, slave and caching-only DNS servers.

## 33

Lightweight Directory Access Protocol (LDAP)

This chapter covers the following major topics:

- ✓ LDAP introduction
- ✓ Features and benefits
- ✓ LDAP terminology – directory, entry, attribute, matching rule, object class, schema, LDIF, DN and RDN
- ✓ LDAP roles – server, replica, client and referral
- ✓ Basic install of Netscape Directory Server software
- ✓ Basic install of LDAP-UX client software

33.1   What is LDAP?

Lightweight Directory Access Protocol (LDAP) is a trivial, simplified networking protocol for obtaining directory information such as email messaging, user authentication and calendar services over a TCP/IP network. LDAP was derived from *Directory Access Protocol* (DAP), which is one of the protocols within X.500 specification developed jointly by the *International Telecommunication Union* (ITU) and the *International Organization for Standardization* (ISO). One of the major disadvantages with DAP was that it required too much computing resources to work efficiently. LDAP (also referred to as *X.500 Lite*), on the other hand, is thinner and requires less client-side computing resources. This protocol is platform-independent which makes it available on a variety of vendor hardware platforms running heterogeneous operating system software.

LDAP is hierarchical and similar to the structure of UNIX directory tree and DNS. It can be based on logical boundaries defined by geography or organizational arrangement. A typical LDAP directory structure for a company, ABC, with domain ABC.com and offices in Canada, USA, UK and Australia, is shown in Figure 33-1.

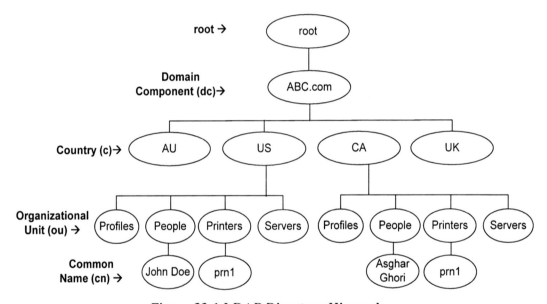

Figure 33-1 LDAP Directory Hierarchy

The top of the company is referred to as the root of the LDAP directory hierarchy. Underneath it is located *domain component* (dc), which is usually the name of the company. *country* (c) falls under domain component. *organizational units* (ou) separate various categories of directory information and may be country-specific. The actual information is at the lowest level of the hierarchy, which may include resources such as users, profiles, people, printers, servers, photos, text, URLs, pointers to information, binary data and public key certificates.

33.1.1   Features and Benefits of Using LDAP

Some of the features of LDAP and key benefits of using it are listed below:

- ✓ Has a hierarchical directory structure that allows organization of information and resources in a logical fashion.
- ✓ Allows the consolidation of common information such as user information within an OU.
- ✓ Has lower overhead than X.500 DAP.
- ✓ Provides users and applications with a unified, standard interface to a single, extensible directory service making it easier to rapidly develop and deploy directory-enabled applications.
- ✓ Reduces the need to enter and coordinate redundant information in multiple services scattered across an enterprise.
- ✓ Enables fast searches, cost-effective management of users and security, and a central integration point for multiple applications and services.
- ✓ Maintains directory-wide consistent information.

33.2   LDAP Terminology

To comprehend LDAP thoroughly, a grasp of the following key terms is essential.

33.2.1   Directory

An LDAP *directory*, a.k.a. *Directory Information Tree* (DIT), is like a specialized database that stores information about objects such as people, profiles, printers and servers. It organizes information in such a way that it becomes easier to find and retrieve needed information. It lists objects and gives details about them. An LDAP directory is similar in concept to the UNIX directory hierarchy.

33.2.2   Entry

An *entry* is a building block of an LDAP directory and represents a specific record in it. In other words, an entry is a collection of information consisting of one or more attributes for an object. An LDAP directory, for instance, might include entries for employees, printers and servers.

33.2.3   Attribute

An *attribute* contains two pieces of information – *attribute type* and *attribute values* – and is associated with one or more entries. An attribute type such as a "jobTitle" represents the type of information the attribute contains. An attribute value is the specific information contained in that entry. For instance, a value for the "jobTitle" attribute type could be "director". Table 33-1 lists some common attribute types.

Attribute Type	Description
CommonName (cn)	Common name of an entry such as cn=John Doe.
DomainComponent (dc)	Distinguished name (DN) of a component in DNS such as dc=ca, dc=ABC, dc=com.
Country (c)	Country such as c=CA.
Mail (mail)	Email address.
Organization (o)	Name of an organization such as o=ABC.
OrganizationalUnit (ou)	Name of a unit within an organization such as ou=Printers.
Owner (owner)	Owner of an entry such as cn=John Doe, ou=Printers, dc=ABC, c=ca.
Surname (sn)	Person's last name such as Doe.

Attribute Type	Description
TelephoneNumber (telephoneNumber)	Telephone number such as (123) 456-7890 or 1234567890.

Table 33-1 Common LDAP Attribute Types

 Long names and corresponding abbreviations can be used interchangeably.

33.2.4   Matching Rule

A *matching rule* matches the attribute value sought against the attribute value stored in the directory in a search and compare task.

For example, matching rules associated with the telephoneNumber attribute could cause "(123) 456-7890" to match with either "(123) 456-7890" or "1234567890", or both. When an attribute is defined, a matching rule is associated with it.

33.2.5   Object Class

Each entry belongs to one or more *object classes*. An object class is a group of required and optional attributes that defines the structure of an entry.

For example, an organizationalUser object class may include commonName and Surname as required attributes and telephoneNumber, UID, streetAddress and userPassword as optional attributes. Minimum required attributes must be defined when an entry is defined.

33.2.6   Schema

schema is a collection of attributes and object classes along with matching rules and syntax, and other related information.

33.2.7   LDAP Data Interchange Format (LDIF)

LDAP Data Interchange Format (LDIF) is a special format for importing and exporting LDAP records between LDAP servers. The data is in text format and consists of entries or alterations to entries, or both.

Each record is represented as a group of attributes with each individual attribute listed on a separate line comprising "name:value" pair. The following is a sample directory entry with attributes representing a record in LDIF:

```
dn: cn=John Doe,ou=People, c=CA,dc=ABC
objectClass: inetLocalMailRecipient
sn: Doe
mail: john.doe@ABC.com
cn: John Doe
givenName: John
uid: jdoe
telephoneNumber: (416) 123-4567
```

33.2.8   Distinguished Name and Relative Distinguished Name

A *Distinguished Name* (DN) uniquely identifies an entry in the entire directory tree. It is similar in concept to the absolute pathname of a file in the UNIX directory hierarchy.

A *Relative Distinguished Name* (RDN), in contrast, represents individual components of a DN. It is similar in concept to the relative pathname of a file in the UNIX directory hierarchy.

As an example, the DN for the printer *prn1* under Printers located in Canada (See Figure 33-1) is:

    cn=prn1,ou=Printers,c=CA,dc=ABC

In this example, the RDN for *prn1* is cn=prn1. Similarly, the RDN for Printers is ou=Printers, the RDN for CA is c=CA and that for ABC is dc=ABC. A DN is thus a sequence of RDNs separated by commas.

33.2.9   LDAP Roles

There are four roles – *server, replica, client* and *referral* – that systems within an LDAP environment may perform. One system may be configured to perform more than one role.

LDAP Server

An LDAP server is a system that holds the LDAP directory information. It may be referred to as the *master* LDAP server. There must be one such server configured to offer directory services.

LDAP Replica

An LDAP replica is a system that contains a copy of the information that the LDAP server maintains. A replica may be referred to as a *slave* LDAP server. It is recommended that at least one replica be configured together with an LDAP server to achieve enhanced availability and load balancing.

LDAP Client

An LDAP client is a system that binds itself with a server or replica to establish a communication session to perform queries on directory entries and carry out necessary modifications.

LDAP Referral

An LDAP referral is an entity on a server that redirects an LDAP client's request to some other LDAP server or replica if it does not contain the requested information. A referral contains names and locations of other LDAP servers where requested information might be found.

33.3   Installing Netscape Directory Server Software

The LDAP directory information is stored on an LDAP server. On HP-UX, *Red Hat Directory Server, Novell eDirectory* and *Netscape Directory Server* software are available that enable a system to be configured and used as an LDAP directory server. The software may be downloaded from *software.hp.com* → Security and manageability. The following procedure demonstrates how to install the Netscape Directory Server software and perform a basic setup. Note that currently this software is only available for HP-UX 11i v1 and 11i v2.

---

1. Download the software for 11i v2 into */tmp*.
2. Install it using the *swinstall* command:

   # swinstall –s /tmp/J4258CA_B.06.21.60_HP-UX_B.11.23_IA_PA.depot

3. Make certain that the SHLIB_PATH environment variable is set for *root* user:

   # export SHLIB_PATH=$(cat /etc/SHLIB_PATH)

4. Run the *setup* command as *root* to configure the software. Choose all the defaults.

   # cd /var/opt/netscape/servers/setup
   # ./setup

Some of the vital data needed during the execution of the *setup* program is given below:

✓ License terms = yes
✓ Choose typical install (option 2)
✓ Machine name = specify full hostname of the system (for example, hp01.getitcertify.com)
✓ System user = www
✓ System group = other
✓ Register with existing Netscape ..... = no
✓ Another directory to store data = no
✓ Directory server network port = 389
✓ Directory server identifier = specify the directory server hostname
✓ Netscape administrator ID = admin (supply a password of your choice)
✓ Suffix = specify a domain name (for example, getitcertify.com)
✓ Directory manager DN = cn=Directory Manager (supply a password of your choice)
✓ Administration domain = specify a domain name (for example, getitcertify.com)
✓ Administration port = 7764
✓ Run administration server as = root

5. After the setup program is finished, the Netscape Directory Server will start. Verify the functionality using the *ldapsearch* command. An example construct of the command would be:

   **# ldapsearch –D 'uid=user1,ou=class,o=getitcertify.com' –w <password> **
   –b 'o=getitcertify.com' uid=user1

33.4   Installing an LDAP-UX Client

To use the Netscape Directory Server software, you need to install and configure the client software called *LDAP-UX Integration* on HP-UX client systems. This software can be downloaded from *software.hp.com*. The following procedure demonstrates how to install it and perform a basic setup. Choose the defaults for most questions.

1. Download the software into */tmp*.
2. Install it using the *swinstall* command:

 # swinstall –s /tmp/LDAPUX_B.04.17_HP-UX_B.11.31_IA_PA.depot

3. Run the *setup* command to configure the software. Respond to setup questions. This command updates the */etc/opt/ldapux/ldapux_client.conf* file.

    # cd /opt/ldapux/config
    # ./setup

4. Edit the */etc/nsswitch.conf* file and make appropriate modifications to have the client system look for information in the LDAP sources. There is a */etc/nsswitch.ldap* template file that can be copied as */etc/nsswitch.conf* if one does not already exist.
5. Edit the */etc/pam.conf* file and make proper modifications to ensure that user logins reference the Netscape Directory Server for authentication. There is a */etc/pam.ldap* template file that can be copied as */etc/pam.conf* if one does not already exist.
6. Start the LDAP-UX client functionality:

    # /sbin/init.d/ldapclientd.rc start

7. Execute the *nsquery* command to verify that the LDAP client is configured and referencing the Netscape Directory Server:

    # nsquery passwd user1 ldap

Summary

In this chapter you were provided with an introduction to LDAP. You looked at features, benefits and definitions of LDAP components such as directory, entry, attribute, matching rule, object class, schema, LDIF, DN, RDN, server, replica, client and referral.

You were presented with high-level information on how to obtain, install and configure Netscape Directory Server and LDAP-UX client software.

## 34

Ignite-UX

This chapter covers the following major topics:

- ✓ Ignite-UX introduction and benefits
- ✓ Install Ignite-UX product
- ✓ Registered and anonymous clients
- ✓ Configure an Ignite-UX server
- ✓ Boot clients and perform HP-UX installation from Ignite-UX server
- ✓ Create golden image and use it to clone another machine
- ✓ Create system recovery archive (or back up the boot disk) and use it to recover a non-bootable system

34.1   Introduction to Ignite-UX

HP Ignite-UX software product is a set of tools that allows installing HP-UX in a variety of ways. The toolset provides the ability to perform local and over-the-network installations. In addition, it offers the capability to clone other systems and create system recovery archives of individual machines. Chapter 09 "HP-UX Installation" described performing a local installation of HP-UX. This chapter covers how to configure an Ignite-UX server, perform over-the-network installations, clone a server, create local and remote system recovery archives, and how to use the archives to recover a corrupted or unbootable HP-UX system.

34.1.1   Benefits of Using Ignite-UX

Ignite-UX supports both 9000 and Integrity client systems and offers several benefits outlined as follows:

- ✓ Install HP-UX on a number of systems concurrently.
- ✓ Have different versions of HP-UX (11i v1, 11i v2 or 11i v3) loaded on different client machines from a single Ignite-UX server.
- ✓ Perform a fully customized and automated installation with no questions for configuration asked.
- ✓ Perform a fresh installation or re-installation.
- ✓ Perform either a push install or a pull install. Push install runs the user interface on the Ignite-UX server, whereas pull install runs the user interface on the client system.
- ✓ Copy the entire image of a running HP-UX system (called *golden image*) and use it to clone other systems.
- ✓ Create a recovery archive of a running HP-UX system and use it in case of emergency when the system becomes unbootable or corrupted.

34.2   Configuring an Ignite-UX Server

An HP-UX system needs to be configured as an Ignite-UX server to provide network installation services. The configuration can be done using GUI (or TUI) or command line. The GUI and TUI interfaces provide identical functionality. The GUI is automatically invoked if the DISPLAY environment variable is set properly, otherwise, the text interface is initiated.

34.2.1   Installing the Ignite-UX Product

If not already loaded, install the Ignite-UX software from the HP-UX media using the *swinstall* command. If the media is unavailable, download the software from *software.hp.com* and install it. The Ignite-UX software bundle is called Ignite-UX-11-31.

34.2.2   Registered and Anonymous Clients

When a client boots up via an Ignite-UX server, the server supplies an available IP address to it from a pool of pre-defined addresses. A client that gets any available IP address in this manner is referred to as an *anonymous client*. The same IP address can be reserved for that client as well so that it cannot be assigned to any other booting client. This is accomplished by associating the MAC address of the client with the IP address. In this case, this client will be referred to as a *registered client*.

For 9000 clients, the IP and MAC information is stored in the */etc/opt/ignite/instl_boottab* file, which is referenced by the Ignite-UX daemon called *instl_bootd*.

For Integrity systems, the */etc/bootptab* file is referenced by another Ignite-UX server daemon called *bootpd*. This file is manually edited to insert entries for booting clients. The same rules that apply to 9000 anonymous and registered client setups, are applicable to Integrity client setups too. A sample entry from the */etc/bootptab* file is shown below. The definition starts with the keyword IADEF and the client name used here is *hp10*.

```
IADEF:\
ht=ethernet:\
hn:\
bf=/opt/ignite/boot/npd.efi\
bs=48:\
sm=255.255.255.0:\
gw=192.168.1.1:\
ds=192.168.1.254:
hp10:tc=IADEF:ip=192.168.1.210:ha=00306A6A4396
```

In this entry, "ht" represents the hardware type, "hn" hostname, "bf" bootfile name, "bs" bootfile size, "sm" subnet mask, "gw" gateway IP address, "ds" DNS server IP address and "hp10" represents the client name with IP adderss and hardware address.

In case an Ignite-UX server is not setup, a DHCP server may be configured instead to respond to boot requests coming from 9000 or Integrity clients. A DHCP server is able to respond and send back an IP address from its pool of available IP addresses. This is the recommended method for assigning IP addresses to booting Integrity clients.

34.2.3   Configuring an Ignite-UX Server from the GUI

To setup an Ignite-UX server from the GUI on *hp01* to boot 9000 clients, follow the steps below:

1. Edit */etc/inetd.conf* file and uncomment the *tftp* entry. This protocol is used by the server to transfer files to a booting client.

    tftp dgram udp wait root /usr/lbin/tftpd tftpd /opt/ignite /var/opt/ignite

2. Force the *inetd* daemon to re-read the configuration file:

    # **inetd –c**

3. Make certain that a *tftp* user entry exists in the */etc/passwd* file. If not, create it.

    tftp:*:510:1:Trivial FTP user:/home/tftpdir:/usr/bin/false

4. Execute the *ignite* command to bring up the GUI:

 # /opt/ignite/bin/ignite

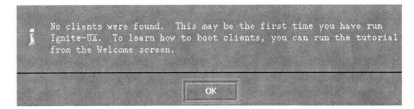

No clients were found. This may be the first time you have run Ignite-UX. To learn how to boot clients, you can run the tutorial from the Welcome screen.

OK

Figure 34-1 Ignite-UX – Message When no Clients are Found

Click OK.

5.   A "Welcome To Ignite UX" screen pops up as displayed in Figure 34-2.

Figure 34-2 Ignite-UX – Welcome Screen

Click "Server Setup". This will execute the *setup_server* command located in the */opt/ignite/lbin* directory. The next screen will display "Server Setup: Overview". Click Next. The following screen will ask whether you wish to choose to configure booting IP addresses now. Choose this option and click Next.

6.   The window shown in Figure 34-3 is where one or more IP addresses and/or MAC addresses for 9000 clients can be defined. It accepts a range of IP addresses as well. Click Add when done and then OK to save the supplied information in the */etc/opt/ignite/instl_boottab* file. For Integrity clients, edit the */etc/bootptab* file manually and insert appropriate information as explained earlier.

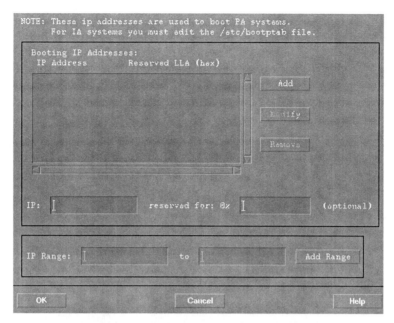

Figure 34-3 Ignite-UX – Configure Booting IP Addresses

7. The next window will bring up the "Server Setup: DHCP (optional)" window. Choose "Skip DHCP Setup" and click Next to go to the "Server Setup: Software Depot Setup" screen as shown in Figure 34-4.

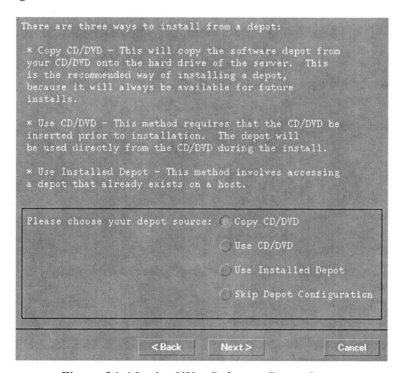

Figure 34-4 Ignite-UX – Software Depot Setup

8. There are four choices available to specify the depot source. The booting client uses the source defined here to pull and *swinstall* the HP-UX software. The four choices are:

✓ **Copy CD/DVD** – This option swcopies the HP-UX software image to the specified directory on the Ignite-UX server. The CD/DVD containing the depot must be loaded in the drive. When the Next button is pressed, the following message will appear prompting to insert the CD/DVD:

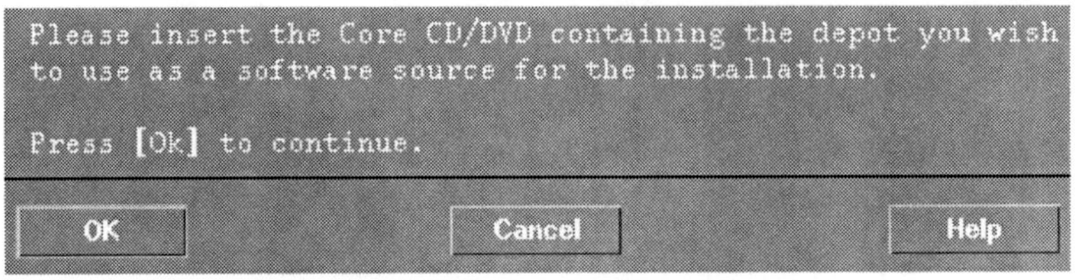

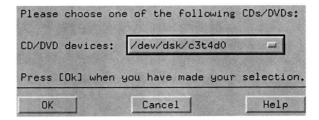

Figure 34-5 Ignite-UX – Prompt to Insert the CD/DVD

Click OK. Confirm the CD/DVD device path as shown in Figure 34-6:

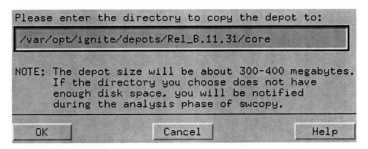

Figure 34-6 Ignite-UX – Prompt for Source Depot Location

Click OK. The CD/DVD is automatically mounted and the default target location to *swcopy* the software will be displayed. See Figure 34-7. You have the option to specify an alternate location.

Figure 34-7 Ignite-UX – Target Depot Location

✓ **Use CD/DVD** – This option installs the HP-UX software directly from the specified CD/DVD drive. The installation CD/DVD must be loaded in the drive.

✓ **Use Installed Depot** – This option is selected when a depot containing the HP-UX installation software is configured and available. You need to supply the hostname of the depot server and the directory location for the depot.

✓ **Skip Depot Configuration** – This option skips the depot setup.

9. Follow the screens to exit out of the GUI.

This completes the procedure for configuring an Ignite-UX server using GUI.

The GUI also presents two tabs to set "Server Options" and "Session Options". See Figures 34-8 and 34-9.

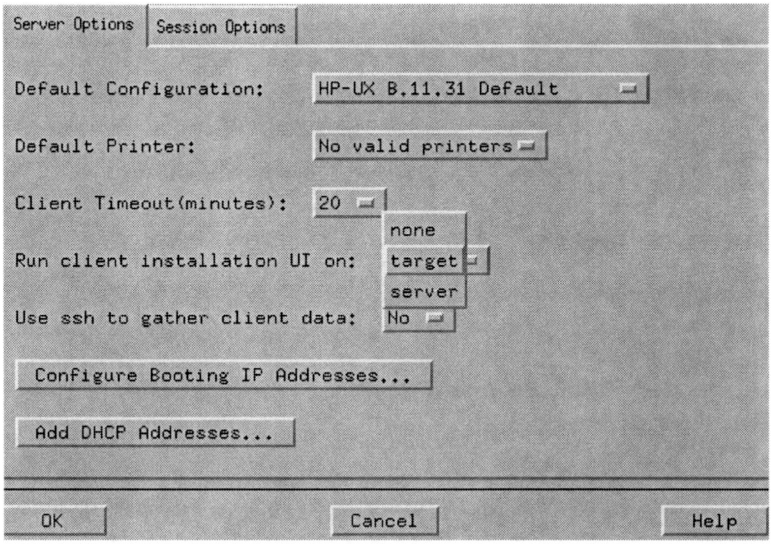

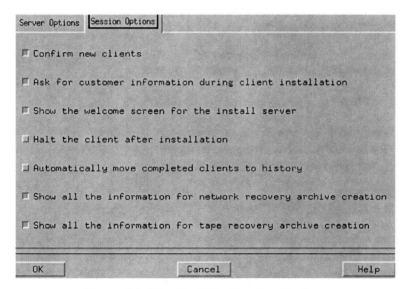

Figure 34-8 Ignite-UX – Server Options

Figure 34-9 Ignite-UX – Session Options

Server options are explained in Table 34-1. Leave the Session options to the defaults.

Server Options	Description
Default configuration	Choose a default configuration for future client installs. This may be overridden for individual clients.
Default printer	Choose a configured printer if you wish to print the history of the install session.
Client timeout (minutes)	Define a timeout value. If turned off, no notification will be generated for the *install.log* file on the client for not being updated. Default is usually good in most cases.
Run client installation UI on	Run user interface on the client in TUI mode or on the Ignite-UX server in either GUI or TUI mode. If disabled, non-interactive installs will be performed.

Table 34-1 Ignite-UX Server Options

34.2.4 Configuring an Ignite-UX Server from the Command Line

To setup an Ignite-UX server from the command line on *hp01* to boot 9000 clients, follow the steps below:

1. Edit */etc/inetd.conf* file and uncomment *instl_boots* and *tftp* entries. These protocols are used for booting and transferring files.

    tftp dgram udp wait root /usr/lbin/tftpd tftpd /opt/ignite /var/opt/ignite
    instl_boots dgram udp wait root /opt/ignite/lbin/instl_bootd instl_bootd

2. Force the *inetd* daemon to re-read the configuration file:

    # **inetd −c**

3. Make sure a *tftp* user entry exists in the */etc/passwd* file. If not, create it. Create */home/tftpdir* as well with proper ownership and group membership:

    tftp:*:510:1:Trivial FTP user:/home/tftpdir:/usr/bin/false

4. Edit */etc/opt/ignite/inst_boottab* file and add either IP addresses only (for anonymous clients) or both IP and corresponding MAC addresses (for registered clients). This file is sourced by the *instl_bootd* daemon. Sample entries are:

    192.168.1.251   # Entry for an anonymous client
    192.168.1.252:070001234567::reserve   # Entry for a registered client

5. Edit */etc/dfs/dfstab* file and add the following entry for */var/opt/ignite/clients* directory, which contains the HP-UX mini kernel to be used by the client when it boots up:

    share −F nfs −o anon=2 /var/opt/ignite/clients

6. Share the directory and ensure NFS server daemons are running:

    # **shareall**

7. Edit the PATH variable to include */opt/ignite/bin* directory:

 # PATH=$PATH:/opt/ignite/bin
 # export PATH

8. Create a depot for HP-UX software at, for example, */var/softdepot/HP-UX11iv3/core*. Make certain that the DVD drive contains the 11i v3 media and is mounted on */dvdrom* directory:

 # make_depots –d /var/softdepot/HP-UX11iv3/core –s /dvdrom

9. Execute the *make_config* command to examine the contents of the depot. Specify the name and location of the configuration file with –c option and the directory location to save the output of this command with –s option.

**# make_config –c /var/opt/ignite/data/Rel_B.11.31/core.conf –s **
/var/softdepot/HP-UX11iv3/core
NOTE: make_config can sometimes take a long time to complete. Please be patient!

Here is some key data extracted from the *core.conf* file:

```
##################
##  Software Sources
##################
sw_source "core" {
    description = "HP-UX Core Software"
    source_format = SD
    sd_server = "192.168.1.201"
    sd_depot_dir = "/var/softdepot/HP-UX11i v3/core"
    source_type = "NET"
    load_order = 0
}
##################
##  HPUX Base OS
##################
sw_sel "HPUXBase64" {
    description = "HP-UX 64-bit Base OS"
    sw_source = "core"
    sw_category = "HPUXBaseOS"
    sd_software_list = "HPUXBase64,r=B.11.31,a=HP-UX_B.11.31_64,v=HP"
    impacts = "/opt" 61011Kb
    impacts = "/usr" 666578Kb
    impacts = "/etc" 22Kb
    impacts = "/var" 98Kb
    impacts = "/sbin" 24636Kb
    impacts = "/" 861Kb
    exrequisite = sw_category
}
(sw_sel "HPUXBase64") {
    _hp_os_bitness = "64"
```

```
}
init sw_sel "OE90BaseOS64" {
  description = "HP-UX 11i Base OS-64bit"
  sw_source = "core"
  sw_category = "HPUXEnvironments"
  corequisite = "HPUXBase64"
  visible_if = can_run_64bit
} = (can_run_64bit)
#########################
##  Operating Environments
#########################
sw_sel "HPUX11i-OE-Ent" {
  description = "HP-UX Enterprise Operating Environment Component"
  sw_source = "core"
  sw_category = "OpEnvironments"
  sd_software_list = "HPUX11i-OE-Ent,r=B.11.31.0612,a=HP-UX_B.11.31_32/64,v=HP"
  (_hp_os_bitness == "32") {
    impacts = "/usr" 3149Kb
    impacts = "/etc" 9419Kb
    impacts = "/var" 58Kb
    impacts = "/sbin" 40Kb
    impacts = "/opt" 157522Kb
    impacts = "/" 12Kb
  }
  (_hp_os_bitness == "64") {
    impacts = "/usr" 3149Kb
    impacts = "/etc" 9419Kb
    impacts = "/var" 58Kb
    impacts = "/sbin" 40Kb
    impacts = "/opt" 157546Kb
    impacts = "/" 12Kb
  }
}
sw_sel "HPUX11i-OE" {
  description = "HP-UX 11i Operating Environment Component"
  sw_source = "core"
  sw_category = "OpEnvironments"
  sd_software_list = "HPUX11i-OE,r=B.11.31.0612,a=HP-UX_B.11.31_32/64,v=HP"
  (_hp_os_bitness -- "32") {
    impacts = "/var" 4Kb
    impacts = "/etc" 2738Kb
    impacts = "/sbin" 16Kb
    impacts = "/opt" 73739Kb
    impacts = "/usr" 1689Kb
    impacts = "/" 1Kb
  }
  (_hp_os_bitness == "64") {
    impacts = "/var" 4Kb
    impacts = "/etc" 2738Kb
```

```
        impacts = "/sbin" 16Kb
        impacts = "/opt" 73763Kb
        impacts = "/usr" 1689Kb
        impacts = "/" 1Kb
    }
}
```

10. The */var/opt/ignite/INDEX* file maintains a list of available configurations that are presented in the user interface after a client successfully boots up. You need to choose from one of them (See Figure 36-8 above). Execute the *manage_index* command with –l option to display the current selected configuration:

> # **manage_index –l**
> HP-UX B.11.31 Default

The default entries for HP-UX B.11.31 in the *INDEX* file look like:

> # **more /var/opt/ignite/INDEX**
> cfg "HP-UX B.11.31 Default" {
>   description "This selection supplies the default system configuration that HP supplies for the B.11.31 release."
>   "/opt/ignite/data/Rel_B.11.31/config"
>   "/opt/ignite/data/Rel_B.11.31/hw_patches_cfg"
>   "/var/opt/ignite/config.local"

Execute the *manage_index* command to update the B.11.31 configuration in the *INDEX* file to reflect the settings created in the previous step:

> # **manage_index –a –f /var/opt/ignite/data/Rel_B.11.31/core.conf –r "B.11.31"**

11. Execute the *instl_adm* command to setup parameters to be used by the client during installation. To check the default entries, use –d option:

> # **instl_adm –d**
> # instl_adm defaults:
> # NOTE: Manual additions between the lines containing "instl_adm defaults"
> # and "end instl_adm defaults" will not be preserved.
> server="192.168.1.201"
> netmask[]="0xffffff0"
> # end instl_adm defaults.

Modify the parameters by saving the defaults into a file and editing the file. Comments follow parameter definitions:

> # **instl_adm –d > /var/tmp/instl_adm.conf**
> # **vi /var/tmp/instl_adm.conf**
> # instl_adm defaults:
> # NOTE: Manual additions between the lines containing "instl_adm defaults"
> # and "end instl_adm defaults" will not be preserved.

```
server="192.168.1.201"              # Ignite-UX server IP address.
netmask[]="0xfffffff0"              # Subnet mask.
# end instl_adm defaults.
sd_server="192.168.1.201"           # IP address of the Ignite-UX server.
route_gateway[0]=""                 # Route gateway.
route_destination[0]="default"      # Route destination.
timezone="EST5EDT"                  # Time zone to be set.
control_from_server=true            # installation process is controlled from Ignite-UX server.
root_password="fn3,d7a.1Bp,."       # copy and paste password from /etc/passwd file for root.
is_net_info_temporary=false         # The TCP/IP parameters supplied are permanent.
disable_dhcp=true                   # Disable DHCP.
_hp_keyboard="PS2_DIN_US_English"   # Keyboard type to be set.
```

Execute the *instl_adm* command again to update the */opt/ignite/data/INSTALLFS* file with the new values:

 # instl_adm –f /var/tmp/instl_adm.conf

Configuration information stored in */var/opt/ignite/INDEX*, */opt/ignite/data/INSTALLFS* and */var/opt/ignite/clients/<client_MAC_address>/config* is used for a client when it is ignited.

This completes the procedure for configuring an Ignite-UX server from the command line.

34.3   Booting Clients and Installing HP-UX

Once an Ignite-UX server is setup, it is ready to be used to install HP-UX on client systems. The client systems may or may not already have HP-UX running. You can initiate a push install from the server or a pull install from a client. There are multiple ways of booting a client and installing HP-UX. Table 34-2 categorizes them in three classes.

Installation Class	Available Methods
Booting and installing with UI running on client console.	Local boot and local install.
	Local boot with HP-UX software located in a network depot.
	Local boot and pull install.
	Remote boot and pull install.
Booting and installing with UI running on Ignite-UX server.	Remote boot and push install.

Table 34-2 Installation Methods

The following sub-sections cover them.

34.3.1   Booting and Installing with UI Running on Client Console

This sub-section outlines installing HP-UX with user interface running on client console.

Local Boot and Local Install

This method employs booting the system locally with the DVD media, performing customization and installing the HP-UX software from the DVD. Refer to Chapter 09 "HP-UX Installation" for details on how to perform installation using local media.

Local Boot with HP-UX Software Located in a Network Depot

In Chapter 09 "HP-UX Installation" a few choices were presented to choose the source location when the "User Interface and Media Options" screen (see Figure 34-10) appeared during HP-UX installation.

The first choice was selected in Chapter 09 to demonstrate local install of the OE. The second choice enables the system to contact a network depot server that has the HP-UX 11i OE image sitting in a depot directory. You need to supply the hostname or IP address of the depot server, and the depot directory location. Choosing this option does not install the OE software locally from the DVD media, instead, it pulls the software over the network from the depot server.

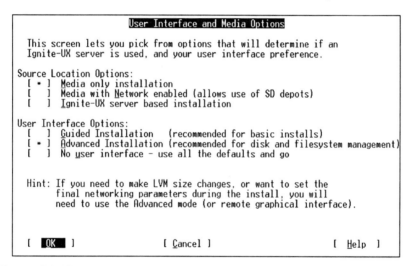

Figure 34-10 HP-UX Installation – User Interface and Media Options

Local Boot and Pull Install

The third option in Figure 34-10 utilizes a configured Ignite-UX server to pull the software image. The system prompts to input the IP address of the Ignite-UX server and the directory location where the HP-UX OE image resides. The next window, Figure 34-11, brings up the itool interface, which allows you to perform any customization. This is the same interface that was used to customize the OE installation in Chapter 09.

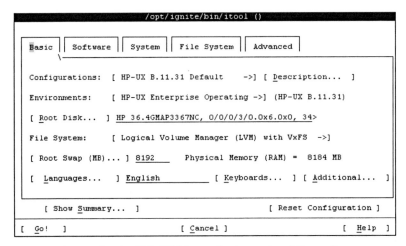

Figure 34-11 HP-UX Installation – itool Interface

Press the Go! button when done to continue the installation process. The client will perform the customization and pull the OE image from the Ignite-UX server.

Remote Boot and Pull Install

Similar to the "Local boot and pull install" method, the user interface with this method runs on the client console. The only difference being that instead of booting the client locally using the DVD media, it is booted remotely from the Ignite-UX server. Make sure that both the Ignite-UX server and the client are on the same subnet, as the *instl_bootd* daemon can only listen and respond to boot requests coming from systems that are on the same subnet. There are two ways to boot a client remotely:

✓ If the client already has HP-UX 11.0 or later running, execute the following on it with –c option and specify the Ignite-UX server name:

   # **bootsys –c hp01**

✓ If the client does not have any OS running, go to the BCH prompt and run the following:

   Main Menu: Enter command > **boot lan.192.168.1.201 install**

Both examples above use the Ignite-UX server *hp01* with IP address 192.168.1.201.

34.3.2   Booting and Installing with UI Running on Ignite-UX Server

This method allows the client to be booted from the Ignite-UX server. You will need to provide input on a few screens that appear on the client console, followed by entering further information on the Ignite-UX server. This method requires that the client already has HP-UX 11.0 or later running.

Here is an example that demonstrates this method of installing HP-UX.

Boot a client such as *hp05* using the *bootsys* command issued on the Ignite-UX server. Alternatively, highlight the client icon in the Ignite-UX GUI and choose the "client boot" option.

bootsys –a hp05:192.168.1.205
Rebooting hp05 now.

This example will keep the existing hostname and IP address of the client. Here is what you would see on the console of *hp05*:

Processor is booting from the first available device.
To discontinue, press any key within 10 seconds.

10 seconds expired.
Proceeding...

Trying Primary Boot Path

Booting...
Boot IO Dependent Code (IODC) revision 1

HARD Booted.
ISL Revision A.00.43 Apr 12, 2000

. . . .

The "Welcome to the HP-UX installation/recovery process!" screen appears on the client console, as shown in Figure 34-12. Highlight "Install HP-UX" and hit the Enter key.

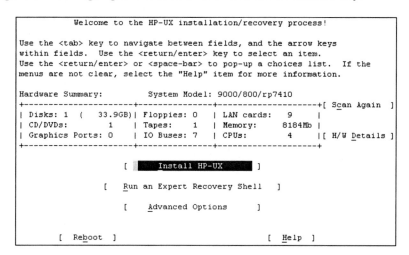

Figure 34-12 HP-UX Installation – Welcome Screen

On the "User Interface and Media Options" window, Figure 34-13, select "Ignite-UX server based installation" and "Remote graphical interface running on the Ignite-UX server" options. Press the OK button.

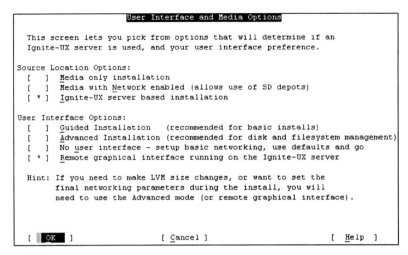

```
                    User Interface and Media Options

     This screen lets you pick from options that will determine if an
     Ignite-UX server is used, and your user interface preference.

  Source Location Options:
     [   ]  Media only installation
     [   ]  Media with Network enabled (allows use of SD depots)
     [ * ]  Ignite-UX server based installation

  User Interface Options:
     [   ]  Guided Installation   (recommended for basic installs)
     [   ]  Advanced Installation (recommended for disk and filesystem management)
     [   ]  No user interface - setup basic networking, use defaults and go
     [ * ]  Remote graphical interface running on the Ignite-UX server

     Hint: If you need to make LVM size changes, or want to set the
           final networking parameters during the install, you will
           need to use the Advanced mode (or remote graphical interface).


     [   OK   ]                    [ Cancel ]                     [  Help  ]
```

Figure 34-13 HP-UX Installation – User Interface and Media Options

A list of all LAN interfaces installed in the system is displayed. Choose the one that has network connectivity and press Enter. A summary of the network information is displayed for review:

NETWORK CONFIGURATION
This system's hostname: hp05
Internet protocol address (eg. 15.2.56.1) of this host: 192.168.1.205
Default gateway routing internet protocol address: 192.168.1.1
The subnet mask (eg. 255.255.248.0 or 0xfffff800): 0xffffff00
IP address of the Ignite-UX server system: 192.168.1.201
Is this networking information only temporary? [No]

Press OK to see the following on the console:

Ignite-UX
Waiting for installation instructions from server: 192.168.1.201   [-]
Icon Name Shown in GUI: hp05
Active System Name/IP: hp05/192.168.1.205
You may now complete the installation using the "ignite" graphical
interface on the Ignite-UX server (See ignite(1M)). If you are not
already running "/opt/ignite/bin/ignite" on the server, do so now.

No further action is required at this console.
[Perform Installation from this Console]
[View Active Network Parameters]
[Change Icon Name Shown in GUI]

At this point, an icon for *hp05* becomes visible in the Ignite-UX server GUI. Select "New Install" by right-clicking on *hp05* icon. See Figure 34-14.

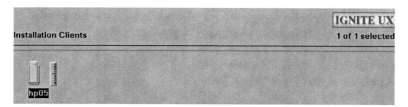

Figure 34-14 HP-UX Installation – Installation Clients

The itool interface appears, as shown in Figure 34-15. Consult Chapter 9 to modify any of the installation parameters. Press Go! when done to complete the installation.

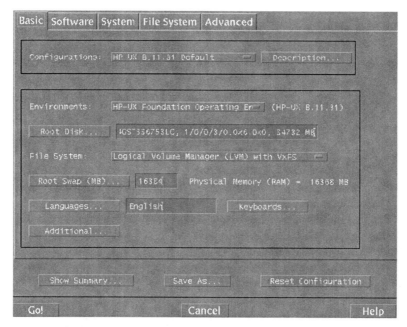

Figure 34-15 HP-UX Installation – itool Interface

34.4   Cloning (Golden Image) / Backing Up the Boot Disk

This feature of Ignite-UX is used to clone multiple systems with identical configuration. It requires that you install HP-UX on one system, install common applications, and configure and patch the system as per requirements. When installation and customization is complete, take a snapshot, called *golden image*, of the entire system either on tape or a network directory. The following sub-sections demonstrate procedures on creating and using golden images.

34.4.1   Creating a Golden Image on Tape

To create a golden image of *hp05* on a tape device at */dev/rtape/tape2_BESTn*, run the *make_tape_recovery* command as follows. The –v option produces detailed output, the "–x inc_entire" option specifies to include the entire volume group and –a option specifies the tape device to be used.

make_tape_recovery –v –x inc_entire=vg00 –a /dev/rtape/tape2_BESTn

    * Creating local directories for configuration files and archive.

======= 04/24/08 15:20:41 EDT Started make_tape_recovery. (Thu Apr 24 15:20:41 EDT 2008)

    @(#)Ignite-UX Revision C.7.3.144

    @(#)ignite/net_recovery (opt) Revision:
/tags/IUX_RA0709w_IC312c/ignite/src@71072 Last Modified: 2007-07-25
08:55:30 -0600 (Wed, 25 Jul 2007)

    * Testing for necessary pax patch.

    * Recovery Archive Description = Recovery Archive

    * Recovery Archive Location   = /dev/rtape/tape1_BESTn

    * Number of Archives to Save = 2

    * Pax type = tar

In?	dsk/vg	name	minor#	Associated disks/mountpoints
2	v	/dev/vg00	0x00	/dev/disk/disk5
				/dev/vg00/lvol1 /stand 2
				/dev/vg00/lvol2
				/dev/vg00/lvol3 / 2
				/dev/vg00/lvol4 /tmp 2
				/dev/vg00/lvol5 /home 2
				/dev/vg00/lvol6 /opt 2
				/dev/vg00/lvol7 /usr 2
				/dev/vg00/lvol8 /var 2

  ** 0 - The Volume Group or Filesystem is Not included in the System Recovery Archive

  ** 1 - The Volume Group or Filesystem is Partially included in the System Recovery Archive

  ** 2 - The Volume Group or Filesystem is Fully included in the System Recovery Archive

  * Checking Versions of Ignite-UX filesets

  * Creating System Configuration.

  * /opt/ignite/bin/save_config –f /var/opt/ignite/recovery/2008-04-24,15:20/system_cfg vg00

  * Backing Up Volume Group /dev/vg00

  * /usr/sbin/vgcfgbackup /dev/vg00

  * Creating Map Files for Volume Group /dev/vg00

  * /usr/sbin/vgexport -s -p -m /etc/lvmconf/vg00.mapfile /dev/vg00

  * Creating Control Configuration.

  * Creating Archive File List

  * Creating Archive Configuration

  * /opt/ignite/bin/make_arch_config -c
/var/opt/ignite/recovery/2008-04-24,15:22/archive_cfg -g
/var/opt/ignite/recovery/2008-04-24,15:22/flist -n 2008-04-24,15:22 -r
64 -d Recovery\ Archive -t -i 3 -m t

  * Saving the information about archive to /var/opt/ignite/recovery/previews

  * Creating The Tape Archive

  * Checking configuration file for Syntax

Adding /opt/ignite/Version file to LIF.

  * Writing boot LIF to tape

48231+0 records in

48231+0 records out

  * Complete writing boot LIF onto tape.

 * /opt/ignite/data/scripts/make_sys_image -c n -d /dev/rmt/6mn -t n –s local -n 2008-04-24,15:20 -m t -w

. . . .

Notice from the output that a utility called *make_sys_image* is invoked during the execution of the *make_tape_recovery* command. This utility is responsible for creating a compressed archive of a running system. This utility may also be invoked directly from the command line. See its man pages on usage.

34.4.2   Creating a Golden Image on a Network Directory

To create a golden image of *hp05* on *hp01* under the */var/opt/ignite/recovery/archives/hp05* directory, you need to create the directory on *hp01*, assign proper ownership and group membership and NFS share it:

> **# mkdir –p /var/opt/ignite/recovery/archives/hp05**
> **# chown bin:bin /var/opt/ignite/recovery/archives/hp05**
> **# vi /etc/dfs/dfstab**
> /var/opt/ignite/recovery/archives/hp05 anon=2,access=hp01
> **# shareall**

Run the *make_net_recovery* command on *hp05* to create its image on *hp01*. The command automatically NFS mounts the directory from *hp01*. The –s option specifies the Ignite-UX server name and –a the directory location to store the archive.

> **# make_net_recovery –v –s hp01 –a hp01:/var/opt/ignite/recovery/archives/hp05**
>   * Creating NFS mount directories for configuration files.
>   * Recovery Archive Name = 2008-04-25,11:21
>   * Lanic Id = 0x00306EA7AC2D
>   * Ignite-UX Server = hp01
> ======= 04/25/08 11:21:13 EDT Started make_net_recovery. (Fri Apr 25 11:21:13 EDT 2008)
>   @(#) Ignite-UX Revision C.6.1.44
>   @(#) net_recovery (opt) $Revision: 10.672 $
>   * Testing for necessary pax patch.
>   * Passed pax tests.
>   * Recovery Archive Description = Recovery Archive
>   * Recovery Archive Location   = hp01:/var/opt/ignite/recovery/archives/hp05
>   * Number of Archives to Save = 2
>   pax type = tar
> . . . .

34.4.3   Cloning a System Using Golden Image on Tape

To clone a 9000 system with identical configuration (except hostname and IP address) using the golden image on tape, do the following:

1.   Power on the system.
2.   Insert the golden image tape into the tape drive.
3.   Interrupt the boot sequence by pressing Esc to go to BCH.
4.   Execute *sea* to get a list of devices.
5.   Execute the *boot* command with proper tape device path specified.
6.   Do not interact with ISL.

7. Interrupt the boot process within 10 seconds when prompted. Follow the screens and set the hostname, IP address and other TCP/IP parameters for the client. Continue the boot process.

Here is the procedure for an Integrity machine:

1. Power on the system.
2. Insert the golden image tape into the tape drive.
3. Interrupt the boot sequence by pressing Esc and go to EFI Boot Manager.
4. Go to "Boot Option Maintenance" menu and select "Add a Boot Option".
5. Select appropriate tape device.
6. Enter an appropriate boot option name at the message prompt.
7. Go back to the main menu. The new boot option appears in the EFI Boot Manager main menu.
8. Select the new boot option and boot the system.
9. Interrupt the boot process within 10 seconds when prompted. Follow the screens and set the hostname, IP address and other TCP/IP parameters for the client. Continue the boot process.

34.4.4 Cloning a System Using Golden Image on a Network Directory

To clone a 9000 system with identical configuration using the golden image on a properly configured Ignite-UX server, do the following:

1. Power on the system.
2. Interrupt the boot sequence by pressing Esc to go to BCH.
3. Execute the following at the BCH prompt:

   Main Menu: Enter command > **boot lan install**

4. Do not interact with IPL.
5. Interrupt the boot process within 10 seconds when prompted. Follow the screens and set the hostname, IP address and other TCP/IP parameters for the client. Continue the boot process.

Here is the procedure for an Integrity machine:

1. Power on the system.
2. Interrupt the boot sequence by pressing Esc and go to EFI Boot Manager.
3. Go to "Boot Option Maintenance" menu and select "Add a Boot Option".
4. Select an appropriate network interface.
5. Enter an appropriate boot option name such as LAN1 at the message prompt.
6. Go back to the main menu. The new boot option appears in the EFI Boot Manager main menu.
7. Select the new boot option and boot the system.
8. Interrupt the boot process within 10 seconds when prompted. Follow the screens and set the hostname, IP address and other TCP/IP parameters for the client. Continue the boot process.

34.5   System Recovery

System recovery is performed in the event of a catastrophic failure of the root disk, root volume group, or when the root disk becomes corrupt. In each of these situations, the system becomes unbootable and cannot continue to function. An Ignite-UX functionality called *system recovery*, which utilizes the same commands and procedures described earlier in this chapter to create and use golden image, may be employed to recover the system. Note that the purpose and usage of system recovery is slightly different from that of golden image's. The key differences are:

✓ A golden image is typically created for the purpose of cloning new servers, whereas, a system recovery archive is host-specific and used primarily to recover an unbootable system.
✓ A golden image is normally produced one time and used many times, whereas, a system recovery archive is made once every week or month via *cron* to capture the root volume group image. A system recovery archive is used only when needed.

From the system recovery standpoint, *make_tape_recovery* creates a bootable system recovery tape archive of either selected, essential files and directories of *vg00,* or the entire *vg00.* This archive is system-specific and includes hostname, IP address, copy of boot area, LVM structures and data in *vg00.*

make_net_recovery performs exactly what *make_tape_recovery* does, with the exception that the archive is stored on a network directory rather than on tape.

In the event a system recovery is required, either of these archives can be used to recover the system. The tape archive boots a system directly from the BCH prompt and requires no further interaction. The network archive requires that you boot the system locally via the HP-UX OE DVD and specify the server and directory location of the archive. Booting from either archive rebuilds the boot area on the root disk, regenerates LVM structures for *vg00,* creates and mounts all file systems and restores data along with all configuration information. Within an hour or two, the system should be back up and running.

34.5.1   Creating and Using Recovery Archives

To create tape and network images for system recovery purposes, follow the procedures outlined in the previous section. A recovery archive should be made on a weekly or monthly basis via *cron.* It should also be made manually if any updates such as kernel modifications are made.

To use tape and network images for system recovery purposes, follow the procedures outlined in the previous section, with the exception of interrupting the boot process.

Summary

In this chapter you learned about benefits and usage of the Ignite-UX product. You developed an understanding of what registered and anonymous clients were. You saw procedures on how to configure an Ignite-UX server via GUI and command line.

You looked at how to install and re-install HP-UX on client systems. You saw how the user interface could be brought up on either client or server.

Finally, you studied how to create golden image and recovery archives on tape and network directory. You used *make_tape_recovery* and *make_net_recovery* tools for these purposes. You saw procedures to clone other machines using golden image. You looked at procedures on how to recover an unbootable system to its previous running state using the tape and network archives.

## 35

Introduction to High Availability and Clustering

This chapter covers the following major topics:

- ✓ Describe high-availability and clustering benefits
- ✓ Traditional and high-availability network computing models
- ✓ Risks with single points of failure
- ✓ Explain key HA/cluster terms – downtime, uptime, reliability, fault tolerance, availability, high-availability, ultra high-availability, cluster, load balancing, rolling upgrade, floating IP address, failover, failback, primary node and adoptive node
- ✓ List and describe types of clusters

35.1 Introduction to High Availability

High Availabililty is a design technique where a computer system is architected and built to recover quickly from a hardware or software failure and restore to normalcy the service it is designed to run. A hardware failure could be a fault in a computer system component that makes the computer unable to deliver the required service. Likewise, a software failure could be a fault in the kernel or an application. In either case, users are unable to access and use the system.

35.1.1 Traditional Network Computing Model

In the traditional network computing environment, a single computer runs user applications, which are accessed over the network. The application data may be located on local drives inside the computer or in an external disk array. In this model, the key hardware components involved are:

- ✓ A hard disk with OS.
- ✓ One or more disks with user data and applications.
- ✓ A SCSI (or fibre) controller card for external disk array connectivity.
- ✓ A network card for network connectivity via a switch or hub.
- ✓ A system power supply connected to a UPS.

And the key software components involved are the OS, and user data and applications. Figure 35-1 illustrates a traditional computer environment.

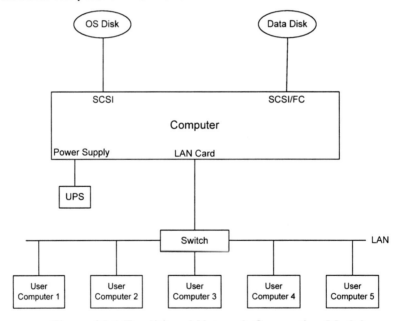

Figure 35-1 Traditional Network Computing Model

In the traditional network computing environment configuration, there are many *Single Points Of Failure* (SPOF). For example, if the OS disk fails, the entire system will crash. Similarly, if the SCSI/FC adapter fails, access to data and applications will be lost. The power supply or the UPS failure will result in no power to the system. A bug in the OS kernel will crash the entire system. In other words, a single hardware or software component failure will cause an interruption to the business that depends on it. The interruption may last for minutes or it could prolong to several hours or even days until the cause of the failure is identified and resolved. Some of the SPOFs are listed below including the ones just described:

✓ SCSI or Fibre Channel adapter
✓ OS disk
✓ Data disk
✓ LAN card
✓ Network connectivity to switch or hub
✓ Power supply
✓ UPS
✓ Computer system itself
✓ Racking
✓ Data

35.1.2   Redundant-Component Network Computing Model

As businesses started to rely more on computing infrastructure, the need arose to reduce the amount of time it took to overcome the interruption and bring the system back to normal operation. This need resulted in designs that led to the deployment of duplicate hardware components in the computer system to minimize the SPOFs. The duplicate hardware components introduce *redundancy*, which increases the overall *availability* of the system. Redundancy allows systems to continue functioning should one of the two redundant components fail. This helps decrease considerably the amount of system recovery time. Figure 35-2 shows the traditional computer model with redundancy added.

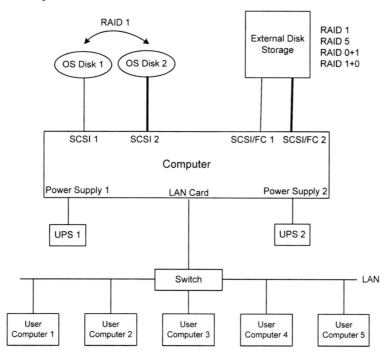

Figure 35-2 Redundant-Component Network Computing Model

The redundant OS disk in the figure is connected using separate SCSI card and cable. Both disks are mirrored using the HP-UX MirrorDisk/UX mirroring software.

Similarly, data and applications are located in a disk array, and are RAID-protected. The disk array is connected to the system via two separate controller cards and cables.

There is a pair of UPS providing power to the computer system. It is very important in an HA environment that both be connected to separate power sources.

35.1.3 High-Availability Network Computing Model

There still are SPOFs in the design. The connectivity to the network is still non-redundant. Similarly, applications in the disk storage are non-redundant. Although the data itself is protected against disk breakdown, but what if the applications crash due to a CPU failure, failure in memory or some other non-redundant component. Generally, when a CPU fails, memory malfunctions, or other system component faults, the system panics and reboots. This results in an interruption to the business service that relies on it. The interruption is over and the applications are restored to normal operation as soon as the system is recovered from the hardware failure.

Figure 35-3 shows more redundancy added to the system environment to overcome remaining SPOFs. Now there are two systems each with redundant OS disks, redundant links to the shared disk array, and connectivity to redundant networks via separate physical switches. The two systems need to be configured in such a manner that both work as a single entity and back each other up. This type of setup creates a *cluster* of systems, whereby failure of one system or a pair of any redundant components within the system, will disrupt the business service for a short period of time only. A cluster of systems (or simply a cluster) is formed using a cluster management software such as HP Serviceguard.

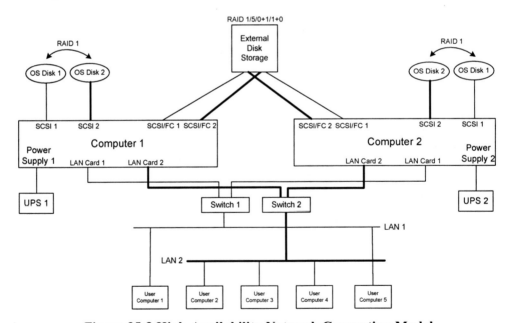

Figure 35-3 High-Availability Network Computing Model

To ensure true HA, both systems should be deployed in separate physical racks. This will remove the SPOF from server racking perspective as well.

35.1.4   Ultra High-Availability Network Computing Model

Although the computer system design is now fully redundant, there is still a SPOF – the data center or the computer room where this setup is deployed. What if the data center becomes inaccessible or destroyed for reasons such as fire, flood or other natural or human-caused disasters? You can have one of the nodes of the cluster placed at an alternate data center, physically apart from the primary data center. The alternate data center could be hundreds or thousands of miles away in another city, country or continent. For this type of setup, standard HP Serviceguard software does not work, and an appropriate version of the software that supports such a setup, must be acquired. Implementing this configuration allows any mission-critical business applications that run on these systems, to become more available. This type of setup may be referred to as *ultra high-availability* or *continuously available* setup.

Ultra HA setup requires intense planning and design consideration from the network and disk storage perspective, requires the implementation of a SAN-based storage solution at each data center to connect cluster nodes, and is very expensive to implement and maintain. The system located in the primary data center will store data on the local disk array. This data will be synchronously or asynchronously replicated in real time to the disk array in the alternate data center. The other node of the cluster will be attached to the second array and the two storage devices will be interconnected via redundant fibre links. If a disaster occurs and renders the primary data center inaccessible, the cluster management software will *failover* the applications running on the *primary* node in the primary data center to the *adoptive* (second) node in the alternate data center. As data was being replicated to the disk storage device in the alternate data center, the adoptive node will have access to the latest data, and hence the applications and services will start up in minutes, allowing remote users to regain access.

35.2   Key HA Terms

This section defines a few common terms used in an HA environment. Some of them have already been covered earlier in this chapter.

35.2.1   Downtime

Downtime refers to the length of time during which a business application is unavailable or non-functional due to a failure. Downtime is of two types – *planned* and *unplanned*. A *planned downtime* is a pre-scheduled maintenance window for performing any hardware, OS or application task. An *unplanned downtime,* on the other hand, refers to a sudden interruption in business application accessibility. It is also referred to as an *outage.*

35.2.2   Uptime

Uptime is the opposite of downtime. It refers to a length of time during which a business application remains up and available for user access.

35.2.3 Reliability

Reliability is the ability of a computer system to carry out and keep up its function in normal as well as abnormal circumstances. Usually, branded computers are manufactured using high quality hardware components. These components are tested and certified, and are used to produce better quality and more reliable computer systems.

35.2.4 Fault Tolerance

Fault tolerance refers to the ability of a computer system to survive and continue to function in the event a sudden hardware or software failure occurs. Fault tolerance is built by adding redundant hardware components to a computer system.

35.2.5 Availability

Availability is a measure of overall system uptime minus any unplanned downtime. It is usually expressed as a percentage of uptime for a given year. The following explains how it is calculated for a given year based on 365 days in the year with total unplanned downtime of 400 minutes:

Total number of minutes in a year (A) (365 * 24 * 60)	= 525,600
Aggregate unplanned downtime (B) for a given year	= 400 (33.33 minutes per month)

===

%age of unplanned downtime in the year (C) = B ÷ A	= 0.076
%age of uptime in the year (D) = 100 – C	= **99.9**

The last line indicates that the availability of the system for the year is 99.9%.

Availability today is typically expressed as a count of 9s. For example:

99.9%	= 43.8 minutes/month or 8.76 hours/year ("three 9s")
99.99%	= 4.38 minutes/month or 52.6 minutes/year ("four 9s")
99.999%	= 0.44 minutes/month or 5.26 minutes/year ("five 9s")

To achieve higher levels of availability, ensure that SPOFs are removed from both hardware and software standpoint, dual data center model is implemented, an appropriate clustering solution is implemented, data is replicated in real time, and so on.

35.2.6 High-Availability

High-Availability (HA) refers to a system design in which failure of a single hardware or software component interrupts only briefly the service offered by the system. The purpose of designing an HA system is to minimize the duration of a possible interruption to the service offered by the system.

35.2.7 Ultra High-Availability

Ultra High-Availability is one level higher than normal HA. It generally includes two or more cluster nodes located in distant data centers with data replicated in real time and continuously available to both or all nodes in the cluster. In the event one of the nodes faults, the cluster management software transfers the control over to another node and starts applications there.

35.3 Introduction to Clustering

Clustering enables a group of two or more independent servers to work cohesively and collaboratively as a single entity under the control of management software to provide high availability to business applications. The management software rapidly responds to failures in a way that minimizes application downtime.

35.3.1 Cluster Benefits

Common benefits of implementing a cluster solution are listed below:

- ✓ **Reduced Downtime** – The overall application downtime is reduced as failure of a single node in the cluster prompts the cluster management software to move the application to another node in the cluster and bring it up there.
- ✓ **Load Balancing** – When several applications require varying amount of compute capacity to run in a multi-node cluster, the cluster is configured in such a way that application load is evenly distributed across all nodes in the cluster. This is called *load balancing* and is done to avoid any single node from being swamped.
- ✓ **Rolling Upgrades** – Within a cluster environment, the OS on a node can be upgraded without requiring a large amount of downtime. Any applications running on the node will need to be manually moved over to some other node in the cluster to free the node up for the upgrade. The applications are moved back after the upgrade is complete. The only downtime required is the time it takes for the applications to move over and back. Performing OS and application upgrades using this method is referred to as *rolling upgrades*.

35.3.2 Types of HP Cluster Software

Several HP clustering software solutions are available depending on need, and availability of required network and storage connectivity. These include:

- ✓ **Serviceguard Cluster** – A group of nodes located within a building, and usually in separate racks.
- ✓ **Extended Distance Cluster** – Contains nodes located in buildings separated by distances of up to 100 km.
- ✓ **Metro Cluster** – Contains nodes separated by distances of up to 300 km, and are usually located within metropolitan area limits or in neighboring cities.
- ✓ **Continental Cluster** – A group of small clusters located in separate data centers and use routed networks for network and storage connectivity. This type of cluster typically has nodes located thousands of kilometers apart in different countries or continents.
- ✓ **Serviceguard Extension for RAC** – Enables a group of up to 16 nodes in a cluster to support Oracle Real Application Cluster (RAC) for increased performance, enhanced data protection and continuous application availability of up to five nines.
- ✓ **Serviceguard Extension for SAP** – Enables a group of nodes in a cluster to support SAP application for increased performance, enhanced data protection and continuous application availability of up to five nines.

35.4 Key Cluster Terms

This section defines a few terms that are commonly used in a cluster environment. Some of them have already been covered earlier in this chapter.

35.4.1 Floating (Virtual) IP Address

When clusters are formed, applications are packaged to run on cluster nodes. Each application package is assigned an IP address, which is associated with a LAN interface on the system where the package is to be run. This IP address is referred to as the *floating* (or *virtual* or *relocateable*) IP address. When the package fails over to another node, the floating IP address goes with the package to that node and is assigned to a LAN interface there. A floating IP address is not tied to a specific system in a cluster.

35.4.2 Failover

The responsibility of cluster management software is to monitor the availability of the hardware and software components within a cluster. If an event occurs that renders a cluster node inoperative, the cluster management software transfers the control of the software package to another configured node in the cluster and starts the package on that node. This stop-transfer-start operation is referred to as *failover*. Clustered nodes in production services are almost always configured to perform failover function automatically without human intervention. The cluster management software does not fix any problems, rather, it monitors hardware and software components and transfers the control to another configured node should a critical fault occurs on the primary node that makes it unable to perform the desired role.

35.4.3 Failback

Failback is the opposite of failover. It refers to the tasks to be performed to transfer the control of the failed over package back to its primary node and bring it up there. Failback is not configured to happen automatically in production environments, it is done manually during a customer-approved scheduled maintenance or specially-arranged window.

35.4.4 Primary (Active) Node

From a package standpoint, a *primary* (or *active)* node is that where the package is configured to start automatically when cluster services are brought up.

35.4.5 Adoptive (Standby or Passive) Node

When a primary node faults, the package running on it fails over to an *adoptive* (a.k.a. *standby* or *passive*) node and starts there. The adoptive node may or may not already be running a different package. Multiple adoptive nodes can be configured for additional redundancy.

HP Serviceguard software can be configured in active/active and active/standby modes. In active/active configuration, each node in the cluster runs at least one package. In contrast, in active/standby configuration, one of the nodes remains idle (standby) until some other node in the cluster dies and the package running there fails over to this standby node.

35.4.6   Cluster Package

A *package* is formed when a *configuration* file and a *control* script are created for an application to start, stop and monitor it. Other required components to support start, stop and monitor functions are also configured in these files. These components include the volume group(s), logical volume(s) and file system(s) which store necessary information to start, stop and monitor the application, references to start, stop and monitor scripts, floating IP address(es) and LAN interface names.

Packages are of two types – failover and non-failover:

  ✓ A *failover package* is installed on multiple nodes in a cluster, but runs only on one at a time.
  ✓ *Non-failover packages* are of two types – multi-node and system multi-node.

    ✓ A *multi-node package* runs concurrently on one or more nodes, and continues to run as long as at least one copy of the package remains up and running on any one defined node.
    ✓ A *system multi-node package* runs simultaneously on all cluster nodes. If any one copy of the package halts on any one node, it brings down all other copies and halts the entire package.

Summary

In this chapter you learned concepts around high-availability and clustering. You looked at various network computing models that helped you understand risks associated with having single points of failure. You saw how those risks could be minimized by adding redundant components.

Several key HA terms such as downtime, uptime, reliability, fault tolerance, availability, high-availability, ultra high-availability, cluster, floating IP address, failover, failback, primary node and adoptive node were presented to enhance your understanding of HA and clustering.

Finally, an overview of some types of HP cluster solutions was presented.

## 36

HP-UX Security

This chapter covers the following major topics:

- ✓ Ways to secure HP-UX systems
- ✓ What is identity management
- ✓ Password aging and how to use it
- ✓ Benefits of shadow password and how to implement it
- ✓ Secure shell benefits and how ssh encryption takes place
- ✓ Access HP-UX systems via ssh
- ✓ Configure single sign-on access
- ✓ Transfer files using scp and sftp
- ✓ Pluggable Authentication Module (PAM) and its use
- ✓ Benefits of HP-UX Bastille and use it
- ✓ Introduction to HP-UX IPFilter firewall
- ✓ Security monitoring, hardening and reporting tools
- ✓ Common HP-UX system hardening tasks

36.1 Securing the HP-UX System

Running an HP-UX system in a networked environment requires that some measures be taken to make the system more secure. Several enhanced and new tools are available in HP-UX 11i v3. You need to identify the type and level of security needed. Security features such as file and directory permissions, user and group level permissions, install-time security, EVFS, system boot security, network access security and NTP/NFS/NIS-level security have been discussed in previous chapters. This chapter covers additional features such as identity management, secure shell, PAM, Bastille, IPFilter firewall, and system hardening and monitoring tools. It also lists recommendations that you might wish to implement to enhance the system security.

36.2 Identity Management Features and Functions

Standard security mechanism is put in place when HP-UX is installed to control user access to the system. User security controls normally cover authentication, authorization and network access into the system.

Authentication identifies a user to the system. When a user enters credentials by entering his username and password, the system checks whether the credentials are valid, and based on the outcome the user is either allowed or denied access.

Authorization determines privileges a user has on using programs and managing resources. The *root* user is authorized to use any program and can manage any system resource. The default authorization is put in place for normal users when HP-UX is installed. Additional privileges may be granted to them by *root*. For instance, SMH is only allowed to be run by *root*, however, *root* can delegate management of a subset of SMH tasks to normal users.

Many incoming client requests from remote systems must pass through the *inetd* daemon on the system in order to be serviced. Security at this level can be controlled in two ways:

- ✓ Disable the service no longer required in the *inetd* daemon's configuration file */etc/inetd.conf*.
- ✓ Limit access into the system for specific systems, networks and domains in the *inetd* daemon's security file */var/adm/inetd.sec*.

The following sub-sections describe methods available to secure a system from user authentication perspective. The later sections explain additional topics surrounding further securing the system.

36.2.1 Setting Password Aging Attributes

In Chapter 12 "Users and Groups", user creation and password setting topics were discussed. Rules that must be adhered to for user password settings were outlined. *Password aging* provides enhanced control on passwords. It allows setting certain limits on user passwords in terms of expiration, warning period, etc. The *passwd* command is used to alter these parameters on a user account. The command has several options in relation to password aging, some of which are listed and explained in Table 36-1.

Option	Description
–d	Unlocks a user account by deleting its password.
–f	Forces a user to change password upon next login by expiring existing password.
–l	Locks a user account.
–n	Specifies the minimum number of days to be elapsed before a user password can be changed.
–r	Specifies the password repository to be updated. Choices include *etc/passwd* and NIS.
–s	Lists password aging attributes.
–w	Defines the number of days a user gets warning messages to change password. If not changed during this period, the user account is locked.
–x	Denotes the maximum number of days of password validity before a user starts getting warning messages to change it.

Table 36-1 *passwd* Command Options

The following example sets password aging on user *bghori*:

passwd –f –n 7 –x 28 bghori
<min> argument rounded up to nearest week
<max> argument rounded up to nearest week

Verify the attributes:

passwd –s bghori
bghori PS 03/21/08 7 28

The output indicates that the user account is passworded and was created on March 21, 2008.

36.2.2   Implementing Shadow Password Mechanism

The default location to store user passwords is the */etc/passwd* file. By implementing *shadow password*, all passwords from the */etc/passwd* file as well as any associated password aging attributes are moved to the */etc/shadow* file, and both files will then be used for user authentication.

To implement the shadow password mechanism, execute the *pwconv* command. This command creates */etc/shadow* file and moves into it all password entries and aging attributes:

pwconv
ll /etc/shadow
-r-------- 1 root   sys   428 Apr 9 12:46 /etc/shadow
cat /etc/shadow
root:xPk1ieoqpwl7E:13612::::::
bin:x:13612::::::
sys:x:13612::::::
adm:x:13612::::::
bghori:UfBFMlhlqXnoM:14077:7:28::::

. . . .

Each line entry in the file contains information about one user account. There are nine fields per line entry separated by colon, and are explained below:

- ✓ The first field contains the login name as appeared in the */etc/passwd* file.
- ✓ The second field contains 13 alphanumeric characters, which represent a user password in encrypted form.
- ✓ The third field contains the number of days since the epoch time (January 01, 1970) that the password was last modified.
- ✓ The fourth field contains the minimum number of days to be elapsed before a user password can be changed. This field is set with –n option of the *passwd* command.
- ✓ The fifth field contains the maximum number of days of password validity before a user starts getting warning messages to change it. This field is set with –x option of the *passwd* command.
- ✓ The sixth field contains the number of days a user gets warning messages to change password. This field is set with –w option of the *passwd* command.
- ✓ The seventh field contains the maximum number of days of user inactivity allowed. This field is set with –f option of the *useradd* or *usermod* command.
- ✓ The eighth field contains the number of days since the epoch time (January 01, 1970) after which the account is no longer valid.
- ✓ The last field is reserved for future use.

To revert to the non-shadow password environment, execute the *pwunconv* command. This command removes the */etc/shadow* file also.

36.2.3 Converting a System to Trusted Mode Security

Trusted mode security implements additional system access protection from user authentication perspective. It complies with C2 level of security and based on *Trusted Computing Base* (TCB). Note that some applications may malfunction if this security level is implemented. Check with application administrators and verify compatibility before implementing it.

Converting a system to trusted mode security provides the following benefits:

- ✓ A user account is locked if it remains dormant for a specified period of time. The default time period is 30 days.
- ✓ If a user attempts to login unsuccessfully, the account gets locked. The default number of unsuccessful attempts after which a user account is locked is 3.
- ✓ *root* user password must be entered in order to get into the single user state.
- ✓ Enhanced password aging attributes such as the minimum time to elapse before a user can change password, warning time before a user account is locked, expiration time for a user account and account lifetime are enabled.
- ✓ A user is provided three options to change the password. These options are "select a randomly generated password string", "select a pronounceable password" and "enter own password".
- ✓ A user can be restricted to login to the system within a specified time period and/or from specific terminals only.
- ✓ Auditing for user activities and system calls is enabled.

To convert the system to trusted mode security, use either command line or SMH. The following example demonstrates how to do it from the command line using the *tsconvert* command:

```
# /etc/tsconvert
Creating secure password database...
Directories created.
Making default files.
. . . . . . . .
. . . . . . . .
Moving passwords...
secure password database installed.
Converting at and crontab jobs...
At and crontab files converted.
```

This command creates a new directory structure */tcb/files/auth* that contains sub-directories named "A" through "Z", "a" through "z" and "system". Each sub-directory holds security files for user accounts that begin with the name of the sub-directory. For instance, user accounts beginning with an "a" have their files under */tcb/files/auth/a* sub-directory, user accounts beginning with a "A" have their files under */tcb/files/auth/A* sub-directory and so on. The "system" directory contains a file called *default*, which contains the default settings applied on all user accounts. All password fields in the */etc/passwd* file are replaced with the * character, and the password and password aging information is moved to this new directory structure. To view the security file for user *bghori*, go to */tcb/files/auth/b*. You will find a file that corresponds to the username. Do a *cat* on the file to view what it contains:

```
# cat bghori
bghori:u_name=bghori:u_id#101:\
    :u_pwd=:\
    :u_auditid#12:\
    :u_auditflag#1:\
    :u_minchg#604800:u_exp#2419200:u_succhg#1132185600:u_pswduser=bghori:\
    :u_suclog#1135355071:u_lock@:chkent:
```

Alternatively, the *getprpw* command can be used to view the contents of the file in addition to any default settings on the account:

```
# /usr/lbin/getprpw bghori
uid=101, bootpw=NO, audid=12, audflg=1, mintm=7, maxpwln=-1, exptm=28, lftm=-1, spwchg=-1,
upwchg=-1, acctexp=-1, llog=-1, expwarn=-1, usrpick=DFT, syspnpw=DFT, rstrpw=DFT, nullpw=DFT,
admnum=-1, syschpw=DFT, sysltpw=DFT, timeod=-1, slogint=Thu Jul 24 14:41:16 2008, ulogint=-1,
sloginy=-1, culogin=-1, uloginy=-1, umaxlntr=-1, alock=NO, lockout=0000000
```

The security file holds all standard and extended password aging attributes for user *bghori*. The numbers in the file are in seconds.

If a user account is activated, a string u_lock@ is displayed as shown in the output of the *cat* command. In case the account is locked, the @ sign will be missing as displayed below:

```
:u_suclog#1135355071:u_lock:chkent:
```

If *bghori* tries to login when the account is locked, the following message will appear:

Account is disabled - see Account Administrator

To unlock a user account, use the *modprpw* command. This command only works in trusted mode security. For example, the following will unlock user *bghori*:

 # /usr/lbin/modprpw –lk bghori

The –w option with the *passwd* command can be used in trusted mode to set warning period on a user account. For instance:

 # passwd –f –w 5 –n 7 –x 28 bghori
<warn> argument rounded up to nearest week
<min> argument rounded up to nearest week
<max> argument rounded up to nearest week

To unconvert the system to standard security level, run the *tsconvert* command with –r option:

 # /etc/tsconvert –r
Restoring /etc/passwd...
/etc/passwd restored.
Deleting at and crontab audit ID files...
At and crontab audit ID files deleted.

To convert the system to trusted mode security and vice versa via SMH, perform the following:

☞ Go to SMH → Auditing and Security → Audited Users → Actions → Convert the System.

36.3   The Secure Shell

You have seen a number of ways so far to make the system secure. This includes setting setuid, setgid and sticky bits, disabling unnecessary services in the */etc/inetd.conf* file, controlling access to the network services via */var/adm/inetd.sec* file, enabling logging for network services by specifying the –l option to the *inetd* daemon in the */etc/rc.config.d/netdaemons* file, setting password aging attributes, implementing shadow password mechanism, converting to trusted mode security and configuring user and host equivalency.

Secure shell (ssh) is a set of utilities that provides remote users with secure login access to the system using hidden encryption. Due to better security features, ssh utilities are preferred over conventional, unsecured *telnet, rlogin, remsh, rcp* and *ftp*. Once ssh is successfully implemented for each individual user including *root*, the *rlogind, rexecd, remshd, ftpd* and *telnetd* services can be disabled in the */etc/inetd.conf* file, provided no user or application functionality is impacted. The secure command that replaces *rlogin, remsh* and *telnet* is called *ssh*. The secure commands that replace *rcp* and *ftp* are called *scp* and *sftp*, respectively.

36.3.1   How SSH Encryption Takes Place

ssh is based on the client/server model where the client piece (*ssh, scp* and *sftp*) makes a connection request and the server process *sshd* responds to it. Here is how a secure communication channel is established when using an ssh utility:

- ✓ The client program sends a connection request to the specified server.
- ✓ The *sshd* daemon on the server receives the incoming request on the pre-defined port. The configuration file for *sshd* is */opt/ssh/etc/sshd_config*. The *sshd* daemon may be controlled via *inetd* daemon.
- ✓ Both client and server processes share ssh protocol versions and switch to a packet-based protocol for communication.
- ✓ The server supplies session information to the client.
- ✓ The client acknowledges the server's session information and responds with a session key.
- ✓ Both client and server enable encryption at their ends.
- ✓ This completes the authentication process and establishes a communication channel.

36.3.2   Accessing HP-UX Server Over SSH

ssh utilities are installed during HP-UX installation, and the *sshd* daemon is enabled and running after the installation is complete. If the daemon is not enabled and running, perform the following two steps:

1. Edit the */etc/rc.config.d/sshd* file and set the variable SSHD_START to 1:

    SSHD_START=1

2. Start the daemon:

    # /sbin/init.d/secsh start
    HP-UX Secure Shell started

On the Windows side, several ssh client programs such as PuTTY, are available. PuTTY can be downloaded free of charge from the internet. Figure 36-1 shows the PuTTY interface.

Supply a hostname or an IP address of the system to login to and check "SSH" under "Protocol". The ssh protocol uses port 22. Assign a name to this session and click Save to save it to avoid retyping this information in future.

The first time you try to ssh into the HP-UX server *hp02,* for instance, information similar to the following will be displayed:

    The authenticity of host 'hp02 (192.168.1.202)' can't be established.
    RSA key fingerprint is d3:a4:4e:c1:9f:de:00:e7:4a:55:ac:a9:e6:5e:ff:a9.
    Are you sure you want to continue connecting (yes/no)? **yes**
    Warning: Permanently added 'hp02,192.168.1.202' (RSA) to the list of known hosts.

Supply "yes" to the question and press Enter. This sets up and saves encryption keys for the client system, and the message will not appear on subsequent login attempts.

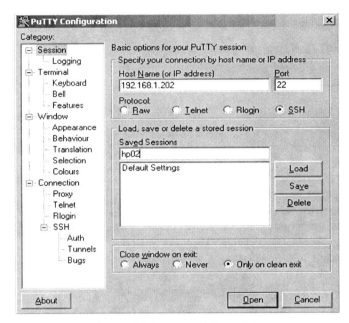

Figure 36-1 PuTTY Interface

36.3.3   Configuring Single Sign-On User Access

Similar to the way user-level trust relationship works for the "r" commands, ssh access can be setup as well for single sign-on (passwordless) user access. The following outlines the step-by-step procedure on how to set this up for *user1* on *hp01*:

1. Login to *hp01* as *user1*.
2. Run the following to create the $HOME/.*ssh* sub-directory along with three files: *id_dsa*, *id_dsa.pub* and *prng_seed* underneath .*ssh*. Press Enter for the three questions asked:

    $ ssh–keygen –t dsa
    Generating public/private dsa key pair.
    Enter file in which to save the key (/home/user1/.ssh/id_dsa):
    . . . .
    Your public key has been saved in /home/user1/.ssh/id_dsa.pub.
    The key fingerprint is:
    7f:21:56:85:70:a8:f6:b9:37:8c:d2:05:cf:10:27:9b user1@hp01

    DSA is an encryption method and stands for *Digital Security Algorithm*. There are a couple of other methods, but DSA is preferred.

3. Change to the .*ssh* sub-directory.
4. Save the key located in the *id_dsa.pub* file into a new file called *authorized_keys*:

    $ cat id_dsa.pub >> authorized_keys

5. Repeat steps 2 through 4 on each system where *user1* requires passwordless access using the *ssh* command. On each system where the *ssh-keygen* command is executed, copy the contents

of *id_dsa.pub* file and append to the *authorized_keys* file on *hp01*. The *authorized_keys* file on *hp01* will eventually contain public authentication keys for all the systems where *ssh-keygen* is run.

$ cat /home/user1/.ssh/authorized_keys

ssh-dss
AAAB3NzaC1kc3MAAACBAPbRCVE820BlPMUNV2VdIKoq/s0tD3hqvIR5z+sarhbbjO218M7i
9AUA6mmvVizC0fxRxIpiNIIdB42H58dK5hvHgeJR/fQTmPkAgvVirXIsJNTfe2x7H7YoV4Fqyn
Em9aG9BuWqxPbVZPty/jawb7mJ9TR+E++k8Xnfnm/lvq5pAAAAFQCuqafHQAz23bQzPJi8HF
YS3SbTbQAAAIB1d3Go+MVEKMs/CbFPItDRowITHlCO/sK6zHnhZhpjY90i5L0EhgbATu2Y2
wImOtZ6BMkeam6sBrdjxj1UtS1vwE9xXjJ3afJBUheVzLjrV4dyaZP6D1P9vjSiBfty/PEQh8gKcql
7rEg+vYBYUao7qRvAL9dSVhEzwNsxApZyiQAAAIEAmiWdn3u7FThSWzbpbd0svu74waYvdq
Fl1Hepj/t23DdLqEBeKsTzslqpx5MSEdgxEIl159zkPdj5PaiD8GCJvJ1+xHBv37ZUVYtY1sDlLSY
Y277T/p0MAEpla73fY8Zgm2ZuadzxuKt5Cx2GGGv2jJH+ZMXtZsNdKxAcRZ2xI= user1@hp01
ssh-dss
AAAAB3NzaC1kc3AAACBAJ2vUeZCBV1nTNJSg8/4vMo+kcrowRDAJzOFM4aokUI5YleFOB
GQrcUwTA+t76j+HNRMkR0375fzf2OjXNcK3jRxJLDUID3aWIp7Ifzh95dHQEvaCV890cIp0IC+
6twapejNLR7gg9dmZglB+3klbNR6qgeI4ddIDFflGHDWA9arAAAAFQD2g7ol+M8XCqqMa0Q
Qqrj/seLnVQAAAB92R3QVPKgv5T7ERWflhrW1rVmJ6X7/davPjoL0PU1ecAmC0zaG5EAwS1
ybZQv4sB0JOcJnloaDWaahb2dYYA2TW6EzDYTXo8tF8CjhTUwo7CA7GMitJZJ7SQ3gQTKY3
GK6c48o14GoWvoAMKxVpneS192kcbvdjmGgm5gAAAIAL3+TEYAhSRdd9LuMHrTEF3FIZV
DqBIMa0nYO5iCLFWRoiLqXqtkz5aJmZSDwhdOEBLd01zDqHEylfVGSXbL2IlFrrm8dSj48utef
uPz8jS/ekAABWQQxg5b52qSksWGW6sicG2sf5a4866Lk8klI+YbnPH9Sq+LIvyg== user1@hp02

6. Ensure that the *authorized_keys* file has 644 permissions. If not, modify them:

   $ chmod 644 authorized_keys

7. Modify permissions on *user1*'s home directory to 755:

   $ chmod 755 $HOME

8. Copy the *authorized_keys* file from *hp01* to *$HOME/.ssh* sub-directory of *user1* on other systems. This way *user1* will have identical file contents for *authorized_keys* across the board.

9. Login as *user1* from *hp01* to *hp02* using the *ssh* command. Answer "yes" to the question asked and supply *user1*'s password:

   $ ssh hp02
   The authenticity of host 'hp02 (192.168.1.202)' can't be established.
   RSA key fingerprint is 25:24:a0:e7:e8:25:96:7d:70:bd:72:db:9b:ff:1c:1b.
   Are you sure you want to continue connecting (yes/no)? **yes**
   Warning: Permanently added 'hp02,192.168.1.202' (RSA) to the list of known hosts.
   Password:
   . . . .

This creates a file called *known_hosts* under *$HOME/.ssh* directory on *hp01*. The *known_hosts* file contains something similar to the following:

```
$ cat /home/user1/.ssh/known_hosts
hp02,192.168.1.202 ssh-rsa
AAAAB3NzaC1yc2EAAAABIwAAAIEAxFjYK353o1fgXMBfySxgPLnhg5oWS+f8nAJx3SO40
pfB3DcA1HLIEV0w2NKmEfgFQYOeoeMfp0IRqYxnyqNo33v3qbRjAxm6emgB2Q0xcUvL55be
m0q6IMEfVn+ycrHsEMu1B1c1pa4b3G1HX1hjcHwp3PA4MmIsyLArRbybWEU=
```

On each subsequent login from *hp01* to *hp02*, this file will be referenced and *user1* will be allowed a passwordless entry into *hp02*.

This completes the procedure for configuring passwordless entry into *hp02* from *hp01* for *user1* for *ssh, scp* and *sftp* commands.

36.3.4   Transferring Files Using scp

To use *scp* to copy *.dtprofile* from *root*'s home directory to */usr/local/etc* directory:

scp $HOME/.dtprofile /usr/local/etc

To use *scp* to copy *.dtprofile* from *root*'s home directory on *hp02* to its home directory on *hp03*, run the following on *hp02*:

scp $HOME/.dtprofile hp03:$HOME

You will be prompted for the user password unless the passwordless authentication is setup.

To use *scp* to copy *.dtprofile* from *root*'s home directory on *hp02* to its home directory on *hp03*, run the following on *hp03*:

scp hp02:$HOME/.dtprofile $HOME

36.3.5   Transferring Files Using sftp

The interfaces of *sftp* and *ftp* are similar. The *sftp* protocol offers more file operation options than does *ftp. sftp* uses encryption methods for user authentication and file transfers.

Here is an example of how to get on to a remote system *hp02* from *hp03*:

sftp hp02
```
Connecting to hp02…
sftp>
```

You will be prompted for the user password unless the passwordless authentication is setup.

Type ? at the *sftp* prompt to list available commands. It will also show what each of these commands does.

```
sftp> ?
Available commands:
cd path                         Change remote directory to 'path'
lcd path                        Change local directory to 'path'
chgrp grp path                  Change group of file 'path' to 'grp'
```

chmod mode path	Change permissions of file 'path' to 'mode'
chown own path	Change owner of file 'path' to 'own'
help	Display this help text
get remote-path [local-path]	Download file
lls [ls-options [path]]	Display local directory listing
ln oldpath newpath	Symlink remote file
lmkdir path	Create local directory
lpwd	Print local working directory
ls [path]	Display remote directory listing
lumask umask	Set local umask to 'umask'
mkdir path	Create remote directory
progress	Toggle display of progress meter
put local-path [remote-path]	Upload file
pwd	Display remote working directory
exit	Quit sftp
quit	Quit sftp
rename oldpath newpath	Rename remote file
rmdir path	Remove remote directory
rm path	Delete remote file
symlink oldpath newpath	Symlink remote file
version	Show SFTP version
!command	Execute 'command' in local shell
!	Escape to local shell
?	Synonym for help

Some of the common commands are *cd/lcd*, *get/put*, *ls/lls*, *pwd/lpwd*, *mkdir/rmdir*, *quit/exit*, *rename* and *rm*.

36.4   Pluggable Authentication Module (PAM)

The *Pluggable Authentication Module* (PAM) is a standard set of library routines that allows using any available authentication service for user authentication, password modification and user account validation purposes. For example, when user authentication is required, the request first goes to PAM which determines the correct verification method to be used and returns an appropriate response. The user authentication methods include the */etc/passwd* file, NIS and trusted mode security. Users and programs that require authentication do not know what method is being used. The PAM framework provides easy integration of additional security technologies into HP-UX system entry commands.

There are two PAM configuration files: */etc/pam.conf* and */etc/pam_user.conf*. The former controls the system-wide user authentication and the latter per-user authentication.

The default */etc/pam.conf* file is shown below:

```
# cat /etc/pam.conf
# PAM configuration
# Authentication management
login        auth     required     /usr/lib/security/libpam_unix.1
su           auth     required     /usr/lib/security/libpam_unix.1

. . . . . . . .
```

```
# Account management
login          account          required          /usr/lib/security/libpam_unix.1
su             account          required          /usr/lib/security/libpam_unix.1

. . . . . . . .
# Session management
login          session          required          /usr/lib/security/libpam_unix.1
dtlogin        session          required          /usr/lib/security/libpam_unix.1

. . . . . . . .
# Password management
login          password         required          /usr/lib/security/libpam_unix.1
passwd         password         required          /usr/lib/security/libpam_unix.1

. . . . . . . .
```

There are four security mechanisms defined in the file for authenticating users: *authentication management*, *account management*, *session management* and *password management*.

Authentication management authenticates a user, *account management* determines if a user's account is valid by checking password and password aging attributes, *session management* establishes and terminates user login sessions and *password management* changes a user's password.

Each line under the four authentication management headings contain five columns. The first column depicts the name of the service such as login, ftp, etc. The second column categorizes the module in one of the four authentication mechanisms. The third column tells how to control more than one definition for the same service: "required", "optional" or "sufficient" keywords can be used. The fourth column lists pathname to the library file to be used to implement the service. The last column is optional and may contain options such as "debug" and "nowarn".

This file must be owned by *root* with 444 permissions.

The default */etc/pam_user.conf* file is shown below:

cat /etc/pam_user.conf

```
. . . . . . . .
# user_name  module_type  module_path options
# For example:
# user_a       auth             /usr/lib/security/libpam_unix.1    debug
# user_a       auth             /usr/lib/security/libpam_dce.1     try_first_pass
# user_a       password         /usr/lib/security/libpam_unix.1    debug
. . . . . . . .
```

This file consists of four columns. The first column contains name of the user, the second column categorizes the service, the third column lists pathname to the library file to be used to implement the service and the last column specifies any options to be used. The second, third and the fourth columns in this file correspond to the second, third and the fourth columns in the */etc/pam.conf* file.

SMH can be used to control system-wide PAM configuration. Follow the links below:

☞ Go to SMH → Auditing and Security → Authenticated Commands. Add, remove or modify a service as desired.

36.5   HP-UX Bastille

HP-UX Bastille is a security hardening and lockdown tool that enhances the system security by implementing various levels of hardening. Some of the hardening tasks that can be performed are:

- ✓ Securing setuid files.
- ✓ Securing user logins and *cron*.
- ✓ Turning off unneeded *inetd* services.
- ✓ Making sendmail, FTP server, Apache web server and DNS more secure.
- ✓ Performing security configuration actions.
- ✓ Configuring an IPFilter-based firewall.

This tool can be integrated with HP System Insight Manager.

HP-UX Bastille can generate reports on system security configuration and allows you to compare current system security settings with saved settings.

36.5.1   Key HP-UX Bastille Files

Several files – configuration, error logs, action logs – are involved when working with HP-UX Bastille. These files are listed and explained in Table 36-2.

File	Description
/etc/opt/sec_mgmt/bastille/config	Configuration file that includes answers to the most recently saved session.
/var/opt/sec_mgmt/bastille/log/error-log	Logs errors generated during executing *bastille*.
/var/opt/sec_mgmt/bastille/log/action-log	Includes steps taken during executing *bastille*.
/var/opt/sec_mgmt/bastille/TODO.txt	Includes manual actions that need to be performed to ensure a secure configuration.
/var/opt/sec_mgmt/bastille/revert/revert-actions	Includes a list of files that were changed when HP-UX Bastille was run.
/var/opt/sec_mgmt/bastille/TOREVERT.txt	Includes manual actions to be performed to finish the revert process.
Under */var/opt/sec_mgmt/bastille/log/Assessment* directory: *assessment-report.html* *assessment-report.txt* *assessment-report-log.txt*	Assessment reports in HTML and txt formats.
/var/opt/sec_mgmt/bastille/log/Assessment/Drift.txt	Includes information about any configuration drift the system had experienced since HP-UX Bastille was last run.

Table 36-2 Key Bastille Files

36.5.2   Working with HP-UX Bastille

HP-UX Bastille may be run interactively using the *bastille* command or non-interactively via GUI. Several options are available with the command and are explained as part of the examples below.

To lockdown an HP-UX system by creating a security configuration file or apply an existing one using GUI, run the *bastille* command. The command will display some messages and bring up the GUI as shown in Figure 36-2.

bastille
NOTE: Valid display found; defaulting to Tk (X) interface.
NOTE: Using Tk user interface module.
NOTE: Only displaying questions relevant to the current configuration.
NOTE: Bastille is scanning the system configuration...
. . . .

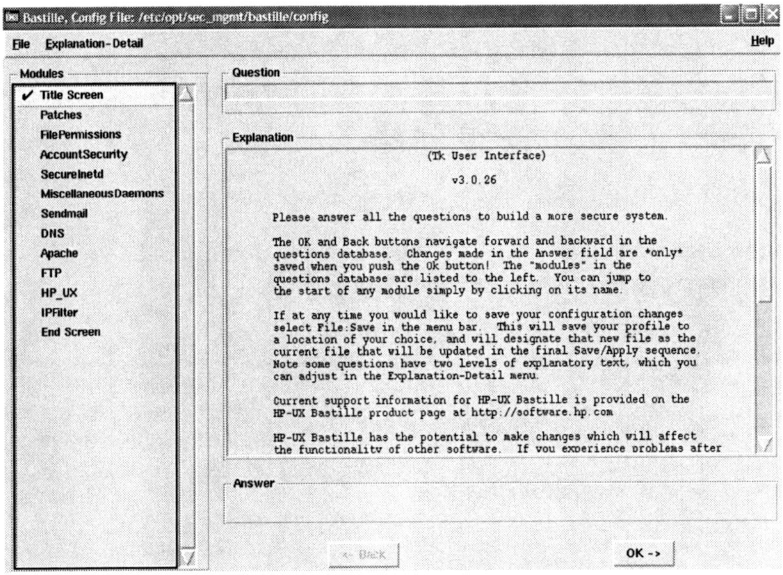

Figure 36-2 Bastille GUI

To apply security settings on the system defined in a security configuration file such as */etc/opt/sec_mgmt/bastille/configs/defaults/SIM.config*. The –b option runs the command in batch mode.

bastille –b –f /etc/opt/sec_mgmt/bastille/configs/defaults/SIM.config
NOTE: Entering Critical Code Execution.
        Bastille has disabled keyboard interrupts.
NOTE: Bastille is scanning the system configuration...
NOTE: Bastille is now locking down your system in accordance with your
        answers in /etc/opt/sec_mgmt/bastille/configs/defaults/SIM.config.
        Please be patient as some modules may take a number of minutes,
        depending on the speed of your machine.
NOTE: Executing File Permissions Specific Configuration
. . . .

To generate reports on security configuration status and display in Mozilla browser (Figure 36-3), use the --assess option. Use the –n option to suppress license information.

bastille –n --assess

NOTE: Using audit user interface module.

NOTE: Bastille is scanning the system configuration...

NOTE: Bastille Hardening Assessment Completed.

You can find a report in HTML format at:

. /var/opt/sec_mgmt/bastille/log/Assessment/assessment-report.html

You can find a report in text format at:

. /var/opt/sec_mgmt/bastille/log/Assessment/assessment-report.txt

You can find a "config" file that will, on the same HP-UX version, similar installed-application set, and configuration, lock-down the Bastille-relevant items that Bastille had completely locked-down on this system below (see html or text report for full detail). In cases where the systems differ, the config file may be either a) contain extra questions not relevant to the destination system, or b), be missing questions needed on the remote system. Bastille will inform you in the first case, and in the second case error. It will then give you an opportunity to answer the missing questions or remove the extra ones in the graphical interface:

. /var/opt/sec_mgmt/bastille/log/Assessment/assessment-log.config

NOTE: Launching /opt/mozilla/mozilla to display report.

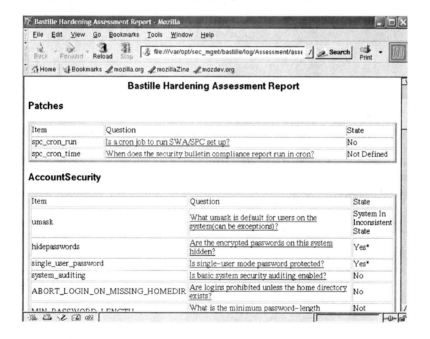

Figure 36-3 Bastille Hardening Assessment Report

To create a baseline and compare the current state of the system with it, use the *bastille_drift* command. The first instance below creates a baseline and saves it to the */etc/opt/sec_mgmt/bastille/sec_config_saved_1* file and the second command compares the current system security configuration with it:

```
# bastille_drift --save_baseline /etc/opt/sec_mgmt/bastille/sec_config_saved_1
NOTE:   Beginning Bastille configuration assessment. This may take a few
        minutes depending on system speed.
NOTE:   Saving baseline to:   /etc/opt/sec_mgmt/bastille/sec_config_saved_1
# bastille_drift --from_baseline /etc/opt/sec_mgmt/bastille/sec_config_saved_1
NOTE:   Beginning Bastille configuration assessment. This may take a few
        minutes depending on system speed.
NOTE:   No drift in bastille security configuration since baseline:
        /etc/opt/sec_mgmt/bastille/sec_config_saved_1.
```

To revert the system security configuration to the pre-Bastille state:

```
# bastille –r
NOTE:   Reverting system state...
. . . . . . . .
```

36.6   Other Security Monitoring, Hardening & Reporting Tools

Several built-in HP-UX and third-party security tools are available that can be employed to enhance the security of a system. These tools include HIDS, IPFilter, Crack, COPS, ISS and SATAN, and are described briefly in the following paragraphs.

36.6.1   HP-UX HIDS

Host Intrusion Detection System (HIDS) is a client/server tool that monitors one or more systems and detects unauthorized access attempts, possible attacks and other suspicious activities that might cause damage to the system(s). HIDS gathers security information from all configured systems and displays results graphically. Some of the activities that HIDS monitors include unauthorized access to system and application programs and their associated configuration and log files, unwanted file additions, deletions and modifications by non-owners, and creation of unnecessary setuid programs and public writable files.

36.6.2   HP-UX IPFilter Firewall

HP-UX *IPFilter* provides system firewall capabilities by filtering IP packets to control traffic in and out of the system.

36.6.3   HP-UX IPSec

HP-UX *IPSec* (IP Security) is a suite of protocols that provides security for IP networks at the host level. The security includes data integrity and authentication to prevent unauthorized creation, modification and removal of transmitted data, data privacy by encrypting data and remote system's identity authentication.

36.6.4   Crack

Crack identifies dictionary-based crackable passwords, and allows to configure different types of password guesses.

36.6.5   COPS

Computer Oracle and Password System (COPS) is a collection of tools that gathers operating system security weaknesses and generates reports for review. In some cases, it automatically fixes one or more weaknesses. It can be configured to send alerts.

36.6.6   ISS

Internet Security Scan (ISS) checks for a number of known security holes such as problems with sendmail and improperly configured NFS.

36.6.7   SATAN

Security Administrators Tool for Analyzing Networks (SATAN) gathers network security weaknesses and generates reports for review.

36.7   Common System Hardening Best Practices

Some HP-UX system hardening best practices are listed below. Many of them have been covered earlier in the book. Not all of these need to be configured on every system, but implementing the ones that suit requirements ensure a safer and more protected system against unknown and outside threats. Before applying any of these, make certain that it does not impact any application functionality.

1.   Convert the system to trusted mode coupled with password aging, or implement the shadow password mechanism with password aging. Force users to change passwords periodically.
2.   Disable or remove dormant user accounts.
3.   Disable the use of the *write* command by defining "mesg –n" in system-wide user profiles.
4.   Create hidden home directory such as */.root* for *root* user with 700 permissions.
5.   Set the umask value to 077 in *root*'s *.profile.*
6.   Set TMOUT variable in *root*'s *.profile* to 600 for instance. This will force *root* to log off if it has been idle for 600 seconds.
7.   Check the contents of the */etc/passwd* and */etc/group* files periodically using the *pwck* and *grpck* commands, for any discrepancies including non-*root* users with UID 0 and users with no passwords and home directories.
8.   Check log files such as */var/adm/sulog, /var/adm/wtmps, /etc/utmps, /var/adm/btmps* on a regular basis for user login activities.
9.   Set 644 permissions on the */var/adm/btmps, /var/adm/wtmps* and */etc/utmps* files.
10. Disable server daemons such as *telnet, rlogin, remsh* and *ftp* in the */etc/inetd.conf* file, or control their access via */var/adm/inetd.sec.*
11. Disable *telnet* and *ftp*, and use *ssh, scp* and *sftp* instead. Perform enough due diligence prior to disabling these services. Many applications rely on them.
12. Disable network services such as *rexec, ident, rusers, finger, tftp, bootps, instl_bootd, uucp, ntalk* and *rpc.ttdbserver* in the */etc/inetd.conf* file if they are not used.
13. Disable network services such as *rbootd, routed, mrouted, gated* and *rdpd* in the */etc/rc.config.d/netdaemons* file if they are not used.
14. If *ftpd* must be used, edit the */etc/ftpd/ftpusers* file and list system usernames such as *root, uucp, nuucp, sys, lp, hpdb, www, webadmin, smbnull, nobody, adm, bin* and *daemon* to prevent them from using *ftp*.

15. Maintain and monitor *$HOME/.rhosts* and */etc/hosts.equiv* files. These files are referenced by *remsh, rlogin, rcp* and *rexec* utilities for passwordless entry into the system. Discourage the use of this trust mechanism especially for the *root* user. Use *ssh* instead.
16. Enable *inetd* logging.
17. Disable direct *root* login. The *root* user should only be allowed to login at the system console. Create */etc/securetty* file with 400 permissions and define "console" in it to disable the access via *telnet*. Update */etc/opt/sshd/sshd_config* file and define "PermitRootLogin no" in it to disable the access via *ssh*.
18. Control the usage of setuid and setgid programs. Use the *find* command to list all files owned by *root* that have setuid and setgid bits set. Analyze the file usage and unset the bits if not needed.
19. Set 777 permissions and sticky bit on world-writeable directories such as */tmp* and */var/tmp*.
20. Disable NFS client, NFS server, PC NFS server and AutoFS functionalities in the */etc/rc.config.d/nfsconf* file. Ensure they are not in use before disabling. If the NFS server functionality must be used, make certain that the shared resources are only available to the specific systems that need access to them.
21. Disable the use of NIS unless there is a dire need to use it.
22. Control the use of *cron* and *at* via user entries in *cron.allow, cron.deny, at.allow* and *at.deny* files in the */var/adm/cron* directory. If *at* is not used, remove the *at.** files. Remove *cron.deny* and update *cron.allow* file with entries for only those users that must require *cron* scheduling.
23. Protect physical access to the system and system console.
24. Change the password for the *Admin* MP user.
25. Implement the use of *sudo*. Force system administrators to login with their user IDs and use *sudo* to run privileged commands. Allow *sudo* access to limited privileged commands to application and database administrators. Update the */etc/sudoers* file accordingly.
26. Implement IPSec and IPFilter to secure IP packets transmitted over the network.
27. Execute security vulnerability tests on a regular basis via *cron* and analyze reports generated.
28. Use Bastille to harden and lockdown the system.
29. Execute software assistant to identify and install missing security patches and updates.

Summary

This chapter discussed various ways of securing an HP-UX system. You looked at the concept of identity management. You understood password aging and set it up on user accounts. You learned benefits associated with shadow password and how to implement it and reverse its implementation.

You looked at benefits associated with using secure shell and how it encrypted information. You saw how to access a remote HP-UX machine via ssh and setup single sign-on for users. You learned the usage of two key ssh file transfer utilities called scp and sftp. You looked at Pluggable Authentication Module and associated benefits, and how to configure its files for authentication purposes.

HP-UX Bastille and IPFilter firewall were two other security tools discussed in the chapter.

At the end of the chapter, a few security monitoring, hardening and reporting tools were discussed. Finally, you were supplied with a list of common system security recommendations that you should look at implementing on your HP-UX systems to elevate security level.

Appendix A – CSA Exam Review Questions

This appendix covers sample questions for HP Certified Systems Administrator exam HP0-A01. Answers to these questions are given in Appendix B. I recommend that you first read and understand the material in this book thoroughly and then take this quiz.

1. What benefit would you get by adding a journal to a file system?

   A. Automatic defragmentation B. Better buffer cache utilization   C. Faster recovery time
   D. Guaranteed data integrity   E. Provides an audit trail

2. Which LVM structure holds a file system?

   A. Volume group   B. VGRA   C. Physical volume   D. Logical volume

3. Why do you use the su command?

   A. To log out of the system   B. To shutdown the system
   C. To switch user id   D. To display a list of logged in users

4. What command is used to display your current group?

   A. newgroup   B. id   C. who   D. whoami

5. Which key combination is used for command line completion in the POSIX shell?

   A. <tab> <tab>   B. <esc> <k>   C. <esc> <esc>   D. <up arrow> <up arrow>

6. Which command determines disks attached to a SCSI controller?

   A. diskinfo   B. lsdev   C. cat /etc/scsiconf   D. pvdisplay   E. ioscan

7. What does the PATH variable contain?

   A. Directories you can cd into
   B. Access paths to a disk
   C. Directory search order when using the find command
   D. Directory search order used when locating a command for execution

8. What is the purpose of the MAC address?

   A. Identifies a LAN interface   B. Points to a location in physical system memory
   C. Controls the processor   D. Locates a block of data on a disk

9. Which THREE ways can you boot a system to install HP-UX?

   A. An NFS mounted file system   B. LAN   C. DVD
   D. Tape   E. IDE drive   F. Mirrored disk

10. Why do you use the CIFS software product?

   A. To share directories between Windows and Mainframe computers

B. To share directories between UNIX and Mainframe computers
C. To share directories between UNIX and Windows systems
D. None of the above

11. What Online JFS command is used to increase the size of a file system without unmounting it?

    A. fsadm   B. lvextend   C. extendfs   D. fsextend

12. Which of the following TWO file transfer protocols are used by the Ignite-UX server?

    A. FTP   B. TFTP   C. NFS   D. CIFS

13. List THREE advantages of Online JFS product.

    A. It can extend the size of a file system online.   B. It defragments a file system automatically.
    C. It can reduce a file system size online.   D. It can increase a logical volume size online.
    E. None of the above.

14. What is the main difference between PCI and PCI-X cards?

    A. PCI-X cards are smaller than PCI cards.
    B. PCI cards are smaller than PCI-X cards.
    C. PCI cards are faster than PCI-X cards (almost double speed).
    D. PCI-X cards are faster than PCI cards (almost double speed).

15. What additional benefit do scp and sftp commands provide over cp and ftp commands?

    A. Enhanced security   B. Enhanced speed
    C. Enhanced command line options   D. None of the above

16. Why quoting is used in shell scripts?

    A. To treat special characters as regular characters   B. To ensure uppercase letters are displayed
    C. To set command substitution   D. To highlight special characters

17. Which of the following extracts all lines from a file that do not contain the specified pattern?

    A. egrep –v pattern filename   B. grep -v pattern filename
    C. grep –n pattern filename   D. fgrep -v pattern filename

18. How would you rename "scripts1" directory to "scripts2" in the present working directory?

    A. ln scripts1 scripts2   B. ren scripts1 scripts2
    C. mv scripts1 scripts2   D. mv scripts2 scripts1

19. What does the command chown do?

    A. Changes user id
    B. Makes you the owner of all files in your home directory
    C. Changes the time stamp on a file or directory
    D. Changes the ownership of a file or directory

20. What signifies the end of an "if" statement in the POSIX Shell?

    A. endif   B. fi   C. }   D. elseif

21. The "break" command in the POSIX shell is used to break out of a:

    A. Shell script   B. Function   C. Loop   D. Sleep routine

22. How would you capture the result of the who and the date commands into a variable called VAR in the POSIX Shell?

    A. VAR=$(who|date)   B. VAR=$(who;date)
    C. VAR=$(who,date)   D. Who>VAR;date>VAR

23. What key in the POSIX shell when repeated twice completes file names?

    A. [space]   B. *   C. [ESC]   D. [TAB]

24. What command counts the number of lines in a file?

    A. fcount   B. wc   C. wordc   D. grep

25. As the root user, what command would you use to influence the priority that a command runs at?

    A. pri   B. priority   C. nice   D. chpri

26. HP-UX _____ swap space for each new process spawned.

    A. Frees   B. Builds   C. Locks   D. Reserves

27. On an HP-UX system the command to view disk space utilization is:

    A. freedisk   B. scandisk   C. bdf   D. diskinfo

28. Which command lists full details of a DSF?

    A. lssf   B. lsdev   C. listsf   D. ls

29. Software Distributor will only run if the following daemon is running:

    A. swinstalld   B. swagent   C. swlogd   D. swagentd

30. Can a user define a default printer for himself (separate from the system's default printer)?

    A. Yes, using SMH   B. Yes, using the lpadmin command
    C. Yes, using the LPDEST environmental variable   D. No

31. The command to submit a cron job is?

    A. cronfile   B. crontab   C. cron.allow   D. /usr/sbin/cron

32. If you create a sub-directory "custom" under /etc/skel, which contains a file "config", then new user accounts created via SMH will:

    A. Contain a symbolic link (symlink) to this file structure
    B. Have a local file ~/config, which is read-only for the account owner
    C. Not have any access to the file "custom"
    D. Have a local file ~/custom/config

33. The which command is used to determine:

    A. The current version and release of an executable
    B. Pseudo terminal your session is running from
    C. The absolute path where an executable is executed
    D. Compiler options used to create an executable

34. The main function of the hpux utility is to:

    A. Load the kernel into memory   B. List the /stand directory contents

C. Execute ISL   D. Rebuild the kernel

35. What command is used to create the whatis database to facilitate keyword search in man pages?

     A. catman   B. man –k   C. echo $MANPATH   D. All of the above

36. Which of the THREE are the main components of an HP-UX system?

     A. Kernel   B. Directory structure   C. Shell   D. User

37. Which of the following are features of HP-UX? Choose THREE.

     A. Multitasking   B. Single user   C. Time sharing   D. Multiuser

38. Which of the following can be used to login to an HP-UX system?

     A. At the CDE console   B. Using the telnet command
     C. At the system console   D. Using the ssh command   E. All of the above

39. What component of the HP-UX structure a user interacts with?

     A. Directory structure   B. Kernel   C. Shell   D. All of the above

40. True or False. A user password is case-insensitive.

     A. True   B. False

41. What is the default length of a user password?

     A. 10 characters   B. 6-8 characters   C. 6-10 characters   D. 7 characters

42. Can a normal user change other users' passwords?

     A. Yes   B. No

43. Match items on the left with description on the right.

     A. nPar   1. software partition that allows to run HP-UX, Linux & Windows
     B. vPar   2. software partition that allows for sharing
     C. Integrity VM   3. hardware partition that allows for electrical isolation
     D. secure resource partition   4. software partition that allows sharing cpu / memory

44. Which directory software come standard with HP-UX 11i v3? Choose TWO.

     A. LDAP-UX integration   B. NIS   C. Red Hat   D. Netscape

45. Which command is used to change a user password?

     A. passwd   B. password   C. pass   D. None of the above

46. How many arguments are in "cal 12 2008" command?

     A. 3   B. 2   C. 1   D. 0

47. The pwd command:

     A. Changes directory path   B. Displays current absolute directory path
     C. Displays current relative directory path   D. Both A and B

48. Where does "cd ~user2" takes you if you run it as user1?

     A. To user1's home directory   B. To user2's home directory
     C. To user2 sub-directory under user1's home directory   D. To root user's home directory

49. What information do logname and whoami commands return?

   A. Home directory path   B. Login information
   C. UID   D. Username

50. Which command only displays a user's group memberships?

   A. id   B. id –a   C. groups   D. usermod

51. Which commands display hardware model of a system? Choose TWO.

   A. model   B. system   C. getconf   D. id

52. Which of the following shows the current system run level?

   A. rwho   B. who   C. uptime   D. who –r

53. Which command compares two text files and displays the differences?

   A. comp   B. diff   C. differ   D. All of the above

54. Which command enables you to view the syntax of the /etc/passwd file?

   A. man 4 passwd   B. man passwd   C. man –k passwd   D. help passwd

55. If lost+found directory is removed, what is the recommended method for recreating it.

   A. mkdir lost+found   B. touch lost+found   C. mklost+found   D. mkdir l+f

56. Which directory is typically used to hold additional software products installed on the system?

   A. /opt   B. /var   C. /etc   D. /usr

57. What is the default location where user home directories are created?

   A. /export/home   B. /home   C. /usr   D. /usr/home

58. Is the path /home/user1/dir1/scripts1 absolute or relative?

   A. Absolute   B. Relative

59. Which command returns the type of file?

   A. filetype   B. filename   C. file   D. type

60. What information does the inode of a symlink contain?

   A. Nothing   B. The creation time of the linked file
   C. The name of the linked file   D. The path to the linked file

61. What type of file contains major and minor numbers in its inode?

   A. Regular file   B. Named pipe   C. Directory file   D. Device File

62. What is the maximum number of alphanumeric characters that a file or directory name can contain?

   A. 128   B. 8   C. 256   D. 255

63. What option with the ls command is used to list hidden files?

   A. –d   B. –l   C. –a   D. –h

64. To create a file of size zero, which command would you use.

A. touch   B. vi   C. cat   D. edit

65. To view all lines in a file beginning line number 100 and onwards, which command would you run.

    A. tail filename   B. tail +100 filename   C. tail –100 filename   D. tail 100 filename

66. Which command displays the legible contents of a non-text file?

    A. strings   B. cat   C. view   D. vi

67. The grep command is used to display lines in a file that match a certain pattern. What modifications does the grep command make in the file?

    A. None   B. Removes the matched lines from the file
    C. Removes the file contents   D. Modifies the file

68. What is not a criteria for finding a file using the find command?

    A. Modification time   B. hostname   C. Directory name   D. File name

69. Can you link files or directories across file systems using symlink?

    A. Yes   B. No

70. Can you link two directories using hard link?

    A. Yes   B. No

71. In vi, which of the following would you use to copy 5 lines and paste them above cursor position?

    A. 5yyP   B. 5yyp   C. 5pyy   D. yy5P

72. What two modes are available to modify file permissions? Choose TWO.

    A. chmod   B. symbolic   C. chown   D. octal

73. To modify permissions on a file to get 751, which of the following would you run? Choose TWO.

    A. chmod +751 filename   B. chmod rwxr-x--x filename
    C. chmod u+rwxrxx filename   D. chmod 751 filename

74. What is the default umask value in HP-UX?

    A. 022   B. 027   C. 000   D. 777

75. What option would you use with the umask command to display umask value in symbolic notation?

    A. –A   B. –B   C. –S   D. –s

76. Which of the following are the default permissions on files and directories?

    A. 777 on files and 666 on directories   B. 666 on files and 777 on directories
    C. 777 on both files and directories   D. 666 on both files and directories

77. What command is used to change a user's primary group temporarily?

    A. chgrp   B. newgrp   C. chsh   D. newgroup

78. What two commands are used to change file ownership and group membership? Choose TWO.

    A. chown   B. chgrp   C. chowner   D. chgroup

79. To prevent users from removing other users' files in a public directory, what would you do?

A. Set setuid bit on the directory   B. Set setgid bit on the directory
C. Set setpid bit on the directory   D. Set sticky bit on the directory

80. Which option with the chmod command enables you to set permissions recursively?

    A. –R   B. –A   C. –r   D. –a

81. To search for all files in the /usr file system with setgid bit set, which of the following would you run?

    A. find /usr –perm 1000   B. find /usr –perm 2000
    C. fine /usr –perm 4000   D. find /usr –perm 4000 –exec rm {} \;

82. Which sftp command would upload several files in a directory?

    A. mput   B. mget   C. uput   D. get

83. Which new feature has potentially improved performance in HP-UX 11i v3?

    A. native multipathing   B. persistent DSFs   C. agile addressing   D. legacy DSFs

84. If the size of a LUN is increased, which command would you use to reflect the change in LVM?

    A. vgchange   B. vgmodify   C. vgextend   D. vgcreate

85. What does]] do in the vi editor?

    A. Takes you to the start of the line   B. Takes you to the first line of the file
    C. Takes you to the end of the line   D. Takes you to the last line of the file

86. What commands are available in the vi editor to get you to the edit mode?

    A. A, a, I, i, o and O   B. A, I and O   C. a, i and o   D. Append, Insert and Open

87. Which command in the vi editor removes a character preceding the current cursor position?

    A. R   B. x   C. X   D. r

88. What does the following do in vi?

    :%s/hpux/HP-UX/g

    A. Replaces the next occurrence of "hpux" with "HP-UX"
    B. Replaces all occurrences of "hpux" with "HP-UX" in the entire file
    C. Replaces all occurrences of "HP-UX" with "hpux" in the entire file
    D. Replaces the previous occurrence of "hpux" with "HP-UX"

89. What does $0 represent with the awk command?

    A. The command name   B. The first command line argument
    C. All command line arguments   D. The last command line argument

90. What does the following sed command do?

    sed –n '/root/p' /etc/group

    A. Displays lines from the /etc/group file containing the pattern root
    B. Displays lines from the /etc/group file not containing the pattern root
    C. Hides lines from the /etc/group file containing the pattern root
    D. Displays lines in duplicate from the /etc/group file containing the pattern "root"

91. Which option is used with the sed command to perform multiple edits in a file?

A. –e   B. –I   C. –s   D. –E

92. Which is the default shell in HP-UX?

    A. Bourne   B. POSIX   C. BASH   D. Korn

93. Which of the following is used to display the value contained in the variable EDITOR?

    A. display $EDITOR   B. display EDITOR   C. echo EDITOR   D. echo $EDITOR

94. Which of the following is not a pre-defined environment variable?

    A. HOME   B. LOGNAME   C. NAME   D.TZ

95. Which of the following alters your primary command prompt to look like the following? Choose TWO.

    < user2@hp01:/usr/bin >

    A. PS2="< `logname`@`hostname`:\$PWD >"   B. PS1="< $LOGNAME@`hostname`:\$PWD >"
    C. PS2="< $LOGNAME@`hostname`:\$PWD >"   D. PS1="< `logname`@`hostname`:\$PWD >"

96. Which symbol redirects error messages to alternate location?

    A. #   B. | C. <   D. >

97. Which command is used to unset an alias?

    A. unsetalias   B. unalias   C. alias rm   D. unset alias

98. What does a pipe do?

    A. Takes the output of one command and pass it as input to the next command
    B. Takes the input from one command and pass it as input to the next command
    C. Takes the output from two files and pass it as input to the next command
    D. None of the above

99. Which command is used to change the priority of a running process?

    A. renicing   B. nice   C. renice   D. niceagain

100. Which of the following are immune to hangup signals? Choose TWO.

    A. nohup cp –rp /dir1 /dir2 &   B. nohup cp /dir1 /dir2 &
    C. cp –rp /dir1 /dir2 &   D. nohup rcp –rp /dir1 server2:/dir2 &

101. Which character when specified at the end of a command runs the command in background?

    A. @   B. %   C. $ D. &

102. Which of the following is not a system administrator resource?

    A. docs.hp.com   B. help.com   C. Online man pages   D. itrc.hp.com

103. How would you run SMH in restricted mode?

    A. smh   B. smh &   C. smh –restricted   D. smh –r

104. Which directory is the samlog file located in?

    A. /var/adm/sam   B. /var/adm/sam/log   C. /var/sam/log   D. /var/adm/log

105. Which command is used to view sam log?

A. sam_view   B. samlog_view   C. samlog_viewer   D. samview

106. What major hardware series capable of running HP-UX are available? Choose TWO.

A. HP Proliant   B. HP Netfinity   C. HP 9000   D. HP Integrity

107. Which feature of HP-UX allows you to replace a PCI card online?

A. PCI/R   B. Card/R   C. OLRAD   D. A/R

108. What is the number of slots in a Superdome PCI I/O chassis?

A. 8   B. 4   C. 12   D. 16

109. What is the maximum number of processors that can be installed on a single cell board?

A. 8   B. 4   C. 16   D. 12

110. What is the minimum and maximum number of node partitions that an HP-UX server can have?

A. 2 and 16   B. 2 and 8   C. 1 and 8   D. 1 and 16

111. What is the maximum number of virtual partitions that an HP-UX server can have?

A. 32   B. 64   C. 128   D. 1

112. What does the CLAIMED status under 'S/W State' of the ioscan command mean? Choose TWO.

A. The software driver for the device is properly bound to it
B. The software driver for the device is not properly bound to it
C. The device is available for use
D. Both A and B

113. Which option with the ioscan command reads and displays device information from running kernel?

A. –H   B. –f   C. –r   D. –k

114. Which option with ioscan command displays logical device file associated with a device?

A. –m   B. –n   C. –k   D. –l

115. Which directories under /dev hold device files for tape devices? Choose TWO.

A. rmt   B. mt   C. rtape   D. tape

116. Major number points to the device driver in the kernel. True or False?

A. True   B. False

117. What kind of information the minor number points to?

A. It points to the type of device
B. It lists a specific device within a category of devices
C. It points to a specific device within a category of devices
D. None of the above

118. Which command displays major numbers for device drivers configured into the kernel?

A. lsview   B. lsdev   C. ioscan   D. lanscan

119. Which of the commands can be used to create device files? Choose THREE.

A. mksf   B. insf   C. mkfs   D. mknod

120. Which command displays diagnostic messages?

    A. dmesg   B. ioscan   C. lsdev   D. lssf

121. HP-UX 11i v3 runs on both HP 9000 and HP Integrity architecture systems. True or False?

    A. True   B. False

122. HP-UX 11i v1 runs on both HP 9000 and HP Integrity architecture systems. True or False?

    A. True   B. False

123. HP Online JFS and MirrorDisk/UX software are included in which OE bundles. Choose TWO.

    A. Foundation OE   B. Enterprise OE   C. Mission Critical OE   D. Both A and C

124. HP Serviceguard software is part of which operating environment software bundle? Choose THREE.

    A. Mission Critical OE   B. Enterprise OE   C. Foundation OE
    D. DC-OE   E. VSE-OE   F. HA-OE

125. Management Processor is also called?

    A. Guardian System Performance   B. Guardian System Processing
    C. General Service Processor   D. Guardian Service Processor

126. Which command at the BCH level on the HP 9000 PA-RISC machine is used to find and display all possible bootable devices?

    A. fi   B. find   C. search   D. se

127. When can network parameters be configured on a new system?

    A. At the installation time
    B. Using set_parms initial after the installation
    C. Using SMH before the installation
    D. Both A and B

128. What is the default primary swap partition size?

    A. Same as the size of system's physical memory   B. Twice the size of system's physical memory
    C. Half the size of system's physical memory   D. Four times the size of system's physical memory

129. By default, HP-UX installation program creates eight logical volumes in vg00 – /, /usr, /var, swap, /tmp, /home, /opt and /stand. True or False?

    A. True   B. False

130. Which command would print the hierarchy of running processes?

    A. ph   B. phierarchy   C. processtree   D. ptree

131. HP Software Distributor is not a client/server software. True or False?

    A. True   B. False

132. At what system run levels does the HP software distributor run?

    A. Power off mode   B. Multiuser mode   C. Single user mode   D. Both B and C

133. What is the smallest unit of software management with SD-UX?

A. Sub-product B. Product C. Bundle D. Fileset

134. What is the location in the directory hierarchy of the Installed Product Database?

A. /var/sw/products B. /var/adm/products
C. /var/adm/sw/products D. /var/adm/sw/software

135. Which SD-UX command uses IPD to search and display installed software information?

A. swlist B. swverify C. swinstall D. swconfig

136. Protected software require customer ID and codeword to be installed. True or False.

A. True B. False

137. What are the two SD-UX agents that make SD-UX utilities to work? Choose TWO.

A. swagent B. swd C. swagentd D. swagentdaemon

138. Which is not an SD-UX command?

A. swpackage B. swinstall C. swunreg D. swreg

139. Where is the HP-UX daemon log file located in the directory hierarchy?

A. /var/adm/sw B. /var/adm/sw/products C. /var/adm/products D. /var/sw/products

140. Which of the two methods can be used to stop the swagentd daemon? Choose TWO.

A. swagentd –k B. swagentd –s C. /sbin/init.d/swagentd shut D. /sbin/init.d/swagentd stop

141. By default, the swlist command displays the following software component:

A. Bundle B. Product C. Sub-product D. Fileset

142. Which is the correct method of using the swinstall command to load software called soft1 located in the depot /opt/depots?

A. swinstall –s soft1 B. swinstall soft1 –s
C. swinstall /opt/depots/soft1 –s D. swinstall –s /opt/depots

143. Which commands are used to package, unconfigure and verify software? Choose THREE.

A. swpackage B. swunconfig C. swconfig D. swverify

144. What is the equivalent of IPD in depot?

A. Software files B. Software installation files C. Log files D. Catalog files

145. Which command copies the perl software from DVD to /opt/depot depot?

A. swcopy –s /dvdrom perl @ /opt/depot B. swcopy –d /dvdrom @ /opt/depot
C. swcopy –s /dvdrom perl –d /opt/depot D. swcopy –p /dvdrom –d /opt/depot

146. Which SD-UX command is used to unregister a software depot?

A. No need to unregister B. swunreg C. swreg D. Either B or C can be used

147. Which command displays all software depots located on the remote system hp02?

A. swlist –l depot @ hp02 B. swlist depot @ hp02
C. swlist –l depots @ hp02 D. swlist –l depot –d hp02

148. Which command removes all software from the /var/depot depot and unregisters it?

A. swremove –d* –d /var/depot
B. swremove –d * @ /var/depot
C. swremove –r * @ /var/depot
D. swremove * –r @ /var/depot

149. What three commands are typically used for user account management? Choose THREE.

A. useradd
B. usermod
C. userrem
D. userdel

150. Hows many fields does the /etc/passwd file contain?

A. Six
B. Seven
C. Eight
D. Nine

151. A user password is saved in encrypted form. How many characters does it contain?

A. 8
B. 11
C. 13
D. 15

152. What permissions should the /etc/passwd file have?

A. 444
B. 555
C. 440
D. 400

153. How many fields do the /etc/group file line entries contain?

A. 3
B. 4
C. 5
D. 6

154. Which commands are used to find syntax errors and verify the consistency of the /etc/passwd and /etc/group files? Choose TWO.

A. passwdck
B. groupck
C. grpck
D. pwck

155. To lock the /etc/passwd file while editing, which command would you use to open it?

A. vi /etc/passwd –l
B. pwvi
C. vi –l /etc/passwd
D. vipw

156. What is the impact of using the –o option with the useradd command?

A. Prevents from assigning duplicate GIDs
B. Allows assigning duplicate GIDs
C. Prevents from assigning duplicate UIDs
D. Allows assigning duplicate UIDs

157. Which of the following command creates a user account called user5 with UID 105, belonging to primary group dba, and secondary groups dba1 and unixadm. The user should have /usr/bin/sh with a new home directory created in /home?

A. useradd –u 105 –g dba –G dba1,unixadm –m –d /home/user5 –s /usr/bin/sh user5
B. useradd –u 105 –g dba,dba1,unixadm –m –d /home/user5 –s /usr/bin/sh user5
C. useradd –u 105 –g dba –G dba1,unixadm –m /home/user5 –s /usr/bin/sh user5
D. useradd –u 105 –G dba,dba1,unixadm –m –d /home/user5 –s /usr/bin/sh user5

158. What does the following command do?

useradd –D –b /u01/home

A. Changes the default home directory to /u01/home for new user accounts created onwards
B. Changes the default home directory to /u01/home for all existing users' home directories
C. Changes the default home directory to /u01/home for all existing and new users
D. None of the above

159. Which command locks user5 and prevents him from logging in?

A. passwd user5 –lock
B. passwd –lock user5
C. passwd –l user5
D. passwd user5 –l

160. To remove a user account along with home directory, which command would you use?

    A. userdel user5   B. userdel –r user5   C. userdel user5 –r   D. userrem –r user5

161. To force a user to change his password at next login, which command would you run?

    A. passwd –m user5   B. passwd –n user5   C. passwd –f user5   D. passwd –c user5

162. Which PAM module restricts login access for a group of users?

    A. pam_access   B. pam_unix   C. pam_validate   D. pam_authz

163. What commands are typically used for group account management? Choose THREE.

    A. groupadd   B. groupmod   C. grouprem   D. groupdel

164. What is the name of the system-wide user initialization file for POSIX and Korn shell users?

    A. /etc/profile   B. $HOME/profile   C. /etc/.profile   D. /etc/swprofile

165. Which command is used to broadcast a message to all logged in users?

    A. write   B. talk   C. wall   D. broadcast

166. Which file does the last command reference?

    A. /var/adm/wtmps   B. /var/adm/btmps   C. /var/adm/utmp   D. /var/adm/ltmp

167. Which file does the lastb command reference?

    A. /var/adm/wtmps   B. /var/adm/btmps   C. /var/adm/utmp   D. /var/adm/ltmp

168. Which file does the who command reference?

    A. /var/adm/wtmps   B. /var/adm/btmps   C. /var/adm/utmps   D. /var/adm/ltmp

169. Which three solutions are available for disk management? Choose THREE.

    A. Logical Volume Manager   B. DiskSuite
    C. Whole disk solution   D. Veritas Volume Manager

170. You can span a file system on two disks using the whole disk solution. True or False.

    A. True   B. False

171. With LVM, you can span a file system on multiple disks. True or False.

    A. True   B. False

172. If you see a message in /var/adm/kc.log file that contains "by daemon", which one of the following would be correct with respect to kernel module?

    A. modified using kcweb/SMH   B. modified at the command prompt
    C. modified by a user with GID root   D. modified using WBEM

173. If you see a message in /var/adm/kc.log file that contains "by root", which one of the following would be correct with respect to kernel module?

    A. modified using kcweb/SMH   B. modified at the command prompt
    C. modified by a user with GID root   D. modified using WBEM

174. Which statement about RAID 0+1 is correct?

A. Mirroring a concatenated volume   B. Striping a mirrored volume
C. Mirroring a striped volume   D. Concatenating a striped volume

175. Which of the following are components of LVM? Choose THREE.

A. Physical volume   B. Disk group   C. Volume group   D. Logical volume

176. Which command below brings a disk under LVM control and also creates BDRA in it?

A. pvcreate –fB /dev/dsk/c1t4d0   B. pvcreate /dev/rdsk/c1t4d0
C. pvcreate –fB /dev/rdsk/c1t4d0   D. pvcreate –f /dev/rdsk/c1t4d0

177. The group file for a volume group in LVM is a block device file. True or False.

A. True   B. False

178. Which LVM structure is used to hold one or more physical volumes?

A. Logical volume   B. Volume group   C. Physical volume   D. Plex

179. What is the default first minor number assigned to a logical volume device file?

A. 0   B. 1   C. 2   D. 3

180. Which of the following is part of the LVM data structure?

A. VGSA   B. PVRA   C. VGRA   D. BDRA   E. All of the above

181. Which command displays all devices visible to the HP-UX system?

A. lsdev   B. lssf   C. ioscan   D. diskinfo

182. Which command displays the boot devices only?

A. lssf   B. diskinfo   C. ioscan   D. setboot

183. Which command at the OS level displays the settings for autoboot and autosearch flags?

A. lssf   B. setboot   C. ioscan   D. diskinfo

184. Which command displays the size and manufacturer information of a disk?

A. diskinfo   B. ioscan   C. lsdev   D. setboot

185. Which one of the following will work?

A. diskinfo /dev/rdsk/c1t0d0   B. diskinfo /dev/dsk/c1t0d0
C. diskinfo c1t0d0   D. diskinfo /dev/vx/rdsk/c1t0d0

186. What is the correct syntax of the mknod command to create a device file?

A. mknod c 64 group 0x010000   B. mknod group 64 c 0x010000
C. mknod group c 64 0x010000   D. mknod group c 0x010000 64

187. Which command displays volume group information in detail?

A. display   B. vgdisplay –v   C. lvdisplay   D. vgdisplay

188. Which three commands (in order) are typically used to display physical volume, logical volume and volume group information?

A. pvdisplay, lvdisplay, vgdisplay   B. vgdisplay, lvdisplay, pvdisplay
C. lvdisplay, vgdisplay, pvdisplay   D. pvdisplay, vgdisplay, lvdisplay

189. Which of the following creates a logical volume, lvol1, of size 500MB in vg01? Choose TWO.

    A. lvcreate –L 500 –n lvol1 /dev/vg01   B. lvcreate /dev/vg01/lvol1
    C. lvcreate –l 500 vg01 lvol1   D. lvcreate –L 500 –n lvol1 vg01

190. Which of the following extends the size of a logical volume, lvol1, located in vg01, to 800MB?

    A. lvextend –l 800 /dev/vg01/lvol1   B. lvextend –L 800 /dev/vg01/lvol1
    C. lvextend –L 800 /dev/vg01 lvol1   D. lvextend /dev/vg01/lvol1 –L 800

191. How would you view the contents of the /etc/lvmtab file?

    A. Using the strings command   B. Using the tail command
    C. Using the more command   D. Using the cat command

192. What is meant by increasing the size of a volume group?

    A. Adding a logical volume to it   B. Adding a physical volume to it
    C. Merging with another volume group   D. None of the above

193. Which command is used to reduce a logical volume and a volume group? Choose TWO.

    A. vgshrink   B. vgreduce   C. lvreduce   D. lvshrink

194. Which of the following are features of BIND 9.3.2? Choose THREE.

    A. Works with IPv6   B. Supports DNSSEC   C. Integrates with IPFilter
    D. New method of listing master DNS servers   E. Allows configuring ordering of records

195. What is the default number of file systems created at HP-UX installation time?

    A. 6   B. 7   C. 8   D. 9

196. How would you list the supported file system types?

    A. fstyp –l   B. showfstyp –l   C. fstype –l   D. cat /etc/vfstab

197. What is the purpose of JFS intent log? Choose TWO.

    A. Keeps file system structural updates log   B. Quick system recovery after a crash
    C. Backs up file system data   D. Maintains file system data

198. Which command is correct to create a JFS file system?

    A. newfs –F vxfs vg01   B. newfs –F vxfs rlvol1
    C. newfs /dev/vg01/rlvol1 vxfs   D. newfs –F vxfs /dev/vg01/rlvol1

199. Which file contains the location information of backup superblocks for an HFS file system?

    A. /etc/sbtab.conf   B. /etc/superblock.conf   C. /etc/adm/sbtab   D. /var/adm/sbtab

200. Which of the following is correct to mount a file system?

    A. mount –F vxfs lvol1 fs1   B. mount –F vxfs /fs1 /dev/vg01/lvol1
    C. mount –F vxfs /dev/vg01/lvol1 /fs1   D. mount –F vxfs /dev/vg01/lvol1 fs1

201. Which file contains file systems to be mounted at system boot?

    A. /etc/vfstab   B. /etc/fstab   C. /etc/sbtab   D. /etc/fs.conf

202. What does the mount command with –a option do?

A. Mounts all CIFS file systems listed in the /etc/fstab file
B. Mounts all file systems that are currently not mounted, but are listed in the /etc/fstab file
C. Mounts all NFS file systems listed in the /etc/fstab file
D. Mounts all CDFS file systems listed in the /etc/fstab file

203. Which file does the umountall command reference to unmount file systems?

A. /etc/mnttab   B. /etc/fstab   C. /etc/vfstab   D. /etc/mnttab.conf

204. What does the mount command do when run without any options?

A. Mounts all file systems listed in /etc/fstab   B. Mounts all NFS file systems listed in /etc/fstab
C. Displays currently mounted file systems   D. Mounts all CIFS file systems listed in /etc/fstab

205. An entry is made into which file when a file system is mounted?

A. /etc/fstab   B. /etc/mnttab   C. /etc/vfstab   D. /etc/mnttab.conf

206. Which command is used to increase the size of an HFS file system online?

A. extendfs   B. fsadm   C. extendhfs   D. None of the above

207. To increase the size of a mounted HFS file system which is listed in /etc/fstab file, what command sequence will you run?

A. lvextend –L 300 /dev/vg01/lvol1, fsadm –F hfs /dev/vg01/rlvol1
B. umount /fs1, extendfs –F hfs /dev/vg01/rlvol1, lvextend –L 300 /dev/vg01/lvol1, mount /fs1
C. umount /fs1, lvextend –L 300 /dev/vg01/lvol1, extendfs –F hfs /dev/vg01/rlvol1, mount /fs1
D. Both B and C

208. Which of the following is correct to reduce the size of a JFS file system /fs2 to 200MB? Assuming OnlineJFS product is installed.

A. lvreduce –L 200 /dev/vg01/lvol2, fsadm –b 200m /fs2
B. umount /fs2, lvreduce –L 200 /dev/vg01/lvol2, fsadm –b 200m /dev/vg01/rlvol2, mount /fs2
C. lvreduce –l 200 /dev/vg01/lvol2
D. fsadm –b 200m /fs2, lvreduce –L 200 /dev/vg01/lvol2

209. Which command is used to list processes using a file system?

A. fuser –cU /fs2   B. fuser –Cu /fs2   C. fuser –ck /fs2   D. fuser –cu /fs2

210. Which command would you use to mount a DVD?

A. mount /dev/dsk/c1t4d0 /dvdrom   B. mount –F cdfs /dev/dsk/c1t4d0 /dvdrom
C. mount –F dvdfs /dev/dsk/c1t4d0 /dvdrom   D. mount –F cdfs /dev/rdsk/c1t4d0 /dvdrom

211. Which command is used to check and repair a damaged CD file system?

A. fsck   B. fsdvd   C. fscd   D. None of the above

212. Which of the following is used to check and repair an entire JFS file system?

A. fsck –F vxfs –o log /dev/vg01/rlvol2   B. fsck –F vxfs /dev/vg01/rlvol2
C. fsck –F vxfs –o full /dev/vg01/rlvol2   D. fsck –F vxfs full /dev/vg01/rlvol3

213. What command would you use to find HFS superblock locations?

A. newfs –N /dev/vg01/rlvol1   B. find / –name sb –print
C. newfs –F hfs /dev/vg01/rlvol1   D. None of the above

214. How would you check the amount of physical memory in your system? Choose TWO.

    A. grep physical /var/adm/syslog/syslog.log   B. grep –i physical /etc/rc.log
    C. dmesg   D. grep –i physical /var/adm/syslog/syslog.log

215. Which type of file system swap area is faster?

    A. Device swap   B. File system swap   C. Both A and B   D. None of the above

216. Which command enables device swap in a logical volume?

    A. lvchange –a y /dev/vg01/swaplvol   B. swapon /dev/vg01/swaplvol
    C. swap /dev/vg01/swaplvol   D. swapon –enable /dev/vg01/swaplvol

217. Which command would display the utilization of all enabled swap spaces?

    A. swapinfo   B. swapon   C. swap –a   D. swapon –a

218. What directory is created in a file system when swap is enabled in it?

    A. fsswap   B. swaping   C. paging   D. None of the above

219. Which of the following TWO entries enable a device swap and a file system swap at system boot?

    A. /dev/vg02/lvol2 /fs2 swapfs defaults 0 0   B. /dev/vg02/rlvol2 /fs2 swapfs defaults 0 0
    C. /dev/vg01/swaplvol … swap defaults 0 0   D. /dev/vg01/rswaplvol … swap defaults 0 0

220. How would you manually enable all swap areas defined in the /etc/fstab file?

    A. swapon –e   B. swapon –a   C. swapon –s   D. swapon –r

221. What is the default number of file system and device swap areas that can be defined on a system?

    A. 5   B. 10   C. 15   D. 25

222. How many run control levels are currently implemented?

    A. 4   B. 5   C. 6   D. 8

223. Which of the following would you run to view the current and previous system run levels?

    A. uptime   B. w   C. who –s   D. who –r

224. What is the default HP-UX run level?

    A. 1   B. 2   C. 3   D. 4

225. To shutdown a system gracefully, which commands are used? Choose TWO.

    A. shutdown   B. init   C. poweroff   D. halt

226. What does the shutdown command by default do which the init command does not? Choose TWO.

    A. Starts the shutdown process right away
    B. Waits for one minute before commencing system shutdown
    C. Broadcasts a message to all logged in users
    D. Both A and C

227. When the shutdown command is run without any options, where does it take the system to?

    A. Displays syntax error   B. Default run level   C. Reboots the system   D. Single user mode

228. To allow a normal user to be able to shutdown a system, which file would you modify?

A. /etc/shutdown.allow   B. /etc/shutdown.enable

C. /etc/shutdown.conf   D. /etc/shutdownallow

229. How would you boot a system to single user state from the ISL prompt?

A. hpux –i   B. hpux –s   C. hpux –is   D. hpux s

230. What script is executed at boot time that checks the root file system and repairs it, if necessary?

A. /sbin/pre_boot   B. /sbin/pre_initial   C. /sbin/init   D. /sbin/pre_init_rc

231. What would you type at the ISL prompt to boot a system to LVM maintenance state?

A. hpux –is   B. hpux –lm   C. hpux –ls   D. hpux –im

232. Which of the following would you type at the command to view the AUTO file contents?

A. lifcp /dev/dsk/c0t4d0:AUTO   B. lifcp –d /dev/rdsk/c0t4d0 AUTO

C. lifcp /dev/rdsk/c0t4d0:AUTO –   D. lifcp AUTO /dev/rdsk/c0t4d0

233. How would you set the alternate boot path to 8/8.12 disk?

A. setboot –h 8/8.12   B. setboot –haa 8/8.12   C. setboot –alt 8/8.12   D. setboot –a 8/8.12

234. Which file determines the default boot level at system startup?

A. /etc/inittab   B. /etc/init.conf   C. /etc/inittab.conf   D. /sbin/init

235. Which file maintains I/O configuration across reboots?

A. /etc/ioconfig   B. /sbin/ioconfig   C. /var/adm/ioconfig   D. /etc/ioconfig.conf

236. Which script checks file systems listed in /etc/fstab file at system startup?

A. /sbin/lvmrc   B. /sbin/bcheckrc   C. /etc/fstab   D. /sbin/inittab

237. Which is the system startup log file?

A. /etc/rc.log   B. /var/adm/startup.log   C. /etc/rc.log.log   D. /var/adm/rc.log

238. Which directory contains configuration files for the startup and shutdown scripts?

A. /etc/init.d   B. /sbin/init.d   C. /etc/rc#.d   D. /etc/rc.config.d

239. Which directory contains the startup and shutdown scripts?

A. /sbin/init.d   B. /etc/init.d   C. /etc/rc.config.d   D. /sbin/inittab

240. Which is not a reason to reconfigure the kernel?

A. Install kernel patches   B. Add/remove device drivers

C. Add/remove subsystems   D. Add swap space

241. Which command can be used to gather running kernel information? Choose TWO.

A. system_prep   B. kconfig   C. kmupdate   D. kmtune

242. What would the following do?

kconfig

A. Displays saved configurations   B. Displays currently running kernel configuration

C. Assigns saved configurations   D. Disables saved configurations

243. Which commands can be used to change the value of a kernel tunable in the system file? Choose TWO.

A. vi   B. system_prep   C. kcmodule   D. kctune

244. Which command can be used to reconfigure a kernel configuration? Choose TWO.

A. kcmodule   B. kconfig   C. mk_kernel   D. kctune

245. Which command can be used to make a saved kernel configuration the running kernel configuration at the next system reboot? Choose TWO.

A. kctune   B. kcmodule   C. system_prep   D. kconfig

246. Which of the following can you use to determine the value of a kernel parameter? Choose TWO.

A. kctune   B. kcmodule   C. sysdef   D. ioscan

247. Which command can be used to query all static and dynamic modules in the running kernel configuration?

A. kcmodule   B. sysdef   C. kcadmin   D. kctune

248. Which version of HP-UX supports kcweb command? Choose TWO.

A. HP-UX 11i v1   B. HP-UX 11i v2   C. HP-UX 11.00   D. HP-UX 11i v3

249. Which command is equivalent to kmsystem in HP-UX 11i v3?

A. kconfig   B. kctune   C. kcsystem   D. kcmodule

250. kcweb provides GUI interface to modify kernel tunable parameters.

A. True   B. False

251. What is system recovery?

A. It is a function that is used to crash a system
B. It is a function that is used to perform a backup
C. It is a function that is used to recover a crashed system to its previous normal state
D. It is a function that is used only to restore data from backup

252. How many levels of backup are supported by the fbackup command?

A. 9   B. 10   C. 8   D. 11

253. Which digit represents an entire file system backup with fbackup?

A. 9   B. 2   C. 1   D. 0

254. What is a graph file?

A. It is a file that contains files/directories to be included in and excluded from a backup
B. It is a log file that is updated for each file/directory that is being backed up
C. It maintains a history of backups performed
D. It maintains backup log information

255. Which one of the following is correct?

A. fbackup –f /dev/rmt/0m –g /home   B. fbackup /home /tmp/index.home
C. fbackup –f /home –i index.home   D. fbackup –f /dev/rmt/0m –i /home –I index.home

256. Where does the fbackup command put a time stamp if the –u option is used with it?

A. /usr/dumpdates B. /var/adm/dumpdates
C. /var/adm/fbackupfiles/dates D. /etc/dates

257. Where does the dump and vxdump commands put a time stamp if the –u option is used with them?

A. /usr/dumpdates B. /etc/dates
C. /var/adm/fbackupfiles/dates D. /var/adm/dumpdates

258. Which command restores only /home file system from a full system backup?

A. frecover –xv B. frecover –f /dev/rmt/1m –i /home –xv
C. frecover –f /dev/rmt/1m –xv D. Any of the above

259. Which TWO can be used to archive the /etc directory to a non-default tape device?

A. tar cvf /dev/rtape/tape2_BEST /etc B. tar –cvf /dev/rtape/tape2_BEST /etc
C. tar cv /etc D. tar c /etc

260. Which of the following would work to backup /etc directory using the cpio command?

A. find /etc –mtime –7 | cpio –icv mod.lst B. find /etc –mtime –7 | cpio –Ocv mod.lst
C. find /etc –mtime –7 | cpio –ocv –O mod.lst D. find /etc –mtime –7 | cpio -itv

261. Which tools are included in HP-UX 11i to perform recovery archives? Choose TWO.

A. make_net_recovery B. create_net_recovery
C. create_tape_recovery D. make_tape_recovery

262. How would you create a recovery archive of hp01 on hp02 at /var/recovery directory and include the entire vg00?

A. create_net_recovery –v –s hp02 –a hp02:/var/recovery/hp01.archive –x inc_entire=vg00
B. make_net_recovery –v –s hp02 –a hp02:/var/recovery/hp01.archive –x inc_entire=vg00
C. make_tape_recovery –v –s hp02 –a hp02:/var/recovery/hp01.archive –x inc_entire=vg00
D. create_tape_recovery –v –s hp02 –a hp02:/var/recovery/hp01.archive –x inc_entire=vg00

263. Which directory in the print spooling system holds temporarily print requests before they are forwarded to a printer for printing?

A. /var/spool/request B. /var/adm/lp/request C. /var/spool/lp/request D. /var/adm/request

264. The lpsched is a local print daemon. Which script starts it at boot time?

A. /sbin/rc3.d/S720lp B. /sbin/rc2.d/S720lp C. /sbin/rc2.d/lp D. /sbin/rc3.d/lp

265. What is the configuration file for the master internet daemon inetd?

A. /etc/inetd.conf B. /etc/inet.conf C. /ctc/internet.conf D. /etc/net.conf

266. What is the range of print request priorities?

A. 1 – 9 B. 0 – 9 C. 1 – 7 D. 0 – 7

267. Which syntax for the lpadmin command is correct to create a local printer named prn3 of type "laserjet" and a printer class prn_class, and add prn3 to the class?

A. lpadmin –pprn3 –v/dev/lp –cprn_class –mlaserjet
B. lpadmin –c prn3 –v /dev/lp –p prn_class –m laserjet
C. lpadmin –p prn3 –c prn_class –m laserjet
D. lpadmin –pprn3 –v/dev/lp –cprn_class

268. Which of the following tool is not used to setup printers?

    A. lpadmin   B. prnadmin   C. SMH   D. None of the above

269. Which of the following sets prn1 as the default print destination?

    A. SMH –d prn1   B. lpadmin –d prn1   C. lp –d prn1   D. lpadmin –p prn1

270. Which sequence of commands is appropriate to offline a printer for maintenance, and then back online?

    A. reject, enable, accept, disable   B. enable, accept, disable, reject
    C. reject, disable, enable, accept   D. reject, accept, disable, enable

271. Which command displays the status of all configured printers?

    A. lpadmin –d   B. lp –t   C. lpadmin –t   D. lpstat –t

272. Which command is used to set printer fence level?

    A. lpalt   B. lpadmin   C. lpfence   D. lp

273. Which command is used to change the print priority of a submitted print request?

    A. lpadmin   B. lpalt   C. lpfence   D. lp

274. Which command is used to cancel a print request?

    A. lpalt   B. lpcancel   C. cancel   D. lpadmin

275. What script is executed at system boot that calls the /sbin/init.d/cron script to start the cron daemon?

    A. /sbin/rc2.d/S730cron   B. /sbin/rc3.d/S730cron   C. /sbin/rc2.d/cron   D. /sbin/cron

276. What happens if neither cron.allow nor cron.deny file exists?

    A. All users excluding root can schedule a cron job
    B. All users including root can schedule a cron job
    C. No users excluding root can schedule a cron job
    D. No users including root can schedule a cron job

277. Which is the log file for the cron daemon?

    A. cron has no log files   B. /var/adm/logs   C. /var/logs/cron   D. /var/adm/cron/log

278. What does the following do if executed at 6pm?

    # at 11pm find / –name core –exec rm {} \;

    A. Executes find command at 11pm next week   B. Executes find command after 5 hours
    C. Executes find command every night at 11pm   D. None of the above

279. Where do at jobs spool?

    A. /var/spool/at/atjobs   B. /var/spool/cron/atjobs
    C. /var/spool/atjobs   D. /var/spool/cron/jobs

280. What does the following crontab entry will do?

    20 1,12 1-15 * * find / -name core –exec rm {} \;

    A. Runs the find command at 20:01 and 20:12 the first fifteen days of the month
    B. Runs the find command at 1:20 and 12:20 the first fifteen days of the month

C. Both of the above
D. None of the above

281. Which option with the crontab command would allow you to modify your crontab file?

A. –e   B. –a   C. –m   D. –l

282. What are the names of the logging daemon and its configuration file?

A. syslog and /etc/syslog.conf   B. syslogd and /etc/syslog.conf
C. syslog and /etc/syslog.log   D. sysloagd and /etc/syslog.log

283. What is the default system logging file?

A. /var/spool/syslog.log   B. /var/adm/syslog.log
C. /var/adm/syslog/syslog.log   D. /var/adm/syslog/log

284. Which of the following cannot be used as a performance monitoring tool?

A. ioscan   B. top   C. iostat   D. uptime   E. glance

285. Which looping constructs are supported in shell scripts? Choose THREE.

A. for-do-done   B. while-do-done C. until-do-done D. if-then-else-fi

286. What is the command that is used in shell scripts to make it interactive?

A. input   B. get   C. write   D. read

287. What logical constructs are supported in shell scripts? Choose TWO.

A. while-done   B. case-esac   C. for-done   D. if-fi

288. Which command quits a running shell script?

A. break   B. exit   C. sleep   D. out

289. Which command suspends a loop execution?

A. break   B. exit   C. sleep   D. wait

290. Which command takes the loop control back to the start of the loop?

A. break   B. continue   C. exit   D. back

291. How would you check the status code of the last running command?

A. echo $*   B. echo $#   C. echo $0   D. echo $?

292. What is the minimum number of nodes required to form a network?

A. 1   B. 2   C. 3   D. Many

293. Which is the most commonly used network topology today?

A. Star   B. Bus   C. Token-ring   D. Ethernet

294. What is the most common network access method in use today?

A. Token passing   B. Ethernet   C. Fibre   D. All of the above

295. How many layers are in the OSI model?

A. 8   B. 9   C. 7   D. 5

296. What is the term used for adding a header message when creating a packet with respect to the OSI reference model?

    A. De-encapsulation   B. Encapsulation   C. Packet-forming   D. Message-forming

297. At what layers the TCP and IP protocols are defined? Choose TWO.

    A. Data link layer   B. Application layer   C. Transport layer   D. Network layer

298. What layers do the routers work at?

    A. Physical   B. Data link   C. Network   D. Transport

299. Which command displays MAC addresses of all available LAN interfaces?

    A. lanscan   B. ioscan   C. lanshow   D. lsdev

300. Which command can be used to change hostname, timezone, IP address, etc.?

    A. ifconfig   B. set_parms   C. hostname   D. timezone

301. Which command is used to configure LAN interfaces?

    A. ifconfig   B. ioscan   C. hostname   D. lanadmin

302. Which command displays routing information?

    A. netstat   B. ifconfig   C. networkstat   D. iostat

303. What is the default netmask for a class B IP address?

    A. 255.255.255.255   B. 255.255.255.0   C. 255.255.0.0   D. 255.0.0.0

304. What is IP multiplexing?

    A. Having a single IP address assigned to multiple LAN interfaces
    B. Having multiple IP addresses assigned to a single LAN interface
    C. Not supported in HP-UX
    D. Both A and B

305. How many useable subnets can be created with 3 host bits in a class C network?

    A. 2   B. 4   C. 8   D. 6

306. What is the netmask for a class C network divided into 6 useable subnets?

    A. 255.255.255.252   B. 255.255.255.248   C. 255.255.255.244   D. 255.255.255.224

307. How many nodes can you have in a subnet with netmask of 255.255.255.128?

    A. 30   B. 126   C. 62   D. 14

308. Which file defines the well-known ports?

    A. /etc/inetd.conf   B. /etc/protocols   C. /etc/services   D. Both B and C

309. Which of the following can be used to display installed LAN interfaces? Choose THREE.

    A. ioscan   B. lanscan   C. iostat   D. netstat

310. What does the following command do?

    # ifconfig lan1:1 150.11.211.100

A. Assigns a logical IP address to lan1
B. Deassigns a logical IP address from lan1
C. Changes the network address to class B for lan1:1
D. Changes the primary IP address of the LAN interface

311. Which file is consulted at system boot to assign IP addresses to LAN interfaces?

A. /etc/rc.config.d/namesvrs   B. /etc/rc.config.d/netconf
C. /etc/rc.config.d/net.conf   D. /etc/rc.config.d/route

312. Which file contains the IP address to hostname mapping?

A. /etc/hosts   B. /etc/rc.config.d/netconf   C. /etc/hostnames   D. /etc/ipnodes

313. Which file contains routing information that takes affect at system boot?

A. /etc/route.conf   B. /etc/rc.config.d/route
C. /etc/rc.config.d/netconf   D. /etc/rc.config.d/route.conf

314. To add a route to network 192.168.5 with gateway 182.0.1.1, which command would you run?

A. route add net 192.168.5.0 182.0.1.1 1   B. route add 192.168.5.0 182.0.1.1 0
C. route add default 192.168.5.0   D. route add 192.168.5.0 net 182.0.0.1

315. Which commands can be used to test physical network connectivity between two nodes? Choose TWO.

A. ping   B. linkloop   C. ioscan   D. nwmgr

316. Which commands would you use to display and modify LAN interface configuration? Choose TWO.

A. nwmgr   B. lanadmin   C. lanadm   D. lanscan

317. Which command would you use to check connectivity between two nodes at the TCP/IP level?

A. linkloop   B. netstat   C. ping   D. linkstat

318. Which command would display TCP/IP parameter information?

A. netstat   B. ioscan   C. ndd   D. lanadmin

319. What would you run after modifying the /etc/inetd.conf file to make the changes take effect?

A. inetd –f   B. inetd –s   C. inetd –c   D. inetd –r

320. Which file defines the port numbers for RPC-based services?

A. /etc/services   B. /etc/rpc   C. /etc/protocols   D. /etc/inetd.conf

321. Which is the security file for the inetd daemon?

A. /var/adm/inetdsec   B. /etc/inetd.sec   C. /var/inetd.sec   D. /var/adm/inetd.sec

322. Which of the following commands use trust relationship defined in $HOME/.rhosts or /etc/hosts.equiv, and without which you cannot get desired results? Choose THREE.

A. rlogin   B. rexec   C. rcp   D. remsh

323. The root user uses the /etc/hosts.equiv file.

A. True   B. False

324. What is the correct syntax for transferring files between two systems? Choose TWO.

A. rcp $HOME/.dtprofile hp02:$HOME   B. rcp hp02:$HOME/.dtprofile .
C. rcp $HOME/.dtprofile $HOME   D. rcp $HOME/.dtprofile .

325. Which line entry in /etc/inetd.conf enables logging for all FTP activities including incoming/outgoing file transfer?

A. ftp stream tcp nowait root /usr/lbin/ftpd ftpd -L
B. ftp stream tcp nowait root /usr/lbin/ftpd ftpd -i -o
C. ftp stream tcp nowait root /usr/lbin/ftpd ftpd –l –i -o
D. ftp stream tcp nowait root /usr/lbin/ftpd ftpd

326. What functions does sendmail provide? Choose TWO.

A. Mail reading   B. Mail transport agent   C. Mail delivery agent   D. Mail display

327. What is the default configuration file for sendmail?

A. /etc/sendmail.conf   B. /etc/mail/sendmail.conf
C. /etc/mail/sendmail.cf   D. /etc/hosts

328. What are alternate secure tools to access the HP-UX system? Choose THREE.

A. ssh   B. telnet   C. sftp   D. scp

329. To setup ssh, which command would you use to generate keys?

A. ssh   B. ssh-keygen   C. ssh.key.gen   D. ssh.keygen

330. What port does ssh use by default?

A. 21   B. 22   C. 23   D. 24

331. Can PAM be used with DNS?

A. Yes   B. No

332. Which is the system-wide configuration file for PAM?

A. /etc/pam.conf   B. /etc/pamconf
C. /etc/rc.config.d/pam.conf   D. /etc/rc.config.d/pamconf

333. Which of the following protocols does the CIFS server support for user authentication? Choose TWO.

A. private/public key   B. Kerberos   C. NTLM   D. ssh   E. EAP

334. What are the common sources of obtaining time for your network? Choose THREE.

A. An internet-based time server   B. A radio clock
C. A hand watch   D. Local system clock

335. Clocks working at what stratum level are considered the most accurate?

A. 0   B. 1   C. 10   D. 15

336. When two time servers work at the same stratum level, they are called Peers?

A. True   B. False

337. What files are typically involved with NTP configuration? Choose THREE.

A. /etc/ntp.drift   B. /etc/ntp.conf   C. /etc/rc.config.d/netdaemons   D. /etc/ntp/ntp.conf

338. Which command can be used at the command line or run via cron to update system time manually?

    A. xntp   B. ntpdate   C. chdatentp   D. ntpchdate

339. Which command is used to check the status of NTP and its associated bindings?

    A. ntpd   B. xntpd   C. ntptrace   D. ntpq

340. Which is the widely used naming service on the internet?

    A. DNS   B. NIS   C. CIFS   D. LDAP

341. Which command would display NFS activities?

    A. nfs –t   B. nfs –s   C. nfsact   D. nfsstat

342. Which daemons do not run on a slave NIS server? Choose TWO.

    A. ypserv   B. ypxfrd   C. ypbind   D. rpc.yppasswdd

343. What script is executed at system bootup to bring up the NIS client functionality, and what startup configuration file it uses? Choose TWO.

    A. /etc/rc.config.d/netconf   B. /etc/rc.config.d/namesvrs
    C. /sbin/init.d/nis.client   D. /sbin/init.d/ypclient

344. Which command does the ypxfrd daemon respond to?

    A. ypserv   B. ypxfr.server   C. nisxfr   D. ypxfr

345. Which command would you use to determine the NIS server your system is bound to?

    A. ypwhich   B. ypwho   C. ypmatch   D. ypcat

346. Which command would you use to list all RPC-based services currently running on the system?

    A. rpc –d   B. rpclist   C. rpcinfo   D. rpc –l

347. Which command would you use to display the contents of an NIS map?

    A. cat   B. ypcat   C. strings   D. ypmatch

348. What commands can be used to change an NIS user password? Choose TWO.

    A. yppasswd   B. yppassword   C. passwd   D. nispasswd

349. What does the following command do?

    # ypset hp03

    A. Nothing
    B. Binds the system to NIS server hp03 in addition to the one the system is already bound to
    C. Unbinds the system from hp03
    D. Binds the system to NIS server hp03

350. Which commands can be used to update NIS maps? Choose TWO.

    A. niscreate   B. ypcreate   C. make   D. ypmake

351. Which file contains network security settings for NIS?

    A. /var/yp/securenets   B. /var/yp/security   C. /etc/securetty   D. /etc/nis/securenets

352. In HP-UX 11i v3, an NFS server _____ a file system and an NFS client _____ it.

   A. shares, accesses   B. shares, mounts   C. exports, mounts   D. exports, accesses

353. NFS is an RPC-based service. True or False.

   A. True   B. False

354. Which is not a benefit of using NFS?

   A. Sharing common application binaries
   B. Multiple NFS client machines can access an NFS file system simultaneously
   C. Sharing user authentication information
   D. Sharing user home directories

355. Which NFS server daemon responds to the mount command request?

   A. rpc.mountd   B. mountd   C. nfsd   D. rpc.nfsd

356. Which NFS server daemon responds to NFS client file access requests?

   A. rpc.mountd   B. mountd   C. nfsd   D. nfs

357. Which NFS daemon has replaced the portmap daemon used in earlier HP-UX versions?

   A. rpc.mountd   B. rpcbind   C. rpc.bind   D. rpc.portmapd

358. Which file is referenced by the shareall command to share listed resrouces?

   A. /etc/share   B. /etc/dfs/dfstab   C. /etc/dfs/sharetab   D. /etc/rc.config.d/namesvrs

359. Which NFS daemons provide crash recovery? Choose TWO.

   A. nfsd   B. rpc.mountd   C. rpc.statd   D. rpc.lockd

360. When an NFS file system is mounted by a client, which file on NFS server stores an entry for it?

   A. /etc/mnttab   B. /etc/dfs/sharetab   C. /etc/rmtab   D. /etc/dfs/dfstab

361. When an NFS file system is mounted by a client, which file is updated on the NFS client?

   A. /etc/mnttab   B. /etc/fstab   C. /etc/rmtab   D. /etc/dfs/dfstab

362. When you execute the mount command with –v option, which file it reads to display the output?

   A. /etc/mnttab   B. /etc/fstab   C. /etc/rmtab   D. /etc/dfs/dfstab

363. When a file system is shared by an NFS server, which file on the NFS server stores an entry for it?

   A. /etc/mnttab   B. /etc/rmtab   C. /etc/dfs/sharetab   D. /etc/dfs/dfstab

364. Which is the startup configuration file for the NFS service?

   A. /etc/rc.config.d/namesvrs   B. /etc/rc.config.d/netconf
   C. /etc/rc.config.d/netdaemons   D. /etc/rc.config.d/nfsconf

365. Which file does the mountall command references to mount unmounted file systems?

   A. /etc/dfs/dfstab   B. /etc/fstab   C. /etc/mnttab   D. /etc/rmtab

366. Which of the following scripts starts the rpcbind daemon?

   A. /sbin/init.d/rpcbind   B. /sbin/init.d/nfs.server

C. /sbin/init.d/nfs.client   D. /sbin/init.d/nfs.core

367. Which versions of NFS are supported in HP-UX 11i v3? Choose TWO.

   A. v0   B. v3   C. v3.5   D. v4

368. What does the following entry in /etc/dfs/dfstab file mean?

   /usr/bin –access=hp03:hp04

   A. Only hp03 and hp04 will be able to mount /usr/bin
   B. All systems other than hp03 and hp04 will be able to mount /usr/bin
   C. All systems including hp03 and hp04 will be able to mount /usr/bin
   D. All of the above

369. What does the following entry in /etc/dfs/dfstab file mean?

   /var/opt/samba –anon=65535

   A. 65535 systems will be able to mount /var/opt/samba
   B. 655535 users can access /var/opt/samba at a time
   C. Anonymous users will be assigned 65535 UID
   D. Both A and B are correct

370. What variables in the /etc/rc.config.d/nfsconf file need to be set to 1 in order to have the NFS server functionality started up automatically at each system reboot? Choose TWO.

   A. NFS_MASTER   B. NFS_SERVER   C. NFS_SLAVE   D. START_MOUNTD

371. Which command shares all resources listed in the /etc/dfs/dfstab file?

   A. allshare   B. share   C. sharetab   D. shareall

372. Which is not one of the default options when sharing a file system?

   A. suid   B. ro   C. rw   D. intr

373. Which TWO when run on hp02 would list resources shared by hp02?

   A. showmount –e   B. cat /etc/dfs/sharetab   C. showmount –a   D. share

374. Which one of the following is correct?

   A. mount –o ro,nfs hp02:/usr/share/man /usr/share/man
   B. mount –o nfs,ro hp02:/usr/share/man /usr/share/man
   C. mount –F nfs –o ro hp02:/usr/share/man /usr/share/man
   D. mount –F ro –o nfs hp02:/usr/share/man /usr/share/man

375. Which TWO when run on an NFS server would list resources mounted by NFS clients?

   A. showmount –a   B. cat /etc/dfs/sharetab   C. share   D. showmount –e

376. Which commands would you use to kill all processes using the /home file system? Choose TWO.

   A. umount –f /home   B. fuser –cg /home   C. fuser –cu /home   D. fuser –ck /home

377. What is the other name for CIFS Server?

   A. Samba   B. CIFS/NFS   C. NFS   D. There is no other name for it

378. Which ones are true for sharing directories using CIFS? Choose THREE.

A. Windows and Windows can share directories   B. UNIX and Windows can share directories
C. UNIX and UNIX can share directories   D. UNIX and UNIX cannot share directories

379. Which is the CIFS server configuration file?

    A. /etc/opt/cifs/smb.conf   B. /etc/opt/samba/smb.conf
    C. /etc/samba/smb.conf   D. /etc/cifs/smb.conf

380. What variable would you set in /etc/rc.config.d/samba file to have CIFS server start at system boot?

    A. CIFS=1   B. RUN_CIFS=1   C. RUN_SAMBA=1   D. SAMBA=1

381. Which of the following would you run to start CIFS server in GUI mode?

    A. /opt/cifs/bin/swat   B. /opt/samba/bin/swat   C. /usr/samba/bin/swat   D. /usr/sbin/swat

382. Which command would you run to check the syntax errors in the CIFS server configuration file?

    A. testcifsserv   B. testparm   C. cifstest   D. sertestcifs

383. Which is the startup configuration file for CIFS client?

    A. /etc/rc.config.d/cifsclient   B. /etc/rc.config.d/samba
    C. /etc/rc.config.d/cifsserver   D. /etc/rc.config.d/sambaclient

384. Which two commands can you use to mount a CIFS share? Choose TWO.

    A. sharemount   B. sambamount   C. cifsmount   D. mount

385. AutoFS requires entries in the /etc/fstab file to work properly. True or False.

    A. True   B. False

386. For how long, by default, an AutoFS file system can remain idle before it is automatically unmounted?

    A. 5 sec   B. 5 min   C. 1 min   D. 10 min

387. What are the AutoFS command and daemon?

    A. automount, autofsd   B. autofs, autofsd
    C. automount, automountd   D. autofs, automountd

388. What two variables in the /etc/rc.config.d/nfsconf file must you set to have AutoFS client funcationality started at each system reboot?

    A. AUTOFS   B. NFS_CLIENT   C. NFS_CORE   D. AUTOMOUNTD

389. What change is required on an NFS server to mount shared resources on a client using AutoFS?

    A. Restart the NFS server daemons
    B. Reboot the NFS server
    C. Re-export the file system to be mounted by AutoFS on client
    D. No change is required

390. What is the directory location for the automount command and the automountd daemon?

    A. /usr/sbin/autofs   B. /usr/lib/netsvc/fs/autofs
    C. /usr/lib/netsvc/fs/automount   D. /opt/autofs/bin

391. Which ones are the AutoFS maps? Choose FOUR.

    A. indirect   B. direct   C. hosts   D. special   E. master

392. Which of the following are true about a direct AutoFS mount? Choose TWO.

    A. Always visible to users
    B. Always invisible to users unless there is an activity inside the mount point
    C. Both local and direct-mounted maps can co-exist under the same parent directory
    D. Both local and direct-mounted maps cannot co-exist under the same parent directory

393. You must run the automount command manually to make the modifications in a direct map take effect. True or False.

    A. True   B. False

394. What does the following mean on an NFS client?

    *   &:/home/&

    A. Mount from an available NFS server only the home directory of the user who logs in
    B. Mount from all configured NFS servers only the home directory of the user who logs in
    C. Mount home directories of all users from all NFS servers
    D. Mount home directories of all users from only one NFS server

395. Which is not true with respect to AutoFS?

    A. It supports files larger than 2GB in size
    B. It supports NFS v3 protocol
    C. It always mounts AutoFS file systems under /tmp_mnt directory
    D. You do not have to restart the automountd daemon everytime you modify any of the map files to take effect

396. Which of the naming services are supported for host name resolution? Choose THREE.

    A. CIFS   B. DNS   C. NIS   D. LDAP

397. In a small environment with a few HP-UX servers, which hostname resolution method would be preferred?

    A. LDAP   B. DNS   C. NIS   D. /etc/hosts

398. Which of the following do not have hierarchical structure? Choose TWO.

    A. LDAP   B. DNS   C. NIS   D. /etc/hosts

399. What is the name of the DNS boot file in BIND version 8.1.2 and later?

    A. /etc/named.dns   B. /etc/named.boot   C. /etc/named.data   D. /etc/named.bind

400. Which of the following DNS server configurations are supported? Choose THREE.

    A. Master   B. Slave   C. Peer   D. Caching-Only

401. Which command is used to create DNS zone files?

    A. createdns   B. converthosts   C. hosts_to_named   D. host_to_named

402. What is the name of the DNS daemon?

    A. named   B. name   C. dnsd   D. inetd

403. On what DNS server would you update host entries to be included in DNS?

    A. Caching-Only   B. Slave   C. Master   D. Client

404. What daemon must run on all types of DNS servers, as well as on clients?

    A. named   B. name   C. dnsd   D. inetd

405. Which file is referenced to determine sources to look up information?

    A. /etc/inetd.conf   B. /etc/nsswitch.conf   C. /etc/resolv.conf   D. /etc/named.boot

406. What is the DNS resolver file name?

    A. /etc/resolve.conf   B. /etc/nsswitch.conf   C. /etc/named.boot   D. /etc/resolv.conf

407. How many nameserver entries can be defined in DNS resolver file?

    A. 1   B. 2   C. 3   D. 4

408. Which of the following entries can be defined in the DNS resolver file? Choose THREE.

    A. defaultdomain   B. search   C. domain   D. nameserver

409. What commands can be used to verify if BIND (DNS) is working? Choose TWO.

    A. nsfind   B. nslookup   C. nsquery   D. nstrace

410. What does the db.cache file contain?

    A. Mapping for loopback address   B. Used on slave servers as /etc/named.conf
    C. Root name server database   D. Used on caching-only server as /etc/named.conf

411. What does the db.127.0.0 file contain?

    A. Root name server database   B. Mapping for loopback address
    C. Used on slave servers as /etc/named.conf   D. Used on clients as /etc/named.conf

412. What is the purpose of the conf.sec.save file?

    A. Used on slave servers as /etc/named.conf   B. Root name server database
    C. Mapping for loopback address   D. Used on master server as /etc/named.conf

413. What is the purpose of the conf.cacheonly file?

    A. Used on slave servers as /etc/named.conf   B. Root name server database
    C. Used on caching-only servers as /etc/named.conf   D. Mapping for loopback address

414. What does the keyword "hint" represent in the /etc/named.conf file?

    A. Points to root DNS servers   B. Points to master DNS server
    C. Points to slave DNS server   D. Points to caching-only DNS server

415. What command is used to restart the DNS daemon?

    A. named restart   B. sig_named restart   C. sig_named start   D. named start

416. What is the name of the configuration file for bootpd daemon?

    A. /etc/bootp.conf   B. /etc/bootpdtab   C. /etc/boottab   D. /etc/bootptab

417. Which command would you use to manually send a message to BootP server to verify if it is setup properly?

    A. nslookup   B. bootpquery   C. bootquery   D. bootqueryp

418. In which file would you define the BootP relay information?

A. /etc/bootp.conf   B. /etc/bootpdtab   C. /etc/bootptab   D. /etc/boottab

419. Which of the following is true about LDAP?

    A. Provides user authentication   B. Provides calendar service
    C. Provides email messaging service   D. All of the above

420. Which protocol is LDAP derived from?

    A. X.500 DAP   B. X.25 DAP   C. TCP/IP   D. NFS

421. What is "directory" in LDAP terminology?

    A. An inode that points to where the directory information is located in LDAP
    B. A file that stores information you type in using the vi editor
    C. A UNIX-like conventional directory that holds file information
    D. A database that stores information about objects

422. What information does an LDAP attribute contain? Choose TWO.

    A. Attribute class   B. One or more attribute values
    C. One or more attribute classes   D. Attribute type

423. Which of the following is a collection of LDAP attributes, object classes, matching rules and syntax, and other related information?

    A. Schematics   B. Object Class   C. Object   D. Schema

424. What is the special format for importing and exporting LDAP data among LDAP servers?

    A. LDAPIF   B. DIF   C. LDIF   D. LIF

425. What identifies an entry starting from the root of the LDAP directory?

    A. Relative distinguished name (RDN)   B. Distinguished name (DN)
    C. Common name (CN)   D. Domain component (DN)

426. What is the purpose of "referral" in LDAP?

    A. Redirects an LDAP request to some other LDAP server
    B. Gets unfound information from another LDAP server and sends back to the client
    C. It is a dedicated machine that performs a referral action in a large environment
    D. None of the above

427. Which statements are true with respect to LDAP "replica"? Choose TWO.

    A. It can be used to provide redundancy
    B. It can be called a referral
    C. It can be referred to as a caching-only LDAP server
    D. It can be referred to as a slave LDAP server

428. What command would you use to configure Netscape Directory server software?

    A. run   B. setup   C. swinstall   D. sh

429. What script is used at system startup to bring the LDAP client services up?

    A. /sbin/init.d/ldapclientd.rc   B. /sbin/init.d/ldapclient
    C. /sbin/init.d/ldap   D. /sbin/init.d/ldapclientd

430. What is the UID of the root user?

    A. 1   B. 0   C. 3   D. 2

431. What is the name and location of the history file for a POSIX shell user?

    A. ~/.history.sh   B. ~/.history_sh   C. ~/.posix_history   D. ~/.sh_history

432. What option would you use with the ls command to display hidden (or dot) files?

    A. –d   B. –l   C. –h   D. –a

433. Which of the following are vi editor modes? Choose THREE.

    A. Edit mode   B. Last line mode   C. Command mode   D. Save mode

434. Which is the default directory location for storing NIS maps?

    A. /var/yp   B. /var/adm/yp   C. /etc/yp   D. /usr/yp

435. What is the default subnet mask for a class A IP address?

    A. 255.255.255.0   B. 255.255.0.0   C. 255.0.0.0   D. 0.0.0.255

436. What is the default subnet mask for a class B IP address?

    A. 255.255.255.0   B. 255.255.0.0   C. 255.0.0.0   D. 0.0.0.255

437. What is the default gateway IP address of 192.168.1.202?

    A. 192.168.1.1   B. 192.168.1.202   C. 192.168.1.255   D. 192.168.1.0

438. What is the loopback IP address of a system?

    A. 0.0.0.127   B. 127.0.0.0   C. 127.0.0.1   D. 1.0.0.127

439. Which option with the netstat command displays the routing information for the system?

    A. –a   B. –i   C. –r   D. –n

440. Which is not another name for the MAC address?

    A. Station address   B. Hardware address   C. IP address   D. Ethernet address

441. What is the lowest priority target ID in a SCSI chain?

    A. 0   B. 7   C. 8   D. 15

442. What would the following command do?

echo $?

A. Echoes the character ?
B. Display the message "command not found"
C. Displays total number of command line arguments specified at the last executed command
D. Displays status code for the last command executed

443. What is the default shell in HP-UX and what is the default shell for the root user?

    A. Korn, POSIX   B. Korn for both   C. POSIX for both   D. POSIX, Korn

444. What is the purpose of output redirection?

    A. Send the output to an alternate destination   B. Take the input from an alternate source

C. Send the output to /dev/null   D. Always send the output to a file

445. What is the major number for the LVM subsystem?

    A. 32   B. 64   C. 96   D. 128

446. What would be the sequence of commands to create a file system on a brand new disk online?

    A. ioscan, insf, pvcreate, vgextend, lvcreate, newfs   B. ioscan, insf, pvcreate, lvcreate, newfs
    C. pvcreate, lvcreate, newfs, vgextend   D. ioscan, pvcreate, vgextend, lvcreate, newfs

447. What is the default root volume group in HP-UX?

    A. vgroot   B. vg01   C. vgboot   D. vg00

448. Which command would put the boot utilities on a disk?

    A. mkdisk   B. mkutil   C. mkboot   D. pvcreate

449. Which command would you use to display the configuration of a volume group in detail?

    A. vgdisplay –a   B. vgdisplay –v   C. vgdisplay –t   D. vgdisplay –o

450. Which command would you use to display the details of a logical volume?

    A. lvdisplay –a   B. lvdisplay –v   C. lvdisplay –t   D. lvdisplay –o

451. Which command would you use to increase the size of an HFS file system?

    A. fsadm   B. lvextend   C. extendfs   D. fsextend

452. Which command would you run to restore a backup made with the fbackup tool?

    A. vxrestore   B. cpio   C. tar   D. frecover

453. Which three layers of the OSI reference model corresponds with the application layer of TCP/IP?

    A. Application, presentation, session   B. Application, session, network
    C. Physical, data link, network   D. Network, transport, application

454. At which layer of the OSI model the TCP and UDP protocols are used?

    A. Transport   B. Network   C. Data link   D. Session

455. Which protocol is used by a BootP client to get its IP address?

    A. RARP   B. ARP   C. TFTP   D. FTP

456. Which command would display information as to which user is using how much space?

    A. du   B. bdf   C. quot   D. ff

457. What is the purpose of the cron daemon?

    A. Run scheduled jobs every hour   B. Run scheduled jobs at specified times
    C. Run all scheduled jobs simultaneously   D. Run all scheduled jobs every hour

458. Which OSI layer does the switch work at?

    A. Transport   B. Network   C. Data link   D. Physical

459. Which OSI layer does the fibre channel cable work at?

    A. Transport   B. Network   C. Data link   D. Physical

460. What is the maximum speed of a fast Ethernet network interface?

    A. 1000 Mbps   B. 100 Mbps   C. 10 Mbps   D. 1 Mbps

461. Which command would display IP and MAC addresses of all systems on the network?

    A. arp   B. bootp –a   C. arp –a   D. None of the above

462. Which command would you use to setup a master NIS server?

    A. setup   B. ypsetup   C. init   D. ypinit

463. At what run level does the NFS client functionality become available?

    A. 4   B. 3   C. 2   D. s

464. What is the well-known port number for ftp?

    A. 21   B. 22   C. 23   D. 25

465. What command can be used to set or modify system hostname, IP address, date/time and root password?

    A. set_parms –m   B. set_parms initial   C. set_parms ip D. ifconfig

466. In which file is the primary group for a user defined?

    A. /etc/passwd   B. /etc/default/useradd   C. /etc/group   D. /etc/profile

467. In which file are the secondary group memberships for a user defined?

    A. /etc/passwd   B. /etc/default/useradd   C. /etc/group   D. /etc/profile

468. What command would you run to set your terminal settings to default?

    A. setterm   B. termset   C. stty   D. stty sane

469. What initializes and loads the HP-UX kernel into memory?

    A. Primary boot loader   B. Secondary boot loader C. The init program   D. /etc/inittab file

470. What commands can be used to display values contained in variables? Choose TWO.

    A. display   B. print   C. show   D. echo

471. Which is the default kernel parameter file?

    A. /etc/system   B. /stand/system   C. /stand/backup/system   D. /stand/system.conf

472. What is the meaning of the character "t" if it appears in the ll command output right after the permissions column?

    A. Setuid bit is set   B. Setgid bit is set   C. Sticky bit is set   D. Nothing special

473. What would the following command do:

chmod a=666 file1

    A. Grants rw permissions to the owner, group members and public
    B. Revokes rw permissions from the owner, group members and public
    C. Grants 666-022=644 permissions to the owner, group members and public
    D. Revokes 666-022=644 permissions from the owner, group members and public

474. Which of the following would display all available tape devices on the system? Choose THREE.

A. ioscan –fnkC tape   B. ioscan –fnkCtape   C. ioscan –fnC tape   D. ioscan –tape

475. Where does the HP-UX system store autoboot information?

     A. PDC   B. Stable storage   C. AUTO file   D. Both B and C

476. Which of the following are metacharacters? Choose THREE.

     A. *   B. \   C. $ D. A tab

477. To bring a disk into LVM control with BDRA created on it, which command would you use?

     A. mkboot –a   B. pvcreate –fB /dev/dsk/c0t2d0
     C. pvcreate –fB /dev/rdsk/c0t2d0   D. pvcreate –f /dev/rdsk/c0t2d0

478. Where is the default file system type defined?

     A. /etc/fs   B. /etc/default/fs   C. /etc/fs.conf   D. /etc/vfstab

479. What is the default file system type for the /var file system?

     A. UFS   B. VxFS   C. LOFS   D. HFS

480. What is the source file for the make utility?

     A. /etc/Makefile   B. /var/yp/make   C. /var/yp/Makefile   D. /var/yp/makefile

481. Which network management tools are deprecated in HP-UX 11i v3 in favor of the nwmgr command? Choose THREE.

     A. lanscan   B. nettl   C. lanadmin   D. linkloop

482. To boot a system to ignore quorum, what would you type at the ISL prompt?

     A. hpux –iq   B. hpux –lq   C. hpux –is   D. hpux –lm

483. Which command would you use to display the contents of the AUTO file at the ISL prompt?

     A. hpux display autofile   B. hpux autofile
     C. hpux show autofile   D. lifcp /dev/dsk/c0t0d0:AUTO –

484. Which shell would you assign to a POSIX shell user who you do not want to change directories?

     A. rsh   B. rksh   C. rcsh   D. sh

485. What is stored in the AUTO file by default?

     A. hpux   B. hpux –lq   C. hpux –is   D. isl

486. Which commands are used to query and set kernel parameters and modules respectively?

     A. kcadmin, kctune   B. kcmodule, kctune   C. kctune, kcmodule   D. kcadmin, kcmodule

487. Which of the following would display the lvmtab information?

     A. pg /etc/lvmtab   B. more /etc/lvmtab   C. cat /etc/lvmtab   D. strings /etc/lvmtab

488. Which command would list running processes?

     A. prstat   B. ps   C. psstat   D. proc

489. Which command would you use to recreate the /etc/lvmtab file?

     A. vgrecreate   B. vgsync   C. vgscan   D. mklvm

490. Which of the following is not a network monitoring tool?

    A. nfsstat   B. netstat   C. nettl   D. top

491. Which free HP tool proactively sends hardware failure notifications to HP?

    A. STM   B. ISEE   C. EMS   D. All of them

492. How many host bits are there in a class A network by default?

    A. 8   B. 16   C. 24   D. 32

493. Which signal is sent by default with the kill command?

    A. 15   B. 9   C. 2   D. 1

494. How many network bits are there in a class B network by default?

    A. 8   B. 16   C. 24   D. 32

495. Which file is created in /var/spool/lp directory to prevent multiple lpsched daemons from running?

    A. .lck   B. LOCK   C. SCHED   D. SCHEDLOCK

496. Which command would display all available signals?

    A. kill –s   B. kill –l   C. kill –a   D. kill

497. What would the following command do?

lp –d prn1 /etc/hosts

    A. Prints the /etc/hosts file on prn1 printer
    B. Sets prn1 as the default printer
    C. Sets prn1 as the default printer and prints the /etc/hosts file
    D. Prints the /etc/hosts file on the default printer and deletes it

498. Where would you start entering the text in vi when you press the A key while in command mode?

    A. Beginning of the current line   B. End of the current line
    C. Middle of the current line   D. Opens up a new line and you insert text there

499. What would the following do in vi?

:%s/old/new

    A. Replaces the first occurrence of the pattern "new" with "old" on the same line
    B. Replaces the first occurrence of the pattern "old" with "new" on the same line
    C. Replaces all occurrences of the pattern "old" with "new" in the entire file
    D. Replaces all occurrences of the pattern "new" with "old" in the entire file

500. What would be the result of the following grep command?

grep ^$ /etc/group

    A. Displays all lines from the /etc/group file that contain at least one character
    B. Displays no lines from the /etc/group file
    C. Displays all lines from the /etc/group file that begin with the character ^ and end with the character $
    D. Displays all lines from the /etc/group file that are empty

501. What command can be used to find help on a command?

A. catman   B. help   C. man   D. Any of the above

502. Which command shows your user ID?

A. id   B. groups   C. usermod   D. uid

503. Which command would you use to navigate within HP-UX directory tree?

A. pwd   B. cd   C. nav   D. id

504. How would you create a symlink?

A. ln −s existing_file link_file   B. ln existing_file link_file
C. ln −c existing_file link_file   D. link −s link_file existing_file

505. What does the execute permission on a directory mean?

A. You can create files in the directory   B. You can execute a command located in the directory
C. You can execute the directory   D. You can cd into the directory

506. Which one is correct to view the value contained in a variable?

A. echo $VAR   B. display $VAR   C. show $VAR   D. echo VAR

507. Which file transfer protocol is used by Ignite-UX?

A. FTP   B. TFTP   C. BootP   D. rcp

508. Which special character would you use at the end of a command to run it in the background?

A. ~   B. ^   C. $ D. &

509. What kind of files are typically stored in the /opt directory?

A. Configuration files   B. Variable files   C. Application files   D. Kernel files

510. What is the recommended way of bringing the HP-UX system down to the power off state?

A. init 6   B. shutdown −h   C. shutdown −6   D. reboot

511. Which script calls and runs startup scripts at boot time?

A. /etc/rc   B. /sbin/init   C. /sbin/rc   D. /etc/init

512. When does the .profile file is executed?

A. When a user logs in   B. When a user logs off
C. When an administrator runs a command   D. At system boot up

513. Which utility allows you to create a bootable system tape?

A. make_net_recovery   B. make_tape_recovery   C. make_tape   D. tape_create

514. What is the most common backup command found on UNIX systems?

A. cpio   B. dump   C. tar   D. fbackup

515. Which of the following gives you number of lines in file15?

A. wc −w file15   B. wc −a file15   C. wc −c file15   D. wc −l file15

516. Which command shows the device files associated with a device?

A. lssf   B. lsdev   C. insf   D. ioscan

517. What happens if you do not specify the size of a logical volume when you run the lvcreate command to create a logical volume?

    A. It will use all space in the volume group   B. It will be created with zero size
    C. It will result in syntax error   D. It will destroy the logical volume

518. Which directory holds the most log files?

    A. /var/logs   B. /var/adm/logs   C. /var/adm   D. /var/adm/syslog

519. Which directory contains the default user startup template files?

    A. /etc/skeleton   B. /etc/default/user   C. /etc/default   D. /etc/skel

520. What is the purpose of using NTP?

    A. Administration files synchronization   B. Time synchronization
    C. Sending packets to test remote connectivity   D. All of the above with proper options and arguments

521. Which of the following is not a correct class C netmask?

    A. 255.255.0.0   B. 255.255.255.128   C. 255.255.255.192   D. 255.255.255.0

522. What permissions does the chmod command set with 755 on file10?

    A. r-wr-wr-w   B. rwxr-wr-x   C. rwxr-xr-x   D. rwxrwxrwx

523. If you assign UID 0 to a normal user, what will happen? Choose THREE.

    A. The user will get root privileges
    B. The user will still be able to do his normal work and will not be able to do anything additional
    C. The user will be able to run SMH with full privileges
    D. The user will be able to run all system administration tasks

524. What kind of file systems can the newfs command create? Choose TWO.

    A. vxfs   B. cdfs   C. hfs   D. swapfs

525. What is the default location for the software depot?

    A. /var/spool/products   B. /var/spool/sw   C. /var/spool/software   D. /var/spool/depot

526. What class does the IP address 199.81.51.231 belong to?

    A. Class A   B. Class B   C. Class C   D. Class D

527. What portions does an IP address contain? Choose TWO.

    A. A protocol portion   B. A network portion   C. A host portion   D. A, B and C

528. Which file is consulted at boot time to configure LAN interfaces?

    A. /sbin/init.d/netconf   B. /etc/rc.config.d/netconf
    C. /etc/netconf   D. /etc/rc.config.d/netdaemons

529. Which directories should not be shared with other systems via NFS? Choose THREE.

    A. /opt   B. /stand   C. /etc   D. /dev

530. What does a direct map contain?

    A. Any number of related mount points   B. Any number of unrelated mount points

C. No related mount points   D. No unrelated mount points

531. What is the alias command used for?

    A. To create nick names for users   B. To create nick names for groups
    C. To create shortcuts to commands   D. To setup cron jobs

532. Which file stores the last software installation log information?

    A. /var/adm/sw/swinstall.log   B. /var/adm/sw/swinstallation.log
    C. /var/adm/sw/install.log   D. /var/adm/software/swinstall.log

533. Which command enables you to make a local variable an environment variable?

    A. echo   B. set   C. env   D. export

534. What does the pipe character do in a command line?

    A. Takes input from an alternate location
    B. Sends output of a command as input to another command
    C. Sends output to the system log file only
    D. Takes input from user

535. Where does the cpio command send its output by default?

    A. stderr   B. stdout   C. stdin   D. stddis

536. Which command would display only the third column from the output of the ls –l command?

    A. ls –l | cut –f2 –d " "   B. ls –l | cut –f3 –d " "
    C. ls –l | cut –d "" –f3   D. ls –l | cut –d " " –f2

537. Which of the following would print the contents of the /etc/profile file on printer prn3?

    A. lp –p prn3 /etc/profile   B. lp –dprn3 /etc/profile
    C. lp –a prn3 /etc/profile   D. lp –pprn3 /etc/profile

538. Which sequence of commands would you run to force unmount a file system? Choose TWO.

    A. fuser –cu, umount   B. fuser –ck, umount   C. umount –f   D. kuser, umount

539. What is the purpose of subnetting?

    A. To create multiple smaller networks out of an IP address
    B. To divide a network portion of an IP address into multiple addresses to create subnets
    C. To create larger networks
    D. To concatenate multiple IP addresses to form a very large network

540. OSI layers provide a set of rules for data transmission. True or False.

    A. True   B. False

541. The lpadmin command is used to create a new printer when the scheduler is running. True or False.

    A. True   B. False

542. Who can change a user password?

    A. Only the user himself   B. Only the root user
    C. Both the user and the root   D. Any users on the system

543. Which file would you modify to prevent users from a specific remote host from printing to a printer on your system?

A. /etc/inetd.sec   B. /etc/securenets   C. /etc/inetd.conf   D. /var/adm/inetd.sec

544. Which kernel parameter defines the maximum number of swap spaces that can be configured?

A. maxswapchunks   B. maxswap   C. maxswapspace   D. maxswapslice

545. What is the meaning of initiator in the output of ioscan?

A. SCSI disk array   B. SCSI bus controller   C. SCSI hard disk   D. SCSI DVD

546. Ethernet and IEEE 802.3 use what kind of network access method?

A. Fibre   B. Token passing   C. CSMA/CD   D. SCSI protocol

547. What is the maximum cable length for a 10BaseT segment?

A. 10 meters   B. 100 meters   C. 1000 meters   D. 10 kilometers

548. At what system run level the NFS server functionality becomes available?

A. 2   B. 3   C. 4   D. 5

549. Which of the following name resolution service will never be used by a system to deliver a packet to the local system?

A. /etc/hosts   B. DNS   C. NFS   D. CIFS

550. Which of the following is the correct $HOME/.rhosts and /etc/hosts.equiv file format?

A. user1 ~   B. ~ user1   C. user1 +   D. + user1

551. What are the default primary command prompts for the root user, POSIX shell users and C shell users?

A. $, $, %   B. #, $, %   C. $, #, %   D. #, %, $

552. What is the default secondary command prompt displayed if a command misses information?

A. >   B. <   C. $ D. #

553. VAR=`hostname` and VAR=(hostname) are examples of:

A. Filename completion   B. Command completion
C. Tilde substitution   D. Command substitution

554. Where does the error messages are sent by default?

A. /var/adm/syslog/syslog.log   B. /var/adm/console
C. Other user's screen   D. Root's screen

555. What is the default UID for user nobody?

A. 1   B. -1   C. 2   D. -2

556. Which of the following is the correct /etc/passwd file entry?

A. username:actual password:UID:GID:Comments:Home directory:Shell
B. username:encrypted password:UID:GID:Comments:Home directory:Shell
C. username:encrypted password:UID:GID:Home directory:Comments:Shell
D. username:encrypted password:GID:UID:Comments:Home directory:Shell

557. What does the following do?

mailx user1 < $HOME/.profile

A. Mail the contents of the sending user's .profile file
B. Mail the sending user's .profile file as an attachment
C. Mail user1's .profile file from his home directory
D. Saves a receiving mail to user1's home directory as .profile

558. What is a socket address?

A. PID appended by an IP address
B. IP address appended by a PID
C. IP address appended by a port number
D. Port number appended by an IP address

559. What would be the DSF for a tape device connected to controller 1 and target 2 with best performance and no rewind?

A. /dev/rmt/c1t2d0BEST
B. /dev/dsk/c1t2d0BESTn
C. /dev/rdsk/c1t2d0BESTn
D. /dev/rmt/c1t2d0BESTn

560. Which command can you use to recreate lost device files?

A. lsdev   B. ioscan   C. insf   D. lssf

561. Which directory does the .rhosts file reside in?

A. $HOME   B. /etc   C. /var   D. /usr

562. What are the ways of saving and exiting vi? Choose THREE.

A. :x!   B. ZZ   C. :wq!   D. :q!   E. :w!

563. Which combination of NFS mount options would reduce the chances of an NFS client hang up when NFS server is unavailable?

A. retry=3,soft,nointr   B. retry=2,soft,nointr   C. retry=2,soft   D. retry=3,soft,intr

564. Given a class B IP address of 171.25.33.0 and subnet mask of 255.255.224.0, how many useable subnets and hosts can you get?

A. 6 / 8192   B. 4 / 16384   C. 8 / 4096   D. 12 / 2048

565. Which LVM command is used to detach a mirrored logical volume?

A. lvsplit   B. lvmerge   C. lvdetach   D. lvattach

566. Which LVM command is used to attach a detached mirrored logical volume?

A. lvsplit   B. lvmerge   C. lvdetach   D. lvattach

567. Which command would you use to synchronize a mirrored logical volume?

A. lvsync   B. lvmerge   C. vgsync   D. vgmerge

568. Which software component must be installed on the system in order to take advantage of the HP-UX mirroring capabilities?

A. OnlineJFS   B. MirrorDisk/UX   C. Both A & B   D. None of these

569. Which of the following statements is true about thread?

A. Process is a component of thread   B. Thread is a component of process

C. Process and thread are identical   D. Process runs in swap; thread runs in memory

570. Which commands identify which hardware address is associated with which device file? Choose TWO.

    A. insf   B. lssf   C. ioscan   D. lanscan

571. What LVM command would you run to form a new volume group?

    A. vgform   B. vgmake   C. vgdo   D. vgcreate

572. What is the sequence of commands to be performed to add memory or cpu to a vpar? Choose TWO.

    A. shutdown –hy now   B. shutdown –ry now
    C. MON> vparmodify –a   D. vparmodify –a

573. Which command would you run to create a mirror of an existing logical volume?

    A. lvmirror   B. lvmir   C. lvcreate   D. lvextend

574. What would be the sequence of commads that you would execute on a mounted, busy file system to run fsck on it? You have to remount the file system.

    1. fsck   2. mount   3. umount   4. fuser
    A. 1,2,3,4   B. 4,1,3,2   C. 3.4,1,2   D. 4,3,1,2

575. The _____ command is used to display the swap space information.

576. In a logical DSF cXtXdX, what does the "t" represent?

    A. Target device   B. Logical unit number   C. Controller number   D. None of the above

577. Bridges can perform translation up to and including which layer in the OSI reference model.

    A. Network   B. Transport   C. Physical   D. Data link

578. The _____ configuration file is referenced at system boot to configure IP address(es).

579. VAR=`pwd` is an example of:

    A. Command aliasing   B. Variable substitution   C. Command substitution D. Function setting

580. Which protocol is used by the Ignite-UX server to transfer files to the client?

    A. FTP   B. BootP   C. SFTP   D. TFTP

581. Which is the preferred and more secure tool to use in place of telnet?

    A. ssh   B. sftp   C. scp   D. rlogin

582. Match items on the left with description on the right:

    A. cimserver   1. Main WBEM daemon
    B. cimserverd   2. Provides PAM authentication to WBEM
    C. cimservera   3. Starts and stops WBEM service

583. HP Online JFS and MirrorDisk/UX software are included in which OE bundles. Choose TWO.

    A. B-OE   B. VSE-OE   C. DC-OE   D. Both A and C

584. Which command can be used to display password aging information?

    A. getprpw   B. modprpw   C. passwd   D. prpwdisp

585. Which command can be used to unlock a user account in trusted mode?

A. getprpw   B. modprpw   C. chprpw   D. setprpw

586. The lpadmin command can be used to define a new printer when:

A. Scheduler is running
C. Does not matter

B. Scheduler is not running
D. None of the above

587. What are the commands to commit superseded patches? Choose TWO.

A. cleanup   B. swremove   C. swunreg   D. swmodify

588. What is the default priority of a child process?

A. It gets the average priority
C. It inherits from the parent process

B. It gets the highest priority
D. It gets the lowest priority

589. Choose TWO. File system swap should be created on:

A. slower disks   B. heavily utilized file systems   C. faster disks   D. less utilized file systems

590. You can view shared memory segment using which command.

A. vmstat   B. ipcs   C. shstat   D. ioscan

591. Which TWO tools may be used for DNS queries?

A. dig   B. nslookup   C. nsswitch   D. resolver

592. Which technology are the Intel Itanium processors based on?

A. Reduced Instruction Set Code
C. Intel Pentium technology

B. Complex Instruction Set Code
D. Explicitly Parallel Instruction Computing

593. Which of the components does every Integrity server have? Choose THREE.

A. PCI I/O card   B. Cell board   C. Itanium processor   D. Core I/O

594. Following is based on the ioscan command. Match the following:

A. Full listing   B. List only disk devices   C. Listing with device files   D. Short listing

1. ioscan –fC disk
2. ioscan
3. ioscan –f
4. ioscan –fn

595. Pluggable Authentication Module (PAM):

A. Enables system administrators to use an available service for NFS
B. Gives system administrators the flexibility for choosing an available authentication service
C. Must be configured, otherwise the system cannot use it
D. None of the above

596. SSH enables:

A. Authentication based on standard 128-bit encryption
B. Authentication based on standard mode security extension
C. Authentication based on hidden keys
D. Authentication based on trusted mode security

597. Which protocol is used by NFSv4?

A. UDP   B. TCP   C. SMB   D. NFSv4

598. Match the following:

A. make_tape_recovery	1.	Bit for bit duplication
B. fbackup	2.	System recovery archive
C. dd	3.	Copies data using the find command
D. cpio	4.	Uses complex criteria to backup data
E. tar	5.	Archives files

599. Choose THREE to view UP status of a LAN interface.

A. ioscan   B. ifconfig   C. lanadmin   D. netstat   E. lanscan   F. nslookup

600. Choose TWO methods to install HP-UX OE using Ignite server.

A. boot lan.<IP address> install   B. boot net – install
C. boot from local media and point to ignite server   D. boot <IP address>

601. What would the following do if dir1 is empty?

ln –f file1 file2 dir1

A. Links file1 with file2 under dir1   B. Links file2 with file1 under dir1
C. Creates file1 and file2 under dir1   D. Creates file1 and file2 under dir1 and linkes them back to file1
and file2

602. Select TWO to trim logfile.

A. cat < /dev/trim > logfile   B. cat < /dev/null > logfile   C. > logfile   D. trim logfile

603. What is the purpose of CIFS server on HP-UX?

A. Share Windows file systems / directories with HP-UX
B. Share HP-UX file systems / directories with Windows
C. Share Windows file systems / directories with HP-UX and vice versa
D. Share OpenVMS file systems / directories with HP-UX

604. Name five VxFS file system structure components:

A. Fragment   B. Inode table   C. Cylinder group
D. Intent log   E. Allocation units   F. Superblock

605. Which of the TWO are correct with respect to HP-UX native multipathing?

A. Native multipathing is included in all HP-UX OE bundles
B. By default, native multipathing only works with persistent DSFs
C. Native multipathing is only included in EOE and MCOE
D. Native multipathing only works with legacy DSFs

606. Which of the following would you use to list installed patches on the HP-UX system?

A. check_patches   B. swlist –l product | grep –i ph
C. list_patches   D. patchinfo

607. Which THREE of the following can be used to software terminate a process with PID 123?

A. kill –s 15 123   B. kill 123   C. kill –s 123   D. kill –s SIGTERM 123

608. What TWO ways are available to fine tune an existing journaled file system?

     A. tunefs   B. mount options   C. vxtunefs   D. vxtune

609. Which of the following correctly describes HP SIM users and authorization?

     A. Users must only exist in /etc/passwd in order to be given authorization to use HP SIM
     B. Users must be defined in HP SIM CMS in order to be given authorization to use HP SIM
     C. Users need not be defined in HP SIM CMS in order to be given authorization to use HP SIM
     D. All normal users are defined in HP SIM by default to perform administrative functions

610. Which of the following would you use to start HP SMH daemon if it is not already running?

     A. smh –s   B. smh start   C. hpsmh –s   D. hpsmh start

611. Which of the following is not a single point of failure (SPOF) in an HP Serviceguard cluster?

     A. Human error   B. Application   C. Electrical power   D. Eetwork card

612. What are TWO HP Serviceguard cluster configurations?

     A. Active/active   B. Active/upgrade   C. Rolling upgrade   D. Active/standby

613. Which command is used to administer and diagnose SCSI devices?

     A. scsiadm   B. scsimgr   C. mgrscsi   D. admscsi

614. Which HP-UX Bastille command is used to compare current and saved Bastille configurations?

     A. bastille_diff   B. bastille_drift   C. bastille_cmp   D. bastille

615. What is the purpose of the lost+found directory in a file system?

     A. Used for JFS intent logging   B. Used to store orphan files
     C. Used to store unnecessary files   D. Used to store unnecessary directories

616. What step-by-step procedure would you follow to run fsck on a file system? List them in sequeunce.

Step 1	A. fsck
Step 2	B. umount
Step 3	C. mount
Step 4	D. Stop all processes using the file system

617. What step-by-step procedure would you follow to install a CPU in a system? List them in sequeunce.

Step 1	A. Shutdown the system to power off state
Step 2	B. Stop all running applications
Step 3	C. Boot the system
Step 4	D. Install the CPU
Step 5	E. Verify the install using the ioscan command
Step 6	F. Open the box

618. What is the sequence to boot and clone a server using an Ignite-UX tape?

Step 1	A. Search for the bootable tape
Step 2	B. Say No to Interact with IPL
Step 3	C. Stop the boot process to go to the BCH

| Step 4 | D. Use the boot command and specify the tape device path |

619. Which of the following are Berkeley services? Choose THREE.

A. telnet　　　　B. BIND　　　　C. ftp　　　　D. rlogin　　　　E. remsh

620. What is the default physical extent size in LVM?

A. 1MB　　　　B. 2MB　　　　C. 4MB　　　　D. 8MB

621. What are the benefits of using the PV Links? Choose TWO.

A. Provide load balancing　　　　　　　　　B. Provide redundancy
C. Provide access to same disk via multiple channels　　　D. Provide access to different disks via single channel

622. Which command would display detailed hardware and OS information?

A. machinfo　　　　B. uname　　　　C. model　　　　D. nwmgr

623. Paths defined in which variable are used for searching man page locations?

A. PATH　　　　B. ECHOPATH　　　　C. MANPATH　　　　D. PATHMAN

624. Which user's privileges a normal user gets if his UID is changed to 0 in the /etc/passwd file?

A. bin　　　　B. root　　　　C. sysadm　　　　D. lp

625. What are THREE benefits of using OnlineJFS?

A. Online resizing　　　　　　　B. Fast resynchronization
C. Automatic deletion of unused files　　　D. Auto defragmentaiton

626. Which THREE statements are true about a logical volume?

A. It is not a file system　　　B. It is a file system　　　C. It may contain a file system
D. It is a swap device　　　　E. It contains a volume group　　　F. It exists inside a volume group

627. When is the information contained in VGRA loaded in memory?

A. When vgsync is executed　　　　　B. When a volume group is activated
C. When vgscan is executed　　　　　D. When a volume group is deactivated

628. Which THREE protocols are used by a PA-RISC client for HP-UX install using an Ignite-UX server?

A. CIFS　　　　B. NFS　　　　C. TFTP　　　　D. instl_bootd

629. What TWO methods can be used to install HP-UX on a new client system using the Ignite-UX server?

A. Boot the client using the bootable HP-UX DVD and point it to the Ignite-UX server
B. Boot the client from the Ignite-UX server
C. Boot the client from the BCH prompt by pointing it to the Ignite-UX server
D. Boot the client using any DVD and point it to the Ignite-UX server

630. Before installing a patch, how would you check if the patch requires a reboot following its installation.

A. All patches require a reboot　　　　B. No patches require a reboot
C. Check the patch's readme file　　　　D. None of the above

631. Which THREE are true for the lanadmin command?

A. Can be used to reset a LAN interface   B. Tells the status of a LAN interface
C. Displays the IP address of a LAN interface   D. Tells the I/O errors of a LAN interface

632. Which of the following services offers file sharing capability between HP-UX and Windows systems?

    A. LDAP   B. CIFS   C. NIS   D. DNS

633. Which of the TWO enables you to end your login session?

    A. ctrl+d   B. out   C. exit   D. quit

634. Which of the following can be used to secure an HP-UX system? Choose THREE.

    A. ssh   B. NIS   C. HIDS   D. PAM

635. How would you force users to change their passwords on a regular basis? Choose TWO.

A. By enabling password aging   B. By disabling password aging
C. By converting the system to trusted mode   D. By using NIS

636. Anonymous user on HP-UX has UID -2 by default?

    A. True   B. False

637. Which THREE are normal user password requirements?

A. Has to be 6-8 characters in length
B. Has to start with a letter
C. Has to use both upper and lowercase letters
D. Has to contain at least one lowercase letter and one numeric or special character

638. When a new process is forked, which of the following statement about swap is true?

A. Kernel reserves memory for the process
B. Kernel creates a new swap space
C. Kernel deletes information about the process's parent process
D. Kernel reserves space for the process

639. What are the steps in sequence to reboot a PA-RISC system gracefully from run level 3 to the single user mode?

Step 1	A. ISL> hpux –is
Step 2	B. Interrupt the boot process
Step 3	C. Stop all applications
Step 4	D. shutdown –ry
Step 5	E. BCH> boot

640. What are the steps in sequence to reboot an Integrity system gracefully from run level 3 to the single user mode?

Step 1	A. HPUX> boot –is
Step 2	B. Interrupt the boot process
Step 3	C. Stop all applications
Step 4	D. shutdown –ry

641. Which variable defines the default printer for a user?

    A. PRNDEST   B. LPDEST   C. PRINT   D. DEFAULT

642. In which file the default system run level is defined ?

   A. /etc/profile   B. /etc/default/inittab   C. /etc/inittab   D. /sbin/inittab

643. What is the purpose of the security patch check tool?

   A. Reports missing security patches   B. Reports missing recommended patches
   C. Tightens system security   D. Checks and installs missing security patches

644. What are the steps in the sequence to extend a busy HFS file system in a logical volume assuming OnlineJFS is installed?

Step 1	A. umount –f
Step 2	B. lvextend
Step 3	C. fuser –cu
Step 4	D. mount
Step 5	E. extendfs

645. Which of the following would run first and last when a system boots up? Choose TWO.

   A. /sbin/rc2.d/S99abc   B. /sbin/rc1.d/s98abc   C. /sbin/rc1.d/S98abc   D. /sbin/rc2.d/s99abc

646. How can a system administrator with root privileges determine a user's lost password?

   A. By decrypting from the /etc/passwd file   B. By decrypting from the /etc/shadow file
   C. By running a password crack tool   D. Cannot determine

647. Which command is used to send a system-wide message to all logged in users?

   A. wall   B. rwall   C. broadcast   D. send

648. Which ftp command would enable you to upload multiple files?

   A. pull   B. mget   C. mput   D. mpull   E. put

649. Which processor families support HP-UX OE? Choose TWO.

   A. Intel Pentium   B. Intel Itanium   C. PA-RISC   D. SPARC   E. Alpha

650. What needs to be done after updating the /etc/mail/aliases file?

   A. Restart Sendmail daemon   B. Run the newaliases command
   C. Run the alises command   D. Reboot the system

651. What are the TWO steps in sequence to extend a busy VxFS file system in a logical volume assuming OnlineJFS is installed?

Step 1	A. umount
Step 2	B. lvextend
Step 3	C. fuser –ck
Step 4	D. mount
Step 5	E. extendfs
Step 6	F. fsadm

652. What is the purpose of the break command in a looping construct?

   A. Breaks out of the shell script   B. Breaks out of the loop
   C. Breaks out of the if statement   D. No effect

653. Which of the following is not an entry in the /etc/passwd file?

　　A. UID　　　　　　B. username　　　　　　C. shell　　　　D. pwd

654. Available memory refers to:

　　A. Available shared memory　　　　B. Memory available after kernel is loaded
　　C. Total system memory　　　　　　D. Available memory for swapping

655. Which daemon responds to the client boot request on an Ignite-UX server?

　　A. bootd　　　　　　B. instl_bootd　　　　　　C. inetd　　　　D. tftpd

656. Which option would you use with the vgscan command to populate /etc/lvmtab file with persistent DSFs?

　　A. –B　　　　　　　B. –A　　　　　C. –N　　　　　　D. –a

657. Which of the following is not a correct subnet mask?

　　A. 255.255.255.255　　B. 255.255.255.192　　　C. 255.255.255.128　　　　D. 255.255.255.224

658. Which IP subnet mask divides a class A IP address into 2000+ networks and 8000+ nodes per subnet?

　　A. 255.255.192.0　　　　　B. 255.255.128.0　　　　C. 255.255.255.128　　　　D. 255.255.224.0

659. If you have a value containing six space-separated fields defined in a variable VAR, how would you extract only the third field?

　　A. echo $VAR | cut –f2 –d" "　　　　B. echo $VAR | cut –f3 –d" "
　　C. cut –f3 –d" " < echo $VAR　　　　D. echo $VAR | grep –f3

660. To start the automounter functionality at each system reboot, where would you define an entry.

　　A. /etc/rc.config.d/netconf　　　　　B. /etc/rc.config.d/nfsconf
　　C. /etc/rc.config.d/netdaemons　　　D. /etc/rc.config.d/automount

661. Match the following:

　　A. Check system's hardware model　　B. Check system's hostname
　　C. Check HP-UX OE version　　　　　D. Check slot information

　　1. uname　　　　　　2. olrad　　　　　3. hostname　　　4. model

662. Given an IP address of 192.168.1.200 and netmask 255.255.255.192, what is the subnet IP?

　　A. 192.168.1.192　　　B. 192.168.1.200　　　　C. 192.168.1.255　　　　D. 192.168.1.0

663. Which command is used to determine the route a packet takes to reach the destination system over the network?

　　A. tracert　　B. traceroute　　　C. route find　　　D. findroute

664. Which option with the swapon command allows you to set a new primary swap for next reboot?

　　A. –a　　　　B. –b　　　　　C. –s　　　　　D. –t

665. Which command is used to report any issues with the installed patches?

　　A. report_patches　　　　B. find_patches　　　　C. check_patches　　　　D. test_patches

666. What is the boot sequence for a vPar on an HP 9000 server? Choose FOUR in the order.

　　A. hpux　　　B. ISL　　　　C. /stand/vpmon　　　　D. /stand/vmunix

667. What is the boot sequence for a non-vPar HP 9000 system? Choose THREE in the order.

    A. hpux   B. ISL   C. /stand/vpmon   D. /stand/vmunix

668. Which protocol is commonly used for network management and monitoring?

    A. SMTP   B. SNMP   C. DNS   D. LDAP

669. What is the boot sequence for a vPar on an Integrity server? Choose FOUR in the order.

    A. EFI   B. hpux.efi   C. /stand/vpmon   D. /stand/vmunix

670. What is the boot sequence for a non-vPar Integrity system? Choose THREE in the order.

    A. EFI   B. hpux.efi   C. /stand/vpmon   D. /stand/vmunix

671. Which command is used to unshar a shar file?

    A. shar   B. unshar   C. sh   D. share

672. Which of the following commands are executed by the create_depot_hpux.11.31 script? Choose THREE.

    A. swcopy   B. swinstall   C. sh   D. swpackage

673. How many nfsd daemon processes run in HP-UX 11i v3 by default to handle NFS client requests?

    A. 1   B. 16   C. 32   D. 64

674. Which commands would find known security issues and vulnerabilities on an HP-UX system? Choose TWO.

    A. swa-report   B. report-swa   C. swa report   D. swa-list

675. Which commands can be used to monitor disk I/O activities? Choose TWO.

    A. top   B. iostat   C. sar   D. ioscan

676. Which is the default packet filtering firewall software in HP-UX 11i v3?

    A. IPFilter   B. Bastille   C. SSH   D. PAM

677. Which command would you use to set, unset and get CIM server properties?

    A. cimserver   B. cimget   C. cimconfig   D. cimconf

678. What is Web-Based Enterprise Management (WBEM)?

    A. A set of software products for multivendor application administration
    B. A set of OS tools for HP-UX administration
    C. A set of standard technologies for multivendor hardware and OS management
    D. A set of tools for Itanium server management

679. Two key components of HP WBEM Services are: Choose TWO.

    A. SIM   B. Client   C. Provider   D. Daemon

680. What is a WBEM provider used for? Choose THREE.

    A. It provides DNS, NTP and NIS configuration information
    B. It provides LVM configuration information
    C. It runs requested action on an HP-UX server
    D. It cannot be used on multiple HP-UX servers

681. What is true about HP WBEM clients?

    A. They are not required for HP WBEM operation   B. They service requests sent by providers
    C. They are purchased separately   D. They are the same as WBEM provider

682. Which WBEM component interacts with WBEM client and provider?

    A. CIM server   B. CIM client   C. CIM provider   D. CIM receiver

683. Which of the following configuration file contents are used if HP WBEM is restarted?

    A. cimserver_reboot.conf   B. cimdaemon_planned.conf
    C. cimdaemon_reboot.conf   D. cimserver_planned.conf

684. Which of the following are true about CIM repository? Choose THREE.

    A. It stores definitions of classes for managed resources
    B. It stores definitions of instances for managed resources
    C. It stores relationship information for managed resources
    D. It stores configuration information for managed resources

685. Which file would you modify to enable the support for NFSv4?

    A. /etc/rc.config.d/nfsconf   B. /etc/default/nfslog   C. /etc/default/nfs   D. /etc/nfs

686. Which variable would you set on the HP-UX server to enable support for NFSv4 also?

    A. NFS_SERVER_VERSMAX   B. NFS_SERVER_VERSION
    C. NFS_SERVER_VERSMIN   D. NFS_SERVER_VERS

687. Which variable would you set on the HP-UX client to enable support for NFSv4 also?

    A. NFS_CLIENT_VERSION   B. NFS_CLIENT_VERSMAX
    C. NFS_CLIENT_VERSMIN   D. NFS_CLIENT_VERS

688. Which variables would you set on the HP-UX server to use NFSv4 only? Choose TWO.

    A. NFS_SERVER_VERSION   B. NFS_SERVER_VERSMAX
    C. NFS_SERVER_VERSMIN   D. NFS_SERVER_VERS

689. How many bits does an IPv4 address contain?

    A. 16   B. 24   C. 32   D. 48   E. 64

690. How many bits does an IPv6 address contain?

    A. 64   B. 96   C. 128   D. 160   E. 192

691. Which command would you use to disable, enable and remove registered CIM providers?

    A. cimclient   B. cimserver   C. cimconfig   D. cimprovider

692. Which of the following would stop WBEM services? Choose TWO.

    A. cimserver   B. /sbin/init.d/cim_server stop   C. cimserver –s   D. cimserver –k

693. HP Systems Insight Manager (HP SIM) is a WBEM-enabled management tool. True or False.

    A. True   B. False

694. Which of the following are true about HP SIM? Choose FOUR.

A. It allows central management of several HP-UX systems
B. It allows managing Windows- and Linux-based systems
C. It allows automatic discovery of networked devices
D. It supports only graphical user interface
E. It generates inventory reports

695. What are the features of HP SIM? Choose THREE.

A. Automatic device identification   B. Supports only manual discovery of devices
C. Fault management   D. Administrative delegation using role-based access control

696. Central Management Server (CMS) of HP SIM is responsible for:

A. HP SIM operation   B. Backup administration
C. Database management   D. Managed systems administration

697. What are the components of HP SIM? Choose THREE.

A. Managed systems   B. Central management server
C. Management domain   D. Hardware

698. Which daemon is responsible for running HP SIM issued commands on remote managed systems?

A. mxdomainmgr   B. mxdtf   C. mxcmd   D. mxcim

699. Which of the following can be used to start and stop HP SIM? Choose TWO.

A. mxstart   B. mxmgr   C. mxadm   D. mxstop

700. Which HP SIM command would you execute to perform initial server configuration?

A. mxstart   B. mxinitconfig   C. mxinit   D. mxtool

701. What is the startup/shutdown script for HP SIM in the /sbin/init.d directory?

A. hpsim   B. sim   C. mxstart   D. mxstop

702. Which variable would you set to 1 in the /etc/rc.config.d/hpsim file to ensure that HP SIM functionality is enabled each time the server reboots?

A. START_SIM   B. START_CIM   C. START_HP_SIM   D. START_HPSIM

703. What is the default HTTP port that HP SIM uses?

A. 270   B. 280   C. 290   D. 300

704. What is the default HTTP port that HP SMH uses?

A. 301   B. 1301   C. 2301   D. 3301

705. Which of the following are correct for Logical Block Addressing (LBA)? Choose TWO.

A. It is a technique used to point to data blocks on a storage device
B. It is replaced by the cylinder-head-sector scheme
C. It has replaced the cylinder-head-sector scheme
D. It is a technique used to point to data blocks on a floppy disk

706. Which operating system cannot be run on the HP BladeSystem?

A. HP-UX 11i v3   B. MS Windows   C. Sun Solaris   D. Linux   E. VMS

707. Which is not a BladeSystem component?

A. Enclosure   B. Server blade   C. Storage blade   D. Modem   E. Interconnect

708. What are the advantages of using BladeSystem technology? Choose FIVE.

A. Less power consumption   B. Redundancy   C. Supports Intel, Itanium and PA-RISC processors
D. Reduced maintenance   E. Affordability   F. Less expensive

709. What is the BladeSystem management software called?

A. Onboard Manager   B. BladeSystem Manager
C. BladeSystem Administrator   D. Onboard Administrator

710. Which commands can be used to run swa step-by-step? Choose TWO.

A. swa   B. swa-report   C. swa-step   D. swa-run

711. Which command would download patches in a depot format identified by swa-report?

A. swa   B. swa-get   C. swa-download   D. swa-clean

712. Which patch management tools have been superseded by Software Assistant? Choose TWO.

A. swpatches   B. patchadm   C. security_patch_check tool   D. patch assessment tool

713. SWA can be integrated with HP SIM. True or False.

A. True   B. False

714. What type of checks does SWA run on a system?

A. Patch warnings   B. Critical defects   C. Security bulletins   D. All of the above

715. What is the main command to manage Pay Per Use (PPU)?

A. ppuadm   B. ppuconfig   C. ppuconf   D. ppuadmin

716. What is Pay Per Use (PPU)?

A. Security tool   B. Load balancer   C. Pricing model   D. Utility meter

717. Which LVM command would you use to convert a volume group to use persistent DSFs that is currently using legacy DSFs?

A. vgconvert   B. vgdsf   C. vgchange   D. vgmodify

718. Which of the following would you run to revert Bastille configuration?

A. bastille   B. bastille --reverse   C. bastille –r   D. bastille –pre

719. HP-UX Bastille supports command line as well as graphical interfaces. True or False.

A. True   B. False

720. What can be controlled/configured using HP-UX Bastille? Choose FOUR.

A. Setuid files   B. User logins   C. cron daemon   D. SMH   E. IPFilter-based firewall

721. What is true about HP-UX Bastille? Choose THREE.

A. Security hardening and lockdown tool   B. Can be integrated with HP SIM
C. Included in all 11i v3 OE bundles   D. Cannot be integrated with HP SIM

722. Which command would you run to lockdown security?

    A. bastille –r   B. bastille –lock   C. bastille –l   D. bastille –x

723. What would the following command do?

    # bastille –b –f /etc/opt/sec_mgmt/bastille/sec_config

    A. Creates sec_config file   B. Removes sec_config file
    C. Duplicates sec_config file on several HP-UX servers   D. Modifies sec_config file

724. What is the name of the node in a cluster where a configured Serviceguard package attempts to start first?

    A. Adoptive node   B. Primary node C. Passive node   D. Standby node

725. What is the name of the node in a cluster where a configured Serviceguard package attempts to failover?

    A. Adoptive node   B. Primary node C. Active node   D. Sleeping node

726. What is the term used for shutting down a Serviceguard package on one node and starting up on the other?

    A. Stopover   B. Failover   C. Reliability   D. Startover

727. True or False. Failback is opposite of failover.

    A. True   B. False

728. What does the term "availability" mean?

    A. Measurement of overall system uptime minus any unplanned downtime
    B. Measurement of overall system uptime
    C. Measurement of overall system downtime minus any planned uptime
    D. Measurement of overall system uptime minus 365 hours

729. What is high availability?

    A. It is the same as fault tolerance   B. A management software
    C. A software product   D. A design technique

730. What is fault tolerance?

    A. Ability of a system to survive and continue to function in the event of a failure
    B. Ability of a system to reboot and continue to function in the event of a hardware failure
    C. Ability of a system to shutdown and power off in the event of a hardware or software failure
    D. None of the above

731. What is uptime?

    A. Time duration when a business application remains up and available for user access
    B. Time duration when a business application remains up, but may or may not be available for user access
    C. Both of the above
    D. None of the above

732. What is downtime?

    A. Maximum 5 hours per day when application is unavailable for user access
    B. Opposite of uptime
    C. Measurement of time when users do not access application
    D. None of the above

733. What is the IP address called that binds itself to a configured LAN interface on the failover server? Choose TWO.

    A. Virtual IP
    B. Floating IP
    C. Network IP
    D. LAN IP

734. Which command would you use to view the version of BIND?

    A. who   B. whereis   C. whence   D. what

735. Which command can you use to unshare all shared NFS resources?

    A. unexport   B. unshareall   C. unshare   D. unexport –a

736. Which command can you use to unshare a shared NFS resource?

    A. unexport   B. unshareall   C. unshare   D. unexport –a

737. Which Serviceguard cluster software product supports cluster nodes located in two continents?

    A. Metro cluster   B. Campus cluster   C. Continental cluster   D. Serviceguard cluster

738. Which Serviceguard cluster software product supports cluster nodes located side by side?

    A. Metro cluster   B. Campus cluster   C. Continental cluster   D. Serviceguard cluster

739. Which Serviceguard cluster software product supports cluster nodes located within city limits?

    A. Metro cluster   B. Campus cluster   C. Continental cluster   D. Serviceguard cluster

740. Which Serviceguard cluster package runs concurrently on one or more cluster nodes?

    A. Failover   B. System multinode   C. Multinode   D. None of the above

741. Which Serviceguard cluster package runs concurrently on all cluster nodes?

    A. Failover   B. System multinode   C. Multinode   D. None of the above

742. Which Serviceguard cluster package runs on one cluster node at a time?

    A. Failover   B. System multinode   C. Multinode   D. None of the above

743. True or False from NFS perspective. Identification establishes identity of systems and users, authentication confirms the identity and authorization controls what information systems and users have access to.

    A. True   B. False

744. True or False. In NFSv4, an exchange of information takes place between NFS client and server for identification, authentication and authorization, and in transit information is encrypted.

    A. True   B. False

745. What features have been added to or enhanced in NFSv4? Choose THREE.

    A. Security   B. WAN support   C. Cross-platform interoperability   D. 256GB file size support

746. NFS is stateless. What does that mean?

    A. NFS keeps track of what a client system is doing on a shared resource

B. NFS does not know what users are doing on NFS client system

C. NFS does not keep track of what a client system is doing on a shared resource

D. NFS does not keep track of when NFS client system reboots

747. What would the following command do?

evfsvol close /dev/evfs/vg00/lvol_evfs1

A. Closes the EVFS volume for block access
B. Unmounts the EVFS volume
C. Closes the EVFS volume for raw access
D. Closes and reopens the EVFS volume

748. What would the following command do?

evfsvol raw /dev/evfs/vg00/lvol_evfs1

A. Opens the EVFS volume for block access
B. Mounts the EVFS volume
C. Opens the EVFS volume for raw access
D. Closes and reopens the EVFS volume

749. What would the following command do?

evfsvol delete –u user1 /dev/evfs/vg00/lvol_evfs1

A. Deletes key record pair for the EVFS volume for user1

B. Deletes recovery keys for the EVFS volume for user1

C. Deletes both user and recovery keys for the EVFS volume for user1

D. Deletes nothing, but displays what would happen if this command is run

750. What would the following command do?

evfsvol delete –u user1 –r /dev/evfs/vg00/lvol_evfs1

A. Deletes key record pair for the EVFS volume for user1

B. Deletes recovery keys for the EVFS volume for user1

C. Deletes both user and recovery keys for the EVFS volume for user1

D. Deletes nothing, but displays what would happen if this command is run

751. What would the following command do?

evfsvol check –a

A. Verifies the integrity of EMD of EVFS volumes

B. Checks the integrity of data in EVFS volumes

C. Verifies if EVFS volumes are open for raw access

D. Checks the status of EVFS volumes

752. What is the default EVFS user account name?

A. evfsadm   B. evfs   C. evfsconf   D. evfs_adm

753. What is the default EVFS group account name?

A. evfsadm   B. evfs   C. evfsconf   D. evfs_adm

754. What is a Logical Unit Number (LUN)? Choose TWO.

A. Physical storage entity defined on RAID arrays
B. Can be created on DVD drives
C. Seen as a physical disk drive by the server arrays
D. Logical storage entity defined on RAID

755. What is a Storage Area Network (SAN)?

A. A network of tape libraries   B. A network of storage devices
C. A local network of servers   D. A network of servers and storage devices connected via switches

756. Which of the following enables CIFS to map Windows and Unix user and group accounts?

 A. winbind   B. smbd   C. nmbd   D. sambad

757. Which is not a benefit of mass storage stack?

 A. Scalability   B. Load balancing   C. Performance   D. Security

758. Which is not a benefit of mass storage stack?

 A. Adaptability   B. Native multipathing   C. File transfer   D. Agile addressing

759. What benefit would you get with agile addressing?

 A. One persistent DSF for all hardware paths to a single device
 B. Two persistent DSFs for each hardware path to a single device
 C. One persistent DSF for each hardware path to a single device
 D. Two persistent DSFs for all hardware paths to a single device

760. Which is not true about persistent binding?

 A. It is enabled by default
 B. It is not enabled by default
 C. No modifications are necessary if any of the paths to a device is altered
 D. It can co-exist with legacy bindings

761. Which of the following are correct about HP-UX IPFilter? Choose TWO.

 A. It is enabled by default
 B. It logs detailed information
 C. It is installed by default
 D. It supports NATting and X.25

762. Match appropriately.

 A. /etc/nsswitch.conf   B. /etc/resolv.conf   C. /etc/networks   D. /etc/rpc

  1. Contains DNS client configuration information
  2. Contains which source to use for looking up information on host, password, group, etc.
  3. Contains mappings for rpc program name and number
  4. Contains mappings for official network name, number and any aliases

763. Which of the following correctly describes when launching a tool using HP SIM?

 A. Users are authenticated using PAM and authorizations are defined in /etc/passwd file
 B. Authorizations are defined in HP SIM CMS and users are authenticated using PAM
 C. Authorizations need not be defined in HP SIM CMS because users are already defined in it
 D. All normal users are defined in HP SIM by default to perform administrative functions

764. Which of the following controls SMH behavior? Choose TWO.

 A. /opt/hpsmh/lbin/envvars   B. /opt/hpsmh/conf/envvars
 C. /opt/hpsmh/conf/timeout.conf   D. /opt/hpsmh/lbin/timeout.conf

765. Which of the following could become performance bottleneck? Choose FOUR.

A. Memory B. CPU C. Disk D. Network E. vPar

766. Which of the following can be used to zero out file1's contents? Choose TWO.

 A. >file1 B. cat /dev/null > file1 C. touch file1 D. zero file1

767. What are the advantages of parallel probing of devices? Choose TWO.

 A. Higher availability   B. Reduced I/O scan time
 C. Reduced system boot time D. No benefit

768. What is the sequence of commands to rename a volume group without removing any data?

 A. vgchange, vgremove, vgimport   B. vgexport, mkdir, mknod, vgimport
 C. vgexport, vgimport   D. vgremove, vgcreate

769. Which command would you use to remove a vPAr which is already shutdown?

 A. vparremove B. parremove C. vpardelete   D. pardelete

770. What is the significance of the letter "x" in the password field of the /etc/passwd file?

 A. Shadow password is enabled B. Shadow password will be enabled at the next system reboot
 C. All user passwords have expired D. All users have been disabled

771. Which feature of HP-UX 11i v3 is not available on PA-RISC servers?

 A. Multiuser dumps B. Fast crash dumps   C. Express crash dumps D. Concurrent dumps

772. Which virtual partition feature was unavailable on HP-UX versions prior to 11i v3?

 A. Dynamic CPU migration   B. Dynamic I/O migration
 C. Dynamic memory migration   D. None of the above

773. What is the significance of /etc/lvmpvg file?

 A. Allows you to control LVM structures   B. Allows you to follow non-strict PVG policy
 C. Allows you to do mirroring   D. Allows you to follow PVG-strict allocation policy

774. What would the following do in POSIX shell?

 2>>file1

 A. Redirects output to file1   B. Redirects error messages to file1
 C. Receives input from file1   D. Redirects input to file1

775. Which command allows you to execute a program using a different user's ID?

 A. privrun B. pubrun C. privexec D. pubexec

776. Which of the following are new security features in HP-UX 11i v2 and 11i v3? Choose THREE.

 A. HP-UX Bastille B. Install-time security C. EVFS   D. NATting

777. Which LVM command can be used to display all logical volumes in a volume group?

 A. vgview B. vgdisplay C. pvdisplay D. lvdisplay

778. Which new features in HP-UX 11i v3 potentially enhance overall I/O performance? Choose TWO.

 A. Persistent DSFs B. Agile addressing   C. Native multipathing D. Unified file cache

779. Which LVM command would you use to reflect the new increased size of a LUN which is part of a volume group?

    A. vgdsf   B. pvextend   C. pvmodify   D. vgmodify

780. Which protocols are supported by the CIFS server for user authentication? Choose TWO.

    A. SSH   B. Kerberos   C. user keys   D. NTLM

781. Which of the following server models do not support HP-UX 11i v3? Choose THREE.

    A. L3000   B. N4000   C. rp3410   D. vPAr version A.03.x   E. BL60p

782. Which of the following can be used to terminate a process? Choose TWO.

    A. kill   B. term   C. pkill   D. pgrep

783. Which sftp command would download several files in a directory?

    A. put/mput   B. get/mget   C. pull/mpull   D. fetch

784. Which of the following security tools can be used to detect an attack on an HP-UX system?

    A. HIDS   B. SSH   C. DNSSEC   D. Bastille

785. Which file provides an extra layer of network security?

    A. /etc/init.d/sec   B. /var/adm/inetd.sec   C. /etc/inetd.conf   D. /var/adm/init.sec

786. Match commands on the left with descriptions on the right:

    A. ioscan   1. Creates device files
    B. machinfo   2. Displays system diagnostic messages
    C. dmesg   3. Displays LAN interface status
    D. uname   4. Performs online replacement of PCI cards
    E. lanscan   5. Scans and displays system I/O devices
    F. olrad   6. Displays OS version
    G. insf   7. Displays detailed machine information

787. What does the /etc/ftpd/ftpusers file contain?

    A. Usernames that are allowed ftp access into the system
    B. Usernames that are not allowed ftp access into the system
    C. ftp configuration information
    D. Usernames that are allowed passwordless ftp access into the system

788. Which file maintains unsuccessful user login attempts history?

    A. /etc/utmps   B. /var/adm/btmps   C. /var/adm/wtmps   D. /var/adm/tmp.log

789. Which file maintains successful user login attempts history?

    A. /etc/utmps   B. /var/adm/btmps   C. /var/adm/wtmps   D. /var/adm/tmp.log

790. Which command would you use on a non-trusted system to determine if a local user account is locked?

    A. userstat   B. userlock   C. userinfo   D. usermod

791. Which of the following are benefits of using EVFS? Choose TWO.

    A. Secures data transfer   B. Supports LVM and VxVM

C. Secures data at rest   D. Secures IP communication

792. How many install-time security bundles are available?

    A. 2   B. 3   C. 4   D. 5

793. What do the whence and which commands do?

    A. Display setuid bit on the specified file   B. Display file information of the specified file
    C. Display absolute path of the specified file   D. Display relative path of the specified file

794. What happens if the telnet command is invoked without an argument?

    A. Nothing   B. Displays telnet prompt   C. Stops telnet daemon   D. Starts telnet daemon

795. What is the order of cron.allow and cron.deny file evaluation when both files contain user entries?

    A. Both are evaluated at the same time   B. cron.allow, cron.deny
    C. cron.deny, cron.allow   D. Only cron.allow is used

796. Which of the following is true about the priority of a child process?

    A. The child process gets lower priority than its parent's
    B. The child process inherits root user's priority
    C. The child process gets higher priority than its parent's
    D. The child process inherits its parent priority

797. Match install-time security bundle definitions with correct bundle names?

    A. Installs security infrastructure with optional security features disabled
    B. Installs a host-based lockdown system without HP-UX IPFilter firewall
    C. Installs a managed lockdown system with HP-UX IPFilter firewall
    D. Installs a full DMZ lockdown system with B and C included

    1. Sec10Host   2. Sec30DMZ   3. Sec20MngDMZ   4. Sec00Tools

798. What does the swlist command display without an argument? Choose THREE.

    A. Software name   B. Software version   C. Software vendor   D. Software description

799. Which of the following cannot be configured using set_parms utility?

    A. Bastille   B. IP address   C. System date/time   D. Timezone

800. In which file in the /etc/rc.config.d directory would you set DHCP_ENABLE variable?

    A. lanconf   B. netconf   C. dhcpconf   D. nfsconf

801. True or false. An alias hostname is just another name for a host?

    A. True   B. False

802. In which file would you set sendmail mail relay information?

    A. /etc/mail/sendmail.cw   B. /etc/mail/sendmail.cf
    C. /etc/mail/sendmail.conf   D. /etc/mail/mail.cf

803. True or false. Mirroring is also referred to as RAID 1?

    A. True   B. False

804. Which default system settings are included in the /etc/default directory? Choose TWO.

A. User attributes   B. File system type
C. Administrator email address   D. System profiles

805. Which of the following is not enabled by WBEM providers instrumentation?

A. Inventory reports   B. Display system properties and health status
C. Automatic discovery   D. Display component health

806. What step can you take to optimize an existing VxFS file system?

A. Upgrade to newer version   B. Create an additional device swap
C. Remount with different options   D. Remove the file system and create another

807. Which file would you consult to check if a service was failed to start during system startup?

A. /var/log/rc.log   B. /etc/rc.log   C. /var/log/syslog.log   D. /etc/syslog.log

808. What are the benefits of using SSH utilities?

A. Use encryption during data transfer   B. Use hidden keys for authorization
C. Log audit trail   D. Both A and B

809. What are the benefits of using SMH? Choose FOUR.

A. Allows to configure and manage HP-UX   B. Allows to view system events
C. Allows to configure and manage several HP-UX systems   D. Allows to view system health
E. Allows to manage WBEM subscriptions

810. What are the best practices for planning a swap area? Choose THREE.

A. Dedicate one disk for all swap areas   B. File system swap should be at lower priority than device swap
C. Use not more than one swap per disk   D. Create several device swap logical volumes

811. alias rm="rm –i" is an example of:

A. Filename completion   B. Alias substitution
C. Tilde substitution   D. Command substitution

812. echo ~user2 ia an example of:

A. Filename completion   B. Command completion
C. Tilde substitution   D. Command substitution

813. Which tool in HP-UX 11i v3 has replaced SAM?

A. SMH   B. SIM   C. WBEM   D. SWAT

814. Which daemon is required to run in order for SMH to function?

A. smhd   B. smhstartd   C. smhsd   D. smh

815. What would you type in a web browser to bring SMH up?

A. http://hostname:301   B. http://hostname:1301
C. http://hostname:2301   D. http://hostname:3301

816. Which of the following SMH cannot do?

A. User/group management   B. Network interface management   C. Kernel administration
D. nPar management   E. Disk/LVM management   F. Software/patch management
G. Remote server management H. Auditing/security configuration   I. Network switch management

---

817. What type of connectivity does a fibre channel card provide?

    A. Wireless   B. Printer   C. Optical   D. Copper

818. Which of the following is true about Multi I/O cards?

    A. Provide LAN interfaces   B. Provide fibre ports
    C. Provide SCSI ports   D. Provide a combination of above

819. How many cores a server will have if it is configured with 4 cell boards and 8 dual-core processor modules?

    A. 8   B. 16   C. 32   D. 64   E. 128

820. What do the commands iobind and iofind do? Choose TWO.

    A. Migrates from agile view to legacy view   B. Migrates from legacy to agile view
    C. Removes specific drivers from system   D. Binds a driver to a LUN

821. What would insf –Lv do?

    A. Displays whether legacy mode is enabled   B. Creates persistent DSFs for LVM
    C. Creates both legacy and persistent DSFs for LVM   D. All of the above

822. What would rmsf –L do?

    A. Displays legacy DSFs   B. Removes legacy DSFs for LVM
    C. Removes all legacy DSFs and associated configuration   D. Removes persistent DSFs

823. What would ioscan –m dsf do? Choose TWO.

    A. Displays mappings between persistent and legacy DSFs
    B. Displays mappings between legacy and persistent DSFs
    C. Displays mappings between lunpath hardware path and LUN hardware path
    D. All of the above

824. What would ioscan –m lun do?

    A. Displays mappings between persistent and legacy DSFs
    B. Displays mappings of a LUN hardware path to its lunpath hardware paths
    C. Displays mappings between persistent DSFs and LUN hardware path
    D. Displays mappings between legacy DSFs and LUN hardware path

825. Which directories store persistent DSFs for disk devices? Choose TWO.

    A. /dev/dsk B. /dev/rdisk   C. /dev/disk   D. /dev/rdsk

826. Which directory stores persistent DSFs for tape devices?

    A. /dev/rmt B. /dev/rtape   C. /dev/rdisk   D. /dev/tape

827. Which option with the ioscan command would you use to view persistent DSFs?

    A. –N   B. –n   C. –P   D. –p

828. What is a lunpath hardware path?

    A. It represents all persistent DSFs to a single LUN
    B. It represents all hardware paths to a single LUN
    C. It represents all LUN hardware paths to a single LUN

D. It represents all hardware paths to all LUNs

829. What is a LUN hardware path?

   A. It represents all legacy DSFs to a single LUN
   B. It represents all persistent DSFs to a single LUN
   C. It represents all LUN hardware paths to a single LUN
   D. It represents all lunpath hardware paths to a single LUN

830. Which option with the ioscan command would you use to list deferred bindings?

   A. –N   B. –n   C. –B   D. –p

831. Which option with the ioscan command would you use to initiate deferred bindings?

   A. –b   B. –n   C. –B   D. –p

832. Which option with the ioscan command would you use to delete deferred bindings?

   A. –N   B. –n   C. –B   D. –r

833. Which option with the lssf command would you use to display stale DSFs?

   A. –N   B. –s   C. –B   D. –p

834. What is the typical prefix that goes with Integrity virtual machines management commands?

   A. ivm   B. vm   C. hpvm   D. hpivm

835. What is the typical prefix that goes with instant capacity management commands?

   A. hpicap   B. icap   C. icaphp   D. ic

836. Which of the following is not an HP virtualtion software management tool?

   A. Capacity advisor   B. Virtualization manager   C. Utility meter   D. vparmgr

837. Which of the following is not an EVFS administration command?

   A. evfsadm   B. evfspkey   C. evfsconfig   D. evfsvol

838. Which is the main EVFS configuration file in the /etc/evfs directory?

   A. evfsadm.conf   B. evfs.conf   C. evfsadm.cf   D. evfs.cf

839. Which command is used to start and stop EVFS?

   A. evfsadm   B. evfsconf   C. evfs   D. evfsexec

840. What would the following do?

   # evfspkey keygen –s –u user1 –k uk100

   A. Creates EVFS keys with an automatically generated passphrase
   B. Creates EVFS keys by the name uk100 for user2 with an automatically generated passphrase
   C. Creates EVFS keys by the name uk100 for user1 with an automatically generated passphrase
   D. Creates EVFS keys by the name uk100 with an automatically generated passphrase

841. What would the following do?

   # evfspkey keygen –r

   A. Creates EVFS recovery keys

B. Creates EVFS recovery keys for user1

C. Creates EVFS recovery keys by the name uk100 for user1 with an automatically generated passphrase

D. Creates EVFS recovery keys with an automatically generated passphrase

842. What would the following command do?

evfsvol enable –k rk100 /dev/evfs/vg00/lvol_evfs1

A. Mounts the EVFS volume
B. Activates the EVFS volume
C. Opens the EVFS volume for raw access
D. Opens the EVFS volume

843. What would the following command do?

evfspkey passgen –u user1

A. Modifies passphrase for a private key
B. Creates passphrase for a private key
C. Unassigns passphrase
D. Removes user private keys

844. Which one best describes pseudo swap?

A. Portion of file system swap
B. Portion of device swap used for faster swapping
C. Portion of LVM disk
D. Portion of physical memory used for swapping

845. When is pseudo swap configured?

A. Automatically when kernel needs it
B. Configured via SIM
C. At system boot
D. Configured via SMH

846. Which of the following is not a kernel configuration tool in HP-UX 11i v3?

A. kcmodule   B. kctune   C. kconfig   D. kcparam   E. kcweb

847. Which command would query shmmni kernel tunable and display detailed information?

A. kctune –v shmmni   B. kcmodule –v shmmni   C. kconfig –v shmmni   D. kctune shmmni

848. Which commands would modify shmmni kernel tunable to 700? Choose TWO.

A. kctune shmmni=700   B. kctune –h shmmni=700   C. kctune shmmni=   D. kctune 700

849. On an Integrity server, what would you type to boot the system into tunable maintenance mode?

A. boot –t   B. hpux –tm   C. boot –tm   D. boot –m

850. What would the following pax command do?

pax –vwf /dev/rtape/tape1_BEST /etc

A. Backs up /etc directory to tape
B. Extracts /etc directory from tape
C. Lists tape contents for /etc directory
D. Removes /etc directory contents from tape

851. What would the following do?

ISL> hpux shmmni=1000

A. Boots the system in tunable maintenance mode
B. Boots the system using the default shmmni value
C. Boots the system with the modified value
D. Boots the system and ignores the value of shmmni

852. What would the following do?

kcmodule cdfs=loaded

A. Unloads the cdfs module   B. Loads the cdfs module
C. Configures the cdfs module to load at next reboot   D. Displays if the cdfs module is loaded

853. What would the following do?

kcmodule –c SC_2

A. Lists SC_2   B. Configures SC_2 tunable
C. Lists all modules defined in SC_2   D. Configures SC_2 module

854. Which of the following can be used to view PID of a specific process? Choose TWO.

A. ps –ef | grep   B. pgrep   C. plist   D. list

855. Which command would you use to convert the contents of /etc/exports file to /etc/dfs/dfstab file?

A. convertexports   B. exp2dfs   C. dfs4exp   D. convexp

856. Which startup/shutdown script in the /sbin/init.d directory is responsible for starting up and shutting down rpc.lockd and rpc.statd daemons?

A. nfslock   B. statlock   C. lockstat   D. lockmgr

857. Which command is equivalent to SMH → Disks and File Systems?

A. fsweb   B. kcweb   C. lvmweb   D. dfsweb

858. Which command is equivalent to SMH → Networking and Communications?

A. fsweb   B. kcweb   C. ncweb   D. dfsweb

859. Which command is equivalent to SMH → Accounts for Users and Groups?

A. fsweb   B. ugweb   C. lvmweb   D. dfsweb

860. Which command is equivalent to SMH → Peripheral Devices?

A. pdweb   B. kcweb   C. ncweb   D. dfsweb

861. Which command is equivalent to SMH → Kernel Configuration?

A. pdweb   B. kcweb   C. ncweb   D. dfsweb

862. Which is the command to administer application core files?

A. coreapp   B. core_manage C. coreconfig   D. coreadm

863. What is the default maximum NFS version used in HP-UX 11i v3?

A. v2   B. v3   C. v4   D. v5

Appendix B – Answers to CSA Exam Review Questions

1. C	2. D	3. C	4. B
5. C	6. E	7. D	8. A
9. BCD	10. C	11. A	12. BC
13. ABC	14. D	15. A	16. A
17. B	18. C	19. D	20. B
21. C	22. B	23. C	24. B
25. C	26. D	27. C	28. A
29. D	30. C	31. B	32. D
33. C	34. A	35. A	36. ABC
37. ACD	38. E	39. C	40. B
41. B	42. B	43. A3B2C1D4	44. AC
45. A	46. B	47. B	48. B
49. D	50. C	51. AC	52. D
53. B	54. A	55. C	56. A
57. B	58. A	59. C	60. D
61. D	62. D	63. C	64. A
65. B	66. A	67. A	68. B
69. A	70. B	71. A	72. BD
73. BD	74. A	75. C	76. B
77. B	78. AB	79. D	80. A
81. B	82. A	83. A	84. B
85. D	86. A	87. C	88. B
89. C	90. D	91. A	92. B
93. D	94. C	95. BD	96. D
97. B	98. A	99. C	100. AD
101. D	102. B	103. D	104. C
105. C	106. CD	107. C	108. C
109. A	110. D	111. C	112. AC
113. D	114. B	115. AC	116. A
117. C	118. B	119. ABD	120. A
121. A	122. B	123. BC	124. ADF
125. D	126. C	127. D	128. B
129. A	130. D	131. B	132. B
133. D	134. C	135. A	136. A
137. AC	138. C	139. A	140. AD
141. A	142. D	143. ACD	144. D
145. A	146. C	147. A	148. B
149. ABD	150. B	151. C	152. A
153. B	154. CD	155. D	156. D

157. A	158. A	159. C	160. B
161. C	162. D	163. ABD	164. A
165. C	166. A	167. B	168. C
169. ACD	170. B	171. A	172. A
173. B	174. C	175. ACD	176. C
177. B	178. B	179. B	180. E
181. C	182. D	183. B	184. A
185. A	186. C	187. B	188. A
189. AD	190. B	191. A	192. B
193. BC	194. ABC	195. B	196. A
197. AB	198. D	199. D	200. C
201. B	202. B	203. A	204. C
205. B	206. D	207. C	208. D
209. D	210. B	211. D	212. C
213. D	214. CD	215. A	216. B
217. A	218. C	219. AC	220. B
221. B	222. C	223. D	224. C
225. AB	226. BC	227. D	228. A
229. C	230. D	231. B	232. C
233. D	234. A	235. A	236. B
237. A	238. D	239. A	240. D
241. AB	242. B	243. AD	244. BC
245. D	246. AC	247. A	248. BD
249. D	250. A	251. C	252. B
253. D	254. A	255. D	256. C
257. D	258. B	259. AB	260. C
261. AD	262. B	263. C	264. B
265. A	266. D	267. A	268. B
269. B	270. C	271. D	272. C
273. B	274. C	275. A	276. C
277. D	278. B	279. B	280. B
281. A	282. B	283. C	284. A
285. ABC	286. D	287. BD	288. B
289. C	290. B	291. D	292. B
293. A	294. B	295. C	296. B
297. CD	298. C	299. A	300. B
301. A	302. A	303. C	304. B
305. D	306. D	307. B	308. C
309. ABD	310. A	311. B	312. A
313. C	314. A	315. BD	316. AB
317. C	318. C	319. C	320. B
321. D	322. ACD	323. B	324. AB
325. C	326. BC	327. C	328. ACD
329. B	330. B	331. B	332. A
333. AB	334. ABD	335. A	336. A
337. ABC	338. B	339. D	340. A
341. D	342. BD	343. BC	344. D
345. A	346. C	347. B	348. AC
349. D	350. CD	351. A	352. B

353. A	354. C	355. A	356. C
357. B	358. B	359. CD	360. C
361. A	362. A	363. C	364. D
365. B	366. D	367. BD	368. A
369. C	370. BD	371. D	372. B
373. AB	374. C	375. AB	376. AD
377. A	378. ABC	379. B	380. C
381. B	382. B	383. A	384. CD
385. B	386. D	387. C	388. AC
389. D	390. B	391. ABDE	392. AD
393. B	394. A	395. C	396. BCD
397. D	398. CD	399. B	400. ABD
401. C	402. A	403. C	404. A
405. B	406. D	407. C	408. BCD
409. BC	410. C	411. B	412. A
413. C	414. A	415. B	416. D
417. B	418. C	419. D	420. A
421. D	422. BD	423. D	424. C
425. B	426. A	427. AD	428. B
429. A	430. B	431. D	432. D
433. ABC	434. A	435. C	436. B
437. A	438. C	439. C	440. C
441. C	442. D	443. C	444. A
445. B	446. A	447. D	448. C
449. B	450. B	451. C	452. D
453. A	454. A	455. B	456. C
457. B	458. C	459. D	460. B
461. C	462. D	463. C	464. A
465. B	466. A	467. C	468. D
469. B	470. BD	471. B	472. C
473. A	474. ABC	475. B	476. ABC
477. C	478. B	479. B	480. C
481. ACD	482. B	483. C	484. A
485. A	486. C	487. D	488. B
489. C	490. D	491. B	492. C
493. A	494. B	495. D	496. B
497. A	498. B	499. B	500. D
501. C	502. A	503. B	504. A
505. D	506. A	507. B	508. D
509. C	510. B	511. C	512. A
513. B	514. C	515. D	516. D
517. B	518. C	519. D	520. B
521. A	522. C	523. ACD	524. AC
525. B	526. C	527. BC	528. B
529. BCD	530. B	531. C	532. A
533. D	534. B	535. B	536. B
537. B	538. BC	539. A	540. A
541. B	542. C	543. D	544. A
545. B	546. C	547. B	548. B

549. B	550. D	551. B	552. A
553. D	554. A	555. D	556. B
557. A	558. C	559. D	560. C
561. A	562. ABC	563. D	564. A
565. A	566. B	567. A	568. B
569. B	570. BC	571. D	572. AD
573. D	574. D	575. swapinfo	576. A
577. D	578. netconf	579. C	580. D
581. A	582. A3B1C2	583. BC	584. A
585. B	586. B	587. AD	588. C
589. CD	590. B	591. AB	592. D
593. ACD	594. A3B1C4D2	595. B	596. A
597. B	598. A2B4C1D3E5	599. BCE	600. AC
601. D	602. BC	603. B	604. ABDEF
605. AB	606. B	607. ABD	608. BC
609. A	610. D	611. A	612. AD
613. B	614. B	615. B	616. DBAC
617. BAFDCE	618. CADB	619. BDE	620. C
621. BC	622. A	623. C	624. B
625. ABD	626. ACF	627. B	628. BCD
629. AC	630. C	631. ABD	632. B
633. AC	634. ACD	635. AC	636. A
637. ABD	638. D	639. CDBEA	640. CDBA
641. B	642. C	643. A	644. CABED
645. CA	646. D	647. A	648. C
649. BC	650. B	651. BF	652. B
653. D	654. B	655. C	656. C
657. A	658. D	659. B	660. B
661. A4B3C1D2	662. A	663. B	664. C
665. C	666. BACD	667. BAD	668. B
669. ABCD	670. ABD	671. C	672. ACD
673. A	674. AC	675. BC	676. A
677. A	678. C	679. BC	680. ABC
681. B	682. A	683. D	684. B
685. C	686. A	687. B	688. BC
689. C	690. C	691. D	692. BC
693. A	694. ABCE	695. ACD	696. A
697. ABC	698. B	699. AD	700. B
701. A	702. D	703. B	704. C
705. AC	706. E	707. D	708. ABDEF
709. D	710. AC	711. B	712. CD
713. A	714. D	715. B	716. C
717. B	718. C	719. B	720. ABCE
721. ABC	722. D	723. C	724. B
725. A	726. B	727. A	728. A
729. D	730. A	731. A	732. B
733. AB	734. D	735. B	736. C
737. C	738. D	739. A	740. C
741. B	742. A	743. A	744. A

745. ABC	746. C	747. C	748. C
749. A	750. C	751. A	752. B
753. B	754. CD	755. D	756. A
757. D	758. C	759. A	760. B
761. AC	762. A2B1C4D3	763. B	764. AC
765. ABCD	766. AB	767. BC	768. B
769. A	770. A	771. D	772. C
773. D	774. B	775. A	776. ABC
777. B	778. CD	779. D	780. BD
781. ABD	782. AC	783. B	784. A
785. B	786. A5B7C2D6E3F4G1	787. B	788. B
789. C	790. A	791. BC	792. C
793. C	794. B	795. D	796. D
797. A4B1C3D2	798. ABD	799. A	800. B
801. A	802. B	803. A	804. AB
805. C	806. C	807. B	808. A
809. ABDE	810. BCD	811. B	812. C
813. A	814. B	815. C	816. G
817. C	818. D	819. D	820. AD
821. A	822. C	823. AB	824. B
825. BC	826. B	827. A	828. B
829. C	830. C	831. A	832. D
833. B	834. C	835. B	836. C
837. C	838. B	839. A	840. C
841. A	842. B	843. A	844. D
845. C	846. D	847. A	848. AB
849. C	850. A	851. C	852. B
853. C	854. AB	855. B	856. D
857. A	858. C	859. B	860. A
861. B	862. D	863. B	

Appendix C – Table of HP-UX Commands

This table provides a list of significant HP-UX commands and their short description. Although there are hundreds of commands available in HP-UX, however only those are covered that are used more oftenly.

File and Directory	
cat	Creates a small file, joins two files and displays contents of a file.
cd	Changes directory.
compress/uncompress	Compresses/uncompresses files.
cp	Copies files or directories.
diff	Compares files or directories for differences.
file	Displays file type.
find	Searches for files in the directory structure.
grep/egrep/fgrep	Matches text within text files.
gzip/gunzip	Compresses/uncompresses files.
head/tail	Displays beginning/ending of a text file.
ln	Links files and directories.
ls/lsf/lsx/lsr/ll/l/lc	Lists files and directories in different formats.
mkdir	Creates a directory.
more/pg	Displays a text file one screenful at a time.
mv	Moves and renames files and directories.
mvdir	Moves and renames directories.
pwd	Displays full path to the current working directory.
rcp	Copies files from one system to another.
rm	Removes files and directories.
rmdir	Removes an empty directory.
shar	Packs data into a bundle file. Unpacks the bundle file.
sort	Sorts text files or given input.
strings	Extracts and displays legible information out of a non-text file.
touch	Creates an empty file. Updates time stamp on an existing file.
vi/edit	Creates or modifies a text file.
view	Displays a text file.
wc	Displays number of lines, characters, words and bytes in a file.
what	Gets SCCS identification information.
whereis	Displays full pathname to a program or command and its manual pages.
which/whence	Displays full pathname to a program or command.
zip/unzip	Compresses/uncompresses files.
Management Tools	

cimconfig	Sets, unsets and gets CIM server properties.
cimserver	Starts, stops and manages WBEM daemons.
cimprovider	Disables, enables and removes registered CIM providers and associated modules.
hpsmh	Starts HP SMH daemon if not already running.
mxagentconfig	Configures HP SIM agent to work with CMS.
mxinitconfig	Performs initial HP SIM server configuration.
mxnode	Adds, lists, identifies, modifies and removes nodes.
mxpassword	Adds, lists, modifies and removes HP SIM user passwords.
mxstart	Starts HP SIM.
mxstop	Stops HP SIM.
mxuser	Adds, lists, modifies and removes HP SIM users.
mxtool	Adds, lists, modifies and removes tools.
osinfo	Gathers information about the operating system.
sam	Runs system management homepage.
samlog_viewer	Displays SAM logs.
smh	Runs system management homepage.
smhstartconfig	Allows you to modify SMH startup mode.
Hardware and Devices	
dmesg	Gathers and displays system diagnostics messages.
insf/mknod/mksf	Creates device special files.
iobind	Binds a specific driver to a LUN.
iofind	Helps migrate from legacy to agile view.
Io_redirect_dsf	Assigns a new disk to an existing DSF.
ioscan	Displays connected hardware devices.
lsdev	Displays device drivers in the kernel.
lssf	Lists special files.
machinfo	Displays machine information.
model/getconf	Displays system hardware model.
mt	Performs tape operations.
olrad	Displays slot status information on select Integrity systems.
rmsf	Removes device special files.
scsimgr	Administers SCSI mass storage devices.
stty	Displays or sets terminal port settings.
tset	Initializes a terminal based on its type.
tty	Displays full device path to the terminal session.
ttytype	Identifies a terminal.
Virtualization Technologies	
hpvmclone	Clones virtual machines.
hpvmcollect	Collects virtual machines statistics.
hpvmcreate	Creates virtual machines.
hpvminfo	Displays information about virtual machines host.
hpvmmodify	Modifies virtual machines.
hpvmnet	Creates and modifies virtual networks.
hpvmremove	Removes virtual machines.
hpvmresources	Stipulates storage and network devices used by VMs.
hpvmstart	Starts virtual machines.
hpvmstatus	Displays guest status information.

hpvmstop	Stops virtual machines.
icapmanage	Manages GiCAP groups.
icapmodify	Activates and deactivates cores, modifies iCAP configuration and applies codewords.
icapstatus	Displays status, allocation and configuration information.
icapnotify	Turns notification and asset reporting on or off.
parcreate	Creates an nPar.
parmgr	GUI tool used to perform nPar operations.
parmodify	Modifies an nPar.
parolrad	Activates and deactivates a cell online.
parremove	Removes an nPar.
parstatus	Displays status information about nPars.
ppuconfig	Displays and configures pay per use computing resources.
psrset	Creates and manages processor sets.
vparboot	Boots a vPar.
vparcreate	Creates a vPar.
vparmodify	Modifies a vPar.
vparremove	Removes a vPar.
vparreset	Resets a vPar.
vparstatus	Displays status information about vPars.
Software and Patches	
check_patches	Checks for any problems with patches.
cleanup	Commits/removes superseded patches.
security_patch_check	Checks for security-related patches.
show_patches	Displays installed patches.
swa	Analyzes a system or depot and generates reports for recommended actions.
swa-report	Reports software and security issues, vulnerabilities and resolutions.
swa-get	Downloads patches to resolve identified issues.
swa-step	Executes swa step-by-step.
swa-clean	Removes any files created by swa command.
swacl	Displays or modifies ACLs that protect software products.
swagent	Starts by swagentd to perform software management tasks.
swconfig	Configures/reconfigures/unconfigures an installed software.
swcopy	Copies software from source to depot.
swinstall/swremove	Installs/removes software.
swlist	Lists installed software.
swmodify	Modifies software.
swpackage	Packages software into a depot.
swreg	Registers a software depot.
swverify	Verifies software.
Users and Groups	
chgrp	Changes group membership on a file or directory.
chmod	Changes permissions on a file or directory.
chown	Changes ownership (and group membership) on a file or directory.
chsh	Changes a user's login shell permanently.
getprpw	Displays user password information including password aging parameters.

groupadd	Creates a group account.
groupdel	Deletes a group account.
groupmod	Modifies a group account.
groups	Displays a user's secondary group memberships.
grpck	Checks /etc/group for consistency.
id	Displays a user's username, UID, groups and GIDs.
last	Displays history of successful user login/logout attempts.
lastb	Displays history of unsuccessful user login attempts.
login	Displays login prompt.
logname	Displays the login name.
mesg	Allows/disallows messages to terminal.
modprpw	Unlocks a user account.
newgrp	Changes a user's primary group temporarily.
passwd	Changes user password.
pwck	Checks /etc/passwd for consistency.
quot	Displays which user is using how much disk space.
rsh/rksh	Restricted POSIX and Korn shells.
sh/ksh/csh	POSIX, Korn and C shells.
su	Switch to a different user.
talk	Invokes an interactive chat session with another logged in user.
umask	Displays or sets file mode creation mask.
uptime	Displays how long the system is up for.
ulimit	Gets and sets user limits.
useradd	Creates a new user account.
userdel	Deletes a user account.
usermod	Modifies a user account.
users	Displays a list of currently logged in users.
vipw	Opens /etc/passwd file in vi and locks it.
w	Displays who is currently logged in, what he is doing and how long the system has been up for.
wall	Broadcasts a system wide message.
who	Displays a list of currently logged in users.
whoami	Displays effective username.
whodo	Displays who is doing what.
write	Chat with another user.
Disks and LVM	
diskinfo	Displays disk size and manufacturer information.
efi_cp	Copies AUTO file contents to and from an EFI partition.
idisk	Creates specified partition information on Integrity servers.
lvchange	Changes the characteristics of a logical volume.
lvcreate/lvremove	Creates/removes a logical volume.
lvdisplay	Displays information about a logical volume.
lvextend/lvreduce	Increases/decreases the number of physical extents allocated to a logical volume.
lvlnboot/lvrmboot	Prepares/removes a logical volume to be a root, swap or dump volume.
lvmerge/lvsplit	Merges/splits mirrored volumes.
lvsync	synchronizes stale logical volume mirrors.

mediainit	Initializes a hard disk.
mkboot/rmboot	Installs/removes boot utilities on/from a disk.
mknod	Creates a device file.
pvchange	Changes characteristics of a physical volume.
pvck	Checks and repairs a physical volume.
pvcreate	Creates a physical volume.
pvdisplay	Displays information about one or more physical volumes.
pvmove	Moves allocated physical extents from one physical volume to another.
setboot	Displays and sets boot parameters.
vgcfgbackup/vgcfgrestore	Saves/restores LVM configuration for a volume group.
vgchange	Changes the status of a volume group.
vgcreate/vgremove	Creates/removes a volume group.
vgdisplay	Displays information about a volume group.
vgextend/vgreduce	Extends/reduces a volume group by adding/removing a physical volume.
vgdsf	Converts a volume group to use persistent DSFs, etc.
vgimport/vgexport	Imports/exports a volume group.
vgmodify	Modifies volume group attributes.
vgscan	Scans physical volumes for volume groups.
vgsync	Synchronizes all stale logical volume mirrors within a volume group.
File Systems	
bdf	Displays disk utilization.
df	Displays disk utilization.
du	Displays directory or file system utilization.
evfsadm	Manages EVFS tasks.
evfspkey	Creates, stores and administers user keys and passphrases.
evfsvol	Performs EVFS volume tasks.
extendfs	Extends an offline file system.
find	Searches for files/directories.
fsadm	Extends an online file system.
fsck	Checks and repairs a file system.
fstyp	Displays file system type.
fuser	Lists/kills processes using a file system.
mkfs	Backend for newfs. Used to create a new file system.
mklost+found	Creates a lost+found directory.
mount/umount	Connects/disconnects a file system to/from directory tree.
mountall/umountall	Connects/disconnects all unmounted file systems listed in /etc/fstab file to/from directory tree.
newfs	Creates file system structures.
tunefs	Tunes an HFS file system.
vxtunefs	Tunes a JFS file system.
Swap	
swapinfo	Displays information about configured swap spaces.
swapon	Enables a configured swap space.
vmstat	Displays virtual memory statistics.
Startup and Shutdown	
From OS Level:	

init	Changes run level of a running HP-UX system.
lifcp	Copies LIF files.
lifls	Displays LIF directory contents.
lifrm	Removes a LIF file.
reboot	Reboots a system.
shutdown	Shuts a system down gracefully.
who	Displays current system run level.
From BCH Level:	
boot	Boots a system using one of the configured boot devices.
path	Displays or modifies boot paths.
search	Searches for all available disks, CD/DVD drives, tape drives and devices using fibre channel protocol.
From EFI Shell Level:	
autoboot	Enables or disables autoboot, and modifies boot wait.
From HPUX Level:	
boot	Boots a system using one of the configured boot devices and to the specified mode.
map	Lists file systems that are known and mapped.
hpux	Boots hpux.efi loader.
showauto	Displays AUTO file contents.
setauto	Modifies AUTO file contents.
From BOOT_ADMIN Level:	
boot	Boots a system using one of the configured boot devices and to the specified mode.
path	Displays path information for boot devices.
search	Searches for bootable devices.
From ISL Prompt:	
display	Displays autoboot and autosearch flag settings.
hpux	Loads the secondary system loader into memory.
hpux /stand/vmunix.prev	Boots a system using an alternate HP-UX kernel file.
hpux −is	Boots a system to single user state.
hpux −lm	Boots a system to LVM maintenance state.
hpux −lq	Boots a system ignoring LVM quorum.
hpux ls	Displays contents of /stand.
hpux set autofile	Sets AUTO file contents.
hpux show autofile	Displays AUTO file contents.
lsautofl	Displays AUTO file contents.
Kernel	
ioinit	Maintains consistency between kernel I/O structures and /etc/ioconfig.
kclog	Kernel log file.
kcmodule	Queries and modifies kernel modules.
kconfig	Performs kernel configuration administration.
kcpath	Displays location of currently running kernel.
kctune	Queries and modifies kernel parameters.
kcusage	Queries the usage of kernel resources.
kcweb	Administers kernel.
mk_kernel	Regenerates a new kernel.

sysdef	Displays kernel parameters.
system_prep	Gathers running kernel configuration.
Backup, Restore and Recovery	
cpio	Creates file archives.
dd	Performs bit by bit copy.
dump/restore	Performs HFS file system backups/restores.
fbackup/frecover	Performs full and incremental file system backups/restores.
ftio	Creates file archives.
pax	Copies files and directories.
rdump	Performs a remote file system backup.
tar	Archives files.
vxdump/vxrestore	Performs VxFS (JFS) file system backups/restores.
LP Spooler	
accept/reject	Allows/disallows users to submit print requests.
cancel	Cancels a submitted print request.
enable/disable	Enables/disables a printer.
hppi	Configures and manages network printers.
lp	Sends a print request to a printer.
lpadmin	Sets up LP spooler system.
lpalt	Alters a submitted print request.
lpfence	Sets minimum priority for printing.
lpmove	Moves one or more or all print jobs from one printer to another.
lpsched/lpshut	Starts/stops lpsched daemon.
lpstat	Displays printer status information.
Performance	
glance (gpm)	Runs HP GlancePus tool.
iostat	Displays I/O statistics.
ipcs	Displays IPC status.
nice	Executes a command at a non-default priority.
renice	Changes priority of a running command.
sar	Reports various system activities.
time/timex	Displays real, user and system time spent on the execution of a command.
top	Displays information about running processes.
uptime	Displays how long a system has been up for.
Scripting and Variables	
awk	A programming language.
break	Breaks a loop.
case	A type of logical construct.
continue	Skips execution of the remaining part of a loop and gives the control back to the start of the loop.
echo	Displays variable values and echos arguments.
env	Displays or modifies current environment variables.
exit	Terminates a process or shell script.
export	Makes a variable a global variable.
expr	Evaluate supplied arguments as an expression.
for	A type of loop.
if	A type of logical construct.

read	Prompts for user input.
sed	Stream editor.
set	Displays set variables.
sleep	Suspends execution of a loop for the specified time period.
test	Evaluates a condition.
trap	Ignores signals.
while	A type of loop.
IP Connectivity and Routing	
arp	Displays and modifies MAC-IP address translation.
hostname	Displays or sets system name.
ifconfig	Displays or configures a LAN interface.
lanadmin	Administers a LAN interface.
lanscan	Displays installed LAN interface.
linkloop	Checks physical level connectivity between two HP-UX machines.
ndd	Tunes network parameters.
netstat	Displays network status.
nettl	Controls network tracing and logging.
nwmgr	Network interface management command.
ping	Tests connectivity between two machines.
route	Manages routing table.
set_parms	Configures TCP/IP parameters.
traceroute	Displays all routes to destination host.
uname	Displays summary information about a system.
Internet Services	
bootpquery	Sends bootrequests to a BootP server.
finger	Displays user information.
ftp	Uploads and downloads files.
mail/rmail/mailq	Sends/reads mail.
inetd	Enables connection logging and forces inetd daemon to re-read its configuration file.
mailx	Sends/receives/reads mail.
newaliases	Rebuilds mail aliases database.
ntpdate	Sets date/time via NTP.
ntpq	Queries NTP daemon.
ntptrace	Displays NTP server hierarchy.
rcp	Transfers files between two UNIX machines.
remsh/rexec	Runs a command on a remote UNIX system without logging in to it.
rlogin/remsh	Logs a user in to a remote UNIX machine.
ruptime/rup	Displays status of remote systems.
rusers	Displays logged in users on remote systems.
rwho	Displays who is logged in on remote systems.
sendmail	Sends mail over the internet.
telnet	Displays login prompt.
tftp	Transfers files to a BootP client.
NFS, AutoFS and CIFS	
automount	Establishes automount mount points and associates automount maps to them.
cifslist	Displays CIFS-mounted resources.

HP Certified Systems Administrator 11i v3

cifslogin	Logs in to a CIFS share.
cifsmount	Mounts a CIFS share.
nfsstat	Displays NFS usage statistics.
rpcinfo	Displays RPC information.
share	Shares a specified resource.
shareall	Shares all resources listed in the /etc/dfs/dfstab file.
showmount	Displays remote NFS mounts.
smbpasswd	Sets password for SAMBA users.
smbstatus	Displays the status of SAMBA shares.
testparm	Checks for any syntax errors in SAMBA configuration file.
unshare	Unshares a specified resource.
unshareall	Unshares all resources listed in the /etc/dfs/sharetab file.
NIS	
domainname	Displays and sets an NIS domain.
nsquery	Queries a specified name service.
ypcat	Displays contents of an NIS map.
ypinit	Sets up an NIS master, slave or client.
ypmake	Builds NIS map files.
ypmatch	Greps for a pattern in an NIS map.
yppasswd	Changes a user password in NIS maps.
yppoll	Queries NIS server for NIS maps.
yppush	Pushes out NIS maps from master NIS server to slave servers.
ypset	Binds to an NIS server.
ypwhich	Displays which NIS domain the client is bound to.
ypxfr	Pulls NIS map files from master NIS server.
DNS and LDAP	
dig	Lookup and troubleshooting utility.
hosts_to_named	Converts /etc/hosts file to DNS zone files.
ldapsearch	Pulls requested inforamtion from an LDAP server.
nslookup	Queries DNS/hosts for name resolution.
nsquery	Queries DNS/NIS/hosts for name resolution.
sig_named	Terminates/restarts named daemon.
Ignite-UX	
bootsys	Reboots remote clients.
check_net_recovery	Compares network-based system recovery archive contents to the running system.
check_tape_recovery	Compares tape-based system recovery archive contents to the running system.
ignite	Configures, installs and recovers HP-UX.
instl_adm	Administers Ignite-UX configuration files.
make_config	Builds Ignite-UX configuration files from software depots.
make_depots	Builds Ignite-UX software depots.
manage_index	Manages the Ignite-UX INDEX file.
make_net_recovery	Creates a system recovery archive on a network directory.
make_tape_recovery	Creates a system recovery archive on tape.
setup_server	Performs management tasks for an Ignite-UX server.
Security	
bastille	Locks down an HP-UX system.

bastille_drift	Creates a baseline and compares the current state of a system with it.
pwconv	Converts to shadow password.
scp	Copies files securely to a remote UNIX system.
sftp	Transfers files securely to a remote UNIX system.
ssh	Opens up a secure login session on a remote UNIX system.
ssh-keygen	Generates keys for ssh passwordless remote login.
Miscellaneous	
alias/unalias	Sets/unsets shortcuts.
at	Executes a command at a later time.
banner	Displays letters in large format.
batch	Executes batched commands right away.
cal	Displays calendar.
catman	Creates a whatis database to facilitate keyword search on man pages.
clear	Clears a terminal screen.
crontab	Schedules user cron jobs.
cut	Extracts selected columns.
date	Displays or sets system date/time.
freedisk	Finds and removes filesets appeared to be not in use.
getty	Sets terminal type, modes, speed and line discipline.
history	Displays previously executed commands.
kill	Sends a signal to a process.
killall	Kills all active processes.
man	Displays manual pages.
nohup	Executes a command immune to hangup signals.
pgrep	Searches a process using its name.
pkill	Kills a process using its name.
pr	Prints a file on the display terminal.
ps	Displays running processes.
r	Repeats the last command executed.
tee	Sends output to two locations.
tr	Translates characters.
uniq	Displays repeated lines in a file.

Appendix D – Table of Important HP-UX Files

This table contains a list of various significant HP-UX files including configuration, startup, log and other important files along with their short description.

Management Tools	
/var/opt/wbem/cimserver_current.conf	CIM server configuration file.
/var/opt/wbem/cimserver_planned.conf	CIM server configuration file.
/var/sam/log/samlog	Logs SMH (SAM) activities.
Hardware and Devices	
/etc/ioconfig	Maintains I/O configuration information.
/stand/ioconfig	A copy of /etc/ioconfig.
Software and Patches	
/var/adm/sw/swagent.log	Logs software agent activities.
/var/adm/sw/swagentd.log	Logs software daemon activities.
/var/adm/sw/swconfig.log	Logs software configuration activities.
/var/adm/sw/swcopy.log	Logs software copy activities.
/var/adm/sw/swinstall.log	Logs software installation activities.
/var/adm/sw/swmodify.log	Logs software modification activities.
/var/adm/sw/swpackage.log	Logs software packaging activities.
/var/adm/sw/swreg.log	Logs software depot registration activities.
/var/adm/sw/swremove.log	Logs software removal activities.
/var/adm/sw/swverify.log	Logs software verification activities.
Users and Groups	
$HOME/.cshrc	Shell initialization file for C shell users.
$HOME/.dtprofile	CDE user initialization file.
$HOME/.exrc	Startup configuration file for the vi editor.
$HOME/.login	User initialization file for C shell users.
$HOME/.profile	User initialization file for POSIX and Korn shells.
$HOME/.shrc	Shell initialization file for POSIX and Korn shells.
/etc/group	Maintains a database of all defined groups on the system.
/etc/logingroup	Contains default group access list for each user.
/etc/passwd	Maintains a database of all defined users on the system.
/etc/profile	System-wide initialization file for POSIX and Korn shell users.
/etc/shadow	Stores passwords and password aging parameters.
/etc/skel/*	Location of user initialization file templates.
/etc/utmps	Contains a list of all currently logged in users.
/var/adm/btmps	Maintains a history of all failed user login attempts.

/var/adm/sulog	Logs switch user activities.
/var/adm/wtmps	Maintains a history of all successful user login attempts.
Disks and LVM	
/etc/lvmconf/*	Stores LVM information.
/etc/lvmtab	Maintains information about volume groups and physical volumes.
File Systems and Swap	
/*/lost+found	Resides in every file system to be used to hold orphan files.
/etc/evfs/evfs.conf	Main EVFS configuration file for setting attributes.
/etc/evfs/evfstab	Lists EVFS volumes to be enabled at system boot.
/etc/evfs/emd	Directory location to store EMD backup copies.
/etc/evfs/pkey	Directory location to store user keys and passphrases.
/etc/rc.config.d/evfs	Startup/shutdown configuration file for EVFS.
/etc/fstab	Contains entries for file systems and swap spaces that are automatically mounted when system boots up.
/etc/mnttab	Maintains information about currently mounted file systems.
/var/adm/sbtab	Contains a list of all superblock location entries for the root file system.
Startup and Shutdown	
/etc/inittab	Source file for the init process.
/etc/issue	Contents of this file are printed as the login banner.
/etc/motd	Contains a message displayed when a user logs in.
/etc/rc.config.d/*	Configuration files for startup scripts.
/etc/rc.log	Logs service startup status at system boot.
/etc/shutdownlog	Logs system shutdown activities.
/sbin/init.d/*	Location of all startup & shutdown scripts.
/sbin/rc*.d/*	Sequencer directories pointing to startup scripts located in /sbin/init.d directory.
Kernel	
/stand/system	Contains drivers, tunable parameters and subsystems whose support is included in the currently running kernel configuration.
/stand/vmunix	Currently running HP-UX kernel.
/stand/current	Keeps currently running kernel configuration.
/stand/backup	Keeps a copy of backup kernel configuration.
/stand/nextboot	Contains kernel configuration to be activated at the next system boot.
/stand/vpdb	Stores all vPar configuration information.
/stand/vpmon	Software piece that sits between the server firmware and HP-UX OE instances running in vPars.
Backup, Restore and Recovery	
/var/adm/dumpdates	The vxdump and dump commands updates this file with backup time stamps if the –u option is used with the commands.

/var/adm/fbackupfiles/dates	The fbackup utility updates this file with backup time stamps if the −u option is used with the command.
LP Spooler	
/etc/lp/*	Contains print configuration information.
/var/adm/lp/*	Contains log files for the printing system.
/var/spool/lp/request/*	Holds print requests temporarily.
IP Connectivity and Routing	
/etc/hosts	Contains hostnames (and optionally aliases) and their corresponding IP addresses.
/etc/rc.config.d/netconf	Startup configuration file that defines hostname, routes, LAN interface configuration information, etc.
/sbin/init.d/net	Startup script that sets hostname, routes, LAN interface configuration as defined in the /etc/rc.config.d/netconf file.
Internet Services	
$HOME/.rhosts	Per user host equivalency file.
/etc/ftpd/ftpusers	Contains a list of disallowed ftp users.
/etc/hosts.equiv	System-wide host equivalency file.
/etc/inetd.conf	Contains internet services information and used by the inetd daemon.
/etc/networks	Contains information about known networks.
/etc/ntp.conf	Configuration file for NTP.
/etc/rc.config.d/netdaemons	Startup configuration file for internet services including NTP.
/etc/rpc	Contains a list of RPC services along with their port numbers.
/etc/services	Contains various services and their corresponding port numbers.
/etc/shells	Contains a list of allowed login shells.
/var/adm/inetd.sec	Security file for the inetd daemon.
/etc/securetty	Disables direct telnet access into a system.
/etc/protocols	Lists available protocols.
/etc/ntp.drift	Helps xntpd keep track of local system clock accuracy.
/etc/ntp.key	Defines NTP encryption to be used.
/var/adm/syslog/mail.log	Logs mail transfer information.
NFS, AutoFS and CIFS	
/etc/auto_master	Contains maps for direct, indirect and special AutoFS maps.
/var/adm/automount.log	Log file for the automount daemon.
/etc/dfs/dfstab	Contains entries for file systems that are NFS shared. This file has replaced /etc/exports in 11i v3.
/etc/fstab	Contains entries for file systems and swap spaces that are automatically mounted when system boots up.
/etc/rc.config.d/nfsconf	Startup script for NFS services.
/etc/rmtab	Maintains a list of shared resources.
/etc/dfs/sharetab	Maintains a list of remotely mounted resources. This file has replaced /etc/xtab in 11i v3.

/sbin/init.d/aufofs	Startup script for AutoFS.
/sbin/init.d/nfs.client	Startup script for NFS client.
/sbin/init.d/nfs.core	Startup script for rpcbind daemon.
/sbin/init.d/nfs.server	Startup script for NFS server.
NIS	
/etc/nsswitch.conf	Name server switch file.
/etc/rc.config.d/namesvrs	Startup configuration file for NIS.
/var/yp/*	Default directory that holds all NIS maps and other related information.
DNS	
/etc/dns/*	Directory that holds DNS zone files.
/etc/named.conf	Boot file on DNS servers.
/etc/nsswitch.conf	Name server switch file.
/etc/rc.config.d/namesvrs_dns	Startup configuration file for DNS.
/etc/resolv.conf	Client-side resolver file.
/sbin/init.d/named	The DNS daemon.
Ignite-UX	
/etc/bootptab	Stores configuration information for Itanium boot clients.
/etc/opt/ignite/instl_boottab	Stores IP address and MAC information for PA-RISC boot clients.
/var/opt/ignite/INDEX	Maintains available configurations for Ignite-UX clients.
Security	
$HOME/.ssh/*	Stores per-user files related to secure shell access into the system.
/etc/default/security	System-wide user security file.
/etc/pam.conf	System-wide PAM configuration file.
/etc/pam_user.conf	Per-user PAM configuration file.
Miscellaneous	
/etc/syslog.conf	Configuration file for syslogd daemon.
/var/adm/at.allow	Allow file for at use.
/var/adm/at.deny	Deny file for at use.
/var/adm/cron.allow	Allow file for cron use.
/var/adm/cron.deny	Deny file for cron use.
/var/adm/cron/log	Logs cron activities.
/var/adm/syslog/syslog.log	Logs all system activities.
/var/spool/cron/atjobs	Spool area for at jobs.
/var/spool/cron/crontabs	Spool area for cron jobs.

Appendix E – Table of HP-UX System Daemons

This table lists several main HP-UX daemon programs and their short description. These daemons are critical to proper service operation.

Management Tools	
cimserverd	WBEM daemon. Interacts with *cimservera* for PAM authentication.
cimservera	Works with PAM to provide authentication services to cimserverd.
mxdomainmgr	Interacts with repository and DTF.
mxdtf	Runs commands remotely on managed systems.
smhstartd	SMH server daemon.
Hardware and Devices	
ioconfigd	I/O configuration daemon.
Software and Patches	
swagent	Invoked by swagentd to perform software management tasks.
swagentd	Software management daemon.
Users and Groups	
pwgrd	Password and group caching and hashing daemon.
Disks and LVM	
lvmkd	Watches LVM queue.
Swap	
swapper	Works with vhand and handles paging and deactivation.
vhand	Works with swapper and handles paging and deactivation.
Startup and Shutdown	
init	Primary Initialization daemon.
LP Spooler	
lpsched	Local print scheduler daemon.
rlpdaemon	Remote print spooling daemon.
Internet Services	
bootpd	Boot server daemon.
ftpd	FTP server daemon.
inetd	Master internet services daemon.
rarpd	Provides a client with its IP address. Responds to ARP requests.
remshd	Remote shell daemon that serves rcp, rdist and remsh.
rexecd	Responds to rexec and remsh commands.
rlogind	Remote login daemon to serve the rlogin client requests.

rpc.rusersd	Responds to rusers command and provides a list of users logged on users.
rwhod	Responds to queries to provide status of the system.
sendmail	Sends and receives mail.
telnetd	Remote login daemon to serve the telnet client requests.
tftpd	Trivial FTP server daemon.
xntpd	Runs on the NTP server where clients and peers have their clocks synchronized.
NFS, AutoFS and CIFS	
automountd	AutoFS daemon that mounts a resource automatically.
cifsclientd	CIFS client daemon.
nfsd	Handles NFS client requests.
rpc.pcnfsd	Provides authentication and printing service to DOS and Mac clients.
rpc.lockd	Provides NFS file locking services.
rpc.mountd	Provides file handle for the file system resource requested to be mounted by a client.
rpc.statd	Works with rpc.lockd to provide crash and recovery services.
rpcbind	Maintains programs-to-address mappings.
smbd	Samba server daemon.
nmbd	NetBIOS name server daemon that provides NetBIOS over IP naming services to clients.
NIS	
keyserv	Stores private encryption keys for users.
rpc.yppasswdd	Manages password change requests in NIS map files.
rpc.ypupdated	Modifies NIS maps based on the updated information.
rpcbind	Maintains programs-to-address mappings.
ypbind	Runs on all NIS servers and clients. Binds the client to an NIS server.
ypserv	Runs on both master and slave NIS servers. The daemon serves client requests.
ypxfrd	Runs on the master NIS server only. Transfers NIS maps over to the slave NIS server when the slave server executes the ypxfr command.
DNS	
named	Runs on DNS servers and clients.
Ignite-UX	
bootpd	Responds to Integrity boot client requests.
instl_bootd	Responds to 9000 boot client requests.
Security	
sshd	Secure shell daemon for ssh utilities.
Miscellaneous	
cron	Executes jobs at scheduled times.
syslogd	Logs system messages.

Bibliography

The following websites, forums and sources were referenced:

1. www.hp.com
2. www.docs.hp.com
3. www.itrc.hp.com
4. www.software.hp.com
5. www.unix.org
6. www.ntp.org
7. www.dmtf.org
8. www.wikipedia.org

Glossary

. (one dot)	Represents current directory.
.. (two dots)	Represents parent directory of the current directory.
9000 systems	A family of HP UNIX systems based on PA-RISC processors.
Absolute mode	A way of giving permissions to a file or directory.
Absolute path	A pathname that begins with a /.
Access mode	See file permissions.
Active node	The node where a package is configured to automatically start when cluster services are brought up.
Address Resolution Protocol	A protocol used to find a system's Ethernet address when its IP address is known.
Address space	Memory location that a process can refer.
Adoptive node	The node to which a package fails over.
Agile view	Representation of LUNs using lunpath hardware paths, LUN hardware paths and persistent DSFs.
Agile addressing	Addressing of a LUN with a single, unique DSF.
Alias substitution	See command aliasing.
Allocation policies	Policies that may be used when configuring a mirror.
Alternate link	A redundant physical path to a disk or LUN.
Anonymous client	A client that gets any available IP address from the Ignite-UX server.
Archive	A file that contains one or more compressed files.
Argument	A value passed to a command or program.
ARP	Displays and changes IP to Ethernet translation mappings.
ASCII	An acronym for American Standard Code for Information Interchange.
Auditing	System and user activity record and analysis.
Authentication	The process of identifying a user to a system.
Authorization	Determines what privileges a user has on using programs and managing resources.
Autoboot	Enables or disables automatic boot of an HP-UX system.
AUTO file	The file that contains boot string.
AutoFS	The NFS client-side service that automatically mounts and unmounts an NFS resource on an as-needed basis.
Autosearch	Enables or disables automatic search for a bootable device.
Availability	A measure of overall system uptime minus any unplanned downtime.
Background process	A process that runs in the background.
Backup	The process of saving data on an alternate media such as a tape.
Backup kernel configuration	A copy of the currently running kernel configuration saved prior to a change in the currently running kernel configuration.
Base OE	OE that contains core HP-UX.
Bastille	A security hardening and lockdown tool.
BBRA	Bad Block Relocation Area contains information specific to the recovery of any bad blocks generated on the PV.

BCH	See Boot Console Handler.
BDRA	Boot Disk Reserved Area contains reserved area on a boot disk.
Berkeley Internet Name Domain	A UC Berkeley implementation of DNS. See also DNS.
BIND	See Berkeley Internet Name Domain.
BladeSystem	An HP hardware technology that provides complete infrastructure out of the box.
Block	A collection of bytes of data transmitted as a single unit.
Block device file	A device special file associated with devices that transfer data in blocks. For example, disk, CD and DVD devices.
BOE	See Base OE.
Boot	The process of starting up a system.
Boot area	A small portion on the boot disk that contains boot utilities necessary to boot the system.
Boot Console Handler	An interface for doing pre-boot tasks.
BootROM	Boot Read Only Memory. BootROM contains stable storage, PDC and other code required to boot an HP-UX system.
Bridge	A network device that connects two LANs together provided they use the same data-link layer protocol.
Broadcast client	An NTP client that listens to time broadcasts over the network.
Broadcast server	An NTP server that broadcasts time over the network.
Bundle	A group of filesets or products, or both, packaged for a specific purpose.
Bus	Data communication path among devices in a computer system.
Campus cluster	A type of cluster whose nodes are located in different buildings that are some distance apart.
Catalog files	Files that hold depot description and software information located in depots.
Cell board	A board that holds processors and memory in n-partitionable servers.
Character	A single letter, digit or special symbol such as a comma or a dot.
Character special file	A device special file associated with devices that transfer data serially. For example, disk, tape, serial and other such devices.
Child process	A sub-process started by a process.
CIFS	Common Internet File System. Allows resources to be shared among UNIX and non-UNIX systems.
CIFS client	A system that accesses a resource shared by a CIFS server.
CIFS server	A system that shares a resource to be accessed by a CIFS client.
Cloning	Building systems with identical configuration.
Cluster	A group of independent systems that work in conjunction with one another under the control of a management software to provide high availability.
Command	An instruction given to the system to perform certain task(s).
Command aliasing	Allows creating command shortcuts.
Command history	A feature that maintains a log of all commands executed at the command line.
Command interpreter	See shell.
Command line editing	Allows editing at the command line.
Command prompt	The OS prompt where you type commands.

Continental cluster	A type of cluster that have nodes geographically located in different continents.
COPS	Computer Oracle and Password System. It gathers OS security weaknesses and generates reports for review.
Core cell board	The cell board in an nPar or server that contains a core I/O.
Core	A processing unit on a processor.
Core I/O	A card that provides console access into an nPar or a server.
Crack	Identifies easily crackable passwords in the /etc/passwd file.
Crash	An abnormal system shutdown caused by electrical outage or kernel malfunction, etc.
Current directory	The present working directory.
Currently running kernel configuration	The kernel configuration that is activated and loaded presently.
Daemon	A server process that runs in the background and responds to client requests.
DAS	See Direct Attached Storage.
Data Center OE	An HP-UX 11i v3 software bundle that includes both VSE-OE and HA-OE.
DC-OE	See Data Center OE.
De-encapsulation	The reverse of encapsulation. See encapsulation.
Defunct process	See zombie process.
Depot	See software depot.
Device	A peripheral such as a printer, disk drive and CD/DVD device.
Device driver	The software that controls a device.
Device file	See device special file.
Device special file	A file associated with an I/O device.
Direct Attached Storage	A disk subsystem connected directly to a server.
Directory structure	Inverted tree-like UNIX directory structure.
Disk array	An external disk storage subsystem.
Disk partitioning	Creating multiple partitions on a given hard drive so as to access them as separate logical containers for data storage.
Distinguished name	A fully qualified object path in LDAP DIT.
DIT	Directory Information Tree. An LDAP directory hierarchy.
DNS	Domain Name System. A widely used name resolution method on the internet.
Downtime	Time period during which a business application is unavailable or non-functional due to a failure.
Driver	See device driver.
DSF	See Device Special File.
Dynamic module	Module that can be loaded and unloaded without system reboot.
Dynamic tunable	Tunable that takes a new value without system reboot.
EFI	Extensible Firmware Interface. It contains boot utilities.
EMD	Encrypted Meta Data stores EVFS volume encryption attributes.
Encapsulation	The process of forming a packet through the seven OSI layers.
Enclosure	The box that holds BladeSystem components.
Enterprise OE	OE that contains Foundation OE plus enhanced components.
Environment variable	A variable whose value can be used in current as well as child shells.
EOF	Marks the End OF File.
EOL	Marks the End Of Line.

EPIC	See Explicitly Parallel Instruction Computing.
EVFS	Encrypted Volume and File System is a virtual device driver used to safeguard data.
Expansion blade	A blade that provides access to additional PCI adapters.
Explicitly Parallel Instruction Computing	A processor technology.
Export	See Share.
Extended PCI	A higher speed PCI bus.
Failback	Opposite of failover.
Failover	The process whereby a cluster management software transfers the control of a software package to another node in the cluster.
Fault tolerant	The ability of a computer system to survive and continue to function in the event a sudden hardware or software failure occurs.
Fibre channel card	An optical adapter that provides servers upto 4Gbps of data transfer speed to and from storage devices.
FIFO file	First In First Out. A special file used to access data on a first-in-first-out basis.
File descriptor	A unique, per-process integer value used to refer to an open file.
File permissions	Read, write, execute or no permissions assigned to a file or directory at the user, group or public level.
File system	A grouping of files stored in special data structures.
Filename completion	Allows completing a filename by typing a partial filename at the command line and then hitting the Esc key twice.
Filename expansion	See filename completion.
Fileset	A set of files and control scripts.
Filter	A command that performs data transformation on the given input.
Floating IP address	The IP address not tied to a specific node in a cluster.
Foundation OE	OE that contains core HP-UX.
Full path	See absolute path.
Gateway	A device that links two networks that run completely different protocols.
Genesis partition	The first nPar created on an n-partitionable server.
GiCap	See global instant capacity.
Global instant capacity	A purchase flexibility to buy cores, memory and cell boards at a reduced price and share among a group of servers.
GID	See group ID.
Global variable	See environment variable.
Golden image	A complete system image that can be deployed on other machines with similar hardware.
Group	A collection of users that requires same permissions on a set of files.
Group ID	A unique identification number assigned to a group.
GSP	See management processor.
Guardian Service Processor	See management processor.
GUI	Graphical User Interface.
HA-OE	See High Availability OE.
Hardening	See Security hardening.
Hard partition	See node partition.

Hardware path	A series of numbers representing the physical or virtualized location of a device.
HBA	Host Bus Adapter. An I/O adapter used to connect to mass storage devices.
HFS	High-Performance File System. A file system type supported by HP-UX.
High availability	A design technique whereby a computer system is built in such a way that it recovers quickly from a hardware or software failure.
High Availability OE	An HP-UX 11i v3 bundle that includes clustering software.
Home directory	A directory where a user lands when he logs into a system.
Host equivalency	Making a system trusted on a remote machine.
Hostname	A unique name assigned to a node on a network.
Hub	A network device that receives data from one or more directions and forwards it to one or more directions.
iCAP	See instant capacity.
Identity management	Set of security tools employed to identify users and systems.
Ignite-UX	A set of tools and techniques that provide various ways of installing HP-UX.
Instant capacity	A purchase flexibility to buy cores, memory and cell boards at a reduced price.
Initialization files	Files executed when a user logs in.
Initial System Loader	Loads HP-UX after POST is complete.
Inode	An index node number holds a file properties including permissions, size, creation/modification time, etc. It also contains a pointer to the data blocks that actually store the file data.
Install time security	Security components that may be selected at 11i v3 installation time.
Installed Product Database	Contains information about all software loaded on a system.
Integrity systems	A family of HP systems based on Itanium processors and capable of running HP-UX, Windows and Linux operating systems.
Intent Log	An area within a JFS file system that holds file system structural information.
Interconnect	A device that provides additional LAN or SAN ports in a BladeSystem.
Interface card	A card that allows a system to communicate to external devices.
I/O chassis	Cage that holds I/O slots.
I/O redirection	A shell feature that gets input from a non-default location and sends output and error messages to non-default locations.
IP address	A unique 32-bit software address assigned to a node on a network.
IPD	See Installed Product Database.
IPFilter	The HP-UX firewall.
IPL	See Initial System Loader.
IP multiplexing	Assigning multiple IP addresses to a single physical LAN interface.
IPSec	The HP-UX implementation of securing IP traffic at the host level.
ISL	See Initial System Loader.
ISS	Internet Security Scan. It checks for known security holes.
Itanium	A 64-bit Itanium processor used in HP Integrity systems. Formerly known as IA-64 and Itanium processor.
Job control	A shell feature that allows a process to be taken to background, brought to foreground and to suspend its execution.
Job scheduling	Execution of commands, programs or scripts at a later time in future.

Kernel	Software piece that controls an entire HP-UX system including all hardware and software.
LAN	See Local Area Network.
LBA	See Logical Block Addressing.
LDAP	Lightweight Directory Access Protocol.
LDIF	LDAP Data Interchange Format. A special format used by LDAP for importing and exporting LDAP data among LDAP servers.
Legacy DSF	The old c#t#d# style of device file naming convention.
Legacy hardware path	Hardware address separated by forward slash characters up to the HBA. After the HBA portion, additional elements are appended, which are separated by period character.
Legacy view	Representation of legacy hardware paths and DSFs.
LIF	See Logical Interchange Format.
Link	An object that associates a file name to any type of file.
Link count	Number of links that refer to a file.
Load balancing	A technique whereby more than one servers serves client requests.
Local Area Network	A campus-wide network of computers.
Local printer	A printer connected directly to a computer.
Local variable	A variable whose value can only be used in current shell.
Logical block addressing	A technique used to point to blocks of data on a hard drive.
Logical construct	A statement in shell scripting whose output relies on a specified condition.
Logical extent	A logical extent points to a physical extent.
Logical Interchange Format	Helps transport media.
Logical Unit Number	A portion of a physical disk (or an entire physical disk) in a RAID array allocated to a server which sees it as a standalone hard drive. A LUN could be a tape or DVD device as well.
Logical volume	A logical container that holds one file system.
Logical volume manager	A disk partitioning solution.
Login	A process that begins when a user enters his username and password correctly at the login prompt.
Login directory	See home directory.
Looping construct	A statement in shell scripting that continuously generates output until a specified condition is met.
LUN	See Logical Unit Number.
LUN hardware path	A virtualized hardware path to a LUN presented as a single persistent DSF representing all lunpath hardware paths.
Lunpath	Physical hardware path leading to a LUN.
Lunpath hardware path	A path that represents a single hardware path to a LUN.
LVM	See Logical volume manager.
MAC address	A unique 48-bit hardware address of a network card or port. Also called physical address, station address, Ethernet address and hardware address.
Machine	A computer, a system, an HP-UX workstation or an HP-UX server.
Major number	Points to a device driver.

Management processor	A hardware module installed on a server for pre-boot system management.
Mass storage stack	A new way of addressing hardware device files.
Metacharacters	Characters that have special meaning to the shell.
Metro cluster	A type of cluster whose nodes are located in or around a city.
Minor number	Points to an individual device controlled by a specific device driver.
MIO card	See Multi I/O card.
Mirror	An exact copy of original data.
Mirroring	The process of creating mirrors.
Mission Critical OE	OE that contains Enterprise OE plus enhanced components.
Mounting	Attaching a device (a file system, a CD/DVD) to the directory structure.
MP	See Management Processor.
Multi I/O card	An interface card that provides two or more different types of I/O connections.
Multimode package	A type of cluster package that runs concurrently on one or more nodes.
Multipathing	Usage of several physical paths pointing to the same LUN.
Name resolution	The technique to determine IP address by providing hostname.
NAS	See Network Attached Storage.
Netmask	See subnet mask.
Network	Two or more computers joined together to share resources.
Network Administrator	Person responsible for configuring and managing networking services on an HP-UX system.
Network Interface Card	A LAN adapter.
Network Attached Storage	A storage subsystem connected to Ethernet LAN to be shared over the network.
Network management	Monitoring, supporting and administering of network devices.
Network printer	A printer connected to a network port and has an IP address and hostname.
Network Time Protocol	A protocol used to synchronize system clock.
NFS	Network File System. Allows UNIX systems to share files, directories and file systems.
NFS client	Enables mounting an exported UNIX resource.
NFS server	Makes available (exports) a resource for mounting by an NFS client.
NIC	See Network Interface Card.
NIS	Network Information Service.
NIS client	UNIX system that binds itself with an NIS server for accessing administrative files.
NIS server	Maintains and makes available shared administrative files.
Node	A device connected directly to a network port and has a hostname and an IP address associated with it. A node could be a computer, an HP-UX workstation, an HP-UX server, an X terminal, a printer, a router, a hub, a switch, a tape library and so on.
Node name	A unique name assigned to a node.
Node partition	A physical partition within an HP UNIX system that can run either a dedicated, standalone HP-UX OE instance within it, or can house one or more vPars.
Npar	See node partition.

NTP	See Network Time Protocol.
Octal mode	A method of setting permissions on a file or directory using octal numbering system.
Octal numbering system	A 3 digit numbering system that represents values from 0 to 7.
OE	See operating environment.
Onboard administrator	A built-in management software in a BladeSystem.
OnlineJFS	Software product that allows to extend the size of a JFS file system online.
Open Systems Interconnection	A layered networking model that provides guidelines to networking equipment manufacturers to develop their products for multi-vendor interoperability.
Operating environment	A collection of core OS and additional tools and utilities including networking software, etc.
Operating system	The core HP-UX functionality.
Orphan process	An alive child process of a terminated parent process.
OS	See operating system.
OSI	See Open Systems Interconnection.
Owner	The user that creates a file or starts a process.
Owner key	The key specified when an EVFS volume is created.
Package (cluster)	A group of software and hardware resources that work together to bring a service online on a cluster node.
PAM	See Pluggable Authentication Module.
Parent directory	A directory one level above the current directory in the file system hierarchy.
Parent process ID	The ID of a process that starts a child process.
PA-RISC	Precision Architecture – Reduced Instruction Set Computing. A RISC-based microprocessor architecture used in HP 9000 systems.
Partitioning	A set of techniques for splitting physical resources of a server into two or more logical servers.
Passive node	See adoptive node.
Password aging	Provides enhanced control on user passwords.
Patch attributes	Attributes associated with a patch.
Pay per use	A pricing model that charges based on actual usage of computing resources.
PCI	See Peripheral Component Interconnect.
PCI-X	See extended PCI.
PCIe	see PCI express.
PCI express	A superior PCI technology intended to replace PCI and PCI-X.
PDC	See Processor Dependent Code.
Performance monitoring	The process of acquiring data from system components for analysis and decision-making purposes.
Peripheral Component Interconnect	A local bus that connects various peripheral devices to the system.
Permission	Right to read, write or execute.
Persistent binding	See agile addressing.
Persistent DSF	The new disk# style of device file naming convention that supports agile addressing.
Persistent LUN binding	See agile addressing.

Physical extent	A physical extent is the smallest allocatable unit of space in LVM.
Physical volume	A hard drive logically brought under LVM control.
PID	See process ID.
Pipe	Sends output from one command as input to the second command.
Plex	Represents one copy of data within a volume.
Pluggable Authentication Module	A set of library routines that allows using any authentication service available on a system for user authentication, password modification and user account validation purposes.
Port	A number appended to an IP address. This number could be associated with a well-known service or is randomly generated.
POST	Power On Self Test. Runs by PDC at system boot time to test hardware.
PPID	See parent process ID.
Primary node	See active node.
Primary prompt	The symbol where commands and programs are typed for execution.
Private variable	See local variable.
PRM	See Process Resource Manager.
Process	Any command, program or daemon that runs on an HP-UX system.
Process ID	An identification number assigned by kernel to each starting process.
Process Resource Manager	A manual resource management tool.
Processor	A CPU. It may contain more than one core.
Processor Dependant Code	Firmware code stored in BootROM and executed at system boot up for performing POST and other necessary boot related tasks.
Processor sets	a set of cores grouped together as an independent entity.
Product	A group of filesets.
Prompt	See primary prompt.
Protocol	A common language that two nodes understand to communicate.
Psets	See pcessor sts.
Pseudo swap	Portion of physical memory used for swapping purposes.
PVRA	Physical Volume Reserved Area holds information specific to the entire VG for which the PV is part of.
RAID	Redundant Array of Independent Disks.
RAID array	A disk storage subsystem that uses hardware RAID.
Reliability	The ability of a computer system to carry out and keep up its function in normal as well as abnormal circumstances.
RDN	Relative Distinguished Name. A relative location of an object in LDAP DIT.
Recovery	Recovering a crashed system back to normal using Ignite system recovery tape. This process may include restoring backed up data.
Recovery key	The key used to change a volume owner key.
Redirection	Getting input from and sending output to non-default destinations.
Redundancy	A technique whereby an alternate device acts for a primary device should it fails. The device could be a server, a boot disk, a network card and so on.
Referral	An entity defined on an LDAP server to forward a client request to some other LDAP server that contains the client requested information.
Registered client	A client that has a dedicated IP addresses defined on the Ignite-UX server.
Regular expression	A string of characters commonly used for pattern matching purposes.
Relative path	A path to a file relative to the current user location in the file system hierarchy.

Reliability	The ability of a computer system to carry out and keep up its function in normal as well as abnormal circumstances.
Remote printer	A printer accessed by users on remote systems.
Repeater	A network device removes unwanted noise from incoming signals, and amplifies and regenerates the signals to cover extended distances.
Replica	A slave LDAP server that shares master LDAP server's load and provides HA.
Resource partition	A software partitioning technique.
Restore	The process of retrieving data from an offline media.
Rolling upgrade	In a cluster environment, rolling upgrade allows for application upgrades with minimal amount of downtime.
Root	See superuser.
Router	A device that routes data packets from one network to another.
Routing	The process of choosing a path over which to send a data packet.
Run control levels	Different levels of HP-UX operation.
SAM	See System Management Homepage.
Samba	See CIFS server.
SAN	See Storage Area Network.
SATAN	Security Administrators Tool for Analyzing Networks. It gathers network security weaknesses and generates reports for review.
Saved kernel configuration	One or more kernel configurations that have been created in stored.
Schema	A set of attributes and object classes.
Script	A text program written to perform a series of tasks.
SCSI	See Small Computer System Interface.
Search path	A list of directories where the system looks for the command specified at the command line.
Secondary prompt	A prompt indicating that the entered command needs more input.
Secure resource partitioning	A partitioning technique intended for resource and workload management.
Secure shell	A set of secure tools to gain access to an HP-UX system.
Security hardening	Implementation of security measures to enhance system security.
Server	A powerful system that runs HP-UX software.
Server blade	A small form-factor computer that goes into the enclosure of a BladeSystem.
Server complex	A complete physical hardware box including server expansion unit.
Server expansion unit	A hardware box that holds extended hardware components of a server.
Set Group ID	Sets real and effective group IDs.
Set User ID	Sets real and effective user IDs.
Setgid	See set group ID.
Setuid	See set user ID.
Shadow password	Mechanism to move passwords and password aging information to secure file.
Share	Making a file, directory or a file system available over the network as a share.
Shared memory	A portion in memory created by a process to be shared with other processes that communicate with that process.
Shell	The UNIX command interpreter that sits between a user and UNIX kernel.
Shell program	See script.
Shell script	See script.
Shell scripting	Programming in a UNIX shell to automate a given task.

SIM	See Systems Insight Manager.
Signal	A software interrupt sent to a process.
Single-user mode	An OS state in which the system cannot be accessed over the network.
Slot	A receptable of an I/O card in a computer system.
Small Computer System Interface	A parallel interface used to connect peripheral devices to the system.
Socket	A combination of an IP address and the port number.
Software assistant	A software upgrade to patch assessment and security patch check tools.
Software depot	A logical repository to store software.
Software distributor	A set of commands to perform software and patch management tasks.
Special characters	See metacharacters.
SPOF	Single Point Of Failure.
Stable storage	A small non-volatile area in PDC that contains hardware paths of system console and boot devices, among other boot-related information.
Standard error	The location to send error messages generated by a command. The default is the terminal screen where the command is executed.
Standard input	The location to receive input from. The default is the keyboard.
Standard output	The location to send output, other than error messages, generated by a command. The default is the terminal screen where the command is executed.
Standby node	See adoptive node.
Stderr	See standard error.
Stdin	See standard input.
Stdout	See standard output.
Sticky bit	Prevents deletion of files in a directory by non-owners.
Storage Area Netwrok	A network of computers that share one or more storage devices.
Storage blade	A small form-factor disk subsystem that goes into the enclosure of a BladeSystem.
Stratum level	The categorization of NTP time sources based on reliability and accuracy.
String	A series of characters.
Subdisk	A logical, contiguous chunk of disk space.
Subnet	One of the smaller networks formed by dividing an IP address.
Subnet mask	Segregates the network bits from the node bits.
Subnetting	The process of dividing an IP address into several smaller subnetworks.
Subproduct	A collection of filesets or subproducts, or both, and control scripts.
Superblock	A small portion in a file system that holds the file system's critical information.
Superuser	A user that has limitless powers on an HP-UX system.
Swap	Alternate disk location for demand paging.
Switch	A network device that looks at the MAC address and switches the packet to the correct destination port.
Symbolic link	A shortcut created to point to a file located somewhere in file system hierarchy.
Symbolic mode	A method of setting permissions on a file using non-decimal values.
System	A machine that runs HP-UX OE software.
System Administrator	Person responsible for installing, configuring and managing an HP-UX system.

System Administration Manager	See System Management Homepage.
System call	A mechanism that applications use to request service from the kernel.
System console	A display device (usually a dumb terminal) connected directly to an HP-UX system.
System Management Homepage	A text/graphical tool for HP-UX system administration.
System multimode package	A type of cluster package that runs simultaneously on all cluster nodes.
System recovery	The process of recovering an unbootable system.
Systems Insight Manager	A management tool that allows to perform system and network administration of several HP-UX centrally.
TCP/IP	Transmission Control Protocol / Internet Protocol. A stacked, standard, suite of protocols for computer communication.
Temporary instant capacity	A purchase flexibility to buy cores, memory and cell boards at a reduced price for predetermined amount of time.
Terminal	See system console.
TiCAP	See temporary instant capacity.
Tilde expansion	See tilde substitution.
Tilde substitution	Using tilde character as short cut to move around in directory tree.
Topology	Ways of connecting network nodes together.
Tty	Refers to a terminal.
UID	See user ID.
Ultra high availability	Design that involes cluster nodes residing in distant data centers.
Unmounting	Detaching a mounted file system or a CD/DVD from the directory structure.
Uptime	The length of time during which a business application remains up and available for user access.
User equivalency	Making a user trusted on a remote machine.
User ID	A unique identification number assigned to a user.
User keys	The keys used to add protection to an EVFS volume.
Variable	A temporary storage of data in memory.
VGDA	Volume Group Descriptor Area contains information that the device driver needs to configure the VG for LVM.
VGRA	Volume Group Reserved Area contains both VGSA and VGDA.
VGSA	Volume Group Status Area contains quorum information for the VG.
Virtual IP address	See floating IP address.
Virtualization technologies	A set of technologies that allows you to group or split physical resources of a large server to function as several virtual resources.
Virtual machine	A partitioning technique used on Integrity servers.
Virtual partition	A logical partition within an HP-UX system complex that runs a dedicated, standalone HP-UX OE instance within it.
Virtual Private Network	A virtual network on the internet to transfer confidential information securely.
Virtual Server Environment OE	A bundle of HP-UX 11i v3 OE that includes virtualization technologies.

Volume group	A logical container that holds physical volumes, logical volumes and file systems.
vPar	See virtual partition.
VSE-OE	See Virtual Server Environment OE.
VxVM	Veritas Volume Manager. A disk partitioning solution.
WAN	See Wide Area Network.
WBEM	See Web-Based Enterprise Management.
Web-Based Enterprise Management	A set of management and internet standard technologies used to integrate the administration of multivendor hardware platforms and operating systems.
Wide Area Network	A network with systems located geographically apart.
Wildcard characters	See metacharacters.
WLM	See WorkLoad Manager
WorkLoad Manager	An automatic resource management tool.
Workstation	A system that runs HP-UX software. These are usually deskside machines used by individuals for specific tasks.
WWID	A unique identifier for a SCSI device.
Zombie process	A child process that terminated abnormally and whose parent process still waits for it.

Index

9 781606 436547